W. D. (William Dool) Killen

The old Catholic Church

Or, The History, Doctrine, Worship, and Polity of the Christians

W. D. (William Dool) Killen

The old Catholic Church
Or, The History, Doctrine, Worship, and Polity of the Christians

ISBN/EAN: 9783337067977

Printed in Europe, USA, Canada, Australia, Japan

Cover: Foto ©Lupo / pixelio.de

More available books at **www.hansebooks.com**

THE

OLD CATHOLIC CHURCH:

OR

THE HISTORY, DOCTRINE, WORSHIP, AND
POLITY OF THE CHRISTIANS

TRACED FROM

THE APOSTOLIC AGE TO THE ESTABLISHMENT OF THE
POPE AS A TEMPORAL SOVEREIGN, A.D. 755

BY

W. D. KILLEN, D.D.

EDINBURGH
T. & T. CLARK, 38 GEORGE STREET
1871

PREFACE.

IN the "Ancient Church" the author has endeavoured to illustrate the ecclesiastical history of the first three centuries. That volume—now several years before the public—has obtained extensive circulation; and though it gives a new view of some matters of importance pertaining to early Christianity, no writer at home or abroad has yet undertaken to set aside its conclusions. "The Old Catholic Church" supplies merely a brief sketch of the history of the Ante-Nicene period. The reader may find the controverted questions which relate to it investigated minutely in the preceding publication; and, in the absence of all attempts to overturn them, the writer feels himself at liberty to take for granted the soundness of his expositions relative to the Ignatian Epistles, the rise of the hierarchy, and the formation of the Catholic system.

During the first three centuries the great struggle of Christianity was with paganism. Pagan philosophy tried to corrupt its creed, and pagan violence sought to accomplish its annihilation. During the period between the age of Constantine and the age of Charlemagne, it passed through another phase of existence. Its theology relative to the Godhead, the Incarnation, and the Fall, was defined by Councils and embodied in carefully prepared formularies; but the Church itself now basked in the sunshine of princely favour, and displayed the relaxing influence of the change. Its simple worship was disfigured by the meretricious adornments of the old pagan ceremonial, and its free constitution was ruined by imperial and papal usurpations. At the close of this period the Western branch of the Catholic Church entered on a new course of development, for then the Bishop of Rome became a temporal potentate.

This work embraces about one-half of the interval between the birth of Christ and the Reformation, and notices the leading ecclesiastical transactions which meanwhile occurred. Original authorities have been carefully consulted; and some new light, it is believed, has been thrown on not a few points of considerable consequence. Special attention is invited to the chapters on the Donatists, the Organization of the Church, and the Ecclesiastical History of England, Scotland, and Ireland. The interpretation here given of Patrick's Confession removes some of the most perplexing difficulties hitherto connected with the career of the great Hibernian missionary.

This work will, it is hoped, supply a want long felt by a considerable portion of the public. Whilst overlooking no ecclesiastical movement of importance which took place during the first seven centuries and a half of the Christian era, and exhibiting the results of original investigation, its size presents no very formidable discouragement to any inquirer. Kindred subjects have been linked together; and the author has studied to maintain a lucid order in his general arrangements. May the reader derive knowledge, comfort, and warning, from a more intimate acquaintance with "The Old Catholic Church!"

OCTOBER 1871.

CONTENTS.

PERIOD I.

FROM THE BIRTH OF CHRIST TO THE CONVERSION OF CONSTANTINE.
A.D. 312.

SECTION I.
THE HISTORY OF THE CHURCH.

CHAPTER I.
THE MINISTRY OF CHRIST.

	PAGE
The Time of Christ's Birth,	1
The State of the World,	1
The Wonderful Works of Jesus,	2
Why so little Notice of Him by Jewish and Pagan Writers,	2
The Memoirs of Him by the Evangelists,	3
The Scene of Christ's Ministry,	3
His Crucifixion,	3

CHAPTER II.
THE APOSTLES, THE EVANGELISTS, AND THE PRIMITIVE PREACHERS.

The Importance of Oral Instruction,	4
Typical Significance of the Twelve and the Seventy,	4
Labours and Sufferings of the Heralds of the Gospel,	5
Thomas, Andrew, Paul, and Peter,	5
The Evangelists,	6
The Early Ministers, how supported,	6
Miraculous Gifts of the Early Preachers,	7
Different Effects of the Building of Babel and of the Building of the Church,	7

CHAPTER III.
THE EARLY FATHERS.

To whom the title Fathers applied,	8
Spurious Writings,	8
The Apostolic Fathers,	8
Justin Martyr,	9
Irenæus and Tertullian,	9

	PAGE
Clemens Alexandrinus and Hippolytus,	10
Origen,	10
Cyprian,	11
Minucius Felix, Gregory Thaumaturgus, and others,	12
Imperfections of the Fathers, and Excellency of Scripture,	13

CHAPTER IV.
THE PERSECUTIONS OF THE CHURCH.

The Weapons of the Church not carnal,	14
Causes of the Early Persecutions,	15
Persecution under Nero and Domitian,	15
Policy of Trajan in regard to the Christians,	16
Rescript of Hadrian,	16
Cruel Policy of Marcus Aurelius,	17
Commodus, Septimus Severus, Alexander Severus, Maximin, and Philip,	18
The Decian Persecution,	18
Valerian, Gallienus, and Aurelian,	19
The Diocletian Persecution,	19
Honours rendered to the Martyrs,	20
Benefits arising from Persecution,	20

CHAPTER V.
THE GROWTH OF THE CHURCH, DOMESTIC AND SOCIAL LIFE OF THE CHRISTIAN.

The Gospel soon spread throughout Palestine,	21
Introduced into Syria, Asia Minor, and Europe,	22
A Revival early in Second Century,	23
Influence of the Church of Rome. The Catacombs,	23
Growth of the Church in Africa,	23
Growth of the Church in Britain, France, Germany, among the Goths, and in Mesopotamia and India,	24
Places of Christian Worship,	25
Success of Christianity not to be ascribed entirely to Miracles,	25
Morality of the Early Christians,	25
Their kindly Treatment of Slaves,	26
Their Conduct at Home. Family Worship,	26
Their Dress. Their Aversion to the Heathen Spectacles,	27
Their Consistency and Loyalty,	27
Their General Benevolence,	28

SECTION II.
THE DOCTRINE OF THE CHURCH.

CHAPTER I.
DOCTRINE OF THE GREAT BODY OF BELIEVERS.

The Messiah Foretold,	29
Perplexity created by the mode of His Appearance	29
Object of his Mission ; and His Dignity,	30

Contents.   ix

	PAGE
Doctrine of the Church not at first exhibited in a fixed Confession of Faith,	31
Introduction of Theological Expressions not found in Scripture,	31
Supreme Authority of the Written Word,	32

CHAPTER II.
EARLY HERESIES, CONTROVERSIES, AND SUPERSTITIONS.

Origin of Gnosticism,	33
Its Doctrines. The Docetæ,	33
Simon Magus, Hermogenes, Carpocrates, Cerinthus, Saturninus, Valentine, and others,	34
Practical results of Gnosticism,	35
Montanus and his Peculiarities,	35
Theodotus, Artemon, Natalius, Noetus, Sabellius and Paul of Samosata,	36
Mani and his Sect,	37
The Nazarenes.	38
The Sign of the Cross,	38
The Paschal Controversy, and the Controversy relative to the Baptism of Heretics,	39
The Novatian Schism, and the Schism of Felicissimus,	40
Lessons to be derived from early Heresies and Divisions,	40

SECTION III.
WORSHIP AND CONSTITUTION OF THE CHURCH.

CHAPTER I.
WORSHIP OF THE CHURCH.

The Fourth Commandment still binding,	42
Psalmody and Prayer,	43
Reading of the Scriptures and Preaching,	43
Baptism and the Lord's Supper,	45

CHAPTER II.
CONSTITUTION OF THE CHURCH.

Extraordinary and Ordinary Office-bearers,	46
The Churches of Jerusalem, Antioch, and Ephesus,	47
Elders in every Church and Popular Election,	49
Timothy, Titus, and the Angels of the Seven Churches,	50
Presbyterial Government supplanted by Prelacy,	51

CHAPTER III.
THE RISE OF THE HIERARCHY AND THE CATHOLIC CHURCH.

The Forerunners of Antichrist,	52
Prelacy begins at Rome,	52
Date of its Commencement,	53
The Change at first not very striking,	54
Presbyters for a time continued to ordain,	55
Prelacy led to Popery,	55
The Catholic Church,	55
The rise of Metropolitans,	56
Danger of tampering with Divine arrangements,	57
Babylon a Type of Papal Rome,	57

PERIOD II.

FROM THE CONVERSION OF CONSTANTINE TO THE ESTABLISHMENT OF THE POPE AS A TEMPORAL SOVEREIGN, A.D. 312 TO A.D. 755.

SECTION I.
GENERAL HISTORY OF THE CHURCH.

CHAPTER I.
THE CONVERSION OF CONSTANTINE AND HIS IMPERIAL RECOGNITION OF CHRISTIANITY. THE PROGRESS OF THE CHURCH BEYOND THE BOUNDARIES OF THE EMPIRE.

	PAGE
Political state of the Empire in the beginning of the Fourth Century,	60
Constantius Chlorus and his son Constantine,	61
The story of the Cross in the sky,	61
Constantine's Conversion to Christianity,	63
His equivocal Proceedings and cautious Legislation,	64
His final struggle with Licinius,	66
His Conduct afterwards in supporting Christianity and discouraging Paganism,	67
Change produced by the Conversion of Constantine,	67
His motives in adhering to Christianity,	69
His Character in advanced Life,	70
Evils connected with his support of the Gospel,	71
Spread of the Truth beyond the bounds of the Empire,	72
The Goths and Ulphilas,	72
Christianity in Persia,	72
The Conversion of the Armenians: Gregory the Illuminator and Miesrob,	72
Christianity in Iberia, Arabia, India, and Abyssinia,	73

CHAPTER II.
THE CHURCH UNDER THE SUCCESSORS OF CONSTANTINE, AND THE FALL OF PAGANISM.

Two of the nephews of Constantine put to death,	74
Misconduct of the sons of Constantine,	74
Constantius left sole Emperor,	74
Laws against Paganism,	74
Julian succeeds Constantius and supports Paganism,	75
Discourages Christianity and attempts to rebuild the Jewish Temple,	77
Jovian succeeds Julian,	78
Valentinian becomes Emperor, his brother Valens Emperor of the East,	78
Gratian succeeds to the Empire,	79
Theodosius the Great,	79
Destruction of the Pagan Temples,	79
The Empire divided between Arcadius and Honorius,	81
Fall of the Western Empire,	81

	PAGE
Social Influence of Christianity,	81
Christian Churches become Sanctuaries,	82

CHAPTER III.

THE ECCLESIASTICAL WRITERS.

Literature of the Fourth Century,	82
Lactantius and Eusebius,	83
Rufinus, Socrates, Sozomen, Theodoret, and Evagrius,	83
Optatus, Epiphanius, Sulpitius Severus and Dionysius Exiguus,	84
Gregory of Tours and Bede,	84
The Correspondence of the Popes, and the Epistles of Boniface,	85
Athanasius,	85
Hilary of Poictiers and Cyril of Jerusalem,	86
Basil of Cæsarea, Gregory of Nyssa, and Gregory Nazianzen,	87
Chrysostom,	88
Jerome,	90
Ambrose,	92
Augustine,	95
Prosper, Marius Mercator, Fulgentius, Cassian, and Vincent of Lerins,	95
Cyril of Alexandria, and Isidore of Pelusium,	96
Gregory I.,	96
Isidore of Seville, Theodore of Canterbury, and John of Damascus,	97
Contradictions and Errors of the Fathers,	97
Influence of Monachism on Literature,	98
False principles of Scripture Interpretation,	99
General integrity of the Fathers,	99

CHAPTER IV.

MONACHISM.

Monachism the Perversion of sound principles,	101
Pagan and Jewish Monachism,	102
Origin of Christian Monachism. Paulus and Antony,	103
Eremites and Cœnobites. Pachomius,	103
Popularity of Monachism,	104
Hilarion and Basil. The Rule of Basil,	105
Nunneries,	106
Monachism in the West,	107
Patronized by Athanasius, Ambrose, Augustine, and Jerome,	107
Martin of Tours and Cassian,	107
Sarabaites, Euchites, Boskoi, and Stylites,	108
Rule of Benedict of Nursia,	109
Folly of the Monastic system,	111
Its Influence on the Church,	112

CHAPTER V.

THE SCHISM OF THE DONATISTS.

Importance of the Proceedings of the Donatists as connected with the Development of the Catholic Church,	113
Death of Mensurius of Carthage, and Election of Cæcilian,	114

xii   *Contents.*

	PAGE
The Election Opposed, and the Numidian Bishops ordain Majorinus,	115
Felix of Aptunga and Donatus the Great,	116
Equivocal position of Cæcilian and injudicious conduct of Constantine,	117
Case of the Donatists examined by Roman commissioners,	118
The Donatists dissatisfied, and their case submitted to the Council of Arles,	119
The Donatists when condemned appeal to Constantine, and are again condemned,	120
Persecution and subsequent indulgence,	121
Prosperity of the Donatists. Their peculiar principles,	122
Persecution of the Donatists by Constantine. The Circumcelliones,	122
Julian encourages the Donatists,	123
Discouraged by Valentinian I. and Gratian,	124
Causes of the Decline of the Donatists,	124
Augustine and the Conference of Carthage in A.D. 411,	125
Errors of Donatists and Catholics,	126
Augustine and the Papacy,	126
Persecuting principles of Augustine,	127
Good Fruits of the Donatist Schism,	127
The African Church long preserved the ancient Ecclesiastical Polity,	128
Its sound Theological creed,	129

CHAPTER VI.

MOHAMMEDANISM.

Birth, Connexions, Personal Appearance, and early History of Mohammed,	129
Originally a fanatic rather than impostor,	132
Circumstances which led him to assume the character of an Apostle of God,	132
Islam and the earliest Converts,	133
Circumstances which recommended Islam to Jews and Christians,	135
Mohammed's Vacillations and the slow progress of Islam,	135
Mohammed is encouraged by strangers from Yathreb,	135
Progress of Islam at Yathreb,	136
Mohammed's dangerous position at Mecca, and his night journey to Heaven,	137
The Hegira or Flight to Yathreb or Medina,	138
Position of Mohammed at Medina,	139
Deterioration in the Character and Doctrine of Mohammed,	139
His Polygamy and the Doctrine of Abrogation,	140
Progress of his Power in Arabia,	140
His farewell Pilgrimage and Death,	141
Extraordinary Career of Mohammed,	142
Causes of his Success,	143
The Paradise and Hell of Mohammed,	143
Doctrines and Usages of Islam,	144
The Koran,	145
The Khalifs and the rapid extension of the Mohammedan Power,	145
Circumstances which may account for the victorious progress of the Khalifs,	146
Their mode of treating the Conquered,	147
Prophecy and Mohammedanism,	148
Mohammed a scourge to degenerate Christians,	148
The success of a cause no sure test of its excellence,	149

SECTION II.

THE DOCTRINE OF THE CHURCH.

CHAPTER I.

THE SCRIPTURES.

	PAGE
Remarkable Characteristics of the Bible,	150
Jewish Canon of the Old Testament,	151
Apocryphal Books of the Old Testament. How received in the ancient Christian Church,	151
Canon of the New Testament,	154
Wonderful care employed in preservation of the Scriptures,	155
Scriptures contain their own Credentials,	157
No Canonical Books lost,	157
The Apostle John and the New Testament Canon,	158
Relation of the Church to the Scriptures,	159
Plenary Inspiration of Scripture,	160
Supreme Authority of Scripture,	161
Tradition and Church Authority,	161
Vacillation and Inconsistency of the Fathers,	163
Attention paid to Scripture an index of the State of the Church,	164
Scripture, and especially the Psalms, largely introduced into ancient Liturgies,	165

CHAPTER II.

THE ARIAN CONTROVERSY.

Rise of the Arian Controversy,	165
Alexander and Arius. Their respective Views,	166
Arius, when excommunicated, applies to Eusebius of Nicomedia,	167
The Council of Nice, and its Creed,	168
Character and History of Athanasius,	169
Refuses to admit Arius to Communion,	170
The Synod of Tyre and the Persecution of Athanasius,	170
Death of Arius,	171
Constantine and Constans support the Nicene Creed, and Constantius opposes it	172
Athanasius, deposed by a Synod at Antioch, repairs to Rome,	172
The Homoousians and the Council of Sardica,	173
Excitement in Alexandria, Assassination of Gregory, and return of Athanasius,	173
Councils of Arles, Milan, Seleucia, and Rimini, and perils of Athanasius,	174
The Heteroousians, Macedonians, and Apollinarians,	175
Tyranny of Constantius,	175
Conduct of succeeding Emperors,	176
Theodosius the Great suppresses Arianism,	176
Ulphilas, the Apostle of the Goths,	176
Results of the Arian Controversy,	177

CHAPTER III.

THE PELAGIAN CONTROVERSY.

Pelagianism, a Western Heresy, and Augustine its Great Antagonist,	178
The Doctrine of the Fall not yet fully Defined,	179

Contents.

Language of Scripture in harmony with the Doctrine of Predestination,	180
Pelagianism propagated by two monks, Pelagius and Cœlestius,	181
Commencement of the Controversy in Africa,	181
Character and History of Augustine. His Conversion,	182
Pelagius in Palestine, Orosius, Heros, and Lazarus,	183
Views of the Pelagians,	185
The Theology of Augustine,	186
Infant Baptism,	186
Innocent of Rome and the African Councils,	188
Vacillation of Zosimus, and firmness of the Africans,	188
Condemnation of Pelagianism by the Emperor Honorius, and the Tractoria of Zosimus,	189
Condemnation by the General Council of Ephesus,	190
Cassian and Semi-Pelagianism,	190
Hilary, Prosper, and Vincentius of Lerins. The Council of Orange,	191
Death of Augustine. His Services to the Church,	192

CHAPTER IV.
THE NESTORIAN CONTROVERSY.

The Constitution of the Person of Christ,	193
Character and History of Nestorius,	193
Refuses to call Mary the "Mother of God."	194
Excitement in Constantinople, and Oration of Proclus,	195
Jealousy of the Bishop of Alexandria towards the Bishop of Constantinople,	196
Character and History of Cyril. His conduct towards Nestorius,	196
Jealousy of the Bishop of Rome. Cyril and Nestorius appeal to Celestine,	198
Conduct of Celestine,	199
The discussion respecting the title "Mother of God" leads to a controversy respecting the union of Divinity and Humanity in Christ,	200
Imperious conduct of Cyril towards Nestorius,	201
The General Council of Ephesus,	202
Memnon and John of Antioch,	202
Diplomacy of Cyril. Mission of Dalmatius to the Emperor,	203
Triumph of Cyril. Deposition and Death of Nestorius,	204
Subsequent History of the Nestorians,	204
Remarks on the Nestorian controversy,	205

CHAPTER V.
THE EUTYCHIAN CONTROVERSY.

Different Schools of Theology at Alexandria and Antioch,	206
Eutyches and his views. The Eunuch Chrysaphius,	206
"Robber Synod" of Ephesus. Violence of Dioscorus and Barsumas,	207
Deposition and Death of Flavian,	208
Leo the Great and his Tome. Treatment of his Legates at the Robber Synod,	209
Anatolius of Constantinople,	210
General Council of Chalcedon,	211
The Monophysites and the Henoticon,	211
Justinian, Theodora, and the Three Chapters,	212
General Council of Constantinople in A.D. 553,	213

Contents. XV

	PAGE
Vigilius of Rome and the Judicatum,	213
The Monothelites, the Ecthesis, the Type, and Martin I. of Rome,	214
General Council of Constantinople in A.D. 680, and Agatho of Rome,	215
Pope Honorius stigmatized as a heretic,	216
Evils of the interference of the State with the Church,	217

SECTION III.

WORSHIP AND CONSTITUTION OF THE CHURCH.

CHAPTER I.

THE LORD'S DAY.

Its name indicates its character,	218
Superseded the Jewish Sabbath,	218
Called Sunday by Christians when addressing heathens	219
Early observance of the Lord's Day,	219
Called the Sabbath,	221
Testimonies of Eusebius, Athanasius, Ambrose, and Augustine,	221
Decisions of Councils,	223
Laws of Constantine, Valentinian and Valens, and Theodosius the Great,	223
Second Council of Maçon, Theodore of Canterbury, and English legislation,	224
Observance of the Lord's Day varied according to circumstances,	225
Blessings connected with keeping the Lord's Day,	225
The spirit of the Lord's Day not ascetic,	225
The Lord's Day is the Sabbath,	226

CHAPTER II.

THE WORSHIP OF THE CHURCH.

Churches of increased splendour built after the Diocletian Persecution,	227
Structure of the Churches. The Chancel, the Nave, the Porch, and the Ambo,	227
Service of the Catechumens, and service of the Faithful,	228
The Psalmody and the Cantors,	229
Prayer and the Reading of Liturgies,	230
The Roman Liturgy and Canon of the Mass,	231
Preaching in the East and West,	232
Baptism, why deferred. Its ceremonies,	233
Unction or Confirmation,	234
The Lord's Supper. Mode of its celebration,	234
Mistakes respecting it,	235
Prayers for the dead. Purgatory,	236
Easter, Whitsuntide, and Christmas,	237
Epiphany, Candlemas, Lady Day, and other Festivals,	237
Origin of Saints' Days,	238
Heathen Rites introduced into the Church,	239
Images and pilgrimages. Worship of the Virgin,	240
Great changes in the outward appearance of the Church,	241

CHAPTER III.

THE HIERARCHY.

	PAGE
Gradual formation of the Episcopal system,	242
Council of Nice established the rights of Metropolitans and the precedence of Rome, Alexandria, and Antioch,	243
Vagueness of the decisions of the Council of Nice,	244
Country Bishops. Their original dignity and gradual suppression,	245
Arrangements of the African Church,	246
Transition from parochial to diocesan Episcopacy, illustrated by a particular case,	247
Bishops decreased as Christians multiplied,	248
Establishment of Exarchs or Patriarchs,	249
Case of the Bishop of Jerusalem,	250
Case of Constantinople,	250
Contentions connected with the organization of the Hierarchy,	251
The Hierarchy culminates in the Papacy,	252

CHAPTER IV.

THE GENERAL COUNCILS.

The Antiquity of Councils,	252
Number of General Councils,	253
Early General Councils all Eastern,	254
Summoned and supported by the Emperor,	254
Numbers in attendance,	254
Order of proceeding. Presidents,	255
Remarkable individuals in the Council of Nice,	257
Erastian interference of the Emperors,	258
Subjects discussed in the early General Councils,	259
Doubtful decisions of General Councils,	259
Violent proceedings in General Councils,	260
Literary attainments of the Members,	262
Strange proceedings in the Sixth General Council,	262
High pretensions of these Councils,	263
Character of the Members,	264
Influence of General Councils on the Emperors,	265
Decline of freedom in General Councils,	265

SECTION IV.

ECCLESIASTICAL HISTORY OF GREAT BRITAIN AND IRELAND.

CHAPTER I.

ECCLESIASTICAL HISTORY OF ENGLAND.

England's early Ecclesiastical History obscure,	267
King Lucius and Pope Eleutherius,	267
Saint Alban and the Diocletian Persecution,	268
British bishops in Councils of Arles, Sardica, and Rimini,	268
Number of bishops in early British Church,	269

	PAGE
Arianism and Pelagianism in England,	271
Germanus and Lupus; Dubritius and Iltutus,	271
English Christianity nearly extinguished by the Saxons,	272
Welsh Church in the Sixth Century. King Arthur, David, and Gildas,	272
Pope Gregory plans a Mission to England,	273
The monk Augustine and his Companions in England,	274
Queen Bertha and King Ethelbert,	274
Kingdom of Kent converted,	274
Establishment of a Hierarchy in England,	275
The old British Church and the Romish Missionaries,	275
Female influence in the Conversion of England,	278
Conversion of East Saxons, Northumbria, West Saxons, Mercia, East Anglia, and Sussex,	278
Superficial conversions and pious frauds,	279
Laurentius and King Eadbald,	280
Great part of England converted by Missionaries from Iona,	280
Superiority of Scottish Missionaries,	281
Excellent character of Aidan,	281
Disputes between Scottish and Romish Missionaries,	282
Synod of Whitby,	283
Theodore, Archbishop of Canterbury. His zeal and learning,	283
Christianity incorporated with the civil Constitution,	284
Influence of the Conversion of England,	285
Devotion of Englishmen to Rome,	285
Division of England into parishes. Church Cess and Tithes,	285
English Missionaries on the Continent,	286
Willibrord and Boniface,	286
Value of even an adulterated Gospel,	286

CHAPTER II.

ECCLESIASTICAL HISTORY OF SCOTLAND.

Christianity in Scotland in the days of Constantine the Great,	287
Nynian the Apostle of the Southern Picts,	287
The mission of Columbkille. His lineage,	288
Ireland called Scotland,	289
Columbkille the apostle of the Northern Picts,	290
The Monastery of Hy. Its organization and educational excellence,	291
Adamnan's Life of Columbkille,	292
Bede's account of the Presbyter Abbot,	293
Bishops ordained by him,	294
Columbkille and the Munster Bishop,	296
Columbkille, Findchan, and Aid,	297
Columbkille ordains a King,	298
Columbkille excommunicated,	299
Columbkille and Robert Bruce,	300
Kentigern of Glasgow,	300
Ancient Scottish Bishops,	300
Decline of the Monastery of Hy. Fame of the island,	301
The Culdees,	302

CHAPTER III.

IRELAND; AND PATRICK ITS APOSTLE.

	PAGE
The Mosaic Narrative, and the early Traditions relating to Ireland,	302
Early colonization of the Country,	303
Early Literature and Civilization,	304
Christianity in Ireland in the fourth century,	304
Cœlestius,	305
Palladius sent to Ireland by Pope Celestine,	305
His want of success, and death,	305
Patrick in Ireland before Palladius,	306
The Confession of Patrick,	307
History of the Apostle of Ireland,	308
His singular dream,	309
True chronology of his life,	311
Difficulties removed by this explanation,	312
Real cause of the Mission of Palladius,	314
Character and great success of Patrick,	314
Sen-Patrick different from Patrick the Apostle,	315
Palladius has been confounded with Patrick,	316
Source of the difficulties connected with Patrick's History,	316
Why misconceptions were promoted,	316
Ordinary Lives of Patrick fabulous,	317
Evidence that Patrick was not sent to Ireland by the Pope,	318
Silence of early writers explained,	319
No evidence of early intercourse between Rome and Ireland,	320
Peculiar usages introduced by Patrick,	321

CHAPTER IV.

DOCTRINE AND POLITY, LITERATURE AND PIETY, OF THE EARLY IRISH CHURCH.

The Hymn of Patrick,	322
Patrick a Trinitarian; held the sovereignty of Grace, and rejected Purgatory,	322
Early Irish Church practised Communion in both kinds, and rejected Transubstantiation,	324
Multitude of Bishops in early Irish Church,	325
Synodical Government,	327
The Bishopric of Armagh. Its origin and progress,	328
Seminaries of the early Irish Church,	330
Irish Missionaries. Columbanus, Gallus, and Kilian,	330
Free spirit of Irish Missionaries,	331
Columbanus and Pope Boniface IV.,	332
Gradual encroachments of Romish principles,	333
Catalogue of old Irish Saints,	333

SECTION V.

PROGRESS OF THE POPEDOM.

CHAPTER I.

PROGRESS OF THE POWER OF THE BISHOPS OF ROME FROM THE CONVERSION OF CONSTANTINE TO THE DEATH OF THEODOSIUS THE GREAT IN A.D. 395.

	PAGE
Great change produced in the condition of the Bishop of Rome by Constantine's conversion,	335
Nicene Canon relating to the Bishop of Rome,	335
The suburbicarian Churches,	336
The Arian controversy, and the Bishop of Rome,	337
Canon of the Council of Sardica,	337
Julius and Liberius, Bishops of Rome,	338
Damasus and Ursinus. Wealth of Roman Bishop,	338
The Roman Clergy and the Ladies,	339
Laws resembling our Statutes of Mortmain,	340
Rescript of Gratian and Valentinian II.,	340
Appointment of Apostolic Vicars,	341
The Decretal Epistles—genuine and spurious,	342
The Bishop of Rome and other metropolitans patronized by the Emperors,	344
Design and fruits of this policy,	345

CHAPTER II.

PROGRESS OF THE POWER OF THE BISHOPS OF ROME FROM THE DEATH OF THEODOSIUS THE GREAT TO THE FALL OF THE WESTERN EMPIRE.—A.D. 395 TO A.D. 476.

Innocent I. and the Apostle Peter,	346
Rome and Constantinople,	347
Pillage of Rome by Alaric and its effects,	348
The Church of Africa and Peter's primacy,	349
The Roman Bishops and the Pelagian controversy,	350
The case of Apiarius, and the Sardican Canon,	351
The Pope and the Gallic Bishops,	353
The Edict of Valentinian III.,	353
Jealousies and contentions of Eastern Patriarchs,	353
Pope Leo the Great,	354
The Bishop of Constantinople, and the Canon of Chalcedon,	354
Attila, Genseric, and the Bishop of Rome,	356
The Pope, and the fall of the Western Empire,	357

CHAPTER III.

PROGRESS OF THE PAPACY FROM THE FALL OF THE WESTERN EMPIRE TO THE PONTIFICATE OF GREGORY THE GREAT, A.D. 476 to A.D. 590.

The Pope and the Fall of the Western Empire,	358
Odoacer and Theodoric,	358
The Greek Emperors and the Pope,	359
The Pope and the Heresies,	360

Contents.

	PAGE
The Henoticon and the Schism between the Greek and Latin Churches,	360
Ennodius and the Papal pretensions,	361
Conversion of Clovis. Its History and Results,	361
The Conquests of Clovis, and the Spread of Papal Influence,	363
The Papal policy—especially in the case of Appeals to Rome,	365
Case of the Bishops of Ambrun and Gap,	365
Conversion of the Arian Kings promoted Papal influence,	366

CHAPTER IV.
THE PONTIFICATE OF GREGORY THE GREAT, A.D. 590 to A.D. 604.

The Early Life of Gregory and His Election to the Popedom,	368
Superstition of the Age and veneration for Relics,	369
The Fame of Rome promoted by Pilgrimages,	369
Attainments and Writings of Gregory,	370
Gregory's Spirit and Policy. He wants peace of conscience,	371
Patronizes Purgatory, and introduces Masses for the Dead,	372
Liturgies, the Gregorian Chant, and the Spread of the Romish Worship,	373
Monachism and the Papacy,	374
The Conversion of England, and the giving of the Pall to Metropolitans,	375
Gregory's Controversy with John the Faster respecting the title of Universal Bishop,	376
Base Conduct of Gregory in the case of Maurice and Phocas,	377
Gregory's character injured by his Creed. His great influence,	378

CHAPTER V.
PROGRESS OF THE PAPACY FROM THE DEATH OF GREGORY THE GREAT TO THE ESTABLISHMENT OF THE POPE AS A TEMPORAL SOVEREIGN, A.D. 604 to A.D. 755.

Causes of increasing Ignorance,	379
Wretched condition of the Clergy,	380
State of the Laity. Disputes respecting Episcopal Elections. Growth of Papal power,	381
The Popes and the Eastern Emperors,	382
Sufferings of Pope Martin,	382
English Missionaries on the Continent,	383
Boniface and his Oath to the Pope,	384
Labours of Boniface in Germany,	384
Effect of revival of Synods,	385
The Metropolitans and the Monasteries,	386
Character of Boniface,	387
The Image Controversy and the Pope,	388
Revolt of Rome and the Exarchate,	388
The Lombards attempt to seize the revolted Territory,	389
Pepin and Pope Zachary,	390
Pope Stephen III. becomes a temporal Prince,	391
State of the Church at this Period,	391
The Little Horn,	392
The Eastern Church and the Saracens,	392
Changes since the Second Century,	393
APPENDIX. Letter of the late Rev. W. Cureton, D.D.,	397

PERIOD I.

From the Birth of Christ to the Conversion of Constantine the Great.—A.D. 312.

SECTION I.

THE HISTORY OF THE CHURCH.

CHAPTER I.

THE MINISTRY OF CHRIST.

ABOUT a thousand years after the dedication of the Temple of Solomon the Lord of Glory was ushered on the stage of human existence. When Jesus Christ was born at Bethlehem—a village near Jerusalem—Augustus, the founder of a new dynasty, reigned over the Roman Empire. Palestine formed part of his wide dominions; and a tributary sovereign—Herod, surnamed The Great—an able but cruel prince of Idumean extraction, was the ruler of the Jewish territory.

It is stated in the New Testament that the Messiah appeared on earth "when the fulness of the time was come."[1] The period of His Advent had been announced by Daniel;[2] and the actual date of its occurrence at once illustrated and confirmed the prophetic intimation. Though the arts and sciences flourished, the aspect of society might have convinced any intelligent observer that the world required "a teacher sent from God." The superstitions of the heathen had become almost effete; licentiousness was prevalent; vice was daily becoming more unscrupulous; and philosophy, after centuries of discussion, had failed to produce any moral reform. The Jews themselves were chiefly noted for their pride, hypocrisy, turbulence, and selfishness; and, as they were widely scattered all over the East and

[1] Gal. iv. 4.   [2] Dan. ix. 24-27.

West, their ritual—intended for a people who could travel three times every year to Jerusalem—was no longer adapted to their condition.

The Divine Being who now sojourned among men derived no factitious importance from wealth or social position. He was the reputed son of a poor mechanic; He never studied in any great school of philosophy or literature; and the associates of His youth were all persons in humble circumstances. But real greatness is revealed by the light of its own excellence. His holy character, His marvellous wisdom, and His mighty works, made Him known as the Redeemer prefigured in so many ceremonies and described in so many prophecies. He quickly excited attention far beyond the boundaries of His native country. "His fame went throughout all Syria: and they brought unto Him all sick people that were taken with divers diseases and torments, and those which were possessed with devils, and those which were lunatic, and those that had the palsy, and He healed them."[1]

The miracles of Christ were distinguished alike by their number, their variety, their utility, and their splendour. He changed water into wine; He opened the eyes of the blind; He walked upon the waves of the sea; and He raised the dead. His keenest assailants were to be met with in the synagogues; and yet He there exhibited some of His most astonishing displays of divine power,[2] and thus submitted His credentials to the severest test of adverse criticism. In cases where vast multitudes were congregated, each individual had positive evidence of the presence of supernatural agency. When five thousand men were fed on five barley loaves and two small fishes, every guest could testify to the bounty of which he had shared.

Our Lord was crucified in the reign of the Emperor Tiberius; and yet several Pagan and Jewish writers who flourished shortly afterwards take scarcely any notice of His career. Tacitus, the Roman historian, makes but one allusion to Him,[3] and that merely incidentally; a single passage respecting Him which appears in Josephus[4] has been suspected of interpolation; and Philo the Jew, who was his contemporary, never even mentions His name in any of his numerous works still extant. Nor is

[1] Matt. iv. 24.
[2] Matt. xii. 9, 10, 13; Mark i. 23-26.
[3] *Annal.* xv. 44.
[4] *Antiq.* xviii. 3, § 3.

this silence extraordinary. Though Christ's ministry produced an immense sensation, He was known chiefly to the common people; for few persons of rank or station cared to come within the circle of His personal influence. Jewish and Gentile writers were disposed to ignore His existence; as they knew that, if they recorded any of His acts, they would be adding to the reputation of a personage whose followers they despised and whose doctrines they pronounced foolishness.

The four Evangelists, each of whom has supplied memorials of the life of Jesus, treat chiefly of His birth and death, of His discourses and miracles. They say nothing of His personal appearance, and little either of His youthful history or His earthly relatives. But their reports of His sermons and conversations are frequent and circumstantial. His instructions shed a new and glorious light on the theology of the Old Testament; whilst His manner of teaching was so dignified, so impressive, and so masterly, as at once to secure the confidence and to excite the wonder of His hearers. "The people were astonished at His doctrine; for He taught them as one having authority, and not as the scribes."[1]

The public life of Christ extends over about three years. He itinerated meanwhile throughout nearly all Palestine; but the towns and cities of Galilee appear to have enjoyed the largest share of His ministrations. As His end approached He was often found in the neighbourhood of Jerusalem, where He was specially exposed to the malice of the chief priests and Pharisees. At length, by "the determinate counsel and foreknowledge of God," He fell into their hands; and, after a hasty trial, was put to death on the Cross.

The Evangelists enter with much minuteness into the details of the Crucifixion. How many predictions did it fulfil! How many types did it illustrate! The passion of Christ was a transaction of momentous import. On Him was laid "the iniquity of us all." Inanimate nature seemed to participate in the travail of the illustrious victim; for, when Jesus hung on the accursed tree, the earth trembled and the sun hid its face. The scene at Calvary excited intense interest among the inhabitants of Heaven, as a new and stupendous display of the Divine perfections was there exhibited. The Apostle Paul speaks of the

[1] Matt. vii. 28, 29.

doctrine sealed by the death of the Great Sacrifice as the key-stone of the Gospel. "We preach," says he, "Christ crucified, unto the Jews a stumbling-block, and unto the Greeks foolishness; but unto them which are called, both Jews and Greeks, Christ the power of God, and the wisdom of God."[1]

CHAPTER II.

THE APOSTLES, THE EVANGELISTS, AND THE PRIMITIVE PREACHERS.

"AFTER that, in the wisdom of God, the world by wisdom knew not God, it pleased God by the foolishness of preaching to save them that believe."[2] The Gospel is the instrument divinely appointed for the regeneration of the world; and it can always be most efficiently promulgated by oral communication. At a time when printing was unknown, the human voice was the only available means of disseminating knowledge among the masses of society. Our Lord assiduously applied Himself to the ministry of the Word; and we are told accordingly that, when He commenced His public career, He "went about all Galilee, teaching in their synagogues, and preaching the Gospel of the Kingdom."[3] Fully aware of the importance of oral instruction, He set apart, first the Twelve, and afterwards the Seventy, to proclaim the great Salvation.

The Founder of our religion was accustomed to teach by typical acts, as well as to speak in parables; and various valuable moral lessons are inculcated by His appointment of the Twelve and the Seventy. The Twelve, in the first instance, were required to confine their labours to "the lost sheep of the house of Israel:"[4] the Seventy, who were subsequently chosen, were commanded to take a wider range, and to go before their Master "into every city and place whither He Himself would come."[5] Our Lord addressed Himself to Samaritans and Gentiles, as well as Jews; and indicated, thus early, that the blessings He dispensed were not to be limited to those hitherto known as the chosen people. According to a tradition then current, and apparently sanctioned

---

[1] 1 Cor. i. 23, 24.   [2] 1 Cor. i. 21.   [3] Matt. iv. 23.
[4] Matt. x. 6.   [5] Luke x. 1.

by certain statements in the Pentateuch,[1] the inhabitants of the earth, after the dispersion at Babel, were divided into seventy nations speaking seventy languages; and whilst the Twelve were the representatives of God's favour to the twelve tribes of Israel, the Seventy symbolized His regard to the whole human race. This arrangement likewise points significantly to the quarter where evangelical charity should first reveal itself. As our Lord sent apostles to His own countrymen before He appointed missionaries to others, He has thus taught us that the condition of those to whom we are more nearly related has the prior claim on our attention and sympathy.

Whilst the Seventy are mentioned only once in the New Testament, the Twelve are again and again presented to our notice. Though we know little of their individual history after their final departure from Jerusalem, it is evident that they must have pursued their labours with singular industry and success; for, long before the fall of the holy city in A.D. 70, some seeds of evangelical truth had been scattered in almost every part of the Roman Empire.[2] But the heralds of mercy were not permitted to preach without disturbance. About A.D. 34 a storm of persecution burst on the mother Church of Christendom: it commenced with the martyrdom of Stephen,[3] a zealous deacon; and so intense was its violence that the disciples in the Jewish metropolis were obliged abruptly to withdraw from the scene of peril, and to disperse themselves all over Palestine. Ten years afterwards, the Apostle James, the brother of John, was put to death at Jerusalem:[4] and Peter, who was thrown into confinement, escaped only by the intervention of a miracle. Meanwhile a new and distinguished convert had joined the missionary band; for Saul, who was also called Paul, a learned Jew, had entered on his labours as the apostle of the Gentiles. This devoted man continued for thirty years to exert himself with amazing energy in propagating the Gospel.

Tradition reports that some of the apostles travelled far into the East; and, according to a writer of the third century, Thomas laboured in Parthia, and Andrew in Scythia.[5] After having

---

[1] Gen. x. 31, 32. See *Ancient Church*, period i. sec. i. ch. 3. May there not be an allusion to this in Deut. xxxii. 8? See Gen. xlvi. 27; Deut. x. 22; and Ex. i. 5. See also Hippolytus, *Refutation of all Heresies*, book x. chap. xxvi.
[2] Rom. i. 8; Col. i. 6. [3] Acts vii. 59. [4] Acts xii. 2. [5] Origen in *Genesim*.

planted Christian churches in Syria and Asia Minor, Paul passed over into Europe and visited the chief cities of Greece. He was subsequently sent a prisoner from Cæsarea to Rome, where he recovered his liberty, probably about A.D. 63. On his release, he fulfilled his long-cherished intention of going into Spain; but the Neronian persecution exposed him to fresh dangers; and, about A.D. 66, he suffered martyrdom in the imperial city. Peter was crucified, about A.D. 67, in the same capital. Philip survived the overthrow of Jerusalem, and died at Hierapolis. John, who lived to extreme old age, finished his career at Ephesus about A.D. 100.

The evangelists mentioned in the New Testament[1] were ordained missionaries trained for the ministry by the apostles themselves, and then sent out by them to preach and organize churches. To this class belonged Timothy—who was requested by Paul on one occasion to oppose false teachers at Ephesus;[2] and Titus—who was left for a time in Crete to make arrangements for the erection of elderships in the cities of that island.[3] In all the Christian societies established by the founders of the Church a local ministry was instituted;[4] and the elders who laboured "in the word and doctrine" occupied the most influential and honourable position.[5]

The apostles, evangelists, and primitive preachers were supported either at their own expense or by the contributions of the faithful. To provide the means of subsistence Paul wrought at the trade of a tent-maker; and that his motives, in a money-making mart, might be above suspicion, he absolutely refused, when on a mission to their city, to receive remuneration from the rich Corinthians.[6] Whilst the apostles declare that those "who preach the gospel should live of the gospel,"[7] they wisely avoid entering into details as to the precise mode or standard of compensation. The early preachers were, no doubt, supported generally by those among whom they ministered; but they were sometimes sustained by the generosity of distant brethren;[8] and there were probably cases not a few in which they were content to labour gratuitously.

The miraculous powers bestowed on the early Christian minis-

---

[1] Acts xxi. 8; Eph. iv. 11; 2 Tim. iv. 5.   [2] 1 Tim. i. 3.
[3] Titus i. 5.   [4] Acts xiv. 23.   [5] 1 Tim. v. 17.
[6] 1 Cor. ix. 12; 2 Cor. xii. 13.   [7] 1 Cor. ix. 14.   [8] 2 Cor. xi. 9.

ters furnished corroborative proofs of their divine mission, and induced many to take a deep interest in their message. Who would not listen with eager curiosity to men able to heal the most inveterate maladies by their touch, and to confer supernatural endowments by the imposition of their hands? Of the extraordinary gifts of the apostolic age that of "divers kinds of tongues" was not the least remarkable. One hundred languages were spoken in the Roman world; and as, with very few exceptions, the first preachers were persons of but little education, the ease with which they could address natives of various regions in their vernacular dialects must have excited much astonishment. Under such auspices no wonder that the Gospel spread with amazing rapidity; and that Paul could assert, several years before his death, that it was known throughout the vast territories subject to the Empire of the Cæsars.[1]

The diversity of languages is one of the evils inherited by our fallen humanity. The stream of knowledge, instead of flowing freely over all the earth, is thus often interrupted; and years must be employed in removing even a few of the barriers which stop the current. But, as the building of Babel led to the confusion of tongues and the dispersion of mankind, the building of the Church promotes the intercourse of nations, and the establishment of a universal brotherhood. The supernatural endowments imparted to the disciples after the Ascension foreshadowed this consummation. The Scriptures, translated into all languages, shall yet form a bond of union for men of every kindred and nation; and the apostles, in their writings, addressing themselves to the whole earth, shall renew the scenes of Pentecost, when "Parthians, and Medes, and Elamites, and the dwellers in Mesopotamia, and in Judea, and Cappadocia, in Pontus and Asia, Phrygia, and Pamphylia, in Egypt, and in the parts of Libya about Cyrene, and strangers of Rome, Jews and proselytes, Cretes, and Arabians," heard them speak in their tongues "the wonderful works of God."

[1] Col. i. 6.

CHAPTER III.

THE EARLY FATHERS.

THE title "The Fathers" is applied, by way of distinction, to the authors of the ancient Church. Though used with considerable latitude, and given often to theologians of the middle ages, it is commonly appropriated by Protestants to the ecclesiastical writers of the first six centuries.[1] Among these are a considerable number of individuals eminent for piety, talent, and erudition.

Many of the works of the fathers of the first three centuries have been lost; and many extant writings attributed to the same period are of little value. The Apostolic Canons, the Apostolic Constitutions, the Ignatian Epistles,[2] the Clementine Homilies, and various other documents ascribed to the apostles or their immediate successors, are apocryphal; and though unquestionably of high antiquity none of them appeared before the third century. The tract known as *The Shepherd of Hermas* —a fanciful composition, in one part of which the Church is presented under the similitude of a tower—was probably written about the middle of the century preceding: and the *Epistle of Barnabas*—a letter remarkable for its allegorical interpretations —may be dated a few years earlier.

The most ancient patristic memorial in existence is an epistle from the Church of Rome to the Church of Corinth, drawn up about A.D. 96 by *Clement*, then senior pastor of the Christians of the Italian metropolis. The Church of Corinth was at that time disturbed by unruly spirits who endeavoured to render their co-religionists disaffected towards certain members of the presbytery: and the object of this communication was the restoration of peace to the distracted community. The author is one of the writers who are said to have been taught by the apostles, and

---

[1] Roman Catholic divines include among the Fathers those who lived down to the thirteenth century. They distinguish between Church *Fathers* and Church *authors*, including in the former class only the most eminent writers of undoubted orthodoxy. See Herzog's *Encyclopedia*, art. *Church Fathers*.

[2] That these epistles are entirely spurious, see *The Ancient Church*, period ii. sect. ii. chaps. ii. iii. See also, in the Appendix to this volume, a remarkable letter from the late Rev. Dr. Cureton.

who have in consequence been called *Apostolic Fathers*. To the same class belongs *Polycarp*, pastor of Smyrna, who, about the middle of the second century,[1] wrote a letter to the Philippians which is still preserved. This epistle, like that of Clement to the Corinthians, abounds with quotations from Scripture, and represents the churches as under presbyterial government. The Epistle to Diognetus, the production of some unknown author, and perhaps of nearly the same date as the Epistle of Polycarp, exhibits a very favourable specimen of the theology of the early Church.

JUSTIN MARTYR is the most ancient father who has left behind him works of such extent as to make a volume. In his youth he was addicted to the study of the heathen philosophy; but he found no satisfaction in its speculations; and it was not until his attention had been turned to the sacred Scriptures that he attained the peace which he had been long endeavouring to secure. His extant publications are his two Apologies addressed to the Emperors, and his Dialogue with Trypho the Jew. In his Apologies he pleads the cause of the oppressed Christians against their heathen persecutors: in his Dialogue he upholds the claims of the Gospel in opposition to Judaism. Whilst his writings bear testimony to the sufferings of the early disciples, they also throw considerable light on the doctrine and worship of the Church of the former half of the second century. This good man earned the surname of Martyr in A.D. 165, when he was put to death at Rome for the profession of Christianity.

IRENÆUS of Lyons wrote towards the close of the second century; and his treatise *Against Heresies*, in five books, illustrates the mode of argumentation then employed when dealing with the sects of the Gnostics. But no author who had yet appeared could wield the pen with such ability as TERTULLIAN of Carthage —who flourished about the beginning of the third century. He is said to have been originally a lawyer, and subsequently a presbyter of the Church of Rome. Taking umbrage at the treatment he received from the clergy of the great capital, he returned to Africa, his native country—where he spent the greater part of his life. His works, which are numerous, treat of a variety of subjects doctrinal and practical; and display much acuteness, learning, and eloquence. But his spirit is ungenial; and, when

[1] As to the date of this Epistle, see *The Ancient Church*, pp. 363, 498.

contending against heretics, he manifests something very like the acerbity of personal hatred.[1] Strange to say, he at length turned Montanist, and thus became obnoxious to the denunciations which he has himself fulminated so frequently against the opponents of the Catholic faith. He is supposed to have died at an advanced age about A.D. 230.

In ancient times the citizens of the Egyptian metropolis were noted for their intellectual cultivation; and, as persons of education began to pass over to the Church when the Gospel was introduced among them, it was soon found necessary to establish an institute in which such candidates for baptism could be prepared for the ordinance by some competent instructor. CLEMENT OF ALEXANDRIA, who was at the head of this catechetical school in the beginning of the third century, is the author of several works which attest his literary accomplishments. Whilst his *Pædagogue*, his *Stromata*, and other publications, supply evidence as to the state of theology in his age, they also contain many incidental observations illustrative of the manners and customs of the Christians about the same period. But his spiritual taste was sadly vitiated by his study of the heathen philosophy; and his tendency to indulge in allegorical interpretations renders him an unsafe guide as an expositor of the Scriptures. HIPPOLYTUS of Portus, near Rome, the contemporary of Clement, was a father of a different type. His recently discovered treatise, *Against all Heresies*, bears a remarkable resemblance to that of Irenæus on the same subject, and displays his uncompromising zeal for orthodoxy. He arraigns even Zephyrinus and Callistus, two of the early bishops of Rome, as holding unsound views in reference to the Trinity. He maintained that those who had lapsed into gross sin should never again be restored to ecclesiastical communion; and closed his career by a decisive proof of the depth of his convictions, for he died a martyr in the reign of the Emperor Maximin.

By far the most voluminous of the fathers of the first three centuries is ORIGEN. He was a native of Alexandria; when very young he gave promise of extraordinary genius, and the high hopes

---

[1] Thus when speaking of the Gnostic Marcion, who maintained that our Lord had no real body, he says—"You may, I assure you, more easily find *a man born without a heart or without brains, like Marcion himself,* than without a body, like Marcion's Christ." *Against Marcion,* book iv. chap. x.

The Early Fathers.

entertained respecting him were in due time fully realized. His father, Leonides, suffered martyrdom when his son was only seventeen years of age; the family property was confiscated; and Origen, the eldest of seven children, was obliged to commence the struggles of life under circumstances of peculiar embarrassment. But he was quite equal to the difficulties of his position, and his wonderful facility in acquiring and communicating knowledge speedily attracted the attention of all classes of his fellow-citizens. Though the greater number of his works are now lost, and a large portion of those which remain exist only in a Latin version, his extant publications are more extensive than those of all the other fathers of the first three centuries combined. On his *Hexapla*—an edition of the Old Testament containing the Hebrew original, with a selection of the Greek versions, including the Septuagint—he expended prodigious labour, and occupied much of his time for eight-and-twenty years; but only a few fragments of this amazing monument of his industry and erudition are now preserved. His most valuable extant production is his treatise in reply to Celsus, a heathen philosopher who wrote against Christianity in the time of the Antonines. Origen was instructed by Clemens Alexandrinus, and the taste for allegorical exposition which distinguished the preceptor disfigures the writings of the illustrious pupil. His intercourse with Ammonius Saccas—an Alexandrian teacher who endeavoured to show that all systems of religion and philosophy contained the elements of truth—exercised a still more injurious influence on his mind; and, in his attempts to reconcile the theology of Scripture with the doctrines of Plato, he involves himself in mysticism, and lapses into dangerous errors. The fame of Origen as a scholar attracted the notice of persons of the most elevated rank; and when Julia Mammæa, the mother of the reigning sovereign Alexander Severus, invited him to visit her at Antioch, he was conducted to that city by an imperial escort. He practised extreme abstinence, and for many years was accustomed to walk barefoot. When far advanced in life he patiently submitted to torture rather than renounce the faith; and at length, at the age of seventy, died at Tyre in A.D. 254.

When Origen was leaving the stage of public life, another father who has since acquired great celebrity was beginning to command attention. This was CYPRIAN of Carthage. As a professor of rhetoric he had occupied a highly respectable position in the capital of the Proconsular Africa, and, when advanced considerably beyond the meridian of life, he created a deep sensation by embracing Christianity. The new convert was hailed by the Church as an important accession; and about two years afterwards—on the occurrence of a vacancy in the bishop's chair—was raised by the enthusiastic suffrages of the people to the episcopal dignity. At this time heresy and sectarianism were rife, and the Catholic hierarchy, which had been gradually acquiring strength, was regarded as the grand bulwark against their encroachments. Cyprian carried its pretensions to a loftier pitch than that to which it had hitherto aspired: he spoke of it as a divine institute, and he denounced the adversaries of the bishop as the enemies of Christ. His aristocratic *hauteur* was evidently gratified by the despotic authority which it challenged; and though he admitted that it had originated at Rome, he imagined that our Lord, in His address to Peter,[1] had in some way endorsed its credentials. Cyprian kept up an extensive correspondence; and many of his productions, including a large number of his letters, are still extant. His style is forcible and eloquent, and he evidently felt powerfully the value of the Gospel; but his theological training was exceedingly imperfect, and his views of divine truth are often jejune, unsatisfactory, or extravagant. After having filled the see of Carthage about ten years, he died a martyr in the Valerian persecution in A.D. 258.

Some other fathers of the first three centuries might here be mentioned, such as *Minucius Felix*, *Gregory Thaumaturgus*, and *Arnobius;* but their contributions to ecclesiastical literature are not extensive, and they exerted comparatively little influence. Enough has been stated to give an idea of the general character of the early writers, and to demonstrate the folly of recognizing them as arbiters of our faith or practice. Many of them were brought up in heathenism, and were not remarkable either for scholarship or grasp of intellect; whilst some who were distinguished for mental culture were so addicted to the study of the pagan philosophy, that the truth, as presented by them, is miserably adulterated. Almost all the fathers of the first three centuries were ignorant of Hebrew; and Origen himself admitted in his old age that he was indifferently acquainted with that lan-

[1] Matt. xvi. 18.

guage.[1] The gross blunders committed by these writers seem to have been providentially designed to teach all open to conviction that they cannot be safely followed. They confound the Scriptures, quoting one book for another,[2] mistake the position of places and the meaning of words, narrate fables for history,[3] and pervert the sacred text by the most foolish and outlandish commentaries. The author of the *Epistle of Barnabas* tells us that the number 318—the amount of Abraham's servants[4]—is a type of Christ, and proceeds, by a most whimsical process, to make good his interpretation. Tertullian maintains that the soul is corporeal; and Origen teaches that the stars are animated beings. "I am aware," says the last-named writer, "that certain critics, in explaining the words used in the Gospel by the Saviour, '*My soul* is sorrowful even unto death,' have interpreted them of *the apostles*, whom He termed His *soul*, as being better than the rest of His body."[5] The learned Alexandrian apparently sanctions this extraordinary exposition.

Surrounded by so many evidences of fallibility, it is consolatory to turn to the Bible, shining from generation to generation with a light of the purest radiance. All the experience of ages, and all the discoveries of science, only reveal more distinctly the wisdom of this wonderful volume. Here there is nothing weak, nothing puerile, nothing that is not good to the use of edifying. As it is designed for the guidance of the whole human family, it is adapted to the wants of men of every clime and of every age; and whilst it instructs the peasant it exalts the spirit of the philosopher. The immense difference between the writings of the New Testament and the works of the early fathers must be apparent to the most cursory reader. "All Scripture is given by inspiration of God; and is profitable for doctrine, for re-

---

[1] See his *Treatise against Celsus*, i. 25.
[2] Justin Martyr, *Apol.* ii. and *Dialogue with Trypho*.
[3] See, for example, the story of the phœnix in the *Epistle of Clemens Romanus*.
[4] "For the Scripture says that Abraham circumcised 318 men of his house. But what, therefore, was the mystery that was made known to him? Mark first the 18, and next the 300. For the numerical letters of 10 and 8 are [the Greek capitals] IH. And these denote Jesus ('Ιησοῦς). And because the cross was that by which we were to find grace, therefore he adds 300, the note of which is [the Greek capital] T [the figure of His cross]. Wherefore by two letters he signified Jesus, and by the third His cross."—§. 9. See Genesis xiv. 14; xvii. 23.
[5] Origen, *De Principiis*, ii. 8.

proof, for correction, for instruction in righteousness; that the man of God may be perfect, thoroughly furnished unto all good works."[1]

CHAPTER IV.

THE PERSECUTIONS OF THE CHURCH.

THE New Testament Church appeared among men under circumstances very different from those which marked the settlement of the Israelites in Canaan. The chosen people entered the land of promise sword in hand, destroyed the inhabitants, and took possession of the depopulated territory. They were the executioners of the Lord's vengeance against a race who had filled up the measure of their iniquities; and, being themselves a typical nation, their very laws indicated truths beyond the range of their literal significance. As they were secured in the enjoyment of their fair and fertile country should they continue to obey their divine code of regulations, all violations, either of its ceremonial or its moral enactments, were visited with condign punishment. The Sabbath-breaker, the blasphemer, the adulterer, and the idolater, were all to be put to death. The precepts of Jehovah were the law of the land, and every transgressor was to be dealt with as a traitor who imperilled the well-being of the commonwealth. But Christ came, not to invest His people with the possession of a temporal kingdom, but to provide for them an eternal inheritance; and He employs for their subjugation, not the weapons of the warrior or the arm of secular authority, but "the word of the truth of the Gospel." This divine word is "mighty through God to the pulling down of strongholds, casting down imaginations, and every high thing that exalteth itself against the knowledge of God, and bringing into captivity every thought to the obedience of Christ."

But though the Gospel seeks to make way simply by appealing to the understanding and the heart, and though its reception is eminently calculated to promote even the temporal happiness of men, it at once encountered the most bitter and severe opposition. Whilst it immediately endangered the emoluments of all who derived a maintenance either directly

[1] 2 Tim. iii. 16.

or indirectly from the established superstitions, its ultimate success implied a change in the whole framework of society. The multitudes, who were enslaved to the grosser vices, were offended by its pure and spiritual requirements; and the thinking few, who valued themselves on their philosophical knowledge, were provoked by its denunciation of the folly of their speculations. Among its most implacable enemies were the unbelieving Jews, who could not brook the thought that their divinely-instituted ritual was ever to be abolished, or that the son of a carpenter was the Saviour of the world. Though their political power was now small, they exerted it to the utmost against the disciples of Christ; and, when they could not succeed by the ordinary processes of law, they had recourse to sedition and tumultuary violence. The intrepid Stephen, one of the seven deacons, soon fell a victim to their rage; and many other instances of their intense antipathy to the faithful are recorded in the Acts of the Apostles.[1] The Roman law looked with jealousy on everything like a new religion, for the rulers of the world apprehended that the supporters of a novel sect either concealed treasonable designs, or might otherwise disturb the settled course of their government. As prudent politicians, they saw the expediency of permitting each nation under their dominion to adhere to its ancient worship; but they had no correct views of the rights of conscience or of the equity of religious toleration. For a time the Christians were confounded with the Jews, and as such they escaped molestation from the Roman authorities; but when their real position, as a distinct religious community, became generally known, they soon experienced a change of treatment. For upwards of thirty years after the passion of our Lord, they were exposed to no imperial persecution. At length, in A.D. 64, they became obnoxious to the cruelty of Nero, who in a fit of recklessness had set fire to Rome, and who sought to escape the odium of the transaction by imputing it to the Christians. The disciples were to be found in considerable numbers in the great metropolis, and the horrid torments inflicted on them by the monster who oppressed the Roman world have been described in the spirit of commiseration even by a heathen historian.[2] They were put to death on the cross; they were disguised in the skins of wild beasts, and then dogs were let loose upon them to tear

[1] Acts xii. 2, 3; xvii. 5; xviii. 12. [2] Tacitus, *Annal.* xv. 44.

them to pieces; when their bodies were smeared with pitch, or covered with other inflammable matter, a torch was applied to them, and thus, during the night, the imperial gardens were lighted up by the flames which issued from the expiring victims. This "fiery trial" of the capital was extended to the provinces; and during the closing years of the reign of Nero, the disciples, throughout all his territories, groaned under the pressure of persecution. At his death they experienced a temporary respite; but, under Domitian, their sufferings were renewed; and towards the end of the reign of that suspicious and bloody sovereign, many of them endured martyrdom. The Apostle John was banished to Patmos,—a rocky island off the coast of Asia Minor,—and there, as he listened to the waves dashing in their might against the shore, he enjoyed sweet fellowship with Him whose voice is sublime and awful, "as the sound of many waters."[1]

After the demise of Domitian the Church again enjoyed peace, and in the beginning of the second century its members quickly increased. So rapid was the progress of the Gospel in Bithynia, that, as appears from the testimony of Pliny, the victims to be offered to the gods found few purchasers, and the pagan temples were comparatively deserted.[2] The votaries of superstition took the alarm; the faithful were dragged before the tribunals of the magistrates, and compelled, under pain of death, to abjure their principles. Though, according to a law promulgated by the Emperor Trajan, they were not to be inquisitively sought after, and though the zeal of persecution was thus to some extent restrained, the profession of the truth was still illegal, and its adherents continued to suffer from the attacks of unfriendly governors. Parties interested in the support of the heathen worship sometimes stirred up the mob to acts of violence; and when the people were assembled in vast multitudes at the public games or spectacles, the cry of "The Christians to the Lions!" was frequently the prelude to scenes of martyrdom. The Emperor Hadrian issued a rescript in which he strongly discountenanced these dangerous ebullitions of popular fanaticism; and provincial rulers were in consequence obliged to resist the rude demands of excited crowds; but, notwithstanding, the condition of the disciples was far from comfortable. Destitute of any legal protec-

[1] Rev. i. 15.   [2] Pliny to Trajan, *Epist.* x. 96.

tion, they were liable to the numberless annoyances and perils which selfishness, malice, or bigotry could create. A debtor could escape payment if he required the Christian creditor to attest his claim by an appeal to the gods; the husband could cast off his wife if she belonged to the Church; the pagan priest convicted any citizen of a capital offence, if he proved him to be a professor of the faith; and an enemy could gratify his thirst for revenge by supplying evidence that a neighbour, against whom he cherished a grudge, was connected with the hated brotherhood. Disciples were to be found everywhere; and whilst their proscription kept them in continual jeopardy, it also generated a feeling of distrust which pervaded almost the whole of the complicated network of society.

Antoninus Pius treated the Christians with forbearance; but his successor Marcus Aurelius, though otherwise an exemplary sovereign, has acquired an unenviable reputation as one of their early persecutors. This prince was a lover of literature, and a devoted student of the Stoic philosophy; yet it never seems to have occurred to him that a Roman emperor was not lord of the conscience, and that some of his poor subjects might understand religion better than himself. The unflinching courage with which the disciples persisted in their adherence to the Gospel only roused his indignation, for he ascribed it to blind and conceited obstinacy. The law of Trajan discouraged all attempts to hunt them down; but Marcus Aurelius gave encouragement to spies and informers; and when the unoffending believers were entangled in his toils, he laboured with hellish ingenuity to force them to recantation. Formerly, when an individual appeared before a magistrate and acknowledged himself a Christian, he was at once condemned to death: now, torture was employed to induce him to withdraw his confession. Humanity shudders at the various modes of torment brought into requisition. Sometimes a delicate female was tossed and torn by a wild bull until ready to expire, and then offered life on the condition of apostasy: sometimes attempts were made to starve the resolute into conformity: and in other cases a prisoner was placed on a heated iron chair and threatened with being roasted alive should he not renounce the Gospel. A contemporary account of the persecution of the Churches of Lyons and Vienne in Gaul in A.D. 177 has survived the oblivion in which many similar records have been buried;[1] and this memorial, which supplies a specimen of the treatment of the faithful in the reign of Marcus Aurelius, contains some of the most revolting details of human suffering to be found in the annals of Christian martyrdom.

Several of the Emperors who flourished towards the end of the second or beginning of the third century were not unfriendly to the Christians. Even the brutal Commodus was indulgent; and though Septimius Severus became ultimately hostile, he evinced a not unfavourable disposition in the commencement of his reign. Alexander Severus admired some of the lessons of the Gospel, and among the statues in his private chapel had a representation of our Saviour;[2] but he thus acted merely in the spirit of an eclectic philosopher who was at liberty to regard Jesus as one of the hierarchy of heaven. Maximin the Thracian was a persecutor. His reign was however brief, and his severity fell chiefly on those brethren who had been distinguishe by the favour of his imperial predecessor. Philip the Arabi. gave the faithful such decided encouragement that he has been described, though erroneously, as one of themselves, and designated the first Christian Emperor.

In the middle of the third century a persecution of unusual violence burst on the disciples. Decius was no sooner seated on the throne than he declared war against the Gospel; the officers of government throughout all the empire were instigated to severity; and the most sanguinary and systematic effort ever yet made by its enemies threatened the ruin of the Church. The pastors were specially marked out as victims: and many of them, including Fabian, bishop of Rome, Babylas, bishop of Antioch, and Alexander, bishop of Jerusalem, met a bloody death. Every one was required to sacrifice to the gods; and whoever refused was consigned to capital punishment, banishment, or slavery. So great was the number of the *lapsed*, or the apostates, who, on the return of better days, sought readmission to communion, that it was found necessary to appoint a special functionary, called *the Penitentiary*, to examine their respective cases, and to deal with them individually according to the rules

---

[1] See Eusebius, v. 1.

[2] This is the first image of Christ mentioned in ancient history. The early disciples altogether condemned the making of any such likeness.

of ecclesiastical discipline. The reign of Decius was abruptly terminated by his defeat and death in the Gothic war; but his successor Gallus continued to harass the Church; and though Valerian, who next assumed the purple, at first seemed disposed to act with leniency, he soon changed his course, and commenced a persecution. At length in A.D. 260, the Emperor Gallienus issued an edict of toleration, under the shelter of which the disciples long enjoyed repose.

The Emperor Aurelian was resolved to revive the penal laws against the Christians; and had actually prepared an edict for their oppression; when, in A.D. 275, death relieved them from impending disasters. For many years of the reign of Diocletian they were undisturbed; and had it not been for the evil influence of his son-in-law Galerius, he would have continued to pursue the policy of forbearance; but the importunity of that stern bigot in the end prevailed; and, in A.D. 303, he was induced to give his sanction to a general persecution. This visitation, which extended with occasional interruptions over ten years, was, in point of ferocity, duration, and loss of life, the most formidable of all the calamities ever yet inflicted on the disciples by the hand of imperial injustice. When it commenced, Diocletian was in Nicomedia; and the prompt demolition of the great Christian church of that city announced the inauguration of the reign of terror. The Scriptures, wherever found, were seized and destroyed; the pastors were imprisoned; the houses of worship were thrown down; those who held government appointments and who refused to repudiate the Gospel were deprived of their places and emoluments; and even slaves who remained Christians forfeited the privilege of manumission. In the Western part of the empire, under the government, first of Constantius Chlorus, and afterwards of his son Constantine, the edicts were not rigorously enforced; and the disciples in that quarter escaped comparatively unscathed: but in the East their sufferings were extreme. When other expedients failed, the gates of the cities were closed; every individual was called on by name to sacrifice to the gods, and presented with the alternative of compliance or martyrdom. Death in its most appalling forms awaited those who continued faithful. Some, after enduring dreadful tortures, were left to pine away in lingering agony; some were thrown into the sea; some were roasted alive; some were crucified; and some were torn to pieces by machinery. But all these inflictions did not break down the constancy of the disciples: the growing power of Constantine, and his increasing regard for them, gave them seasonable encouragement; the persecutors themselves became weary of the work of butchery; and, in A.D. 313, an imperial edict placed all the Christians throughout the Roman world under the shield of an authorized toleration.

The persecutions of the early Church form one of the most prominent features in its history. Long before the reign of Constantine its members, in various parts of the empire, constituted a body numerically formidable; and yet it does not appear that the cruel treatment they experienced from the state ever tempted them to waver in their allegiance. They never rose up in rebellion. They vanquished their oppressors literally by patience and prayer. As they were yet only a minority of the whole population, and without military organization or equipments, every attempt to obtain a redress of their wrongs by insurrection must have signally failed; and defeat would have prejudiced their cause and aggravated their sufferings.[1] The atrocities to which they were exposed were most discouraging; but the honours lavished on the martyrs by the Church animated the fortitude of many who might otherwise have recoiled from the fatal ordeal. Tickets of recommendation from brethren doomed to die for their religion, when presented by *the lapsed*, at once secured readmission to communion; the anniversaries of the days on which the martyrs suffered were devoutly celebrated; and the faithful in the hour of agony were described as "washing away their own iniquities."[2] No wonder, under such circumstances, that some fanatically courted death by appearing spontaneously before the tribunals of the magistrates and avowing their Christianity.

By deterring many from entering the Church, persecution contributed to purify its fellowship. The insincere and the time-serving did not care to join a society with which they

[1] They certainly did not hold the doctrine of passive obedience. Origen declares that "it is not irrational to form associations in opposition to existing laws, if done for the sake of the truth." He adds that, "those persons do well who enter into a secret association to put to death a tyrant who has seized on the liberties of the state." Origen, *Against Celsus*, i. 1.

[2] Tertullian, *De Pudicitia*, c. 22.

might be obliged to maintain their connection at the peril of their lives. But the sufferings of the early disciples made a deep impression on their contemporaries, and powerfully advanced the cause of the Gospel. The heathen in general had no strong attachment to their superstitions, so that they readily passed from one form of idolatry to another; and they were overwhelmed with amazement as they saw the Christians dying for their faith, or heard them singing hymns of praise on the eve of martyrdom. Whilst every persecution drove away from the brotherhood multitudes of the timid and the temporizing, it enlisted new bands of earnest disciples. On the return of better days the lapsed sought restoration to the position they had forfeited, and thus a time of trial was commonly the precursor of a season of abundant enlargement. Tertullian could boast that the blood of Christians was "their harvest seed."[1] The Diocletian persecution—the most frightful and protracted attack ever made on the Church—had scarcely passed away, when the tide of prosperity began to flow; and all gazed with wonder as they saw a Christian sovereign seated on the throne of the empire.

CHAPTER V.

THE GROWTH OF THE CHURCH. DOMESTIC AND SOCIAL LIFE OF THE CHRISTIANS.

THE followers of our Lord, immediately after the Ascension, were not confined to the one hundred and twenty assembled in the upper room at Jerusalem. During the preceding forty days of His sojourn on earth, He was "seen"—perhaps in Galilee—"of above five hundred brethren at once;"[2] and it is not improbable that, even at this early period, little groups of His adherents were to be found all over Palestine. But the death of the Master terrified the disciples; and if, in the chief city of Israel, only one hundred and twenty were willing openly to espouse His cause, we may infer that the number of His avowed friends was not yet considerable. The outpouring of the Spirit on the day of Pentecost gave an immense impulse to the Church; and the three thousand converts who were then gathered in were

[1] *Apol.* 50.   [2] 1 Cor. xv. 6.

only the firstfruits of an abundant harvest. The disciples multiplied in Jerusalem greatly; and Christian societies were soon organized throughout all Judea, Galilee, and Samaria. The increase of the brethren beyond the boundaries of the Holy Land began to excite Jewish jealousy even before the conversion of Saul; for that zealot was sent to Damascus with authority from the chief priests to bind all that called on the name of the Lord.[1] At an early date a Christian Church was formed at Antioch, the capital of Syria; soon afterwards the Gospel was proclaimed in the principal towns of Asia Minor; and about A.D. 52, Paul crossed the Ægean Sea, and commenced his European ministry at Philippi. He subsequently preached at Thessalonica, Athens, Corinth, and "round about unto Illyricum."[2] Meanwhile, the truth had found its way to Rome;[3] and, when the Apostle arrived there as a prisoner in A.D. 61, he was permitted to expound it for two whole years in his own hired house to "all that came in unto him."[4] Long previously, others had travelled eastward from the holy city bearing the precious seed of the Word; whilst the evangelist Mark is said to have planted it successfully in the capital of Egypt.

On the release of Paul from his first imprisonment at Rome, he was enabled to fulfil his intention of preaching the Gospel in Spain;[5] but, in a short time, the Neronian persecution interposed, and arrested its advancement. In a few years the death of the tyrant put an end to his oppression; and the fall of Jerusalem, soon afterwards, gave a fresh impetus to the Christian cause. The overthrow of the metropolis of the Israelites had been predicted by our Lord; he had announced it as to occur *in that generation*;[6] the prophecy had been made known throughout the empire in the Gospels of Matthew, Mark, and Luke;[7] and the exact accomplishment of all its details produced a deep and extensive impression. Towards the end of the first century the persecution of Domitian again cast a cloud over the Church; but, as this passed away, the disciples took courage, and proceeded with new zeal and energy to diffuse their principles. In the beginning of the second century their prospects were most hopeful; something like what in modern times has been called a

---

[1] Acts ix. 14.   [2] Rom. xv. 19.   [3] Rom. i. 7, 8.   [4] Acts xxviii. 30.
[5] Rom. xv. 28.   [6] Matt. xxiv. 34; Mark xiii. 30; Luke xxi. 32.
[7] The Gospel of John, written after the event, does not mention it.

revival of religion was experienced; in particular districts the heathen temples were deserted; and the priests trembled as they contemplated the threatened subversion of the established worship. Though persecutions ever and anon attempted to stop the victorious movements of the faith, these terrors created only a temporary suspension of activity; and when they were withdrawn, the Church, with recovered elasticity, moved forward in its triumphant career. Its onward course may be tracked even by the blood of the martyrs. We might have found it difficult to prove that it had numerous adherents in the south of France, in the reign of Marcus Aurelius, did we not possess the record of the sufferings of the Churches of Lyons and Vienne.

The constant intercourse kept up between the imperial city and the provinces supplied facilities for the dissemination of the Gospel; so that, when it had obtained a firm footing at Rome, it was sure soon to find its way from thence throughout the empire. There is clear evidence that the Church of the capital, shortly after the middle of the second century, was flourishing and opulent. It willingly employed a portion of its wealth in assisting needy brethren abroad; its advice was eagerly solicited by surrounding communities; and, about the close of the century, it was strengthened by a large accession of influential converts.[1] Even in times of persecution this Church was not absolutely helpless; for its members obtained shelter in the Catacombs— those vast subterranean labyrinths which still exist under the ecclesiastical metropolis of Italy. Their excavators—the sand-diggers or quarrymen—were, from a very early period, the friends of the disciples; and the officers of government, bewildered amidst their endless mazes, could seldom hope to overtake a Christian fugitive who there sought an asylum. Even in the second century the Catacombs began to be the great cemetery of the Roman Church; and the inscriptions on their earlier tombstones are among the most interesting memorials of antiquity. These inscriptions, still to be seen on their original slabs, and now arranged in the Lapidarian Gallery in the Vatican, ignore prayers for the dead, the worship of Mary, and the doctrine of purgatory.

From Rome, Christianity was conveyed into the Proconsular Africa. Many churches are found there in the beginning of the third century; and a contemporary writer, who was a native of

[1] Euseb. v. 21.

the district, tells the imperial magistrate that its chief city would be decimated should the disciples be proscribed.[1] Carthage was soon known as one of the great centres of Christian influence; among the Churchmen of the west in the reign of Decius its presiding pastor was only second in importance to that of Rome; and on a particular occasion eighty-seven bishops met in it for consultation.[2] In a different quarter of the world, the Gospel had been long before propagated. It is not improbable that it had gained some adherents in England about the close of the apostolic age; and there can be no doubt that it had made considerable progress in the island at the end of the second century. Tertullian, writing a few years afterwards, asserts that "the places of Britain inaccessible to the Romans were subject to Christ;"[3] and though the statement is obviously an exaggeration, it supplies evidence that the new faith had already penetrated into Scotland. Irenæus also speaks of its promulgation among barbarous nations[4]—apparently alluding to those on the outskirts of Roman civilization. In the middle of the third century seven eminent missionaries are said to have introduced it into seven of the principal towns of France;[5] and about the same period it appears to have been preached with success in some parts of Germany. Soon afterwards, the Goths inhabiting Mœsia and Thrace were partially evangelized by ecclesiastics whom they had carried captive in one of their predatory incursions into the Empire. In the East, as early as A.D. 170, a Christian prince reigned over a little state at Edessa in Mesopotamia;[6] and in the following century there were churches in Parthia, Armenia, India, and other oriental countries.

[1] Tertullian, *Ad Scapulam*, 5.
[2] Cyprian. Council of Carthage on the baptism of heretics.
[3] *Adversus Judæos*, 7.   [4] *Adv. Hæres*, lib. i. c. x. § 2.
[5] Gregory of Tours, *Hist. Ecc. Franc.* i. 28.
[6] This is proved by existing coins. See Assemanni *Bibl. Or.* i. 423; Wichelhaus, *de N. T. ver. Syr. Antiq.* l.l. iv. 1850, p. 50. The "Ancient Syriac Documents relative to the earliest establishment of Christianity in Edessa and the neighbouring countries," edited by the late Dr. Cureton (London, 1864), are little better than a mass of legends. Witnesses who describe the Edessians in the apostolic age as keeping "*the festivals of the Church at their proper seasons,*" and continuing "*every day in the vigils of the Church,*" and who represent Fabian, bishop of Rome, who flourished in the third century, as living in the reign of Trajan, clearly attest their own imposture. See these Documents, pp. 16, 63, 71. The Orations of Mar Jacob are probably genuine.

At first the Christians held their religious meetings in private dwellings; and, for a considerable time, they had very few buildings exclusively devoted to social worship. When the profession of the faith was a capital crime, and when those interested in upholding the old superstitions were continually endeavouring to hunt down the disciples, it was not wonderful that they did not wish to obtrude their places of assembly on public observation. But necessity soon compelled them to make permanent provision for their ecclesiastical accommodation; and, in some places, perhaps by purchasing the forbearance of the local magistrates, they at length ventured to erect edifices for the stated celebration of their religious ordinances. In the beginning of the third century these structures were well-known to the heathen; and, shortly afterwards, a decision of the Emperor Alexander Severus, conceding to them a plot of ground for the building of another meeting-house in Rome, must have greatly contributed to their encouragement. The publication of the edict of toleration by Gallienus, in A.D. 260, gave them a still more secure position; and, during the forty years immediately succeeding, their numbers rapidly increased. In many of the great cities the old churches were now taken down, and their places supplied by others at once more elegant and more capacious. About the close of the third century, not a few of the highest officers of government were Christians; the wife of Diocletian and his daughter Valeria are said to have professed the Gospel; the tide even of fashion was almost beginning to turn in favour of the Cross; and the vessels of silver and of gold, employed by some pastors at the administration of the Sacraments, betokened the wealth and prosperity of the faithful.

The rapid spread of Christianity in the face of so many discouragements cannot be ascribed entirely to the miracles by which it was accompanied. These miracles served, no doubt, to awaken attention to the truth and to support its claims: but they gradually disappeared; and, after those on whom the Apostles conferred supernatural gifts had passed away, we have no satisfactory evidence that any one was to be found who could speak with tongues or raise the dead.[1] The exemplary lives of its professors contributed far more than their wonder-working powers to advance its interests. Among its adherents were

[1] See Kaye's *Tertullian*, pp. 98—101.

always some who disgraced their creed; but, as a body, they were elevated far above the rest of society as upright and useful citizens. A system which was known to improve all the relations of life—which made kind husbands and chaste wives, sober parents and dutiful children, honest servants and faithful friends—could not fail to attract the notice of every serious observer. Nor was it difficult to obtain a knowledge of its principles; for the Sacred Books, as well in various versions as in the originals, were soon extensively disseminated. Their doctrines, when candidly examined, exhibited their own credentials, and, by manifestation of the truth, commended themselves to every man's conscience. Like the light of the sun, their excellence could be appreciated by all save those whose eyes were closed against the illumination.

When Christianity appeared in the world, slaves constituted a large proportion of the population of the Empire. Many of these children of oppression were soon brought under the influence of the Gospel, and enrolled as members of the Church. Nor was it strange that they were attracted to a system which revealed to them a God who is "no respecter of persons," and proclaimed a Saviour who can sympathize with those who "labour and are heavy laden." A slave, when transferred to a Christian owner, must have felt his position wonderfully ameliorated. The pagans, no doubt, had their household deities; and religious ceremonies were associated with almost all their domestic arrangements. But paganism produced no improvement on the temper or character; it restrained no furious bursts of passion; and, when any untoward incident disturbed the equanimity of a heathen master, he was ready to give vent to his ill-humour by flagellating alike his slaves and his idols. The Gospel exerted its vital power by renovating the inner man, and by completely changing the tone of social fellowship. The Christian home was the abode of peace, purity, and kindness; the feelings of all the inmates were respected; the servants were treated as heirs of immortality; and the spirit of prayer hallowed the household atmosphere. In the morning, the father gathered his family around him, and commended them to God; the children were taught to pray apart, and to commit portions of the Holy Word to memory;[1] a blessing was sought before meals, and a hymn was often sung as the

[1] See the case of Origen, Euseb. vi. 2.

repast proceeded;[1] after dinner, a passage of Scripture was read, and sometimes made the theme of conversation;[2] and family prayer closed, for the day, the intercourse of the domestic circle.[3]

The dress is frequently an index of the character. It reveals the habits of the wearer, whether slovenly or exact; and guides to a knowledge of his ruling passion, whether vanity, parsimony, or ambition. The early Christians endeavoured to commend their religion by the modesty of their apparel. They did not make themselves singular by assuming any peculiar garb; but they eschewed gaudy colours, sumptuous robes, and expensive ornaments. There were, indeed, among the wealthy members some who still continued to indulge a love of finery and display;[4] but these votaries of fashion were regarded with coldness and suspicion by the more zealous and decided. The brotherhood as a body kept aloof from the heathen spectacles. They could not approve either of the profane rehearsals of the theatre or the brutal fights of the gladiators.[5] Though their religion taught them cheerfulness, they could not laugh at what was sinful: and they were denounced by the multitude as austere because they declined to take part in the popular amusements.

Aware that any post of prominence added to their perils, the Christians of the first three centuries were deterred from courting rank or power. Even the honours paid to the sovereign on the occasion of a victory savoured of idolatry: and as the disciples did not feel at liberty to join, in the usual manner, in the celebration, they were stigmatized by their enemies as disloyal. But they avoided political intrigues, and approved themselves industrious and faithful subjects. In their religious assemblies they remembered their earthly rulers, praying that the emperor might have "a long life, a secure dominion, a safe home, valiant armies, a faithful senate, a righteous people, and a world at peace."[6]

To all who marked the conduct of its professors, Christianity

---

[1] See Kaye's *Writings of Clement of Alexandria*, p. 453. See also Cyprian to Donatus, § 14.
[2] See Cave's *Primitive Christianity*, part i. chap 9. See also Tertullian, *Ad Uxorem*, lib. ii. 6.
[3] Clem. Alex. *Pædag*. lib. ii. c. 4; *Strom*. lib. vii. e. 7.
[4] Clem. Alex. *Pæd*. lib. ii. 3, 8.
[5] Tertullian, *Apol*. xxxv. xxxviii.
[6] Tertullian, *Apol*. xxx.

must have appeared a religion of love. Though, for the first three centuries, comparatively few of the mighty, the noble, or the wealthy, belonged to its communion, it provided systematically for the wants of all its indigent adherents. In the middle of the third century, the Church of Rome alone supported fifteen hundred paupers, many of whom were widows.[1] The newly-born children of pagans were left to perish in the open field, when the parents were unwilling to undertake the expense of their sustenance and education; but the Christians took charge of these poor infants, and brought them up in the bosom of the Church. They sometimes expended large sums on the redemption of captives;[2] they delighted in the liberation of slaves; and certain officials were appointed by them to look after the destitute sick, and to see that they were nursed with assiduity and tenderness.[3] Nor were their charities confined to those who made a profession of the faith; for, in times of pestilence, when the heathen deserted their dying co-religionists, the Christians stepped forward and ministered to their wants. Such works of mercy could not fail to bear good fruit; and many who might otherwise have continued to listen with indifference to the claims of the Gospel were won over by its large-hearted, unostentatious, and unremitting benevolence.

[1] Euseb. vi. 43.
[2] Basil, *Epist.* 220.
[3] They are afterwards known in Church history as the *Parabolani*. See Bingham, bk. iii. 9, § 2.

SECTION II.

THE DOCTRINE OF THE CHURCH.

CHAPTER I.

THE DOCTRINE OF THE GREAT BODY OF BELIEVERS.

IMMEDIATELY after the transgression of our first parents, the advent of a Saviour, the Seed of the woman,[1] was foretold. The sacrifices of the patriarchal economy and of the Mosaic ritual all announced His approach. The predictions relating to Him gradually became more copious and circumstantial, so that, as the time of His manifestation drew nigh, the students of prophecy could venture to declare not only the nation, the tribe and the family from which He was to spring, but also the place of His birth and the age in which He was to make His appearance. But, when He actually became incarnate, faith alone could recognize the Divine Deliverer; and after His resurrection, the first point pressed by the apostles on the consideration of their countrymen was the fact that He was the promised Shiloh. "Let all the house of Israel," said they, "know assuredly that God hath made *that same Jesus*, whom ye have crucified, both Lord and Christ."[2]

At a time when many were expecting an extraordinary personage, the very announcement that the Christ, or the Messiah, had entered on His mission was sure to awaken curiosity; and yet few, if any, were prepared to form a correct estimate of the Saviour's character. Multitudes, who had heard with wonder of the miracles of Jesus, were filled with blank disappointment when they saw Him; for they could not believe that an individual in such lowly circumstances could be the great liberator of Israel. How, they were disposed to ask, can this son of a carpenter be the King of Zion? How can one who has not where to lay his head be the Desire of all nations? To those who judged merely according to the outward appearance such questions were no doubt sufficiently perplexing, but more earnest

[1] Gen. iii. 15.   [2] Acts ii. 36.

and accurate observers, who pondered the marks of the Messiah indicated in the Old Testament, and who compared them with the life and actions of the Son of Mary, could scarcely fail to discover the correspondence; for Isaiah had described Him as "despised and rejected of men, a man of sorrows, and acquainted with grief;"[1] and others of the prophets had mentioned additional tokens, all of which were realized in the Prophet of Nazareth.

As the whole system of New Testament theology rests on the fundamental fact that "Jesus is *the Christ*," we are led at once to inquire, What is the teaching of Scripture respecting the Messiah, or the Lord's Anointed?[2] What was the object of His mission? What is His rank? What benefits may we expect from Him? The writings of the apostles and evangelists enable us to answer all these questions, and thus to ascertain the doctrines of primitive Christianity.

The object of the mission of the Son of God is clearly stated in the book of inspiration, where we are told that He came to "save His people from their sins."[3] The Gospel contemplates man as a transgressor exposed to punishment, and sets forth Jesus Christ as a Redeemer who has made atonement for iniquity. He saves us by restoring us to the divine favour and enlisting us in the divine service. When we were enemies, we were reconciled to God by the death of His Son, who was sent to bless us in turning away every one of us from our iniquities.[4]

The essential dignity of the Saviour befits the office He sustains. He acts as Mediator for sinners with God; and between parties thus estranged, and placed at an infinite distance, who is competent to interfere? The Intercessor must be One who is "higher than the heavens," and yet "bone of our bone and flesh of our flesh." Such is Christ, as He is exhibited in the sacred volume. In Him "dwelleth all the fulness of the Godhead bodily."[5]

The benefits to be derived from the mediation of the Son of God are sufficient to meet our spiritual wants and to satisfy our noblest aspirations; for He gives to all who believe on Him a

---

[1] Isa. liii. 3.
[2] It can scarcely be necessary to inform even the English reader that the *Christ* from the Greek and the *Messiah* from the Hebrew signify the *Anointed*.
[3] Matt. i. 21.   [4] Rom. v. 10; Acts iii. 26.   [5] Col. ii. 9.

free pardon, a holy nature, and an eternal inheritance. "Being justified by faith," says the apostle, "we have peace with God through our Lord Jesus Christ; by whom also we have access by faith into this grace wherein we stand, and rejoice in hope of the glory of God."[1]

These doctrines and others which flow from them constituted the theology of the early Church, but for some time they were not embodied systematically in any ecclesiastical symbol. All adults who received baptism were previously made acquainted with its spiritual meaning, and when they submitted to the ordinance they openly professed their attachment to the Gospel;[2] but originally no confession of faith was in existence to which they were required formally to declare their adherence. Even the first draft of the symbol known as *The Apostles' Creed* was not drawn up until perhaps about a century after the demise of all the inspired teachers of Christianity.[3]

We have strong presumptive evidence of the soundness of a system of theology when we find that its great outlines can be appropriately described in Scripture language, and that it does not require us to explain away or ignore any of the phraseology of the sacred penmen. Such a system will treat " of the Father, and of the Son, and of the Holy Ghost,"[4] of " propitiation "[5] and " redemption,"[6] of " justification "[7] and of " the gift of righteousness,"[8] and of " election " to salvation " through sanctification of the spirit and belief of the truth."[9] But a doctrine may be recognized in the word of God though the technical name by which it is now known was not in use in the days of the apostles. When heresies became rife it was sometimes found convenient to introduce a nomenclature in which a disputed question of theology was represented by a single vocable. Hence it was that, though the New Testament teaches the subsistence of three Persons in the Godhead, the word *Trinity* was not introduced into Church literature until the close of the second century, when the doctrine of which it is the index began to be considerably controverted.

---

[1] Rom. v. 1, 2.   [2] 1 Pet. iii. 21.
[3] Some of the articles found in it are of a still later date. See Goode's *Divine Rule of Faith and Practice*, i. 108, London, 1853.
[4] Matt. xxviii. 19.   [5] 1 John ii. 2.   [6] Eph. i. 7.   [7] Rom. v. 16, 18.
[8] Rom. v. 17.   [9] 1 Thess. i. 4 ; 2 Thess. ii. 13.

In a case such as this the use of a term not found in Scripture served greatly to abbreviate discussion; but in other instances the appearance of new modes of expression could not be viewed with the same approval. Whilst the teaching of the Gospel relative to the being, unity, and perfections of God commended itself to the more intelligent heathen, and induced many of them to renounce their superstitions, it was often, as a whole, imperfectly understood; and, in particular, the place which it assigns to faith in the scheme of salvation was very indistinctly apprehended. This subject, which transcends the sphere of natural reason, can be studied to advantage only by those who enjoy the higher illumination of the Spirit of God: it was a stumbling-block to self-righteous Jews, and foolishness to conceited philosophers; it was foreign to all the current modes of thought; and it was here that the first successful attempts were made to adulterate the pure theology of the apostles and evangelists. Salvation by faith was admitted in words, but salvation by works was substantially acknowledged; and forms of expression, endorsed by ecclesiastical authority and compromising the truth of Scripture, soon became prevalent. As early as the third century Christian writers speak of "sins *cleansed* by repentance"[1] and "*expiated* by due satisfactions and lamentations."[2] At the same time, repentance began to be confounded with penance, and the blood of Christ to be superseded by the blood of martyrdom.

But whilst error commenced so soon to poison the fountains of instruction, there was still an antidote at hand in the holy Scriptures; and, throughout the first three hundred years, the Church firmly maintained their supreme authority. With the exception of a few of the smaller epistles, which do not seem to have been so early in general circulation, the whole of the New Testament was received as inspired at the close of the first century, and was publicly read, along with the sacred books handed down by the Jews, in all the congregations of the faithful. Thus the whole body of the people had an opportunity of hearing the great truths of God's law proclaimed, from week to week, in the words of the lively oracles.

[1] Tertullian, *De Pœnitentia*, c. 3.
[2] Cyprian, *Epist.* 55, ed. Baluz, Venice, 1728.

CHAPTER II.

EARLY HERESIES, CONTROVERSIES, AND SUPERSTITIONS.

THE visible Church suffers from the disturbing influences incident to other earthly associations. It may be annoyed by self-conceit, perplexed by ignorance, or agitated by faction. The Gospel, when first promulgated, was foolishness to the Greeks; disputatious speculators were confounded by the very simplicity of its announcements; and those who spurned the grace of a crucified Redeemer could not appreciate the grandeur of its salvation. But philosophy, purblind as it was, soon discovered traces of divinity in the doctrine of the cross; and some of its votaries submitted to baptism in the hope of attaining a higher illumination by incorporating their favourite theories with the Christian theology. The incongruous mixture—attempted even in the first century—was condemned by the tongue and pen of inspiration; and the Apostles point to it when they denounce "philosophy and vain deceit," "the wisdom of this world," and "oppositions of science falsely so called."[1] In the second century, this tendency to adulterate the truth was fully developed; and, as those who thus signalized themselves pretended to the possession of superior knowledge or intelligence, they were distinguished by the designation of GNOSTICS.

The creed of Gnosticism was a coat of many colours; for almost every new teacher valued himself on some peculiarity of doctrine; but, as a system, it was marked by the recognition of certain leading principles. The origin of evil was one of the difficult problems it attempted to solve; and its abettors based their explanations on the philosophy of Plato—alleging, with the Athenian sage, that *matter* is eternal and essentially corrupt. As the Gnostics maintained that the soul is contaminated by the body, they inferred that it cannot attain perfection whilst connected with such a tabernacle. Hence, some of them denied the incarnation of Christ. According to their ideas, it is an imputation on His purity to suppose that He came "in the flesh." These transcendentalists, who were called *Docetæ*, affirmed that His visible frame was a mere phantom, and that, even on the

[1] Col. ii. 8; 1 Cor. i. 20, 21; 1 Tim. vi. 20.

cross, He suffered only in appearance. The resurrection of the body contradicted their fundamental positions, and they rejected it altogether—contending that the restoration accomplished by their *Gnosis* is the great fact of spiritual existence, and that "the resurrection is past already."[1] The Godhead furnished them with a field for boundless speculation; and, with fancy on the wing, they invented strange "fables and endless genealogies"[2]— teaching that many æons, or inferior deities, of gradually decreasing excellence emanated from the Fountain of Divinity. One of these æons, named the Demiurge or Achamoth, was represented by them as the Maker of the world; for they refused to admit that the Supreme God could come in contact with this earth's debasing elements. The soul in its present state is, as they conceived, in bondage to materialism; and the illumination of their doctrine was proclaimed as the grand panacea for spiritual maladies.

Simon Magus, mentioned in the 8th chapter of the Acts of the Apostles, is commonly reputed the father of Christian Gnosticism. From the statements of Luke it is apparent that he was actuated by sinister motives in making a profession of the Gospel; he was cunning, conceited, and selfish; and he continued, throughout the whole of his career, to pursue a tortuous policy. Long after his baptism in Samaria, he travelled to Rome, where he attracted considerable attention. Hymeneus, Phygellus, Hermogenes, and others named in the New Testament,[3] have also been classed among the Gnostics; and, towards the close of the first century, Carpocrates, Cerinthus, and Ebion are said to have propagated the system. There is a tradition that the Apostle John designs to bear special testimony against the errors of Cerinthus, when he declares in the beginning of his Gospel that "the Word was made flesh." But heresy gained few disciples during the lives of the primitive heralds of the cross. Subsequently its advocates became much more formidable, as well from their numbers and zeal as from their ability and erudition; and, before the middle of the second century, the Church from east to west was excited by their discussions. Saturninus at Antioch, Basilides at Alexandria, and Marcion, Cerdon, Valentine, and Marcus at Rome, are still remembered as the chiefs of the errorists; and the Christian literature of at least a century is, to

[1] 2 Tim. ii. 18.   [2] 1 Tim. i. 4.   [3] 2 Tim. i. 15; ii. 17.

a great extent, occupied with the task of their refutation.[1] Among the most accomplished of these heresiarchs was Valentine, who died at an advanced age in the island of Cyprus, and who had many disciples in various countries.

Whilst Gnosticism involved a denial of the Supreme Deity of Christ, representing Him as an Æon or Emanation of the Primal Essence; it also discarded the atonement, exhibiting the Gospel rather as a revelation of light than as a revelation of mercy. Its supporters did not scruple to disown the authority of Scripture, when it directly contradicted their opinions. Many of them entirely rejected the Old Testament, and received only certain portions of the writings of the Apostles and Evangelists. Some of them fabricated gospels, which they circulated with much assiduity. Their practical theology revealed the absurd and dangerous character of their system—some of its teachers insisting on the most severe abstinence, and others recommending the most shameless self-indulgence. According to the one party, the flesh is incorrigible, and it is useless to curb its inclinations; according to the other, it should be kept constantly mortified by the chastisement of ascetic discipline.

Temperance is unquestionably favourable to the cultivation of all the virtues; but many of the heathen philosophers held extreme views on the subject of the appetites, asserting that the highest type of spiritual excellence can be attained only by a life of carnal austerities. The Eastern theology sanctioned the same principle; and, long prior to the Christian dispensation, monasticism was extensively established among the disciples of Buddha. The leaven of this doctrine was soon introduced into the Church; and before the end of the second century celibacy and protracted fasting were supposed by many to be essential to exalted piety. Such sentiments at length found a most energetic advocate in an individual connected with an obscure Phrygian village—a fanatic named Montanus—who made a vigorous attempt to secure their general adoption. This man, without erudition or extraordinary talent, created a wonderful impression; for the amazing earnestness with which he announced his convictions compelled attention, and persons of a certain temperament were prepared to listen approvingly to his pretensions. He imagined that he had a special mission from heaven, that he was the apostle of an age

---

[1] See particularly Irenæus, *Contra Hæreses*, and the *Philosophumena* of Hippolytus.

of purer spiritualism, and that he was empowered to supplement the defects of the system of Christianity. He delivered gloomy predictions, interdicted flight in times of persecution, imposed rigorous fasts, and condemned second marriages. Two females of distinction became his ardent partisans, and greatly contributed, by their wealth and personal influence, to assist him in the dissemination of his sentiments. But it was at length discovered that he was the dupe of his own folly; the Councils of the Church condemned his extravagance;[1] and the signal failure of some of his most remarkable predictions consigned him to contempt. The false principles he so senselessly exaggerated were not, however, brought into disrepute by his disgrace; for, soon afterwards, they reappeared in the theology of the Church, where they exercised an extensive and most pernicious influence.

Montanus did not deny any of the cardinal doctrines of the Gospel; and his system had a "shew of wisdom" in "neglecting of the body;" but others, who disturbed the Christian community towards the close of the second century, advanced more boldly in the path of speculative innovation. Theodotus, a native of Byzantium, who about that time came to Rome and maintained the simple humanity of Christ, was excommunicated. Shortly afterwards, an individual, named Artemon, also taught that our Lord was a mere man; and Natalius, another heresiarch of the same class who settled in the great metropolis, is said to have received a monthly salary for acting as pastor to what would now be called a Unitarian congregation.[2] Noetus, a native of Smyrna, confounded the first and second persons of the Godhead;[3] and, as it apparently followed from his theory, that the Father suffered on the cross, those by whom it was supported were called *Patripassians*. Sabellius, an African ecclesiastic who confounded all the distinctions of the Trinity, and taught that the terms Father, Son, and Holy Spirit, merely indicate different phases or manifestations of the same Divine Person, broached an hypothesis, which found some advocates, and which is still known under the designation of Sabellianism. But the most influential assailant of the commonly received doctrine of the Godhead was the celebrated Paul of Samosata,[4]

---

[1] Euseb. v. 16.   [2] *Ibid.* v. 28.
[3] Hippolytus, *Philosophumena*, lib. ix.
[4] So called because Samosata was his birthplace.

Bishop of Antioch. He maintained that the Logos, or Word, is not a Divine Person, but the Reason of God; and that Jesus was the greatest of the sons of men because the Logos dwelt in Him more abundantly than in any other of the children of Adam. Paul's high position in the Church, and his commanding talents, rendered him peculiarly formidable; but the dangerous character of his creed was quickly perceived even by those whom he was appointed to instruct; and, though he dexterously endeavoured to elude investigation, a council was specially convened in A.D. 269 at Antioch to sit in judgment on his heresy; and he was finally deposed and excommunicated. The decision, which was officially announced by the assembled fathers to the chief pastors of Christendom,[1] was received with general approbation.

About the time that Paul of Samosata was cut off from catholic communion, another individual in the farther east began to attract notice as the founder of a new school of theology. This was Mani, or as he is sometimes called Manichaeus. He was a Persian by birth, and a proficient in several arts and sciences; for he excelled as a painter and a physician, a mathematician and a mental philosopher. Entering on public life at a time when two rival forms of traditional faith were struggling for ascendency in Persia, and when the progress of the Gospel was stimulating the activity of religious inquiry, it occurred to him that, by blending the creed of his ancestors with the creed of Christianity, he could concoct a system acceptable to his countrymen; and, confident in the resources of a fertile genius, he attempted to overcome the difficulties of amalgamation. He adopted the Persian doctrine of two First Principles as the fundamental idea of his theory, teaching that a Good and an Evil Deity existed from eternity. Christ came to liberate souls from the dominion of the Evil Deity, or the Power of Darkness; and Mani was the Paraclete commissioned to proclaim His will. He rejected the greater portion of the canon of Scripture, and published a book, rich in Oriental imagery, as the Gospel which his followers were to acknowledge. His disciples were divided into two classes— the *Elect*, or the Sacred order; and the *Auditors*, or the ordinary members. To each section he prescribed ascetic and dietary regulations—requiring the elect to abstain from marriage, as well as from wine, milk, and flesh-meat. His system embodied

[1] Euseb. vii. 30.

several very popular elements; and though the sect which he organized was soon exposed to persecution, it was remarkable alike for its longevity and its extensive diffusion.

Missionaries in all ages have admitted that it is often easier to secure the acknowledgment of theological truths than to destroy the influence of hereditary ceremonies. The history of Christianity supplies countless illustrations of this position; and the annals of the early centuries continually remind us of its importance. The believing Jew could not readily give up his national usages; neither could the converted Gentile at once lay aside those habits in which he had been trained from infancy. Thus it was that so many observances, unsanctioned by divine authority, found their way into the Church. Not a few of the posterity of Abraham who embraced the Gospel continued for a time to keep Saturday as a Sabbath; and, in the former half of the second century, a portion of the members of the Church of Jerusalem, rather than give up the Mosaic ritual, withdrew from their brethren, and formed themselves into a distinct community—known by the title of the Nazarenes. Before the end of the second century a large portion of the Church became involved in a controversy relative to the proper mode of holding an annual festival corresponding to the Passover. Pagan rites also were soon copied by the Christians. Heathenism was a religion of images, of gestures, and of incantations; and some of its little forms were so constantly in requisition that they were often performed almost unconsciously by its votaries. Among these the touching of the forehead in a particular fashion was one of the most common; and, when idolaters in large numbers passed over to the Church, they speedily discovered that they could sanctify the ceremony by showing that it involved the making of a cross. The gesture was forthwith adopted as the sign manual of the professors of the Gospel; and, in some places, before the close of the second century, when the Christian sat down to table, or went to bed—when he put on his shoes, or put out his candle—he did not neglect the sealing of his forehead.[1] The cross was one of the emblems of pagan superstition;[2] but

---

[1] Tertullian, *De Corona*, c. 3.

[2] Socrates, *Hist.* v. 17. One of the symbols of San, or Sansi, the sun-god of the Chaldeans, was a circle with a cross inscribed. Rawlinson's *Ancient Monarchies*, i. 161. This very symbol ⊕ may be seen reproduced in the crosses on some of

the disciples boldly appealed to this fact as a providential testimony in support of their theology; and as the sacred figure was usually seen in the hand of the statue of the goddess of victory, they interpreted the coincidence as a token of the prospects of their system, and as a typical prediction of its ultimate success. Those who, when heathens, had believed that the touching of the forehead operated as a charm, could not be easily persuaded that it had less potency when executed by a Christian; and accordingly the making of the sign of the cross was supposed to be invested with extraordinary virtue; for it was understood to protect against the infection of disease, to affright dæmons, and to propitiate the favour of the Almighty. Even the divine ordinances appointed in the New Testament were at length misrepresented by superstition. Baptism—not faith—was extolled as a shield wherewith we may quench all the fiery darts of the wicked; and the Lord's Supper was described as if, irrespective of the spiritual condition of the recipient, it was endowed with some magic efficacy.

It has been already intimated that, before the close of the second century, the Church was agitated by a controversy relative to the mode of keeping a festival corresponding to the Jewish Passover. The chief pastor of Rome and the chief pastor of Ephesus took the lead in the discussion; and advocated respectively the sentiments of their co-religionists in Italy and Asia Minor. Fasting and feasting were conjoined in the commemoration; and whilst the Easterns insisted on partaking of the Paschal Lamb at the same time as the Old Testament church, their Western brethren imagined that they would have compromised their Christianity by so far conforming to Judaism. They also disputed concerning the time of observing what was called the Festival of the Resurrection, or the anniversary of the day when our Lord issued from the grave. The questions controverted were intrinsically unimportant; but a spirit of contradiction was aroused; and the parties refused to agree to any terms of reconciliation. About sixty years afterwards the same churches came again into collision on the subject of the baptism of heretics—the Asiatics, now allied with the Africans, contend-

---

the old Irish churches. See Petrie's *Ecclesiastical Architecture of Ireland*, p. 174, 403-4, Dublin, 1845. See a curious article on "The Pre-Christian Cross" in the Proceedings of the Royal Irish Academy, vol. viii. part v. p. 322, Dublin, 1863.

ing that the ordinance when dispensed by sectaries was a nullity, and the Italians asserting its validity. In both instances the Bishop of Rome threatened his antagonists with excommunication; but he had as yet no power to carry out such a sentence, so that he thus only gave note of warning of those high pretensions which he was afterwards to assert so successfully.

Immediately before the commencement of the baptismal controversy the Church of Rome was disturbed by the first of the many schisms which form such a conspicuous feature in its history. A party within it maintained that those who had fallen into gross sins should never again be admitted to ecclesiastical fellowship; but as Cornelius, who was then at the head of the church of the capital, refused to act on this austere principle, its supporters renounced his jurisdiction; and Novatian, a presbyter of contracted spirit but blameless character, was ordained their bishop. The separatists were joined by others in various quarters of the Empire, and, under the designation of Novatians, long existed as a sect, noted alike for their orthodoxy and their over-scrupulous discipline. About the time of their secession, another division, promoted chiefly by Felicissimus, an influential deacon, occurred at Carthage. The dissentients insisted that the recommendation of a martyr[1] was a sufficient title to church-fellowship; but Cyprian, the bishop, declined to acknowledge this test of qualification, and the schism thus originated.

Poets have sung of a golden age of the world when men lived in peace, purity, and love; but history dissolves the pleasing illusion, as it tells that no such age has been registered in its records. Many are willing to believe that in the early centuries there was also a golden age of the Church; but facts attest that they thus indulge only a fond imagination. Christ found the earth a moral wilderness, and it would have been extraordinary had the fairest fruits of the Gospel been the earliest products of sacred culture. The truth, no doubt, at once revealed itself as a light from heaven, and shed, all around, its holy and genial radiance; but dense clouds of prejudice and superstition struggled against the influence of its penetrating beams. Scarcely had Christianity appeared, when Gnosticism sought to supersede

[1] These certificates were sometimes written after the martyr's death by parties who pleaded his authority. See Cyprian, *Epist.* 22, ed. Baluz.

it by its "darkness visible:" subsequently, Montanism attempted to spread over it the shade of a gloomy fanaticism: and afterwards, Manichæanism interposed the exhalations of its folly and extravagance. Meanwhile, Humanitarianism, Noetianism, and Sabellianism, tried to obscure its divine testimony. Even where there was no fundamental difference of creed, diversity of sentiment as to ceremonies and discipline led to ecclesiastical separation. The Nazarenes formed themselves into a distinct community when their brethren declined to continue the observance of the Mosaic law: the Novatians seceded because, as they conceived, transgressors were not punished with due rigour: and the party of Felicissimus withdrew on the ground that weak disciples were not treated with becoming indulgence. The sectaries often gave unequivocal proofs of the depth of their convictions; for the Montanists courted martyrdom; the Manichæans passed through many a bloody ordeal; and the Novatians made unflinching constancy in persecution a condition of church membership. But all these separatists set up a standard of duty unknown in the Word of God; and error cannot be converted into truth, either by the dogged pertinacity with which it is asserted, or by the ingenuity of the arguments which may be urged in its vindication. The highest credentials of the Gospel are, not those derived from exhibitions of zeal or genius or determination, but those written on the hearts of believers. It achieves its noblest triumphs when it converts the soul, and clothes with the beauty of holiness. In early times evidences of its power were not wanting among those who discarded some of its heavenly doctrines; but, in all ages, the purest type of godliness has been found in connection with the purest faith. As a remedy for the healing of the nations, the Gospel is still as efficacious as in the days of the apostles; and, if we are to believe the sure word of prophecy, it is destined to produce in states and kingdoms even more glorious changes than it has ever yet accomplished.

SECTION III.

WORSHIP AND CONSTITUTION OF THE CHURCH.

CHAPTER I.

THE WORSHIP OF THE CHURCH.

THE observance of one day in seven as a sacred rest dates from the beginning of the history of our species.[1] Whilst the arrangement tends to refresh the body and invigorate the mind, it provides likewise for the regular maintenance of public religious ordinances. The division of time into weeks, mentioned in the book of Genesis,[2] attests its existence from the earliest antiquity. When giving the law from Sinai, the Heavenly Legislator refers to it as a well-known institute, saying significantly, "*Remember* the Sabbath day to keep it holy."[3]

It cannot be shown that this law expired with the Jewish dispensation. The Sabbath did not originate with the Mosaic ritual; its bodily as well as its spiritual comforts are still required as urgently as ever by the human family; and the fact that the fourth commandment occupies so prominent a position in the Decalogue attests at once its vast importance and its perpetual obligation. But its Divine Author can substitute one seventh day for another; and, as Christ was in the grave on the Jewish Sabbath, it was not fitting that a season associated with such melancholy recollections should henceforth be a church festival. Jesus changed many other portions of the ritual, and, being "Lord of the Sabbath," He altered the time of its observance. His disciples commemorated His resurrection by meeting for worship on the first day of the week; and this holy rest, designated in the New Testament "The Lord's Day,"[4] has ever since

---

[1] Gen. ii. 2, 3.   [2] Gen. xxix. 27, 28.

[3] "The word (Remember) always presupposes antecedent knowledge." See *Scripture Account of the Sabbath*, by Archbishop Stopford, p. 159, London, 1837.

[4] Rev. i. 10. See also Acts xx. 7; 1 Cor. xvi. 1, 2. "In every case in which the first day of the week is mentioned in the Greek (of the New Testament) it

The Worship of the Church.

been set apart to the stated performance of the public services of the Christian religion.

For several years after the death of our Saviour all the adherents of the Gospel were converts from Judaism; and, for a considerable part of the first century, the Christians were confounded by many with the posterity of Abraham. Nor was it strange that the mistake was made, as the worship of the early Church closely resembled the worship of the synagogue. The service consisted of psalmody,[1] prayer, reading the Scriptures and preaching. The Old Testament psalms were generally sung, but they were not exclusively employed. No instrumental music was heard in the congregation during the first three centuries. The prayers, which were delivered in the vernacular tongue, and which in the infancy of the Church were distinguished by their evangelical fervour, had special reference to the spiritual wants, the peculiar temptations, or the prevailing sins of the petitioners; and the phraseology varied according to the gifts of the individual who officiated. A portion of Scripture, either from the Old or the New Testament, was read; and, as books were comparatively rare and the sacred manuscripts in the hands of very few, this public exercise was the chief opportunity enjoyed by multitudes for obtaining a knowledge of the written word; and thus the attention of the auditory to the lesson for the day was quickened and sustained. Exposition, or preaching, followed the reading of the Scriptures.

The custom of discoursing from a text, or from a few words of holy writ, was not known during the first three centuries. The sermon—an address partly didactic and partly hortatory—had reference to the whole portion of Scripture read at the time to

---

is called by the name of Sabbath. . . . . The expression which in English is translated 'the first day of the week' occurs eight times in the New Testament. In Mark xvi. 9, in the Greek, it is πρώτῃ σαββάτου, literally 'first of the Sabbath.' And also Matt. xxviii. 1; Mark xvi. 2; Luke xxiv. 1; John xx. 1, 19; Acts xx. 7; 1 Cor. xvi. 2; in all of which the Greek is μιᾷ τῶν σαββάτων, literally, 'one of the Sabbaths.'"—Stopford, 228, note. See, in the Septuagint, Gen. xxix. 27, and Dan. ix. 27.

[1] As to the mode of singing in the synagogue, see Vitringa, *de Synagoga Vetere*, lib. iii. pars. 2, cap. 16, p. 1070, Franeq. 1696. The mode of singing in the primitive Church was probably the same. The testimony of Isidore of Seville, though not of the highest historical value, is remarkable. "Primitiva autem ecclesia ita psallebat, ut modico flexu vocis faceret resonare psallentem, *ita ut pronuncianti vicinior esset quam canenti.*"—*De Ecclesiast. Officiis*, i. 5.

the congregation. And the mode in which ministers of the Gospel proceeded to disseminate their views very soon arrested the attention of intelligent pagans. Unlike the heathen philosophers—who were wont, in the first instance, to exact a pecuniary reward for their instructions, and who confined their prelections to the wealthy and the educated—the missionaries of the cross ignored the love of gain; and, in their anxiety to leaven the whole community with their principles, addressed themselves indiscriminately to the rich man and the beggar, the young and the old, the learned and the illiterate. In every country persons of humble rank constitute the bulk of the people; and the early Christian teachers could urge, like their divine Master, as part of the credentials of their mission, that the poor had the Gospel preached to them. A Roman citizen, when present for the first time at the worship of the Church, might have remarked how profoundly it differed from the ritual of paganism. The services in the great heathen temples were but an imposing scenic exhibition. The holy water for lustration, the statues of the gods with wax tapers burning before them, the officials robed in white surplices, and the incense floating in clouds and diffusing perfume all around, could only regale the senses or light up the imagination. No stated time was devoted to instruct the assembly; and the liturgy—often in a dead language—as it was mumbled over by the priest, merely added to the superstition and the mysticism. But the worship of the Church was, in the highest sense, a "reasonable service." It had no parade, no images, no fragrant odours; for the first hundred years it was commonly celebrated in private houses or the open fields; and yet it addressed itself so impressively to the understanding and the heart that the congregations of the faithful frequently presented scenes incomparably more spirit-stirring and sublime than anything ever witnessed in the high places of Greek or Roman idolatry. As the Christians prayed together they realized the presence of the Great King, and tears often flowed profusely as they rejoiced in the precious promises. Or, as the minister expatiated on the terrors of the law or on the love of the Redeemer, the word was felt to be the voice of Omnipotence, and the whole auditory was intensely moved. Whilst the Christian preacher wielded the sword of the Spirit, the unbeliever felt himself subdued. "Thus," says Paul, "are the secrets of his heart made manifest; and so, falling down on his face, he will worship God, and report that God is in you of a truth."[1]

As originally administered, baptism and the Lord's Supper— the two symbolic ordinances of the New Testament—were distinguished by their extreme simplicity. In baptism, the initiatory rite, water was applied to the body either by affusion or immersion;[2] and when an adult convert had his children baptized along with him, he was thus pledged to "bring them up in the nurture and admonition of the Lord."[3] In the Eucharist bread and wine were dispensed to the faithful seated around a table; and, as they partook of these memorials, they celebrated their communion with Christ and with each other. The Lord's Supper was administered on the Lord's day; and, though the point cannot be established by decisive evidence, the ordinance was perhaps generally observed weekly. In the New Testament the word sacrament is not employed to designate either baptism or the Eucharist, and about the end of the second century, when it was introduced into the ecclesiastical nomenclature, it was not applied exclusively to those two institutions.[4]

No individual or Church court is warranted to tamper with symbolic ordinances of divine appointment; for, as they are the typical embodiment of great truths, any change essentially vitiates their testimony. But their early administrators, overlooking this grave objection, soon ceased to respect the integrity of baptism and the Lord's Supper. In the third century a number of frivolous and superstitious ceremonies—such as exorcism, unction, the making of the sign of the cross on the forehead, and the kiss of peace—were already tacked to baptism; so that the beautiful significance of the primitive observance could not be well seen under these strange trappings. Before the middle of the second century the wine of the Eucharist was mixed with water; fifty years afterwards the communicants participated standing; and at length the elements themselves were treated with awful reverence. The more deeply to impress the

[1] 1 Cor. xiv. 25.

[2] In cases where delicacy of health interfered, sprinkling was always considered sufficient. See Cyprian, *Epist.* 76, ed. Baluz. According to the decision of a Synod held in Africa about the middle of the third century, infants might be baptized before the eighth day after birth.

[3] Eph. vi. 4.   [4] Kaye's *Tertullian*, p. 357.

imagination, baptism and the Eucharist began to be surrounded with the secrecy of the heathen mysteries, and none save those who had received the ordinances were suffered to be present at their dispensation. The ministers of the Church sadly compromised their religion when they thus imitated the meretricious decorations of the pagan worship. As might have been expected, the symbols[1] so disfigured were misunderstood and misrepresented. Baptism was called regeneration, and the Eucharist was designated a sacrifice. Thus a door was opened for the admission of a whole crowd of dangerous errors.

CHAPTER II.

THE CONSTITUTION OF THE CHURCH.

WHEN attempting to trace in the New Testament the constitution of the Church, some have been perplexed by confounding its ordinary and its extraordinary ministers. The apostles, prophets, and primitive evangelists, held a position which other heralds of the Gospel cannot occupy; they were endowed with supernatural gifts; and, as they were raised up for an emergency, they left behind them no successors. Authority which cannot be legitimately exercised over an association when its organization is complete, must often, from the necessity of circumstances, be assumed by the founders of the institute. We form a most erroneous estimate of the constitution of the Lutheran Church if we think that its office-bearers may act as did the father of the German Reformation; and we sadly misrepresent the polity of English Methodism, if we argue that any member of the Conference possesses the power wielded by the venerable Wesley. The missionary who succeeds in collecting congregations of Christian converts in a heathen country, feels at liberty to give advice, and to guide by supervision in a way which, if adventured on by any other, would be resented as intrusive. We are to overlook neither this element of influence, nor their gifts of miracles and inspiration, when judging of the relation in

[1] It is however abundantly clear that the sacramental elements were still considered as but symbols. Thus Tertullian says: "Having taken the bread and given it to his disciples, He (Christ) made it His own body by saying, 'This is my body,' that is, *the figure of my body*."—*Against Marcion*, book iv. chap. 40.

which the original ambassadors of the Gospel stood to the primitive Churches. The apostles and evangelists were the founders of these societies; by them the disciples were collected and organized; from their lips they first heard the glad tidings of mercy; and by them were promulgated laws for the guidance of the children of God in all succeeding generations. They are therefore placed far above the ordinary functionaries of the Christian commonwealth. "God hath set in the Church, *first*, apostles; *secondarily*, prophets; *thirdly*, teachers."[1]

But, making due allowance for the peculiar circumstances of a new brotherhood, we may distinctly trace certain elements of uniformity in the constitution of the primitive churches. The great outlines of their polity may be discovered in the Church of Jerusalem. We learn from the book of the Acts,[2] that the apostles remained a considerable time in the holy city after the resurrection of our Lord; and it is plain that they stood, meanwhile, on a footing of perfect equality. They had already been rebuked for striving who among them should be the greatest;[3] they had been told that one was their Master, even Christ;[4] and they had been taught to treat each other as brethren. If, according to a tradition resting apparently on a sound foundation,[5] they sojourned twelve years in Jerusalem after the effusion of the Spirit on the day of Pentecost, they must, all this time, as a common council, have ruled the mother Church of Christendom. The community over which they presided consisted of many thousands of souls;[6] it must have formed several worshipping societies; and yet it presents no trace either of Episcopacy or Congregationalism. The apostles—a united body incorporated by divine authority—constituted the primitive presbytery of Jerusalem. Their office, as described by themselves, and so far as the holy city was concerned, involved merely the performance of the ordinary duties of the pastorate; for they were to give themselves continually to prayer and to the ministry of the word.[7] They were assisted by a body of deacons whose business it was to relieve them from secular anxieties by taking charge of the distribution of alms—the only monetary care with which the infant Church was encumbered.

[1] 1 Cor. xii. 28. [2] Acts i. 4; viii. 1. [3] Luke xxii. 24.
[4] Matt. xxiii. 10-12. [5] Clem. *Strom.* vi. p. 742, note, ed. Potter.
[6] Acts ii. 41; iv. 4. [7] Acts vi. 4.

The Apostles acted together in their government of the Church of Jerusalem. They admitted converts to their society by baptism; they had one faith, known as "the apostles' doctrine;" and they belonged to one brotherhood, known as "the apostles' fellowship."[1] They united in the ordination of the deacons;[2] and, when they heard that the people of Samaria had also received the word of God, "they sent unto them Peter and John."[3] Thus they were subject one to another; and, in the administration of internal discipline as well as in the management of missions, they ruled the Church conjointly. When about to withdraw from Jerusalem they established there a body of elders to occupy their place and to perform their functions.[4] These elders were recognized as members of their common council; and even when the question of the circumcision of the Gentiles was discussed, "the apostles and elders came together" for its consideration.[5] The elders did not all perform exactly the same duties. Some preached; some confined themselves to the communication of private instruction; some attended specially to the visitation of the sick; and some were distinguished by their zeal in the maintenance of discipline.[6] This distribution of duty was in accordance with Jewish usages; for whilst every synagogue had its bench of elders, the care of public teaching devolved on one or two, and the rest merely assisted in the inspection or government of the community.[7]

The other Christian fraternities throughout the Roman Empire had the same organization as the parent society. The Church of Antioch—perhaps only second to that of Jerusalem in numbers and influence—was under the care of "prophets and teachers,"[8] who co-operated in its supervision. They were banded together

---

[1] Acts ii. 42.   [2] Acts vi. 6.   [3] Acts viii. 14.
[4] Acts xi. 30.   [5] Acts xv. 6.
[6] Rom. xii. 6-8. In Heb. xiii. 7, the Apostle speaks of rulers who teach, and in Heb. xiii. 17, of rulers who govern.
[7] See Lightfoot's Works, iii. 242, and xi. 179. The *elders of the people*, as distinguished from *the elders of the Church*, seem to have disappeared almost everywhere before the fifth century. The system, introduced early in the third century, of requiring every ecclesiastic to commence with the lowest church office, and to ascend through all the gradations, soon effectually excluded them. In apostolic times old men were at once ordained as elders; but when the position could not be attained without passing through the subordinate offices of porter, reader, exorcist, acolyte, subdeacon, and deacon, the original arrangement was destroyed.
[8] Acts xiii. 1.

in their ministry; and when Barnabas and Paul were to be set apart to the work of foreign missions, these prophets and teachers were associated in the act of ordination.[1]

The Church of Ephesus—another of the most famous of the early Christian societies—was fashioned after the same model. It had its bishops or elders and its deacons—all chosen by popular election.[2] Its elders were required "to take heed to all the flock over the which the Holy Ghost had made them bishops," and to watch particularly against the intrusion of false teachers.[3] Some of them only ruled, whilst others "laboured in the Word and doctrine."[4] These elders were the only governors of the Church of Ephesus; and Paul, in his farewell address to them, ignores the existence of any ecclesiastical superior. He assumes that they possessed the power of self-government, and that they were officially responsible for each other's proceedings.

Throughout the whole of the Apostolic age the churches remained under the same form of polity. The first Epistle of Peter was written at an advanced period of the reign of Nero; and the brethren scattered throughout Pontus, Galatia, Cappadocia, Asia, and Bithynia, to whom it was sent, were then associated under presbyterial government. The Apostle there speaks to his fellow-rulers as one of themselves—not in the language of command, but in the humbler tones of exhortation. "The elders which are among you," says he, "I exhort, *who am also an elder*, ... feed the flock of God which is among you, taking the oversight thereof, not by constraint, but willingly; not for filthy lucre, but of a ready mind; neither as being lords over God's heritage, but being ensamples to the flock."[5]

At the close of the first century, and for a considerable part of the second, the same ecclesiastical regimen was everywhere established. We learn from a letter written about A.D. 96, in

---

[1] Acts xiii. 3.
[2] 1 Tim. i. 3; iii. 1, 2; iii. 10; Acts xx. 17, 28.
[3] Acts xx. 28-31.
[4] 1 Tim. v. 17. Even Vitringa, perhaps the most learned opponent of the distinction between teaching and ruling elders, is constrained to admit that, in point of fact, some of the Ephesian elders did not teach. "Neque nos negamus Paulum quosdam presbyteros hic laudare, ut docentes, *alios vero ut non docentes.*"—*De Synagoga Vetere*, p. 491.
[5] 1 Pet. v. 1-3.

the name of the Church of Rome to the Church of Corinth, that it was then the order of the West. The Epistle rebukes the Corinthians for their quarrels, and exhorts them to submit to the rule of their presbyters or elders; but it never even hints that they were amenable to any other authority. We may infer from this ancient memorial that presbyterial government was then administered as well in Rome as in Corinth. The Epistle of Polycarp to the Philippians, written probably about the middle of the second century, bears testimony to the continuance of the same polity; for, at that time, the Churches of Smyrna and Philippi were unquestionably governed by their presbyteries.

All the functionaries of the Church were elected by general suffrage;[1] and even appointments to temporary offices were sanctioned by the authority of the people.[2] All the arrangements for the government of the ecclesiastical community were unfavourable to the existence of arbitrary power. The disciples were taught to regard each other as members of a holy brotherhood, where the common edification was properly promoted only when the various parts of the spiritual body were pervaded by a loving sympathy, and disposed to act in harmonious combination. Every one was led to feel that he had privileges to enjoy, graces to cultivate, and gifts to exercise. Without united action persons even of high endowments can accomplish little, for the sagacious and profound can make small progress when destitute of the co-operation of the energetic and the active. "The eye cannot say unto the hand I have no need of thee, nor again the head to the feet I have no need of you. Nay," says the Apostle, "much more those members of the body which seem to be more feeble are necessary."[3]

The statement that Timothy and Titus were bishops respectively of Ephesus and Crete is a fiction handed down from the fourth century. The postscripts in which they are so designated,[4] and which are appended to the Epistles addressed to them, are spurious additions: and the letters themselves supply proof that these eminent evangelists were not permanently located in the places where they are thus supposed to have exercised exclusive jurisdiction.[5] The assertion that the angels of

---

[1] Acts i. 23; xiv. 23.   [2] 2 Cor. viii. 19.   [3] 1 Cor. xii. 21, 22.
[4] 2 Tim. end of 4th chap., and Titus, end of 3d chap.
[5] 1 Tim. i. 3; iii. 14, 15: iv. 13; 2 Tim. iv. 10, 21; Tit. i. 5; iii. 12.

the Seven Churches were diocesans is equally unfounded. There is no evidence whatever that the name angel was given to any functionary of the ancient Church: and the individuals mentioned in the Apocalypse were simply messengers sent by seven Christian communities of Asia Minor to visit John in his island of exile.[1]

But though, if we are to judge from the earliest ecclesiastical records, as well as from the Scriptures, it is plain that the Church was placed by the Apostles under presbyterial government, it must be admitted that this state of matters was not of long continuance. Some time before the middle of the second century heresy began sadly to distract the Christian community; and, to avoid the imminent danger of schism, it was deemed expedient, in a few great towns, to arm the chairman of the eldership with additional power. A modified form of prelacy was thus introduced. This change, inaugurated at Rome, was speedily adopted in other cities of the Empire; and, during the succeeding half century, the episcopal system was extensively engrafted on the ecclesiastical constitution.[2] But as yet little more than its germs were visible; for, even at the time of the establishment of Christianity by Constantine, the jurisdiction of a bishop seldom extended beyond the city or parish in which he lived; and, in the middle of the third century, the Bishop of Rome, the greatest churchman in existence, had only forty-two or forty-six presbyters[3] under his supervision. The chief pastors of the capital towns were now, however, in a position for extending their influence; and, in due time, the parochial bishops were obliged to succumb to the diocesans. The fourth century witnessed the accomplishment of this ecclesiastical revolution.

[1] See this more fully illustrated in the *Ancient Church*, period i. sec. iii. chap. iv.
[2] See this more fully illustrated in the next chapter.
[3] Euseb. vi. 43. Some MSS. read 42 presbyters; others 46.

CHAPTER III.

THE RISE OF THE HIERARCHY AND THE CATHOLIC CHURCH.

"LITTLE children," says the Apostle John, "it is the last time: and, as ye have heard that Antichrist shall come, even now are there many antichrists; whereby we know *that it is the last time*.[1] . . . Beloved, believe not every spirit, but try the spirits whether they are of God; because many false prophets are gone out into the world. . . . Every spirit that confesseth not that Jesus Christ is come in the flesh is not of God: and this is that *spirit of Antichrist*, whereof ye have heard that it should come; and *even now already is it in the world.*"[2]

These words suggest that, even in the days of the beloved disciple, there were indications of the approach of a great apostasy. The many false prophets abroad in the world were viewed by the inspired writer as ominous of the appearance of a still more formidable power known by the designation of THE ANTICHRIST. They are described as possessed of his spirit, and as antichrists in miniature. The history of the second century wonderfully illustrates these announcements; for, in point of fact, the rise of heresies led to the formation of that ecclesiastical tyranny which eventually enthralled Christendom. This revolution commenced within less than fifty years after the death of the Apostle John; and though it had small beginnings it proved more influential than any other recorded in the annals of the Church.

The origin of the movement is thus narrated by one of the most erudite of the ancient Fathers: "Before that, by the prompting of the devil, there were *parties in religion* . . . the churches were governed by the common council of the presbyters. But after that each one began to reckon those whom he baptized as belonging to himself and not to Christ, *it was decreed throughout the whole world that one elected from the presbyters should be set over the rest*, that he should have the care of the whole Church, that the seeds of schisms might be destroyed."[3]

The place where this change commenced is mentioned by a

[1] 1 John ii. 18.   [2] 1 John iv. 1, 3.
[3] Jerome, *Comment. in Titum.*

Father of the third century, who states that *from Rome* "the sacerdotal unity took its rise."[1] The disciples in the great capital, from their position at the seat of civil government, from their numbers, their wealth, their zeal, and their intelligence, soon acquired influence among their brethren all over the world; and when "parties in religion" threatened to rend the Christian commonwealth, they took the lead in appointing a prelate as a means of preventing ecclesiastical divisions. The dominion of the Cæsars had not been long established when the Romans began to contrast the peace enjoyed under the imperial dynasty with the civil wars which convulsed the last days of the Republic: and it occurred to the friends of the Church, in some of the principal cities, that a similar alteration in its polity would be an antidote against schism. Nor was it strange that those who loved the truth were now filled with alarm; for the heresiarchs were numerous and plausible, learned, acute, and eloquent. Appearing almost simultaneously in the chief towns, they propounded their theories with the utmost assurance; and artfully mingling the popular elements of the heathen philosophy with a portion of the Gospel, they deceived the hearts of the simple. The Church, hitherto noted as a haven of peace, was suddenly converted into a scene of disputation; and multitudes sighed for deliverance from the strife of tongues. Under these circumstances, it was deemed expedient to appoint a bishop, who was to be the centre of ecclesiastical unity, and to whom all parties were to yield submission.[2]

The time when this new arrangement was introduced can be easily determined. The writers of antiquity concur in asserting that, towards the close of the administration of the Emperor Hadrian, who died in A.D. 138, or in the earlier years of his successor, Antoninus Pius, a crowd of errorists first seriously disturbed the Roman Church.[3] About that period Cerdon, Marcion,

---

[1] Cyprian, *Epist.* 55, ed. Baluz.
[2] The celebrated Isidore of Seville, who wrote in the early part of the seventh century, gives the same account of this matter as Jerome. "Ac sola *propter auctoritatem* summo sacerdoti clericorum ordinatio et consecratio servata est, *ne a multis Ecclesiæ disciplina vendicata concordiam solveret, scandala generaret*. Nam Paulus apostolus eosdem presbyteros, ut vere sacerdotes, sub nomine episcoporum asseverat."—*De Ecclesiasticis Officiis*, lib. ii. cap. 7, § 2. *Patrol. Curs.* lxxxiii. 787.
[3] Irenæus, i. 27, § 1; Clemens Alexandrinus, *Strom.* p. 764, ed. 1688.

Valentine, and other Gnostic leaders, arrived in the imperial city, and created commotions which may still be traced in ecclesiastical history. Hyginus, who was at the head of the Roman presbytery, endeavoured promptly to quell the dangerous excitement. At a meeting specially convened to concert measures for guiding the brethren in this crisis of difficulty, it was resolved that "one elected from the presbyters should be set over the rest, that he should have the care of the whole Church," and that whoever refused to be amenable to his authority should be excluded from ecclesiastical fellowship. As Hyginus was mainly instrumental in procuring this enactment, an ancient document declares that he "arranged the clergy and distributed the gradations."[1]

Where the Christians constituted but a single congregation, it often happened that only one of those entrusted with their spiritual oversight was competent to preach; and in such cases this elder already stood at the head of the community, inasmuch as, according to apostolic rule, the labourer in the word and doctrine was entitled to precedence. The disciples were still thinly scattered over the empire, and in few even of the great cities were they sufficiently numerous to form more than one worshipping association. The change now inaugurated was not therefore immediately productive of any very extensive results. It affected chiefly a comparatively small number of the towns, investing the president of the presbytery with a certain amount of absolute authority. But owing to the place where it originated it was specially influential. Before taking this decisive step, the ministers of the metropolis appear to have obtained the sanction of those of some other large churches which had also been thrown into confusion by the heretics; and thus it was that the system introduced at Rome was soon after adopted at Alexandria, Antioch, Ephesus, and elsewhere. The example of these leading communities was generally followed; and, as Christians multiplied, the chief pastor of every mother church obtained jurisdiction over the ministers of all the new congregations erected in his locality. At length in councils held, as it would seem, about the end of the second century, "it was decreed throughout the whole world" that "the plants of dissensions" should be rooted up by transferring "all care to one."[2]

[1] *Liber Pontificalis.*
[2] "Ut dissensionum plantaria evellerentur, ad unum omnem solicitudinem esse delatam."—*Jerome on the Epistle to Titus.*

Though the presbyters were thus subjected to the bishop, they were not at once stripped of their ancient prerogatives. At first he was expected to consult them as to all matters of public interest; they sat with him in councils, and joined with him in laying on hands in ordination. Until about A.D. 230 the presbyters of Alexandria, the second see in the empire, performed all the ceremonies connected with the investiture of their ecclesiastical chiefs.[1] About that period even a bishop was ordained by the imposition of the hands of a bishop and a presbyter.[2] But as prelacy advanced all these marks of primitive equality were gradually obliterated.

The principle of the new polity, when carried out to its legitimate consequences, led to the establishment of a universal episcopate; for, if it was necessary to set up a bishop to prevent a schism among the presbyters, it was also necessary to appoint a higher functionary to serve as a bond of union among the bishops. Hence a general confederation, comprehending what was called *The Catholic Church*, was formed by the new hierarchy; and the chief pastor of Rome was placed at the head of the association.[3] The object of this league was to ascertain and unite the friends of orthodoxy, so that they could effectively employ their combined influence for the suppression of sectarianism. Several ingenious reasons were soon discovered for assigning to the Roman prelate the first place among his brethren. It was alleged that Peter had once presided over the Church of the capital; that he is said to have been "first"[4] among the apostles; and that the successors in his see should therefore be first among the bishops. All now believed that such a centre of union was required; and the arguments brought forward in his favour were not very scrupulously canvassed, as every supporter of the Catholic system was interested in exalting the honour of its most distinguished ecclesiastical representative. A text of Scripture was at length adduced which was supposed to settle his claims on an impregnable basis, for our Lord had said to

---

[1] Jerome, *Epist.* 101, *Ad Evangelum.*

[2] Origen, *Commentaries on Matthew, Opera,* iii. 535, Delarue's edition. See also Bunsen's *Hippolytus,* iii. 43.

[3] The reader may find this point, and the whole question relative to the origin of the hierarchy, fully investigated in *The Ancient Church.* See especially period ii. sect. iii. chaps. v. vi. vii. viii. ix. x.

[4] Matt. x. 2.

Simon Barjona, "Thou art Peter, and upon this rock I will build my Church."[1] It had been hitherto believed that the rock was no other than Christ Himself,[2] and that Peter was a living *stone* built upon the sure foundation; but this interpretation was now ignored, and the Rock of Rome was substituted for the Rock of Ages! When the Church was prepared quietly to listen to such an exposition, surely intimations were not wanting that Antichrist was already preparing to erect his throne.

Though the occupant of the "See of Peter" was acknowledged to be first among the bishops as early as the close of the second century, the doctrine of the parity of all members of the episcopal order was still jealously maintained. The deference paid to the Roman chief pastor was considered more complimentary than otherwise, amounting merely to the honorary precedence required by a regard to order among so many peers. Any act of his which was understood to imply that he was disposed to assume the position of an archbishop, or a "Bishop of Bishops," was treated as a piece of intolerable arrogance.[3] But, about the middle of the third century, another step was taken towards the organization of the hierarchy. The Church was then involved in new difficulties by the schisms of Felicissimus and Novatian;[4] the bishops took opposite sides in these dissensions; and the arguments which had previously been used for setting up chiefs among the presbyters were found to be equally potential for placing these chiefs themselves under ecclesiastical supervision. This new arrangement of the hierarchy led to fresh discord, as the more influential prelates of each province were forthwith engaged with each other in a struggle for pre-eminence; and the Church history of the latter part of the third century is little better than the record of a general war among the bishops.[5] The controversy was not settled till the establishment of Christianity by Constantine, when the title *Metropolitan* first occurs in ecclesiastical documents.

Meanwhile the Catholic Church was gradually extended and consolidated. It was still a great voluntary association, held together by the mutual agreement of its members; and the dread

---

[1] Matt. xvi. 18.
[2] "Petra hæc . . Filius Dei est."—*Hermæ Pastor*, lib. iii. sim. ix.
[3] Tertullian, *De Pudicitia*, c. 1; Cyprian, *Concil. Carthag.*
[4] See preceding chapter, p. 40.   [5] Euseb. *Hist. Ecc.* viii. 1.

of schism was the predominating principle which gave it vitality and strength. But, as time passed on, it grew into a compact body, guided by new principles and submitting to despotic dictation. The word *Catholic*[1] was originally descriptive of an evangelical believer who cherished wide and generous sympathies, and who abhorred the endless divisions of sectarianism: in a thousand years it had completely changed its significance, and had become the designation of a slave who dared not even *think* for himself, and who was prepared to destroy the very word of God at the bidding of an ecclesiastical superior.

Under the Jewish dispensation the Almighty insisted on strict obedience to His will, and death was the penalty of a violation of merely ceremonial ordinances. Under the New Testament economy He is equally jealous of the honour of His law, and, in attempting to check the growth even of error, we are not at liberty to tamper with the integrity of any of His institutions. When the rulers of the spiritual commonwealth sought to put down heresy by endowing one of themselves with despotic power, they only increased the perplexities in which they were entangled; and by making obedience to the bishop a condition of church membership, they prescribed a term of communion of which the Scriptures know nothing. The Gnostic teachers were Antichrists,[2] as they substituted their own vain philosophy for the Saviour; and well may the Bishop of Rome be styled *The Antichrist*, for he broadly asserts that he is *the vicar* of the Son of God. He stands at the head of a system which presents a dead ritual instead of the living word, and which clothes a priest with the attributes of the Redeemer. It is not strange that the Apostle John was dismayed when he saw a brood of false prophets spreading themselves over the Church, for he knew that they were the harbingers of "*the last time*" of Antichrist's dominion. The unwise means employed for their suppression issued in the establishment of that vast scheme of spiritual slavery.

It is believed by not a few commentators on prophecy that papal Rome is the Babylon of the Apocalypse; and, assuming the correctness of this interpretation, the preceding statements

---

[1] *i.e. General* or *Universal*. It was introduced in the latter half of the second century.

[2] Hence we find Tertullian speaking of "the Antichrist Marcion."—*Against Marcion*, book iii. c. 8.

remind us of several interesting points of resemblance between the type and the antitype. Babylon commenced with the building of Babel, a great tower, erected as a centre of union for the people of the plain of Shinar, lest they should be "scattered abroad upon the face of the whole earth."[1] But, as time rolled on, the tower became a monument of antiquity; a mighty metropolis surrounded it, and from that seat of empire an absolute sovereign issued laws to many kindreds, and tongues, and people. So it has been with the place whence "the sacerdotal unity took its rise." Hyginus of Rome built an ecclesiastical tower when he "arranged the clergy and distributed the gradations;" and in process of time his see became the capital of a spiritual empire whose ecclesiastical potentate could make kings hold his stirrup and tremble at his mandates. It has appeared extraordinary to many readers of the Old Testament that an undertaking so gigantic as the building of Babel was attempted so soon after the flood; for as the deluge stained the pride of all human glory, its remembrance might have long continued to check the aspirations of ambition. And to others it may seem quite as singular that a graduated hierarchy was commenced so soon after the days of the apostles. Christ taught that no "lordship,"[2] such as that exercised by the princes of the Gentiles, should be acknowledged in His Church; but, in less than a century after the close of the canon of Scripture, bishops were beginning to be entrusted with power which rendered them "lords over God's heritage," and whoever declined their authority was cast out of the Catholic Church. Another point of resemblance between Babylon and papal Rome was only partially illustrated at the great Reformation. As the capture of Babylon led to the liberation of the Israelites and the rebuilding of the temple of God, the downfall of papal Rome is connected with the emancipation of the Church. The overthrow of her tyranny shall usher in the day of millennial glory. Jeremiah thus predicted the fate of the Eastern metropolis: "As God overthrew Sodom and Gomorrah, and the neighbour cities thereof, saith the Lord, so shall no man abide there, neither shall any son of man dwell therein.[3] .... Babylon hath been a golden cup in the Lord's hand that made all the earth drunken; the nations have drunken of her wine; therefore the nations are mad.[4] .... Babylon shall become heaps, a dwelling-place for

[1] Gen. xi. 4. [2] Mark x. 42-45; 1 Pet. v. 3. [3] Jer. l. 40. [4] Jer. li. 7.

dragons, an astonishment, and an hissing, without an inhabitant.[1] How is the praise of the whole earth surprised! How is Babylon become an astonishment among the nations!"[2] Such, too, shall be the fate of Rome, the mystical Babylon. "I saw," says John, "an angel come down from heaven, ... and he cried mightily with a strong voice, saying, Babylon the great is fallen, is fallen, and is become the habitation of devils, and the hold of every foul spirit, and a cage of every unclean and hateful bird. For all nations have drunk of the wine of the wrath of her fornication, and the kings of the earth have committed fornication with her, and the merchants of the earth are waxed rich through the abundance of her delicacies. . . . For her sins have reached unto heaven, and God hath remembered her iniquities."[3]

[1] Jer. li. 37.   [2] Jer. li. 41.   [3] Rev. xviii. 1, 2, 3, 5.

PERIOD II.

From the Conversion of Constantine to the Establishment of the Pope as a Temporal Sovereign.—A.D. 312 TO A.D. 755.

SECTION I.

GENERAL HISTORY OF THE CHURCH.

CHAPTER I.

THE CONVERSION OF CONSTANTINE AND HIS IMPERIAL RECOGNITION OF CHRISTIANITY. THE PROGRESS OF THE CHURCH BEYOND THE BOUNDARIES OF THE EMPIRE.

THE difficulty of governing the vast territories included within the bounds of the Roman Empire led Diocletian to divide the sovereign power among four rulers. Two of these, under the designation of *Augusti*, possessed supreme and co-ordinate authority; and the two others, who were called *Cæsars*, occupied a somewhat lower position. Time soon proved that the arrangement was impolitic. The support of so many regal establishments added to the burden of taxation, and aggravated popular discontent; jealousies and distrust prevented the cordial co-operation of the Augusti and the Cæsars; the unity of the imperial administration was destroyed; and the executive power, no longer grasped by one vigorous hand, lost the influence it had hitherto commanded.

In A.D. 305, Diocletian retired from public life; and, when the State ceased to be guided by so skilful and experienced a director, the evils of the system he had organized were speedily developed. Three years after his abdication, no less than six princes, ruling contemporaneously, claimed authority in the empire. A series of civil wars succeeded; disease and violence gradually reduced the number of regal personages; and, after many struggles and intrigues, Constantine, surnamed the Great, at length found himself in sole possession of the sovereignty.

Constantius Chlorus, the father of Constantine, was one of the associates with whom Diocletian shared his government. The western provinces of Europe, including Britain, Spain, and Gaul, were allotted to his supervision; he discharged the duties of his high trust with much ability; and his subjects awarded him the praise of a prudent and equitable ruler. He saw clearly the folly of the pagan theology; and, though he did not embrace the Gospel, he was disposed to treat its professors with indulgence; so that, when persecution raged throughout the rest of the Roman world, the Christians under his authority escaped comparatively uninjured. In A.D. 306, he died at York in England; and his soldiers immediately, and by acclamation, appointed his son Constantine Emperor. The other princes, though dissatisfied with the proceeding, found it expedient to acquiesce. The new Emperor, at the time of his election, had reached his thirty-second year; and his mind had already been vigorously disciplined by a variety of trials. His personal appearance commended him to the admiration of the multitude, for he was tall, robust, dignified, and handsome; the troops had ample confidence in his courage and capacity as a general; and, during his reign, he evinced his political sagacity by many efforts of bold and successful statesmanship. In A.D. 312, he became involved in a war with Maxentius, one of his colleagues who ruled over Italy and Africa; and the hostile armies came to a decisive engagement at the Milvian bridge in the neighbourhood of Rome. On the eve of the battle Constantine was deeply anxious; for he had to fight against superior numbers, and in the adverse ranks were the veteran Prætorian guards, who were deemed almost invincible. At this crisis he is said to have seen in the heavens a cross of light, bearing the inscription—"*By this Conquer.*" As night drew on, according to the legend, Christ appeared to him in a dream, directed him to prepare a standard corresponding to the pattern exhibited in the sky, and assured him that, under the sacred banner, he should never sustain defeat. Constantine obeyed; and a glorious victory immediately followed.

This story, as handed down from the days of Eusebius,[1] is not

---

[1] *Life of Constantine*, i. 28, 29.

to be received with implicit confidence. The idea that Constantine now witnessed a veritable miracle—that he actually saw in the firmament the figure of a cross, with an inscription in gigantic letters describing it as the pledge of victory—and that he was instructed by Christ Himself to frame the celebrated standard called the Labarum—cannot for a moment be entertained. The instrument of torture on which our Saviour suffered was already regarded with undue reverence; and it is not to be thought that the Prince of Peace at once prescribed it as a warlike banner, and sanctioned the superstition with which it was associated. But though the tale, as related by the imperial biographer, is self-contradictory and preposterous,[1] it is quite possible that it may rest on some substratum of truth. The Christians of that age could detect the figure of a cross in many objects which suggested no such comparison to other observers;[2] and, not improbably, on the day before the battle of the Milvian bridge, the clouds presented an appearance bearing some resemblance to the venerated symbol. And if either the sun itself or a solar halo[3] surmounted the fleeting image, there were individuals in the army on the watch for supernatural intimations, who would point to the cross and the crown of light as a divine and auspicious omen. Whilst, therefore, the ordinary account of this transaction cannot be fully accredited, neither should it be rejected as utterly destitute of foundation. Admitting that selfishness or vanity may have tempted Constantine and others to embellish or exaggerate, it is highly probable that something occurred[4] about the time of the decisive struggle which arrested the attention of the troops, and made a lasting impression on the mind of the Emperor.

Constantine had never been much attached to the worship of

[1] Eusebius himself ignores it in his *Ecclesiastical History*. Even in his *Life of Constantine* he records it with apparent hesitation; stating that he would not have believed it had not the Emperor confirmed the recital of it by an oath—a somewhat suspicious certificate.

[2] As in trees and flowers, fishes and fowls. See Justin Martyr, *Dial. with Trypho*, and *Apol.* ii.; Tertullian, *Adv. Judæos*, c. 10, and the *Octavius* of Minucius Felix.

[3] See a remarkable plate in Sir Edward Belcher's *Arctic Voyages*, i. pp. 168, 169, for a similar phenomenon—a paraselene.

[4] For a similar portent in 1848, see Stanley's *Eastern Church*, p. 224. See also in the *Proceedings of the Royal Irish Academy*, iii. 18, an account of "a cross of light" seen in Dublin on the 27th June 1844.

the gods; and, on his accession to power, he pursued the tolerant policy of his father. He thus conciliated the favour of the members of the Church; and it may be presumed that a considerable number of his soldiers were Christians. The cross was regarded by them as the badge of their faith; and whilst the announcement that they were to fight under its auspices must have stimulated their military enthusiasm, it served, at the same time, to inspirit their heathen comrades—as the cross was also a pagan emblem not unfrequently exhibited in the hand of the statue of Victory.[1] The Emperor, even when advanced in life, was greatly under the influence of superstition; and if he now saw in the clouds some appearance resembling the well known figure, it is not strange that he hailed it as a sign of success. Recent events had prepared him for entertaining the idea of embracing the Gospel. He had marked the indomitable constancy with which its adherents endured the Diocletian persecution; and he had observed how his colleague Galerius, the real author of that terrible scourge, had died in lingering agony of a most loathsome distemper. He could not well divest himself of the feeling that the sufferings of the unhappy prince were inflicted by the God of the Christians. If Jesus was mighty to destroy, he was also mighty to save; and if, at a period of intense excitement, when Constantine was looking all around for help, he saw the sun shining forth in splendour, and an opening in the clouds forming something like a cross of light, he might recognize the spectacle as a celestial intimation, and interpret it as the token of an approaching triumph. And when, immediately afterwards, he vanquished a most powerful enemy, he would be still the more encouraged to cherish the conviction that Christ had interposed in his behalf and assured him of victory.

Whatever may have been the origin of the story which describes Constantine as receiving a revelation from heaven, it is certain that, about the date of the battle of the Milvian bridge, he was induced to become the patron of Christianity. It has, indeed, been alleged that his conduct is to be entirely

---

[1] As may be seen on coins and medals of pagan times. The military ensign of heathen Rome was a species of cross, or "a spear with a transverse piece on the top." Kennett's *Antiquities of Rome*, p. 207, Dublin, 1767. See also Tertullian, *Apol.* xvi. See a remarkable article on the "Pre-Christian Cross" in the *Edinburgh Review* for January 1870, p. 222.

attributed to state policy. He saw that the professors of the faith were a great and united body; that it was in vain to attempt extirpating them by persecution; and that the time was come when a statesman must acknowledge their importance, and tolerate their religion. But we cannot in this way fairly account for his proceedings. It is exceedingly improbable that the Christians now constituted nearly one-half of the subjects of the empire; and they were comparatively uninfluential; for the pagans were in possession of almost all the civil and military offices. The Church, oppressed by a proscription of unprecedented length and severity, was in a state of extreme exhaustion. Had the Emperor simply desired to conciliate the faithful, he could have done so effectually by licensing their worship, as he would thus have bound them to his throne by the double tie of self-interest and of gratitude. But, when he joined their ranks, he took a step of which no mere politician would have deliberately approved. Whilst he thus gained little support which he could not have otherwise secured, he provoked an opposition which might have overturned his government. The sovereign had hitherto been the high priest of heathenism; and the immense array of individuals who derived their means of subsistence from its ritual, as well as the multitudes who were attached to it by education and by prejudice, must have been deeply mortified and provoked by the defection of the imperial pontifex.

If, as is asserted, Constantine became a convert about the time of the battle of the Milvian bridge, he did not, very distinctly and at once, proclaim his convictions. For several years after that event his public acts relating to matters of religion were equivocal and vacillating. He commemorated the defeat of Maxentius by causing his own statue to be erected in the forum of Rome, with a cross in the right hand, and bearing the inscription,—"By this salutary sign, the true symbol of valour, I have delivered your city from the yoke of the tyrant;" but he did not thus offend the prejudices of any portion of his subjects; for the cross, as we have seen, was the index of the goddess of Victory, so that pagans and Christians would concur in recognizing the propriety of the imperial decoration. Even the famous edict of Milan, bearing date March A.D. 313, in which he announced toleration to the Church, is the manifesto of a sovereign apparently very undecided as to the truth of the Gospel. According to this enactment the sacred edifices and other ecclesiastical properties wrested from the disciples during the Diocletian persecution were to be forthwith restored; and, that none might complain of spoliation, the legitimate claims of those thus deprived of possession were to be paid out of the public treasury; but the Emperor significantly adds,—"We grant to the Christians, *and to all*, freedom to follow the mode of worship they prefer, *that whatever divinity exists in heaven may be propitious to us and to all who live under our government.*"[1]

Several other legislative acts of Constantine, intended to promote the interests of the Church, were so cautiously or ambiguously expressed that even his pagan subjects could not well object to their propriety. Thus, in laws enjoining the observance of the first day of the week as a sacred rest, the festival is styled, not as designated in the New Testament, "The Lord's Day," but, as known to the heathen, "the day of the Sun," or Sunday, so that it is left doubtful whether it should be kept in honour of the Lord Christ or of the sun-god Helios.[2] On this day no business was to be transacted in the courts of judicature; and workshops were to be closed; but many of the labouring poor were not relieved by his enactment, as he permitted husbandmen to pursue their agricultural operations without interruption.[3] The knavery of the itinerant haruspices was notorious; and even princes, such as Tiberius and Diocletian, had discountenanced their impostures. When Constantine ordained that a soothsayer who entered into a private house and practised his magical arts should be burned alive, he did not therefore necessarily come into collision with paganism; for not a few of its adherents would applaud such legislation. Various public pro-

---

[1] Euseb. x. 5.
[2] Neander has remarked that we find the god of the Sun represented on coins as the patron god of Constantine.—*Hist. of Christian Religion and Church*, iv. 514, Edinburgh, 1849.
[3] See Jortin's *Remarks on Ecclesiastical History*, i. 425, London, 1846. The following is the brief edict of A.D. 321—" On the venerable day of the sun let all the judges and people residing in cities rest, and let all workshops be shut. In the country, however, persons engaged in the work of husbandry may freely and lawfully continue their pursuits; because it often happens that another day is not so suitable for grain-sowing or for vine-planting; lest by neglecting the proper moment for such operations the bounty of Heaven should be lost. Given the 7th day of March, Crispus and Constantine being Consuls, each of them for the second time."

ceedings bearing date long after the battle of the Milvian bridge attest that he still professed a very adulterated Christianity. So late as the year 317, if not later, the marks of the pagan state worship are displayed on his coins. After his alleged conversion he attended the sacred games, and observed some of the heathen ceremonies. One of the rescripts of the august proselyte encourages the people to frequent the temples, that they may there ascertain from the priests and diviners the secrets of futurity.[1] Nay more—should lightning strike his own palace, the Christian Emperor directed that the Deity should be propitiated according to the forms of the ancient superstition, and that the haruspices should be consulted as to the meaning of the portent!

Some laws made by Constantine a few years after the defeat of Maxentius evince a growing disposition to foster Christianity; and yet he could vindicate his legislation by pleading that he wished to place all his subjects on a footing of religious equality. The fact that the heathen priests enjoyed various privileges, supplied an apology for the extension of similar favours to the ministers of the Gospel. They were, therefore, released from the performance of burdensome municipal duties; their lands were, to a certain extent, freed from taxation; and, whilst a testator was permitted to convey to the Church any amount of every kind of property, the bequest was not encumbered with the charges paid by the inheritor of an ordinary legacy. Under the tyranny of Maxentius, the Church of Africa suffered considerably; and when Constantine gave a large sum of money to assist in repairing or rebuilding the places of Christian worship in that country which were ruined or dilapidated, he could plead that the donation merely involved equitable restitution to an injured community.

Constantine seems to have been led almost imperceptibly, by the current of events, to assume a more decided position as a professor of the Gospel; and his final conflict with his colleague Licinius may be regarded as the second grand crisis in his religious history. As the patron of the Christians he already enjoyed their universal sympathy; and his rival was prompted by policy, as well as by prejudice, to link himself closely with the abettors of the old worship. During the struggle all felt that the two competitors represented the antagonist interests of Christianity

[1] See Milman's *History of Christianity*, ii. 360.

and Paganism. Each party sought to fortify itself by celestial aid. The Christian pastors offered up earnest and unceasing prayer for the success of Constantine; and, as he marched to battle, the Labarum, which displayed so conspicuously the sign of the cross, was guarded by fifty of his best soldiers. The heathen priests anxiously performed the various ceremonies of their ritual; and Licinius himself, having assembled his most distinguished officers in a consecrated grove and presented the accustomed sacrifices, thus addressed the company: "He who leads the troops now opposed to us has proved false to the religion of his forefathers, and adopted the sentiments of those who deny the existence of our divinities. He is so infatuated as to honour some strange and unheard-of Deity, with whose contemptible standard he disgraces his army. Confiding in this aid he has engaged in war, and is now advancing, not so much against us, as against those very gods he has despised. But the present occasion must prove who is mistaken, and decide between our divine guardians and the Deity of our adversaries."[1]

The result of the war was interpreted as the answer of an appeal to Heaven. From A.D. 324, when Constantine became sole emperor, he relinquished the comparatively neutral ground he had hitherto occupied, and boldly adopted measures for the general spread of Christianity. In A.D. 325, the first General Council was convened, and the Roman world looked on with astonishment as the pastors, who had so lately been proscribed, were conveyed on their way to Nice, the place of meeting, in carriages supplied by government. Nor was this all. The emperor took the ordinary ecclesiastical courts under his patronage. His biographer informs us that "he added the sanction of his authority to the decisions of bishops passed at their synods, and forbade the provincial governors to rescind any of their decrees."[2] The pagans still constituted a large portion of the middle and upper classes of society, and sometimes the public interest imperatively required their services; but, except under special circumstances, Constantine bestowed on his new co-religionists the highest offices of trust, authority, and dignity. Nor did he otherwise neglect their interests. Connected with the imperial residences were Basilicæ, or halls of justice, well

[1] Euseb. *Life of Constantine*, ii. 5.   [2] *Ibid.* iv. 27.

adapted for the accommodation of large assemblies; and as many of these were seldom required for the service of the state, they were now devoted to the celebration of Christian worship. The sovereign invited distinguished pastors to his court; admitted them to his confidence; and encouraged the building of new and beautiful churches everywhere throughout his dominions. The ministers of the Gospel had hitherto subsisted chiefly on the voluntary oblations of the faithful; and, in consequence of the improved social position of their flocks, many of them now enjoyed considerable emoluments, so that Constantine did not require to make any general provision for their maintenance. But he frequently contributed largely to their support, and in particular instances established something like missionary stations in the midst of a heathen population.[1]

Whilst endeavouring to promote the growth of Christianity, the Emperor adopted measures for the discouragement or suppression of heathenism. The civil magistrate, who had till this time acted as one of the ministers of the gods, was no longer permitted to add the weight of his official dignity to the pagan worship; for a law was now promulgated forbidding all holding any public appointment to engage in sacrifice. Had Constantine required the indiscriminate overthrow of the heathen temples, he would have found it impossible to secure obedience to his orders; and hence prudence suggested that many of them, at least for a time, should be suffered to remain uninjured. He contrived, however, to give an effective blow to the system which they represented, by pulling down a few of the high places of idolatry; and he exhibited no little tact in the selection of the buildings singled out for demolition. Two temples of Venus, at Aphaca and Heliopolis in Phœnicia,[2] had long outraged common decency by their abominable ceremonies; and Constantine performed a service which all the friends of social order could not but applaud when he issued orders for destroying these dens of licentiousness. A temple in Cilicia dedicated to Æsculapius had been noted as the scene of extraordinary cures; but, by razing it to the ground and exposing the tricks and jugglery of its priesthood, the credit of the old religion was vastly lowered.[3] Images which popular credulity had invested with supernatural powers were stripped

---

[1] For an example of this see *The Life of Constantine*, iii. 53.
[2] Euseb. *Life of Constantine*, iii. 55, 58.   [3] *Ibid.* iii. 56.

of their outward finery, and their rude materials displayed to the mocking multitude. Towards the end of his reign, Constantine commanded all the heathen temples to be closed;[1] but there is good evidence that the order was not generally carried into execution.

The government of this prince extended over a period of upwards of thirty years—more than thirteen of which he was sole emperor. Meanwhile the Roman world was the theatre of a wonderful revolution. In A.D. 306, when the soldiers invited him to assume the purple, Christianity was struggling under the most sanguinary persecution it had ever encountered; many of its churches lay in ruins; its pastors were oppressed and dispirited; and even its resolute adherents met in secret to celebrate its ordinances. In A.D. 337, when he died, it basked in the sunshine of imperial favour; its professors had so multiplied that they probably formed a majority of the whole population; its bishops were to be seen in the palace of the sovereign, mingling on equal terms with the most favoured of the courtiers; and not a few of its religious edifices, in magnificence and amplitude, rivalled the splendid structures of heathenism. But, after all, there is no very satisfactory evidence of the vital piety of the man who was instrumental in bringing about this momentous transformation. The success of Constantine, when contending against Licinius and other enemies of the Church, was obviously regarded by him as the best proof of the Divine origin of the Gospel. "To this truth," he exclaimed, "bear testimony the happy issue of all my endeavours, my battles, and triumphs.[2] . . . Everywhere preceded by Thy sign have I led on a victorious army. . . . *For this cause* I have consecrated to Thee my soul. . . . I venerate Thy power which Thou hast revealed to me by so many proofs, and by which Thou hast confirmed my faith."[3] Had Constantine been less successful as a general, he would, probably, have been less zealous as a patron of Christianity. He professed its creed not, as it would appear, because he had experienced its renovating power, but because, as he believed, its Divine Author had been his Protector, and had fought for him against rival sovereigns. Many passages in the history of his life may well suggest the painful conclusion that his religion was

---

[1] Theodoret, *Ecc. Hist.* v. 21. [2] *Constant. Oratio*, 22.
[3] *Life of Constantine*, ii. 55.

little better than a refined superstition. He was convinced of the folly of polytheism; he saw that the Christian system had many practical advantages; he was led on, step by step, till he was completely committed to its recognition; but the great reason why he supported it so steadfastly was because he feared that, were he ever to act otherwise, he would soon cease to be a victor and an emperor.

From his constant intercourse with eminent pastors this prince must have acquired a considerable knowledge of the doctrines of the Gospel; and, under the advice of some of his Christian counsellors, he enacted several excellent laws; but we still lack decisive evidences of his own spiritual enlightenment. His conduct in the Arian controversy[1] was such as might have been expected from a prudent politician who cared little for the question in dispute, and who was mainly anxious to promote the unity and strength of the party with which he was identified. In an address to the Council of Nice, delivered immediately before its separation, he urged the propriety of seeking to attract converts to the Church by holding out to them the prospect of secular advantages. "Some," said he, "who hear are glad to secure the supply of their bodily necessities; others court the patronage of their superiors; some fix their affection on those by whom they are hospitably entertained; others, again, who are gratified by presents, love their benefactors in return; but few really desire instruction, and it is rare indeed to find a friend of the truth. Hence we must endeavour to meet every individual case, and try, physician-like, to administer to each what may tend to the health of the soul, that the saving doctrine may by all be fully honoured."[2] A man who had felt that "the law of the Lord is perfect, converting the soul" would have been slow to recommend so prominently to an assembly of Christian ministers such methods of conversion. It was not thus that the Gospel originally triumphed.

The personal conduct of Constantine in advanced life did not exhibit Christianity as a religion fitted to effect a marked improvement in the spirit and character. In A.D. 326, he put to death his son Crispus, a youth of the highest promise, who had in some way disturbed his suspicious temper. His nephew Licinius and his own wife Fausta shared the same fate. His

---

[1] See Sect. II. Chap. II. of this Period.   [2] *Life of Constantine*, iii. 21.

growing passion for gaudy dress betrayed pitiable vanity in an old man of sixty; and, towards the end of his reign, the general extravagance of his expenditure led to an increase of taxation of which his subjects complained. He desired to be a dictator of the Church, rather than a disciple; and, with a view to share its privileges without submitting to its discipline, deferred his baptism until the near approach of death. He then received the ordinance from the Arian bishop of Nicomedia.

The defects in the religious character of Constantine greatly impaired his moral influence. Though he did much to promote the extension of the visible Church, his reign forms an era in the history of ecclesiastical corruption. His own Christianity was so loose and accommodating that it seemed to consist chiefly in the admiration of a new ritual; and the courtiers who surrounded him, and who complimented him by the adoption of his creed, seldom seemed to feel that it taught the necessity of personal reformation. All at once the profession of the Gospel became fashionable: crowds of merely nominal converts presented themselves at the baptismal font; and many entered even the clerical office who had no higher object in view than an honourable or a lucrative position. Ecclesiastical discipline was relaxed; and, that the heathen might be induced to conform to the religion of the Emperor, many of their ceremonies were introduced into the worship of the Church. The manner in which Constantine intermeddled with ecclesiastical affairs was extremely objectionable. He undertook not only to preach but also to dictate to aged and learned ministers. Had any other individual who had never been baptized appeared in the Nicene synod, and ventured to give counsel to the assembled fathers, he would have been speedily rebuked for his presumption; but all were so delighted to see a great prince among them, that there was a general unwillingness to challenge his intrusion. He sometimes indeed declared that he left spiritual matters to Church courts; but his conduct demonstrated how little he observed such an arrangement. He convened synods by his own authority; took a personal share in their discussions; required their members to appear before him, and submit their proceedings to his review; and inflicted on them civil penalties when their official acts did not meet his approval. Had Constantine given his sanction and encouragement to the Church, and yet permitted her to pursue her noble mission in the full enjoyment of the right of self-government, he might have contributed greatly to promote her safe and vigorous development; but, by usurping the place of her chief ruler, and bearing down with the weight of the civil power on all who refused to do his pleasure, he secularized her spirit, robbed her of her freedom, and converted her divine framework into a piece of political machinery.

During the reign of Constantine Christianity made considerable progress beyond the bounds of the Empire. The Goths, who had previously obtained some knowledge of its doctrines, now appear more prominently in Church history. Their chief pastor Theophilus was present at the Council of Nice; but the converts were still comparatively few; and Ulphilas, or Wolf, who flourished in the succeeding generation,[1] has been commonly designated their *Apostle*. His labours among them produced a great and permanent impression. He invented an alphabet for their use, and translated almost the whole of the Scriptures into their language.

Whilst the Gospel was spreading among these fierce warriors, other nations outside the Roman frontier were beginning to enjoy its illumination. It had already extended into Persia, and a flourishing church existed in the capital of that country; but political jealousies interfered to impede its advancement. The government looked with extreme suspicion on the intercourse of the native believers with their brethren within the Roman territory, and the conversion of Constantine vastly increased this distrust. In the fourth and fifth centuries the disciples in Persia endured two persecutions of long continuance and of almost unparalleled severity. At these trying seasons many Christians of high station chose to meet death in the most frightful form rather than relinquish their religion.

Towards the commencement of the fourth century Tiridates, King of Armenia, was converted by the instrumentality of Gregory, surnamed *the Illuminator*. The monarch immediately took steps to plant the Gospel throughout his dominions: no less than four hundred bishops were forthwith ordained: churches were built all over the land: and Armenia is said to have em-

---

[1] Ulphilas died, aged 70, in A.D. 388. See Neander's *General History*, iv. 539, note.

braced Christianity as the religion of the sovereign, the nobles, and the people, even before the new faith was publicly recognized by Constantine.[1] But the old pagan worship long lingered in many of its provinces, and in the beginning of the fifth century still retained no small number of adherents. About that time Miesrob, an eminently devoted missionary, supplied the Armenians with an alphabet, translated the Scriptures into their language, and contributed greatly to weaken the influence of the ancient superstition.

In the early part of the fourth century Christianity was introduced into Iberia, a country bordering on Armenia. It was also successfully diffused in Arabia and India. About the same time it made rapid progress in Abyssinia, a portion of Africa in which it has never since been entirely extinguished. In A.D. 316, a Tyrian navigator, engaged in exploring the countries south of Egypt, was murdered with all his ship's crew, except two, by the savage inhabitants. Frumentius and Ædesius, youths of superior intelligence, who escaped the carnage, were taken to court and entrusted with the education of the heir to the throne. The young prince thus became a convert to the faith, and many of the Abyssinians speedily followed his example.

CHAPTER II.

THE CHURCH UNDER THE SUCCESSORS OF CONSTANTINE, AND THE FALL OF PAGANISM.

CONSTANTINE the Great, whose reign terminated in A.D. 337, was succeeded by his three sons, Constantine, Constantius, and Constans. Constantius, the last survivor, died in A.D. 361, so that the government of these princes continued about twenty-four years. Throughout the whole of this period the Church was visibly enlarging its boundaries; but the example of the children of the first Christian emperor contributed nothing to its real advancement. Though educated in the faith of the Gospel, they exhibited little of its spirit, and their history is a melancholy record of perfidy and discord. They had not yet entered on the cares of government when the troops protested against a portion

[1] Milman, *History of Christianity*, ii. 318.

of their father's will—which directed that their cousins Dalmatius and Hannibalianus should be associated with them in the administration of the empire. This manifestation of discontent among the soldiers awakened the alarm of the two royal youths whose promotion was disputed; and Constantius, the second son of Constantine, and the only one present to interfere, pledged his oath for their protection; but he soon basely permitted both his relatives to fall victims to military violence. Within three years after their father's death, the eldest and the youngest of the sons of Constantine commenced a fratricidal war, in which Constantine the Second perished. Meanwhile controversy continued to distract the Church; and, whilst Constans in the West supported the Nicene Creed, Constantius, in the East, was the abettor of Arianism. The reign of Constans closed abruptly in A.D. 350. His profession of the Nicene faith was dishonoured by his immoralities; his worthless character tempted Magnentius, an ambitious soldier, to aspire to the imperial dignity, and the youngest son of the great Constantine was slain as he fled from the usurper. Constantius, now sole Emperor, was the dupe of unworthy favourites; and, though he took no small credit to himself as the patron of the Gospel, his religious zeal was expended chiefly in fruitless efforts to establish the ascendency of Arianism.

All these princes were desirous to strengthen the political position of the Church, and endeavoured, in pursuance of their father's policy, to discourage or suppress paganism. A law promulgated by Constantius in A.D. 341 is couched in the following peremptory language: "Let superstition cease! let the folly of sacrifices be abolished. Whoever, after the publication of this law, continues to sacrifice shall be punished in accordance with his deserts."[1] Five years afterwards Constans and Constantius published still more stringent enactments. They directed the temples to be everywhere closed, and sacrifices to cease on pain of death and confiscation of goods. In A.D. 356, Constantius issued another edict, in which sacrificing is again pronounced a capital offence. These laws did not enjoin the *profession of Christianity* under pains and penalties—and in so far they are somewhat less objectionable than later acts of intolerance—but they all overlooked the rights of conscience, and they were all conceived in a spirit

[1] *Cod. Theodos.*, l. xvi. t. x. 2, ed. Gustavus Haenel, 1842, c. 1012.

intensely persecuting. There were districts of the empire in which it would have been unsafe to attempt their enforcement, so that in some quarters they operated only in the way of intimidation, and they were nowhere very rigorously executed, as large numbers, including not a few persons of high rank, continued long after their promulgation to adhere to paganism. But still, combined with the influence of fashion and the policy pursued by the imperial court in the distribution of its patronage, they produced a wonderful impression. Multitudes, who had no deep religious convictions and who were guided merely by secular considerations, submitted to baptism, and thus rapidly augmented the nominal amount of the Christian population.

On the death of Constantius, in A.D. 361, the superficial character of much of the Christianity he patronized was soon painfully apparent. His cousin Julian, now sole monarch of the empire, accomplished in a very short reign another great ecclesiastical revolution. This prince, commonly known as *The Apostate*, though brought up within the pale of the Church—in which for a time he officiated as a lector, or reader of the Scriptures—had secretly imbibed an inveterate prejudice against the Gospel, and at length became an avowed and ardent abettor of the pagan worship. It is not difficult to account for his backsliding. The Church, torn by the violence of disputation during the Trinitarian controversy, excited the derision of the pagans. In an age when an insincere profession of the Gospel was so common, Julian seldom, or perhaps never, enjoyed a very favourable opportunity of observing the consistent excellence of a life of faith, the most effective argument of Christianity. The cruelty with which many members of his family were treated by their imperial relatives inspired him with a settled antipathy to the religion of the Court; and his leanings to paganism were encouraged and confirmed by his intercourse with certain heathen philosophers attached to the ancient superstition. A large portion of the literati still supported the worship of the gods. Adopting the system called *New Platonism*, they gave to the legends of the heathen deities a mythical interpretation, and assigned to the various parts of the pagan ritual something like a spiritual significance. According to their views the gods were so many emanations from one Supreme Being; each exerted a special influence, and each felt gratified by homage paid to his image or visible representative. Many of the old aristocracy of the empire, who adhered to heathenism under the impression that the glory of Rome was in some way bound up with the preservation of the ancient religious services, willingly adopted expositions of its worship which appeared to relieve it of much of its grossness and absurdity. And the philosophers, thus left at liberty to invent as many theological allegories as they pleased, were delighted with the exercise of grafting their own speculations on the old stock of the pagan ceremonial.

When Julian became emperor he at once re-established the religion of Jupiter and the gods. The facility with which he effected this ecclesiastical change supplies satisfactory proof that Christianity had yet a very feeble hold on the mass of the population. The profession of the Gospel made by myriads in the days of Constantine and his sons was dictated by purely secular motives; and under the auspices of the new emperor such parties were quite ready to return to idolatry. Julian exerted himself to the uttermost to increase the attractiveness of the old ritual. He renovated the dilapidated temples, restored their endowments, and, as the supreme pontiff of paganism, sacrificed with his own hand multitudes of victims. He appointed persons of the highest distinction to the priesthood, required the officiating ministers to wear sumptuous vestments, and embellished the service by the music of bands of choristers. He recommended the priests to imitate the Christians—or, as he contemptuously styled them, *the Galileans*—by attending to the wants of the poor and the afflicted; exhorted them to study to advance their cause by the decency of their behaviour; and encouraged them to endeavour to gain possession of the public mind by introducing into their worship something like preaching or popular instruction.

Whilst Julian was diligently labouring to revive the pagan interest, he did not neglect to take measures for weakening the cause of Christianity. Though he professed to extend to it the privilege of toleration, he contrived to harass it by various petty modes of annoyance. Summoning before him the chiefs of the parties into which the disciples were divided, he invited them to discuss their principles in his presence, and, whilst listening to them with affected candour, sought, by an artful distribution of praise and blame, to foment and perpetuate their dissensions. But he did not confine himself to this sly amusement. As the Christians were now fully equal to any other class of the community in literary culture, he attempted to degrade their children by restricting them to an inferior course of education. He accordingly prohibited the brethren from acting as teachers in the public seminaries, and from cultivating the study of Homer and the other ancient classic authors. Some of his acts were of a still more hostile character. In many cases where heathen temples had been destroyed in the preceding reigns, Christians were compelled to undertake the expense of their restoration. He also confiscated the wealth of the Church, withdrew the endowments of the clergy, and deprived them of immunities which they had enjoyed since the days of Constantine.

Julian was a prince of no mean capacity, of blameless morals, learned, and brave; but he was unequal to the task of the resuscitation of paganism. Though seconded in his efforts by a crowd of so-called philosophers, and though multitudes, guided by self-interest or fashion, returned to the worship of the gods, the Gospel lost little substantial influence. Professing to deride the religion of those whom he nicknamed Galileans, the emperor borrowed from it almost all the reforms he introduced into the pagan discipline and ritual, so that by some of the wits of his generation he was styled "The Ape of Christianity." The failure of his attempt to rebuild the temple of Jerusalem made a deep impression on the public mind. He imagined that, by erecting a new structure on the foundation of the old, he would in some way invalidate the prophecies of our Saviour; but balls of fire, bursting from various parts of Mount Moriah, terrified his workmen, and induced them eventually to give up the undertaking. The fact of these fiery eruptions is attested by heathen as well as Christian evidence;[1] and though we may now find it easy to account for them on scientific principles,[2] they were at the time deemed miraculous, and regarded as indications of the wrath of God against those who sought to overturn the divine testimony.

Julian was sole emperor only about twenty months, and during his short reign he laboured with amazing diligence for the ad-

---

[1] Ammianus Marcellinus, xxiii. 1; Chrysostom, *Adv. Jud. et Gent.*: Gregory Nazianzen, Orat. iv. *Adv. Julian;* Ambrose, *Epist.* xl.

[2] See the life of this emperor in the *Encyclop. Metropol.*

vancement of his favourite designs; but all his efforts to revive paganism were as abortive as his attempt to build the Jewish temple. Though possessed of various accomplishments, he had an ill-balanced mind; he was pedantic and vain, as well as singularly deficient in discernment and common sense. His opposition to the Gospel was obviously dictated rather by passion than by reason; and his credulity as a devotee of the heathen superstition was as singular as his want of faith in everything pertaining to Christianity. The old idolatry and the philosophy of New Platonism were incongruous elements, and the experiment of their combination only hastened the disappearance of both. Paganism in the reign of Julian was like a dead body under the influence of galvanism: all at once it displayed signs of life, it stood up, and it appeared as if prepared to enter on a new career of existence; but, when the power of the imperial operator was withdrawn, it suddenly fell, and betrayed the secret of its artificial restoration.

Jovian, who was called to occupy the throne left vacant by the death of Julian, made a profession of the Christian faith; and though he deemed it prudent to tolerate the religion of his predecessor, the Church, during his short reign of little more than seven months, quietly recovered its ascendency. Under the government of his successor it continued to gain strength. Its position is indicated by the fact that the adherents of the old idolatry began about this period to be designated *Peasantry* or *Pagans*. The name, as descriptive of the worshippers of the gods, occurs for the first time in one of the laws of Valentinian,[1]—a circumstance from which we may infer that heathenism now maintained its ground only in places far away from the great thoroughfares of men, and that Christianity was generally professed throughout the cities and towns of the Empire.[2]

In the reign of Julian, Valentinian had signalized himself as a despiser of the ceremonies of the heathen ritual. On one occasion, when entering a temple at Antioch in company with his sovereign, he struck a priest proceeding to sprinkle him with

---

[1] In A.D. 368. *Cod. Theodos.* l. xvi. tit. ii. 18, ed. Haenel, c. 1491.

[2] Neander has remarked that Paganism maintained itself so long among the country people, partly in consequence of the indifference or selfishness of Christian landholders, who were anxious to allow the pagan temples to stand for the sake of the income derived from the taxes on them. Neander, iv. 519.

lustral water, and thus grievously offended his imperial master.[1] But, when he succeeded to the throne, he adopted the policy of toleration; and even his heathen subjects acknowledged the impartiality of his government. His brother Valens, who ruled over the Eastern portion of the empire, was a feeble prince; and, though a bitter advocate of Arianism,[2] could be controlled by fraternal influence. During his reign paganism in the East was well nigh crushed to death; but it suffered chiefly on account of its political delinquencies; as a rebellion[3] which threatened to subvert the authority of Valens, and in which almost all the leaders of the heathen party were understood to be implicated, provoked him to treat them with excessive severity.

Though Christianity had, at this time, been professed by so many rulers of the Roman world, Gratian, who succeeded his father Valentinian in A.D. 375, was the first emperor who refused to permit himself to be arrayed in the official robes of the high priest of heathenism. This act of the young prince indicated the policy he subsequently pursued. Guided by the advice of Ambrose, the celebrated bishop of Milan, he soon afterwards[4] removed the altar of Victory from the Roman senate-house; confiscated the property of the temples; and withdrew the privileges of the priesthood.[5] Under the government of Theodosius the Great, who succeeded Valens in the East in A.D. 379, and who subsequently became sole monarch, the proscription of paganism continued with unabated severity. Crowds of monks traversed the country, and occupied themselves with the demolition of the idolatrous edifices. A rescript issued by Theodosius, in A.D. 391, commanded the destruction of the heathen temples of Alexandria; and in other places these structures were pulled down without the express sanction of any imperial enactment.

Of all the buildings consigned to ruin no one has more attracted the notice of historians than the temple of Serapis in the capital of Egypt. This high-place of superstition was scarcely surpassed, as to extent and magnificence, by any other pile of architecture in the Roman Empire. It was of a quad-

---

[1] Sozomen, vi. 6; Theodoret, iii. 16.
[2] As an instance of his cruelty, see Sozomen, vi. 14.
[3] The rebellion of Procopius. See Milman's *Hist. of Christianity*, iii. 119.
[4] A.D. 382.   [5] *Cod. Theodos.* xvi. t. x. 20.

rangular form, and placed on an artificial elevation ascended by one hundred steps. The outer buildings, which were of vast dimensions, accommodated the priests and the devotees. Within was a spacious square surrounded with a range of galleries; and in the middle stood the habitation of the idol, built of marble, and supported on pillars of immense magnitude and beautiful symmetry. The idol itself was a human form of colossal proportions made of gold, silver, iron, and other metals, fused together, and inlaid with precious stones. It was asserted that the demolition of this statue would involve the ruin of the world, and that any one who attempted to do it injury would forthwith be swallowed up by an earthquake. These statements had made such an impression even on the minds of the Christians that when the multitude came together to destroy the image, all stood before it for a time silent and fearful. At length a soldier, urged on by the bishop Theophilus, ventured to strike it with a hatchet on the knee; and the blow resounded through the temple without producing any visible catastrophe. The assailant, emboldened by the result of his first attack, climbed up to the head; and, exerting all his strength, succeeded in cleaving the jaw asunder. A swarm of mice rushed out of the aperture, and scampered off in all directions. The appearance of these unexpected colonists excited universal laughter; and the mob, now relieved from their fears, entered in right earnest on the work of destruction. Serapis was soon reduced to fragments, and the temple itself converted into a heap of ruins.[1]

A few of the more famous of the religious edifices of the heathen were preserved as noble specimens of architecture; some became Christian churches; but many were levelled to the ground. Towards the end of his reign Theodosius prohibited the celebration of the heathen rites by the most stringent enactments. Any landowner who tolerated their performance forfeited the estate on which the offence was committed; and any individual who sacrificed a victim was liable to the punishment of death.[2] Paganism was professed at Rome by an influential section of the old aristocracy; but the emperor refused to permit the public revenue to contribute to its maintenance; and, though its votaries were still at liberty to visit its shrines, these were soon almost completely deserted.

[1] Theodoret, v. 22; Socrates, v. 16.   [2] *Cod. Theodosiani*, lib. xvi. t. x. 12.

and the Fall of Paganism.

The Empire had long been exhibiting unmistakeable indications of decay, and Theodosius was the last monarch under whom it remained united. At his death, in A.D. 395,[1] it was divided between his two sons Arcadius and Honorius; the barbarians from the North burst into some of its most fertile provinces; and, after a struggle of about eighty years' continuance, the line of Western sovereigns closed, in A.D. 476, with the deposition of the feeble Augustulus. Odoacer, a barbarian chief, now assumed the designation of king of Italy; and, though acknowledging a species of nominal subjection to the Emperor of the East, occupied the position of an independent potentate.

Throughout the period we have just reviewed we see a new element exerting an increasing influence in the affairs of the Roman Empire. Christianity was no sooner recognized by the State than it began to confront and to curb the imperial despotism. Asserting the great principle that all men are equal in the sight of God, it taught the humblest member of the community to cherish a higher idea of his individual importance, and abated that overweaning regard for rank and official position so common in states destitute of a popular constitution. The Christian emperors soon found that the Church checked and embarrassed them in the exercise of tyrannical authority. It brought a discipline to bear upon them by which even they were intimidated, and created a public opinion before which they were constrained to succumb.

As the Church continued to gain strength, it ventured to assume a bolder attitude; and, at length, fairly overstepping the limits of its proper province, exercised the oppression of a spiritual despotism. But for some time—though its proceedings were occasionally characterized by insolence or caprice—its influence, on the whole, was extremely salutary. As soon as it was incorporated with the State, its ministers were advanced to a high social position; and were, in consequence, not unfrequently employed by persons in distress to act as intercessors with magistrates, with military chiefs, and even with the emperors themselves. In this way their interference was often very seasonable and useful. The harsh governor or the enraged prince found it difficult to resist the appeals of an eloquent and

---

[1] According to some this is a great prophetic era. See Elliott's *Horæ Apocalypticæ*, i. 344.

pious pastor, as he expatiated on the merciful spirit of Christ, and inculcated the duties of forbearance and forgiveness. In A.D. 387, when the people of Antioch had committed various acts of outrage and sedition, Theodosius determined to punish them in such a way as would at once vindicate his insulted authority and intimidate all the disaffected. The inhabitants heard of his intentions; and the whole city was a scene of mourning and dismay. But the aged bishop Flavian, who undertook the work of mediation, was able, on his return from court, to announce a free and universal pardon.

In the days of paganism offenders fled for protection to its fanes; and when Christianity became the established faith, its sacred edifices began to be regarded as places of refuge. By an enactment made in A.D. 431, this right of asylum was legally recognized.[1] Pastors often interposed with effect on behalf of those who sought shelter in their sanctuaries. And when the barbarians overran the Empire, the Church, degenerate as it was, still proved a blessing of singular excellence. Its ministers, permitted, in the first instance, to act as mediators between the victors and the vanquished, eventually united both in the bonds of Christian brotherhood.

CHAPTER III.

THE ECCLESIASTICAL WRITERS.

THOUGH Christianity was introduced into the world in an age noted for intellectual activity and literary culture, it was at first embraced by but a very small number of scholars, philosophers, or persons of distinction. "Not many wise men after the flesh, not many mighty, not many noble," were "called."[2] For several generations after the days of the apostles, the ecclesiastical memorials are scanty and meagre; and the fathers of the first three centuries seldom ranked high among contemporaries as men of classic taste or superior erudition. The fourth century witnessed a wonderful revolution, as well in literature as in religion. The pagan writers of that time are few and of inferior merit; whilst a whole multitude of Christian authors, some of

---

[1] *Cod. Theodos.* ix. t. xlv. 4, ed. Haenel, c. 966.   [2] 1 Cor. i. 26.

The Ecclesiastical Writers.   83

them of much ability and eloquence, adorn the literary firmament. Early in the century, LACTANTIUS, whose polished style has earned for him the title of the *Christian Cicero*, published his *Divine Institutions*. In this work, which is divided into seven books, he discusses the claims of heathenism and Christianity. EUSEBIUS, in his *Evangelical Preparation* and *Evangelical Demonstration*, enters more largely into the same argument, and asserts in opposition to both pagans and Jews the divinity of the Gospel. Both these writers moved in the highest circles of society. Lactantius was the tutor of Crispus,[1] son of Constantine; and Eusebius was one of the confidential advisers of the first Christian Emperor.

Eusebius has been called *the father of Church history;* and his work on the subject, in which he describes some of the ecclesiastical transactions of the first three centuries, is that by which he is best known. It is, however, a very unsatisfactory performance; it supplies no information respecting many of the most important occurrences of the period; but, as it is almost the only volume from which we can learn anything of the annals of the early Church, it has acquired a celebrity to which it has little intrinsic claim. RUFINUS,[2] a presbyter of Aquileia, has reproduced it in a loose Latin translation, and carried it down to the death of Theodosius the Great.[3] Three Greek historians—SOCRATES and SOZOMEN, both of whom belonged to the legal profession, and THEODORET, bishop of Cyrus, in Syria—take up the narrative in the reign of Constantine, and continue it through a portion of the fifth century; and, as they all illustrate nearly the same interval, we may, from their combined statements, form a tolerably correct idea of the transactions of the period. Theodoret brings his relation to a close somewhat earlier than either of his contemporaries, as he stops at A.D. 428. He was personally involved in the discussions which agitated the Church during the next quarter of a century; and, among all the assailants of the heresy of Eutychianism, he may be pronounced the most for-

---

[1] His mother Minervina, a person of obscure birth, was the first wife of the Emperor. Crispus was a prince of great promise. As to his death, see p. 70.

[2] That Rufinus, not Ruffinus, is the true orthography, see Migne, *Patrol. Curs.* xxi. 76.

[3] This Emperor died, as already stated, in A.D. 395. The history of Eusebius closes before the Council of Nice in A.D. 325. Eusebius has also left behind him a Life of Constantine, and other works.

midable and accomplished. He has written on a great variety of subjects; and his expository works hold a high place among patristic commentaries. EVAGRIUS, a lawyer who resided at Antioch, has left behind him a Church history extending from the Council of Ephesus, in A.D. 431, to nearly the end of the sixth century.

Various other contemporary works throw light on the ecclesiastical movements of the period before us. OPTATUS, bishop of Milevi, in Numidia, has bequeathed to us a history of the Donatists; and, though he writes in the spirit of a partisan, he is well acquainted with the transactions he describes, and has preserved much valuable information relative to the Church of Africa in the fourth century. EPIPHANIUS, bishop of Salamis, in Cyprus, in his treatise *On Heresies*, and elsewhere, has illustrated the events of his age; but his style is uncouth and his judgment imbecile.[1] SULPITIUS SEVERUS, a Gallic presbyter who flourished about the beginning of the fifth century, shared in the admiration of asceticism characteristic of his generation; and, in his *Life of Martin of Tours*, has detailed with wonderful simplicity the alleged miracles of that apostle of monachism. The style of this work, as well as of his *Sacred History*, is excellent; and hence he has acquired the name of the *Christian Sallust*. DIONYSIUS EXIGUUS, who lived in the reign of Justinian,[2] rendered an important service to ecclesiastical literature by publishing a collection of the Canons of the Councils. GREGORY OF TOURS is the author of the *Annals of the Francs;* and, though a barbarous writer, he assists us in tracing the history of Gallic Christianity during the second, third, fourth, fifth, and sixth centuries. A monk of Northumberland, the presbyter BEDE, surnamed the VENERABLE, has given us an ecclesiastical history of England. This work comes down to A.D. 731—the year before his death. Bede was one of the most learned men of his day; and his writings, which discuss a wide range of topics, contributed to sustain the lamp of Christian knowledge in Europe during the long night of the Middle Ages.

A considerable part of the ecclesiastical literature of the time

---

[1] Epiphanius is a rare example of a convert from Judaism among the Fathers. He was acquainted with five languages, Hebrew, Syriac, Egyptian, Greek, and Latin.

[2] A.D. 527 to A.D. 565.

of Constantine, and of the four succeeding centuries, consists of the correspondence of churchmen and others. The bishops of Rome now stand out prominently among their contemporaries, and many of their letters are documents of much importance. Several epistles written by DAMASUS[1] are still extant; and SIRICIUS, his immediate successor, who occupied the papal chair from A.D. 384 to A.D. 398, commenced the *Decretals*,—or those episcopal circulars in which the great Italian pontiff undertakes to propound ecclesiastical law to the other prelates of Christendom. The letters of INNOCENT I., LEO I., GREGORY I., GREGORY II., GREGORY III., and ZACHARY, are of special historical value. A large portion of the correspondence of persons in an humbler position has also been preserved; and, among these remembrancers of the past, not the least interesting are the epistles of BONIFACE, the apostle of the Germans.

The disputes relating to the Trinity, which convulsed the Church during the greater part of the fourth century, produced a large amount of theological literature. ATHANASIUS, bishop of Alexandria, the champion of orthodoxy, was an indefatigable writer. As the intellectual features of this distinguished father will be exhibited in the history of the Arian controversy,[2] a particular description of his character is at present unnecessary. His works, especially his *Apology against the Arians*, his *Apology addressed to the Emperor Constantius*, his *Epistle to Serapion* concerning the death of Arius, and his *Encyclical Epistle* addressed to all the bishops, as well as others of his letters, throw much light on the progress of the struggle in which he was the chief athlete. Many of the productions ascribed to him, including the creed which bears his name,[3] are unquestionably spurious. He had profoundly studied the question of the Deity of Christ, so that he felt himself strong in the truth; and, when required to enter into disputation, his tact, acuteness, and eloquence gave him an immense superiority over all antagonists. He possessed other qualities which won for him the sympathy and the admiration of the multitude. Whilst the Arians disgraced themselves

---

[1] A.D. 366 to A.D. 384.   [2] Section II. Chap. II. of this Period.
[3] See Cave's *Lives of the Fathers*, ii. 242, Oxford, 1840. According to some, this Creed was written by Vigilius, bishop of Tapsus in Africa, who flourished towards the close of the fifth century. See Hagenbach's *History of Doctrines*, i. 267, Edinburgh, 1846. According to others, it is of French origin. See Schaff's *Hist. of the Christ. Church*, iii. 696.

by shuffling and tergiversation, Athanasius always asserted his convictions, and always appeared bold as a lion. But his sound logic was not always rendered palatable by the milk of human kindness, and some of his vindications of the great doctrine of the Saviour's Godhead exhibit but little of the meekness of wisdom. The evangelical reader will peruse many of his controversial treatises with a degree of disappointment; for, whilst he displays wonderful argumentative ability, his polemic bitterness is intense;[1] and he rarely dwells on the practical application of his glorious theme, or points out the overflowing comfort which faith can draw from the doctrine of an Almighty and Eternal Saviour.

Among the most resolute advocates of the Supreme Deity of Christ in the Western Church was HILARY OF POICTIERS.[2] He has written commentaries on the Psalms and on the Gospel of Matthew. His work *On the Trinity*, divided into twelve books, is considered the most comprehensive and systematic treatise on the subject which antiquity has produced. But, as his style is involved and obscure, and his manner abrupt, he is by no means an attractive author. He is supposed to have died about A.D. 367.

Another bishop, invested with the episcopal office about the same time as Hilary, and also involved in the commotions created by the Arian controversy, was CYRIL OF JERUSALEM. When only a deacon he delivered those *Catechetical Lectures*, in which he expounds to us so fully his views respecting baptism. For six-and-thirty years he presided over the mother Church of Palestine; and, during his episcopate, the Emperor Julian made that attempt to rebuild the Jewish temple which at the time proved

---

[1] He describes his adversaries as "the Ariomaniacs" with "a whore's forehead," "equally unlearned and irreligious." *Against the Arians*, Oratio ii. 58; iii. 1. He does not scruple to denounce the Emperor himself as "the most impious Constantius," as a being who "does not possess common understanding," and as the tool of persons who "have trampled his brains under the soles of their feet!" *History of the Arians*, 69, 70. *Epistle concerning the Councils of Ariminum and Seleucia*, 55. See also *History of the Arians*, 38. These references may be found in Migne's edition of *Athanasius*, tom. ii. 270, 322; i. 775; ii. 790; i. 738. In his *Apology addressed to the Emperor* he had adopted quite a different tone, styling Constantius "your Piety" and "godly by descent," § 1.

[2] Hilary the Deacon, sometimes called *Ambrosiaster*, and the reputed author of a commentary on the Epistles of Paul, was contemporary with Hilary of Poictiers. Pope Hilary, who has left behind him a few letters, flourished in the fifth century. Hilary, bishop of Arles, who was a semi-Pelagian, and who has often been confounded with a layman of the same name who held different sentiments, died in A.D. 449.

so disastrous, and which has since led to so much discussion. Cyril witnessed its failure with unmingled satisfaction. He has been charged with semi-Arianism; and the imputation may not be unfounded; but, towards the close of his career, he certainly professed the orthodox creed, for he was present in Constantinople at the second Œcumenical Council in A.D. 381, and there attested his belief in the Supreme Godhead of the Son and of the Spirit.

Contemporary with Cyril, and connected also with the Eastern Church, were three remarkable men who have usually been named together—BASIL OF CÆSAREA, GREGORY OF NYSSA, and GREGORY NAZIANZEN. All the three were bishops, natives of Cappadocia, and persons of superior education. Basil was one of the patriarchs of monachism; he had vast social influence; and his numerous letters supply much information respecting the ecclesiastical affairs of the fourth century. To distinguish him from others of the same name[1] he has been called *The Great;* and so widespread was his reputation that EPHRAEM SYRUS, a deacon of Edessa, who was himself one of the best writers of his age,[2] took a journey to Cæsarea that he might see and hear a preacher so much extolled by the voice of fame. Gregory of Nyssa, the younger brother of Basil, possessed a more vigorous and original mind; he was a staunch defender of Trinitarianism; and, of his various works, his treatise *Against Eunomius,* the Arian, may be pronounced the most valuable. Though a church leader, he was married;[3] and when he entered on his episcopal office he did not, like some others, put away his wife; he visited Jerusalem, but he discovered that the sight of a city so noted in sacred history added nothing to his sanctity; and, in one of his letters,[4] he has denounced most energetically the folly of pilgrimages to holy places. In the second General Council, where he acted a conspicuous part, he was honoured as one of the pillars

---

[1] Such as Basil of Ancyra, who is said to have been a semi-Arian; and Basil of Seleucia, a writer of the fifth century, many of whose Homilies are still extant.

[2] Ephraem wrote in Syriac, and was a voluminous author. His works were so highly valued that they were publicly read in some churches. An English version of a portion of them has been supplied by the Rev. J. B. Morris, Oxford, 1847. Dr. Burgess has also translated some of his works.

[3] See Cave's *Lives of Fathers,* iii. 432, Oxford, 1840. See also Gregory's own testimony, *De Virginitate,* iii., *Opera,* tom. iii. 326, ed. Migne.

[4] *Epist.* ii. *De euntib. Hieros., Opera,* iii. 1010, ed. Migne.

of orthodoxy.[1] Gregory Nazianzen, another member of this Synod, who, as bishop of Constantinople, presided for a time over its deliberations, was a celebrated pulpit orator. His discourses, many of which are extant, procured for him the title of *the theologian*. Like Basil, with whom he was on terms of intimacy, he loved retirement; he sometimes writes in the spirit of a disappointed man; and his temper ill-fitted him either to bear with equanimity the rough trials of life or to heal the wounds created by ecclesiastical divisions. During the sittings of the second General Council he left the chair in a pet, and resigned the second bishopric in Christendom. He died about thirteen years afterwards.

Gregory was succeeded in the see of Constantinople by Nectarius, an aged senator who owed his appointment to the partiality of the Emperor Theodosius. He was but a catechumen at the time of his advancement, so that he required to be baptized before he could be invested with episcopal authority. He is the reputed author of a single tract of little value; and, though he occupied the bishopric for fifteen or sixteen years, he was miserably qualified for such a high position. But on his death, in A.D. 397, the most distinguished prelate ever connected with the capital of the Eastern Empire was elevated to the patriarchal office. This was JOHN, a presbyter of Antioch, known to after ages as CHRYSOSTOM, or the Golden-mouthed. To his mother, the excellent Anthusa, he was indebted for his youthful religious training. It soon appeared that the lessons of the Gospel had made a saving impression on his heart; and, under the care of a skilful and accomplished literary teacher, he gave early indications of that extraordinary genius which was yet to astonish and delight the Church. In personal piety, in Christian benevolence, and in pastoral efficiency, few of the fathers can be compared to this illustrious man. Among the preachers of antiquity he stands unrivalled; and so fascinating was his eloquence that, even on an ordinary week-day, the theatres and other places of public amusement were deserted when he delivered a sermon. His voice, his countenance, his graceful elocution, his immense enthusiasm, all added to his power as a speaker. Such was his popularity at Antioch, that it was feared his removal would lead

---

[1] He is supposed, though erroneously, to have composed the Creed usually attributed to that Council. See Schaff's *History of the Christian Church*, iii. 906.

to a civil commotion. He was accordingly summoned to meet an imperial officer in the suburbs of the city; and the messenger, after informing him of his promotion, put him, on the spot, into a carriage and conveyed him directly to the scene of his future labours. He did not enjoy much comfort in his new situation. His abstemious mode of living was disliked by the voluptuous magnates; his strict discipline provoked the clergy; his unsparing denunciations of vice offended the court, especially the Empress Eudoxia; and his superior influence irritated Theophilus, the proud and unscrupulous bishop of Alexandria. Five years after he attained the primatial dignity his enemies preferred against him a series of frivolous or unfounded accusations, and he was condemned to exile. The attempt to execute the sentence threw all Constantinople into an uproar; an earthquake which shook the city was interpreted as a manifestation of the wrath of God evoked by the unrighteous treatment of the holy pastor; and, terrified by the storm of public indignation, Eudoxia herself was constrained to beg the recall of the banished patriarch. The day of his return was celebrated as a general jubilee; the Bosphorus was covered with barges filled with his rejoicing friends; and the bishop, amidst the acclamations of the multitude, was conducted in triumph to his cathedral. But his enemies, though foiled for the time, were still bent on his ruin; and the Empress, provoked afresh by the bold language of the preacher, at length succeeded in effecting his overthrow. He was once more driven from Constantinople; another bishop was ordained; and, after years of privation and anxiety, Chrysostom, at the age of sixty, died in Pontus in the autumn of A.D. 407.

Chrysostom is the most voluminous of the Greek Fathers. As an interpreter of Scripture he holds a very high place among ancient expositors; for, instead of continually seeking, like many others, to find out allegories in the word of God, he applies himself to the investigation of the grammatical meaning. In some cases he apparently leans towards Pelagianism, but the controversy relative to the corruption of human nature commenced after his death; and, as his attention had never been turned particularly to the doctrine of the fall of man, he occasionally uses language which more mature consideration might have taught him to avoid. In his earlier years he was a great admirer of monasticism; but, as he advanced in life, he regarded it with less favour; and, when bishop of Constantinople, he induced many who had been long immured in cloisters to engage in missionary labours.

JEROME, AMBROSE, and AUGUSTINE, three of the great Fathers of the Latin Church,[1] flourished in the time of Chrysostom. Though Jerome never attained any high official position, he possessed much influence, and was by far the most learned ecclesiastic of his generation. When he had received a good elementary training in his native town of Stridon, on the borders of Pannonia, he was sent to Rome to complete his education, and there, under the tuition of a very excellent teacher, became a great proficient in classical literature. After travelling into France—where he cultivated an acquaintance with some eminent scholars and divines—he returned to the Italian capital, with the intention of devoting himself to a life of retirement. But, as the great city did not afford him sufficient seclusion, he set out for the East, and took up his abode in a desert of Syria. In that dreary solitude he submitted, without much benefit, to the rugged discipline of the cloister. Still harassed by the law of sin in his members, he resolved to chasten himself by tasking his application to the uttermost; and, commencing the study of Hebrew, he hoped, by the drudgery of acquiring a difficult language, more effectively to mortify his corruptions. At Antioch he received ordination as a presbyter, and passed from thence to Bethlehem, his favourite residence. At this time he did not remain long in that retreat, for we find him soon afterwards at Constantinople, where he enjoyed much pleasant and profitable intercourse with its eloquent bishop already mentioned, the far-famed Gregory Nazianzen. He next repaired to Rome, where he was well received by Pope Damasus, and where he spent about three years. Religious ladies, including some of the richest of the Roman matrons, gathered round the learned presbyter, and were delighted, as well with his expositions of Scripture as his laudations of monasticism. But he was by no means a favourite with the clergy of the metropolis. The honours lavished on the erudite monk excited their jealousy; their manner of living outraged his ideas of propriety; their ignorance provoked his scorn; he was

---

[1] The four great Latin Fathers are Ambrose, Augustine, Jerome, and Gregory the Great. There are also four great Greek Fathers—Athanasius, Basil the Great, Gregory Nazianzen, and Chrysostom.

harsh, arrogant, and sarcastic; and the freedom with which he animadverted on their proceedings roused their indignation. On the death of Damasus, he left Rome in disgust, and returned to the East. In Cyprus he met with Epiphanius, the learned but credulous bishop of the chief city of that island, whose works have been before noticed; and in Egypt he spent some time very pleasantly in the society of Didymus—teacher, for more than half-a-century, of the catechetical school of Alexandria—a man who had been blind from early youth, and who was, notwithstanding, one of the best informed and most profound theologians of antiquity. Jerome finally settled in his monastery at Bethlehem, where he died, according to some accounts, about A.D. 420, at the age of fourscore-and-ten.[1]

The works of Jerome are voluminous, including letters and tracts on various subjects, versions of Scripture, and commentaries. By translating the Old Testament from the original Hebrew into Latin, he rendered an invaluable service to the cause of Christian literature; and yet the performance was not appreciated in his own time; for, as it revealed numerous errors in the current text, many complained that it shook the confidence of the Church in the Word of God. But, as its merits were better understood, it gradually supplanted other translations; and it is, substantially, the version known as *the Vulgate*, and recognized by the Council of Trent in the sixteenth century as "authentic."[2] Though so ripe a scholar, so acute, and so ingenious, Jerome cannot be trusted as a sound and independent thinker. He had nothing of the spirit of an ecclesiastical reformer; for, when Jovinian, an Italian monk, and Vigilantius, a Gallic presbyter, attacked monasticism, the celibacy of the clergy, and other innovations, the recluse of Bethlehem repelled their assaults with a pen dipped in gall, and poured forth on them torrents of audacious ribaldry. Rufinus, the Latin interpreter of the ecclesiastical history of Eusebius, experienced from him quite as rough handling. The indefatigable monk had himself translated several of the works of Origen, and had spoken in commendation of the author; but, when the divines of the West began to denounce the Alexandrian father as a heretic, Jerome changed his tone and concurred in

---

[1] According to Prosper, in his *Chronicon*, he lived to the age of ninety-one; Bede represents him as ninety-eight years of age; but Baronius computes that he lived only to the age of seventy-eight. [2] Sessio. iv.

the condemnation. Rufinus, who has left behind him a garbled version of the Treatise of Origen, *De Principiis*, exposed this exhibition of inconsistency; and a literary warfare of long continuance and extreme acerbity commenced between these two scholars. After passing through various trials, Rufinus died in Sicily in A.D. 410; but Jerome did not cease to load him with opprobrious epithets, and to execrate his memory. "The scorpion," says he, "is buried under the soil of Sicily, with Enceladus and Porphyrion; the many-headed hydra has at length ceased to hiss against us."[1]

When Jerome, in a convent, was pursuing his literary labours, another celebrated Doctor of the Latin Church was preaching to admiring auditories in one of the chief cities of Italy. In the days of the Emperor Theodosius the Great, Ambrose of Milan was by far the most distinguished prelate of the West. At the time of his birth, his father was Prætorian prefect, or principal magistrate, of Gaul, and thus it happened that the future bishop was nursed in a palace; but, though he afterwards acquired such popularity as a pulpit orator, he was not originally trained for the clerical profession. Entering public life as a lawyer, his superior talents were soon recognized; and he was made governor of the district to which Milan belonged. The bishopric, meanwhile, became vacant; and the election of a prelate created such disturbance that Ambrose found it necessary to repair to the cathedral and address the contending factions. As he proceeded, in eloquent terms, to recommend peace, a child present, supposing that he was preaching, and knowing that such a duty then usually devolved on the chief pastor, artlessly exclaimed—"Ambrose is bishop." The hint was at once caught up by the bystanders; and the whole multitude, forgetting their divisions, joined enthusiastically in the choice. Ambrose, though a professing Christian, had not yet received baptism; for many, like the Emperor Constantine, were inclined to postpone the ordinance under the superstitious idea that, as they might fall into mortal sin, it was well to keep what they deemed an infallible antidote as long as possible in reserve. In vain the governor protested against the determination of the multitude; in vain he urged that, as a catechumen, he could not even be nominated a candidate for episcopal promotion. The citizens would sustain no

[1] *Comment in Ezech.* i. 1, *Opera*, v. 16, 17, ed. Migne, Paris, 1845.

apology; and at length Ambrose was reluctantly obliged to yield to their solicitations. He was forthwith baptized, and, eight days afterwards, ordained bishop.[1] As he was wholly unprepared for an office with which he was so unexpectedly invested, he was obliged to send to Rome for an able and erudite presbyter, named Simplician, by whom he was instructed in theology, and taught how to perform his episcopal duties. The new bishop applied himself with amazing industry to his professional studies, and soon attained such proficiency that he began to be consulted as an oracle in matters of faith and discipline.

The rhetorical ability of Ambrose had been already exhibited at the bar; and in the pulpit he had a far nobler sphere for its exercise. He preached with great frequency, and crowds thronged to his sermons. Milan was at this time the residence of the imperial court; and, as the Empress Justina, the mother of the younger Valentinian, was a keen abettor of Arianism, it was no easy matter to counteract her intrigues and withstand her influence. But, supported by the popular feeling, Ambrose succeeded in defeating all her machinations. Accustomed from childhood to move in the higher circles of society, he was distinguished by the grace and dignity of his deportment; his talents were well known, and his character generally respected; and when the usurper Maximus disputed the possession of the Empire, the bishop of Milan was employed more than once to negotiate with that able diplomatist. His enforcement of discipline in the case of Theodosius the Great is perhaps the most striking and memorable incident in his history. On a festive occasion the mob of Thessalonica demanded the release of a favourite charioteer who had been thrown into prison for infamous conduct. When their importunities were resisted, they rose up in insurrection, and killed, not only the imperial lieutenant who refused to liberate the criminal, but also many soldiers and others who came in their way. Though the outrage was so aggravated, Ambrose obtained from Theodosius a promise of pardon for the insurgents. The imperial counsellors took a different view of the transaction—they argued that government must become contemptible if such wholesale butchery, including the murder

---

[1] Without passing through the inferior orders, he was at once invested with the episcopal dignity. Such cases of ordination were not uncommon even after the recognition of Christianity by Constantine. See 2d Canon of the Council of Nice.

of a high state functionary, were not punished with severity; and they induced their master to give them a secret warrant for chastising the rioters. The vengeance was terrible. The people, invited to the circus to witness some public sports, were attacked suddenly by the military; for three hours the work of slaughter was continued; and seven thousand persons perished in the massacre. When Ambrose heard the sad intelligence, he consulted with a synod of his brethren then in session as to the course to be pursued; and determined, with their concurrence, to teach the Emperor that he must be amenable to discipline. Theodosius was accordingly informed, by letter, that he could not now be admitted to communion. Soon afterwards the monarch presented himself at the door of the church; but the bishop laid hold of his robe, and desired him to withdraw. The Emperor submitted; and, divested of his princely ornaments, remained for eight months in the condition of a penitent. When he again appeared among the worshippers to be restored to fellowship, he threw himself on the pavement, and with tears and sighs bewailed the enormity of his transgression. To obviate the dangers of sudden passion, as well as to testify his repentance, he agreed, at the suggestion of Ambrose, to make a law that no decrees, involving loss of life or forfeiture of property, should in future take effect for thirty days after their adoption; so that time might be given for their reconsideration, and, if necessary, for their reversal.[1]

In this transaction Theodosius displayed the spirit of a true penitent. He confessed his crime, attested his sorrow, and provided against a repetition of the transgression. Ambrose also acted the part of a zealous and conscientious pastor; and, though his bearing throughout is not fully susceptible of vindication, it obviously commanded the respect of the imperial offender. A minister of the gospel, presuming on his position, should beware of acting towards his earthly superiors with anything like arrogance; and Ambrose had no right, either to insist on the free pardon of the rioters of Thessalonica, or to dictate a law to guide the future course of his sovereign. But though his conduct has often since been quoted in support of the caprices of papal tyranny, it does not legitimately admit of any such application.

Ambrose was busy with his pen. His extant works comprise

[1] Theodoret, v. 17, 18.

an ample collection of letters, hymns, commentaries, and other treatises. As an author, he does not possess much originality; he has borrowed largely from his Greek contemporaries; he unduly extols the power of the priesthood; and his admiration of monasticism is most extravagant. After a laborious episcopate of three-and-twenty years, he died, aged fifty-seven, in A.D. 397.

Among those who flocked to the sermons of Ambrose was a clever African who had settled at Milan as a teacher of rhetoric. This literary gentleman was a Manichæan; but the fame of the bishop as an orator attracted him to the cathedral. The preaching of Ambrose gradually removed his objections to the Catholic doctrine; and the foreigner, whose name was Augustine, submitted to baptism. Shortly afterwards he returned to his native country, where he eventually became bishop of Hippo.

When we proceed to discuss the history of the Pelagian controversy,[1] our attention must be directed to the life and character of Augustine, so that we need not at present particularly discuss his merits. In breadth of intellect, in metaphysical acuteness, and in holy skill as a spiritual comforter, as well as in the extent of his contributions to patristic theology, he is pre-eminent among the Fathers. In his publications he treats of not a few philosophical questions, examines various points of doctrine, expounds many portions of Scripture, and investigates the claims of Manichæanism, Donatism, Pelagianism, and Semi-Pelagianism. His great work, "The City of God," occupied his leisure for thirteen years. On the taking of Rome by Alaric, in A.D. 410, the pagans alleged that the calamities of the Empire were to be ascribed to the spread of the Gospel; and Augustine wrote this treatise to demonstrate the fallacy of the argument. It is by far the most valuable defence of Christianity which ancient ecclesiastical literature supplies.

The Pelagian controversy, in which Augustine took so prominent a part, employed many other writers. Among these, two laymen, PROSPER of AQUITAIN and MARIUS MERCATOR, or Marius the merchant, ardently supported the doctrine of the bishop of Hippo. FULGENTIUS of RUSPE, who flourished about a century after the time of the great African Father, was also a strenuous advocate of his theological principles. On the other side,

[1] Section II. Chapter III. of this Period.

CASSIAN of MARSEILLES and VINCENT of LERINS pleaded the cause of Semi-Pelagianism.

The Nestorian and Eutychian controversies[1] likewise called forth not a few authors. Among these one of the most noted is CYRIL, the tyrannical bishop of ALEXANDRIA. His works, though voluminous, are now little studied; he was an acute disputant; in synodical meetings his high station and forensic talent gave him preponderating influence; but he is an indifferent writer, and his large contributions to theological literature are comparatively worthless. ISIDORE of PELUSIUM,[2] another African Father, had the faithfulness to expostulate with the Alexandrian primate; and to condemn, in very decided terms, the unchristian spirit in which he upheld what he professed to regard as the faith delivered to the saints.

Very few of the ancient bishops of Rome were distinguished by their literary labours; but, in the beginning of the seventh century, the chair of the great Western see was occupied by a prelate who plied his pen with marvellous industry. GREGORY I., or Gregory the Great, ranks among the most eminent of the Latin Fathers. In some respects he bears a remarkable resemblance to Ambrose of Milan. Like him he was an admired preacher and a prolific writer—of high birth, of great energy of character, and of much dexterity in the management of political affairs. But he did nothing to arrest the flood of superstition which was overspreading the Church. His works rather contributed to increase the intensity of spiritual ignorance. As we must however hereafter notice this extraordinary man,[3] we shall not dwell at present on the consideration of his writings.

Contemporary with Gregory was ISIDORE, bishop of SEVILLE. This prelate, who was the grandson of Theodoric, king of Italy, possessed much of the learning of his age. In his *Ecclesiastical Offices* he has illustrated the worship and constitution of the Church of Spain; and in his *Sentences* he treats of the faith, the duties, and the temptations of a Christian. Thirty-three years after his death,[4] a Greek monk, and an accomplished scholar, arrived in England as archbishop of Canterbury.[5] The stranger,

---

[1] See Sect. II. Chapters IV. V. of this Period.
[2] At the mouth of the Nile, near Damietta or Damiat.
[3] Sect. V. Chapter IV. of this Period.
[4] Isidore died in A.D. 636.
[5] See Sect. IV. Chapter I. of this Period.

whose name was THEODORE, was a zealous patron of literature in his adopted country; and his *Penitential,* or Directory on the subject of penance,—a work now existing only in an imperfect form—long enjoyed extensive celebrity. About half a century afterwards flourished the famous JOHN DAMASCENUS—so called from Damascus, the place of his birth. Because of his eloquence he was designated *Chrysorrhoas,* or the *Golden Stream;* but his works, which are numerous, are deeply tinged with superstition; and among the early advocates of image worship he was one of the most learned and influential.

Even the brief sketches now given are enough to convince any candid mind that these ecclesiastical writers are not to be trusted as guides in matters of religion. How can men who differed from each other in doctrine be arbiters of our faith? Eusebius was the theological antagonist of Athanasius; Jerome denounced Rufinus as a heretic; Augustine condemned the views of Cassian; and Cyril of Alexandria was the persecutor of Theodoret. The fathers were far from regarding their own writings as above challenge; for even Augustine, when advanced in life, published a work, entitled *Retractations,* in which he modified or disavowed not a few sentiments he had previously promulgated. Some of the most venerated of those ancient worthies inculcate principles which few professing Christians of the present day of any denomination would acknowledge. Hilary of Poictiers affirms that the soul is corporeal,[1] and that our Lord, when on the cross, had no sense of pain.[2] Jerome teaches that the providence of God does not extend to all His creatures.[3] Lactantius asserts that the souls of all men after this life are immured in a common prison, where they are to remain till the final judgment;[4] and Ambrose maintains that the apostles themselves are to be proved by fire at the last day.[5] John Damascenus places the so-called Canons of the apostles among the books of the New Testament;[6] and even councils contradict each other in reference to the writings which we are bound to recognize as divine. The third

---

[1] *Comment. in Mat.* cap. v. *Opera,* i. 946, ed. Migne, Paris, 1844.

[2] *De Synodis, Opera,* ii. 516; *De Trinitate,* x. 23, *Opera,* ii. 362.

[3] He thinks that gnats, flies, and such things are beneath the special notice of the Almighty. *Comment in Abac.* i. 1, *Opera,* vi. 1286.

[4] *Inst. Divin.* vii. 21.

[5] *In Ps.* cxviii. *Serm.* xx. 12, *Opera,* ii. 1487, ed. Migne.

[6] *De Fide Orthodoxa,* lib. iv.

Council of Carthage, held in A.D. 397, inserts The Maccabees, Ecclesiasticus, Wisdom, Tobit, and Judith among the Old Testament Scriptures: whilst the Council of Laodicea, held about A.D. 360, rejects them as apocryphal.[1]

The monastic system, organized in the beginning of the fourth century, quickly displayed its influence in the department of ecclesiastical literature. The fathers of the period before us unanimously commend a single life; Athanasius, Theodoret, and others published memoirs of the most remarkable of the ancient monks, in which they describe their proceedings with enthusiasm; and Jerome speaks of marriage in terms which imply that it is little less than a mortal sin.[2] These writers, in their absurd laudations of the artificial piety of the cloister, gravely relate legends of the most puerile or extravagant character. They were prepared to believe that men who lived like wild beasts were the special favourites of heaven, and that these crazed sons of the desert could deliver prophecies, work miracles, and teach senators wisdom. Monasticism impaired the vigour of the mind, discouraged that healthful exercise of the faculties so essential to intellectual progress, and fostered credulity and mysticism. The works of some of the most famous of the fathers, and particularly those of Gregory the Great, are stuffed with "old wives' fables" of which even Roman Catholic writers are ashamed.[3]

It has often been asserted that those fathers who lived nearest the times of the apostles must, therefore, be the best expositors of Scripture. It might with equal propriety be affirmed that the most ancient philosophers are the most enlightened interpreters of the works of creation. The age of a father can in

---

[1] Dupin has observed that, appended to the canon of the third Council of Carthage, is a "*postil that is very remarkable:* 'Let the Church beyond sea be consulted before this canon be confirmed.'"—*History of Ecclesiastical Writers*, i. 17, Dublin, 1723. These African fathers evidently distrusted their own judgment.

[2] *Adv. Jovin.* i. 29, *Opera*, ii. 251, ed. Migne; *Epist.* liv. 1. *Ad Furiam, Opera*, i. 550.

[3] Thus Dupin says of his *Dialogues:* "This work does not appear worthy of the gravity and discretion of this holy Pope, it is so full of extraordinary miracles and histories almost incredible. . . . . The histories related in it are many times grounded only on the relations of ignorant old men, or common reports. Miracles are so frequent, so extraordinary, and oftentimes for matters of so small consequence, that it is very difficult to believe them all. . . . . I do not believe any man will warrant all these relations."—*Ecclesiastical Writers*, i. 580, ed. Dublin, 1723.

itself be no test of the excellence of his commentaries. Divines who flourished towards the end of the fourth or beginning of the fifth century are often much safer guides as expositors than any of their predecessors. Earlier writers, such as Origen or Clement of Alexandria, frequently expound the word of God in the way in which Neo-Platonists explained the pagan mythology—that is, they regard it as an allegory from which they extract whatever meaning happens to be most agreeable to themselves; and too many continued to adopt the same system of interpretation. But among the fathers of the fourth century there were some who followed sounder principles of exegesis, and carefully investigated the literal sense of the holy oracles. Still, comparatively few of the Christian writers even of this period are very valuable as biblical interpreters. These authors occasionally contradict themselves; and, without acknowledgment, copy most slavishly from each other.[1] Jerome argues that the great duty of an expositor is, not so much to exhibit the mind of the Spirit, as to set before the reader the conflicting sentiments of interpreters. "What," says he, "is the business of a commentary? .... It represents the several opinions of others, and says—Some expound the passage in this way, and others in that way. ... The intelligent reader, having a number of expositions before him, ... may judge which among them has the greatest amount of truth, and, like a wise banker, may refuse all adulterated coin. Now I would ask whether he ought to be accounted guilty of diversity in his interpretations, or of contradictions in the senses given, who in one and the same commentary delivers the expositions of divers expounders?"[2]

But though we discover in these fathers so many traces of human infirmity, we must make allowance for the times in which they lived, and for the prejudices in which they were educated. Christianity passed through a terrible ordeal when it suddenly became the religion of the Empire. Society was by no means prepared for so vast a change. Already the Gospel had suffered sadly from adulteration, and now it was more rapidly deteriorated. Many who were quite uninstructed became pastors of the Church; pagan forms and ceremonies were incorporated

---

[1] Thus the works of Ambrose contain many long passages taken from his contemporary, Basil the Great.

[2] *Apologia adv. Lib. Rufin.* i. 16, *Opera*, ii. 409-10, ed. Migne.

with its ritual; pagan superstitions were recognised as principles of action; and pagan philosophy corrupted theological science. A dense cloud of errors soon overspread the whole spiritual firmament. But though the light of truth was thus obscured, and though the fathers sometimes erred egregiously; they often exhibited, withal, noble specimens of meekness, integrity, self-denial, and Christian earnestness. We may mourn over the folly which prompted Athanasius to write an admiring biography of the hermit Antony, and yet we cannot but applaud the ecclesiastical hero who so frequently imperilled his life in the cause of Trinitarianism. We may well wonder how it was that Ambrose was tempted to indulge in such laudations of monasticism; but assuredly the Bishop of Milan was no puling sentimentalist or fawning courtier; and too seldom since his time have the rulers of the spiritual commonwealth imitated the lofty consistency with which he insisted on the observance of the discipline of the Church by the first personage of the Empire. We may see cause to distrust the wisdom of the fathers, and we may be satisfied that they were fallible as ourselves; but in many instances we must recognize and honour the fidelity with which they acted up to their convictions. We cannot doubt the honesty of men who, in obedience to what they believed to be the call of duty, were prepared to submit to poverty or to martyrdom.

CHAPTER IV.

MONACHISM.

IN the very commencement of the book of revelation, when the Divine Lawgiver declares—" It is not good that the man should be alone"[1]—He enunciates one of the great principles essential to human well-being. Without society the tongue cannot exert its power of fascination: the health fails: the spirits sink: the intellect degenerates: and even the features lose their expression. God gave Adam a helpmate of a different sex: and, as in every country males and females exist in nearly equal proportions, He thus continues to indicate the arrangement by which He desires them to be united. The New Testament teaches that "marriage

[1] Gen. ii. 18.

is honourable *in all;*[1] and the voice of Providence attests from age to age that this holy bond is specially conducive to individual comfort, to domestic peace, and to national prosperity.

But general rules admit of limitations and exceptions. There are times when solitude is more profitable than society, and cases in which celibacy may be more expedient than marriage. As the religion of the heart is nourished by the perusal of the Scriptures, by meditation, and by secret prayer, occasional retirement is required for the cultivation of personal piety. Many have been ripened for glory by long confinement to a lonely chamber. And there are circumstances in which individuals may feel it to be their duty to lead a single life that, unentangled by domestic cares, they may either more efficiently occupy peculiar spheres of usefulness, or be better prepared for persecution. Paul lays down the normal principle for the regulation of society when he says—" Let every man have his own wife, and let every woman have her own husband;"[2] and yet, in the prospect of a day of trial, he recommends some of the Corinthians to remain unmarried.

But, as Satan can transform himself into an angel of light, almost every false system can be made to assume the appearance of something great and godlike. Monachism owes much of its influence to its exaggerated representations of the importance of solitude and abstinence; and, for a certain class of minds, it possesses wonderful attractions. Though the monk in his cell may be a cold misanthrope, nourishing spiritual pride, by vigils and fasting, he may imagine, and he may induce others to believe, that he is an eminent saint moving forward rapidly on the highway to perfection. There is, however, a wide difference between the tendency of a system and the character of some of its supporters; and there is no inconsistency in saying that, whilst asceticism is based on principles essentially anti-evangelical, not a few of its abettors have laboured earnestly, and no doubt acceptably, to serve God in their generation. Monachism errs by changing the exception into the rule, and by making what may be occasionally expedient the standard of duty. The Christian in the world is a city set on a hill: the pious ascetic in his cloister is a candle under a bushel. By pushing the practice of devout retirement to an extreme, he makes himself

[1] Heb. xiii. 4. [2] 1 Cor. vii. 2.

useless to society, and converts the cheerful religion of the Son of God into a system of gloom and repulsiveness.

Monachism is not the native growth of Christianity. The old Romans showed their superstitious regard for celibacy by the establishment of the vestal virgins: and monasteries existed among the Buddhists of the East hundreds of years before the birth of our Saviour. The Essenes and Therapeutæ of the ancient Jews observed a species of monastic discipline.[1] As early as the second century there were ascetics here and there among the Christians; but though these individuals practised abstinence, and in some cases refrained from marriage, they lived in society, and assiduously endeavoured to promote the progress of the gospel. The infusion of the pagan philosophy into the theology of the New Testament first infected the Church with a sickly pietism. Some of the heathen sages laid great stress on solitude, silence, and the maceration of the flesh; and certain Christians who aspired after a higher excellence soon began to signalize themselves by their peculiar garb[2] and their bodily austerities. In the early part of the third century the single clergy were by many esteemed more holy than their married brethren; and this false sentiment quickly gained such currency that males and females who declined to enter into wedlock, and who lived in comparative seclusion, were commended by their pastors as worthy of all honour. When the Decian persecution obliged vast numbers to withdraw from places of public concourse, a new impulse was given to the spirit of asceticism; and at least one individual, who then fled into the desert, has acquired a distinguished reputation among the fathers and founders of

---

[1] See Prideaux's *Connections*, pt. ii. bk. v. In the sixteenth century, when the celebrated Jesuit missionary Francis Xavier visited Japan, an island then only recently known to Europeans, he was astonished to find many pagan monasteries in the country. The pagan monks of Japan were dressed in grey or black gowns, had their heads shaved, and recited prayers by the help of beads. Venn's *Missionary Life and Labours of Francis Xavier*, pp. 186, 187, London, 1862.

[2] Some of them wore the dress of pagan philosophers. Their discipline was called *philosophy*. At a later period the monks assumed a symbolic costume. Thus Sozomen says—"The peculiar vestments of the Egyptian monks had reference to some secret connected with their philosophy. . . . They wore their tunics without sleeves to teach that the hands should not be ready to do evil. They wore a covering on their heads called a cowl, to show that they ought to live with the same innocence and purity (as infants) who are nourished with milk, and wear a covering of the same form." *Ecc. Hist.* iii. 14. See also Cassian, *De Cænob. Institutis.* lib. i. cap. iv.

Christian monachism. This was Paul, or Paulus. He was a native of Thebes in Egypt, and only sixteen years of age when Decius proclaimed war against the Church. Retiring to the wilderness, he eventually took up his abode in a cave, where he spent the remainder of a life protracted to upwards of a century. Antony, another Egyptian and the heir of a considerable fortune, holds a still higher position in the history of monachism. When he had barely reached manhood he was so impressed by the account of the young ruler[1] who had great possessions, and some other statements in the Gospels, that he relinquished all his property and devoted himself to poverty and seclusion. He died about the middle of the following century at the advanced age of one hundred and five; and meanwhile attracted great attention by the fame of his sanctity. His place of abode was in the depths of a trackless desert; but he issued on two memorable occasions from his retreat, and presented himself to the astonished gaze of the people of Alexandria. When the Emperor Maximin, in A.D. 311, renewed his persecution of the Church of the Egyptian capital, Antony hastened to the city, and exhorted the prisoners to submit cheerfully to suffering. These days of terror only stimulated the zeal of the dauntless hermit: he boldly threw himself in the way of the officers of government: and yet, when he appeared in the company of the accused Christians even before the tribunals of the magistrates, so great was the awe inspired by his presence, that no one ventured to harm the unearthly visitor. Again, in A.D. 352, when Arianism was in the zenith of its power, the saint, now an hundred years of age, repaired to Alexandria, and earnestly pleaded for Trinitarianism.

The appearance of Antony in the metropolis of Egypt during the persecution under Maximin led many to imitate the mode of living adopted by this poor visionary. The desert around him was soon peopled by solitaries of a kindred spirit, and the old man found employment in instructing the members of the new brotherhood. Not a few of the early monks were *Eremites*,[2] or Hermits, who dwelt alone in the wilderness, seeking by fasting, meditation, and prayer, to attain a more exalted spiritualism. Antony is said to have united the separate cells of these anchor-

---

[1] Matt. xix. 16; Luke xviii. 18.
[2] So called from ἔρημος, a desert.

ites[1] into batches, called *Lauræ*.[2] Pachomius, who was also an Egyptian, and who flourished in the fourth century, was the father of the *Cœnobites*,[3] or of the brethren associated in monasteries. The system spread rapidly in Africa and the East; and Pachomius himself, at the time of his death, is reported to have had several thousands of these ascetics under his jurisdiction.

The climate of Egypt, Palestine, Syria, and various other adjacent countries, was peculiarly favourable to the indulgence of the monastic spirit; for there the solitary could support himself on a very slender stock of food, and remain night and day in the open air under the shade of a rock, a bank, or a mountain. Seated by a running stream or a well of pure water, he could live on a little grain and a few wild fruits; and gazing on the rugged scenery around him, or on the serene sky above him, could gratify abundantly his taste for contemplation. In a short time the monastic system acquired immense popularity, as it had charms for a great variety of characters, including the morose, the disappointed, the romantic, and the indolent. The monks all at once commanded unwonted reverence, and crowds of the lower classes embraced the profession; for, whilst it scarcely interfered with any of their usual comforts, it greatly elevated their social position. In the monastery persons of the meanest grade mingled on equal terms with the rest of a community to which, in many instances, members of the most distinguished families belonged. About the middle of the fourth century the mania for monachism in various oriental regions assumed something like the form of an epidemic; and, so great was the disturbance it created, that the Council of Gangra,[4] held about A.D. 369, was obliged to interpose, and check its extravagance. This council denounced the folly of those who, in their zeal for celibacy, refused to receive the Eucharist from the hands of married presbyters;[5] and forbad husbands and wives, under pretence of piety, to separate from each other and desert their families. In A.D. 365, the Emperor Valens found it necessary

---

[1] So called from ἀναχωρέω, to retire.

[2] A Laura consisted of many cells divided from each other—a Cœnobium was but one habitation where the monks lived together. See Bingham, ii. 246, London, 1840.

[3] From κοινὸς βίος, common life.

[4] The metropolis of the Province of Paphlagonia in Asia Minor.

[5] Canon iv.

to discourage monachism by a law, requiring that all who had betaken themselves to what was called a religious life through sloth or with a view to evade their social obligations, should be dragged from their seclusion.[1]

Among those most celebrated in the fourth century in connexion with the spread of monachism in the East are Hilarion of Palestine and Basil of Neocæsarea. Hilarion founded a society of Cœnobites near Gaza, and the branches of this establishment were soon extended over all Syria. Basil is still more widely known as one of the patrons of the institute. This eloquent and accomplished man had in early life visited Egypt, conversed with its solitaries, and surveyed with admiration the arrangements of its monasteries. Some time afterwards he introduced the system into Pontus, and provided his monks with a code of written regulations. Almost all the monasteries of the East continue to the present day to observe the rule of Basil.

The monks were originally laymen, and those of them who were hermits could not enjoy the privilege of social worship; but the brethren collected in monasteries were placed under the superintendence of an *Abbot* or *Archimandrite*, to whom they were expected to yield implicit submission. It was arranged, at an early period in the history of the institute, that this abbot must be a presbyter, and of course authorized to administer the various ordinances of the Church.[2] Each monastery was subject

---

[1] *Cod. Theodos.* lib. xii. tit. i. 63, Hænel, c. 1224.

[2] It is obvious, from the Rule of Benedict, that the abbot, though only a presbyter, had the power of ordination. "In illis locis ubi ab eodem sacerdote, vel ab eisdem abbatibus, qui abbatem ordinant, ab ipsis etiam et præpositus ordinatur." *Reg.* cap. lxv. See also cap. lxiv., where, through a corrupt text, the same fact still appears, as the neighbouring abbots are empowered to interfere when an abbot is to be ordained in an adjacent monastery. "Prohibeant pravorum prævalere consensum, sed domui Dei dignum constituant dispensatorem." Migne's *Latin Fathers,* lxvi. 881. Cassian represents a monk named Daniel as ordained, first a deacon, and then a presbyter, by the presbyter abbot Paphnutius. "A beato Paphnutio solitudinis ejusdem presbytero, et quidem cum multis junior esset ætate, ad diaconii est prælatus officium. In tantum enim beatus Paphnutius virtutibus ipsius adgaudebat, ut quem vitæ meritis sibi et gratiam parem noverat, coæquare sibi etiam sacerdotii ordine festinaret; siquidem nequaque ferens in inferiore cum ministerio diutius immorari, optansque sibimet successorem dignissimum providere, *superstes cum presbyterii honore provexit.*" Cassian, *Collatio* iv. cap. i. Even abbesses at length asserted their right to consecrate and ordain, and councils were obliged to interfere and restrain them. See Dean Waddington's *History of the Church,* p. 400, London, 1833. An old ritual, in use before the time of Theo-

to the jurisdiction of the bishop of the district. According to the rule of Basil, the monks could not lead a life of idleness. Some were employed in agriculture, some in weaving, some in shoemaking, and some in other mechanical occupations. Their time was parcelled out into sections, each of which was in some way appropriated, but a large portion of it was devoted to religious exercises. The tenants of the cloister wore a uniform dress, and at certain hours repeated psalms, offered up prayers, or listened to the exposition of the Scriptures. One class of the Cœnobites—the *Akoimetoi*, or the *sleepless*—kept up religious exercises, without intermission, night and day—some of them retiring to rest when others were prepared to resume the service. The monasteries supplied refreshment to travellers, served as asylums for orphans, and shed around them a few rays of spiritual instruction. Basil recommended that the monks should be bound by a vow to adhere to their profession; and though this part of the system was not at first strictly enforced, yet from his time any one who entered the order and subsequently deserted it was reputed scandalous.

Nunneries are almost of as high antiquity as monasteries. Syncletica, a lady of Alexandria, and the contemporary of Pachomius, is commemorated as their foundress. The ascetic life had not equally powerful attractions for females as for males, and hence in point of numbers the brethren generally far exceeded the sisters. About the beginning of the fifth century, when the nuns of Egypt amounted to little more than 27,000, the monks of the same country were reckoned at from 70,000 to 80,000.[1] The rules by which the nunneries were regulated were much the same as those established in monasteries; but, instead of the axe and the spade, the nuns plied the needle and the distaff.

Monasticism was brought into the West by the great Athanasius. The champion of Trinitarianism, when driven from his see, was more than once hospitably entertained by the bishop of

---

dore of Canterbury, attests that abbots anciently ordained: "Congregatio debet sibi eligere abbatem, post mortem ejus, aut eo vivente, si ipse discesserit vel peccaverit; ipse non potest *aliquem ordinare* de suis propinquis, neque de alienis, nec alio abbati dare, *si non voluerint fratres.*" *Patrol. Curs.* clvi. 1113, ed. Migne. Some such arrangement obviously existed among the monks of Iona. See Sect. IV. Chap. II. of this Period.

[1] Milman's *Hist. of Christianity*, iii. 306.

Rome, and other pastors in the same quarter of the Empire; and, during his stay among them, he dilated with his wonted enthusiasm on the advantages of the new discipline. His Life of Antony, the Egyptian hermit, was very soon translated into Latin;[1] and its popularity contributed much to promote asceticism in Italy and Gaul. Other bishops who, as well as Athanasius, were forced by the persecutions of the Arians to seek an asylum in the West, were equally zealous in proclaiming the praises of fasting, celibacy, and retirement. Thus it was that establishments such as those founded in Egypt and Palestine by Pachomius and Hilarion soon afterwards appeared in Europe. Ambrose, the famous bishop of Milan, recommended the monastic life with all the power of his fervid and persuasive eloquence. The celebrated Augustine, bishop of Hippo, was also among its patrons. He introduced a modification of the institute among the ecclesiastics over whom he presided; for his clergy lived in the same dwelling, partook of their meals at the same table, and assembled at stated hours for religious exercises. At these reunions Augustine occasionally expounded the Scriptures to his auditors; and his house thus became a species of seminary where candidates were educated for the higher functions of the ministry. Jerome, the brightest literary star in the Latin Church, was a most extravagant advocate of celibacy; and laboured assiduously, when at Rome in the time of Pope Damasus, to diffuse the ascetic spirit. So great was his influence that a number of the richest females in the city embraced his views; and, when he withdrew to the East, some ladies followed him, and spent the rest of their lives in the retirement of the nunnery. Many of the secluded districts of Italy, as well as the little islands along its coasts, were studded over with monasteries. Martin, bishop of Tours, in France, was a zealous propagator of the system; and such was its progress in his neighbourhood before his death, that two thousand monks were present at his funeral. Cassian, a native of the East who settled at Marseilles in the early part of the fifth century, was another most successful disseminator of monachism in Western Europe.

In addition to the hermits, who lived each apart in a solitary cell, and the Cœnobites, or brethren of the common life, who

---

[1] An English translation of the Life of Paulus by Jerome, and of the Life of Antony by Athanasius, may be found in the American *Bibliotheca Sacra* for 1844.

resided in monasteries, there were various other classes of individuals who passed under the name of monks. Such were the *Sarabaites*,[1] a species of ascetics who wandered about from city to city, trading in relics, and often attempting by jugglery and impudence to impose on popular credulity. The *Euchites*,[2] or the Prayerful, who appeared in Mesopotamia about A.D. 360, exhibited perhaps more modesty, but certainly as little discretion. Renouncing every species of labour as sinful, or of the earth, and professing to give themselves wholly to devotion, they lived on alms and in idleness. The *Boskoi*,[3] or Graziers, though more absurd fanatics, were not so burdensome to the community. In a state of almost complete nudity—sometimes creeping on all fours and overgrown with hair—they wandered about in deserts or on mountains, feeding on such roots and herbs as grew spontaneously in the places they frequented. The *Pillar Saints* were another class of monks quite distinct from all the rest of the fraternity. Of these by far the most famous was Simeon the Stylite,[4] an ascetic of the fifth century, who dwelt on a mountain of Syria in the neighbourhood of Antioch. Perched on the top a pillar at length elevated sixty feet high,[5] he was visited by admiring multitudes. He is said to have been able to remain seven days at a time without food; and his body must have possessed extraordinary flexibility, for, when engaged in his devotions, he often bowed so profoundly that his head touched his toes. Strange to tell, this wretched visionary, who occupied his pillar upwards of thirty years, was deemed one of the lights of his age; and Roman emperors were not ashamed on important occasions to solicit his counsel!

Though there were ascetics in Europe perhaps as fanatical as any of the Eastern Stylites, the more rigid climate of the West restrained their folly, so that the order of the Pillar Saints was confined to Oriental regions. When a devotee, named Wulflaich, attempted, in the sixth century, to introduce this form of superstition into Germany, he met with nothing but discouragement. The pastors of the district condemned his folly and pulled down his pillar. Had they not been sustained by public opinion, they

---

[1] This word is said to have been of Egyptian origin, and various interpretations of it have been given. See Migne's *Latin Fathers*, lxvi. 254.
[2] From εὐχή, a prayer.
[3] From βόσκω, to graze.
[4] So called from στύλος, a pillar.
[5] Evagrius, i. 13.

would scarcely have acted with such decision. Common sense here prevailed over the dreams of mysticism; and no one in the same part of the world ever afterwards ventured to repeat the folly of Wulflaich.

The monks of the West could not subsist on the slender diet sufficient to sustain their brethren in Palestine or Syria; they always used more substantial fare; and, though they were partially guided by the rule of Basil, their discipline was somewhat lax and capricious. In the early part of the sixth century an individual, named Benedict, a native of Nursia in the diocese of Rome, greatly improved their organization. Benedict bound his monks by an irrevocable vow to persist in the perpetual observance of his regulations. This vow pledged the undertaker to poverty, celibacy, and obedience. To prevent rash engagements, those who entered the order were obliged to pass through a lengthened noviciate. After remaining several days at the gate of the monastery supplicating admission, the candidate was received, first into the chamber of strangers, and then into that of novices. At the end of two months, the rule of the fraternity was read to him, at the end of six months it was read again, and once more at the end of the year. If he passed satisfactorily through this ordeal, he was then formally admitted into the society.

The Rule of Benedict is still extant;[1] and, though not wanting in strictness, is mild when contrasted with the system of austerities practised by some of the Egyptian ascetics. His monks assembled twice every day at a common table—first at noon, and then in the evening. To each was allowed daily a pound of bread and a small quantity of wine.[2] The rest of their fare was very simple; and, except to invalids, the use of flesh-meat was interdicted. In winter they were obliged to rise every morning about two o'clock for *Vigils*. At this time twelve psalms were sung or chanted, and certain lessons from the Scriptures were read or recited. The remainder of the morning till daybreak was spent in committing to memory portions of the psalms, in reading, and in meditation.[3] At sunrise they assembled for *Matins*, or morning worship. Seven hours each

---

[1] It may be found in Migne's *Latin Fathers*, t. lxvi.
[2] *Regula*, cap. xl.
[3] They were allowed to retire to rest for some time after noon. *Reg.* cap. xlviii.

day were devoted to manual labour, and two to reading. Under the charge of an inspector they slept, without undressing, in common dormitories large enough to accommodate ten or twenty individuals.[1] When at table, some one read aloud; and all conversation was prohibited. The abbot, on certain occasions, was instructed to solicit the counsel of the monks; but his authority was absolute,[2] for he was not required to act according to their directions. Implicit obedience to his injunctions was one of the first duties of a devout Benedictine.

About A.D. 529, Benedict established at Monte Cassino, in Campania, the monastery which served as a model for the institutions of his order. He does not seem to have anticipated that his rule was so soon to become popular; but, as it removed some of the most obvious defects of existing systems, it speedily commended itself to general acceptance. For many centuries its authority was acknowledged throughout almost all the monasteries of Europe. Though the Benedictines took a vow of poverty, it so happened that many of their fraternities gradually acquired immense riches. Princes and persons of rank deemed it meritorious to give them large donations; and as the resources thus placed at their disposal were not the property of any individual monk, the brethren professed to believe that, though wallowing in wealth, they were still adhering to their original principles. But opulence generated a taste for luxury; the rule of Benedict was silently relaxed; and, within two centuries after his death, the revenues of some of his establishments were miserably perverted. The needy favourites of princes were thrust on them as abbots; and these minions of royalty, who had no higher object in view than the indulgence of their appetites, converted the cloisters into the haunts of dissipation and licentiousness.

Something may be said in favour of almost any institution which folly or fanaticism may contrive; and even among Protestant writers there have been admirers and advocates of the monastic system. Monks, it has been urged, have cultivated

---

[1] *Regula*, cap. xxii.

[2] *Regula*, cap. iii. "Ut aliquid imperatum a majore fuerit, *ac si divinitus imperetur*, moram pati nesciunt in faciendo," cap. v. The same blind submission to the abbot was enjoined in the Egyptian monasteries. "Sic universa complere quæcunque fuerint ab eo præcepta, *tanquam si a Deo sint cœlitus edita, sine ulla discussione* festinant." Migne's *Latin Fathers*, lxvi. 352.

waste lands, caused the desert literally to "blossom as the rose," copied the Bible and other valuable books, and carried the gospel into regions never before trodden by the feet of the missionary. This form of will-worship made its appearance about the time when the Northern barbarians commenced to pour their countless hordes over the Roman Empire; and the abodes of the ascetics have been represented as so many sanctuaries where religion and literature found protection when most of the memorials of civilization were overwhelmed in a common ruin. But others, as well as monks, have reclaimed deserts, transcribed the Scriptures, and cheered the dark places of the earth with the blessings of revelation. The Christian teachers of Asia Minor, carried captive by the Goths in the latter half of the third century,[1] accomplished at least as signal a spiritual conquest as any ever achieved by monachism; for they won the hearts of those by whom they were enslaved, and induced them to embrace Christianity.[2] Frumentius and Ædesius, the two Tyrian youths spared when the savages on the shores of the Red Sea murdered all the rest of the crew of their vessel,[3] were equally successful in imparting a knowledge of the truth to the people of Abyssinia. The services rendered to religion by the monks when the Northern barbarians subdued the Roman Empire have been absurdly exaggerated. The monasteries presented Christianity under a false aspect, and thus prevented it from exerting its proper influence. Men who rudely severed all domestic ties—who shut themselves up in a kind of prison—who declined to bear the burdens of ordinary life—and who were seldom permitted to open their lips in conversation—were miserable representatives of Him who went about doing good, and who instructed His disciples to cause their light so to shine before men that others seeing their good works might glorify their Father in heaven. The gospel is designed for social and for active beings; and the barbarians could see little of its genial spirit in the moody mysticism of the monasteries. Many of the early monks were, no doubt, men of true piety; but they buried their talents, and were comparatively useless. Had they imitated the example of our Lord and His Apostles, and, taking their lives in their hands, had they gone forth individually, or two by two as missionaries,

---

[1] Period I. Sec. I. Chap. V. p. 24. [2] Sozomen, ii. 6.
[3] Sect. I. Chap. I. of this Period, p. 73.

they would have exhibited more Christian wisdom, as well as more self-denial, and more spiritual heroism. No wonder that the dark ages supervened, when the best specimens of the beauty of holiness were to be found in the monasteries! "God setteth the solitary in families," and the graces of the gospel never appear more attractive than in the domestic circle. But the monks, by aiming at a higher spiritualism than the New Testament recognizes, did violence to some of the very best feelings even of sanctified humanity, and stunted the growth of genuine godliness.

The introduction of monachism contributed greatly to promote clerical celibacy. As soon as it was generally believed that those who led a single life were more pious than husbands and fathers, the higher orders of ecclesiastics were deterred from matrimony; for they could not afford to be considered less holy than any other section of the community. The monastic system had been established only a few years when it began to control public opinion; and at the Council of Nice, in A.D. 325, a proposal was made that the married clergy should be separated from their wives! This overture was there successfully resisted by Paphnutius,[1] an Egyptian confessor—a man who, though himself an ascetic, was too enlightened to impose his own austerities on others,—but it was ruled that bishops, presbyters, and deacons, *after ordination*, should not be at liberty to enter into wedlock. Before the close of the fourth century the monastic system was held in such repute that the pastors of the Church began to be chosen from the inmates of the cloister; and, for upwards of a thousand years afterwards, the monastery supplied the surest and shortest pathway to ecclesiastical promotion. Ministers thus educated were ill fitted to guide their generation, or elevate the condition of society. Under such tuition the human mind well nigh lost its power of independent thought; legends the most puerile were delivered as the truth of God; the endowment of convents was extolled as superlatively meritorious; and a worse than Egyptian darkness overspread Christendom. It required a terrible convulsion to awaken the Church out of the spiritual stupor which monkery superinduced.

[1] Socrates, i. 11.

CHAPTER V.

THE SCHISM OF THE DONATISTS.

THE great schism which rent the Church of Africa in the fourth century supplies materials for an interesting and instructive chapter in ecclesiastical history.[1] The Donatists have often been described as bigots who created immense disturbance by their senseless fanaticism; but a candid investigation of their rise and progress may lead us to think somewhat more charitably of these ancient nonconformists. They constituted at one period the majority of the Christian population of a large section of the empire; they professed a sound theological creed; and, after having remained for generations in a state of ecclesiastical secession, the Catholic Church was still willing to recognize the standing of their bishops, and to receive them within her pale without either re-ordination or penance. They cannot therefore have been regarded by sober contemporaries as a body of contemptible or mischievous zealots. Whilst their annals throw light on some important points of polity and discipline, they also reveal certain curious facts relating to early Christianity which might have remained otherwise unknown.

The schism of the Donatists commenced before the conversion of Constantine. It originated at Carthage. A deacon of that place had written a tract in which he had attacked Maxentius, the reigning sovereign; and Mensurius, the bishop, who was suspected of concealing the obnoxious ecclesiastic, was required to repair to Rome and give an account of himself before the imperial tribunal. There were then connected with his Church, as well as with other Christian communities, certain office-bearers, called *seniors*, whose counsel was always sought in matters of consequence;[2] and, when the aged pastor was about

---

[1] We derive most of our information relating to the Donatists from Optatus and Augustine, both of whom were in personal collision with them. Their statements must consequently be received with caution. Tillemont, in the "Histoire du Schisme des Donatistes," given in his *Memoires*, has investigated this subject with great care, and pointed out some of the mistakes of these writers.

[2] Christianity was yet proscribed, and these seniors, or elders, could not therefore have been, as some suppose, civil functionaries, such as our churchwardens or aldermen. Neither were they, as some imagine, confined to Africa; for they

to set out on his journey, he handed over to these elders some pieces of gold and silver plate—probably used on great occasions when the Eucharist was celebrated.[1] Mensurius died on his way back from Rome, and the haste with which the election of a successor was precipitated led to the Donatist schism. In cases of importance the Numidian clergy had long been accustomed to meet for consultation with their brethren of the Proconsular Africa;[2] and Secundus, the primate, or senior Numidian bishop, now considered it his privilege to preside at the ordination of the chief pastor of Carthage; but the vacancy was abruptly supplied without any reference either to him or his comprovincials. As soon as the death of Mensurius was known, Cæcilian, the archdeacon, contrived to obtain the suffrages of the multitude; some bishops of the neighbourhood, who had assembled on short notice at Carthage, sanctioned his election; and Felix of Aptunga, one of their number, invested him with the episcopal dignity.

According to some accounts the choice was unanimous,[3] but several well-known facts are at variance with these representations. It is admitted that Lucilla, a lady of great wealth and influence, was opposed to the nomination, and it is certain that she soon had extensive support. Her hostility was ascribed by the other party to a rebuke administered to her by Cæcilian, when archdeacon, because she kept by her some bone, the supposed relic of a martyr, which she kissed before she partook of the communion.[4] It is also acknowledged that at least some of the Carthaginian presbyters were among the malecontents. Personal grounds have also been assigned for their dissatisfaction—they are said to have been disappointed candidates. It appears likewise that the elders of the Church[5] were adverse to

---

are mentioned by Hilary the deacon, who was connected with the Church of Rome. See *Ancient Church*, 585, 586, note. They corresponded to what in some Protestant Churches are called *ruling elders*. See Dr. Samuel Miller, *On the Office of the Ruling Elder*, pp. 70, 71, Glasgow, 1835.

[1] Optatus, *De Schismate Donat.* i. xvii. Migne's *Patrologiæ Cursus*. xi. 918.
[2] In one of his letters to Cornelius, we find Cyprian expressly saying: "Our province is of very wide extent, for it has Numidia and Mauritania annexed to it."
[3] Optatus says: "Suffragio totius populi Cæcilianus eligitur."
[4] Optatus, i. 16.
[5] It is admitted by Archbishop Potter that, even in the days of Cyprian, there were connected with this Church of Carthage presbyters who taught (*doctores*), "by way of distinction from other *presbyters who did not exercise this office of public teaching.*" See Potter's *Discourse of Church Government*, p. 155, London, 1839.

the new bishop, as it is related that, when, immediately after his
ordination, he called for the plate deposited with them by Mensurius, they declined to surrender possession. The refusal has
been ascribed to a dishonest intention of appropriating the treasure; but this is apparently a party calumny. It is not to be
supposed that a whole body of men holding an honourable
position yielded so shamefully to the temptations of avarice—
more especially when we remember that, in days of persecution,
they were selected by the late bishop as the most trustworthy
conservators of these precious articles. It is much more probable that they questioned the right of Cæcilian to the bishopric,
and that they were disposed to retain the plate merely until the
proper ecclesiastical authorities had adjudicated on his title.[1]

At this time the Christian population of Carthage was greater
than that of any city in the West except Rome, and Cæcilian
may have managed to carry his election by packing some particular building[2] with his own partisans; but it is quite clear
that his appointment created a large amount of popular dissatisfaction. Immediately after his elevation to the episcopal chair,
seventy Numidian bishops held a Synod at Carthage, condemned
the indecent hurry of his ordination, and summoned him before
them to answer for his conduct. Cæcilian, on the pretence that
his judges were prejudiced, declined to appear:[3] but at the
same time professed his willingness to be re-ordained by them
should a defect be discovered in his previous consecration.[4] This
reply, which obviously betrayed a consciousness of something
wrong, was very unsatisfactory to the Council, and they accordingly pronounced the ordination invalid. But they could not
stop here. Majorinus, a reader of the Church, and in some
way connected with the household of Lucilla, was elected
bishop, and clothed by them with episcopal authority. Circular
letters were written to the other bishops of Africa notifying his

---

[1] It would appear from Optatus that they were forced to give it up to Cæcilian
—probably by an appeal on his part to the civil power.

[2] According to his advocates, he had possession of the Cathedral Church.

[3] He afterwards absurdly complained that he was condemned in his absence.

[4] Iterum a Cæciliano mandatum est, ut *si Felix in se, sicut illi arbitrabantur,
nihil contulisset,* ipsi tanquam adhuc diaconum ordinarent Cæcilianum. Optatus,
i. 19. At this period, when a deacon or archdeacon was made bishop, it was not
considered necessary, in the first place, to make him a presbyter. The archdeacon
was now simply the chief deacon.

appointment; and thus, in A.D. 311, the schism was formally inaugurated.

No record of the acts of this Synod has been preserved, and our knowledge of its proceedings is derived chiefly from the garbled narrative of its adversaries; but, among the reasons assigned for the course pursued by it, we are told that Cæcilian had exhibited want of feeling for some of the sufferers during the Diocletian persecution, and that Felix, who ordained him, had purchased immunity in time of trial by giving up the Scriptures, and thus earning the designation of a *traditor*. The charges were vehemently denied; and the members of the Council, in their turn, were accused[1] of the offence imputed to Felix of Aptunga; but, with the evidence now available, it is impossible to determine the exact amount of truth or falsehood contained in these criminations. It is however unquestionable that the Numidian bishops enjoyed a large amount of popular sympathy; and that "the party of Majorinus," as their adherents were originally called, was soon numerically stronger than the party of Cæcilian. Majorinus himself died about two or three years after his election, and was succeeded in the bishopric by Donatus, surnamed the Great, a man of superior ability, energy, and eloquence. From him the Separatists were called Donatists,[2]—the name by which they are still known.

When Cæcilian was condemned and deposed by the Council of bishops assembled in Carthage, we do not find that he appealed for redress to any other ecclesiastical tribunal.[3] As if aware that the mode of his election could not be justified, and that the

[1] The minutes of the Synod of Cirta, quoted by Augustine (*Contra Cresconium*, iii. c. 27) as evidence that in the Diocletian persecution the leading Donatists themselves had been traditors, are not above suspicion. The Donatists objected to them for reasons which cannot be easily refuted. See Neander, iii. 248, 249, note. The Synod of Cirta is said to have been held in A.D. 305. Augustine himself is not very positive in denying the charges brought against the ordainers of Cæcilian. "Utrum Cæcilianus a traditoribus divinorum Codicum fuerit ordinatus, nescio."—*Epist.* clxxxv. § 5.

[2] Donatus was now a very common name in this part of Africa, and another bishop of the party—Donatus of Casæ Nigræ—acts a prominent part in this controversy; but there is no reason to doubt that the sect derived its designation from the successor of Majorinus. In A.D. 348, when far advanced in life, he was sent into banishment by Constans.

[3] Augustine virtually makes this admission when he intimates that Cæcilian expected justice from the Church on the other side of the Mediterranean. *Epist.* xliii. 18, *Opera*, tom. ii. 168, Migne's edition.

general feeling was against him, he did not venture to demand farther investigation. He contrived, however, to fortify his position by securing the recognition of the bishop of Rome and some other influential Churchmen.[1] The value of their support was soon apparent. When Constantine triumphed over Maxentius, and thus virtually became Master of Africa, these Italian friends gained the ear of the victor, and filled his mind with prejudices against the Donatists. Several epistles written by the conqueror show how soon he displayed the spirit of a partisan in this unhappy controversy. In an edict issued early in A.D. 313,[2] and addressed to Anulinus, his proconsul or lieutenant in Africa, he announces that the Catholic clergy are henceforth to be exempt from municipal services; but he provides that this privilege is to be confined to "the Church over which Cæcilian presides."[3] In a letter to Cæcilian himself, Constantine speaks out still more explicitly. He states that he had sent money to be distributed among the African pastors—who had suffered much during the recent persecutions—but that no encouragement was to be given to the abettors of "a certain vile delusion." "If," said he, "you see any of these men *persevering in their madness*, you are required, without hesitation, to report them to the judges, that they may be dealt with according to instructions which I have already given."[4]

At this time Constantine must have been very imperfectly acquainted with ecclesiastical affairs, and his inexperience may supply some apology for his rashness; but the course he pursued is utterly incapable of vindication. When he bestowed on one party favours which he withheld from the other, he decided without examination; he had no right to treat the majority of the African clergy as schismatics; neither was he warranted, in a public document, to denounce them either as mad or as the supporters of a vile delusion. No wonder that, when thus stigmatized, they appealed to the justice of the Emperor. They have been bitterly assailed because they were afterwards opposed to the alliance between Church and State; and it has been alleged that they were now the first to crave the interference of civil authority; but a candid examination of their history must show

---

[1] Augustine, *Epist.* xliii. 19.
[2] See Tillemont, *Memoires*, vi. prem. par. art. x.
[3] Euseb. x. 7.   [4] Euseb. x. 6.

that they have suffered greatly from misrepresentation. Constantine had prejudged their case, and had subjected them to invidious disadvantages before they made any complaint. And, when they at length remonstrated, they had every reason to say that they were treated unfairly and disingenuously.

When the African clergy found themselves condemned without trial by their sovereign, they requested him to submit their case to the judgment of the bishops of Gaul.[1] As these bishops had been under the government of tolerant princes—the present Emperor and his father—they had suffered little during the Diocletian persecution; and few of them could be suspected as traditors. The party of Majorinus therefore reckoned on them as impartial arbiters. But, without directly rejecting this proposal, Constantine managed to neutralize it, by committing the examination of the matters in dispute to a court very differently constituted. Nineteen bishops, of whom only three were beyond the Alps,[2] assembled by his directions at Rome, in October A.D. 313, to investigate the charges against Cæcilian. Miltiades, or Melchiades,[3] the chief pastor of the Italian metropolis, was the president and the most active member of this commission. He is said to have been an African by birth;[4] his antecedents were not unknown to the Donatists; and he was suspected by them as a time-server. And the proceedings of the commissioners certainly indicate their anxiety rather to quash the controversy than to pronounce an honest decision. Ten bishops from each party in Africa appeared before them as plaintiffs and defendants; Cæcilian was acquitted; the most zealous of his prosecutors—Donatus of Casæ Nigræ, who confessed that he had rebaptized some who had passed over from the opposite faction—was summarily condemned; and the disputants were exhorted to live at peace. The judges recommended that the status of all the bishops on both sides should be recognised, that the pastor first ordained in any place should there continue to occupy his position,

---

[1] Optatus, i. 22.

[2] These were Marinus of Arles, Reticius or Reticus of Autun, and Maternus of Cologne.

[3] Tillemont remarks that the manuscripts of Augustine and other ancient authorities give the name Miltiades, and that by more modern writers he is called Melchiades. See also August. *Contra Epist. Parmen.*, i. 5, note, Migne's edition.

[4] Tillemont, *Memoires*. vi. prem. par. art. xiii.

and that those thus left without episcopal charges should, as soon as possible, be inducted into vacancies.[1]

It is not strange that the Donatists were dissatisfied with this award. Miltiades, the chairman of the Commission, had long before acknowledged Cæcilian as bishop of Carthage; most of his colleagues were, no doubt, in the same position; and the judges were thus practically committed to a particular verdict. The Africans asserted that these so-called arbiters examined the charges against Cæcilian very superficially, and that, in condemning Donatus, they had violated all the principles of ecclesiastical order. If he had done anything improper, he should, at least in the first instance, have been tried by a tribunal in his own country; and it was monstrous to pronounce him guilty for the performance of acts which the Church courts of Africa deemed perfectly legitimate.[2] Nor were these the only grounds on which the Donatists objected to the proceedings of this judicatory. They had not, they alleged, sought its decision; they had appealed to the arbitration of the brethren in Gaul; and it was vain to imagine that the hasty deliverance of nineteen commissioners met in Rome should outweigh the decision of seventy bishops convened in Carthage.

Constantine could not well meet these arguments; and, when he discovered that the interference of Miltiades and his colleagues had rather strengthened than weakened the schism, he resolved to comply so far with the original request of the Donatists as to assemble a large Synod in Gaul to examine the controversy. This council, which, according to some authorities, consisted of two hundred bishops,[3] and, according to others, of a still greater number,[4] met at Arles in August A.D. 314. No Church judicatory on a scale so extensive had ever before assembled; its members were conveyed to the place of convocation at the public expense;

[1] Augustine, *Epist.* xliii. 16.

[2] The propriety of rebaptizing heretics was the current doctrine of the African Church from the time of Cyprian. Some other charges of a similar kind were preferred against Donatus of Casæ Nigræ.

[3] This is the number given in a considerable portion of the MSS. of Augustine (*Contra Epist. Parmeniani*, i. 5), and adopted by Baronius, Cave, Routh, and many others. Some MSS. have a different reading. See August. *Opera*, ix. 40, note, Migne's edition.

[4] According to some, 600. See Hefele, *Conciliengeschichte*, 1. 170. Some have maintained that there were only about 30 bishops at Arles, because only so many names are found appended to its canons. See Spelman's *Concilia*, i. 42. But

and among them were bishops from Italy, Sicily, Spain, and Britain, as well as from France. The Donatists found little favour at this Synod. A strong prejudice against them already existed; for it was well known that the Emperor regarded them with dislike, that the bishop of Rome, the most influential prelate in the West, had all along been opposed to them, and that, more recently, other Italian Churchmen and some of the most eminent Transalpine bishops had pronounced an adverse verdict. Marinus of Arles, one of the Roman commissioners, presided in this Council.[1] The fathers agreed that no bishop should be found guilty as a traditor who could not be convicted on the evidence of public documents; and, as Felix of Aptunga, who ordained Cæcilian, could not be reached by this species of testimony, the catholic prelate of Carthage was triumphant, and his opponents were again condemned. The Donatists, now, as a last resource, appealed to the Emperor himself, hoping, perhaps, that his innate sense of justice would at length prevail over his prejudices. With considerable reluctance, he consented to examine an affair which did not properly pertain to his jurisdiction; and, in A.D. 316, the parties were permitted to plead before him at Milan. Here, once more, however, the Donatists were defeated.

The party opposed to Cæcilian had already been greatly discouraged by the State; but, after the decision given against them at Milan, they experienced still more rigorous treatment.

---

the names of only 23 bishops are found annexed, according to Spelman, and of a still smaller number, according to Binius ; and the order in which they are arranged indicates that some one, when transcribing the canons at a subsequent period, has capriciously annexed as many signatures as he could recollect ; for Marinus, the president of the Council, stands pretty far down in the catalogue. There can be no doubt that the Council numbered at least 200 bishops. Constantine was most anxious that it should be numerously attended. (See his letter to Chrestus, bishop of Syracuse, Euseb. x. v.) The Donatists boasted that they were sustained by the authority of a Synod of 70 bishops. The Emperor, therefore, wished that a far larger number should meet at Arles. I do not know on what authority Mr. Bright asserts that the members amounted to 400. *History of the Church*, 7, Oxford and London, 1860. It is remarkable that the learned Irishman Cummian, writing in the seventh century, asserts that there were six hundred bishops at Arles. See his letter in Ussher's *Sylloge, Epist.* xi., Ussher's Works, iv. 435, edition by Elrington.

[1] This Council was convened by Constantine, though he was not yet baptized ; and its canons were sent to the bishop of Rome and others to be observed as the laws of the Church. The Roman bishop, who was not present, was represented by two presbyters and two deacons.

Their churches were taken from them; their property was confiscated; they were driven into banishment; and, in some cases they were threatened with capital punishment. We do not know that the penalty of death was ever actually inflicted; but there can be no doubt that they suffered much from intolerant legislation. Constantine soon began to have misgivings as to the equity or policy of this course; and, accordingly, in A.D. 317, he relaxed the severity of persecution. Four years afterwards, the Donatists presented to him a memorial praying for religious liberty, and declaring their determination to have nothing to do with his "scoundrel of a bishop," as they bitterly designated Cæcilian. When he was convinced that oppression only aggravated their obstinacy, he repealed the laws against them, and, whilst testifying his abhorrence of their turbulence, declared that he was determined to leave them to the judgment of God. They had meanwhile rapidly increased, and it is admitted that they already formed the major part of the Christian population. In A.D. 330, they held a celebrated Synod at Carthage, where no less than two hundred and seventy of their bishops took part in the deliberations.[1] So large a Church judicatory had never before been seen in that quarter of the Empire.

Though the irregular ordination of Cæcilian was the immediate cause of the great African schism, a substantial diversity of sentiment prolonged and embittered the controversy. There were principles involved in it which had long been struggling for ascendency. Donatism was in fact a new development of the spirit of Novatianism,[2] or a new phase of an austere system of church discipline. Its advocates maintained that the value of an ordinance depends on the character of its administrator; and, according to their views, no one could receive any pastoral authority from bishops who had been traditors; for they argued that all the official acts of such men were invalid. Immediately after the commencement of the schism, the Church began to enjoy the sunshine of imperial favour; and many, prompted by merely secular motives, sought ecclesiastical promotion; but, as the Donatists were understood to guard the door into the ministry with peculiar vigilance, the more serious Christians in many places joined their ranks, and increased their moral influence.

---

[1] Augustine, *Epist.* xciii. x. 43, *Opera*, t. ii. 342.
[2] See Period I. Sect. II. Chap. II.

They carried their ideas of the purity of Church communion to excess; the Catholics leaned to the side of laxity. As the controversy continued, other principles appeared in sharp antagonism. The Donatists had reason to complain of the harshness of a Christian emperor; and, when they saw him lavishing benefactions on their adversaries, they were tempted to believe that religion must necessarily be injured by princely patronage: the Catholics, delighted with the wonderful improvement in their social position, maintained that the Church and the State should be incorporated. Both parties were equally narrow in their religious sympathies. The Donatists have been blamed for asserting that all grace pertained to themselves; but in this they did not differ from their opponents, who held that there was no salvation out of the Catholic Church.[1]

Constans, the son of Constantine the Great, tried to lure the Donatists back to Catholicity by offering them pecuniary rewards; but comparatively few were won over by his largesses. The nobler spirits among them spurned his gifts, and asked indignantly—what right had the Prince to tamper with the Church?[2] The emperor then changed his policy, and the nonconformists were exposed to persecution of unusual severity. Troops of armed men rushed in among them when engaged in worship: blood flowed profusely: and, at the point of the sword, they were driven from their religious edifices. But they were not all prepared to submit quietly to oppression. A class of persons, inheriting some of the morose principles of the Montanists,[3] had sprung up in Africa; and, wandering idly about the country, soon began to attract attention by their ascetic extravagance. These gloomy devotees, who sustained themselves by begging, imagined that all things were out of course; they believed that, in certain cases, they had a divine commission to root out and to destroy; and they hailed martyrdom as the highest honour of humanity. They called themselves *Agonistici*, that is, the *Contenders* or the *Prizemen*, for they considered themselves the Lord's champions; but the Catholics gave them the less complimentary title of *Circumcelliones*—a name by which they are better known, and which implies that they were at once *Eaves-*

---

[1] See Neander iii. 272-4.   [2] Optatus, iii. 3.
[3] See Section II. Chap. II. Period I.

droppers and *Waylayers*.[1] They sympathised with the Donatists, for they admired their strict views of discipline; and, delighting in the "wild justice of revenge," they made terrible reprisals on all who injured these nonconformists. They attacked the churches and the houses of the Catholics; and, armed with heavy bludgeons which they styled *Israelites*, beat their victims to death. Regular soldiers were perplexed by the movements of these furious vagabonds; for they were scattered in small companies all over North Africa. They rather courted than avoided death. When driven to desperation, they threw themselves from precipices, leaped into the fire, or hired others to kill them. In A.D. 348, they appeared together in formidable numbers at Bagai in Numidia,[2] where they were defeated in battle by Macarius, the lieutenant of the Emperor Constans. The more sober Donatists repudiated any alliance with them, and denounced their lawless acts: but others of less forbearance and Christian wisdom sought their co-operation. Hence their connection with the Circumcelliones has sadly stained the reputation of the African nonconformists.

After the battle of Bagai, the imperial yoke pressed more heavily than ever on the Donatists; and for thirteen years they were treated with extreme cruelty. During this period their worship was proscribed; and those of them who escaped death were sent into exile. But when Julian became sovereign of the empire, all sectaries obtained encouragement; and the Donatists, after their return from banishment, were admitted to ample privileges. Their numbers now rapidly increased, but their stern bigotry was unabated; and, when brought into personal collision with their ecclesiastical foes, they too frequently exhibited much brutality and recklessness. On various occasions their fanaticism assumed a very extravagant form. If they obtained possession of a church which had been occupied by their rivals, they washed the floor, scraped the walls, burned the communion table, and cast the Eucharistic elements to the dogs.[3]

---

[1] They were called Circumcelliones because they wandered *Circum cellas*, that is, about the cottages of the peasantry. "Hoc genus hominum . . . victus sui causa cellas circumiens rusticanas, unde et Circumcellionum nomen accepit." Augustine, *Contra Gaudentium*, i. c. 28.

[2] Tillemont, vi. prem. p. art. 46. Optatus, iii. 4.

[3] Optatus, ii. c. 19; vi. c. 6.

Valentinian I. was unfriendly to them, and Gratian gave orders that they should be deprived of their churches; but the dread of the terrible Circumcelliones interfered with the general enforcement of this decree. Towards the end of the fourth century they enjoyed peace; and their bishops amounted to between four and five hundred.[1]

From this period we may date their decline. Divisions now began to appear among them; for, after the death of Parmenian,[2]—their bishop of Carthage, in A.D. 392,—a schism occurred in that see, and two rivals—Primian and Maximian—contended for the episcopal dignity. These disputes exposed them to much ridicule, weakened their influence, and led not a few to return to Catholicity. About the same time several imperial acts of uniformity, designed to compel them to return to the established Church, added to their difficulties. The labours of the great Augustine also contributed to diminish their popularity and reduce their strength. When this distinguished pulpit orator was ordained bishop of Hippo, the Donatists formed the bulk of the inhabitants; and so intense was their bigotry, that a baker of their communion would not supply bread to a Catholic household.[3] Augustine was led to apply his vigorous mind to the consideration of the most effectual means of healing the schism; and, before the close of his life, he had the satisfaction of seeing his efforts crowned with wonderful success. Confident in the goodness of his cause, and in his own powers of forensic eloquence, he challenged them to engage in public discussion, and in this way to test the merits of their respective principles. Dreading his argumentative skill and his rhetorical superiority, they were exceedingly reluctant to grapple with him in debate; but at length, in A.D. 411, they consented to hold a conference at Carthage. At this meeting 565 bishops were present[4] of whom

---

[1] When Primian and Maximian disputed, a council of one hundred bishops supported the latter, and another council of three hundred and ten bishops maintained the cause of the former. Augustine, *Contra Epist.* Parmen. i. 4. There were doubtless Donatist bishops who were not present at either of these meetings.

[2] Parmenian was the immediate successor of Donatus the Great, and was thus the third Donatist bishop of Carthage. He was the contemporary of Optatus, who wrote against him. After his death Augustine wrote a work in three books in reply to one of his publications.

[3] Augustine, *Contra Lit. Petiliani.* ii. c. lxxxiii. § 184.

[4] Though great exertions were unquestionably made to secure a large attend-

286 were Catholics, and 279 were Donatists. The Catholic bishops declared that if the Donatists lost their cause, and yet consented to join the established Church, they should be recognized in their episcopal character, and stand on the same level with themselves in the exercise of their functions.[1] Should this arrangement prove unsatisfactory to the people, it was proposed that both Catholics and Donatists should resign, and that the congregations should be permitted to choose new pastors. "Be brothers with us in the inheritance of the Lord," exclaimed Augustine. "Let us not, for the sake of preserving our own honours, hinder the peace of Christ."[2]

The Conference of Carthage was kept up for three successive days;[3] and Marcellinus, a high officer of government under the Emperor Honorius, presided over the meeting. Seven bishops on each side conducted the discussion; the history of the schism was canvassed; and the theological questions on which the parties were divided supplied topics for keen debate. Marcellinus, as might have been expected, pronounced in favour of the State Church; but many of the Donatists remained unconvinced. Some of their leaders, who relinquished their principles of separation, were recognized, in accordance with previous arrangements, as Catholic bishops; and those who persisted in their views were subjected to a persecution of fearful violence. Slaves and peasants were beaten into conformity; persons of wealth were deprived of all their possessions; the clergy were banished; and the churches, with other ecclesiastical property, were confiscated. During these days of trial, some of the sufferers, in their despair, were tempted to commit suicide. When the Vandals invaded Africa, the Donatists experienced a relaxation of the perse-

---

ance, it may be fairly questioned whether much more than one-half of the bishoprics were represented at the meeting. Distance, age, and other causes must have kept many away, and a considerable number of sees were vacant. At this time the entire population of this part of the empire amounted only to about nine millions (according to Merivale, in his *History of the Romans under the Empire*, iv. 451), or little more than the census of Ireland before the famine of 1847, and a large portion of this population was still pagan, as the writings of Augustine abundantly testify.

[1] Augustine, *Epist.* cxxviii. 2, 3.
[2] *Sermo.* ccclviii. 4.
[3] Augustine has given an account of it in his *Breviculus Collationis cum Donatistis*.

cution, and, though in greatly reduced numbers, continued to exist till the seventh century. They then disappear from history.

When reviewing the controversy between the Catholics and the Donatists, we must confess that both parties deserve condemnation; but, if required to decide where the greater blame rested, we may find it impossible to pronounce an award. The ordination of a successor to Mensurius was rash and disorderly; the conduct of Constantine in at once identifying himself with Cæcilian was unwarrantable; and yet the doctrine of the Donatists—that an ordinance of God becomes a nullity when dispensed by an unworthy pastor—is thoroughly untenable. Truth remains truth though uttered by unhallowed lips; and a divine institution is not necessarily invalid because celebrated by a minister who wants the spirit of his high calling. The violence with which the Catholics persecuted the nonconformists is incapable of vindication; and yet the fury with which the Donatists avenged themselves is appalling. The Catholics and the Donatists were equally wrong when they maintained respectively that the true Church was only with themselves. The true Church rises out of God's Word; his children are found wherever the Gospel is appreciated; and any visible community is entitled to expect the blessing of Christ only in so far as it obeys the voice of its heavenly Monitor. The Catholics could not carry out consistently their theory of exclusiveness; and when, at the Conference of Carthage, they expressed their readiness to recognize the ecclesiastical status of the Donatist bishops, if united to themselves, they broadly admitted a principle which they had all along professed to ignore. The Donatists had been in a state of secession for a century, and it was now acknowledged that, if they would at length conform, their pastors were competent, without re-ordination or any further ceremony, to administer all the ordinances of the Catholic Church.

According to the current theology of the fourth century, the Catholic Church should be regarded as a great visible confederation, with the bishop of Rome as its centre of unity; and as, in his disputes with the Donatists, Augustine pressed this doctrine to its logical conclusions, he was led unduly to exalt the claims of the Italian pontiff. In the controversy relative to the rebaptizing of heretics, the African clergy of the third century scouted the idea of the Roman Pope's dictation; and at the commencement of the Donatist schism the majority appealed, not to his arbitration, but to the judgment of the bishops of Gaul; the minority, however, enjoyed his patronage, and were thus tempted to connive at the advancement of pretensions which they would have otherwise opposed. Augustine fell into this mistake; and though when Zosimus, in the Pelagian controversy,[1] attempted to overbear the African fathers, the bishop of Hippo apparently modified his views,[2] he seems never to have been fully aware of the dangerous tendency of papal assumptions. Nor was this the only error he committed in the affair of the Donatists. He was originally indisposed to employ compulsion in matters of religion; but observing that the obstinacy of the Separatists often gave way before the flashing swords of the imperial soldiery, he adopted the notion that, in the cause of truth, force might be legitimately added to persuasion.[3] He is thus unhappily known among the fathers as one of the earliest apologists and advocates of religious persecution.

Ecclesiastical divisions have produced much mischief: they have fostered prejudices and engendered sectarian bitterness; but, in the wonderful providence of Him who can bring good out of evil, they have often contributed to check the progress of corruption. In this respect the Donatists were singularly useful; for it was owing to their influence that various parts of the structure of the ancient Church were so long preserved. Their schism commenced before the conversion of Constantine; it arose from a dispute relative to a matter of discipline; and when the ecclesiastical framework was elsewhere undergoing a silent transformation, the Catholics of Africa dared not attempt any considerable departure from existing regulations. They knew that the Separatists were waiting for their halting, and ready to denounce innovation. In many districts the Catholics were the weaker

---

[1] See Section III. Chap. II. of this Period.

[2] As to the vacillation respecting the interpretation of Matt. xvi. 18, see Barrow *on the Pope's Supremacy*, by M'Crie, p. 78, Edinburgh, 1852. It is worthy of note that, in a sermon preached immediately before the Conference of Carthage, Augustine gives the Protestant interpretation. We may presume that the Donatists thus expounded the text. See Augustine, *Serm.* ccclviii. § 5.

[3] "Cur ergo non cogeret Ecclesia perditos filios ut redirent? . . . . Annon pertinet ad diligentiam pastoralem . . illas oves . . . . si resistere voluerint, flagellorum terroribus, vel etiam doloribus revocare?"—*Epist.* clxxxv. § 27.

party, and they could not afford to hazard a diminution of their strength by tampering with the ecclesiastical constitution. Hence the church polity of Africa at length differed widely from that of the rest of the Roman Empire, as it remained much the same amidst surrounding changes. The title *chorepiscopus* was here unknown;[1] for, though village pastors abounded, they exercised all the functions of the episcopal office. The bishop, as to spiritual power, was simply the moderator of a small church judicatory. When he engaged in ordination his presbyters all laid on hands along with him,[2] and he could do nothing of importance without their special advice and concurrence.[3] The bishops of the Catholic Church in Africa amounted to at least 500,[4] and those of the Donatists were not less numerous. With one exception,[5] the system of metropolitans, properly so called, had no existence in that part of Christendom. The senior bishop for the time being was president of the provincial synod;[6] and as he was generally far advanced in life when he attained the primacy, he seldom continued long to occupy his position. To defeat any attempt to break in on the proper order of succession, as well as to obviate all disputes relative to seniority, two distinct registries, each specifying the name of every bishop in the province and the date of his ordination, were carefully preserved.[7] The primate was often nothing more than a parish minister.[8] As his rank was humble, his power was limited; for he was not at liberty to act without the concurrence of his brethren; and by a special law he was forbidden to assume any other name but that of "Bishop of the First See."[9] The Church

---

[1] Leydecker, *Hist. Ecc. Africanæ Dissert. Prælim.* § vii.
[2] Fourth Council of Carthage, Canon 3.
[3] Fourth Council of Carthage, Canons 22 and 23.
[4] According to Victor Vitensis, a contemporary and himself a sufferer, 466 Catholic bishops appeared on one occasion before Hunneric, king of the Vandals, at Carthage in A.D. 484.
[5] That of the Proconsular Africa, of which province Carthage was the capital.
[6] This system continued for nearly two hundred years afterwards. See *Epistles of Pope Gregory the Great,* lib. i. 74. *Opera,* tom. iii. 529, Migne edit.
[7] Bingham, book ii. c. xvi. § 8.
[8] The fact that nine hundred or a thousand bishops ministered to six or seven millions of Christians is itself a sufficient indication of the position of an African bishop. The diocesan system had commenced at Carthage, and now prevailed, perhaps, to a considerable extent in the Proconsular Africa; but elsewhere almost all the bishops must have been parochial.
[9] Third Council of Carthage, Canon 26.

of Africa was noted for its sound creed no less than for its ancient polity. When doctrinal error had made extensive progress in other parts of Christendom, this section of the Empire still remained pure. Pelagius and Cœlestius passed without rebuke at Rome; but, when they ventured across the Mediterranean to propagate their errors, the African bishops at once took the alarm: the heresy was condemned; and its authors were cut off by synodical authority from Catholic communion. Thus Donatism, on the whole, seems to have exercised rather a healthful influence as well on the doctrine as the polity of the African Church.

CHAPTER VI.

MOHAMMEDANISM.

WE cannot well narrate the history of the Christian Church without noticing the rise and progress of the system taught by the false prophet of Arabia. Mohammedanism[1] spread with amazing rapidity; swept away the professors of the Gospel from whole regions; and, though a scheme of monstrous delusion, reasserted some great principles well nigh suppressed by superstition. Nor can it be regarded as a temporary effervescence of fanaticism. After the lapse of twelve centuries it retains its ascendency over a large section of the family of man.

Mohammed was born about A.D. 570.[2] He was of the tribe of Koreish—a noble Arabian clan; and his ancestors, for several

---

[1] The name of its founder has been variously written Mahomet, Mohammed, Mohammad, and Muhammed, as well as in some other forms. It signifies "Praised." Among the most recent and valuable contributions to the literature of this subject may be mentioned Dr. Sprenger's *Life of Mohammad*, Part I. of which was printed at Allahabad (India) in 1851. Dr. Sprenger has since undertaken a larger work on the same subject in German—*Das Leben und die Lehre des Mohammad*,—the first volume of which appeared in Berlin in 1861, and the second the following year. William Muir, Esq., of the Bengal Civil Service, has also published a most important work in 4 vols. (London 1861) entitled *The Life of Mahomet*.

[2] According to Sprenger, Mohammed was born at Mecca in April A.D. 571. According to M. Caussin de Perceval and Muir, the date is August 20th A.D. 570. The event is said to have taken place on a *Monday*. Many of the most remarkable incidents of his life occurred, according to tradition, on that day.

I

generations, had been entrusted, as well with the care of the Kaaba, or great temple of Mecca, as with the government of the city. His countrymen—some of whom occupied fixed habitations, whilst others led a wandering life amid sandy deserts of vast expanse—were addicted to idolatry, and, to a great extent, unacquainted with the elements of literature. Deprived at a very early age of both his parents, Mohammed was brought up under the care of his uncle Abu Talib, with whom he was a special favourite. When a child, he was subject to fits like those of epilepsy;[1] and, as he advanced in life, he was thoughtful, somewhat given to despondency, and constitutionally timid. He was afraid to sit down in the dark; an unpleasant dream, or an omen, deemed unlucky, gave him much uneasiness;[2] and he was of an inactive or languid temperament; but, withal, he was shrewd and sagacious. He was rather above the middle size; though slightly stooped, his frame was well knit together; he had fine black eyes, an ample forehead, and an aspect at once benevolent and dignified. He was generally silent; but, when he began to speak, his auditors were constrained to admire his melodious voice, his graceful elocution, and the outpourings of his native eloquence. In his twenty-fifth year he was engaged as factor, or commercial agent, for a rich widow of Mecca. The wealthy matron soon bestowed on him her affections; though fifteen years his senior, she still retained much of the bloom of beauty;[3] and, by his marriage with the prudent and intelligent Khadija, he became one of the most opulent inhabitants of the city.

This portion of the history of Mohammed is involved in no little obscurity,[4] so that we have not the means of ascertaining what first suggested to him the idea of assuming the character

[1] The statement that he was subject to such fits, though denounced by Gibbon as "an absurd calumny of the Greeks," is now supported by the highest authorities. See Sprenger's *Life of Mohammad*, pt. i. 77, 78, and Muir, i. 23.

[2] Muir, iv. 312.

[3] She was now nearly thirty-nine solar years of age. She had six children by him.

[4] In addition to hints supplied in the Koran, there are still extant biographies of Mohammed written by Ibn Hisham, who died early in the ninth century, by Wackidi, who was a Cazi of Baghdad about the same period, by Muhammad ibn Saad, the secretary of Wackidi, and by Tabari, who also flourished in the ninth century. See Muir, i. 89-103. Such works as *The Life of Mahomet* by Prideaux, based chiefly on later authorities, are now nearly obsolete.

of a prophet. As pilgrims annually assembled from all parts of the country to perform their devotions in the Kaaba, he had frequent opportunities of witnessing the grossest forms of Arabian superstition; and he probably soon discovered some of the absurdities of the current idolatry. He had twice visited Syria; first, when only twelve years of age, and afterwards, when in the service of Khadija; and, though these journeys were undertaken for mercantile purposes, they must have stimulated the intellectual activity of a youth gifted with exceedingly quick powers of observation. At the great fairs, held in the neighbourhood of Mecca,[1] he was also supplied with much food for thought; for he was there brought into contact with the professors of various creeds—including Jews and Catholics, Nestorians and Monophysites. It is not improbable that he derived from some of these strangers certain sound principles which he subsequently inculcated. A Jew could teach him the doctrine of the unity of God, as well as the folly of the worship of images; whilst either a Catholic or a sectary might convince him that the author of the Christian religion exhibited indubitable proofs of a divine commission. Nor was he, as we may presume, altogether indisposed to listen to statements from the Old Testament; for Abraham, the father of the faithful, was reputed the common ancestor of the Arabians and the Israelites; and Mohammed might naturally feel interested in the scriptural history of his great progenitor. Though he gloried in the title of the "Illiterate Prophet," he could read and perhaps write;[2] and, in the elaboration of his doctrine, he could avail himself of various accessible sources of information. But his system possessed very marked and peculiar features; he was ambitious to distinguish himself as a religious reformer; the conviction of the unity of God and of the absurdity of image worship seized on his mind with a power which he mistook for inspiration; and we can well believe that, like Montanus or Manes, he proceeded in the earlier stages of his career very much under the promptings of fanaticism. The comparative purity of his life till he passed middle age; the discouragements under which he prosecuted his mission for eight or ten years; and the deference with which he was

---

[1] Such as at Ocatz, within three days' journey of Mecca, where Mohammed is said to have heard Coss, the bishop of Najran, preach. Muir, ii. 7.

[2] Muir, i. ix.; iv. 271; Sprenger, *Das Leben und die Lehre*, ii. 398.

treated when he appeared as a prophet by his most upright and intimate acquaintances—all forbid the inference that he acted from the first the part of an impostor. He was naturally pensive and reserved; he continued to suffer occasionally from the paroxysms of some strange disease;[1] and, as he approached his fortieth year, he became deeply meditative. Frequently retiring to a cave at Mount Hira, about three miles from Mecca, he spent much time in solitude, contemplation, and fasting. Shortly afterwards he entered on his mission—in obedience, as he alleged, to a divine vision, in which he was assured that he was chosen as the apostle of God.

Mohammed passed through many severe mental struggles before he ventured to claim the attention of his countrymen in the character of a prophet. The resolution to renounce the idol-worship of Arabia must have cost him many an anxious thought; but, when had proceeded thus far, he could not be content with such an amount of reformation. He had grasped certain sound theological principles—he had attained a knowledge of the vanity of images and of the unity of God—and prompted, partly perhaps by the conscious possession of truth, and partly by the hope that he might thus elevate himself to power, he was desirous to impart his own convictions to his fellow-citizens. But, when at this stage of his career, he proceeded to promulgate his views, he at once encountered the objection that he had no divine call, and that he had therefore no right to interfere with the established faith. He was in consequence thrown into dreadful despondency, and sometimes even tempted to destroy himself.[2] There was a wonderful sympathy between his mind and his body; and, as amid the solitudes connected with Mount Hira, he brooded over his position, he seems at length to have been wrought up to such a pitch of excitement that one of the paroxysms of his nervous malady supervened. When in this state he imagined that the angel Gabriel appeared to him in the sky, and commanded him to speak in the name of the Lord. He regarded the communication as divine, and forthwith commenced

---

[1] By means of hysteria—a disease, as it appears, not confined exclusively to females—Sprenger endeavours to account for various physical as well as mental phenomena exhibited by Mohammed. *Das Leben und die Lehre des Mohammad*, i. 207.

[2] Muir, ii. 84.

his mission. And often afterwards when he delivered *Suras*, or *portions* of his revelations, he was under the same nervous influence. All at once, and in the coldest day, large drops of perspiration would bedew his forehead, his countenance would express deep disquietude, and he would fall to the ground. If he happened at the time to be riding on his camel, even the poor brute would be affected and would be thrown into a state of wild excitement.[1] Some of his fits may have been brought on designedly to give greater impressiveness to his communications; but his health suffered seriously from these convulsions; and he is said to have ascribed the increasing number of his grey hairs to the influence of the "*terrific* Suras."[2]

The religion of the prophet has been called *Islam*—a word which denotes the *surrender* of the soul *to God*; and its professors are known as Musalmans, Mussulmans, or Moslems.[3] For a long time Mohammed made but slow progress. His wife Khadija was his first disciple. His young cousin Ali, the son Abu Talib, likewise became a proselyte. Zeid, who had formerly been his slave, but who had been adopted by him as his son, was another of his earliest converts. Abu Bakr, one of the richest and most influential inhabitants of Mecca, also joined him; and several respectable citizens soon followed the example. These men had probably been previously convinced of the folly of polytheism, so that their adoption of Islam involved little substantial change in their sentiments.[4] Mohammed now began to preach more publicly—announcing that he was sent to deliver his countrymen from their errors, and to propagate the true faith. He professed not to teach any new religion, but merely to restore to its original purity the theology professed by Abraham. The primitive creed of the Arabians, he affirmed, was sound; for Ishmael, their ancestor, had been instructed by his father "the

---

[1] Muir, ii. 87.
[2] *Ibid.* 88.
[3] "Islam is the verbal noun, or infinitive, and Moslim, which has been corrupted into Musalman, is the participle of the causative form of salm, which signifies immunity, peace. The signification of Islam is, therefore, to make peace, or to obtain immunity, either by compact, or by doing homage to the stronger, and acknowledging his superiority, and surrendering to him the object of the dispute. It also means simply to surrender. In the Koran it signifies in most instances to do homage to God, to acknowledge him as our absolute Lord to the exclusion of idols." Sprenger's *Life of Mohammad*, p. 168-9.
[4] Sprenger's *Life of Mohammad*, pt. i. p. 174.

friend of God;" but, in process of time, corruptions had multiplied, and thus the ancient religion of the country had miserably deteriorated. Neither did Mohammed ignore either the Old or New Testament.[1] He seems, indeed, to have known almost nothing of the Christian Scriptures. He revived the Gnostic fable that Jesus was taken up into heaven without having suffered any real crucifixion,[2] and otherwise so adulterated the testimony of the Evangelists as to warrant the conclusion that he must have obtained much of his information relative to our Lord through very corrupt channels. But though he admitted that both Moses and Jesus were divine messengers, he intimated that they merely prepared the way for his own dispensation, and that he was invested with a higher commission than either the Jewish or Christian lawgiver. Whilst he wished the Israelites to believe that he was the Great Prophet whose coming they had expected for so many generations, he sought to persuade the Christians that his appearance was indicated in the New Testament and in some way identified with the Second Advent of their Messiah.[3] It is easy to see that such views, promulgated at a time of great religious degeneracy by a man of rank, ability and eloquence, were calculated to make an impression. Instead of wounding the prejudices of his countrymen by proposing to overthrow their ancient traditions, he rather flattered their pride by representing himself as the restorer of the faith of their fathers; and by asserting that he was merely appointed to inaugurate another economy, he was the more likely

---

[1] The statements so often made, that he condemned the current copies of the Jewish and Christian Scriptures as corrupt, cannot be sustained. See Muir, i. lxx. The Mohammedans, at a later period, found it convenient to fabricate the tradition. The prophet was too ignorant to be a Biblical critic, and he unquestionably admitted the genuineness of both the Jewish and Christian Scriptures.

[2] Koran, Sura iv., "They killed Him not, neither did they crucify Him, but He was simulated unto them. . . . But God raised Him up unto Himself."

[3] Muir, ii. 313. We read in the Koran—"And when Jesus, the Son of Mary, said, O children of Israel, verily I am the apostle of God sent unto you, . . . *bringing good tidings of an apostle who shall come after me*, and whose name shall be AHMAD," Sura lxi. "The passage to which this verse of the Koran alludes is St. John xvi. 7, where Christ said, I go to my Father, and the Paraclete shall come. It appears from Ibn Ishaq, . . . that the Syriac translator read Periclyte, the illustrious or praised, instead of Paraclete; and that the word was rendered in the Arabic version, which was made from the Syriac, by Ahmad, *i.e.* praised. The meaning of Mohammed is the same." Sprenger's *Life of Mohammad*, pt. i. 97, note.

to obtain the support of "the People of the Book,"—the designation by which he was wont to distinguish the Jews and the Christians.

Notwithstanding the zeal with which Mohammed promulgated his creed, his converts, towards the close of the fourth year of his public career, barely amounted to forty individuals. His preaching offended many of his countrymen; his attacks on the national idolatry were heard with indignation; and, as he wrought no miracles in confirmation of his claims, his position became daily more uncomfortable. At this crisis he betrayed signs of vacillation—recognized the intercessory power of the false gods of Arabia,[1]—and prepared the way for a reconciliation with his alienated fellow-citizens. But he soon withdrew this concession, and thus added to the irritation he had already created. In spite of all his efforts to advance Islam, his adherents increased slowly; and had not the state of matters in another city of Arabia opened up a new prospect, and led him to adopt new measures, he might have sunk into obscurity, and, in a few generations, been forgotten. A casual meeting with some pilgrims at Mecca formed a turning-point in his history.

Crowds of worshippers from all parts of Arabia annually repaired to the Kaaba to go through their religious ceremonies; and at these great gatherings Mohammed had been long accustomed to urge his claims on the devotees. In A.D. 620, when the visitors were about to set out homewards, the prophet entered into conversation with a group of six or seven individuals lingering in the suburbs of the city. These strangers were from Yathreb—distant, northwards, between two and three hundred miles from Mecca, and on the route by which caravans often travelled on their way to Syria. Though the mass of the population of this city practised the superstitions of Arabia, there were Jews in the district who had diffused some vague hopes of a Messiah; but the place had been sadly distracted by party spirit, and a recent civil war had rather exasperated than allayed the hatred of opposing factions. Worn out by discord apparently interminable, the people of Yathreb were fully prepared to entertain any proposition likely to promote peace; they had already heard of the proceedings of Mohammed; he was the near kinsman of one of their most influential families;[2] and

---

[1] Muir, ii. 150. Sprenger's *Life of Mahommad*, pt. i. 184 5.   [2] Muir, ii. 213.

some of them were not indisposed to cherish the idea that such a Prophet or Messiah would put an end to their divisions. The little company of pilgrims now listened attentively to his statements; and, before the close of the interview, embraced the faith of Islam. In consequence of his growing insecurity at Mecca he felt that he must soon withdraw from it; and he anxiously asked his new proselytes whether, in the event of his removal to Yathreb, they would be accountable for his protection? For the present, they declined the responsibility. Determined, however, to do their utmost to propagate the religion of the prophet among their townsmen, they promised to return, at the next annual pilgrimage, and report the result of their exertions.

The labours of these converts soon produced fruit. The simple and sublime doctrine of the unity of God cannot well be rejected when fairly presented to the mind; the intercourse of the men of Yathreb with Jews and Christians had long since led some of them to doubt the propriety of their idol-worship; there were a few among them looking out for the appearance of a Great One who would extinguish their bloody feuds; and when Mohammed was proclaimed as the apostle of God, a goodly number were ready to listen with favour to his pretensions. Next year, when the time of pilgrimage came round, twelve men, from the two great political factions hitherto at such enmity in Yathreb, met Mohammed at Mecca, and pledged themselves to support Islam.

From this date the new religion made rapid progress in Yathreb. Islam was the topic of general conversation, its merits were discussed in every house, and its adherents soon formed a large section of the inhabitants. At the request of the proselytes a more advanced believer was sent from Mecca to superintend their religious instruction; and under the care of this teacher they met for prayer and the reading of the revelations of Mohammed. The creed of the prophet became popular; the Jews looked on with astonishment as the pagans demolished their images and professed their belief in the unity of God; men who had long been deadly foes were now seen holding peaceful fellowship; and a great change was visible in the general aspect of society.

Meanwhile the prospects of Islam at Mecca were anything but encouraging. The adherents of Mohammed constituted a mere fraction of the citizens; his own life was in peril; for years he had gained scarcely a single convert; and he had almost ceased to attempt proselytism. But the news of what was passing in Yathreb soon reached him, and led him to revert to the idea of repairing to that place as a safer and more promising field for missionary operations. When ruminating on this project he had a dream which forms one of the most remarkable episodes in his history. He imagined that a white steed was brought to him, and that, mounted on this mysterious animal, which was conducted by the angel Gabriel, he was carried, in the twinkling of an eye, past Yathreb to Jerusalem. From thence, still accompanied by Gabriel, he ascended a ladder of light which led to the upper world, where he traversed the seven heavens, each distant from the other, according to the ordinary rate of travelling on earth, no less than a five hundred years' journey. On his way through these celestial regions he saw Adam, Moses, Abraham, Jesus, and others, whose salutations he acknowledged. On all the gates of the seven heavens were inscribed the words " There is no God but God—Mohammed is the Prophet of God." As he approached within two bowshots of the Eternal Presence, he saw the Most High sitting on His throne. When he drew nearer, the divine hand was laid on him, and immediately an intense chill ran through his body. The Lord then talked to him familiarly, revealed to him many mysteries, and made him acquainted with the whole of His law. At first he was required to pray fifty times a day; but, after repeated remonstrances, the burden was relaxed, and the Creator agreed to be satisfied with five daily acts of devotion. Mohammed now descended to Jerusalem, mounted again his fleet steed, and was forthwith transported to Mecca.

In its original form this story of the night journey to heaven contained few details, but it has been wonderfully embellished by oriental fancy, and furnished with a strange variety of incidents which the Moslems delight to recapitulate. Though the most ancient traditions describe it as a vision,[1] many Mahommedan authorities set it forth as a real transaction; and the followers of the prophet have often appealed to it as an illustration of the regard paid to him by the Sovereign of the universe. Though noticed,[2] it is not narrated in the Koran; but it is given

---

[1] Muir, ii. 221, 222.
[2] Koran, Sura, xvii. at the beginning.

in the *Sonnah,* or books of traditions,[1] volumes revered by the Mohammedans as the depositaries of the sayings and doings of the founder of Islam. When the apostle himself first repeated the story, it was received with incredulity, and for a time it exposed him to scorn; but when the trusty Abu Bakr affirmed his faith in it, others ceased to persist in their scepticism.

Shortly after the promulgation of this account of the night journey, Mohammed was enabled to make arrangements for a real removal from his native city. At the next annual pilgrimage seventy-three men from Yathreb, the representatives of a still larger number, met him privately in the vicinity of Mecca, undertook to be accountable for his protection, and pledged themselves by oath to defend him at the hazard of their lives and properties. The labours of from ten to twelve years had collected around him about 150 adherents, including men, women, and children;[2] and in a few weeks these disciples were sent forward to the place of his intended residence. He and Abu Bakr soon followed. The prophet and his friend were obliged to conceal themselves for several days in a cave, and then to escape by night to elude their pursuers; and hence the Mahommedan Era, which dates from this period, has been called the *Hegira,* that is, *Flight* or *Emigration.*[3] The announcement of the approach of the fugitives to Yathreb created general joy: multitudes went out to meet them; and, on Friday, the 2d of July, A.D. 622,[4] Mohammed, mounted on his camel, entered the city in the midst of an immense concourse of spectators, and surrounded by a goodly array of Arabian warriors in glittering armour. Friday has ever since been observed by the Moslems as the day on which they meet for worship.

The settlement of Mohammed at Yathreb—henceforth known as *The Town of the Prophet,* or *Medina* [5]—immensely improved

[1] See Prideaux, 53, London, 1723.

[2] Muir, ii. 247. Mecca at this time contained 12,000 inhabitants. Sprenger's *Life of Mohammad,* part i. 44.

[3] The Hegira was instituted by Omar, the second of the Caliphs. According to the common computation, it dates from July 16th, A.D. 622. The Mohammedan year consists of 354 days and a few hours.

[4] This is the calculation of some of the highest authorities, such as M. Caussin de Perceval. See Muir, ii. 261, iii. 6.

[5] "Yathreb was called Medinato 'l Nabi, the town of the prophet, and at last Medina, the town, by way of eminence."—Ockley's *History of the Saracens,* p. 31, London, 1848.

his position. At first only a portion of the inhabitants professed his creed; but his appearance in the place put an end to the factions by which it had so long been distracted; few ventured openly to challenge his claims as the apostle of God, and in some years the whole population was gained over to his religion. He thus became master of the second city in Arabia; for he exercised the kingly as well as the prophetic office, and his authority was absolute. Shortly after his arrival he built a *mosque*—the first edifice ever erected for the celebration of the rites of Islam. In this rude temple—which was in form a square, each side being about 150 feet in length—he officiated as the presiding minister, the service consisting chiefly of prayer and preaching. Often did the congregation here hang on the lips of Mohammed, as he poured forth streams of fiery eloquence; as, with awful solemnity, he professed to speak in the name of the Eternal, and as he descanted on the miseries of hell and the joys of paradise. But the mosque was often used for other purposes. When the prophet entered on his career of conquest, it was the news-room to which the citizens resorted for intelligence; and when chiefs and princes began to send representatives to Medina, it was the hall of audience in which their ambassadors were received.

A decided change for the worse appears in the character of Mohammed after his removal to his new residence. When in Mecca he had submitted with wonderful forbearance to the indignities heaped on him, and had sought to solace himself by prayer; but the bitter remembrance rankled in his heart, and, as soon as circumstances permitted, he determined on revenge. He now taught that his religion must be propagated by the sword; and this terrible method of conversion was first tried on his kinsmen and former fellow-citizens. "Kill the idolators wherever ye find them," says the Koran—the Bible of the Moslems—" take them prisoners and besiege them, and lay wait for them in every convenient place. . . . . Go forth to battle, both light and heavy,[1] and employ your substance and your persons for the advancement of God's religion. . . . . O Prophet! wage war against the unbelievers and the hypocrites, and be severe to them. . . . . O true believers! wage war against such of the infidels as are near you."[2]

[1] That is, "light and heavy armed."—Rodwell. [2] Koran, Sura ix. Sale's version.

Though the earlier public movements of this singular personage may be attributed to a fanatical abhorrence of idolatry, mingled with a delusive conviction that he was the apostle of God, it is clear that when success began to crown his efforts he yielded to less spiritual and to baser impulses. Man is an awful self-deceiver: Mohammed wanted the sterling honesty which would have prompted him to recoil from a pious fraud, and, on more than one occasion, he stands convicted of treachery and imposture. When this false prophet, in advanced life, gave almost unbridled license to his lusts and acted the part of a leader of banditti, he still maintained that he was acting under the guidance of the Almighty. He was not originally a polygamist, and during the life of Khadija, his only partner until he was nearly fifty years of age,[1] he appears to have given no cause for scandal; but afterwards he threw off all restraint, and before his death he had at one time no less than ten wives and two concubines.[2] In justification of his licentiousness, he published revelations said to have been made by the angel Gabriel; nor was he ashamed to confess that his highest enjoyment consisted in sexual indulgence. As the tide of prosperity continued to flow in upon him his views continued to change, so that the inconsistencies to be found in the Koran are too palpable to admit of denial. The Mohammedan expositors endeavour to account for them by the rather awkward doctrine of *abrogation*, alleging that what was taught at one time was revoked by a new revelation.[3]

During the last ten years of his life, Mohammed was almost perpetually engaged in military enterprises. His position for a time was very much that of the captain of a gang of freebooters. After his settlement in Medina, he commenced his aggressive movements by attacking the passing caravans; but, as his power increased, he entered on a course of more systematic and extensive conquest. The political circumstances of Arabia peculiarly favoured his designs, as its government was divided among a multitude of petty chiefs, who were soon either compelled or persuaded to receive his creed and submit to his authority. Within little more than seven years after the Hegira, he became master of his native town, Mecca, the civil and ecclesiastical metropolis of the country. He had already ordained that his disciples should turn towards the Kaaba when they engaged in their de-

---

[1] She died Dec. A.D. 619, aged 65.   [2] Muir, iv. 89.   [3] Ockley, 65.

votions,[1] and he now accomplished the purification of this celebrated temple by the destruction of all the images either in it or around it. Mecca has ever since been the holy city of his followers.

The subjugation of Arabia was not sufficient to satisfy his ambition. By his letters or ambassadors he invited the neighbouring potentates to embrace Islam; and the murder of one of his envoys gave him an apology for invading the Greek Empire; but, before his death, the Mohammedan power had made little impression beyond the territories of the tribes of the desert. In the tenth year of the Hegira the prophet proceeded from Medina to Mecca, accompanied by all his wives and an immense train of devotees. On this occasion, known as his "Farewell Pilgrimage," he observed all those ceremonies which every good Mussulman is expected to perform once during his life. After kissing the black stone[2] fixed in a corner of the Kaaba, and reputed one of the stones of Paradise which fell down with Adam from heaven, he passed seven times round the sacred edifice, and drank of the water of the adjacent spring Zemzem—according to Arabian tradition, the very well discovered by Hagar when she wandered in the wilderness of Beersheba.[3] He also shaved his head, pared his nails, and slew with his own hand many camels which he had brought with him for sacrifice. During this visit to his native city he was impressed with the conviction that he was closely approaching the end of his apostleship; and he was not mistaken, for in the following year he was attacked by a bilious fever, which terminated fatally. When he expired, his friends could not believe that the vital spark was extinct. "Mohammed, the prophet of God, is not dead, as the infidels declare," exclaimed one of his most distinguished disciples, "he is gone to his Lord, like Moses, the son of Amram, who was absent from his people

---

[1] This arrangement was made about sixteen months after his arrival in Medina. Prior to this his adherents had been taught to pray towards Jerusalem. Muir, iii. 43.

[2] "This mysterious stone is semicircular, and measures about 6 inches in height and 8 in breadth; it is of a reddish-black colour, and bears marks in its undulating surface, notwithstanding the polish imparted by a myriad kisses, of volcanic origin.—Muir, ii. 35.

[3] Ockley, 3, 4, 59, 60; Gen. xxi. 19. In point of fact this well was sunk by 'Abd-al-Motalib, who died when Mohammed was eight years of age, Sprenger, *Life of Mahommad*, part i. 31.

forty days, and then returned to them again." All, however, were soon constrained to admit that he had really tasted death. His remains, wrapped in perfumes, were laid in a grave prepared in the apartment where he expired. He died on Monday,[1] the 8th of June A.D. 632, in the eleventh year of the Hegira.

The prophet of Arabia must have been no ordinary man. The firm hold he retained to the last over his proselytes, and the reverence with which he continued to be treated by the friends of his youth, attest the possession of attractive and remarkable endowments. Even when success had clothed him with extensive authority he cultivated the simpler habits of earlier life; and the chief who ruled with despotic sway over his countrymen might have been seen assisting his wives in the performance of their household duties, sweeping the floor, tying up his goats, mending his garment, or cobbling his sandals. But, whilst maintaining none of the more pretentious forms of regal state, he contrived to surround himself with associations which challenged far higher consideration; and he did not neglect to insist on the observance of certain outward tokens of respect indicating a recognition of his exalted character. All who addressed him were required to speak in a subdued tone; and no one was permitted to venture on anything like an approach to familiarity. The prophet of God was a sacred personage. The faithful attached peculiar value even to his spittle, and to the water used by him in his lustrations.[2] A deputy from Mecca, who visited the victorious apostle in Medina, was heard to exclaim—"I have seen the Chosroes of Persia, and the Cæsar of Rome, but never did I behold a king among his subjects like Mohammed among his companions."[3]

Khadija, his first wife, was a person of excellent understanding; after their marriage she still retained in her own hands the management of her property; and, while she lived, he was very much guided by her advice. But, soon after her death, the more odious features of his character were rapidly developed. The man who had heretofore appeared so mild began to display the spirit of a fiend incarnate. With sanctimonious words on his lips, the Apostle of God became a monster of cruelty and licen-

---

[1] The reader may remember that Monday has been considered a remarkable day in the history of Mahommed.
[2] Gibbon, ch. 50.   [3] *Ibid.*

tiousness; the ambition of empire took full possession of his soul; perfidy and malignity marked his career; and the progress of Islam was indicated by fields of carnage, by the cries of orphans, and the wailing of widows.

The success of Mohammed has frequently excited wonder; but, when all the details are maturely weighed, the rapid extension of his power is not so very extraordinary. In the world's history we have other instances of petty adventurers becoming mighty kings, and of delusions spreading like wild-fire. The husband of Khadija had great force of character, as well as various eminently popular qualities; and a fortunate concurrence of circumstances enabled him to establish and to maintain his position. Neither was the system he propounded destitute of plausibility. By professing to honour Adam, Abraham, Moses, and Jesus, he contrived to gain the attention of several classes of religionists; and the ignorance of the age was exceedingly favourable to his pretensions. It is not strange that, in a series of years, a few proselytes were secured by a man of noble birth and dignified appearance—respected for his devotional habits and the generous distribution of his charities—who possessed superior genius as well as much rhetorical ability—and who promulgated certain great principles which neither Jews nor Christians could venture to gainsay. And when success began to dawn upon him, it stimulated his fanaticism, and confirmed the faith of his followers. When he adopted the policy of propagating his religion by the sword, the progress of his cause was suddenly accelerated. The day of death, he affirmed, was so fixed that no precaution on the part of any individual could add one moment to existence; and this doctrine of fate, which was cordially believed by his followers, rendered them reckless of danger. The courage of a naturally brave people was raised to the highest pitch of fanaticism, and they rushed into battle determined to conquer or die.

Every one who died fighting for the faith, according to Mohammed, was sure of a place in paradise. And the joys which he promised to his warriors in the world to come were such as their gross minds could best appreciate; for his heaven is a scene, not of spiritual, but of sensual enjoyment.[1] The Prophet tells

[1] "These delights of paradise were certainly at first understood literally, however Mohammedan divines may have since allegorized them into a spiritual sense." Ockley, p. 69.

his disciples that they shall enter into pleasant gardens, where rivers of milk, rivers of wine, and rivers of clarified honey flow;[1] that they shall recline on couches adorned with gold and precious stones, under the shade of trees yielding all manner of delicious fruit; that fair damsels, "refraining their eyes from any but their own spouses," shall be given to them;[2] and that they shall drink most luscious wines, administered by handsome boys, in cups of gold and glasses adorned with diamonds.[3] In paradise the ear shall be regaled, not only with the sweetest songs of the angel Israfil—who has the most melodious voice of all the creatures of God—but even the trees themselves shall give forth enchanting harmony; whilst the bells, hanging on the trees, and put in motion by the wind proceeding from the throne of God, shall swell the chorus, as often as the blessed wish for music.[4] And the hell of Mohammed corresponds to his heaven; for its torments are all corporeal. He declares that such as refuse to believe in him shall drink nothing but boiling and fetid water; that they shall dwell amidst burning winds; that they shall be surrounded with a black, hot, and salt smoke, as with a coverlet; and that they shall eat nothing but briers and thorns, and the fruits of a tree inflicting intolerable anguish.[5]

Mohammed was, in the strictest sense, a Unitarian; for he rejected even the doctrine of the Trinity.[6] According to his teaching, images or pictures are not to be employed in worship; a fast is to be observed during the whole month Ramadan;[7] at this season no food is to be eaten from daybreak to sunset—but at night it is lawful to partake of refreshment; prayer, preceded by ablution, is to be offered up at appointed hours five times daily; and alms, amounting in some cases to a tenth of the personal property,[8] are to be distributed. The Moslems practise polygamy, abstain from wine, observe the rite of circumcision, divide the year into weeks of seven days each, and meet on

---

[1] Koran, Sura xlvii. [2] Koran, Sura lv.
[3] Koran, Suras lxxvi. lxxvii.
[4] Sale, *Preliminary Discourse*, § iv. [5] Koran, Suras lv. lvi.
[6] He apparently refers to this in Sura iv. The passage is thus translated by Rodwell: "Say not 'Three,' (there is a Trinity). Forbear—it will be better for you."
[7] This fast took place originally in winter, when the days were comparatively short; but the lunar year of the Moslems gradually shifted its position.
[8] Mills, *History of Mohammedanism*, p. 314, London, 1818.

Friday for religious exercises.[1] The Koran is made up of alleged revelations delivered from time to time by Mohammed, and committed to memory by his disciples. These announcements were written down on the leaves of the palm-tree or the skins of animals; and the manuscripts, under the care of one of his wives, are said to have been deposited in a receptacle called "The chest of the apostleship." The prophet asserted that he received the Koran from the angel Gabriel—that the original was laid up in the archives of heaven—and that his celestial visitant supplied him with chapter after chapter as occasion required. Part of it was published by him at Mecca, and part at Medina. Shortly after his death, the whole was put together in a volume; but the copies in circulation soon exhibited such startling discrepancies that one of his early successors deemed it necessary to collect and destroy them all, and supplied a new text sanctioned by his own authority. In the Koran there is nothing like classification of topics, or chronological arrangement; and, though the first revelations made by Mohammed were distinguished by their brevity, the longest chapters, or Suras, are placed towards the commencement of the volume, and the shortest towards the close. This dislocation of subjects, connected by the order of time or otherwise, has greatly perplexed the Mohammedan doctors, as it increases the difficulty of passages otherwise sufficiently obscure.[2]

On the death of Mohammed, Abu Bakr, his constant friend and the father of his favourite wife Ayesha, became *Khalif*, or *Successor*.[3] This first heir of his royal and pontifical authority had a triumphant career. Shortly after his accession, he sent an army into Syria; and, on the day of his death—Friday, the 23d of August, A.D. 634—the city of Damascus was taken by Kaled, his distinguished general. Within eighty years after the death of the prophet, the Khalifs were masters of a more extensive dominion than Rome had been able to acquire in eight centuries. Syria was subdued; Jerusalem was captured; Persia was attacked and reduced to obedience; and Constantinople itself was endan-

---

[1] The Moslems also transact business on this day, so that it does not exactly occupy the position of the Lord's day of Christianity.

[2] Mr. Rodwell, in his recently published translation of the Koran, with the Suras arranged in chronological order, has endeavoured to diminish this difficulty.

[3] Khalif, or Khalifah, signifies successor or *vicar*. The Khalif claims to be "Vicar of God:" the Pope, to be "Vicar of Christ." See Ockley's *Hist. of the Saracens*, Bohn's edition, note, p. 79.

gered. Egypt was invaded about six years after Mohammed's death; a siege of fourteen months secured the surrender of Alexandria,[1] and the whole province was soon in the hands of the Saracens. Pursuing their course along the northern shore of Africa, the victors, before the end of the century, were in possession of Carthage. Still continuing to advance westwards, their authority was established, in A.D. 709, over the whole country from Egypt to the Atlantic Ocean. The vicinity of Spain and the factious dissensions of its nobility invited them to attempt its subjugation. Accompanied by a force of 7000 men, Tarik, an intrepid soldier, crossed the strait, and formed his first camp on Mount Calpe, one of the Pillars of Hercules. The spot was hence called Gebel-Tarik, or *the mount of Tarik*;[2] and, after the lapse of upwards of eleven hundred years, the name, in the altered form of Gibraltar, still preserves the memory of the first Saracen invader. The Mohammedans then crossed the Pyrenees, and overran, with little opposition, the south-western provinces of France; but when they marched forward into the heart of the kingdom, they were encountered, between Tours and Poictiers, by the famous Charles Martel, and defeated in a decisive engagement. This battle—which lasted for seven successive days, and issued in the expulsion of the Saracens from the Gallic territories—was fought in A.D. 732, exactly a century after the death of Mohammed.

A few of the early Khalifs were chosen by election; and, in this manner, some of the most distinguished companions of the prophet were appointed his successors. But the elective system was soon abandoned; and the Khalifate became hereditary in the family of the Ommiades. It afterwards passed into the family of the Abassides,[3] where it remained till the end of the empire of the Saracens.[4] The victories of the early Khalifs were perhaps quite as extraordinary as those of Mohammed himself. Some have thought it strange that the uncivilized tribes of Arabia so quickly subdued such immense tracts of

---

[1] At this time the famous Alexandrian library is said to have been consumed by command of the Khalif Omar. As to the truth of this story, see Ockley, Bohn's edition, p. 264, note.

[2] Mill's *History of Mohammedanism*, p. 111. Calpe, according to Sir William Betham (*Gael and Cymbri*, p. 103), is from the Celtic word *calb*, signifying *bald head*.

[3] About A.D. 749.   [4] In A.D. 1258.

Asia, Africa, and Europe; but the state of the world at the time accounts for the triumphs of Islam. Long before the seventh century, the strength and glory of the Cæsars had departed. In the West, the Empire had been overwhelmed by hordes of barbarians; and, in the East, it exhibited symptoms of feebleness and decay. The brave and hardy veterans who had extended the terror of the Roman name to the ends of the earth were now no more; and luxury had introduced sloth, pusillanimity, and lax discipline. At the death of Mohammed, the Persian empire also was exhausted by wars foreign and domestic. There was thus no powerful antagonist to make head against the Khalifs; and hence it was that success so long continued to crown their military enterprises. The Arabians were full of energy, fierce, and courageous; they had always been a nation of soldiers; they were well fitted to endure the privations of a camp and the fatigues of a campaign; and now that their strength was concentrated under one leader, and roused to its utmost exertion by the excitements of a warlike creed, they were all but invincible.

The success of the Saracens was very much promoted by the divisions of the Christians. Multitudes, scattered by persecution throughout Asia and oppressed as heretics—rather than remain under the yoke of sovereigns whose injustice they daily experienced—were prepared to submit to the dominion of a foreign master who gave them liberty of conscience. In Egypt the mass of the native population suffered from a sentence of ecclesiastical proscription; and these followers of Eutyches rejoiced in the victories of the Moslems; for, from them, they expected indulgences which Catholic potentates denied. Though the Saracens avowedly propagated their religion by the sword, and at first offered to the idolatrous heathen nothing but the alternative of death or the reception of Mohammedanism, they granted toleration to " the people of the book," that is, to those Jews and Christians who could not be tempted to apostatize. If they consented to pay a certain tax for their nonconformity, they were permitted to remain unmolested. The Christians of the time of Mohammed, as has already been intimated, were a very degenerate race; and many of them fell an easy prey to the delusions of the Arabian impostor. Within a century after his appearance, the boundaries of the visible church were sadly curtailed; and along the whole Northern coast of Africa, where Cyprian, Optatus, and Augustine had once preached to overflowing audiences, the Christian name was almost completely extinguished.

Many of our most eminent commentators on prophecy maintain that the appearance of the Mohammedan power is foretold in the ninth chapter of the Apocalypse. According to the views of these expositors, the warlike followers of the Arabian apostle are there described as "locusts;" and, in the picture drawn by the inspired seer, the Saracens are apparently delineated with wonderful accuracy. "The shapes of the locusts," says John, "were like unto horses prepared unto battle; and on their heads were, as it were, crowns like gold, and their faces were as the faces of men. And they had hair as the hair of women."[1] The military strength of the Mohammedans consisted mainly in their cavalry, or their "horses prepared unto battle:" these warriors had on their heads turbans, or "*as it were* crowns like gold:"[2] they wore long beards, so that "their faces were as the faces of men;" and they had "hair as the hair of women," for it was flowing and plaited. Nor is it strange that the followers of the false prophet are thus presented to our notice in the prophetic history of the Church: for, in the triumphs of the Saracens, we may recognize the visitations of a retributive providence. Christians had already become paganized; idolatry in almost every form was patronized by them; images of saints and of the Virgin supplied the places of the images of the gods; the doctrine of the Trinity, instead of being contemplated with holy reverence, was dissected and distorted by a spirit of curious speculation; its advocates exposed themselves to the scorn of the heathen by their interminable factions and divisions; and they received a tremendous rebuke from the founder of Islam. How humiliating to think that a false apostle was commissioned to chastise them for their idol-worship; and that, on the very spot where the temple of the Lord once stood, and where the great Teacher in the days of His flesh exhibited His wisdom, a mosque was erected a few years after the death of Mohammed!

[1] Rev. ix. 7, 8.
[2] It is remarkable that Ezekiel (xxiii. 42) thus describes the turbans of the Arabs, when he speaks of "Sabeans from the wilderness which put *beautiful crowns* upon their heads."

The history of the prophet of Mecca demonstrates that the success of a cause is no decisive test of its excellence; for perhaps no form of religion ever spread with such rapidity as Mohammedanism. But the means employed for its propagation explain its extraordinary progress. It was indebted for its success partly to the amount of truth which it contained, partly to the degeneracy of the times, but still more to the terrible valour of its armed missionaries. The annals of the Saracens show how much, even in matters of faith, men may be influenced by mere fear; for, at the point of the sword, the soldiers of the so-called apostle of God imposed their creed on myriads of the human family. It is the glory of the Christian religion that it can make its way without the aid of any carnal weapons of warfare—that it never shines with so bright a lustre as in the time of severest trial—that when other systems, such as Mohammedanism, are ready to vanish away, it is still as vigorous as in the days of its youth—and that, after a struggle of eighteen centuries, it is warranted more confidently than ever to expect the fulfilment of the promise, "I shall give thee the heathen for thine inheritance, and the uttermost parts of the earth for thy possession."

SECTION II.

THE DOCTRINE OF THE CHURCH.

CHAPTER I.

THE SCRIPTURES.

THE Bible is, beyond comparison, the most wonderful book in existence. Some parts of it are in one language, and some in another; its writers occupied various positions in society—some were peasants, some kings, some courtiers, and some fishermen; it consists of histories, biographies, letters, poems, and prophecies, exhibiting great diversity in length, style, and subject-matter; upwards of fifteen hundred years passed away from its commencement to its completion, and meanwhile the greatest potentates of the earth, as well as the nations most remarkable for their philosophical attainments, were ignorant of the true God; and yet every part of it teaches a pure and sublime theology which commends itself by the light of its own evidence, and, as a whole, it is distinguished by unity of doctrine and unity of design. The sacred writers could not have proceeded according to any preconcerted plan, for they were separated from each other by hundreds of years; some of them possessed a very small share of education; and yet they display a knowledge of divine things incomparably superior to the wisdom of Plato or of Aristotle; and they concur in promulgating a scheme of salvation remarkable for its grace and consistency, simplicity and grandeur. The book of revelation presents much the same features as the book of creation and providence; some parts of it are more interesting or more intelligible than others, and some are more mysterious; but it addresses itself to the wants of all men—it is emphatically "reading for the people," and its serious perusal is eminently calculated to invigorate the understanding and to improve the heart. Thus the Scriptures attest that they have all emanated from the High and the Holy One, even from "the Father of Lights, with whom is no variableness neither shadow of turning."

The Scriptures.

The Word of God is made up of two grand divisions—the Old Testament and the New. The books found in the Bible are said to be *canonical*, because they are constituent elements of the canon, or *rule* of faith, recognized as of divine authority. At the time of our Lord's appearance the Jewish Church reckoned only two and twenty books in the canon of the Old Testament.[1] These two and twenty books are the same that are still found in the Hebrew Bible and in our authorized English version; but some of the smaller works, now counted separately, were formerly grouped together. The Twelve Minor Prophets constituted only one book, as did also Ezra and Nehemiah, First and Second Samuel, First and Second Kings, and First and Second Chronicles, respectively. Ruth formed part of Judges, and the Lamentations were appended to Jeremiah. It thus appears that the ancient Church of Israel did not acknowledge any of the books now known among Protestants as apocryphal;[2] and whilst, in the New Testament so many charges are preferred against the Jews by our Lord and His apostles, they are never accused of any neglect or dishonesty in regard to the care of the sacred records. Though, as we are told, they had the high privilege of keeping the oracles of God,[3] it is never hinted that they in any way abused their trust; and though they were commanded to "search the Scriptures,"[4] they were never upbraided for ignoring any portion of the divine testimony. We are thus warranted to infer that the writings admitted into the canon of the Old Testament by the Jews in the days of our Saviour are the only writings entitled to occupy such a position.

The books usually termed apocryphal, and appended to some copies of the Old Testament, are of obscure origin. One of these works, the Book of Wisdom, has by some been ascribed to Philo Judæus;[5] towards the close of the Second Book of Maccabees the unknown writer claims the indulgence of his readers;[6] and

---

[1] Josephus, *Against Apion*, i. 8.
[2] It is noteworthy that the Church of Rome acknowledges as canonical only a portion of those apocryphal writings approved in the 6th article of the Church of England to be "read for example of life and instruction of manners." Romanists reject as apocryphal the third and fourth books of Esdras (sometimes called the first and second) and the prayer of Manasses.
[3] Rom. iii. 2.   [4] John v. 39.
[5] As by Basil in *Epist.* 406, to Amphilochius. See also Jerome, *Præf. in Lib. Salom.*
[6] 2 Macc. xv. 38, 39.

Ecclesiasticus, the most respectable of the apocryphal productions, contains various unmistakable evidences of its want of inspiration.[1] Though not in the Hebrew Bible, these writings at length found their way into the Greek translation of the Seventy; and thus, though condemned as uncanonical by the most eminent of the early fathers, they gradually obtained consideration. Melito of Sardis, a Christian writer who flourished towards the close of the second century, and who travelled extensively to obtain exact information respecting the Old Testament canon, has left behind him a catalogue of the sacred books[2] from which the Apocrypha is excluded. This witness is corroborated by Origen, the most learned Christian of the first three centuries. "We should not be ignorant," says he, "that the canonical books are the same which the Hebrews delivered to us, and are twenty-two in number, according to the number of the letters of the Hebrew alphabet.[3] Athanasius,[4] Hilary of Poictiers,[5] Cyril of Jerusalem,[6] Gregory Nazianzen,[7] and Chrysostom[8] bear substantially the same testimony. Jerome, the most learned of the fathers—who published a new Latin version of the Scriptures under the auspices of Pope Damasus—also denies the divine authority of these writings. He tells us that the book of Daniel "among the Hebrews has neither the history of Susanna, nor the Song of the Three Children, nor the fables of Bel and the Dragon;"[9] that "the Book of Baruch, the scribe of Jeremiah, is not read in Hebrew, nor esteemed canonical;"[10] and that "as the Church reads the Books of Judith, Tobit, and the Maccabees, but does not receive them among the canonical Scriptures, so also she may read Wisdom and Ecclesiasticus for the edification of the common people, but not as authority to confirm any of her doctrines."[11] What is more, the Council of

---

[1] See, for example, the Prologue.
[2] Euseb. *Ecc. Hist.* iv. 26.
[3] Quoted by Eusebius, *Ecc. Hist.* vi. 25.
[4] In his *Paschal Epistle*. See Lardner, iv. 154.
[5] *Prolog. in Lib. Psalm.* § 15.
[6] *Cat. Lect.* iv. § 33.
[7] *Carm.* 33.
[8] *Synopsis Scripturæ.* The genuineness of this document has been disputed, but Lardner has proved that its testimony is sustained by the undoubted works of Chrysostom. *Credibility of the Gospel History*, ch. cxviii.
[9] "Apud Hebræos nec Susannæ habet historiam, nec hymnum trium puerorum, nec Belis Draconisque fabulas."—*Præf. in Dan.*
[10] *Prol. in Jerem.*
[11] *Præf. in Lib. Salom.*

Laodicea, held about A.D. 360, rejects all these books,[1] and its canons are adopted by the fathers of Chalcedon, assembled in A.D. 451 in the fourth Œcumenical Council.[2]

Several parts of the Apocrypha tend to nourish superstition, whilst others, of a fabulous character, are well adapted to the taste of a credulous age; and probably for such reasons, when the Church began to decline in spirituality, these writings became increasingly popular. They are quoted even by some of the apostolic fathers,[3] and, though not acknowledged as canonical, they were, as Jerome and others inform us, read occasionally in the public congregations for the instruction or entertainment of the multitude. But Augustine is the first Christian writer of distinguished reputation who classes them among the books of the Old Testament.[4] Though a profound thinker, this father was an indifferent critic; he knew nothing of Hebrew and little of Greek; and, as he found the apocryphal writings mixed up with the Latin version of the Bible used in Africa, he was thus induced to permit them to pass unchallenged. His testimony respecting them is, however, far from consistent or conclusive. Though he sometimes speaks of them as a portion of the Old Testament, he elsewhere objects to their authority, and tells us that, when used in the Church, they were not read from the same desk as the canonical Scriptures.[5] In his day their authority was acknowledged by several African councils; and the Trullan Synod, held at Constantinople in A.D. 692, adopted the African canons.[6] But meanwhile they were only very partially recognized. Even Pope Gregory the Great, when quoting from Maccabees, apologizes for referring to "a book which is not canonical;"[7] and John of Damascus, the ablest Greek writer of the eighth century, adheres to the Hebrew canon of two and twenty books.[8] He makes no mention of Maccabees, Judith, or Tobit; and speaks of wisdom and Ecclesiasticus as elegant and virtuous writings, yet not to be numbered among the canonical books of Scripture, having never been laid up in the ark of the covenant.[9]

---

[1] Canon 60. [2] Canon 1.
[3] Clemens Romanus, *Epistle to the Corinthians*, § 55 ; *Epistle of Barnabas*, § 19.
[4] *De Doctrinâ Christianâ*, ii. 8.
[5] *De Prædest. Sanct.* xiv. See Cosin's *Scholastical History of the Canon*, 160.
[6] In Canon 2d this Synod recognizes the Canons of Carthage ; but it also acknowledges those of Laodicea, so that its testimony is inconclusive.
[7] *Moralia*, book xix.   [8] *De Fide Orthodoxâ*, iv. 17.   [9] *Ibid.*

The Scriptures.

Though many apocryphal writings appeared in the early Christian Church, there never was any great diversity of sentiment as to the canon of the New Testament. Some doubts existed for a time respecting the Epistle to the Hebrews, the Epistle of James, the Second and Third Epistles of John, and the Epistle of Jude. The contents of the Epistle to the Hebrews were, in the first instance, offensive to Judaizing brethren, and afterwards to those disposed to assert the priestly character of Christian ministers. The very brevity of the other epistles perhaps prevented them from at once attracting the attention which they could rightfully claim; and when they obtained more general circulation, it was not strange that they were regarded with suspicion by churches to which they had been previously unknown. But all these documents gradually established a title to universal confidence. When the Apocalypse was written it was immediately placed among the sacred books; when, however, the Montanists, towards the end of the second century, began to appeal in support of their doctrine of a millennium to certain obscure passages it contains, some who opposed the errors of these fanatics were tempted rashly to question its genuineness. With these exceptions, the canon of the New Testament, as at present owned both by Romanists and Protestants, was at once universally accepted. No doubts were ever entertained by what was called the Catholic Church respecting the four Gospels, the Acts of the Apostles, thirteen of the Epistles of Paul, the First Epistle of Peter, and the First Epistle of John. And the canonicity of the various parts of our present New Testament, including the Apocalypse and all the Catholic epistles, is attested by the most able and erudite of the fathers. Origen has given us a catalogue of the books belonging to it, in which he mentions the four Gospels, the Acts of the Apostles, fourteen Epistles of Paul, two of Peter, three of John, and the book of Revelation.[1] He here passes over the Epistles of James and Jude, but the omission is perhaps to be attributed to a lapse of memory, as he elsewhere acknowledges the claims of these letters.[2] Eusebius also, in a catalogue to be found in his *Ecclesiastical History*,[3]

---

[1] Euseb. vi. 25.
[2] Hom. 7th, *On Joshua;* *Com. on John.* See the remarks of Lardner, *Works*, ii. 497.
[3] iii. 25.

enumerates every book at present in our canon; and though he admits that doubts existed as to the authority of the Apocalypse and a few of the epistles, he intimates that the objections were not sufficiently weighty to overbalance their claims. Athanasius, too, has left us a list of the books of the New Testament[1] which exactly corresponds to that of our authorized English version. Jerome[2] and Augustine[3] adopt precisely the same catalogue. The list sanctioned by the Council of Laodicea[4] leaves out the Apocalypse, but is otherwise the same as our canon. The Council of Carthage, which met upwards of thirty years afterwards, has endorsed a catalogue the same as our own, including the book of Revelation.[5]

It thus appears that the canon of the New Testament was quietly settled all over the Church. The books reputed of authority were read in a fixed order in the religious assemblies of the faithful, and the omission of an epistle or other record from these Scripture lessons was tantamount to its rejection as not being part of holy writ. The question of canonicity was at first kept constantly before the whole ecclesiastical community; the character of every book and letter claiming inspiration was submitted to the scrutiny of the pastor of every congregation; and yet the utmost unanimity always prevailed with regard to the divine original of more than six-sevenths of our present New Testament. Even the refusal of some Christian societies to admit certain memorials as a portion of the rule of faith affords proof, as well of the scrupulosity which was exercised, as of the liberty allowed to those who, through deficiency of information or otherwise, could not go so far as their brethren. The doubts entertained as to the claims of a few documents were gradually removed, and at length all sections of the Church concurred in the recognition of the same New Testament canon.

The wonderful care employed in the preservation of the Scriptures may well excite our admiration and gratitude. Though we have but few old manuscript copies of the works of many of the classic authors of antiquity,[6] we do not doubt their

---

[1] Fragment of Paschal Epistle, *Athanasii Opera*, tom. ii. 1178, Migne's edition.
[2] *Epist. ad Paulinum*, 50. [3] *De Doctrinâ Christianâ*, ii. 8.
[4] Canon 60. [5] Third Council of Carthage, Canon 47.
[6] " About fifteen manuscripts of the history of Herodotus are known to critics, and of these several are not of higher antiquity than the middle of the fifteenth century..... This amount of copies may be taken as an average number of ancient

genuineness; neither have we any reason to believe that they have been extensively interpolated. The *Orations* of Demosthenes and the *Æneid* of Virgil speak for themselves; they supply internal proof that they deserve the fame they have acquired; and were it asserted that the originals have been lost, and that the works now attributed to the Athenian orator and the Mantuan bard are nothing more than fabrications, who would be so silly as to give credence to the tale, or to imagine that any mere impostor could have forged such masterpieces of genius? But the care expended on the conservation of the Scriptures has been so continuous and so watchful, that we have immeasurably better security for their freedom from mutilation than for the integrity of any other writings whatever. Since the beginning of our era the Old Testament has still been in the keeping of the Jews as well as of the disciples of the Saviour; and could there be such a disaster as the destruction of all the copies of it in the possession of the Christians, the want could be forthwith supplied by those in the hands of the posterity of Abraham. Meanwhile an attempt by either party to corrupt the text could be immediately detected. Of the New Testament we have copies extant that can claim an antiquity of fourteen or fifteen hundred years;[1] so that if all the intermediate ages had conspired for its adulteration, these ancient witnesses would be forthcoming to expose the fraud. But no variations of importance—none that may not be ascribed to the inadvertence or the ignorance of copyists—can be traced between manuscripts of the fourth or fifth century and those written a thousand years afterwards. And, in the early ages, how could the text of the sacred writings have been successfully falsified? It existed in innumerable transcripts: at least one copy of it—to be read in the assembly—should have been found in every congregation;[2] it was translated into various languages, and some of these versions—made very soon after the days of the apostles—have descended to our times; it is quoted so largely

manuscripts of the classic authors; some few have many more, but many have fewer."—Isaac Taylor's *Hist. of the Transmission of Ancient Books*, ch. vii. We have only one ancient MS. copy of the *Epistle of Clemens Romanus*, the earliest of the apostolic fathers; and of not a few patristic productions we have only two or three codices.

[1] As the *Codex Vaticanus*, the *Codex Alexandrinus*, and the *Codex Sinaiticus*.

[2] It is probable, however, that many congregations were obliged to be content with a portion of the sacred canon.

by the early fathers that, if lost, the major portion of it could be made up from their citations; it was in possession of heretics of all classes, so that any deviation from it could have been at once discovered and proclaimed; and its precious words were so graven on the memories of multitudes that, when it was rehearsed at social or public worship, even a change of phraseology would at once have attracted observation. The very discrepancies in the hundreds of manuscripts transmitted to us assist us in determining the true readings; and, in regard to every verse of the New Testament, we can speak of the original text with an amount of confidence which we are scarcely warranted to assume when dealing with any uninspired document of antiquity.

The Scriptures, handed down to us under such circumstances, possess internal tokens of divinity which should commend them to our acceptance. If the eloquence of Demosthenes is recognized in his *Orations*, something higher than the wisdom of this world may be traced in holy writ. There is a spirituality and a power in the word of God by which it is essentially distinguished. The simplicity and gravity of its style, the harmony of its parts, the excellence of its moral instructions, the beauty and elevation of its views of the works and ways of God, the exceeding grace of its communications relative to man, and the holy and happy influence it invariably exerts over the hearts and lives of believers, all avouch it to be a revelation from heaven. Those who reject a volume which presents such credentials may well be accused of wilful blindness. "If our Gospel be hid," says the apostle, "it is hid to them that are lost; in whom the God of this world hath blinded the minds of them which believe not, lest the light of the glorious Gospel of Christ, who is the image of God, should shine unto them."[1]

There is no authority for the statement that writings which once formed part of the canon of revelation have been lost. The Hebrew Bible in our possession contains exactly the same documents found in it in the days of our Lord; and the most ancient lists of the contents of the New Testament do not include any gospels, epistles, or other tracts, which are not yet forthcoming. In the Old Testament,[2] as well as in the New,[3] there are references to productions either not now in existence

---

[1] 2 Cor. iv. 3, 4. [2] Numb. xxi. 14; 1 Kings iv. 32.
[3] 1 Cor. v. 9; Jude 14.

or not deemed worthy of a place in the canon; but a prophet or evangelist may quote a book, when it gives correct testimony, without thereby endorsing its inspiration. It is, too, quite possible that the apostles penned some letters which have perished;[1] their ordinary communications were very much like those of other men; they did not always speak—and they may not always have written—as they were moved by the Holy Ghost;[2] and if anything that they produced has passed into oblivion, we may presume that it never was intended to form part of the permanent rule of faith. Many things uttered by our Lord Himself have not been recorded; and it was not necessary that every word spoken by the evangelists, or that every familiar note which they dictated, should be transmitted to the latest generations. All that was considered needful for the ends of redemption has been conserved—so that the Scriptures, as we have them, are able to make "the man of God perfect, thoroughly furnished unto all good works."[3]

The apostles, no doubt, knew when they wrote under the guidance of inspiration; and were quite competent to declare whether any letter, or gospel, really possessed divine authority. The whole New Testament appeared before the termination of the apostolic age; the latest documents belonging to it are from the pen of the beloved disciple; and John, in the close of the Apocalypse, sternly warns against spurious additions. "If any man," says he, "shall add unto these things, God shall add unto him the plagues that are written in this book."[4] We find Paul quoting from the Gospel of Luke,[5] and Peter classing the epistles of Paul with "the other scriptures."[6] According to an early tradition[7] the three narratives of the life of our Lord by Matthew, Mark, and Luke were in general circulation before the destruction of Jerusalem; and John wrote his supplementary gospel that the Church in future generations might be made duly acquainted with matters of importance not recorded by the other evangelists. We have, indeed, reason to believe that all the parts of our present New Testament were known to John, and that they all

---

[1] What our Lord Himself wrote on the ground has not been preserved, John viii. 6.
[2] See Gal. ii. 14.   [3] 2 Tim. iii. 17.   [4] Rev. xxii. 18.
[5] 1 Tim. v. 18; Luke x. 7.   [6] 2 Peter iii. 16.
[7] Euseb. iii. 24. See also Routh, *Reliq. Sac.* i. 394.

had the sanction of his approval. And as many who had the gift of "discerning of spirits" lived toward the close of the first century, it is not improbable that the faith of the Church in the inspiration of the Scriptures of the new canon was confirmed by their attestations.

In some respects the relation of the Church to the Scriptures is very much akin to that of the scholars of succeeding generations to the works of the great poets, philosophers, and historians of antiquity. Literary men have always taken a deep interest in the writings of their gifted predecessors; they have studied their remains with care; endeavoured, by transcripts or otherwise, to preserve them from oblivion; commended them to public admiration; and illustrated their peculiar excellences. But nothing has been meanwhile added to the essential value of the original publications. Their descriptions, so true to nature—their reasonings, so subtle and so sagacious—their narratives, so lucid and so instructive—remain unchanged. And though the Church from age to age has preserved the Scriptures, and borne witness to their worth, and been quickened by their saving influence, it has added nothing to their divine authority. Its testimony to their excellence may commend them to its own children as well as to those beyond its pale, and may secure for them a degree of attention which they could not otherwise obtain; but it can impart nothing to their intrinsic weight as inspired records. And the vacillation of fathers and councils in reference to the extent of holy writ demonstrates that they have only been fallible conservators of infallible oracles. The Apostle John lived to the close of the first century; and there is every reason to believe that he gave his sanction to all the parts of our present New Testament; but within one hundred years after his demise his own Apocalypse was challenged as a forgery; and by many it was long excluded from the canon. Before the death of John the Church of Rome admitted the claims of the Epistle to the Hebrews;[1] and yet the same Church in the fourth century rejected the same epistle.[2] The Council of Laodicea condemned the apocryphal books of Tobit, Judith, Ecclesiasticus, and the Maccabees; but soon afterwards the Council of Carthage—con-

[1] It is repeatedly quoted as Scripture by Clement in his epistle written in the name of the Church of Rome, § 36.
[2] Euseb. vi. 20, iii. 3. Jerome, *Epist. ad Dardanum.*

taining perhaps not one member competent to read the Hebrew letters, and very few acquainted with Greek—pronounced the same writings inspired. The Council of Laodicea refused to acknowledge the Apocalypse, and the General Council of Chalcedon subsequently endorsed the decision; and yet the most eminent fathers recognized its canonicity; and it is now admitted into the sacred volume by both Romanists and Protestants. The claim of any book to a place in the Bible is to be determined by the application of the principles of sound and enlightened criticism; but it is apparent from the history of the Scriptures that, whilst they have remained unchanged, those who have been entrusted with their keeping, and who should have been able to determine their extent, have committed very grave blunders.

Whilst there was some difference of opinion among the ancient Christians as to the canonical authority of a few books or tracts, there was none whatever as to the amount of deference due to those which they acknowledged. The Scriptures themselves uniformly claim plenary inspiration; it can be shown that one or two passages,[1] which have been supposed to suggest another conclusion, have been misunderstood; and unquestionably the early ecclesiastical writers utter no uncertain sound when adverting to the subject. They describe the sacred books, not merely as *containing* the Word of God, but as the Word of God itself. The variety of style presented in Holy Writ is no more antagonistic to the principle of unity of inspiration, than is the variety of plants and animals around us incompatible with the doctrine of a common Creator; and the fathers firmly believed that one unerring Spirit moved and guided all the sacred writers. "The holy and divinely inspired Scriptures," says Athanasius, "are sufficient to express the truth."[2] Chrysostom speaks of the Apostle Paul as "the temple of God, the mouth of Christ, the lyre of the Spirit."[3] "What avails it," says Theodoret, "to know whether all the Psalms were written by David, it being plain

---

[1] See Lee's *Inspiration of Holy Scripture*, 297-299, third ed. Dublin, 1864. In reference to 1 Cor. vii. 10, 12, 40, Dr. Lee remarks,—"St. Paul does not distinguish between his own commands and those received by an immediate revelation from Christ; but between his own commands and those which Christ had given when on earth, and which were now *historical*."

[2] *Oratio contra Gentes*, § 1, *Opera*, i. 3, Migne's ed.

[3] *De Lazaro. Concio.* vi.

that all were composed under the influence of the Divine Spirit?"[1] "It is needless to inquire who wrote the book of Job," says Gregory the Great in the same strain, "since we may honestly believe that the Holy Ghost was its author."[2]

The ancient Church also asserted most distinctly the supreme authority of Scripture. The heretics, feeling that they could not sustain their cause by the evidence of holy writ, commenced, as early as the second century, to appeal to tradition; and alleged that the apostles had privately communicated a higher wisdom to certain select disciples. The Catholics, such as Irenæus and Tertullian, met this argument by the counter testimony of the same witness, and maintained that the tradition of all the apostolic Churches was opposed to the teachings of the errorists; but they did not thereby intend to abandon the principle that the Word of God is the only decisive arbiter. They merely meant to show that they could confront the subverters of the faith on their own territory, and beat them with their own weapons.[3]

Nothing can be more evident than that, according to the views of the early Christians, the reports of tradition, and the opinions of churchmen, however eminent, should not, for a moment, be brought into competition with the utterances of the Word of God. The faithful were, in various ways, kept constantly in recollection of its paramount claims. It was read as often as they met for worship; it was studied by them in their private dwellings;[4] it was committed to memory; and it was largely incorporated with the language of their prayers. When a bishop was ordained, a copy of the holy book was presented to him;[5] when a synod was held, the volume was placed on an elevated seat in the midst of the convocation,[6] that all might be kept in remembrance of the rule to which their proceedings should be conformed. When the first Œcumenical Council assembled at

---

[1] *Proth. in Psalmos.*   [2] *Præf. in Moralia in Lib. Job.*

[3] By *Apostolical* or *Evangelical Tradition* the fathers often mean the Gospel *handed down in the New Testament*. Hence their testimony has often been quoted in favour of tradition when it really refers to Scripture. See Goode's *Divine Rule of Faith and Practice*, i. 13, 68, 72, 73, iii. 5, London, 1853.

[4] In one of his famous discourses Chrysostom presses on the laity the command to search the Scriptures, and exposes the excuses by which they sought to apologize for their neglect of the duty. *Concio in Lazar.* iii. See also *Opera*, iii. 86, ed. Paris, 1835. Many other fathers inculcate the same duty.

[5] Palmer's *Origines Liturgicæ*, ii. 302.

[6] Stanley's *Eastern Church*, 139, 140.

Nice, the Emperor himself, in an address to the members, emphatically called their attention to the divine standard. "We are," said he, "discussing sacred things, and have the teaching of the most Holy Spirit fully committed to writing. For the evangelical and apostolical books, and the oracles of the ancient prophets, clearly and fully teach us what should be our views respecting the Godhead. Let us therefore banish hostile contention, and take the solution of the points in question from the words of divine inspiration."[1] The most distinguished fathers of the fourth and fifth centuries echo the same sentiments. "The doctrine of the Church," says Jerome, "may be found in the fulness of the divine books.[2] . . . There is no argument so forcible as a passage from the Holy Scriptures."[3] "As an earthly father," says Optatus, "when he perceives himself to be near death—fearing lest, after death, the brothers should quarrel with one another and go to law—calls witnesses, and transfers his wishes from his dying breast to the tablets that will endure; and, if a contention arises between the brothers, the grave is not applied to, but the will is sought; and he who rests in the grave speaks in silence from the tablets, so it is with us. He whose will we have is alive in heaven, therefore let His directions be sought in the Gospel as His will."[4] The testimony of Augustine is even still more precise and ample. "We must not," said he, "allow even Catholic bishops, if at any time perchance they are in error, to hold any opinion contrary to the canonical Scriptures of God."[5] . . . "Who is ignorant that the holy canonical Scripture is limited to certain bounds, and is so *far above all the later writings of bishops* that, of it, it cannot be doubted or disputed, whether, it is true or right, whatsoever shall appear to be written in it; but that, as to the writings of bishops, which either have been written or are being written since the confirmation of the canon, they may be found fault with, both by the wiser discourse of any one more skilful in the matter, and by the weightier authority and more learned wisdom of other bishops and by councils; and that local and provincial councils yield without any doubt to the authority of those plenary councils that are assembled together from the whole Christian world; and that, as to these very œcumenical councils, the former are

[1] Theodoret, *Ecc. Hist.* i. 7. [2] *Epist. ad Paulun.* [3] *In Zach.* c. 10.
[4] *De Schism. Donat.* v. 3. [5] *Epist. ad Cathol. vulg. De Unit. Eccles.*

often corrected by the latter."[1] The great African father here distinctly teaches that the decision of the Word of God is incomparably superior even to the deliverance of an œcumenical council.

But it must be acknowledged that all the fathers do not speak consistently when referring to the sacred oracles; and, as we descend from apostolic times, we may trace a gradual declension in the clearness and fidelity of their evidence. The writers of the second century express themselves very strongly when treating of the internal marks of divinity to be found in the Scriptures. "I was brought to believe them," says one of these ancient witnesses, "on account of the simplicity of the style, and the freedom from artifice in the authors, and the plain account given of the creation of the universe, and their foreknowledge of things to come, and the superiority of their precepts, and the majesty of all that is written in them."[2] But in the fifth century even Augustine is tempted to declare—"I would not believe the Gospel, if the authority of the Catholic Church did not move me to do so."[3] This assertion, made in the excitement of controversy, certainly does not quadrate with other statements of the same writer already quoted; but its utterance by this celebrated African divine, under any circumstances, is a sign of the times, and betokens the growth of a spirit of servile submission to ecclesiastical authority. Already tradition had risen into a position of importance; and, in matters not directly relating to the cardinal doctrines of the Church, it was deemed a safe and sufficient guide. It was adduced as affording a warrant for rites and ceremonies ignored in the written word—such as the use of the symbol of the cross, the turning to the East in prayer, and the anointing with oil in baptism.[4] It was also found to be a most convenient voucher for the observances of monkery. "The holy Apostles," says Epiphanius, "delivered some things by writing and some by tradition. . . . The holy Apostles of God delivered the precept to the holy Church of God that it was sinful for any one, after having vowed virginity, to betake himself to marriage."[5] The claims of synods were silently added

[1] *De Bapt. cont. Donat.* ii. 3. [2] Tatian, *Cont. Græc.* § 29.
[3] *Contra Epist. Man. quam voc. Fundam.* c. 5.
[4] See Basil's *Treatise on the Holy Spirit addressed to Amphilochius*, 27.
[5] *Hær. Apos.* 61, § 6.

to those of tradition; and at length, in the beginning of the seventh century, we find Gregory the Great speaking of the four Gospels and the first four œcumenical councils as of co-ordinate authority.[1]

The amount of attention bestowed on the Scriptures is an index of the spiritual condition of any community. How can we expect God to be truly honoured where His will is unknown or disregarded? If the Bible is the Word of the Most High, it has a title to consideration possessed by no other volume. It is a revelation of truth and holiness pertaining to the most precious interests of man, and able to make him wise unto salvation through faith which is in Christ Jesus. Our Lord Himself, in the synagogue of Nazareth,[2] acted as a reader of the Scriptures; and He has thus taught His ministers that they should deem themselves honoured when performing the same holy office. It was a sad token of defection when, towards the close of the second century,[3] the pastors of the Church delegated to subordinates the performance of a duty so necessary for the instruction of the congregation. In the fourth century children of seven or eight years of age were employed as lectors;[4] and the people could expect comparatively little benefit when they were obliged to depend, for a knowledge of the Scriptures, on persons incompetent to read intelligently and impressively. The reading of the divine records in the Church is one form in which the truth should always be proclaimed: it is part of the duty of the minister of the Word; it is a service which should not be handed over to inferior functionaries; and, when efficiently discharged, it is eminently fitted to interest and to improve the worshippers.

In the times of the early Christians the Scriptures were read to the people in the vulgar tongue that they might be understood by all. The various versions then prepared tended much to a diffusion of a knowledge of divine things; and several of these translations which remain, and which show how disputed passages were interpreted at the period of their execution, afford valuable assistance to the biblical expositor. And the amount

---

[1] "Quatuor Synodos sanctæ universalis ecclesiæ, sicut quatuor libros sancti Evangelii recipimus." *Epist.* lib. iii.; *Epist.* x.; *Opera*, tom. iii. 613, ed. Migne.
[2] Luke iv. 16, 17. [3] See *Ancient Church*, 590.
[4] Bingham, book iii. chap. v. § 5.

of Scripture embodied in the ancient liturgical formularies contributed greatly to keep alive a spirit of true godliness. Even when, because of the decay of the language, the ritual ceased to convey information to the multitude, it was understood by the clergy; and thus its Bible lessons continued to send forth some rays of spiritual light into the dark places of ignorance and superstition. And the benefits conferred in this way on the Church universal by the Book of Psalms cannot well be overestimated. From this hallowed repository the children of God for nearly three thousand years have been furnished with the noblest poetry, and the sweetest songs of praise. The Psalms have entered largely into the composition of all Christian liturgies. They speak to the inner man in strains of inimitable beauty, tenderness, and power. They are still as grateful to the devout spirit, whether penitent or thankful, bereaved or comforted, in days of darkness or in seasons of rejoicing, as when they were poured forth in all their freshness from the lips of the holy penman. They are more ancient than the age of Homer, and yet the saint can still say of them, "How sweet are thy words unto my taste, yea sweeter than honey to my mouth."[1] They illustrate the substantial unity of feeling and of faith which has characterised the true Church in all generations; and as the rich utterances of a heart renewed and animated by the spirit of the living God, they shall never cease to be relished by the heirs of salvation.

CHAPTER II.

THE ARIAN CONTROVERSY.

DURING the first three centuries the relations of the Father, Son, and Holy Spirit had been the subject of various discussions; but diversity of sentiment had not hitherto produced any considerable schism, or even awakened any deep and general excitement. In the early part of the fourth century these disputes assumed a more formidable aspect. All at once they broke out in Alexandria with extraordinary violence; the theological strife extended rapidly to the East and to the West; and the whole of

[1] Ps. cxix. 103.

Christendom was soon involved in an earnest and bitter controversy. The Church had never before been the scene of such intense intellectual agitation.

About A.D. 318, as Alexander, the bishop of the Egyptian metropolis, was discoursing, in presence of some ecclesiastics, on the question of the Trinity, one of his auditors objected to the positions advanced by him, on the ground that they savoured of Sabellianism,[1] or that they confounded the persons of the Godhead. The individual who signalized himself on this occasion, by challenging the teaching of the chief pastor, was a presbyter named Arius—a man somewhat advanced in life, and rather noted for his pugnacious and restless temperament. Nor was this the first instance in which he had come into collision with his ecclesiastical superior. Melitius, an Egyptian bishop, dissatisfied, as is alleged, with what he considered the lax discipline of the Church, had separated from his brethren;[2] and by his irregular proceedings had given some annoyance to the Alexandrian prelate. Arius had joined this schismatic; but after some time had repented of his folly and had been restored to catholic communion. Undeterred by past experience, he now again prepared to pursue a divisive course; and from this period till the end of his life, kept himself in a state of perpetual turmoil.

The aged bishop of Alexandria taught that the first and second persons of the Godhead existed in the relation of Father and Son from all eternity. Arius denied this proposition; and maintained that, though the Son was generated before all worlds, He had a beginning of existence. Alexander held what is known as the doctrine of *Eternal Generation*.[3] As the "Son of man" is one who has all the attributes of man; so, according to this view, the only-begotten Son of God is one who has all the attributes of Deity. He is, therefore, Omnipotent, Omniscient, Eternal, and Self-existent. Arius was prepared to admit that the Son should be called God, and that, in various respects, He

---

[1] Socrates, i. 5.
[2] His views are said to have been akin to those of the Novatians. According to Socrates (i. 6), he lapsed in time of persecution, and for this, along with other reasons, was excommunicated.
[3] The English reader may find this question of theology well expounded in Treffry's *Inquiry into the Doctrine of the Eternal Sonship*, London, 1839.

is the Father's representative;[1] but he denied His self-existence; he affirmed that He is not of the same substance or essence as the Father, and that He was created out of nothing.

The position of the heresiarch, as a presbyter of the Church of Alexandria, gave him considerable influence. He had the charge of one of the nine Christian congregations already established in the Egyptian capital;[2] he was a popular city minister, and the versatility of his talents supplied him with special facilities for the dissemination of his sentiments. He composed heterodox songs adapted to the taste of the lower classes; he was enthusiastically supported by seven hundred female devotees; a section of the clergy espoused his cause; and the venerable bishop Alexander was exceedingly perplexed by his energy, subtlety, and perseverance. Arius was a man of blameless morals; his spare habit betokened that he was addicted to asceticism; he was tall, though not erect; and his pale and thoughtful countenance, which was not without lineaments of beauty, produced altogether a pleasing impression. His manner was ordinarily calm, but he broke out occasionally into wild passion; and he was distinguished more by acuteness than by breadth or vigour of intellect. When engaged in disputation he had an odd habit of twisting his body; and as he was deemed rather a slippery antagonist, his enemies tauntingly declared that he wriggled like a snake.[3]

In A.D. 321, Arius was deposed from his office, and excommunicated by a synod held at Alexandria.[4] He now addressed himself to Eusebius of Nicomedia, his former fellow-student[5]— a prelate of great ability and influence, and an ardent abettor of his own principles. With the aid of this distinguished man, he secured the support of a large number of Eastern bishops. The affair thus assumed quite a new form; it was no longer a dispute between the Egyptian primate and one of his presbyters; a considerable portion of the Church was involved in the discus-

---

[1] He says in a letter still extant that the Son "in will and purpose existed before all times and before all worlds, *perfect God*, the only Begotten, *unchangeable*; and that before He was begotten, or created, or purposed, or established, *He was not.*" See Dorner, div. i. vol. ii. p. 237; and Theodoret, i. 5.
[2] See Fleury's *Ecclesiastical History*, book x. 28.
[3] Stanley's *Eastern Church*, p. 115, London, 1861.   [4] Socrates, i. 6.
[5] Dorner's *Doctrine of the Person of Christ*, div. i. vol. ii. p. 231, Edinburgh, 1862.

sion; and society, throughout all its gradations, was disturbed by the din of the theological warfare. Dealers in the market places and artisans in the workshops, as well as ministers in the churches, entered keenly into the argument. Constantine attempted to put an end to the contention by representing the question as of little consequence, and by exhorting the disputants to peace; but the advice of the imperial mediator produced little impression. Finding that all his endeavours to restore concord were abortive, he at length called a council to examine and decide the controversy.

This assembly, known as the First Œcumenical or General Council, met at Nice in Bithynia in A.D. 325, and remained together about two months. It soon appeared that there were three parties in the synod—those who maintained the soundness of the teaching of Alexander—those who were ready to defend the doctrine of Arius, if not to go farther—and those who were desirous to effect an adjustment by some species of compromise. To this third party belonged Eusebius, bishop of Cæsarea in Palestine, the ecclesiastical historian—a man who stood high in the favour of the Emperor, and whose prudence, volubility, and erudition, gave him much weight among his contemporaries. He proposed, for the acceptance of the council, a creed then long in use in the Church of Cæsarea, and which he had himself been taught in childhood. In this formula, which is still extant, the Son is described as—"God of God, Light of Light, Life of Life, the only-begotten Son, the First-born of every creature, begotten of the Father before all worlds, by whom also all things were made"[1]—though no precise deliverance is pronounced by it as to the particular point in controversy. This overture, therefore, proved unsatisfactory; but after much disputing, the compound Greek word *Homoousios*,[2] that is, *consubstantial*, was adopted as providing a suitable test of orthodoxy. The Son was thus declared to be *of the same substance* as the Father; and the congregated legislators, with a few exceptions, signed a symbol in which this doctrine was proclaimed. Arius and some others, who persisted in objecting to the finding, were sent into exile by the Emperor;[3] but the decree of banishment seems to have been soon reversed. The heresiarch was, however, forbidden to return to Alexandria.

[1] Socrates, i. 8.   [2] Ὁμοούσιος.   [3] Socrates, i. 8.

Among those present at Nice, not as members of the council but as deeply-interested spectators, was a young ecclesiastic destined shortly to act a conspicuous part in the history of the Church and of the Empire. His name was Athanasius. In the wealthier and more populous churches, one of the deacons, called the archdeacon—who was entrusted with the chief management of the temporalities of the see, and known as the bishop's high steward and confidential adviser—had already become an important functionary. This post was now filled by Athanasius. The archdeacon, though only twenty-five years of age, had distinguished himself as well by dexterity in business as by skill in disputation. He was of slender frame and of diminutive stature —circumstances to which he was indebted for many wonderful escapes. Once, long afterwards, when the soldiers burst into a church of Alexandria where he was engaged in conducting worship, and when it was thought that his capture was inevitable, he contrived to disappear among the crowd; and his admirers believed that his deliverance was miraculous. On another occasion when he fled up the Nile and when every stroke of the oars only placed him nearer to his enemies, he managed to escape, almost out of the very grasp of his pursuers, by taking advantage of a bend in the river. Commanding the boatmen, at the critical spot, instantly to turn and to row in the opposite direction, he lay down in the bottom of the tiny vessel and awaited the issue. When the parties met, and when the pursuers made inquiries respecting Athanasius, they were satisfied with the reply—"He is not far off"[1]—not perceiving that the little theologian was at their mercy. But, though almost of dwarfish size, it could not be said that his bodily presence was contemptible; for there was an air of dignity about him which commanded the respect even of the magnificent Constantine. His features were comely; his eye beamed with intelligence; and, when he opened his small but well-formed mouth, he convinced and captivated his auditors. Before the meeting of the Council of Nice he had, no doubt, measured his strength with Arius at Alexandria, and had discovered that he was more than a match for the plausible errorist. At the council itself, to which he was taken by the old bishop Alexander, he displayed consummate address in detecting the fallacies and ex-

[1] Theodoret, iii. 9; Socrates, iii. 14.

posing the inconsistencies of heresy. Shortly after the dissolution of the council, Alexander died; and the youthful archdeacon, amidst the acclamations of the clergy and people,[1] was elevated to the episcopal throne. He survived his appointment forty-six years; and, though meanwhile driven repeatedly from his see and obliged to encounter persecution in a variety of forms, he exhibited a courage, energy, and penetration, as well as a nobility of character, which won for him immense applause.. He died, at an advanced age in A.D. 373, in undisputed possession of the primatial dignity; and left behind him a reputation scarcely, if at all, inferior to that of any other father of the Church.

Constantia, the sister of Constantine and widow of the Emperor Licinius, was a supporter of Arianism. Some time after the Council of Nice, her brother was induced, it is said partly by her dying exhortations, to think better of the party she patronized and to restore them to his favour. But, when he required Athanasius to re-admit Arius to communion, he quickly discovered that the Christianity which could not be constrained to crouch throughout three centuries of suffering, would not bow to the despotism of a prince whom it ranked among its proselytes; and that there was at least one individual in his Empire prepared to disobey his arbitrary mandate. The bishop of Alexandria respectfully intimated to his sovereign that the keys of the Church did not belong to the civil magistrate; and that, when he gave orders for the restoration of Arius to ecclesiastical fellowship, he was intruding into a province beyond his jurisdiction.

Irritated by the firmness of the Egyptian primate, Constantine now listened complacently to the representations of his enemies. At the Synod of Tyre, held under the Imperial sanction in A.D. 335, several charges were trumped up against Athanasius. He was accused of incontinency; arraigned as a magician; and indicted for cutting off the hand of a bishop, named Arsenius, that he might use the dried and salted member for purposes of incantation. Arsenius himself, with both hands uninjured, was produced before the council; and a woman brought forward to convict him of impurity was shown to be a vile impostor.[2] But

---

[1] There could have been no ground for the charge that his election was irregular. He was obviously the man of the people.
[2] Socrates, i. 29; Sozomen, ii. 25.

his judges were determined not to permit the great champion of orthodoxy to escape. He was said to have deported himself in a violent and disorderly manner when visiting a certain church in the neighbourhood of Alexandria; and the council agreed to send into Egypt a deputation, consisting exclusively of hostile bishops, to investigate the transaction. When Athanasius saw that none of his friends were to be put on the commission, he embraced the bold resolution of proceeding directly to the Eastern capital, and of appealing in person to the justice of the Emperor. As Constantine passed through the great street of the city, a petitioner, who attempted to approach him, was repelled promptly by the guards; but the stranger, nothing daunted, announced himself to be the bishop of Alexandria, and earnestly pleaded for an opportunity of explanation. His sovereign, impressed by his tone and bearing, listened to his address; and was so far moved by his statements, that he summoned the members of the Synod of Tyre, by whom the Egyptian prelate had in the meantime been deposed, to appear before him and to account for their proceedings. His accusers now shifted their ground—alleging that another charge remained to be examined; and that the fleet, which brought supplies of grain from Alexandria to Constantinople, had been detained by the influence of Athanasius. This was a point on which the Emperor was peculiarly sensitive, as he was aware that his own popularity in New Rome depended much on the regular arrival of the corn ships from Egypt; but, though nothing like proof could be adduced to substantiate the accusation, suspicion was aroused; and, to quiet his fears, Constantine deemed it prudent to banish the primate into Gaul. The triumph of the Arian party did not stop here. Arius was brought to Constantinople; and Alexander, the orthodox bishop of that city, was required to readmit him to communion. Greatly perplexed by this order, and yet destitute of the decision of the Egyptian metropolitan, Alexander retired to his church, and prayed that either Arius might be taken out of the way, or that he himself might not be spared to participate in the scandal about to be perpetrated. The bishop was soon relieved from his perplexity; for the heresiarch died suddenly on the eve of the day on which he was to be restored to catholic fellowship. Some, without any evidence, attributed his demise, under such peculiar circumstances, to poison; whilst others recognized in it the finger of a rebuking and righteous Providence.[1] It is probable that the excitement of the occasion proved too much for a body weighed down by age, and debilitated by years of contention.[2]

Shortly after the death of Constantine, in A.D. 337, the banished primate was permitted to return to Alexandria. Constantine and Constans, the emperors of the West, espoused his cause; but their brother Constantius, the emperor of the East, was the devoted advocate of Arianism. Athanasius was not long suffered to remain unmolested. His zeal—his eloquence—his extraordinary popularity—his vigorous attacks on their theology —rendered him most obnoxious to the opponents of the Nicene Creed; and the means by which they sought to circumvent him betray at once the violence and the blindness of their antipathy. By a Council held at Antioch in A.D. 341 a sentence of deposition was pronounced against him, upon the ground that he had returned to his see without any proper ecclesiastical warrant, as well as for other reasons equally trivial and vexatious. He now fled to Rome, where he enjoyed the sympathy of Julius, the bishop of the great western metropolis; and a synod held there shortly afterwards absolved him from all the charges previously preferred against him, and declared the condemnation of the fathers of Antioch unjust and invalid.

We cannot well avoid the conclusion that personal feeling entered largely into the disputes between the Homoousians and their adversaries, and that, after all, the Christian world was not really very much divided in sentiment on the doctrine of the Trinity. Several creeds drawn up at Antioch about this period demonstrate that many of those opposed to Athanasius maintained the perfect deity of Christ. Thus one of them describes the Son as " God of God, Whole of Whole, an only One of the Only One, Perfect of Perfect, . . . Unchangeable and Inconvertible, the unalterable Image of his Father's Godhead, Substance, Power, Will, and Glory;" and anathematizes those who say that He is " a creature, as one of the creatures," or that " there was any

---

[1] Athanasius, *Letter to Serapion concerning the Death of Arius*, § 1; Sozomen, ii. 30.

[2] Authorities differ as to the age of Arius at the time of his death. According to some, he was upwards of eighty. See Kurtz, *History of the Christian Church*, p. 189, Edinburgh, 1860.

time or age before the Son was begotten."[1] There is apparently much truth in the statement of an ancient writer who avers that the parties were often ignorant of the meaning of each other's terms, and that they were like combatants fighting in the dark.[2] The word Homoousios was a terrible stumbling-block to not a few; for, fifty years before the Council of Nice, it was the symbol of heterodoxy;[3] and it involved, as some conceived, a virtual annihilation of the distinctions of the Godhead. Had Athanasius consented to add one letter to the Nicene Creed—to say that the Son is, not *Homoousios*, or *of the same substance*, but *Homoiousios*, or *of like substance* as the Father—their scruples would have been satisfied; but the orthodox chief rejected a concession involving, as he believed, a logical absurdity; and his firmness exposed him to much obloquy. The extent to which personal hostility to Athanasius was mixed up with the discussion appeared at the opening of the Council of Sardica in A.D. 343,[4] where the question, whether he should be allowed to take part in the deliberations as a bishop in full standing, abruptly produced a schism. His partisans, who constituted the majority, remained in Sardica, and enacted various canons; whilst the minority retired to Philoppopolis in Thrace, and passed counter-resolutions.

The Egyptian metropolis was kept in almost constant excitement when Athanasius was an exile in the West. The Council of Antioch, which confirmed his degradation, had overstepped the limits of all legitimate authority by appointing a Cappadocian, named Gregory, his successor;[5] but the greater number of the clergy and people of Alexandria refused to acknowledge a functionary thus set over them without their concurrence; and the intruded prelate, after struggling for a few years against the stream of popular dissatisfaction, was assassinated in A.D. 349. The Emperor Constans now insisted peremptorily on the restoration of Athanasius to his see; Constantius was constrained to acquiesce; and the primate, so long banished, entered Alexandria like a conqueror celebrating a triumph. The clergy and people went out to meet him; bishops assembled to

---

[1] Socrates, ii. 10.   [2] *Ibid.* i. 23.
[3] It was so used by Paul of Samosata. See Dorner, div. i. vol. ii. p. 489.
[4] Some place this council in A.D. 344. The later date—A.D. 347—is evidently inadmissible.
[5] This is one of the earliest cases in which the election of a bishop was wrested out of the hands of the people.

tender their congratulations; alms were liberally distributed; incense perfumed the air; the city was illuminated; and joy lighted up every countenance.

The death of Constans, in A.D. 350, led to new complications. Constantius, now sole emperor of the East and West, soon renewed his attacks on the most powerful antagonist of Arianism; the Councils of Arles and Milan were induced, by bribery and intimidation, to sanction the sentence of deposition previously pronounced on him; Athanasius was forced to seek an asylum in the deserts of Egypt; and a Cappadocian, named George,[1] was appointed to the Alexandrian primacy. The six years spent in concealment[2] by the Trinitarian leader form the darkest period in his ecclesiastical career. Arianism was rampant; the weak Constantius had set his heart on securing its ascendency; and, to effect his object, he called into requisition all the resources of an absolute government. The Councils of Seleucia[3] and Rimini[4] were compelled by violence to acknowledge heterodox creeds; Liberius, bishop of Rome, was tempted to express his approval of the degradation of Athanasius, and to subscribe an Arian confession; and even Hosius of Cordova—now more than a hundred years of age, and one of the most distinguished and faithful pastors of his generation[5]—was seduced into apostasy. Almost every great city of the empire became a scene of strife between the Arians and the orthodox; thousands perished in attempts to force Anti-Nicene bishops on reluctant flocks; and the floors of many cathedral churches literally ran with blood. Athanasius, sheltered among the monks of the desert, though hunted from place to place, could never be captured; and his writings, discussing the theories of the Arians with the unsparing severity of an iron logic, found their way throughout the Church, and imparted to others his own indomitable resolution. The divisions of his adversaries contributed greatly to strengthen his cause. A few of his own supporters inspired him with uneasiness; for some,

---

[1] This individual is not to be confounded with the famous St. George, another Cappadocian said to have been martyred about the beginning of the Diocletian persecution. But doubts have been entertained respecting the very existence of this patron saint of England.
[2] From A.D. 356 to A.D. 362.   [3] A.D. 359.   [4] A.D. 359.
[5] He was employed confidentially by Constantine the Great, and was one of the most distinguished members—perhaps the president—of the Council of Nice. See Athanasius, *History of the Arians*, § 42, 45, 46.

such as Marcellus of Ancyra and Photinus of Sirmium, carried their principles to excess and verged towards Sabellianism; but, before the death of the Trinitarian leader, many new shades of doctrine had appeared among the Arians. To the Homoiousians, or Semi-Arians of various classes, were added the *Heteroousians* or *Anomœans*,[1] who held that the Son is in nature *dissimilar* to the Father; the *Macedonians*,—so called from Macedonius, bishop of Constantinople, who denied the divinity and personality of the Holy Spirit; and the *Apollinarians*, deriving their name from Apollinaris, bishop of Laodicea, who taught that the Logos, or Word, supplied the place of the human soul in Christ, and who consequently rejected the doctrine of His perfect humanity.

Constantine the Great interfered most unwarrantably in the government of the Church, and his example was only too closely copied by his sons. Constantius in particular, by his oppressive treatment of all who opposed his theological views, has left a deep stain upon his memory. This prince, who favoured a section of the Arian party, acted as if ecclesiastical courts were bound to yield implicitly to his will; and, when they appeared disposed to assert their independence, nothing could exceed the truculence with which he insisted on submission. Thus, at the synod of Milan, where he occupied the chair as moderator,[2] he endeavoured, by the weight of his personal authority, to compel the members to subscribe decrees agreeable to his own sentiments; and when individuals ventured to plead the existing canons of the Church as an apology for their hesitation, he fiercely exclaimed, "What I command, let that be your canon."[3] When some still remained refractory, he started up, grasped his sword, brandished it in the face of the assembly, and ordered the most pertinacious of the recusants to go forthwith into exile. Though Constantius possessed but a feeble intellect, he was most impatient of contradiction, and he is said to have carried out his intolerance of orthodoxy so barbarously that the Church suffered more under this nominally Christian sovereign than under any one heathen emperor.[4]

[1] From ἑτεροούσιος and ἀνόμοιος.
[2] He was not yet even baptized. Like his father, he received baptism shortly before death.
[3] Athanasius, *Hist. Arian.* 33, *Opera*, tom. i. 731, Migne's ed.
[4] Cave's *Lives of the Fathers*, ii. 332.

On the death of Constantius in A.D. 361, the banished pastors who supported the Nicene faith were permitted to return from exile. Athanasius now resumed possession of the bishopric of Alexandria, but, towards the end of the short reign of Julian, he was again obliged to retire. The death of the Apostate led to a new ecclesiastical revolution; and the Trinitarian chief, after an absence of some months, appeared once more in the Egyptian metropolis. The remainder of his life was spent in comparative tranquillity, as, with the exception of a short interval during the reign of Valens, he experienced no farther disturbance. Valens was a zealous Arian; his temporal power was employed to support his creed, and his orthodox subjects were in some cases treated with shameless inhumanity; but he was restrained by his brother Valentinian, emperor of the West; and the other princes, who ruled the Roman world from Julian to Theodosius, either acted on the principle of toleration or promoted the cause of Trinitarianism. In A.D. 381, Theodosius convened at Constantinople a council, commonly called the Second Œcumenical or General Council, by which the Nicene creed was reaffirmed, and the Macedonian and Apollinarian heresies rejected.[1] Arianism was already on the decline, and Theodosius nearly effected its extinction by refusing toleration to its professors. "Throughout my dominions," said he to the Arians, "I will not permit any other religion than that which obliges us to worship the Son of God in unity of essence with the Father and Holy Ghost in the adorable Trinity. As I hold of Him the empire and the power which I have to command you, He likewise will give me strength, as He has given me the will, to make myself obeyed in a point absolutely necessary to your salvation and to the peace of my subjects."[2]

Ulphilas, the apostle of the Goths, when on a visit at the court of the Emperor Valens, was induced to adopt the Arian theology; and thus it was propagated among the barbarians living along the banks of the Rhine and the Danube. When these fierce warriors subsequently invaded Southern Europe and North

---

[1] That which is commonly known as the Nicene Creed, and which is used in the Communion Service of the Church of England, is an expansion of the formula adopted at Nice. The chief additions were made by this Council of Constantinople. See Pusey on the Councils, p. 312, and Stanley's *Eastern Church*, 163, 164, 174.

[2] Waddington, p. 99. See *Cod. Theod.* lib. xvi. tit. i. § 2, xvi. tit. v. § 6.

Africa, they carried their creed along with them, and Arianism for a time recovered its ascendency in several of the dismembered provinces of the Roman Empire. In Africa the Catholics were treated by these savages with horrid barbarity; but in the course of a few centuries all the descendants of the conquerors were induced to embrace the Nicene faith, and to submit to the authority of the bishop of Rome.

The breaking out of the Arian controversy, so soon after the conversion of Constantine, was well-fitted to discourage the illustrious proselyte. On many of the more intelligent pagans it produced a very unfavourable impression. The proceedings of the Council of Nice awakened general interest; not a few so-called philosophers resorted to the place of meeting; and these sophists exulted exceedingly as they witnessed the violence with which the Christians disputed respecting the object of their worship. But the controversy was inevitable; as the speculations of those addicted to the study of Platonism had obscured the simplicity of divine truth; and the manner of speaking of the Persons of the Godhead was, in consequence, often loose and inaccurate. The controversy fixed the attention of the ablest men in the whole Church on the subject; led to a more careful examination of the testimony of the Word of God; and resulted in more perspicuous views and a settled terminology. Arius illogically held that the Son possesses all the divine attributes *except one or two;* but Athanasius demonstrates that such a position is untenable; and the followers of the heresiarch, in endeavouring to make out a more consistent system, deviated farther and farther from the truth, and were brought into more direct antagonism with the evidence of Scripture. The decision of the Council of Nice attests that the Church, in the early part of the fourth century, adhered firmly to the doctrine of the supreme Deity of Christ. Before the meeting, Constantine did his utmost to quash the discussion; and, at Nice, Eusebius of Cæsarea, who had a leaning to Semi-Arianism,[1] was his confidential counsellor; but so determined were the pastors who had borne the brunt of the Diocletian persecution to assert, in the most explicit terms, the co-equality of the Father and the

[1] He at length signed the Nicene Creed with an explanation. According to Dorner (div. i. vol. ii. p. 218), his doctrinal system is "a chameleon-hued thing, a mirror of the unsolved problems of the Church of that age."

Son, that neither the intrigues of courtly prelates nor the personal influence of the Emperor could divert them from their purpose. At a subsequent period Arianism predominated in ecclesiastical courts; but it was indebted mainly for its position to the props of princely favour, and it never seemed able to stand alone. When the support of the sovereign was withdrawn, it pined away and disappeared. In the day of its power it deported itself with all the insolence of tyranny; but, when threatened with persecution, it betrayed a craven spirit, and could seldom be provoked to encounter the perils of martyrdom.

CHAPTER III.

THE PELAGIAN CONTROVERSY.

THE Eastern Church soon developed its speculative tendencies, and most of the discussions which agitated the early Christian communities originated within its borders; but, in the fifth century, a controversy, commencing in the West, excited intense and general interest. Hitherto the doctrines of the Gospel chiefly disputed were those relating to the Godhead: now, the subject of *Anthropology*, or the state and prospects of man, began to attract much attention. Athanasius, a prelate of vast influence, a subtle logician, a powerful debater, and a tactician of wonderful firmness and energy, was raised up to defend the Trinitarian cause; Augustine, a bishop of less elevated rank,[1] but a more indefatigable writer and a more profound thinker, expounded and vindicated that system of theology with which his name has ever since been associated. After the lapse of fourteen centuries he is quoted with respect; and, from his own time till the Reformation, the doctrines usually denominated evangelical found no more able and successful advocate.

Church writers had not yet undertaken minutely to determine how far the eating of the forbidden fruit by Adam affected

---

[1] He was Bishop of Hippo, a maritime city of Numidia—designated, by way of distinction, *Regius*, because formerly the residence of the Numidian kings. Augustine had several congregations under his care, and yet it does not follow that his jurisdiction extended over a district more extensive than some of our modern parishes. There were certainly other bishops in the region of Hippo. See the *Select Works* of David Clarkson, p. 88, London, 1846.

himself and his posterity. It was generally admitted that Christ appeared "to seek and to save *that which was lost*,"[1] and that "*by the offence of one* judgment came upon all men to condemnation;"[2] but the doctrine of the Fall had not been presented in a dogmatic form by any ecclesiastical council. Tertullian had described original sin as the "vice of our origin;"[3] Cyprian and others had expressed themselves in similar language;[4] and all acknowledged that we are indebted to *grace* for our salvation. But no church judicatory had promulgated any definite decisions either as to the extent of man's apostasy or as to the amount of his obligations to the Saviour. The language of Scripture on these points is sufficiently precise, and no one had ventured very broadly to deny its literal significance. As, however, the heathen philosophers taught the doctrine of fate, and as the Gnostics and Manichæans attributed our sinfulness to matter or an evil deity, Christian apologists, when insisting on human responsibility, had often spoken unguardedly on the subject of the freedom of the will. When treating of this topic in some of his earlier disputations, Augustine himself made use of phraseology which he was afterwards obliged to explain;[5] for, as he advanced in life, he acquired clearer views of several doctrines which he had not before so narrowly investigated. Controversy is in itself not to be desired; and yet, if managed by advocates of ability, its results may be eminently advantageous. As conducted by Augustine and his opponents it tended to the illustration of truth, brushed away inaccurate or meaningless forms of speech, and imparted greater precision to the ecclesiastical terminology. Inquiries into the origin of evil, the mode of the Spirit's operation, and the compatibility of the perfect prescience of Him who declareth the end from the beginning with the accountability of man, present questions of portentous difficulty; and it is not strange if the more ancient fathers, when discoursing of such mysteries, occasionally employ terms either vague

---

[1] Luke xix. 10.   [2] Rom. v. 18.

[3] Originis vitium. *De Anima*, c. 41.

[4] Cyprian, *De Habitu Virginum*, c. iv.; see also a quotation from Ambrose in Augustine, *Contra Julianum*, ii. 6, *Opera*, t. x. pars prior. 684.

[5] Some statements on the subject of free-will, made by him in the controversy with the Manichæans, were afterwards quoted against him by Pelagius. See Wigger's *Historical Presentation of Augustinism and Pelagianism*, by Emerson, p. 111, Andover, 1840.

or exceptionable. When approaching these subjects we feel the weakness of our faculties; and we may well acknowledge that creatures such as we are can but feebly comprehend what may be truly called the philosophy of the infinite. In the formation of our theological views it becomes us to beware of seeking to be wise above what is written, to avoid vain theorizing, to attend to the simple facts of our religious experience, and to adhere closely to the testimony of the Book of God. The spirit of the true disciple is exhibited in the prayer, "Teach me, O Lord, the way of Thy statutes."[1]

The general character of any system, whether of religion or philosophy, may be inferred from the words and phrases most prominently employed by its expositors. Modern writers on astronomy are as silent respecting crystalline spheres as are the ancients in reference to telescopic phenomena or the law of universal gravitation. If we apply this test to the theology of the sacred record, we cannot well mistake its peculiar features. In the New Testament the words "grace," "chosen," "elect," "ordained," and "predestinated," are of frequent occurrence; and it is not very easy to conceive how many passages of Scripture, such as our Lord's Prayer in the seventeenth chapter of the Gospel of John, or the Epistles to the Romans and Ephesians, could have been dictated by any other than a Predestinarian. The Scriptures represent the work of redemption as devised before the earth itself came into existence—as intended to exhibit God's abounding mercy—and as carried out, in all its arrangements, according to his sovereign will. "He hath chosen us in Christ, before the foundation of the world," says the apostle, "that we should be holy and without blame before Him in love, having predestinated us unto the adoption of children by Jesus Christ to Himself according to the good pleasure of His will, to the praise of the glory of His grace."[2]

The distinction between *precepts* and *counsels*—or those requisitions obligatory on all, and those to be obeyed only by such as aspire after a higher piety—had been long recognized; and its results were now presented ostentatiously in a practical form in the system of monachism. The pride of self-righteousness was greatly encouraged by the new institute; for, if the monks believed that their religion was of an essentially superior type,

[1] Ps. cxix. 33.   [2] Eph. i. 4-6.

they were strongly tempted to boast of its peculiarities, and to plead a special claim to the favour of heaven.[1] Many of the inmates of the cloister have, indeed, been distinguished by their evangelical humility; but their discipline has an altogether different tendency; and it is a memorable fact that Pelagius, a member of the monastic brotherhood, has given a name to that scheme of theology which most highly estimates man's ability, and describes him as least indebted to the grace of God for his salvation. This noted heresiarch, who was advanced in life when he began to attract public attention, was a British monk[2]— probably a Welshman—and known among his own countrymen by the name of Morgan. He was not attached to any particular community; for, in the beginning of the fifth century, the monks were not bound by very stringent regulations, and passed frequently from one monastery to another. The morals of Pelagius were pure; he was of lofty stature, of dignified appearance, and of bland address; in Rome, where he sojourned for several years, he was known as a man of superior erudition; and, in that ancient metropolis of the Empire, he promulgated his theological sentiments in commentaries on Paul's Epistles. He was intimately associated with an individual named Cœlestius, a tall and robust Irishman.[3] Cœlestius, originally an advocate or lawyer, had been induced by Pelagius to relinquish his profession, and devote himself to a life of asceticism. He was much younger than the Welshman, of a more ardent temperament, and of a more sprightly genius. About A.D. 411 these two monks passed over into North Africa; and from thence Pelagius proceeded to Palestine. Cœlestius sought to be admitted as a presbyter of the Church of Carthage; but Paulinus, a deacon of Milan who happened to be in the country and who was acquainted with his peculiar views, opposed his advancement on the ground of his heterodoxy; and, by an African synod, held in

---

[1] Isidore, one of the early ascetics, affirmed that "he had not been conscious of sin, *even in thought, for forty years!*" Socrates, iv. 23. How different from the experience of the Apostles Paul and James! Rom. vii. 21-23; James iii. 2.

[2] Prosper, a contemporary, has thus described Pelagius and his heresy:
"Dogma quod antiqui satiatum felle draconis,
 Pestifero vomuit *coluber* sermone *Britannus*."
Carm. De Ingratis. pars prima.

[3] Cœlestius is described by Vicent of Lerins as "prodigious." *Commonitorium*, i. 24. See some observations bearing on this subject by the present writer in the *British and Foreign Evangelical Review* for Oct. 1864, p. 669.

A.D. 412, before which he was arraigned, he was condemned as an errorist. Augustine, who had not yet interfered in the discussion, now published several works in which he examined the points in controversy; and, as he was already reputed the most eminent divine in the Western Church, his statements produced a profound impression.

When the controversy fairly commenced, Augustine was on the verge of sixty years of age; for a quarter of a century the Christian system had been his incessant study; and the views he now propounded are of especial value as the fruit of his matured convictions. This extraordinary man, in the well-known volume entitled his *Confessions*, has left behind him a piece of autobiography where he has described, with graphic pen, a most interesting portion of his spiritual history. In A.D. 354 he was born of reputable parentage at Tagaste, in Africa. His mother, the pious Monica, has been long celebrated as a bright specimen of maternal love, and a precious example of the success of persevering prayer. The youth of Augustine was not promising; though possessed of high talent, he did not diligently avail himself of his means of instruction; he could not be induced to apply, with becoming industry, to the acquisition of Greek literature; and, in consequence, in all his subsequent controversies, he laboured under great disadvantages as compared with his antagonists. He was quite ignorant of Hebrew, as well as deficient in a critical knowledge of the language of the New Testament. As he advanced to manhood he discovered a taste for philosophy and poetry; but, instead of exhibiting symptoms of moral improvement, he fell into open licentiousness. He now became a teacher of rhetoric—a vocation which trained more than one eminent father for the Church. He had meanwhile joined the Manichæans, because their system appeared to him more philosophical and promised him a deeper insight into the mysteries of theology than any other; and he remained nine or ten years involved in its delusions. But his excellent mother never ceased to pray for his conversion, and never despaired as to the issue. In due time her petitions were answered. Removing to Milan in the way of his profession, Augustine was attracted to the cathedral by the fame of bishop Ambrose; he was desirous to ascertain whether common report had not given an exaggerated account of the eloquence of that distinguished preacher; and, for some time, his attention was confined to the sermon considered merely as a display of rhetoric. But the momentous truths delivered from the pulpit soon began to create anxiety; and Augustine experienced the misery of an awakened and guilty conscience. In this state of mental anguish he turned to Paul's Epistles, and there eagerly sought for light and comfort. A spiritual crisis, marked by some extraordinary circumstances, speedily followed. As he lay on the ground, deeply dejected, with a portion of Scripture beside him, he heard, or thought he heard, a voice saying to him—"Take and read, take and read."[1] Opening the Epistle to the Romans, in obedience to what he deemed the heavenly dictate, his eye lighted on the words—"Not in rioting and drunkenness, not in chambering and wantonness, not in strife and envying; but put ye on the Lord Jesus Christ, and make not provision for the flesh to fulfil the lusts thereof."[2] He had long hesitated to make that spiritual surrender which the divine law requires, but his resolution was now fixed; he gave himself up to God; a peace he had never felt before beamed into his soul, and in a short time he received baptism. At this period he was upwards of thirty years of age; and, for the remainder of his life, his great powers, some of which had heretofore been little cultivated, were devoted with amazing industry to the service of the Gospel. His own spiritual experience had taught him well how to minister to minds diseased; and he stands out conspicuously among the writers of the ancient Church as *the father* who can best explore the depths of human depravity, and portray most skilfully the exceeding riches of God's grace.

Pelagius, as has been stated, had passed from Africa to Palestine; and, when there, he was accused of heterodoxy by a young Spanish presbyter, named Orosius,[3] then on a visit to Jerome. That famous scholar, the most erudite of the fathers, had, as we have seen,[4] previously lived for some time at Rome, where he aspired to the popedom; but he had long since left the great city in disgust; and he was now residing in a monastery at Bethlehem. He was far advanced in life; but he retained his intellectual vigour, and continued to take a lively interest in

---

[1] *Conf.* viii. 12. [2] Rom. xiii. 13, 14.
[3] Orosius has left behind him several works—including a history in seven books.
[4] Sec. I. Chap. III. of this Period.

everything pertaining to the Church. Pelagius, it seems, had spoken disrespectfully of his writings—an offence which the old monk could not readily forgive—and Jerome encouraged his young friend and visitor Orosius to press his accusation. The matter was investigated by a synod[1] held in July A.D. 415; but Pelagius, who was sadly deficient in candour, contrived to furnish such a plausible account of his opinions that he escaped without censure; and to add to the mortification of his adversaries, he was permitted, though a layman, to take a seat, during the trial, with John, bishop of Jerusalem, and his presbyters. No definite sentence was, however, pronounced by this judicatory; and, as both the accused and the complainant belonged to the Western Church, the court agreed, at the request of Orosius, to refer the case for final decision to Innocent of Rome—a prelate under whose supervision the errorist had long lived, and to whose tribunal he was properly accountable. At the instigation of two Western bishops, Heros and Lazarus, a second attempt was made, before the end of the year, to convict Pelagius of heresy; and a synod, consisting of fourteen bishops, was held at Diospolis, or Lydda, in Palestine, to reconsider the indictment. On this, as on the former occasion, his superior scholarship was of good service to the Welshman. One of his assailants was prevented by sickness from appearing; the others failed to attend; and, as the judges did not understand Latin, the charges could scarcely be made intelligible. The heresiarch equivocated, and again escaped. His partisans now exulted; but Augustine, who had received an accurate report of the proceedings, and who was aware of the circumstances to which the errorist was indebted for a favourable judgment, announced the true cause of the exculpation. "The heresy," said he, "is not justified, but the man who denied the heresy."[2]

Pelagius, with all his plausibility, was but a superficial thinker; and, as he more than once attempted to keep some of his doctrines in abeyance, he seems to have had a lurking conviction that they were fitted to excite alarm by their novelty

---

[1] This, though commonly called a synod, was properly a meeting of presbytery, as it consisted only of John of Jerusalem and his presbyters. See Mar. Mercator. *Opera*, 324, 325, ed. Migne.

[2] See Wiggers, p. 154. See also Augustine, *De Gestis Pelagii*, cap. xiv.

and extravagance. He was quite prepared to subscribe the creed of the Church respecting the Trinity and the Supreme Deity of Christ, as taught by the general councils of Nice and Constantinople; but he denied altogether the doctrine of original sin; he held that the moral nature of every one who comes into the world is as good as that of Adam when in Paradise; and he maintained that eternal, not physical, death is the punishment of sin—that our first parent would have died even if he had not sinned—that man, by his free-will, can choose good as readily as evil—and that, if he pleases, he can be perfectly free from sin. He fortified this last proposition by quoting, among others, the case of Mary, the mother of our Lord; and he is one of those who supported thus early the dogma of her immaculate conception.[1] According to the Pelagians, grace is not absolutely necessary to the attainment of eternal life; but, by means of it, we may *more easily* secure the kingdom of heaven. The term *grace* was understood by them in a peculiar sense—not as indicating the operation of the Holy Spirit on the will, but rather as denoting the assistance afforded to us by the light of the Gospel. "God works in us to will what is good, to will what is holy," said Pelagius, "while, *by the greatness of the future glory and the promise of rewards*, he inflames us who are devoted to earthly desires and delighting, like dumb beasts, only in the present—while he excites the stupid will to longing after God *by the revelation of his wisdom*—while he counsels us to all goodness."[2] The heresiarch could not brook the idea of the all-sufficiency of grace; as, according to his views, man is indebted for his salvation to the right use of his free-will. Hence he is said to have been exceedingly dissatisfied when he heard a bishop once offering up the prayer of Augustine—"My God! give me what Thou commandest, and command what Thou wilt."[3] Pelagius also discarded the principle that the title to an inheritance in heaven is derived solely from the good pleasure and

---

[1] Augustine said of our Lord—"Sine peccato *solus* est natus." *De Nuptiis et Concup.* i. cap. 24, *Opera*, tom. x. pars prior. 429. He was, however, unwilling to speak of Mary as an actual sinner. He says of her—"De qua *propter honorem Domini* nullam prorsus, cum de peccatis agitur, haberi volo *quæstionem*." *De Natura et Gratia*, cap. 36, *Opera*, tom. x. 267.

[2] August. *De Gratia Christi*, i. 10, *Opera*, tom. x. pars prior. 365, 366, Migne, Paris, 1861.

[3] *Conf.* x. 29.

grace of the Almighty; for he taught that men are elected to glory on the ground of their foreseen obedience.

The theology of Augustine was intensely opposed to that of Pelagius. The great African father maintained that all men are by nature dead in sin; and that, without special grace, we cannot think a right thought or perform a good action. "That man is able to will and to do good, is of God alone."[1] . . . "Adam perished, and in him we have all perished."[2] The will, by nature, is in bondage to sin; and men, if left to themselves, will go on from iniquity to iniquity. But God has mercy "on whom He will have mercy;" from eternity He chose a certain number of the race of Adam as heirs of heaven;[3] and, in pursuance of His everlasting counsels, He gathers them, in the fulness of time, into His Church. He gives them grace to believe the Gospel, and keeps them, by His mighty power, through faith unto salvation. "If we inquire for that which deserves mercy," said Augustine, "we find it not, for it has no existence . . . . because if we say that *faith* precedes, in which there should be what deserves grace—what merit had the man before faith, in order to his receiving faith ? . . . If we say the merit of *prayer* precedes, that we may obtain the gift of grace . . . even prayer itself is found among the gifts of grace."[4] Grace is imparted to man, not *because* he believes, but *that he may believe,* for faith is the gift of God.

The ordinance of infant baptism, and the language employed in its administration, greatly perplexed the advocates of the new doctrine. The germ of a liturgy first appeared in connexion with the baptismal service;[5] and the Pelagians themselves were in the habit of using a current formula which stated that little children are "baptized for the remission of sins."[6] Some doubts

---

[1] *De Gratia Christi,* i. 4, tom. x. 362.

[2] *Opus Imperfectum cont. Jul.* i. 47, tom. x. pars alt. 1069. Augustine quotes these words from Ambrose.

[3] Milner has asserted (*Hist. of the Church of Christ,* cent. v. ch. ix.) that "the notion of particular redemption was *unknown to the ancients.*" This is a very grave misrepresentation, as the doctrine is taught explicitly by Augustine himself. Thus he says,—"Every one who has been redeemed by the blood of Christ is a man; but not every one who is a man has also been redeemed by the blood of Christ." *De Conjug. Adulter.* i. 15, *Opera,* tom. vi. 461. See also various other testimonies equally decisive in Wiggers, pp. 254, 255.

[4] *Epist.* 194, iii. iv. tom. ii. 879.   [5] See *Ancient Church,* p. 479.

[6] Perhaps in reference to Acts ii. 38.

might be entertained as to the precise meaning of these words—but they unquestionably implied that infants are sinners, and consequently in need of salvation. Had the Pelagians been able to prove that infant baptism is not a divine appointment they could have escaped the difficulty; but they were obliged to acknowledge its apostolicity;[1] and their attempts to answer the argument it supplied in support of original sin were weak and sophistical. To meet some of the objections urged against their doctrine, they invented a distinction between *eternal life* and *the kingdom of heaven*. By eternal life they understood the ordinary happiness of the blessed; by the kingdom of heaven, the higher salvation of the Christians: infants dying unbaptized were, they alleged, made partakers of eternal life; but infants baptized were admitted into the kingdom of heaven. Out of their own distinction Augustine dexterously framed an argument to demonstrate that, in the case of twin children, one of whom died baptized and the other unbaptized, they could not vindicate the equity of the divine procedure. Whilst they rejected the idea that posterity suffer for the sin of Adam, they thus admitted that children may be punished for the neglect of their parents or guardians. Is it right, asked the African father, that one child should gain by baptism the salvation of Christians, and another, who has not received baptism, be excluded from the kingdom of God? What merit have those infants, who are received by baptism as the children of God, acquired for themselves above such as die without obtaining this favour? Why is one twin brother accepted by baptism as the child of God, and the other not? "The unbaptized twin brother comes to you and inquires softly—why he has been separated from his brother's good fortune? Why he has been punished with this mishap that, while the other is to be received as a child of God, he has not received the sacrament needful to all?"[2]

As Pelagius and his accusers all belonged, not to the Greek, but to the Latin Church, it had been arranged in Palestine, as

---

[1] The Pelagian leaders were among the most learned men of the age, and therefore their admission is all the more important. See Bright's *History of the Church*, 285, 286, Oxford and London, 1860.

[2] Augustine, *Contra Duas Epistolas Pelag.* ii. 7, *Opera*, tom. x. pars prior. 583. Augustine often recurs to this argument. See, for example, *De Peccant. Merit. et Rem.* i. 21, tom. x. pars prior. 125, and *Contra Julian.* lib. sex, iv. 8, tom. x. pars prior. 758.

already stated, that the questions in dispute should be submitted to the judgment of the Roman bishop Innocent. Meanwhile two African Councils, which met in A.D. 416, one at Carthage and another at Milevis, condemned the Pelagian doctrine. Their resolutions, accompanied by a letter from Augustine and a few of his brethren, were forwarded to the Roman patriarch; and Innocent, professing to be well pleased with this recognition of what was called the see of Peter, promptly signified his approval of their conclusions. But Pelagius and Cœlestius were not idle. Pelagius transmitted to Rome a confession of faith, in which he artfully concealed the more obnoxious features of his system; and Cœlestius himself soon appeared in the great ecclesiastical metropolis to vindicate his reputation. Innocent died before his arrival, and before the creed of Pelagius reached its destination; but Zosimus, who now occupied the papal chair, gave a courteous reception to the eloquent Irishman. Cœlestius pleaded his cause with address and ability; and his defence was pronounced satisfactory. Pelagius was equally successful. Heros and Lazarus, the two bishops who opposed him at the Synod of Diospolis, in Palestine, were known to the pontiff as turbulent and ill-conditioned individuals, so that their interference had rather enlisted his sympathy on the side of the accused; and a letter from Pelagius himself, presented along with his confession of faith, produced a most favourable impression. Another letter from Praylus, now bishop of Jerusalem, attested his orthodoxy. Zosimus accordingly wrote to the North African bishops announcing his acquittal of the two heresiarchs, and expressing his astonishment that their soundness in the faith had ever been challenged. "How I wished," said he, "that one of you had been present when the letter was read! How rejoiced and surprised were all the pious who heard it! Scarcely could some refrain even from tears to find that men so thoroughly orthodox could be defamed. Has any point relating to grace or the assistance of God not been recognized by them?"[1] Zosimus also intimated to his correspondents that the questions in dispute were too knotty and obscure to be investigated, and that no profit could arise from their discussion. There had been all along at Rome a party favourable to the views of Pelagius and Cœlestius; and the bishop, an indifferent theologian and quite

[1] *Patrologiæ Cursus Complet.* tom. xx. 655, Migne, Paris, 1845.

incompetent to grapple with the questions brought before his tribunal, was probably persuaded by this faction to depart so widely from the course pursued by his predecessor. But the Africans, led on by Augustine, refused to yield to any such dictation. Whilst professing all respect for the apostolic see, they complained of its inconsistency, and protested against its decision. Determined to show that they were prepared at all hazards to maintain their principles, they met at Carthage in A.D. 418,[1] and again condemned the doctrines of the two heresiarchs. A few extracts from their resolutions may suffice to illustrate the intrepidity and dialectic skill of these African churchmen. By the grace of God the Pelagians understood, as had been shown, not the special aid of the Holy Spirit, but rather the additional knowledge supplied in the sacred volume. Even with Zosimus for their antagonist, the Carthaginian Synod did not hesitate to declare :—" Let him be accursed who teaches that grace helps to keep us from sinning only as it opens our minds to a knowledge of the divine commands . . . but that it does not bestow a disposition to love, and a power to practise such commands. For whereas the apostle says—' knowledge puffeth up, but charity edifieth,' it would be very impious to believe that we have the grace of Christ to puff us up and not to edify us—while in truth both are given of God, not only that we may know what we must do, but also that we may love it so as to perform it—that thus, where love edifies, knowledge may not puff up."[2] The Pelagians affirm, as we have seen, that grace enables us *more easily* to do the divine will. "Christ has not said," argued the divines of Carthage, "without Me ye would find it *more difficult* to do anything, but without Me ye can do *nothing.*"[3]

The Africans had taken steps to invest their views with an authority before which, as they well knew, the bishop of Rome himself must succumb. The Western Emperor now held his court at Ravenna; and the Count Valerius, one of the most influential of his ministers, was the friend of Augustine. Honorius was thus prepared to support the African bishops by giving

---

[1] Another synod, animated by the same spirit, and consisting of 214 bishops, met at Carthage in Nov. A.D. 417.
[2] August. *Opera*, tom. x. pars alt. 1729.
[3] *Ibid.*

to their doctrine his imperial sanction. An edict was issued[1] denouncing Pelagius and Cœlestius, condemning them to banishment, and threatening their supporters with exile and loss of property. Zosimus, already beginning to betray signs of indecision, quailed before this demonstration. Pretending that he had been deceived by false statements, he summoned Cœlestius before him to undergo a new examination; and when the monk, convinced of the hopelessness of his position, failed to appear, the bishop anathematized his doctrines, and pronounced him and his friend excommunicated. Nor did he stop here. In a circular letter, known as the *Tractoria*,[2] addressed to the bishops of Christendom, he virtually adopted the decrees of the Council of Carthage. Subscription to the doctrine set forth in this encyclical epistle was enjoined by the State, and eighteen bishops of Italy who refused to sign were deposed and driven from their sees. Of these the most eminent was Julian, bishop of Eclanum, —a man no less distinguished for his learning than for his disinterestedness, courage, and candour.

The Pelagian cause was completely prostrated by these proceedings. Pelagius and Cœlestius soon afterwards disappear from history, and we cannot tell under what circumstances they finished their earthly career. By the third General Council, held at Ephesus in A.D. 431, they were stigmatized as heretics; and thus the doctrines of which they were the most prominent advocates were virtually condemned by the highest ecclesiastical authority.

Another theological system, since known as Semi-Pelagianism, found strenuous supporters before the death of Augustine. Its chief champion was Cassian—a monk who had travelled from the East and settled at Marseilles in France. Some represented the doctrine of predestination as calculated either to render men careless or to drive them to despair: and, though Augustine laboured to prove that such are not its legitimate consequences —that it is fitted simply to inspire believers with humility and confidence in God—he could not induce all to adopt his conclu-

---

[1] This rescript appeared on the last day of April A.D. 418. The Synod of Carthage met the day following. It consisted of more than 200 bishops. See Wiggers, p. 11.

[2] This document is not now extant, but some fragments of it may be found in Migne's *Patrol. Curs.* tom. xx. 693.

sions. Cassian maintained, despite the reclamations of the great African divine, that the disputed article makes the Most High the author of sin, and, on this ground, joined with Pelagius in its rejection. But he imagined that, by attributing to grace somewhat more than was conceded by the British monk, he could avoid the difficulties in which that errorist had involved himself. Without special grace we may, according to Cassian, *commence* a course of obedience; but, without it, we cannot *persevere*—so that its necessity must be acknowledged. In some, conversion is accomplished by the interposition of grace; in others, by the power of free-will. According to Augustine, Christ died for the elect;[1] according to Cassian, he died for all men.

The last works of Augustine were written in reply to the Semi-Pelagians. After his death the argument was sustained by Hilary and Prosper, two of his ardent admirers. Others subsequently engaged in the controversy—among whom, on the side of the semi-Pelagians, was Vincentius of the monastery of Lerins, who, in a work which acquired much celebrity,[2] asserted the principle that nothing is to be received as catholic doctrine except what has been believed "always, everywhere, and by all." By the aid of this proposition he might have proved that Augustine himself was not a teacher of the Catholic faith! He did not, however, venture on such an invidious application.

Prosper and Hilary endeavoured to obtain from Celestine, one of the successors of Pope Zosimus, a condemnation of Semi-Pelagianism; but, whilst the wary pontiff acted towards them in a friendly spirit, he was not led by their importunity to commit himself by any very distinct deliverance. The system gained extensive support; and when condemned by the fathers assembled at Orange in A.D. 529,[3] it had meanwhile received encouragement even from several provincial councils. But, long before it acquired much strength, Augustine had gone to his reward; for the bishop died in the place of which he was chief pastor, in A.D. 430, at the age of seventy-six. Hippo was invested

---

[1] Hos noverat qui prædestinaverat ; noverat qui redimere sanguine suo fuso venerat. *Serm.* cxxxviii. 5, tom. v. p. pr. 765, 766. See also preceding note 3, p. 186.

[2] His *Commonitorium*. The work now exists only in an imperfect form. On this subject see Neander, iv. 399.

[3] This condemnation of Semi-Pelagianism was ratified by Pope Boniface II.

by the Vandals, and for upwards of a year it resisted their attacks; but, in the third month of the siege, the man known to all after ages as its most illustrious citizen was carried off by fever. Augustine stands at the head of the Latin fathers; and in his writings, which discuss a vast variety of subjects, we find many of the errors of his age. He participated with his contemporaries in the admiration of monasticism; but his good sense pointed out to him the folly of some of its austerities. Persisting in the use of shoes, he said to those who thought that they displayed a loftier piety by walking barefoot—"I admire your fortitude—endure my weakness."[1] He held that the sin of intermediate progenitors, as well as of Adam, is imputed to posterity[2]—not considering that our first parent was in a position, as our representative, different from that of any of his offspring. Augustine unhappily did much to give currency to the principle that brute force may be employed for the advancement of religion; and, with his concurrence, the civil power attempted to compel the submission of both the Pelagians and the Donatists. Justification, according to this father, includes the infusion of grace, as well as pardon and acceptance; and, in consequence, his account of the way of salvation is occasionally obscure; for he confounds the forensic act, by which we are recognized as members of the body of Christ, with the work of the Spirit by which we are made meet for the inheritance of the saints in light. But Augustine did immense service to the Church by illustrating the work of redemption, and by showing how the truths of theology all combine in one grand and harmonious system. He possessed a comprehensive mind, a large amount of general knowledge, great metaphysical acuteness, a ready elocution, and a lively fancy. As a preacher, there are few to be compared with him in the Latin Church. He was of an ardent temperament; and when treating of his favourite theme —the grace of God—he pours forth the fulness of his heart in strains of tender and commanding eloquence. His life was a beautiful commentary on his doctrines, as he was eminently holy. A sentence inscribed on his table warned his guests against evil speaking; and, when strangers indulged in detraction, their attention was called to "the law of the house."

[1] *Serm.* ci. cap. vi. ; *Opera*, t. v. 699.
[2] *Enchiridion*, 46, 47 ; *Opera*, tom. vi. 254, 255.

Augustine was gentle, placable, and generous. The greatest statesmen of the age did not disdain to cultivate the acquaintance of the bishop of Hippo; he counselled them with the wisdom of a Christian patriarch; and, when needful, he pointed out to them their faults, or reminded them of their duty. By those who love the truth he will be honoured to the end of time as a master in Israel, who has done more than any other father to demonstrate how grace reigns, in the election of believers, "according to the foreknowledge of God the Father, through sanctification of the Spirit unto obedience, and sprinkling of the blood of Jesus Christ."

CHAPTER IV.

THE NESTORIAN CONTROVERSY.

THE controversy with Pelagius had scarcely gone to rest, when the discussions pertaining to the Godhead, which had occupied so much attention in the fourth century, revived in a new form, and created immense excitement. The questions now agitated related to the constitution of the Person of the Mediator—and particularly to the union of His Divinity and Humanity. The conclusions adopted have ever since been regarded as substantially sound;[1] but though they must all be more or less interesting to the systematic theologian, they are established by processes of reasoning rather too abstruse to be easily appreciated. Strange as it may appear, the debates respecting these sublime and subtle theorems were carried on with extreme acrimony, and were not unfrequently connected with scenes of uproar, violence and bloodshed.

Nestorius, who has given a name to a controversy and a sect, was the patriarch of Constantinople. He had been a presbyter of Antioch; he was noted for his ability and eloquence; and his advancement to the great Eastern see had disappointed a crowd of other candidates. He owed his elevation to the will of the Emperor, who resided at Constantinople and virtually selected its chief pastor; and the metropolitan clergy, dissatisfied that

[1] See XXXIX. Articles of the Church of England, Art. II. ; and Westminster Confession of Faith, chap. viii. § 2.

the office had not been conferred on one of themselves, looked with coldness on the Syrian stranger. Nestorius became patriarch in A.D. 428; and his first public acts were not calculated to conciliate opposition. New Rome contained a considerable number of Arians, Novatians, and other nonconformists; and the patriarch, in his inaugural discourse, implored the civil power to aid him in accomplishing the annihilation of the sectaries. "Give me a country purged of heretics," he exclaimed, addressing his sovereign, "and, in exchange for it, I will give you heaven. Help me to subdue the heretics, and I will help you to conquer the Persians."[1] When he uttered these words little did he imagine he was himself soon to undergo the penalties he invoked. In his zeal for what he deemed sound doctrine, he came into collision with popular prejudice, and roused a storm of opposition he was unable to withstand. Three years after his promotion he was obliged to resign his see; when he retired to a convent, he was not permitted to enjoy its seclusion; and, still hunted by the malice of his enemies, he died in poverty and exile.

Superstition had already magnified the reputation of the mother of our Lord. Pelagius was not the only individual prepared to maintain the doctrine of her sinless perfection; and in some places she now inherited the honours previously paid to one or other of the goddesses of paganism. She had long been known as the "Mother of God:"[2] and even the great Athanasius had sanctioned the use of the designation.[3] But divines of the school in which Nestorius had been educated objected to the title—because, as they conceived, it absurdly confounded the divine with the human nature of the Saviour. It was currently used in Constantinople; and Anastasius, a presbyter who accompanied the new patriarch from Antioch, ventured, in one of his sermons, to point out its inaccuracy. Mary, he declared, was not the mother of God, but the mother of the man Jesus.[4] His hearers listened with perplexity; the language sounded strangely in their ears; it seemed to be disrespectful to the Virgin; and they were still farther disturbed when told that Nestorius himself concurred with his Syrian presbyter. The views of the patriarch were soon well known. In a series of discourses he expounded the subject, and fully explained his sentiments.

---

[1] Socrates, vii. 29.   [2] Θεοτόκος.
[3] Discourse III. against the Arians, xxv. 8, and xxvi. 7.   [4] Socrates, vii. 32.

"Can God," said he "have a mother? ... If so, Paul erred concerning the Deity of Christ, when he speaks of him as 'without father, without mother.'[1] ... A creature cannot bear the Uncreated. ... God was not born of Mary: He dwelt in Him who was born of her."[2]

The religious meetings of the Christians, especially in some of the great towns, had long lost much of the grave decorum of the days of the Apostles; for the preacher was now treated like any other public speaker, and the assembly testified its interest in his sermon by tokens of disapprobation or applause. When the sacred orator gratified his congregation, he was often forced to pause by clapping of hands, shouts of enthusiasm, and like noisy demonstrations; and when he addressed an adverse auditory, he was not unfrequently assailed with hisses, or mortified by other rude interruptions. Nestorius had now to pass through this rough ordeal. His rhetorical ability gave him influence with the crowds who flocked to his cathedral; and, when he commenced his ministrations in the Eastern capital, he enjoyed extensive popularity. The citizens compared him to the greatest preacher of antiquity—their favourite bishop Chrysostom, to whom many of them had listened only five and twenty years before—and a goodly number of his hearers were willing to sustain their patriarch in his criticisms on the language applied to Mary. But, from the first, he had to struggle against a party envious of his exaltation and ready to seize on any circumstance that might operate to his prejudice. This faction, composed largely of the monks and clergy, now saw their opportunity. Mingling with the multitude, and scattering abroad dark insinuations, they soon created a popular ferment. Nestorius was not permitted to proceed with his discourses unopposed. As he was one day contrasting the eternal generation of the Logos and the nativity of the man Christ Jesus, a person of rank who was present caused great confusion by abruptly vociferating "No! the eternal Logos himself condescended also to the second birth."[3] Part of the audience applauded the objector, and part cheered the patriarch; so that a considerable interval elapsed before the preacher could continue his discussion. At another time, when he was about to go into the pulpit, a monk stood in his way,

[1] Heb. vii. 3, 17.
[2] Mar. Mercat. *Opera*, 760, 761, 769, edit. Migne.   [3] *Ibid.* 769.

and attempted to prevent his entrance on the pretence that a heretic should not be permitted to teach in public. The city ministers, in their sermons, pleaded the claims of Mary with amazing zeal; and a bishop, named Proclus,[1] on the day of a festival in her honour, delivered in Constantinople a discourse which produced a wonderful sensation. "Behold," said Proclus in this sermon, as he quoted some not very appropriate passages of Scripture, "Behold the divine approbation of the holy Mother of God,"[2]—the very title condemned by the patriarch. The preacher at the same time described Mary as "the spotless vase of virginity—the living Paradise of the Second Adam—the workshop in which the (two) natures were annealed—the bush which the fire of the Divine Birth did not burn."[3] As Proclus produced, one after another, these flowers of rhetoric, the building echoed with applause. The excitement at length rose to such a pitch that many of the clergy and people renounced the communion of Nestorius, and a schism seemed inevitable.

Nestorius was supported by the emperor; and, as his own eloquence and the influence of his station also secured him many friends, he might have overcome this opposition, had he been sustained by his brethren elsewhere: but those who could have given him most efficient aid had an interest in aggravating his difficulties. The Bishop of Alexandria had long observed, with ill-suppressed jealousy, the increasing power of the Bishop of Constantinople. The Egyptian primate once presided over the second see in Christendom; and New Rome had suddenly sprung up, and interfered with his ecclesiastical honours. He could ill brook the idea that he must occupy a lower position than the prelate of the Eastern capital; he had repeatedly vented his mortification in attacks on the new dignitary; and, in the hope of weakening his authority, he lost no opportunity of giving him annoyance. From the present Egyptian patriarch Nestorius could expect no sympathy; for Cyril was one of the proudest and most unscrupulous of churchmen. When a youth,

---

[1] The practice of episcopal non-residence had already commenced. A number of bishops whose sees were at a considerable distance spent most of their time in the Eastern capital. Proclus had been ordained Bishop of Cyzicum, but the people had refused to receive him as their pastor. He afterwards became patriarch of Constantinople.

[2] Marii Mercat. *Op.* 781, ed. Migne.

[3] *Ibid.* 777. See also *Binii Concilia,* tom. i. par. ii. pars. i. p. 6, ed. 1618.

he had spent five years with the monks in the Nitrian desert; but, though he had acquired among them a knowledge of polemic theology, he had made little progress in that higher wisdom which is " pure, then peaceable, gentle, and easy to be entreated." Cyril had an excellent voice, a pleasing exterior, a good address, and a vigorous intellect; and, as he was a stern assertor of the orthodox faith, he contrived so to recommend himself to the clergy and people that, on the death of his uncle Theophilus, he was elected his successor in the see of Alexandria. When he attained this dignity he acted more like an absolute prince than a Christian pastor. Nor is it very strange that he was forgetful of the spirit of his profession; for he had strong temptations to domineer. Placed in a great metropolis—in the granary of the empire—at a distance from the court—in the enjoyment of ample revenues—and the dispenser of all the public charities—the Egyptian patriarch wielded vast influence: and when an ecclesiastic of commanding talent, such as Cyril, was seated on the episcopal throne, the emperor himself was unwilling to quarrel with such a spiritual potentate. In addition to a city mob ever ready to commit deeds of violence, he could, on any emergency, avail himself of the aid of swarms of monks alike ferocious and fanatical. Nor did Cyril hesitate to employ these auxiliaries. Immediately after his advancement to the primacy he assailed the Novatians, closed their meeting-houses, and stripped them of their property.[1] The Jews, who had been provoked by his partisans into sedition, next experienced his intolerance. At the head of an immense multitude of his adherents, he laid their synagogues in ruins, gave up their houses to pillage, and drove the whole race out of the city. Orestes, the prefect of Alexandria, who incurred his displeasure, was waylaid and wounded by a rabble of five hundred monks. Ammonius, one of their ringleaders, who had hurled a great stone at the head of the imperial functionary, was put to death by the hand of the public executioner; but Cyril conferred on the criminal the honours of martyrdom, and named him Thaumasius, or the *Wonderful*.[2] A pagan lady of high rank and extraordinary talent—the celebrated Hypatia—offended the haughty patriarch; and a crowd of miscreants, among whom an ecclesiastic of his party was conspicuous, dragged her from her chariot, and rent her limb from

[1] Socrates, vii. 7.   [2] *Ibid.* vii. 14.

limb.[1] The majesty of the law was never properly vindicated by the punishment of those concerned in the horrid outrage; for the officers of justice were induced, by bribes, to stop the progress of inquiry. But Cyril was too closely allied to the rioters to escape suspicion.

Such was the man who stepped forward to interfere in the theological controversy which disturbed Constantinople. He had his agents at the imperial court, as well as among the monks of the capital, who reported to him from time to time the details of the struggle and the increasing embarrassment of Nestorius. Cyril now perceived that he could at once signalize his zeal for orthodoxy and humble the Bishop of New Rome; and he did not fail to take advantage of the occasion. He wrote to the monks of Egypt, to the clergy of Constantinople, to the Emperor Theodosius II., to other members of the imperial family, and to Nestorius himself,[2] defending the use of the designation "Mother of God;" and either insinuating or affirming, according to circumstances, the enormity of the heresy into which his reverend brother had fallen. A concern for the truth, he alleged, compelled him to speak out, and publish his protest against the false teaching of Nestorius. These letters, which were widely circulated, stimulated the opposition to the new patriarch.

There was another great prelate who viewed with perhaps even livelier jealousy the growing influence of the see of Constantinople. This was the Bishop of Rome. When the empire was undivided, and the sovereign resided in its ancient metropolis, the Italian primate was acknowledged as first in dignity among the clergy of Christendom; but a rival had appeared in New Rome, who might, at no distant day, set up a claim to precedence. He had already asserted his ecclesiastical equality, and it was to be feared that he would soon adopt a tone of loftier assumption; for Constantinople was the metropolis of the Eastern Empire, whereas Old Rome had been long deserted by the Western court, and was fast sinking into the condition of a provincial city. But it had for ages been called the See of Peter; and its prelates, who were celebrated as supporters of the orthodox faith, were most desirous to be known as arbiters in

---

[1] Socrates, vii. 15.

[2] These letters may be found in *Binii Concil.*, tom. i. p. ii. pars. i. pp. 9, 20, 43, 119, 120, 126.

matters of controversy. A golden opportunity for making good
their pretensions was now presented. Cyril had taken care to
supply the Roman bishop with information respecting the proceedings of Nestorius; and, along with various false statements,
had been so considerate as to furnish him with Latin translations
of some important documents bearing on the dispute.[1] These
translations were all the more necessary, as Celestine, who now
filled the papal chair, was ignorant of Greek—a fact probably
not unknown to his Alexandrian brother. The complimentary
language addressed by Cyril to Celestine must have been extremely grateful to the pontifical ear; for the artful Egyptian
requested the Italian patriarch to determine whether Nestorius
ought or ought not to be excluded from the communion of the
Church, and begged him to announce his decision, by letters, to
all the bishops of the East, that they might act together as conservators of the orthodox doctrine. Nestorius also had been
writing to Rome,[2] but neither the matter nor tone of his epistles
was well fitted to recommend him to his western correspondent.
Four Italian bishops, deposed for Pelagianism, had taken up
their abode in his diocese; they complained of unjust treatment,
and implored his interference. He reported their statements to
Celestine, and sought an explanation; but, coming from such a
quarter, the pontiff probably deemed the inquiries impertinent,
and declined an answer. Nestorius addressed other letters to his
brother in Rome, detailing the history of the disputes in Constantinople; but he wrote in Greek,[3] and expressed himself in
the style of an independent bishop conveying intelligence to a
dignitary of equal authority. Celestine, who regarded the
designation "Mother of God" as part of the current language
of orthodoxy, had no difficulty in coming to a decision. At a
synod convened in Rome it was resolved that, if, within ten days
after the reception of the sentence, Nestorius did not, by a written
recantation, renounce his doctrine, he should be deposed from his
patriarchal station and excommunicated. Celestine transmitted
circular epistles to the East announcing this deliverance. In a

[1] "Misi tomos aliquot, capitum quorumdam fragmenta continentes, quos quo-
que, quantum quidem per illos fieri potuit qui Alexandriæ vivunt, Latine reddi
curavi."—*Binii Concilia,* tom. i. p. ii. pars. i. p. 131.

[2] See his first letter in *Binii Concil.* t. i. p. ii. pars. i. p. 133.

[3] The pope, it appears, was obliged to send all the way to Cassian of Marseilles
for a translation of these documents.

letter to Cyril, eulogizing most extravagantly his fidelity as a pastor of the Catholic Church, he is instructed to act as the representative of the apostolic see, and empowered to carry into execution the sentence of the Roman synod. Its resolutions were duly communicated to Nestorius himself, and to the clergy of Constantinople who had renounced his fellowship.

Two powerful parties were now arrayed against each other in resolute antagonism. On one side was Nestorius, supported by the emperor and a portion of the clergy and laity of his ecclesiastical metropolis: on the other was an excited faction of presbyters, deacons, monks, and people, backed by the two great prelates of Rome and Alexandria. Nestorius, it must be admitted, had not hitherto passed through the controversy entirely without reproach. He had sometimes lost his temper; he had sanctioned the flogging of refractory citizens and preachers; on one occasion he had, with his own hand, inflicted corporal chastisement on a monk who obstructed him;[1] and he had thus failed to deport himself with becoming dignity and forbearance. Though the opposition of Cyril and Celestine was conducted with passion and quickened by ecclesiastical jealousy, it would be unwarrantable to assert that it is to be attributed altogether to such influences. Before Nestorius was elevated to the patriarchal throne, the Egyptian primate had written a treatise on the incarnation promulgating the principles he now reaffirmed.[2] The title, "Mother of God," had, in various quarters, been so long in use that many distinguished churchmen were startled by the attempt to remove it from the ecclesiastical vocabulary, and the question of its propriety or impropriety impinged on another controversy. According to Nestorius, the two natures in Christ are rather *related*, or *conjoined*, than *united;* according to Cyril, they are so united that, though we can distinguish between them, they are no longer specifically different. Mary, said Nestorius, was not the mother of God, because God can neither be born nor die. If, rejoined Cyril, the Son of God had not been born—if Mary had not given birth to him—there would have been no real incarnation. If we are forbidden to deny that the Son of God was born, we are equally forbidden to deny that He suffered.[3] "The Council of Nice," argued Nestorius, "acknow-

---

[1] *Binii Concil.* t. i. p. ii. p. i. p. 160.
[2] Dorner's *Doctrine of the Person of Christ*, div. ii. vol. i. p. 55.   [3] *Ibid.* p. 62.

ledged an incarnation, but did not allow that God suffered, or that the Son of God was born of Mary." To attempt to conceive of the one nature apart from the other, replied Cyril, would be as perverse as for any one to represent the human body as a man in and by itself, or to say that a mother had brought forth a body, instead of that she had brought forth a man.[1] Nestorius so distinguished the two natures in Christ that some imagined he taught the existence of two persons; and Cyril so confounded them that they seemed to be but one. The teaching of Nestorius was really offensive to both Cyril and Celestine; but, had they been personally his friends and anxious to promote peace, they might, no doubt, have obtained satisfactory explanations, and put an end to the contention. Nestorius himself, indeed, soon began to make advances towards a settlement. He proposed that Mary should be called "Mother of Christ,"[2] and, if permitted to expound his meaning, he was even willing to continue the use of the designation "Mother of God." He denied that he had any intention of teaching the existence of two sons of God, or of impugning the doctrine of the incarnation. The whole controversy was, in fact, very much a war of words; and, if a calm conference had been possible, it must have issued in a reconciliation. But it was soon discovered that the enemies of Nestorius were determined not to accept of any compromise.

When Cyril received the communication from Constantine empowering him to act as the representative of the apostolic see, he lost no time in proceeding according to his instructions. In A.D. 430 he wrote a letter to the bishop of Constantinople, in the name of a Synod held at Alexandria, requiring him to recant, and, as a test of his orthodoxy, to anathematize all who held twelve propositions he enumerated relative to the points in dispute. A deputation of Egyptian prelates, bearing this epistle, appeared in the Eastern capital. Nestorius treated the commissioners with contempt, ascended the pulpit, expatiated on the heresies of Cyril, and published twelve counter-propositions which he called on his adversaries to condemn. The breach was thus made wider than ever.

[1] Dorner's *Doctrine of the Person of Christ*, div. ii. vol. i. p. 66.
[2] Χριστοτόκος. He also proposed the designation Θεοδόχος, or "Receiver of God." *Serm.* vii. Mar. Mercat. *Op.* 800. As to his willingness to continue the use even of "Mother of God," see Socrates, vii. 34.

At an early stage of the controversy Nestorius himself had suggested the meeting of a synod as a means of extinguishing the strife; and the Emperor Theodosius II. now summoned such a convention. This synod, known as the third Œcumenical Council, assembled at Ephesus in A.D. 431. The place of meeting was unfavourable to Nestorius, for Memnon, the bishop, was as unscrupulous as Cyril, and as jealous of the growing power of the patriarch of Constantinople. According to a current tradition, Mary, whose title was so much controverted, lay buried at Ephesus; and the populace, wrought up almost to frenzy by Memnon's exhortations, were persuaded that the honour of their city was involved in the condemnation of an errorist who even dared to question the dignity of the mother of God. Nestorius and Cyril reached the place of meeting at the appointed time; but the Alexandrian primate, who travelled by sea, had taken care to bring with him a far greater number of bishops than were in the train of his antagonist, and commanded, besides, a large force of stout Egyptian sailors, prepared, with formidable weapons, to overcome the timid and decide the wavering. John of Antioch, one of the most influential of the Eastern prelates,—who travelled by land, and who, on account of the unsettled state of his metropolis,[1] was unable to set out in due time,—had not yet arrived; and, as he was understood to be friendly to Nestorius, Cyril resolved to take advantage of his delay, and to commence the proceedings before his appearance. The imperial commissioner, deputed to be present, protested against this movement; Cyril, supported by Memnon, carried his point and opened the meeting. The result might have been easily anticipated. In a single day the whole business was transacted; the doctrine of the One Person in Christ was affirmed; the designation, "Mother of God," was approved; and Nestorius, who declined to sanction the meeting by his attendance, was condemned and degraded. On the arrival of John of Antioch, some days afterwards, a rival council was held, which awarded to Cyril and Memnon the sentence they had already pronounced on the bishop of Constantinople.[2] Thus every turn in the progress of the controversy seemed only to place at a greater distance the prospect of an adjustment.

[1] A famine at Antioch had led to popular tumults, and delayed his departure.
[2] Evagrius, i. 5.

Cyril, who had hitherto been sternly discountenanced by the Emperor, clearly saw that, if he could produce no impression at Court, he could not ultimately prevail; but arrangements had been made to prevent intercourse between his partisans in the council and their friends at Constantinople, so that he could obtain no access to the palace. He at length hit on a scheme for surmounting this difficulty. A beggar, or rather perhaps a bishop in disguise,[1] made his way to the capital, and presented to a monk, named Dalmatius—a personage of unrivalled fame for sanctity—a hollow staff in which was concealed a letter reporting the condemnation of Nestorius, and the hardships to which his judges were, in consequence, exposed. This monk was a bitter enemy to the patriarch; and an epistle, conveyed to him by so strange a messenger and through a channel so mysterious, kindled his imagination, and led him to believe that the friends of orthodoxy were suffering a grievous persecution. The Emperor himself had not deemed it beneath his dignity on another occasion to visit and consult this solitary in his cell; but, for eight and forty years, Dalmatius had not been induced to go beyond its precincts. The bearer of the letter probably suggested to him that it was now his duty to interfere; the idea soon took full possession of his soul; and, accordingly, he proclaimed his determination to proceed on a mission of remonstrance to Theodosius. The announcement of this resolution threw all Constantinople into a ferment. The monks and abbots hastened to join the venerable man; and Dalmatius, accompanied by a prodigious concourse of citizens of all classes, and at the head of a deputation of his brethren singing hymns and bearing lighted torches, advanced to the imperial residence. Whilst the crowd remained without, the monk and a select party were ushered, before a crowded court, into the presence of the sovereign. Unabashed by the brilliant throng, Dalmatius boldly complained that none opposed to Nestorius could obtain the ear of the Emperor; and, towards the close of the interview, the feeble prince consented to permit deputies from the party of Cyril to appear in Constantinople. When this answer was reported to the waiting multitude, the whole procession joined in a song of praise.

The mission of Dalmatius to the palace was the turning-point

[1] See Neander, iv. 182.

in this controversy. Cyril now distributed large sums of gold among the courtiers; and, partly corrupted by bribes, and partly gained over by other influences, the ministers of Theodosius gradually deserted the cause of their patriarch. John of Antioch and the Egyptian primate were reconciled; Cyril consented to sign a formula recognizing two natures in Christ; and Nestorius, at the request of Theodosius, withdrew to a Syrian monastery. At a subsequent period he was banished to Egypt, from which he never returned. He lingered out his last days in wretchedness; but the exact date of his death cannot now be ascertained.[1]

The party adhering to the bishop of Constantinople throughout this struggle was not extinguished by his fall. Persecuted within the Roman Empire, they found refuge in Persia, where they soon became a flourishing community. Pushing their principles farther than they were carried by Nestorius, they declared in their creed that there are in the Saviour two Persons —a divine and a human—yet that these Persons constitute but one *Aspect*.[2] The Nestorians may be found at the present day scattered throughout various countries in the East. They refuse to call Mary the "Mother of God," worship no images—venerate Nestorius and his teacher Theodore of Mopsuestia, and still execrate Cyril.[3]

The Nestorian controversy forms a melancholy and yet an instructive chapter of Church history. Though the conduct of the patriarch of Constantinople was not above censure, it was far less exceptionable than that of his Egyptian adversary. Nestorius often exhibited violence of temper; but he was comparatively free from ambition; for, when required to relinquish the patriarchal dignity, he readily obeyed; and he never afterwards made any effort to recover his position. Neither do we ever find him descending to the falsehood and bribery by which Cyril disgraced himself. The Egyptian primate scattered his gold so profusely among the courtiers of Theodosius, about the time of the Council of Ephesus, that the rich Church of Alexandria long felt the effects of his extravagance.[4] The intense

[1] Evagrius (i. 7) has given a sad account of his last days.
[2] Πρόσωπον. See Murdock's *Mosheim* by Soames, i. 489.
[3] *Ibid.* Some of them have been tampered with by the agents of Rome. See Dr. *Grant and the Mountain Nestorians* by Laurie, p. 44, Edinburgh, 1853.
[4] See Neander, iv. 190, 191.

acrimony displayed by the disputants in this controversy cannot be too strongly reprobated. When, in the spirit of the Gospel, we contend for its great truths, we are improved by the effort. We thus become better acquainted with the precious things of God, with the wonders of His law, and with the glory of His character. But when we dispute in the spirit of mere partisans, and when our strife is but logomachy, the heart is hardened, and the intellect is debased. Nestorius and Cyril debating respecting the Person of the Mediator, and hurling anathemas against each other, present a most humiliating spectacle. The union of the Godhead and the Manhood in the Saviour is a sublime and awful theme; but the subject should lead us rather to wonder and adore, than to carp and quarrel. When the sun shines on us in his noontide splendour, we survey with pleasure the radiant scenery; but it is dangerous to gaze on his own bright orb. There are times when the light around us is so faint that we cannot read, and the sight is injured by exertion; and again the illumination may be so singularly brilliant that the eye is dazzled by the glare. As we contemplate the wonders of redeeming love through the glass of revelation, we grow in grace and in the knowledge of Christ; but if we push our inquiries beyond the range of our faculties, or into regions where the Bible supplies no light, we can expect nothing but vexation and bewilderment. "Who by searching can find out God? Who can know the Almighty to perfection?" Who can fully comprehend how Deity is united to Humanity in the Lord Jesus? Who can pretend exactly to define their relations? Instead of fulminating their anathemas when discussing this mystery of mysteries, Cyril and Nestorius should have mutually confessed their ignorance; and sought, either to remove each other's difficulties, or to check each other's vain curiosity. Whilst the Eastern Church was convulsed by this controversy, superstition and ungodliness advanced apace. The worship of relics, the invocation of saints, and the senilities of monachism, now made vast progress. In a few centuries the countries where the Nestorian controversy was carried on with greatest bitterness were overrun by Mohammedanism; and the religion of the False Prophet was established in the sees of Cyril, of Nestorius, of Memnon, and of John of Antioch.

CHAPTER V.

THE EUTYCHIAN CONTROVERSY.

NESTORIUS and Cyril were the representatives of two schools of theology which flourished in the fifth century. The tendency of the school of Antioch, in which Nestorius was educated, was to push to an extreme the distinction between the Son of God and the man Christ Jesus; the tendency of the school of Alexandria, to which Cyril belonged, was so to mingle the two natures that they could not be discriminated. The disciples of the school of Antioch were not willing to say that *the Son of God suffered* on the cross; the disciples of the school of Alexandria threw the whole church into confusion rather than change the language of a favourite hymn which contained the expression "*God* was crucified." Cyril, as we have seen, after the Council of Ephesus had consented to sign a formula which recognized, though somewhat ambiguously, the two natures of the Saviour; but many of his adherents were disobliged by his subscription, and the controversy soon broke out afresh. It commenced, as before, in Constantinople.

Eutyches, from whom Eutychianism derived its name, was abbot of a monastery in the neighbourhood of the Eastern capital. He rarely left his cloister; as a devout ascetic he was second in reputation only to the monk Dalmatius who had rendered such aid to Cyril and his friends in the Council of Ephesus; and Eutyches himself had taken a very prominent part in opposition to Nestorius. Flavian, now Bishop of Constantinople, had offended a most influential courtier; and this imperial favourite, the eunuch Chrysaphius, formed the design of removing the obnoxious prelate, and of placing the abbot, who was his godfather,[1] in the episcopal chair. A counterplot was concocted to disqualify Eutyches for promotion. At a synod held in Constantinople in A.D. 448, he was charged by a bishop, named Eusebius, with heresy; and though Flavian, who presided, and who foresaw the

---

[1] In primitive times parents presented their own children for baptism; but, when monachism was established, the inmates of the cloister often acted as sponsors for foundlings and others. According to ecclesiastical law, only *one* sponsor was admitted in each case. Bingham, xi. 8, § 2, 9, 11.

confusion which such a process must create, attempted to stop it in its preliminary stages, he was unable to prevail on the complainant to withdraw the accusation. The result showed that his fears were not unfounded. When first summoned to answer for himself, Eutyches refused to leave his cloister; but the firmness of his judges at length compelled submission; and he then appeared before the synod attended by an imperial officer, and a large escort of monks and soldiers. In reply to the interrogatories addressed to him, he endeavoured, at the commencement of his examination, to avoid any more positive statement by declaring that " he did not permit himself to wish to comprehend the essence of the Lord of heaven and earth "[1] but, when more closely pressed, he admitted his belief of *only one nature* in the Saviour. The body of Christ, as was well known, had been usually designated by him *the body of God*; and when questioned on this subject, he admitted that it was not of the same substance as other human bodies.[2] Eutyches was a presbyter as well as an abbot; and, when he persisted in refusing to renounce his sentiments, he was deposed from both offices, and excommunicated.

The monk was not to be put down by any such sentence. He was now the most influential personage of his order at Constantinople; he could reckon on the support of an immense multitude of his brethren; and his godson, the great courtier Chrysaphius, was his steady patron.[3] After having in vain applied for a new trial, he resolved to submit the case to a higher ecclesiastical tribunal. The interference of Theodosius II. was solicited and secured; and a council, to pronounce a decision on the views of Eutyches, was summoned, by imperial authority, to meet at Ephesus in A.D. 449.

This convention, known as the "Robber Synod,"[4] from the fraud and violence by which it was characterized, holds a bad

[1] See Neander, iv. 223.

[2] Evagrius, i. 9. *Liberatus Diaconus*, cap. xi. This dispute respecting the two natures led to various discussions concerning the body of Christ—some maintaining that it was not liable to decay; and others, that it was not subject to hunger, thirst, and pain.

[3] *Liberatus Diaconus Breviarium*, cap. xi.

[4] Leo I. appears to have suggested this title, when he speaks of "quidquid in illo Ephesino non judicio sed *latrocinio* potuit perpetrari." *Epist.* xcv. 2, *Opera*, tom. i. 943, edit. Migne.

pre-eminence among ecclesiastical convocations. Its president was Dioscorus, the successor of Cyril in the see of Alexandria. This prelate, in point of intellect, was much inferior to his predecessor; but he had equal ambition and far greater recklessness. The proceedings were conducted without much regard to law, precedent, or decency; and the council often presented the appearance rather of a meeting of hostile political factions than of a grave Christian judicatory. When a report was read stating that, at the Synod of Constantinople, Bishop Eusebius had asked Eutyches whether he acknowledged the doctrine of the two natures, the uproar reached a climax. "Away with Eusebius!" shouted the reverend judges—"Banish Eusebius! Let him be burned alive! As he cuts asunder the two natures in Christ, so let him be cut asunder!"[1] All the members were not, however, prepared to join in this fierce outcry. There were some utterly opposed to the views of Eutyches, and means were taken to compel these dissentients to concur with the rest of the assembly. A mob kept up a system of intimidation outside the church; for a whole day the bishops were immured within its walls; soldiers and brawny bullies were introduced into the church itself, and placed on benches immediately behind those whose resistance was anticipated; and votes were thus extorted by the influence of sheer terror. Flavian, Bishop of Constantinople, is said to have received all manner of insults, and even blows, from the furious Dioscorus; and a monk, named, Barsumas,[2] who was admitted to a seat in this council, is reported to have shouted "Strike him! Strike him dead!" as the president was employed in the undignified exercise of beating and kicking his brother patriarch.[3] It is certain that Flavian died a few days afterwards, in consequence of the bodily and mental sufferings he endured at this disreputable synod.[4]

All the proceedings of the second Council of Ephesus were dictated by its tyrannical chairman. Eutyches was acquitted of the charge of heresy, and restored to his former position as a

[1] *Binii Concilia*, ii. 49, 76, edit. 1618.
[2] This Syrian abbot sat and voted in this council as the representative of the monks. Hefele, *Conciliengeschichte*, ii. 332. Abbots began now to sit in councils. See Bingham, vii. c. iii. § 13; and Döllinger's *History of the Church*, ii. 164.
[3] Evagrius, ii. 2. See also Milman's *Latin Christianity*, i. 205.
[4] Hefele, *Conciliengeschichte*, ii. 363; *Liberatus Diaconus*, cap. 12. Liberatus, who was a deacon of Carthage, flourished in the sixth century.

presbyter and abbot: Flavian—so soon to close his earthly course—was deposed from the patriarchal dignity; and Eusebius also was degraded. An imperial edict confirmed these decisions.

The triumph of Eutyches was short. Leo I., distinguished from all his successors of the same name by the title of *The Great*, now filled the episcopal chair at Rome; and never before had it been occupied by a prelate of so lofty pretensions, or of such address, eloquence,[1] and political ability. At this time the Western Empire was tottering to 'its fall; but its increasing weakness was favourable to the growth of the papal power—as the sovereign was often obliged to crave the aid of the Church, and, in consequence, to submit to the dictation of its most influential functionary. Leo had sagacity to see that the theological divisions in the East could be made available for the maintenance of his claims as the heir of Peter; he had no reason to apprehend the encroachment of the Bishop of Constantinople so long as that dignitary was engaged in a deadly struggle with the Bishop of Alexandria; and, as his aid was eagerly sought by each of the contending patriarchs, he might contrive to obtain from both an acknowledgment of his ecclesiastical pre-eminence. He was decidedly opposed to the views of Eutyches; but, to a memorial transmitted from the abbot, at an early stage of the proceedings, he had returned, indirectly, a mild answer.[2] When a General Council was proposed, after the deposition of Eutyches by the synod of Constantinople, Flavian also had appealed to the Pope by sending him an epistle deprecating the idea of such a meeting, and requesting his co-operation in an effort to prevent its convocation. Leo replied in a document displaying consummate tact and talent. This letter, or *Tome*, as it is sometimes called,[3] is an elaborate exposition of the subject in controversy, setting forth, as the faith of the Church respecting Christ, the doctrine of one person in two distinct natures. Leo assumes that, as the bishop of the apostolic see, he had a right to issue such a manifesto; that the ecclesiastical belligerents were bound

[1] Preaching had fallen into disuse in Rome long before the time of this prelate, but he revived the practice. See Bingham, book xiv. c. iv. § 3.

[2] See Dorner, div. ii. vol. i. 405. See also a letter addressed to him by Leo in *Binii Concil.* tom. ii. p. 6.

[3] It is Epistle xxviii. in Migne's edition of Leo's *Works*, where it may be found, tom. i. 755-782.

to submit to his decision; and that, with such a judgment for the guidance of the Church, the meeting of a General Council was unnecessary. We may well suppose that Flavian must have been sadly puzzled by this missive. Though disposed, under the circumstances, to defer to Leo, and to accept an arbiter so unfavourable to Eutyches, he must have felt that, by this mode of settlement, the claims of his see would be compromised, and the bishop of Rome distinctly acknowledged as the authoritative arbiter of ecclesiastical controversies. He was not, however, obliged to submit to this alternative. The second Synod of Ephesus was held in despite of his remonstrances; and when an attempt was made in that assembly to read the letter or tome of Leo, it was set aside, on the pretence that certain other official communications of higher importance were entitled to precedence.[1] Nor was this all. The legates of the Pope who appeared on the occasion were treated with marked indignity: and one of them, who conveyed the earliest intelligence of the proceedings to Rome, escaped with difficulty from Ephesus. After such a public affront, Leo was bound to exert himself, with all his influence, to subvert the acts of the "Robber Synod."[2]

The Italian patriarch had not long to wait for an opportunity of testifying his dissatisfaction with the movements of the Eutychians. It was desirable that Anatolius, the new Bishop of Constantinople, should be acknowledged in the Western Church; and Leo was accordingly requested to bestow on him the usual recognition. But the pontiff insisted, in the first instance, on the production of clear proofs of his orthodoxy. Anatolius must condemn the heresies of both Eutyches and Nestorius, and subscribe, in addition to several other formularies, the letter of Leo to Flavian. Commissioners entrusted with this negotiation, who were sent from Rome to Constantinople, enabled the Pope to maintain a correspondence with those who supported his theological views in the Eastern capital. The progress of political events hastened the overthrow of the party of Eutyches. His godson, Chrysaphius, fell into disgrace, and soon afterwards Theodosius II. died. Marcian, the new emperor, inaugurated an

---

[1] Evagrius, ii. 18. *Liberatus Diaconus*, cap. 12.
[2] This synod, according to some authorities, consisted of one hundred and thirty-five members; and, according to others, of three hundred and sixty. See Hefele, ii. 351.

ecclesiastical revolution. A synod called by his authority, and known as the fourth Œcumenical Council, assembled at Chalcedon in A.D. 451, deposed Dioscorus of Alexandria, condemned Eutychianism, and adopted the letter of Leo to Flavian as a symbol of orthodoxy. This famous convention, which was attended by six hundred and thirty bishops,[1] affirmed that Christ is " true God and true man; that He was like us in all things, yet without sin; that, according to His divinity, He was begotten from all eternity, and equal to the Father; that, according to His humanity, He was born of Mary the Virgin, and Mother of God; and that He has two natures unmixed and unchanged, undivided and not separated—the distinction of natures being by no means taken away by their union."[2]

The Council of Chalcedon did not restore peace to the spiritual commonwealth. Its resolutions were strenuously opposed by many, especially in Palestine and Egypt; and the dissentients, who were called *Monophysites*,[3] or Believers in One Nature, and who are still represented by the Copts, separated from the Catholic Church. For many years these malecontents continued to create much political disturbance, and at length, in A.D. 482, the Emperor Zeno issued an edict of union—the *Henoticon*[4]—by which he hoped to put an end to the controversy. This formula, which contains no recognition of the Council of Chalcedon, adopts the creed sanctioned at Constantinople in A.D. 381, and condemns Nestorians and Eutychians. The *Henoticon* obtained the approval of the patriarchs of Constantinople, Alexandria, and Antioch; but the bishop of Rome, on the ground that it involved an unholy compromise, gave it the most determined opposition; and, in consequence, a schism, commencing in A.D. 484, divided for thirty-five years the Eastern and Western Churches.

In A.D. 476 the Western Empire fell; and in the same year a usurper, named Basiliscus, mounted in the East the throne of the

---

[1] *Binii Concilia*, ii. 411. Pope Leo makes the number somewhat less: "*Sexcentorum fere* fratrum coepiscoporum nostrorum synodus."—*Epist.* cii. *Ad. Epis. Gall.*

[2] Hefele, ii. 453, 454.

[3] The Monophysites were subsequently called *Jacobites*, from one of their bishops, Jacobus Baradæus, who died at Edessa A.D. 578, after having greatly promoted their cause. The orthodox Greeks were called *Melchites*, or *King's Men*, as they adhered to the religion of the emperor.

[4] Ἑνωτικὸν, *i.e. uniting or making one*. Evagrius, iii. 12.

successors of Augustus. Basiliscus was able to maintain his position only for a year; and Zeno, who then recovered the sovereignty, was too much occupied at home to think of engaging abroad in a war of aggression. But, though the Eastern princes always considered that, as the legitimate heirs of the Western Empire, they had a right to wrest it from its barbarian conquerors, it was not until the early part of the sixth century that they practically asserted a title to any of its dismembered provinces. They then saw, however, that they could scarcely hope for the recovery of Italy without conciliating the bishop of Rome; and accordingly, to prepare the way for the restoration of fellowship between the Greek and Latin Churches, the *Henoticon* was superseded. But in the East the Monophysite controversy kept up a perpetual commotion. The Emperor Justinian, who reigned from A.D. 527 to A.D. 565, imagined that his great mission was to re-establish ecclesiastical peace; and yet he acted with so much indiscretion, that his interference only tended to aggravate existing divisions. His queen—the intriguing Theodora—by whom he was governed, was secretly attached to the Monophysites; and he was led by her to believe that the enemies of the Council of Chalcedon would be satisfied if certain parties, whose memory was peculiarly obnoxious to them, were publicly stigmatized. The individuals thus singled out for ignominy were Theodore of Mopsuestia, the theological teacher of Nestorius; Theodoret, bishop of Cyrus, the ecclesiastical historian, who had written much in support of the ill-treated patriarch; and Ibas of Edessa, a distinguished scholar and divine, who had published a letter reflecting on Cyril which the Monophysites could neither forgive nor forget. All these bishops were now dead nearly a century, but theological hatred still continued to pursue them with unabated acerbity. In A.D. 544 Justinian published an edict, which has acquired an unhappy notoriety from what has been called its " Condemnation of the *three Heads* or *Chapters*,"—that is, its anathema on the person and writings of Theodore, its anathema on the writings of Theodoret against Cyril, and its anathema on the letter of Ibas. Many loudly complained of this edict as rash and unwarrantable; for it seemed to them absurd that men who had died in the communion of the Church should be held up in this way to reprobation; but Justinian rewarded the monk Eutychius with the patriarchal throne of Constantinople,[1] because he supplied his sovereign with a new, and, as it was thought, an unanswerable argument in support of his anathemas—alleging that he thus followed in the footsteps of the good king Josiah, who ordered the very bones of the dead priests of Baal to be reduced to ashes.[2] This imperial edict did not at all improve the state of public feeling; and therefore, to add to its authority, Justinian convened, at Constantinople in A.D. 553, a synod, known as the fifth General Council—which ratified his condemnation of the Three Chapters. Vigilius, bishop of Rome, consented, after some hesitation, to give his sanction to the decisions of this assembly.

The Western Church had quietly concurred in the decrees of the General Councils of Ephesus and Chalcedon, and yet had hitherto evinced little interest in the Eutychian or Monophysite[3] controversy. It now entered into the dispute with all the alacrity of an eager partisan. The skill and valour of his great general Belisarius had established the dominion of Justinian in Italy; and the Pope soon felt the effects of the political revolution. The influence of the court of Constantinople at once predominated in Rome, and the Italian patriarch could no longer maintain that tone of independence he had been so long accustomed to assume when addressing the Eastern Emperor. Vigilius owed his appointment as bishop of the apostolic see to a base compact made with the Empress Theodora, by which he pledged himself to the condemnation of the Council of Chalcedon.[4] In a letter still extant he also undertakes to support Eutychianism. For some time after his elevation to the papal throne he did not venture to commit himself by any open avowal of the sentiments he had promised to uphold, as he found that public opinion in the West was vehemently opposed to the Egyptian school of theology; and when he was induced, by the pressure of imperial importunity, to act more decidedly, he encountered a most resolute resistance. The celebrated document, entitled his JUDICATUM, in which he approved of the condemnation of the Three Chapters, raised a storm of indignation. By the decree of a North African

---

[1] Evagrius, iv. 38.   [2] 2 Chron. xxxiv. 5.
[3] The Egyptian dissenters soon refused to be called Eutychians, alleging that they did not adopt all the views of Eutyches.
[4] *Liberatus Diaconus*, cap. 22. *Binii Concil.* tom. ii. pars. ii. 191, 192.

synod he was formally excommunicated.[1] When it was known that he had sanctioned the canons of the fifth General Council held at Constantinople, the dissatisfaction extended. But he died soon afterwards; and Pope Pelagius, who succeeded him, and who adhered to his policy, was deserted by many even of the bishops of Italy. The Church of Istria, and all connected with the metropolitan of Aquileia, renounced the fellowship of the Roman patriarch.[2]

In the seventh century the controversy relating to the constitution of the Person of the Mediator assumed a new aspect. Some, who maintained that Christ has two natures, were prepared to admit that he has only *one will;* and as the Monophysites, of course, held this doctrine, it was thought that a basis of union might here be found for the reconciliation of parties so long alienated. The Emperor Heraclius was most desirous to bring about a settlement; for the Mohammedan power was advancing with amazing rapidity, and the oppressed Monophysites were disposed to hail the Saracens as liberators. The divisions of the Church were, therefore, a source of great political weakness; and could the various parties be induced to unite in the recognition of this new statement of doctrine, the dangers which threatened the Empire from the followers of the false prophet might be averted or mitigated. The patriarchs of Constantinople, Alexandria, and Antioch, approved of the project; and Honorius, Bishop of Rome, also bestowed on it his sanction. Heraclius accordingly published, in A.D. 638, the well-known edict, called the ECTHESIS, or Exposition of the Faith, in which the doctrine of One Will is promulgated by imperial authority. But though many were anxious to terminate a controversy which had been carried on with so much bitterness for about two hundred years, this scheme proved unsuccessful; it was soon obvious that the views of the believers in the One Will—designated the *Monothelites*—were not destined to meet with general acceptance; and the opposition to them at length became so formidable that, in A.D. 648, the Emperor Constans II. deemed it expedient to issue an edict, known as THE TYPE, or Model, in which the Ecthesis was repealed, and silence imposed on the

---

[1] *Victoris Tununensis Chronicon.* Migne, *Patrol. Curs.* tom. lxviii. 958. Victor was an African bishop of the sixth century, and a contemporary witness.

[2] Döllinger, *History of the Church,* ii. 188. Neander, iv. 281.

contending theologians. This new law rather prompted than checked the zeal of the adversaries of Monothelitism; as they argued that the interests of orthodoxy were not to be betrayed by any such inglorious peace. Pope Martin I., a most arrogant and litigious churchman, led the opposition; and in a synod held at Rome in A.D. 649—called by some the First Council of the Lateran—anathematized both the Ecthesis and the Type, and all the abettors of Monothelitism.[1] His insolence met with a tremendous chastisement. He was seized, by order of the enraged Emperor, and carried in chains to Constantinople—where he would have been beheaded as a traitor, had not the Eastern patriarch, who was then on his deathbed, succeeded with difficulty in obtaining a commutation of the sentence. He was, in consequence, banished to the Crimea, where he died, shortly afterwards, in extreme wretchedness.

These severe measures succeeded for a time in compelling obedience to the caprice of the sovereign; but it became gradually more and more apparent that the Type could not secure tranquillity. At length the Emperor Constantine Pogonatus resolved to summon a council for the decision of the question of Monothelitism; and this convention, known as the sixth General Council, assembled at Constantinople in A.D. 680. The Roman Bishop Agatho, who was desirous to act, like his predecessor Leo I., as the arbiter of ecclesiastical controversies, looked forward to this meeting with deep anxiety; and, as he was opposed to the doctrine of the One Will, he laboured assiduously to secure its condemnation. In a letter to the Emperors[2] he expounded his views on the much litigated subject. "We assert," says he, "that as our Lord Jesus Christ has two natures, so also has He wills—a divine and a human; that from eternity He had the divine will and activity in common with the co-essential Father; and that He assumed the human will from us in time along with our nature. . . . We assert that these wills are not contrary to, and do not conflict with each other. . . . . When Christ says: 'Father, if it be possible let this cup pass

---

[1] See his Encyclical Epistle on the subject in Migne's *Patrol. Curs.* tom. lxxxvii. 120-134.

[2] The letter is addressed to Constantine, Heraclius, and Tiberius—as Constantine Pogonatus conferred on his two brothers the name of the imperial dignity, reserving all the real power to himself. See Gibbon, chap. xlviii.

from Me, nevertheless not as I will, but as Thou wilt,'[1] . . . He shews here two wills, and that the one is indeed human, or of the flesh, whilst the other is divine. . . . He who denies a human will in Christ will not acknowledge His human soul."[2] Another letter addressed by Agatho to the fathers of Constantinople, and written in the same style, was adopted by the assembled theologians as the symbol of orthodoxy. "We believe," said they, "that our Lord Jesus Christ is our true God; and we say that His two natures appeared in His one Person; . . . that He exhibited in this Person both His miracles and sufferings, the distinction of natures being preserved, inasmuch as each nature, in conjunction with the other, willed and wrought that which was proper to itself. Thus we confess two natural wills and operations mutually concurring for the salvation of the human race."[3]

The letter of Agatho would not have been so signally honoured by this Eastern Synod, had not the aspect of the political horizon suggested to the Greek Emperor the prudence of cultivating the favour of the Western patriarch. The Saracens were still extending their conquests; the Imperial power in Italy was on the decline; and the social influence of the Pope was, therefore, not to be disregarded. But the gratification derived by Agatho from the condemnation of the doctrine of the One Will was not without alloy; for, among the Monothelite heretics anathematized by this œcumenical council, was his own predecessor Pope Honorius.[4] The decision now adopted almost put an end to the controversy. From this date Monothelitism languished; and though, about thirty years afterwards, the Emperor Philippicus Bardanes endeavoured to promote its revival, the attempt was soon abandoned.[5]

[1] Matt. xxvi. 39.
[2] *Epistola ad Augustos Imperatores. Patrol. Cursus*, tom. lxxxvii. 1168, 1176, 1180, edit. Migne.
[3] *Binii Concilia*, iii. 185.
[4] The Roman Catholic Dupin defends the acts of this council against the groundless attacks of Pighius and Baronius. "These writers," says he, "could not endure to see Pope Honorius' name among the heretics condemned in this council, and that was the cause that moved the one openly to attack the acts of the council very rudely, and the other to charge them with corruption." *History of Ecclesiastical Writers*, Seventh Century, Third Council of Constantinople. See also Döllinger, ii. 196, 202; and Hefele, iii. 264-284.
[5] See Dorner, div. ii. vol. i. 206.

The great apostle has taught us that the weapons of the Christian's warfare are not carnal; but the Church has been slow to learn this important, though simple, lesson. When it has been ignored, how much misery has been the result! The sanctuary of conscience has been violated; brute force has supplied the place of conviction; and civil war has converted smiling landscapes into fields of blood and terror. Had the parties in the Eutychian controversy been confined to the use of spiritual weapons, the Church would have avoided much scandal, and the State would have escaped much confusion. History would not have been obliged to record the disgraceful scenes of the "Robber Synod," or to report the base tergiversation of Pope Vigilius. By their wanton interference in ecclesiastical affairs the Greek Emperors kept themselves in a state of almost perpetual turmoil. Every one of their theological edicts generated new heart-burnings and new disorders. The Henoticon rent asunder the Eastern and Western Churches; the condemnation of the three chapters embroiled whole provinces; in ten years it was found necessary to repeal the Ecthesis; and the publication of the Type only made "confusion worse confounded." The Empire was weakened by the absurd means employed to promote religious peace, and the Nestorians and Monophysites hailed the Saracens as their deliverers from Christian oppression. By foolishly dabbling in matters which they should have left to the courts of the Church, and by employing the secular power in support of ecclesiastical decisions, the Emperors compassed themselves about with sparks of their own kindling, and aggravated the rancour of theological contention. Christ came to promote peace on earth and good will towards men; and every system of policy which aims at the advancement of His kingdom by the establishment of a reign of terror is condemned by the spirit of His religion.

SECTION III.

WORSHIP AND CONSTITUTION OF THE CHURCH.

CHAPTER I.

THE LORD'S DAY.

THE controversy relating to the Lord's Day, which has been revived from time to time in England since the reign of Queen Elizabeth, involves some very grave issues; but, as occasionally conducted, it may seem little better than a war of words. It must be admitted, on all hands, that the day has been kept, without interruption, since the age of the apostles; and it is equally clear that, in the times of primitive Christianity, it was regarded as a divine institute. A heathen author,[1] writing immediately after the close of the first century, mentions its observance by the professors of the new faith; one of the earliest of the fathers speaks of it as the Sabbath of the Church;[2] and another, a few years later, tells us that it was honoured by the disciples, wherever found.[3] Its very name indicates its character. As the "Lord's House"[4] is a building dedicated to His service, and as the "Lord's Supper"[5] is an ordinance celebrated in remembrance of His mercy, so the "Lord's Day"[6] is a season which He claims as His own, and which is to be employed in the public and private exercises of His worship.

Whatever may be our explanation of the fact, we must acknowledge that, as the dispensation of the gospel superseded the dispensation of the law, so the Lord's Day supplanted the Jewish Sabbath. For a time, the Christians of Jewish descent kept the last as well as the first day of the week; and even in the fourth or fifth century there are traces of this double ob-

---

[1] *Plinii Epist.* x. Ep. 97.
[2] "Consider what He means by it—*the Sabbaths*, says he, which ye now keep are not acceptable unto Me. . . . For which cause we observe the eighth day." *Epist. of Barnabas*, xv.
[3] Justin Martyr, *Apol.* ii.
[4] Οἶκος Κυρίου, Septuagint, 1 Sam. i. 7, 24.
[5] Κυριακὸν δεῖπνον, 1 Cor. xi. 20.
[6] ἡ Κυριακὴ ἡμέρα, Rev. i. 10.

servance;[1] but, from the apostolic age downwards, the Lord's Day alone was respected by the great majority of believers. It has often been taken for granted that the Jewish Sabbath was a day of gloom—whereas, when celebrated by a pious Israelite, it was far otherwise; to him it suggested bright hopes and pleasant recollections; he called it "a delight"[2] and rejoiced before the Lord his Maker; and, from the beginning, the Lord's Day was also deemed a holy festival. "Sunday we give to joy," says Tertullian.[3] "On the Lord's Day," says he again, "we should avoid every care-inspiring habit and duty, and postpone even worldly business, that we may not give any place to the devil."[4] The Jewish Sabbath was "the holy of the Lord;"[5] "the Lord's Day" is the same. The Jewish Sabbath was the day of "holy convocation;"[6] the Lord's Day is the season appointed of God when we are not to forsake "the assembling of ourselves together."[7] The Jewish Sabbath was a *rest* from bodily labour; so is the Lord's Day.

When addressing the heathen, the early Christians called the first day of the week *Sunday;*[8] but, among themselves, it was known by the name given to it in the Apocalypse.[9] They preferred this designation to any other, and it was specially appropriate. Many of them had been accustomed from infancy to speak of the last day of the week as the Sabbath; it still retained that title; and the sudden transference of the Jewish nomenclature would have been attended with inconvenience and confusion. But it is abundantly clear that they considered the Lord's Day as *their* Sabbath—their weekly rest—their stated time for special fellowship with God, for religious instruction, and for Christian intercourse. They maintained that all the ten commandments are still obligatory;[10] and though, for the first

---

[1] As in the Apostolic Constitutions, bk. v. See also Bingham, xiii. ch. ix. § 3.
[2] Isa. lviii. 13.   [3] *Apol.* xvi.   [4] *De Orat.* xxiii.
[5] Isa. lviii. 13.   [6] Levit. xxiii. 3.   [7] Heb. x. 25.
[8] Kaye's *Ecc. Hist. illustrated from the writings of Tertullian*, 412.
[9] Rev. i. 10.
[10] Thus we read in Irenæus—"Decalogi quidem verba ipse per semetipsum omnibus similiter Dominus locutus est; et ideo similiter *permanent apud nos, extensionem et augmentum, sed non dissolutionem accipientia* per carnalem ejus adventum," lib. iv. 16, § 4, *Opera*, 1018, Migne ed. In like manner Tertullian speaks of our Lord as "imparting to the Sabbath Day itself, which from the beginning had been consecrated by the benediction of the Father, *an additional sanctity* by His own beneficent action." Tertullian, *Against Marcion*, iv. 12.

three centuries—when they were under heathen governors, a minority of the population, and a proscribed sect—they must have often been prevented from duly observing their sacred ordinances, they always recognized the first day of the week as a season which they should remember to keep holy. "For the eighth," says Clemens Alexandrinus, "comes to be properly the seventh, and the seventh manifestly the sixth; and *the one* (the eighth) *to be properly a Sabbath, and the seventh a working day.*"[1] In various appointments of the Old Testament, such as in the time for circumcision, the early fathers found types and shadows of the Christian institute.[2] Melito of Sardis, one of the most distinguished theologians of the second century, wrote a treatise "On the Lord's Day;"[3] and, though the work is now lost, the fact of its composition attests the importance then attached to the discussion of the subject. According to Origen, one of the marks of "the perfect Christian" is "the keeping of the Lord's Day;"[4] and the same writer undertakes to show that the weekly festival of the Church is better than its Jewish predecessor. "I wish," says he, "to compare our Lord's Day with the Sabbath of the Jews. For from the divine Scriptures it appears that on the Lord's Day the manna was first given to the earth. For if, as the Scripture says, it was collected in six continuous days, but on the seventh day, which is the Sabbath, it ceased, it undoubtedly began on the first day, which is the Lord's Day; so that if, from the divine Scriptures it appears that on the Lord's Day, God rained manna from heaven, and did not rain it on the Sabbath, let the Jews understand that even then our Lord's Day was preferred to the Jewish Sabbath—even then it was indicated that on their Sabbath no grace of God would descend on them from heaven, no celestial bread, which is the word of God, would come to them."[5]

---

[1] *Strom.* lib. vi. tom. ii. 366, Migne's ed.
[2] Justin Martyr, *Dialogue with Trypho*, 41.
[3] Euseb. iv. 26.   [4] *Contra Celsum*, viii. 22.
[5] *Hom.* vii. § 5, *in Exod. Opera*, ii. 345, ed. Migne. The sophistry of this reasoning is quite transparent; but it is plain from it that, in the opinion of Origen, the Lord's Day has even higher claims than the Jewish Sabbath. Another passage from this writer has sometimes been quoted in illustration of this subject. (Hom. xxiii. § 4, in *Num. Opera*, ii. 749-50.) He there speaks of "the observation of *the Christian Sabbath;*" but it cannot be clearly shown that he refers to the Lord's Day. It is, however, remarkable that in the Church of Ethiopia—a daughter of the Church of Alexandria to which Origen belonged—the Lord's Day

During the long night of persecution which preceded the recognition of the Gospel by Constantine, the disciples often painfully felt that their position interfered with the enjoyment of their weekly rest; and the first Christian Emperor, by the promulgation of an edict enjoining its observance, rendered them a most substantial service; for they were thus no longer subject to the mercantile and other disadvantages under which a sect, abstaining from business on a day kept only by itself, must necessarily labour. The edict was, no doubt, cautiously expressed; it did not even acknowledge their religion;[1] and yet in places where the Christians most abounded—in the towns and cities of the Empire—its beneficial operation must at once have been appreciated; as it required the courts of law and the workshops to be closed, and business to be discontinued. The agricultural population—still almost entirely pagan—were permitted on Sunday to pursue their husbandry; but, in granting this license, Constantine appears to have acted in accordance with his own views of political expediency, and not in obedience to the promptings of Christian advisers. His confidential ecclesiastical counseller, Eusebius the historian, would have taught him that the law of the fourth commandment applied to the first day of the week. "The Word," says he, "by the New Testament has *transferred and transposed the feast of the Sabbath*[2] . . . and handed down to us, as an image of the true rest, the [day] of salvation, the Lord's [Day], the first day of light. . . . On this day, being the day of light, and the first [day], and [the day] of the true sun, we ourselves also, assembling after an interval of six days, celebrate the holy and spiritual Sabbath."[3] Athanasius, another contemporary of Constantine and the greatest theologian of his age, also bears unequivocal testimony to the

---

was designated "*the Christian Sabbath*" at an early period. See Platt's *Ethiopic Didascalia, or Ethiopic Version of the Apostolical Constitutions*, p. 99, London, 1834.

[1] See Sect. I. Chap. I. of this Period, p. 65.

[2] Μετήγαγε καὶ μετατέθεικε τὴν τοῦ Σαββάτου ἑορτήν.

[3] Dr. Hessey affirms that "in no passage" of any writer of the fourth or fifth century "is there any hint of the transfer of the Sabbath to the Lord's Day." *Bampton Lectures for* 1860, p. 114. The testimony in the text, taken from Eusebius on the Psalms [Psa. xci. (xcii.), *Opera*, v. 1169, Migne ed.], as well as other passages quoted in this chapter and entirely overlooked by the Bampton lecturer, may convince every candid reader that he has not carefully consulted original authorities.

claims of the Lord's Day. According to this father, the Sabbath was originally instituted, not as a season of inactivity, but as a means of attaining a better knowledge of the Creator.[1] He tells us that the Jewish Sabbath—the end of the old creation—has become defunct; and that the Lord's Day—the commencement of the new creation—has taken its place.[2] He discovers an allusion to the Christian institute in the title of the sixth Psalm.[3] In the 24th verse of the 118th Psalm he recognizes a still more distinct reference. "This," says the Psalmist, "is the day which the Lord has made." "What can this be," asks Athanasius, "but the day of the resurrection of the Lord—the day which brought salvation to all nations—the day on which the stone rejected by the builders became the head of the corner?"[4]

Ambrose of Milan, another of the most eminent divines of the fourth century, expresses himself in much the same strain. He contrasts the existing Lord's Day of the Gospel with the obsolete Sabbath of the law; and occasionally applies to the Christian ordinance the name given to the seventh day in the fourth commandment.[5] Epiphanius speaks even more explicitly; for he transfers to the first day of the week the language of the decalogue. "This," says he, "is the day which God blessed and sanctified, because in it He ceased from all His labour, when He had perfectly accomplished the salvation, as well of those who are on the earth, as of those under the earth."[6] In the same spirit, Gregory of Nyssa, writing towards the close of the fourth century, describes the festival of the resurrection as "the Sabbath, the day of rest, which God blessed above other days."[7] Augustine also speaks of the Lord's Day as an ordinance of Divine appointment;[8] though he believed that the fourth com-

---

[1] *De Sabbatis et Circumcisione*, § 3, *Opera*, iv. 136, Migne ed.

[2] *De Sabbat*. § 4, 5.

[3] Upon Sheminith, or *Upon the Eighth*. Athan. *Expositio in Ps*. vi. *Opera*, iii. 75.

[4] *Expositio in Ps*. cxvii. (cxviii.) v. 24, *Opera*, iii. 479, Migne ed.

[5] *In Ps*. xlvii. § 1.

[6] *Hom. in Die Resur. Christi*, *Opera*, iii. 468, Migne ed. Petavius is of opinion that this Homily is not the work of the bishop of Salamis, but of another writer of the same name. Dupin and others are disposed to receive it as the genuine production of the bishop of Salamis.

[7] *In Christ. Resur. Orat*. i. *Opera*, iii. 601, Migne ed.

[8] "Eum Dominus suæ resurrectionis gloria consecravit." *Sermo*. ccxxi. *Opera*, v. 1090.

mandment applied literally only to the Jewish Sabbath.[1] Chrysostom maintains the divine authority of the seventh day festival. "God," says he, " has *taught us from the beginning* that, within the compass of a week, one whole day is to be set apart and consecrated to spiritual works."[2]

These views of the day of rest were sustained by the decisions of the Church and the laws of the Empire. The Council of Eliberis, held in A.D. 305, decreed that any one who absented himself from public worship for three Lord's Days in succession should be suspended from ecclesiastical privileges.[3] The Council of Nice, assembled twenty years afterwards, ordained that, on the Lord's Day, the people should pray *standing*[4]—a posture deemed more suitable than kneeling for those who celebrated a church festival. The Council of Laodicea interdicted manual labour, except in cases of necessity, on the first day of the week.[5] Constantine anticipated the law relating to it, already noticed, by ordaining that slaves, instead of being required, as in times past, to go before the magistrate for manumission, might formally obtain it on the Lord's Day at the church in presence of the Christian congregation.[6] He also required his soldiers at this season to rest from military exercises.[7] According to an enactment of Valentinian and Valens no debt could be legally exacted from a Christian on the sacred day.[8] Theodosius the Great still farther provided for its observance by prohibiting the transaction of all secular business, and by abolishing the Sunday games and spectacles which had so long afforded amusement to the multitude.[9] But it was found exceedingly difficult to enforce such legislation. The people loved their sports more than their religion; and, even when the prince of Christian orators was preaching in Constantinople, many of the citizens sometimes resorted to the

---

[1] "In lege, quæ duabus lapideis tabulis conscripta est, solum inter cætera in umbra figuræ positum est, in qua Judæi Sabbatum observant." *De Spiritu et Litera*, xv. *Opera*, x. 218, Migne ed. See also x. 594.
[2] In cap. i. *Genes. Homil.* xi. *Opera*, iv. pars prior. 89, Migne ed.
[3] Canon 21.
[4] Canon 20. "In Dominico die *stantes* oramus, quod est signum *futuræ resurrectionis*." Isidore of Seville, *De Eccles. Officiis*, lib. i. c. 24.
[5] Canon 29.
[6] This law was made in A.D. 316.
[7] Euseb. *Life of Constantine*, iv. 18.
[8] *Cod. Theod.* viii. 8, 1, ed. Haenel, 1842, c. 754.
[9] *Cod. Theod.* xv. 5, 2, ed. Haenel, c. 1452.

theatre rather than the Church. Chrysostom bitterly complains that, during his ministry in the Eastern capital, the holy day was thus desecrated.[1]

In the sixth, seventh, and eighth centuries, the keeping of the weekly rest was inculcated by divines, enjoined by councils, and made compulsory by royal regulations. The second Council of Maçon, held in A.D. 585, forbids any one "on the Lord's Day, under plea of necessity, to put a yoke on the necks of his cattle;" and declares that all should then be occupied "with mind and body in the hymns and the praise of God. For this," say these fathers, "is the day of perpetual rest—this is shadowed out to us by the seventh day in the law and the prophets."[2] Theodore, archbishop of Canterbury, who flourished about a century later, assures us that the Greeks and Latins agreed in their mode of keeping Sunday—that they neither baked nor bathed on it—that they then made no use of a vehicle, except to convey themselves to church—and that they did not indulge on that day in boating or riding.[3] Ina, king of Wessex, who commenced his reign shortly before the death of Theodore, guarded the observation of the day, by very stringent enactments.[4] An English council, held in A.D. 697, affixed a severe penalty to its violation by a freeman, and imposed a fine on any master who compelled his servant to work between sunset on Saturday and the corresponding hour on Sunday.[5] In several parts of Western Europe the Lord's Day was then understood to be comprehended within these limits.[6]

The multiplication of holidays interfered greatly with the due observance of this weekly religious festival; but still, even in ages of increasing darkness, its claims were, to some extent

---

[1] See his *Life* by Neander, i. 209, London, 1845.

[2] Canon I. Isidore of Seville, writing in the early part of the seventh century, thus speaks on this subject: "Quique ideo Dominicus dies appelatur, ut in eo a terrenis operibus vel mundi illecebris abstinentes, tantum divinis cultibus serviamus, dantes scilicet huic diei honorem, et reverentiam propter spem resurrectionis nostræ, quam habemus in illo." *De Eccles. Offic.* lib. i. cap. xxiv. § i.

[3] *Pænitentiale*, cap. viii.; *Patrologiæ Curs.* xcix. 931, edit. Migne. See this confirmed by Gregory of Nyssa, in *Resur. Orat.* iii.; *Opera*, iii. 657, Migne edit.

[4] See Sect. IV. Chap. I. of this Period.

[5] Spelman's *Concilia*, i. 195, 196.

[6] The Druids with the Gauls and Germans, as well as the Jews, reckoned time from evening to evening. Jackson's *Chronological Antiquities*, i. 19, London, 1752.

acknowledged both theoretically and practically. It was kept more or less strictly according to the state of piety in the Church, or the zeal and enlightenment of the instructors of the people—for the Christian teachers in all places did not equally appreciate its character and obligations. But, because in the seventh and eighth centuries the legislation relating to it was so stern and so exacting, it does not follow that it was then held in greater reverence than in the ages preceding; for the Sunday statutes of that period are rather evidences of the advancing barbarism of the times, and of the growing authority of ecclesiastics as statesmen and law-makers.

The blessings which this holy day has conferred upon the world are as varied as they are solid and enduring. The wearied beast, as well as the worn-out hireling, feels its advantages. Its influence, even as a sanitary ordinance, illustrates the wisdom and benignity of its divine author. The Lord's Day is a perpetual remembrancer of the duties which we owe to Him in whom we live, and move, and have our being. Without it a worse than Egyptian darkness would speedily overspread the Christian community. Without it, neither could the communion of saints be maintained, nor could religious knowledge be systematically and readily disseminated. No wonder that sceptics and infidels have ever cherished such a bitter antipathy to the institute! They constantly feel its power as the muniment of a hated faith. The Lord's Day, the ministry of the Gospel, and the Bible, are the three grand ordinances set up by the God of heaven for the enlightenment and renovation of a world lying in wickedness.

The spirit of the Lord's Day has often been strangely misconceived. By some the day has been frittered down into little better than a time of recreation; by others it has been converted into a season of oppressive austerity. Its very name attests that it is desecrated when dissipated in amusement; and the fact that it was kept originally as a day of joy proves that its character is misunderstood when it is made a day of mortification. Let it not be deemed unseemly should a smile now irradiate the countenance; and let it not be thought unwarrantable should the admirer of the beautiful and the good now gaze with delight on the glory of creation. If the day commemorates the rest of God when He finished the works which He had made, is it not most appropriate that we should now survey these works with wonder, love, and praise? The Lord's Day is not a fast,[1] but a festival; and why, therefore, should the body now fare worse than at other times? The day should be given to God; it should be devoted to religious improvement; but the outward appliances needful to promote health and cheerfulness should not be neglected, so that we may enjoy it at once as a day of rest from bodily labour and of earthly care, and as a day of spiritual refreshment. If rightly spent, it should be the happiest day of all the seven.

Those who maintain that the Lord's Day is not the Sabbath find it difficult to explain wherein these institutions substantially differ. The Lord's Day, according to the literal meaning of the designation, is to be kept holy to the Lord; and, as a divine appointment, its claims have been acknowledged from the earliest antiquity. The seventh day of the Israelites was, no doubt, to be observed with minute care, and its violation was to be visited with a tremendous penalty. A Jew could not kindle a fire on the Sabbath;[2] and, according to the judicial law, the transgressor of the fourth commandment was to be stoned to death.[3] These, however, were arrangements confined to the peculiar people; and they have accordingly passed away along with the other regulations of the Mosaic economy. But "the Sabbath was made *for man;*"[4] in an age when the hum of industry is heard all over the world its rest is even more required than when the Israelites were settled in the land of promise; and, as a portion of time set apart for spiritual improvement, it is still absolutely necessary. All the other precepts of the decalogue are confessedly of perpetual obligation, and, if the fourth commandment is no longer binding, why has it been placed among them? Why, like the others, was it pronounced by God Himself, and written on a table *of stone?* and why, since the days of the apostles, has it been recognized by the Church Catholic as a part of the moral law.[5] To such questions, those

---

[1] "It is a great scandal to fast on the Lord's Day." Augustine, *Epist.* xxxvi. 12; *Opera*, ii. 148, Migne edit.

[2] Exod. xxxv. 3.

[3] Exod. xxxi. 15; Numb. xv. 32-36.

[4] Mark. ii. 27.

[5] Even Augustine, who speaks as loosely on this subject as any of the fathers, does not venture to say that the fourth commandment has ceased to be obligatory.

who hold that the fourth commandment is a merely ceremonial ordinance have never been able to give anything like a sufficient answer. The title "The Lord's Day" reminds us that one day in seven is still to be given to our Creator; and that therefore "there remaineth the keeping of a Sabbath to the people of God."

CHAPTER II.

THE WORSHIP OF THE CHURCH.

THE recognition of the Gospel by Constantine inaugurated a new era in the history of sacred architecture. During the Diocletian persecution, places of Christian worship had been everywhere pulled down; but the adoption of their religion by the sovereign inspired the disciples with fresh zeal; and forthwith more spacious and ornamental edifices appeared all over the empire. Ecclesiastical architecture was generously patronised by Constantine. He erected not a few buildings at his own expense; and some of these churches emulated the magnificence of the far-famed temples of heathenism.[1]

The ecclesiastical structures of this period exhibited no little variety in the details of their arrangement; but they consisted, generally speaking, of three principal divisions—the *Chancel* or Sanctuary, the *Nave* or body of the building, and the *Porch* or Vestibule. The Chancel, which was commonly the eastern extremity of the church and of a semi-circular form, was surrounded by an enclosure of lattice-work,[2] and occupied by the clergy. Here, at the wall and in the middle, stood the episcopal

---

But he virtually sets it aside by teaching that it is now to be understood only spiritually. "Præceptum de Sabbato, quod carnaliter Judæi celebrant, nos spiritualiter agnoscamus." *Sermo.* ix. *Opera*, v. 80. He inculcates the observance of the Lord's day; but he does not see that this day is the Sabbath under another name. His idea is, "Ille vere observat Sabbatum, qui non peccat." *Serm.* cclxx. *Opera*, v. 1242. He insists, notwithstanding, most strenuously on the continued authority of the decalogue. "Quis est tam impius, qui dicat ideo se ista legis (Decalogi) non custodire præcepta, quia est ipse Christianus, nec sub lege, sed sub gratia constitutus?" *Contra duas epistolas Pelag.* lib. iii. 10, *Opera*, x. 594, Migne ed.

[1] See Eusebius, *Ecc. Hist.* x. 4; and *Life of Constantine*, iii. 50.
[2] From this lattice-work (*cancelli*) the word *chancel* is derived.

throne; on each side of it were the seats of the presbyters. Immediately in front of the bishop's chair, and at a short distance from it, was the communion table, better known by the designation of the altar. The preacher usually placed himself before it when he addressed the congregation. The Nave was appropriated to the use of the members of the church; the sexes were separated;[1] and, where galleries were not provided for the females, the seats allotted to them on the ground floor were not unfrequently distinguished by their somewhat higher elevation. Near the middle of the Nave was a platform ascended by steps called the *Ambo*.[2] There the lectors appeared when they read the Scriptures to the people, and there the singers stood when they conducted the psalmody. The Vestibule—separated by a railing from the Nave—was assigned to those who did not enjoy the privilege of church fellowship. Here might be seen one grade of penitents, and such Jewish and Gentile strangers as were induced by curiosity, or some other motive, to attend the service. At the entrance was a laver, or fountain, where the worshippers washed their hands[3] before going into the interior of the edifice. One of the side buildings was the *Baptistery*, in which the initiatory rite of the Christian Church was administered.

In the apostolic age baptism was often dispensed before a promiscuous multitude;[4] and no law prevented individuals unconnected with the Church from witnessing the observance of the Lord's Supper. But, towards the close of the second century, these ordinances began to be called *mysteries;* and, the more effectually to hedge them round with awe, none save communicants were suffered to be present at their celebration. Thus it was that, in the fourth century, the ritual was divided into two parts—*the service of the catechumens* and *the service of the faith-*

---

[1] Chrysostom admits that originally the males and females sat together. See Bingham, book viii. c. v. § 6.

[2] From ἀναβαίνω, to ascend.

[3] This custom was perhaps taken originally from the Jews. See Ex. xl. 31. As the heathen entered their temples they were sprinkled with lustral water, and the Church eventually adopted this rite. The holy water of the heathen was simply "a mixture of salt with common water, and the form of the sprinkling brush, called by the ancients *aspersorium*, or *aspergillum*, much the same" as Romish priests now use. Middleton's *Letter from Rome.*

[4] Acts ii. 41, xvi. 15.

ful.[1] The service of the catechumens consisted chiefly of the reading of the Scriptures and preaching. Strangers, whether Pagans or Jews, as well as candidates for baptism, might attend this part of the worship. At its close they withdrew, and the service of the faithful proceeded. Devotional exercises of praise and prayer prepared the members of the Church for approaching the communion table and partaking of the Eucharist. But when time had brought about other changes, the distinction between the service of the catechumens and the service of the faithful also became obsolete.

In primitive times the whole congregation joined in the psalmody; but, as zeal declined, a fastidious taste found undue encouragement; and the ordinary worshippers became more and more disposed to remain silent during this service. About the beginning of the fourth century, a new class of church officers, called *cantors*, was instituted; and the singing was gradually appropriated by these trained choristers. Ambrose, Bishop of Milan, patronised a style of sacred music which soon became exceedingly popular, as it was distinguished by its superior melody and modulation; and, upwards of two centuries later, Gregory the Great of Rome introduced the chant with which his name is still associated. The Gregorian chant could only be performed by a carefully educated choir; so that, when it came into use, the people could no longer blend their voices in the service of song. The Psalms of David were still commonly employed;[2] but the poetry of uninspired authors was not excluded; for hymns composed by Hilary, Ambrose,[3] Augustine, and others, were often heard in the congregation.[4] During the period before us organs were generally unknown at least in the Western Church,[5] and the psalmody was conducted without the aid of any instrumental accompaniment.

---

[1] Missa catechumenorum et missa fidelium. The word *missa*, from which our *mass* is derived, came into use as early as the fourth century. It is employed by Ambrose. When the service of the catechumens ended, one of the clergy made the announcement: "Ite, missa est," *i.e.* Go away, the congregation is dismissed. Hence the service itself began to be known by this technical designation.

[2] Bingham, book xiv. c. i. § 2.

[3] See Isidore of Seville, *De Ecc. Off.* i. 6.

[4] Bingham, xiv. i. § 17. The *Te Deum* was composed in the fifth or sixth century, probably by some Gallic poet. See Palmer's *Orig. Liturg.* i. 256, and Stillingfleet's *Orig. Britannicæ*, 227, London, 1840.

[5] Bingham, book viii. c. vii. § 14; Kurtz, p. 347. The organ is said to have

The early Christian ministers were not restricted to any prescribed forms of prayer. Their petitions varied according to circumstances, and, when the heart was full, they did not find it difficult to pour forth their feelings in appropriate utterances. But they generally adhered to a certain order of worship;[1] and as they repeated from time to time such prayers as they deemed seasonable, there was a considerable amount of sameness in the language of their public devotions. When heresies became rife, the catholic clergy, to guard the purity of communion, agreed on a common formula of questions to be addressed to candidates for baptism; and thus something like the germ of a liturgy originated; but, during the first three centuries, the reading of prayers was still unknown among Christians.[2] The first prayer prescribed by public authority was probably a formula drawn up by Constantine for the use of his army.[3] The new position acquired by ministers of the Gospel in the reign of this emperor led to extensive changes. Crowds of merely nominal converts, who carried their heathen tastes and prejudices along with them, flocked into the Church; and not a few of them at once gained admission into ecclesiastical offices.[4] These hireling pastors,

been known in England towards the close of the seventh century. See Soame's *Anglo-Saxon Church*, p. 275, and Hook's *Archbishops of Canterbury*, i. 198.

[1] Bunsen has done much to mystify this subject by confounding an order of worship and a liturgy; but surely there is a wide difference between a fixed form of prayer and a general arrangement of the service. Whilst Bunsen admits that "free prayer" was anciently and generally used even in the communion service (*Hippolytus and his Age*, iii. p. 63), he speaks of liturgies as possessing an antiquity of "upwards of seventeen hundred years" (*ibid.* iv. 139). He tells us that "in the second century, and even in the third, every town of any consideration had certainly its own service" (*ibid.* iv. 160), and yet he has published what he calls the "Church and House-Book of the Early Christians," as if they all adhered to one formulary. This Church and House-Book is merely his own version of the spurious Apostolical Constitutions; but some writers, who should have known better, have recently quoted it as a genuine document of the Ante-Nicene period!

[2] Palmer's *Origines Liturgicæ*, i. 9, 121, London, 1845. If no liturgy was then written, none could have been read.

[3] Eusebius, *Life of Constantine*, iv. 18, 19. Every Lord's Day the troops, drawn up in order in the open field were, on a signal given, to repeat this prayer all together. The prayer asserts the Being, Unity, Power, and Goodness of God; and the pagan soldiers were all obliged to repeat it. The Christian soldiers were at liberty to attend the Church. The Pagans were in the habit of repeating their liturgies after the officiating minister. See Peter Heylin's *Eccles. Vindic.*, p. 83, London, 1681.

[4] See Second Canon of the Council of Nice. See also Neander, iii. 203-5.

destitute of scriptural knowledge and spiritual experience, were obliged to borrow the forms of prayer employed by others; but they could not so readily commit them to memory; and as they were accustomed in the days of their paganism to the reading of a liturgy,[1] they imported that usage into the assemblies of the faithful. The growth of the hierarchical spirit and the jealousies created by the theological controversies of the times contributed to recommend the arrangement; for, with a view to promote uniformity and check heresy, metropolitans began to insist that only such prayers as had their special approbation should be rehearsed by the ecclesiastics within the bounds of their jurisdiction.[2] Some of the petitions offered up by the more illiterate clergy were not very agreeable to persons of education and refinement; and thus an additional argument was supplied for the adoption of carefully prepared formularies. Ambrose, Basil, Chrysostom, and other distinguished fathers of the fourth century are the reputed authors of ancient liturgies; and, though perhaps they had only a share in their compilation,[3] it is certain that such helps to devotion were then quite current. Churchmen maintained that the general use of a common Prayer Book tended much to advance the cause of catholic unity; and thus it happened that the liturgies of Rome, Milan, Constantinople, and a few other great sees, were by degrees very widely adopted. The first draft or outline of the Roman liturgy is said to have been made by a scholastic, or man of learning, of whom nothing more is known.[4] Pope Leo the Great, who died in A.D.

---

[1] "The magic and thoroughly formal character of the Roman religion . . . is discerned . . . in the contents of the *Roman formulæ of prayer*. Everything here depended on the words used—a mistake might render the whole prayer inoperative; but, if the formula was pronounced correctly, without a wrong word, an omission or addition, all disturbing causes and things of evil import being kept at a distance the while, then was success assured, independently of the intention of the person praying. Hence, as Pliny tells us, the highest officers of state, during religious acts, *had the formula read before them from a ritual*, one priest being obliged to follow attentively each word as it was pronounced, and another to keep silence among the assistants. *The Gentile and the Jew* by Döllinger, ii. p. 75, London, 1862.

[2] Bingham, ii. c. xvi. § 22. Isidore of Seville tells us that the Greeks were the first to compose prayers—"quasque (preces) primi Græci cœperunt componere." *De Ecc. Off.* i. 8.

[3] Palmer's *Orig. Liturg.* i. 68, 74, 75.

[4] Palmer, i. 114. Gregory I. apparently refers to this scholastic in his letter

461, probably composed some of its parts,[1] and Gelasius, one of his successors, submitted it to a thorough revision;[2] but Pope Gregory, who flourished about the beginning of the seventh century, made still more extensive alterations. His *Canon of the Mass* was much admired; and owing partly to this circumstance, and partly to the powerful influence of the great Italian bishop, this form was at length generally used throughout Western Christendom.

Oral instruction formed originally the most prominent duty of Apostles and Evangelists. In the New Testament, most of the names by which those admitted to the pastoral office are known, such as teachers,[3] ministers of the Word,[4] and preachers of the Gospel,[5] specially refer to its highest function. In the ancient Church bishops were ordinarily the only preachers; and, as such dignitaries were to be found only in the towns after the establishment of diocesan episcopacy, a sermon was rarely to be heard in a rural district. But, in the course of ages, a great change took place in all the arrangements of the Church. Presbyters began to preach;[6] and then deacons were permitted to undertake the same service.[7] In some places, however, this part of public worship gradually fell into abeyance. As free prayer was superseded by a liturgy, ritualism nearly extinguished preaching. Even in the beginning of the fifth century, an exposition of the Gospel, in an address from the pulpit, was never heard in Rome.[8] Leo the Great, who revived the practice of sermonizing in the ecclesiastical metropolis of the West,

---

to the Bishop of Syracuse, *Epist.* lib. ix. *Ep.* xii. Migne's *Patrol Curs.* lxxvii. 957. It is said that there was no written liturgy in use at Rome in the beginning of the fifth century. Hence the Greeks boast that their liturgy—that ascribed to Basil—is more ancient than the Roman. See *The Origin and Composition of the Roman Catholic Liturgy*, by Ivan Borovnitsky, p. 12, London, 1863.

[1] Palmer, i. 118.
[2] *Ibid.* i. 116.
[3] Eph. iv. 11; Acts xiii. 1.
[4] Luke i. 2.
[5] Matt. iv. 23; 1 Tim. ii. 7.
[6] Augustine is said to have been the first African presbyter who preached when the bishop was present. See Potter on *Church Government*, p. 154, London, 1839.
[7] Bingham, ii. c. xx. § 11.
[8] *Ibid.* xiv. c. iv. § 3.

acquired much reputation by delivering discourses—seldom more than from eight to ten minutes long.[1] Gregory the Great also signalised himself by his labours as a preacher; but few popes followed their example, and, throughout the West, the teaching of the people, by means of addresses in the Church, was very much neglected. In the East, where pulpit oratory was more cultivated, and where the preacher sometimes occupied the attention of his auditory for upwards of an hour,[2] the sermons were often calculated rather to entertain than to edify. When narrating the history of the Nestorian controversy, we have seen how, during this part of the service, the people sometimes deviated far from the sobriety so becoming in the house of God. As the speaker proceeded with a popular discourse he was greeted with stamping of feet, waving of handkerchiefs, and shouts of acclamation; and, when he happened to offend his congregation, he had to encounter a volley of contradictions or a storm of hisses.[3] When the Church was thus transformed into a theatre, and when the Gospel was treated as an ordinary message, it was not to be expected that the auditors could derive much profit from the service, or depart under very serious impressions.

In relation to baptism, the Church of the fourth century was in a rather anomalous position. Many infants were baptized; but the children of Christian parents often reached maturity, and sometimes old age, before they received the ordinance. Since the rise of Montanism an impression prevailed that grievous sins committed after baptism could scarcely be obliterated; and, therefore, that, if the rite could safely be delayed, so much the better. The example of Constantine himself, to whom it was administered immediately before his death, exercised a very unhappy influence; for others, who professed a belief in the Gospel, were thus encouraged to remain, all their days, in the condition of catechumens. Many never thought of applying for baptism until either overtaken by some alarming sickness, or about to enter on a life of monasticism. Some of the most eminent pastors who flourished about the close of the fourth and beginning of the fifth century protested against this

---

[1] Bingham, xiv. c. iv. § 21.
[2] Some of the sermons of Chrysostom were of this length.
[3] Bingham, xiv. c. iv. § 27. See also Sect. II. Chap. IV. of this Period, p. 195.

irregularity,[1] as they saw that the children of the faithful were thus deprived of spiritual advantages which they might have otherwise enjoyed. Their remonstrances led to the more general observance of infant baptism; but the increasing superstition of the times sadly obscured its true import and disfigured its scriptural simplicity. It was almost universally believed that it washed away the guilt of sin, and that it was tantamount to regeneration.[2] In addition to exorcism and signature with the sign of the cross, the candidate was anointed; salt or milk and honey were then administered:[3] and the act of immersion or sprinkling was followed by what was called the kiss of peace and several other frivolous ceremonies. Parents were originally sponsors for their own children;[4] but godfathers and godmothers were now introduced; and the parties united by this species of spiritual relationship were treated by the Church, in the article of marriage, as if within the prohibited degrees of kindred.[5]

In the ancient Church baptism was immediately followed by unction and the imposition of hands. In some cases olive oil was employed; and, in others, a perfumed ointment composed of various ingredients.[6] When there had been some informality in the baptism previously administered, this ceremony—whether performed by a bishop or a presbyter—was understood to supplement the deficiency. It was at first merely an appendage to the initiatory rite of the Christian Church, and was therefore dispensed to infants as well as to adults; but, by degrees, it assumed the rank of a distinct ordinance, known by the name of Chrism or Confirmation.[7]

The Lord's Supper, as celebrated in the early Church, was a very beautiful yet simple ceremony. After an exhortation and a prayer by the bishop, bread—perhaps in a basket of osier—and

[1] Gregory Nazianzen, *Oratio*, 40, *Opera*, tom. i. p. 648.

[2] Augustine sometimes makes the distinction—as when he says that "the sacrament of baptism is one thing and the conversion of the heart another." See Wiggers, *Augustinism and Pelagianism*, p. 77.

[3] Isidore of Seville, *De Ecc. Off*. ii. 21. See also Neander, iii. 435, 436; and *Apost. Constit.* lib. viii. 43.

[4] Bingham, xi. c. viii. § 2.

[5] Guericke's *Manual of the Antiquities of the Church*, by Morrison, p. 241, London, 1851.

[6] Coleman's *Antiquities of the Christian Church*, p. 130. See also Covel's *Account of the Present Greek Church*, 183-4.

[7] In the Greek Church confirmation is still administered to infants.

wine—in a cup of wood or horn—were distributed to the worshippers. But in process of time the Eucharist began to be considered as a grand mystery; the rites connected with it were multiplied; the uninitiated were carefully excluded from the place where it was dispensed; in the wealthier churches the elements were presented in vessels of silver or of gold adorned with jewels; and the accidental dropping of a particle of bread, or the spilling of a drop of wine, was deprecated as a dreadful profanation. But, throughout the period before us, the cup, as well as the other symbol, was given to those admitted to the holy table,[1] and the recipients participated standing.[2] During the time of communicating a Psalm was sung;[3] the clergy partook first, and the people afterwards. Some communicated daily, some weekly, and some only once a year.[4]

Many of the fathers speak of the Eucharist in the most exalted strains; but their language is often vague and rhetorical, and perhaps they themselves attached no very definite ideas to several current forms of expression. Their object was to magnify the mystery; and they did not therefore scrupulously weigh their figures of speech. Some of them, indeed, when referring to the ordinance, use phraseology which would still be adopted by evangelical Protestants. Thus Eusebius of Cæsarea describes Christians as celebrating "the remembrance of Christ's sacrifice by the symbols of His body and blood."[5] Augustine, when explaining the words uttered by our Saviour at the institution of the Supper, tells us that by Christ's body is meant "the symbol of His body;"[6] and even Pope Gelasius, who lived in the fifth century,[7] asserts that what is used in the sacrament "does not cease to be the substance or nature of bread and wine."[8] But others

---

[1] Pope Gelasius strenuously condemns the use of the bread without the cup. Migne's *Patrologiæ Cursus*, lix. 141.

[2] Hence the deacon says, in what is called the *Liturgy of St. James*, "Let us *stand* decently, let us *stand* devoutly, let us *stand* with the fear of God and contrition." *Greek Liturgy of St. James*, by Trollope, p. 142, Edinburgh, 1848. See also Augustine, *Epist.* lv. c. 15, *ad Jan.*

[3] Often the thirty-fourth Psalm.

[4] *Guerike's Antiquities*, by Morrison, p. 249-251.

[5] *Demonst. Evang.* i. c. x. p. 39.

[6] *Contra Adimant.* c. 12. See also *De Doctrina Christiana*, iii. c. ix. xvi.

[7] He occupied the papal chair from. A.D. 492 to A.D. 496.

[8] "Certe sacramenta, quæ sumimus, corporis et sanguinis Christi, divina res est, propter quod et per eadem divinæ efficimur participes naturæ *et tamen esse non*

treat the subject very differently, and something like the doctrine of consubstantiation seems to have been floating in the minds of not a few of these authors. After the rise of the Nestorian and Eutychian controversies, the Lord's Supper was frequently employed to illustrate the theories of the disputants; and from this date the views entertained respecting it became more precise and intelligible. It was believed that Christ's body and blood are united to the bread and wine in the Eucharist in much the same manner as divinity is united to humanity in the Person of the Redeemer.[1] The way was thus prepared for the admission of transubstantiation—but that dogma was not established until long afterwards.

The honours paid to the martyrs in early times generated much superstition. The disciples—assembled in the Catacombs, or other cemeteries, to keep the anniversaries of their sufferings—partook of the Lord's Supper at their graves; and the fervid prayers offered up on such occasions not unfrequently contained petitions for the happiness of the faithful departed. In the Eucharist believers were understood to hold communion with the whole Church, whether on earth or in heaven; and warm-hearted preachers of a poetic temperament might see nothing very incongruous in the expression of a desire for the felicity of those who were already glorified. The idea of an intermediate state where souls are purged from the stains of venial sin now found encouragement; it was sanctioned somewhat equivocally by Augustine,[2] and afterwards very decidedly by Gregory the Great;[3] and as it furnished a doctrinal basis for prayers for the dead, it is not strange that such prayers appear in the ancient liturgies. The notion that the Lord's Supper is a real sacrifice also became prevalent; its mysterious efficacy was supposed to extend into the world of spirits; at the instigation of surviving relatives it began to be celebrated on behalf of the deceased; and thus what have been called *masses for the dead* were silently established.

The Paschal festival, now known as Easter, was introduced very soon into the Church; and we have seen how, towards the

---

desinit substantia vel natura panis et vini." See Hagenbach's *History of Doctrines*, i. 372, 373.

[1] See Neander, iv. 448.
[2] *Enchiridion ad Laurentium*, c. 68, 69.   [3] *Dialog.* iv. 39.

close of the second century, all Christendom was agitated by a controversy relative to the mode of its observance.[1] The question was settled in A.D. 325, when the Council of Nice required conformity to the Roman practice. Pentecost, or Whitsuntide,[2] was kept by some in the early part of the third century; but Christmas was of much later origin. It began to be celebrated in the West about the middle of the fourth century, and twenty-five years afterwards it found its way into the East.[3] According to ancient traditions our Lord was born in spring, or in the month of May;[4] but that portion of the year was already occupied by two great anniversaries, and it was desirable that a different season should be allotted to another commemoration. In December, during the heathen holidays called the *Saturnalia*, the people had long been accustomed to all manner of merry-making, and the 25th of that month was distinguished as the *Feast of the winter solstice*. When Christianity became the religion of the multitude there was still a hankering after the old pagan jubilee, and an attempt was therefore made to supersede it by the institution of a new festival in honour of the birth of our Saviour. The experiment was only partially successful, for many traces of former superstitions still remained, and even to the present day they are perpetuated as part of the rites of a merry Christmas.[5]

The feast of Epiphany, kept on the 6th of January, was brought from the East into the West during the fourth century. An idea prevailed in some quarters that our Lord's birth and baptism took place on the same day of the year;[6] and this festival seems to have been originally intended to commemorate both these occurrences; but, when Christmas was established, Epiphany was invested with another significance, and was said to be a remembrancer of the *manifestation* of Christ to the Magi, or to the Gentiles, or of His first miracle in Cana of Galilee.[7] Other festivals were subsequently instituted. Among these may be mentioned the feast of Stephen, on the 26th of December, to

---

[1] Period I. Sect. II. Chap. II. p. 39.

[2] Baptism was then usually administered, and, as the newly baptized wore white garments, the Lord's day when it was celebrated was called *White-Sunday*.

[3] See Neander, iii. 416.

[4] Clemens Alexand. *Strom.* lib. i. p. 340, ed. Coloniæ, 1688. See also Greswell's *Dissertations*, i. 461-462; and Coleman, 189.

[5] Coleman, 190, note.   [6] Some drew this inference from Luke iii. 23.

[7] See Neander, iii. 415.

commemorate his martyrdom; the feast of John the Evangelist, on the 27th of December; the feast of the Innocents, on the 28th of the same month, in remembrance of the slaughter of the infants at Bethlehem; the feast of the Circumcision of Christ, on the 1st of January; the feast of the Purification of the Virgin, or Candlemas, on the 2d of February; the feast of the Annunciation of the Virgin, or of the Conception—perhaps better known as *Lady Day*[1]—on the 25th of March; the feast of John the Baptist, commemorative, not of his martyrdom, but of his birth, on the 24th of June;[2] the feast of the Apostles Peter and Paul, on the 29th of June; and the feast of All Saints, finally appointed for the first of November.[3]

Various writers have exhibited much anxiety to show that some of these feasts may be traced up to the age of the apostles, but they have entirely failed to prove that any of them can claim such a high origin. They were obviously instituted to satisfy Jewish or Gentile prejudices, and not a few of them supplied the place of festivals previously observed by the converts to Christianity. Easter and Whitsuntide, the two most ancient, corresponded to the Passover and Pentecost; and we cannot suppose that they had the sanction of Him who instructed His apostle to say to the Judaizing disciples: "Ye observe days, and months, and times, and years. I am afraid of you, lest I have bestowed upon you labour in vain."[4] . . . . Let no man judge you in meat, or in drink, or in respect of an holy day, or of the new moon, or of the Sabbath days, which are a shadow of things to come; but the body is of Christ."[5] The feast of the Innocents was apparently a substitute for the heathen "festival of infants," when little children received presents of wax dolls;[6] the feast of the Circumcision was fixed for New Year's Day, a festival which the old Romans celebrated by the interchange of gifts and compli-

---

[1] See Hislop's *Identity of Babylon and Rome*, p. 22-3. Cybele was called *Domina*, or our Lady.

[2] The festival of a saint is usually celebrated on the day of his death.

[3] Boniface IV., in A.D. 610, obtained by gift the Pantheon at Rome, and consecrated it to the honour of Mary and all the martyrs, as it had before been sacred to Cybele and all the gods. The feast of all the martyrs was celebrated originally on the 12th of May. Large crowds congregated in Rome at this festival; and in consequence Gregory IV., in A.D. 834, transferred it to the 1st of November—when provisions are more easily obtained—and called it the feast of All Saints. It is preceded by Hallowe'en, *i.e.* Holy Eve.

[4] Gal. iv. 10, 11.   [5] Col. ii. 16, 17.   [6] Kurtz, 219; Neander, iii. 419.

ments;[1] the feast of the Purification of the Virgin anticipated by a few days the festival of the *Lupercalia*, when the purification of the land was symbolically celebrated;[2] and the feast of John the Baptist occurred about the time of the festival of Vesta, or the day of the summer solstice. At an earlier period some of the more zealous disciples kept the heathen holidays as seasons of fasting and humiliation; but subsequently the rulers of the Church were disposed rather to strip them of their pagan dress and convert them into Christian festivals. Thus, about the beginning of the seventh century, when the monk Augustine was officiating in England as a missionary, Pope Gregory the Great recommended him to permit the inhabitants, under certain restrictions, to enjoy their old celebrations. Their heathen temples were to be changed into places of Christian worship, and, on their ancient festival days, the people were permitted to congregate round these edifices, to erect booths, and to indulge in feasting and joviality.[3]

Nothing, indeed, can be more evident than that, as soon as Christianity became the religion of the State many of the forms and appendages of heathenism were adopted by the Church. The mitre of a bishop was the apex, or official head-dress, of a flamen or pagan hierophant;[4] his episcopal crosier was the lituus or divining staff of an augur;[5] and the patriarch of the West assumed the designation of Pontifex Maximus, the very name of the high-priest of Jupiter.[6] In the days of Tertullian, or in the

---

[1] Neander, iii. 423.

[2] Smith's *Dictionary of Greek and Roman Antiquities*, article *Lupercalia*.

[3] Bede, i. 30. "This circumstance may account for the retention of many Saxon names in matters connected with religion. Thus Yule, the old name for Christmas, is derived from Jule, a Saxon feast at the winter solstice; and Easter from the goddess Eostre, who was worshipped with peculiar honours in April. Lent signifies spring. From the deities Tiw, Woden, Thunre, Friga, and Saterne, are derived the names of the days of the week." Short (bishop of St. Asaph's), *History of the Church of England*, note, p. 7. In Ireland there are still traces of the two great heathen festivals of Samhain and Belltaiuc, or Belltine, celebrated at May Day and Hallowe'en. See Todd's *St. Patrick*, 134, 500, and Moore's *History of Ireland*, i. 205, London, 1836.

[4] See Smith's *Dictionary of Greek and Roman Antiquities*, art. *Apex*.

[5] Murdock's *Mosheim*, by Soames, i. 369. See also a curious fact mentioned in *Scotland in the Middle Ages*, by Cosmo Innes, p. 285, Edinburgh, 1860.

[6] See Middleton's *Letter from Rome*. This writer remarks that "Caligula was the first who ever offered *his foot to be kissed* by any who approached him." The Roman emperor acted as Pontifex Maximus.

early part of the third century, a seller of frankincense was deemed unworthy of church-fellowship, because he supported himself by vending an article employed so largely in the heathen worship;[1] but, within little more than a hundred years afterwards, the Christian temples were filled with odours which till then had issued from the altars of superstition.[2] The use of wax lights at worship during the day was also of pagan origin.[3] Nor were the Christians ashamed to ape the religious processions of the heathen; so that a crowd of disciples, as they moved along singing litanies,[4] and headed by professing ministers of the Gospel in white surplices, might have been almost mistaken for a pagan mob,[5] headed by their priests, on the way to offer sacrifice. Even some of the favourite petitions introduced into the prayers of the sanctuary were borrowed from the pagan offices;[6] and to the same source may be traced the vain repetitions to be found in so many of the ancient liturgies.[7]

The imperial court had scarcely embraced the Christian faith, when the dangers with which the Church was threatened by this new alliance began to appear. Constantia, the sister of Constantine, expressed a desire to possess a likeness of Jesus; and though the request was withdrawn when Eusebius, the ecclesiastical historian, condemned it as unlawful,[8] and as leading to a violation of the second commandment, there was from this period a growing disposition to clothe the ritual with meretricious decorations, and to make it equally fascinating to the senses as the worship of the heathen. Before the close of the fourth century, representations of the Saviour were ostentatiously displayed in several

---

[1] Tertullian, *De Idolatria*, xi.   [2] *Apostol. Canons*, iii.; Evagrius, vi. 21.
[3] Middleton's *Letter from Rome*.
[4] As to the origin of Litanies, see Rawlinson's *Herodotus*, ii. 84.
[5] "At these solemnities (of pagan Rome) the chief magistrate used frequently to assist, in robes of ceremony, attended by the priests in surplices, with wax candles in their hands, carrying upon a *pageant* or *thensa* the images of their gods, dressed out in their best clothes. These were usually followed by the principal youth of the place, in white linen vestments, or surplices, singing hymns in honour of the god whose festival they were celebrating."—Middleton's *Letter from Rome*.
[6] See Covel, *On the Greek Church*, p. 90, where, speaking of the *Kyrie Eleison*, he says: "This ejaculation or short prayer was used by the heathen in their auguries or divinations, as we find in Arrian's *Epictetus*." See also Murdock's *Mosheim*, by Soames, i. 347.
[7] Thus the *Kyrie Eleison* is sometimes repeated fifty times in succession. See Covel, p. 90, Cambridge, 1722.
[8] See Guerike's *Antiquities*, by Morrison, p. 111.

churches, and the remonstrances of eminent bishops failed to put a stop to their exhibition. The multitude, never thoroughly divorced from paganism, were unwilling to give up the use of images; their predilections were indulged; and, in the beginning of the seventh century, we find Pope Gregory the Great pleading for the presence of pictures in places of worship.[1] Another practice sanctioned by the example of the imperial family soon became exceedingly popular. In A.D. 326, Helena, the mother of the Emperor, visited Palestine, was baptized in Jordan, and discovered, as was believed, the very cross on which our Lord suffered.[2] Crowds of pilgrims now commenced to move towards Judea, that they might see what have been called "the holy places;" and the strangers returned home bearing relics of various kinds, to which they ascribed wonderful virtues. These relics brought high prices; without some of them, to impart the benefits of their reputed sanctity, new churches could not be well dedicated; they were enclosed in precious cases, and treated with extraordinary reverence. Other superstitions soon multiplied. Prayers for the dead were followed by the invocation of saints and angels; and the number of deceased persons deemed worthy of this species of worship rapidly increased. Mary, the mother of our Lord, received the honours of a goddess. Even in the latter part of the fourth century, a female community in Arabia, known as the Collyridians,[3] offered cakes to her as to the Queen of heaven. At the time their gross impiety was condemned; but, after the Nestorian and Eutychian controversies, she was generally acknowledged as the "Mother of God," and invoked, in both the East and West, as a divine mediator of singular potency.

The worship of the sanctuary, as celebrated towards the close of the period before us, contrasts most unfavourably with the simple and spirit-stirring services of the days of the Apostles. The "joyful noise" of the whole congregation was superseded by the singing of the choir; and the variety of free prayer was supplanted by the sameness of a liturgy. The exposition of the Word—the most prominent portion of the ritual in primitive

---

[1] *Epist.* cv. *ad Serenum.*

[2] This story of the cross was probably invented after the death of Constantine. Eusebius, who mentions Helena's visit, takes no notice of it. See Jortin, i. 385-390, London, 1846.

[3] Murdock's *Mosheim*, by Soames, i. 414. They derived their name from the small round cakes (κολλυρίδες) which they offered. See Jer. xliv. 18, 19.

times—was very much neglected; for, in many cases, the officiating minister was incompetent to preach, and the reading of "one of the homilies of the holy fathers"[1] supplied the place of a popular discourse. The Eucharist, dispensed with so little of anything like parade in the first century, was now converted into a grand scenic exhibition, at which the multitude stared in mute bewilderment. Had a Roman Christian of the days of Paul awoke, after a sleep of seven centuries, and entered one of the churches of the city, he might well have thought that he was still in the old pagan capital; for the clouds of incense, and the groups of statuary, and the priests in splendid vestments reading the prayers, would have been quite sufficient to generate the impression that he was the spectator of some heathen solemnity.

CHAPTER III.

THE HIERARCHY.

WHEN Constantine the Great embraced Christianity, the Episcopal system on a small scale was already an ancient institute. But, though introduced in a few cities one hundred and eighty years prior to the Council of Nice,[2] it prevailed only partially even at the close of the second century.[3] Originating in the great towns, it steadily extended itself from these centres of influence. For a time the members of the new order jealously maintained the principle of episcopal parity, and protested against a "bishop of bishops;"[4] but they could not well carry out their idea of Catholic unity without a graduated hierarchy; and, in the latter half of the third century, there are various traces of the commencement of archiepiscopal government. In the beginning of the fourth century, the strife among the bishops for pre-eminence created much scandal.[5] In various places, the chief pastor of the provincial capital claimed the dignity of moderator or chairman; in others, the senior bishop presided over the remaining bishops of the district; and elsewhere

[1] Bingham, ii. 20, § 11.   [2] *Ancient Church*, 535-558.
[3] *Ibid.* 514, 515.
[4] Tertullian, *De Pudicitia*, i.; Cyprian, *Con. Carth.*
[5] Euseb. viii. 1.

neither custom nor positive agreement had yet settled the order of official precedence.[1]

The bishop of the civil metropolis began to be generally acknowledged as the president of the provincial synod about the period of the recognition of Christianity by Constantine. Convenience[2] and the wish of the Emperor, no doubt, recommended the arrangement. But the whole system of ecclesiastical polity was in a very crude and unsatisfactory condition at the time of the first General Council; and several questions of jurisdiction were submitted for determination to the Nicene divines. Their decision might have been anticipated. The leading members of the council had a personal interest in the sustentation and advancement of primatial power; and, as they were supported by the sovereign,[3] they contrived to obtain a favourable deliverance. The Nicene fathers did not, however, venture to define the prerogatives of the great prelates, neither did they pretend to base them either on the canons of the Church or on the authority of Scripture. Aware that they were the growth of circumstances, that they were sanctioned neither by divine nor statute law, and yet that, in some quarters, they could plead the prescription of perhaps three-fourths of a century,[4] they confirmed them on the ground of long-established usage. "Let,"

---

[1] *Ancient Church*, 599, 600.

[2] The metropolis was usually the largest town in the province; it was most accessible by the public roads; and its bishop was the churchman with whom his brethren could most readily correspond. The metropolitan at first derived no emolument from his office. He was simply constant moderator of the provincial synod.

[3] Eusebius admits that Constantine took a very active part in Church judicatories. He often performed the duty of a metropolitan. "He exercised a peculiar care over the Church of God; and whereas in several provinces there were some who differed from each other in judgment, he *assumed as it were the functions of a general bishop constituted by God, and convened synods of his ministers.* Nor did he disdain to be present and sit with them in their assembly, but *bore a share in their deliberations,* endeavouring to minister to them all that pertained to the peace of God. . . . Those whom he saw inclined to a sound judgment, and exhibiting a calm and conciliatory temper, received his high approbation, for he evidently delighted in a general harmony of sentiment; while he regarded the refractory and obstinate with aversion." *Life of Constantine,* i. 44. After such a statement it is easy to understand how the structure of the Church assumed the form of the political fabric in the days of Constantine.

[4] Since the time of Cornelius of Rome in the middle of the third century. See *Ancient Church*, 597-8.

said they, "the *ancient customs*[1] be maintained which are in Egypt, and Libya, and Pentapolis, according to which the bishop of Alexandria has authority over all these places. For this is the *custom* in the parallel case of the bishop of Rome. In like manner in Antioch, and in the other provinces, the privileges are to be preserved to the churches. But this is clearly to be understood that if any one be made a bishop without the consent of the *metropolitan*, the great synod declares that he shall not be a bishop. If, however, two or three bishops from private contention oppose the common choice of all the others, it being a reasonable one and made according to the ecclesiastical canons, let *the choice of the majority* hold good."[2]

The singularly vague style of expression here employed by these ecclesiastical legislators is all the more remarkable when contrasted with the precision of several of their other canons. It is impossible to tell what degree of authority was thus secured to the Egyptian primate; and the language might be interpreted as conveying the absurd allegation that the admitted existence of a custom at Rome settled the disputed question of custom at Alexandria. On the subject of ecclesiastical jurisdiction these Nicene judges betray an unwillingness to enter into details, or to commit themselves to any very positive statement. They could not well avoid the discussion; for it was forced on them by the disorderly acts of the Melitians—a party who held much the same views as the Novatians,[3] who disowned the bishop of Alexandria, and who ordained ministers in places over which he claimed supervision. But the word *metropolitan* occurs for the first time as the designation of a church functionary in the canons of this council—a fact which proves that, though a very few leading prelates may have exercised something like primatial power for two or three generations, the system was only beginning to be generally developed. The last clause of the canon just quoted appears to have been added partly with a view to curb archiepiscopal tyranny, for it seems to include the metro-

---

[1] The Council of Chalcedon based certain rights of the see of Constantinople on ancient custom, though that see had acquired its position only in the latter half of the preceding century. See Cave, *Prim. Christianity, Dissert.* pp. 418, 419. The same council ruled that a prescription of *thirty years* settled the question of custom. See Canon xvii.

[2] Canon vi.   [3] See Sect. II. Chap. II. Period I., p. 40.

politan himself among the two or three dissentients who are not to be permitted to overbear the will of the majority.¹ Still, the language is so ambiguous that it may admit of a different exposition; and we know that, not long afterwards, the primate claimed a veto on all episcopal appointments.

After the conversion of Constantine we hear, for the first time, of *country bishops*. In the preceding century all the members of the episcopal order were at least theoretically equal; the pastor of the poorest village in the province had the same ecclesiastical status as the prelate of the chief city; and in an African synod of eighty-seven bishops, held in A.D. 256—though some of these brethren had the care of very small flocks—Cyprian of Carthage distinctly acknowledges that each individual among them was as independent as himself.² But the appearance of a new nomenclature in the early part of the fourth century marks the establishment of a real and invidious distinction. About that time pastors of rural districts begin to be known as *chorepiscopi*;³ and in the Synod of Ancyra, in A.D. 314, they were forbidden to ordain presbyters or deacons.⁴ Thirty years afterwards a vigorous attempt was made to suppress them altogether; for the Council of Sardica, in A.D. 343, decreed that "a bishop be not ordained in a village, or small city, where a single presbyter is sufficient, lest the name and authority of a bishop be brought into contempt."⁵ This canon did not, however, effect their total extinction. Hence the Council of Laodicæa, held about A.D. 360,⁶ declared that "bishops ought not to be appointed in villages and rural districts—but visiting presbyters—and that those already appointed do nothing without the sanction of the city bishops."⁷

The recognition of Christianity by the State produced a vast change in the position of the bishops of the great capitals; for they soon acquired important civil privileges,⁸ their revenues

---

¹ The 2d Council of Arles, held in the fifth century, required the metropolitans to obey the will of the majority. See Canon v.

² *Con. Carthag.* See also Hefele's *Christian Councils* by Clark, pp. 17, 18, Edinburgh, 1871.

³ *i.e.* τῆς χώρας ἐπίσκοποι, or bishops of the country.

⁴ Canon xiii. ⁵ *Ibid.* vi.

⁶ The exact date cannot be well ascertained. It certainly took place between A.D. 343 and A.D. 387. See Hefele, *Conciliengeschichte*, i. 724.

⁷ Canon lvii.

⁸ They acted as secular judges. Bingham, book ii. c. 7, § 1. They sat also in

rapidly increased, and they mingled on equal terms with the highest officers of government. Meanwhile the bishops of villages, or rural districts, remained in comparatively humble circumstances. This state of things could not continue; for, except in name and order, the poor minister of a country parish was *not* the ecclesiastical peer of the opulent chief pastor of the provincial metropolis; and the prelates contrived to put an end to the anomaly by gradually extinguishing the rural dignitaries. But they did not succeed without determined opposition; and, far down in the middle ages, we find the chorepiscopi sometimes performing the act of ordination.[1]

In Africa, ancient arrangements were long maintained. There, as has been stated in a former chapter,[2] though parishes might be small, no pastor was ever styled a chorepiscopus: there, the bishop was the only preacher:[3] and there, all ministers of the Word were of the same power and dignity. There, a bishop with only one presbyter was nothing unusual:[4] and the metropolitan might be a country parson who dispensed the ordinances of religion every Lord's day to his little flock in an humble meeting-house. The African primate succeeded to his position by seniority; and in all his proceedings he was amenable to his brethren. Such, no doubt, were the ecclesiastical arrangements common before the time of Constantine: and their preservation here is to be ascribed to the agitation created by the Donatists. These ancient Puritans arraigned their adversaries as the abettors of corruption; and, in the face of watchful rivals supported by the mass of the Christian population, the Catholics dared not venture on extensive innovations. Hence it is that in Africa we recognise so many of the more ancient outlines of the Church constitution.

The Sardican canon of A.D. 343, enacting that "a bishop be not ordained in a village, or small city," where a single presby-

---

civil conventions or councils. See *Rise and Progress of the English Commonwealth* by Sir Francis Palgrave, part i. 337, London, 1832.

[1] Thus, in the ninth century, the famous Gottschalk was ordained by a chorepiscopus.

[2] Section I. Chap. V. of this Period, towards the end.

[3] Optatus, vii. 6; *Life of Augustine* by Possidius, c. v.

[4] See the objection of Posthumian to the claim of the bishop of Carthage, and the argument based on this fact in the third Council of Carthage. *Binii Concilia*, tom. i. p. 577, *Coloniæ Agrippinæ*, 1618.

ter could perform all the necessary duty, was totally neglected in Africa;[1] but, in other parts of the Empire, it was systematically carried into operation. The result soon appeared in a gradual transition from parochial to diocesan episcopacy. A few of the chief pastors had long before extended their jurisdiction beyond the walls of the cities in which they were located; but in many places a parish and a bishopric were still synonymous. Owing to peculiar circumstances some small sees were preserved; but most of them disappeared in little more than half a century; and it is interesting to trace the progress of their suppression. The history of a single case will better illustrate the subject than any more general statement.

When the Council of Sardica decreed the extinction of the minor bishoprics, there was at least one member of the assembly who must have felt humiliated as he signed its canons. This was the individual who subscribes himself Dioscorus, *Bishop of Tenedos*.[2] The little rocky island in the Ægean Sea which enjoyed his pastoral inspection was barely the size of an ordinary parish;[3] at present it contains a population of from six to seven thousand souls; in the former half of the fourth century, the census was probably much less; and a considerable number of its inhabitants were pagans. If Dioscorus lived in a central position, he was distant little more than two miles from the most remote family under his episcopal jurisdiction. But his see did not long survive the date of the Sardican canon; and he himself was perhaps the last of the bishops of Tenedos. Less than ninety years afterwards, or in A.D. 431, a somewhat singular signature appears among the subscriptions to the canons of the General Council of Ephesus. It is that of John, who styles himself *Bishop of all Lesbos*.[4] This island, which is more than one hundred miles in circumference, at present supports about forty thousand inhabitants. At one time it contained several

---

[1] Part of the bishops summoned to meet at Sardica retired to Philippopolis, so that its canons, in consequence of this schism, had not the authority they would have otherwise possessed. In the early part of the fifth century they seem to have been unknown in Africa. The fathers who retired to Philippopolis endeavoured to open up a correspondence with the Donatists.

[2] Bingham, book ix. c. iii. § 18.

[3] According to Bingham it is "ten miles *in compass*." *Antiquities*, book ix. chap. iii. § 18.

[4] Johannes Episc. *totius Lesbi*. See Maurice's *Defence of Diocesan Episcopacy*, p. 405, London, 1691. In some copies of the subscriptions the word *all* is omitted.

bishoprics, among which were those of Mitylene and Methymna;[1] but the signature of this John testifies that a new system had been inaugurated, as he had the episcopal oversight of the whole population. Within the next twenty years prelacy made another stride in the Ægean; for, appended to the Acts of the General Council of Chalcedon in A.D. 451, we find the subscription of Florentius, "Bishop of Lesbos, Tenedos, Proselene, and the Ægiali islands."[2] Proselene, or Poroselene, a small island near Lesbos, had at one time a bishop of its own as well as Tenedos;[3] it is probable that the Ægiali islands had also enjoyed the same privilege: Lesbos, as we have seen, had several bishops—and John, in A.D. 431, seems to have considered he had attained no common distinction when he could sign himself bishop of it all; but the system still continued to advance, and hence Florentius, in A.D. 451, had the charge of so considerable a diocese. Another remarkable circumstance connected with this subscription remains to be told. Florentius subscribes the canons of the council by proxy, that is, by Euelpistus, *his chorepiscopus*.[4] We thus see that an inferior functionary was set up where a bishop had formerly been established.

The progress of diocesan episcopacy accounts, as well for the disappearance of the chorepiscopi, as for the gradual diminution in the number of the ancient bishoprics.[5] Some have

[1] Bingham, ix. iii. § 18.
[2] *Binii Concilia*, ii. pars. pri. 337; Maurice, 405.
[3] Bingham, ix. iii. § 18.
[4] *Binii Concilia*, ii. p. pr. 337. In another place he signs by another chorepiscopus named Eulogius. *Bin. Con.* ii. p. pr. 212.
[5] Gibbon, guided by Bingham, has estimated the number of bishops in the fourth century at 1800, giving 1000 to the Greek and 800 to the Latin provinces of the Empire (*Decline and Fall*, chap. xx.). This is very far below the true reckoning. In that part of Africa alone which belonged to the Western Church, there were at least 900 or 1000 Catholic and Donatist bishops. See Sect. I. Chap. V. of this Period, p. 125. In the fifth century, when many of the smaller sees had disapppeared, the Abbot Dalmatius reckoned the number of bishops at 6000, following, no doubt the common estimate. See *Binii Concil.* tom. i. pars. ii. 290. Italy, comprehending the whole country under the jurisdiction of the *Præfectus urbis* and the *Vicarius Italiæ*, was somewhat more extensive than the section of Europe now so designated, and contained, according to Bingham (ix. 5, § 1), 300 bishoprics. But there is every reason to believe that the number was much larger; for we know the names of so many sees only by the attendance of their bishops at synods or councils; and there was not anything like a full representation on such occasions. Bingham asserts that the bishops were most thickly planted about Rome. This is obviously a mistake. Rome was the place where

The Hierarchy.

alleged that the country bishops were originally subordinate to the city bishops; but all the historical evidence we possess is quite opposed to such a statement; and the theory that these humble dignitaries were primarily but episcopal assistants is contradicted by the fact that the prelates were all along impatient of their existence, and did not rest until they had accomplished their extirpation. The country bishops were most numerous where the city bishops were also most thickly planted; and we read of one prelate in the fourth century who had no less than fifty chorepiscopi under his jurisdiction.[1] The Bishop of Rome himself, in the middle of the third century, had not the charge of so many presbyters.[2] But the diocesan system was meanwhile gradually extended; and, though the Church gained immense accessions of numbers after its recognition by the State, bishops decreased as Christians multiplied.

The one hundred and eighteen provinces of the Roman Empire were grouped, about the time of Constantine,[3] into thirteen or fourteen larger sections called *Dioceses*. The arrangements of the Church were accommodated to these civil divisions,[4] for the chief pastor of the chief city of each diocese, under the title of *Exarch* or *Patriarch*, stood at the head of all its metropolitans. Rome, Constantinople, Alexandria, and Antioch, surpassed in wealth, population, and political influence, all the other cities of the Empire; and the chief pastors of these places were soon exalted above all the other exarchs or patriarchs. The Bishop of Jerusalem, or Ælia Capitolina,[5] after a protracted struggle, attained

---

councils generally met, and these conventions would, of course, be most numerously attended by the bishops of the neighbourhood. But it does not follow that in more remote districts there were fewer bishops. At a time when travelling presented so many difficulties, the more indigent bishops could not attend distant councils.

[1] Such, according to Gregory Nazianzen, was the case of Basil of Cæsarea, *Carmen. de Vita sua, Opera*, tom. ii. 8, Coloniæ, 1690.

[2] According to the testimony of Cornelius, the bishop, there were only forty-six presbyters connected with the Church of Rome at that time. See Euseb. vi. 43.

[3] Cave, *Primitive Christianity*, dissertation appended, 372, Oxford, 1840.

[4] "It is very plain," says Bingham, "that the Church took the model in setting up *metropolitical* and *patriarchal* power from this plan of the state," ix. i. § 4.

[5] This name, given in the time of the Emperor Hadrian, was used less frequently after the age of Constantine. The place then began to resume its former designation.

the same high position. By the decision of the first Council of Nice a certain amount of honour was conceded to him;[1] but he was still left subject to his metropolitan, the Bishop of Cæsarea. About this time the holy city began to attract great notice; it was visited by Helena, the mother of Constantine; and, at her instigation, splendid ecclesiastical edifices were erected on those spots connected with it which are specially memorable in the history of our Lord. The pretended discovery of the true cross,[2] and the marvels ascribed to it, gave new encouragement to superstition; pilgrimages were now made to the holy places; and all these circumstances contributed to add to the glory of the bishop of the mother church of Christendom. At the General Council of Ephesus in A.D. 431, his metropolitan, the Bishop of Cæsarea, was absent; and, as the patriarch of the Syrian metropolis was on the unpopular side, the Bishop of Jerusalem, who took a prominent part in opposition to Nestorius, openly ventured to maintain that Antioch should be subject to the ancient capital of Palestine. But he was unable to obtain support for so bold a proposition. At the Council of Chalcedon, in A.D. 451, he was somewhat more successful; for, though the Bishop of Antioch was permitted to retain his rank, he was obliged to give up a portion of his charge to his aspiring neighbour; and the Bishop of Jerusalem was placed fifth among the patriarchs.[3]

The history of New Rome shows clearly the intimate connection between the ecclesiastical and the political status of a city. At the time of the Council of Nice, Heraclea was the metropolis of the province to which Byzantium belonged; but, when this latter place was converted into Constantinople, Heraclea succumbed to the new capital of the Eastern Empire. The importance of Constantinople as the seat of government was at once universally acknowledged; and the second General Council, held in A.D. 381, placed its chief pastor above all other churchmen in Christendom except the Bishop of Rome. Had not

---

[1] "Since custom and ancient tradition have ruled that the Bishop of Ælia should be honoured, let him have the second place of honour, saving to the metropolis (Cæsarea) the authority which is due to it." Canon vii. of the Council of Nice.

[2] *Now* aptly designated in the calendar of the Book of Common Prayer for the 3rd of May—"*Invention* of the cross."

[3] Act vii. *Binii Concilia*, ii. p. pr. 272. The Bishop of Jerusalem had the charge of the three Palestines.

peculiar circumstances interfered, New Rome would have eventually supplanted even the ecclesiastical metropolis of the West as the centre of catholic unity.[1]

The establishment of metropolitans was preceded by ecclesiastical convulsions; for, towards the close of the third century, when the system was in process of formation, the bishops struggled with each other most pertinaciously for pre-eminence. When the patriarchs proceeded to distribute the metropolitans among themselves, the strife was renewed. The bishops of Cyprus, for instance, peremptorily refused to submit to this new supervision; and, assisted probably by their insular position, succeeded, not without a sharp controversy, in maintaining their independence.[2] The Bishop of Jerusalem was recognized as a patriarch only after a long and bitter warfare with his brother prelates of Alexandria and Antioch: the Bishops of Alexandria and Constantinople contended for generations; and the Church was at length rent in twain by the contests of the Bishops of Rome and Constantinople. No wonder that a good man of the order, wearied with these episcopal broils, exclaimed in agony of spirit, "How I wish we had no primacy, no precedence of place, no tyrannical prerogative of station! that we might be known by virtue alone! But, as the case now stands, the distinction of a place on the right or on the left or in the middle, a higher or a lower position, the going before or aside of each other, has given rise to many disorders among us to no good purpose whatever, and plunged multitudes in ruin."[3]

When the Apostles strove for official pre-eminence, our Lord said to them: "Ye know that the princes of the Gentiles exercise dominion over them, and they that are great exercise authority upon them; but it shall not be so among you: but whosoever will be great among you, let him be your minister; and whosoever will be chief among you, let him be your servant; even as the Son of Man came, not to be ministered unto, but to minister, and to give His life a ransom for many."[4] The greatest

---

[1] Immediately after the fall of the Western Empire, it began to claim precedence.

[2] Bingham, book ii. c. 18, § 1. They refused also to submit to the canon of Sardica ordaining the suppression of small bishoprics, and hence village bishops continued to be found in the island. See Sozomen, vii. 19.

[3] Gregory Nazianzen, *Oratio* xxviii. *Opera*, tom. i. 484.

[4] Matt. xx. 25-28.

minister of Christ is he who is most faithful, most humble, and most laborious. But this principle was completely set at nought when the hierarchy was fully organized; for the bishops occupied much the same position as the princes of the Gentiles, and exercised a lordship quite as oppressive and unscrupulous. The metropolitans and patriarchs had power to preside in synods, to ordain their suffragans, to hear appeals from inferior judicatories, to take charge of the affairs of vacant sees, to interfere between contending prelates, to visit bishoprics which were said to be neglected or mismanaged, and even to dictate the forms of worship to be used by those over whom they claimed jurisdiction.[1] Such authority in the hands of a despot or an enemy made his yoke intolerable. The tyranny of the great prelates culminated in the Papacy. Rome, the birthplace of the system, soon began to claim the rights of the first-born, and continued to assert her title until she had established her supremacy over the greater part of Christendom. The moderator of her small presbytery was transformed into a city bishop: this bishop, whose jurisdiction did not originally extend beyond the walls of the Italian capital, became at length a metropolitan who swallowed up all the country bishops around him; the metropolitan soon obtained the dignity of a patriarch; and then the patriarch appropriated the title of pope. Thus, from inconsiderable beginnings, the most gigantic spiritual despotism ever known was gradually consolidated.

CHAPTER IV.

THE GENERAL COUNCILS.

SOME modern writers have asserted that synods or councils commenced in Greece about the middle of the second century. This statement, based on the misinterpretation of a passage in Tertullian,[2] is destitute alike of probability and of historical evidence. As soon as we can trace the progress of the Church by the aid of documentary testimony, we find councils in operation all over the Roman Empire; and there is every reason to believe that they were established in the days of the Apostles.

---

[1] Bingham, book ii. c. 16, § 22.   [2] See *Ancient Church*, 610-614.

The General Councils. 253

At first they met in private and on a very limited scale; but, as persecution subsided, they assembled more openly; and, immediately after the promulgation of the edict of toleration by the Emperor Gallienus in A.D. 260, pastors from distant countries were seen sitting together in large ecclesiastical judicatories. The Council of Antioch, which deposed the celebrated Paul of Samosata in A.D. 269, was attended by some bishops from remote provinces.[1]

Latin theologians have dignified nineteen or twenty councils[2] with the name of œcumenical or general; but the propriety of the title is not very obvious. These synods, beginning with the Council of Nice and ending with the Council of the Vatican, are not particularly distinguished either by the authority under which they acted—by the multitude, learning, and piety of their members—or by the extent of the churches over which they exercised jurisdiction. The more ancient councils known as œcumenical[3] were all convened by the Roman Emperor; but similar meetings assembled under the same auspices, even though more largely attended,[4] have not been honoured with the same designation. The first seven general councils—which are also acknowledged by the Greek Church as œcumenical—all met in the

---

[1] Euseb. vii. 27, 28, 30.

[2] Bellarmine recognizes eighteen General Councils. *De Conciliis et Ecclesia*, i. c. v. Hefele acknowledges nineteen, at least partially. The following is his list: 1st, 1st Nice, A.D. 325; 2d, 1st Constantinople, A.D. 381; 3d, Ephesus, A.D. 431; 4th, Chalcedon, A.D. 451; 5th, 2d Constantinople, A.D. 553; 6th, 3d Constantinople, A.D. 680; 7th, 2d Nice, A.D. 787; 8th, 4th Constantinople, A.D. 869; 9th, 1st Lateran, A.D. 1123; 10th, 2d Lateran, A.D. 1139; 11th, 3d Lateran, A.D. 1179; 12th, 4th Lateran, A.D. 1215; 13th, 1st Lyons, A.D. 1245; 14th, 2d Lyons, A.D. 1274; 15th, Vienne, A.D. 1311; 16th, Constance, A.D. 1414-18; 17th, Basil and Florence, A.D. 1431-42; 18th, 5th Lateran, A.D. 1512-17; 19th, Trent, A.D. 1545-63. *Conciliengeschichte*, i. 57-8. Bellarmine and Hefele are agreed as to the first fifteen in this list. Bellarmine omits Constance and Basil, but acknowledges Florence. To these must now be added the Vatican Council of 1869.

[3] The title *œcumenical* (σύνοδος οἰκουμενική) occurs for the first time in the 6th Canon of the 1st Council of Constantinople. Bellarmine thus defines a General or Œcumenical Council: "Generalia dicuntur ea, quibus interesse possunt et debent Episcopi totius orbis, nisi legitime impediantur, et quibus nemo recte præsidet, nisi summus Pontifex, aut alius ejus nomine. Inde enim dicuntur œcumenica, id est, orbis terræ Concilia." *De Conciliis et Ecclesia*, i. 4.

[4] Such as the Council of Arles, the Council of Sardica, or the Council of Rimini. At Rimini there were at least 400 bishops—according to some above 1,000. See Cave's *Fathers*, ii. 313, Oxford, 1840.

East: among the three hundred and eighteen ministers[1] who sat in the first Council of Nice only eight or nine can be discovered who belonged to the Western Empire;[2] the first Council of Constantinople was attended by but one bishop from Western Christendom:[3] and other œcumenical synods contained no greater proportion of Latin members. The bishop of Rome was, perhaps, not even consulted before the calling of some of these early councils, and certain of their decisions gave him intense dissatisfaction; but, as their doctrinal decrees met with his approval, the Church of which he is the representative has taken them under its special patronage, and recognizes them as guides in the determination of theological controversies.

As the early general councils were summoned by the reigning sovereigns, the expenses of the ecclesiastical legislators were defrayed out of his treasury; and, when the fathers journeyed to the place of conference, the public conveyances were at their service. The wits of antiquity amused their contemporaries by describing the movements of the clerical travellers—telling how the imperial posting establishments were scarcely able to provide accommodation—how bishops, in their anxiety to be present in due time, galloped most uncanonically along the Roman roads—and how horses and mules were knocked up by their reverend riders. These convocations were very unequally attended; for, in the fourth General Council held at Chalcedon in A.D. 451, there were six hundred and thirty members,[4] or about double the number congregated at Nice; but the second which met at Constantinople, in A.D. 381, reckoned only one hundred and fifty

---

[1] This is the number commonly alleged, but perhaps it is merely a fancy estimate, as the number 318 was supposed to possess peculiar virtue. See Gen. xiv. 14. The signatures found in Binius only amount to about 225. Of these 15 are of chorepiscopi. Other lists do not contain so many signatures. See Cowper's *Syriac Miscellanies*, pp. 25-30. Eusebius (*Life of Constantine*, iii. 8) speaks of them as more than two hundred and fifty. Athanasius, who was also present, calls them "more than three hundred." *Epist. Def. Nic. Def.* ii. § 2.

[2] Stanley's *Eastern Church*, p. 127. Of these were Hosius of Corduba, Cæcilian of Carthage, Marcus of Calabria, Nicasius of Dijon, Domnus of Stridon in Pannonia, and the two Roman presbyters Victor and Vincentius.

[3] Acholius of Thessalonica. Pusey's *Councils of the Church*, p. 319.

[4] In the Definition of the Faith of the 3d Council of Constantinople, held in A.D. 680, the number of bishops in attendance on the first four General Councils is given as in the text. See Sect. II. Chap. V. of this Period, and *Binii Concilia*, iii. pars. i. 182.

members; and the third, assembled at Ephesus in A.D. 431, consisted of not more than two hundred.[1] The fifth and sixth General Councils, held respectively in A.D. 553 and A.D. 680, were attended each by about one hundred and sixty members. We cannot tell in what way the right to sit in either the first Council of Nice or the first Council of Constantinople was determined; nor how many who were summoned to either of these conventions, failed to appear.[2] Before the third General Council, the Emperor Theodosius the younger issued a circular letter, in which he required each metropolitan to bring with him as many bishops as he deemed expedient;[3] but complaints were made that an undue proportion of members from the neighbourhood of Ephesus were introduced into the assembly. As there were one hundred and eighteen provinces in the eastern and western sections of the Empire, and nearly as many metropolitans, it is obvious, even from an announcement of the numbers, that the Christian Church was very inadequately represented in most of the general councils. In the days of Constantine and Theodosius there did not exist the facilities for locomotion which are provided in the nineteenth century; and as very few bishops were willing to encounter the fatigue and inconvenience of a journey to a distant city, a large proportion of those who took part in these convocations resided not far from the place of meeting.

The general councils did not always hold their sessions in houses of worship. Some of them, including the first Council of Nice, assembled for deliberation in a spacious chamber of the imperial residence. The business even of the provincial synods soon began to be conducted with considerable formality; the members sat in a semicircle around their chief in the order of their seniority; and the oldest bishop occupied the most honourable place next to the chairman.[4] In œcumenical councils there was, of course, still greater ceremony; and the metropolitans and patriarchs claimed peculiar honours; but, with certain exceptions, the arrangements established in inferior judicatories were

[1] It thus appears that the Vatican Council of 1869 stands very high in point of numbers. It was attended by upwards of 700 prelates.
[2] The Emperor probably acted very much according to his discretion. To later synods some were specially summoned on the ground of their theological reputation—as Augustine to Ephesus. Death prevented his attendance.
[3] *Binii Concilia*, tom. i. par. sec. p. 158.
[4] *Ordo de Celebrando Concilio*, Isid. Mercat. ii. Mig. *Patrolog. Cursus*, cxxx.

here, no doubt, generally observed.[1] A prayer yet extant—remarkable, in times of increasing superstition, for its evangelical simplicity—is said to have been used from an early period at the opening of these conventions.[2] A copy of the Gospels, exhibited on an elevated seat or throne in the middle of the apartment, reminded every one who entered it that the Word of God, the great arbiter in all questions of faith and duty, was acknowledged as of supreme authority.[3] In later œcumenical synods the Pope claimed the right to preside either in person or by deputy, but such pretensions were unknown in the fourth century. The Roman bishop was not present at any of the earlier councils; the age and infirmities of Sylvester were assigned as the reason why he did not appear at Nice; and two of his presbyters, by whom he was represented, occupied there only a secondary position.[4] Meletius, bishop of Antioch, presided at the opening of the second General Council; and Cyril of Alexandria at the third. In several cases a number of individuals presided jointly; and at Chalcedon, in A.D. 451, the

---

[1] At the Council of Nice each member had a seat assigned to him "*according to his rank.*" Euseb. *Life of Constantine*, iii. 10. In this way Constantine may have managed quietly to settle the precedence of metropolitans.

[2] This prayer was used at the opening of the Vatican Council in 1869. It is as follows: "We are here, Holy Spirit, we are here—kept away from Thee, indeed, by the exceeding greatness of sin, but brought together specially in Thy name; come to us, be present with us, and deign to flow into our hearts; teach us what we should do, show us the way in which we should walk, work in us what we should perform. O Thou, who alone with God the Father and the Son possessest a glorious name, be Thou alone both the suggester and the framer of our judgments. O Thou, who supremely lovest equity, suffer us not to be the overthrowers of justice. Let not ignorance draw us to the left hand, let not favour lead us from the right path, let not the consideration of reward or of persons corrupt us, but join us effectually to Thyself by the gift of Thy grace alone. Let us be one in Thee, and in nothing let us deviate from the truth. As we are collected in Thy name, so in all things let us hold fast that which is right with well regulated piety, that our mind may differ from Thee in nothing, and that we may hereafter, for acts well done, obtain eternal rewards. Amen." This prayer, here given entire, may be traced back to the fourth Council of Toledo in A.D. 633, and contains internal marks of even a higher antiquity. It may be found in the works of Isidore Mercator, *Patrol. Cursus*, tom. cxxx. 11, and the *Pontif. Roman.* iii. 142, Paris, 1852.

[3] Stanley's *Eastern Church*, 139, 140.

[4] In the ordinary statements of the proceedings of the council, they are represented as subscribing immediately after Hosius, but it has been alleged that originally they occupied only the *fourth* place. See Grier's *Epitome of the General Councils*, p. 36, Dublin, 1828. See also Stanley's *Eastern Church*, pp. 143-4.

deputies of the Roman prelate sat, for the first time, as assessors with others.[1]

The meeting at Nice in A.D. 325 was in some respects distinguished above all the other general councils. Never was an ecclesiastical judicatory convened under circumstances more intensely interesting. The vital doctrine of the supreme deity of Christ had been assailed; the discussion had disturbed almost the whole of the Eastern Church; and the fathers of the Christian commonwealth were assembled to settle the controversy. Not a few of the members of the council were far advanced in life, and their earnest piety had been attested by the sufferings they had endured for their attachment to the faith. In one part of the meeting might be seen an aged bishop who had lost the use of his hands during the Diocletian persecution; elsewhere others were sitting who could have uncovered their backs or sides and exhibited the prints of torture; here and there were venerable confessors whose right eyes had been dug out by the heathen, and whose countenances were thus horribly disfigured; and, as several of the fathers entered the assembly, they halted or walked with difficulty, for they had been condemned to work as slaves in the mines, and the sinews of their legs had been seared to prevent them from escaping. These good men must have felt deeply as they gazed on everything around them. Not many years before, some of them had been immured in dungeons—now they found themselves in a palace; their scars and mutilations, once marks of ignominy, were now badges of honour; they could vividly call to recollection the reign of terror, when the approach of a band of soldiers would have thrown their whole assembly into consternation—now, on a gilded seat in the midst of them, with scarlet shoes and purple robe sparkling with jewels, sat the great Emperor himself, taking a kindly interest in their debates, whilst his guards were at hand to protect them from the slightest annoyance. Constantine was not yet baptized; but notwithstanding he acted on some occasions as chairman of this œcumenical council.[2] The ordinary president was Hosius

---

[1] As these deputies could not speak Greek, they were obliged to communicate with the council through an interpreter. See Dupin, *Eccles. Writ. Council of Chalcedon*, and Binius, ii. 73.

[2] Euseb. *Life of Constantine*, i. 44, iii. 10, 13.

of Cordova,[1] his confidential spiritual adviser; whilst Eusebius of Cæsarea, the ecclesiastical historian, and probably some others, assisted in preserving order.

The meeting of this first general council virtually celebrated the recognition of the Gospel by the first Christian emperor. The attention of men of all ranks throughout the Roman world was attracted to the great assembly; scholars, philosophers, and statesmen mingled in the crowd of onlookers; and there was a universal feeling that a spiritual revolution of portentous significance had just been accomplished. Constantine now deeply pledged his imperial power to the support of his adopted creed; and the system of enforcing religious uniformity by civil pains and penalties was immediately inaugurated. An idea prevailed in the ancient Church that, whilst matters of discipline might be decided by a majority of suffrages, questions of faith should be settled unanimously;[2] and the attempt strictly to carry out this principle led not unfrequently to harsh or violent proceedings. Unanimity was sometimes secured, as at Nice, by the deposition or banishment of dissentient members, and sometimes it was brought about by bribing the venal and overawing the timid. The aid of the State was often employed to reduce the hesitating or refractory to submission. The civil magistrate did not give these services for nothing. His ecclesiastical influence was felt to be very formidable. He convened synods when and where he pleased, intermeddled with their deliberations, and treated refractory bishops in a spirit of capricious tyranny. None of the canons of the early general councils were deemed valid until they had obtained his sanction; and when thus confirmed they had all the authority of the other laws of the Empire.

The assertion of the equality of the Father and the Son—the

---

[1] His name stands at the head of the members who subscribed its creed, and he is expressly distinguished by Athanasius as "the *president* of councils," as he presided both at Nice and Sardica. Athan. *Hist. Arian.* 42, *Opera*, tom. i. 743. Hefele maintains, without reason, that Hosius represented the bishop of Rome. No writer of the fourth century says so; and the authority of Gelasius of Cyzicus —on which he relies—is worthless. Hosius was appointed president by Constantine because of the high estimation in which he was held by him. There is nothing improbable in the story that the bishop of Cordova had been the means of the Emperor's conversion to Christianity.

[2] Kurtz, p. 156. Even the fathers of Trent, in the sixteenth century, are found appealing to this ancient arrangement. See Father Paul's *History*, book vi. p. 538, London, 1676. This principle was ignored in the Vatican Council of 1869.

doctrine decided by the theologians of Nice—involved various other questions which occupied the succeeding general councils of the fourth, fifth, sixth, and seventh centuries. The first Council of Constantinople, in A.D. 381, followed up the deliverance of the Council of Nice by proclaiming the Personality and Godhead of the Holy Spirit; and the Councils of Ephesus and Chalcedon still further developed the doctrine of the perfect deity and the perfect humanity of Christ, by affirming His existence as One Person in two natures. The second General Council of Constantinople, in A.D. 553, tried to conciliate the Monophysites, but the attempt proved unsuccessful. The sixth General Council consistently completed the system of theology already promulgated relative to the Person of the Saviour, by maintaining the perfection of His two natures, and by its condemnation of Monothelitism. All these decisions have since been approved by the voice of Christendom; and hence some have been led to speak in very extravagant terms of the synods by which they were adopted. Even by certain professing Protestants the first four general councils have been placed, in point of authority, almost, if not altogether, on a level with the Holy Scriptures.[1] But their promulgation of right views on matters of doctrine forms no essential difference between them and other ecclesiastical conventions; for many modern Church judicatories, advancing no claim to inspiration, have supported the same theological conclusions.

A perusal of all the canons of the early general councils is sufficient to reveal the fallibility of these assemblies. No enlightened student of Scripture would now venture to anathematize every one who hesitates to call Mary "the Mother of God;" and yet the General Council of Ephesus committed this folly. The Council of Chalcedon endorsed the system of monasticism; and even the Council of Nice sanctioned the division of the congregation into *Auditors, Prostrators, Co-standers,* and *Communicants.* The auditors were penitents required to withdraw from the Church when they had heard the Scriptures read and

[1] "The Act I. Elizabeth, c. i. § 36, in laying down rules for the judgment of heresy by the Court of High Commission, constitutes the decrees of these councils a requisite part of the rule whereby the court was to guided. And this law, though since repealed, has generally been taken to *govern the judgments of the ecclesiastical courts* in such cases." Bricknell's *Judgment of the Bishops upon Tractarian Theology,* p. 234, Oxford, 1845.

the sermon preached; the prostrators remained behind and knelt, or fell prostrate, as prayer was being offered for themselves; and the co-standers, who had nearly finished their course of penance, stood at prayer along with the faithful, but were not permitted to partake of the Eucharist. Each class occupied a certain place in the house of worship; and, according to the decision of the Nicene fathers, the lapsed were to remain *three years* among the auditors, *seven* among the prostrators, and *two* among the co-standers.[1] There is always great danger in such minute legislation; and we may question the wisdom even of a general council in excluding for *twelve years* from sealing ordinances those who had meanwhile exhibited satisfactory evidences of repentance.[2] In its zeal for religious uniformity, the Council of Nice condescended to make a law respecting the *posture* of the worshippers on the Lord's day. "That all things may be done uniformly in every parish, the holy synod decreed that all should offer up their prayers to God *standing*."[3] The Presbyterians and the Lutherans are almost alone among occidental Christians in observing the only rubric relative to worship prescribed by the first œcumenical council.

The assembly at Nice contained a larger proportion of pastors eminent for piety than any other of these general synods; but, though its proceedings have been very imperfectly recorded, there is ample evidence that its members too frequently betrayed indications of human infirmity. As soon as the bishops reached the place of convocation they began to criminate each other, and their very first public meeting was a war of angry personalities. The theological belligerents wrote down their mutual accusations and addressed them to the Emperor; but Constantine wisely refused to read the parchment rolls, and threw them all into the fire. According to tradition the disputants sometimes acted with the utmost violence; for, when Arius was propounding his sentiments, an orthodox father is said to have been so provoked by what he deemed the impudent blasphemy of the heresiarch, that he started up and struck him on the jaw.[4] The next general

---

[1] Canon xi.

[2] Bishops commenced the system of *Indulgences* by relaxing the severity of such canons.

[3] Canon xx.

[4] This incident is represented in the traditional pictures of the Council. See

The General Councils. 261

council—the first of Constantinople—was probably disfigured by quite as many scenes of uproar. Gregory Nazianzen, who presided over a portion of its deliberations, compared its members to wasps and magpies—to a flight of cranes and to a flock of geese.[1] The next two general councils—those of Ephesus and Chalcedon—were still more disorderly. The factious spirit by which they were disgraced has been already described when treating of the Nestorian and Eutychian controversies; and it has been shown that those who prevailed at the former of these synods secured their ascendency by physical force, intrigue, bribery, and courtly influence. The Emperor Theodosius the younger addressed to the fathers of Ephesus, immediately before their separation, a rebuke memorable for its caustic severity. "God is my witness," he declared, "that I am not the author of this confusion. His providence will discern and punish the guilty. Return to your provinces, and may your private virtues repair the mischief and scandal of your meeting."[2] The business of the Council of Chalcedon was completely interrupted when Theodoret, the ecclesiastical historian, made his appearance. This excellent man, one of the ablest writers of the age, had given deadly offence to the abettors of Eutychianism, and his right to sit[3] among the ecclesiastical judges was keenly disputed. The discussion of his claims had been already introduced, and the opposing factions were giving utterance to their feelings in tumultuous shouts, when the bishop himself walked into the council. His presence was the signal for increased excitement. His friends welcomed him with enthusiastic acclamations, and his adversaries lustily called out: "Cast forth the Jew—the enemy of God—the blasphemer of Christ."[4] In the midst of this Babel of jarring sounds the imperial commissioners were obliged to interfere; and, after sternly reprimanding the bishops

---

Stanley's *Eastern Church*, p. 153. The striker is said to have been Nicolas of Myra, but some doubts exist as to his presence at the council.

[1] *De Vita sua Carm. Opera*, tom. ii. p. 27; *Carm.* x. *De Div. Vit. Gen. Opera*, tom. ii. p. 81, Coloniæ, 1690.

[2] The version of Dean Waddington is here adopted. See his *History of the Church*, p. 183.

[3] According to Athanasius (*Hist. Arian.* § 36), "it is wrong that those who maintain an impious creed should be admitted as members of a council," and on this ground attempts were often made to exclude theological opponents.

[4] *Binii Concilia*, tom. ii. 44.

for behaviour so disreputable, required them to proceed calmly and at once with their proper deliberations. The resolutions finally passed were exactly the reverse of those previously adopted by the assembly since so unhappily known as the "Robber Synod;" and yet a large number of the same fathers sat and voted in both these conventions. The legislators of Chalcedon thus repudiated the principles supported by many of themselves only two years before at Ephesus!

An individual acquaintance with the members of the third and fourth general councils is not at all calculated to heighten our respect for their ecclesiastical authority. Though the points submitted to these fathers for decision required the exercise of very nice discrimination, and involved some of the most difficult questions in theology, not a few of them were exceedingly illiterate. All were expected to sign the doctrinal decisions, but a considerable number had not acquired so much proficiency in the rudiments of penmanship as to be able to write even their own names. Such subscriptions as the following occur again and again: " I "—such an one—" have subscribed by the hand of " such an one, " *because I cannot write;*" and—such a bishop—" *having said that he could not write*, I," whose name is underwritten—" have subscribed for him."[1]

As we descend the stream of time in the history of Church courts, we are continually presented with proofs that we are receding farther and farther from apostolic simplicity; and, when we arrive at the sixth general council, it at once becomes apparent that we have reached an age of dense superstition. An occurrence, which created no small sensation in the fifteenth session of this synod, gives us an idea of the mode of argument now occasionally employed by the contending theologians.[2] A monk, named Polychronius, presented himself to the assembly, and declared that there had appeared to him a band of men in white garments encircling a personage radiant with surpassing glory. This personage directed him to go to the palace and to caution the Emperor against the denial of Monothelitism, assuring him that those opposed to it—that is, those who did not hold

---

[1] Jortin's *Remarks on Ecclesiastical History*, ii. 111, London, 1846.
[2] When Augustine the monk arrived in England, he proposed also to settle his controversy with the British bishops by appealing to a miracle. See Sect. IV. Chap. I. of this Period.

the doctrine of One Will and One Operation in the Saviour—were no Christians. The monk then offered to prove by a miracle the truth of his theology. He undertook to restore a dead man to life by means of a Confession of Faith embodying the doctrine of the One Will and the One Operation. The challenge was accepted; and, in an open plain into which a dead body was brought, the entire synod, with the highest officers of state, surrounded by an immense concourse of spectators, met to decide, by this most extraordinary experiment, what was henceforth to be deemed orthodoxy. Polychronius laid his confession on the corpse, and continued for several hours to whisper into its ear. But he could not wake the dead; and the announcement of his failure was a signal for the populace[1] to load him with execrations. It is somewhat difficult to determine whether the monks or the synod acted the more absurdly on this occasion. Polychronius was at least an honest zealot; he firmly believed he could work miracles; and the bishops, by consenting to assemble with so much ceremony to witness his proceedings, showed that they were themselves bewildered by the pretensions of the crazed fanatic.

Though the general councils presented so many scenes of truckling, diplomacy, and discord, the invariable tone of their canons is sufficiently pretentious. The divines sitting in these judicatories had ever before them the idea that they represented the Catholic Church; that they, therefore, acted under the direction of Him who has promised to guide His people continually; and that, of course, what seemed good to them also seemed good to the Holy Ghost. The epithet "Holy" is a title which they all assume. The sixth general council employs this word with stately redundancy as it acknowledges and confirms the proceedings of its five predecessors. "This our *Holy* and Œcumenical Synod, having driven away the *impious* error which had prevailed for a certain time until now, and following closely the straight path of the *holy* and approved fathers, has *piously* given its full assent to the five *holy* and œcumenical synods."[2] Whilst these arbiters of the faith thus eulogize themselves, they denounce their theological adversaries in terms of unmeasured severity.

[1] *Binii Concilia*, iii. pars. i. 172.
[2] *Definition of the Orthodox Faith, Binii Concilia*, iii. pars. i. 182.

Those whom they deem errorists are "impious heretics" who stand convicted of "madness and blasphemy." The views of Nestorius were in reality scarcely distinguishable from those of his antagonists, and yet they are described as his "frenzied imaginations" and as "monstrous doctrine." The question decided by the sixth œcumenical council, relating to the volitions of Christ, is of a metaphysical character, and has apparently no direct bearing on personal godliness; but the fathers of Constantinople deliberately stigmatize the Monothelites as "suitable instruments for working out the will of the devil." This bitter and contemptuous language contrasts strangely with the strains of high flown adulation in which the councils always speak of the reigning monarch. No matter what was his character, he is described as "most religious." The members of the third Council of Constantinople very complacently compliment both the Emperor Constantine Pogonatus and themselves. "Our God has raised up our faithful sovereign—a new David—having found him a man after his own heart, who, as it is written, has not suffered His eyes to sleep or his eyelids to slumber, until he has found a perfect declaration of orthodoxy by this our divinely collected and holy synod."[1]

Though it is preposterous to place even ancient general councils on a level with the Word of God, they are entitled to respectful consideration. They reflected the spirit of the times in which they met for consultation; and they are memorials of the primitive Church polity, or of government by Church judicatories. We are not to infer that piety had forsaken the earth, because we see so few indications of its holy and happy influence in the history of these conventions. We cannot always judge of individual character from the proceedings of great meetings, where questions which have already created heart-burnings and divisions are the topics of debate; for comparatively few can preserve unruffled equanimity amidst the excitement and provocations of public discussion; and, when the spirit of party is intensely moved, even good men are sometimes tempted to perform acts from which they would otherwise recoil. Notwithstanding the folly perpetrated in the general councils, all of them contained individuals who were the leaders of thought in

[1] *Binii Concilia,* iii. par. i. 184.

their generation. Some of those who figured in them most prominently were remarkable rather for tact or rhetorical ability than for private worth or pastoral excellence; but most of these assemblies contained a considerable number of men of true godliness, though, it may be, of narrow views or of little intellectual culture.

The commencement of the general councils constituted a new era in the history of the Roman Empire. Before the time of the recognition of the Gospel by Constantine, the sovereign was the high priest of heathenism,—the supreme director of the worship of his subjects, as well as their civil ruler. But, when Christianity became the religion of the State, the monarch ceased, in one department, to possess absolute power. Athanasius, backed by the decision of the Council of Nice, dared to disobey the mandate of Constantine himself, and refused to admit Arius to communion. The authority of the Church now began to control the authority of the Emperor. The will of the prince seemed indeed to dominate in the councils; but his influence was frequently more apparent than real. There were times when he was borne along by the current, and merely took the lead in movements which he could not restrain.

The fathers who met at Nice, in A.D. 325, were permitted to speak and act more freely than the members of any other general councils. When the first Council of Constantinople assembled upwards of fifty years afterwards, the authority of metropolitans was fully established; and the ordinary bishops were trammelled by their ecclesiastical superiors. In succeeding councils the suffragans generally voted with their spiritual chief, as they no longer held that position of personal independence essential to freedom of discussion.[1] The patriarchs had at their command so many means of annoyance and oppression, that their wishes rarely encountered any very resolute opposition. At length either the imperial commissioners, or these great prelates, originated all the resolutions submitted for consideration. As

---

[1] In the diocesan synod, the bishop alone at length usurped all the substantial power. The presbyters had only a "*votum consultativum*, a right to be present and speak, but not to vote on the decrees. Here the bishop alone decides, the others are only his councillors, and the decision is pronounced in his name." Hefele's *Christian Councils* by Clark, p. 16.

ecclesiastical tyranny advanced, councils became little better than assemblies for the registration of the wishes of the princes of the Church; and eventually the Pope claimed the exclusive privilege of introducing all questions brought before them for examination.[1] Still they retained some of the elements of constitutional liberty; and in the fifteenth century, by asserting their own ecclesiastical supremacy, they gave a stunning blow to the spiritual despotism of Rome.

[1] As in the Council of Trent.

SECTION IV.

ECCLESIASTICAL HISTORY OF GREAT BRITAIN AND IRELAND.

CHAPTER I.

ECCLESIASTICAL HISTORY OF ENGLAND.

THE early ecclesiastical history of the country now known as England is involved in much obscurity. As the Gospel quickly reached the other parts of the Roman Empire, we may presume that it soon found its way into Britain; but no remaining records enable us to trace the circumstances under which it was first announced in this corner of Europe. The tales told of its diffusion by Joseph of Arimathea are manifestly fabulous; and, though it has often been asserted that Claudia—spoken of by Paul in one of his letters to Timothy [1]—was a native of the island, a woman of rank, and the wife of Pudens mentioned in the same passage—little reliance can be placed on statements so imperfectly authenticated, more especially as the proofs of the identity of Pudens, the Roman senator, and Pudens, the friend of the Apostle, are by no means satisfactory. The story that the new faith was first preached in England by missionaries sent there in compliance with the request of Lucius, a British monarch, may safely be pronounced apocryphal. There may have been, in the second century, some petty British chieftain, named Lucius, who signalized himself by his encouragement of Christianity; but the letter, still extant,[2] purporting to be the reply of Eleutherius, bishop of Rome, to the application of this prince, is an impudent forgery; the tradition itself, as it has been handed down to us, presents chronological difficulties apparently insuperable; and other objections quite as formidable are opposed to its reception.[3]

[1] 2 Tim. iv. 21.
[2] It may be found in both Fuller and Collier. See also Spelman's *Concilia*, i. 34. There was a chieftain of Glamorganshire named Lleurwg, surnamed Lleufer Mawr, "the Great Luminary;" and this title may have been latinized Lucius. Todd's *St. Patrick*, 266.
[3] Fuller and Collier state a number of these difficulties.

Eusebius reports that some of the Apostles proclaimed the Gospel in the British isles;[1] but the bishop of Cæsarea is a witness of the fourth century; and his testimony cannot confidently be accepted when supported by no other solid evidence. The truth had unquestionably made some progress in England early in the third century, as several contemporary Christian writers attest the fact.[2] The British Church did not escape the perils of the Diocletian persecution: some of its houses of worship were then demolished by command of government;[3] Alban, commonly reputed the first British martyr, and several others of his countrymen, were put to death; but the monkish legends mixed up with the account of their sufferings have shaken the credit of the whole narrative. When the persecution commenced, Constantius Chlorus, who governed England in the capacity of Cæsar, could not directly disregard the imperial orders; and yet, as he was averse to measures of severity, he contrived in various ways, without openly opposing the will of Diocletian, to mitigate the horrors of the reign of terror. The disciples in Britain thus suffered comparatively little; and it has been thought that meanwhile their numbers were recruited rather than diminished by the visitation, as brethren driven from other quarters of the Empire here found a species of asylum.

The Council of Arles was held in A.D. 314; and the names of three British bishops, among the few signatures appended to the record of its proceedings, may be interpreted as an index of the importance of their Church in the beginning of the fourth century. This council, which aimed at the extinction of the schism of the Donatists, failed to accomplish its design; but otherwise it exerted no small influence; and its canons are among the most ancient ecclesiastical regulations preserved from primitive ages. Very few churchmen from Europe sat in the Council of Nice; and none appeared there from its Western isles, as the extreme distance and the crossing of a boisterous sea interfered with their attendance. In the Council of Sardica, which met in A.D. 343, there were some bishops from Britain; and the Council of Ariminum, or Rimini, assembled in A.D. 359, contained a considerable number of representatives from the same country.

[1] *Demonst. Evang.* iii. c. 7. [2] Tertul. *Adv. Judæos*, c. 7; Origen, *in Ezek. Hom.* 4.
[3] *De Mortibus Persecutorum*, c. 15.

All the information we possess relative to the British Church concurs to prove that its original constitution differed considerably from its framework in later ages. Even the traditions concerning Eleutherius and Lucius point to this conclusion; for they indicate that, when England contained a population of not more than from one-half to three-quarters of a million,[1] it was furnished with a more numerous staff of bishops than it can reckon in the nineteenth century. At that time, instead of twenty-eight flamens and three archflamens, an equal number of Christian overseers—or twenty-eight bishops and three archbishops—are said to have been entrusted with the supervision of the subjects of King Lucius.[2] According to another account, no less than sixty-five bishops were set up in England when it first received the Gospel.[3] Paganism long lingered within its borders; and, at the outset, sixty-five pastors dispersed over the island must have been sufficient to minister to its Christian inhabitants. Other testimonies lead us to infer that there was a still larger supply of bishops in the country about the time of the conversion of Constantine; for, according to various authorities,[4] the Council of Arles, held in A.D. 314, contained several hundreds of these dignitaries; and it is admitted that most of the members were

---

[1] See Henry's *History of Great Britain*, i. 190, Dublin, 1789. In the beginning of the seventh century it is probable that the population scarcely reached this amount, as meanwhile the country had been sadly depopulated by wars, especially by the wars of the Saxons.

[2] Geoffrey of Monmouth, iv. 19. Geoffrey was bishop of St. Asaph in the twelfth century. His history is full of fables. The story was probably suggested by the fact that there were more than thirty towns of some note at an early period in Britain. See Sharon Turner's *History of the Anglo-Saxons*, i. 83, London, 1807.

[3] Giraldus Cambrensis, quoted by Spelman, *Concilia*, i. p. 15. According to this writer there were five provinces in Britain and five metropolitans—each metropolitan having twelve suffragans under him. Cambrensis flourished towards the close of the twelfth century. These statements of Geoffrey and Giraldus, though of little consequence in themselves, concur to prove that, according to tradition, there were, at the first planting of Christianity in Britain, more bishops than afterwards. The work attributed to Richard of Cirencester (*Ancient State of Britain*, i. 7) tells us that the Britons had formerly ninety-two cities, of which thirty-three were more noted than the rest. The rule of the ancient Church was to have a bishop in every town where there was a Christian congregation. But great doubts exist as to the genuineness of Richard's Chronicle.

[4] See Sect. I. Chap. V. of this Period, p. 119. See also Pusey's *Councils of the Church*, p. 98. The law requiring all the members to subscribe the decrees was not generally observed until long afterwards; and hence the signatures to these early Councils supply no test whatever as to the number of bishops in attendance.

from Gaul and Britain.[1] Only a portion of the bishops who flourished in these regions could have been present at that convocation; and, if only so many as two hundred, chiefly from France and England, found it convenient to attend, we may reasonably infer that such Church functionaries were then very thickly planted. We cannot tell how many British bishops were in the Council of Ariminum, held in A.D. 359; but it is recorded [2] that three of the party incurred the displeasure of their brethren by living on a government allowance. Ecclesiastics did not then object to receive gifts from the hand of an emperor, and not a few pastors rejoiced in the bounty of the great Constantine; but the gratuities distributed by Constantius at Ariminum were regarded as bribes intended to secure votes for Arianism; and hence their acceptance by these three fathers gave so much offence to their associates. In Britain, as in most other places, the ancient bishops were ordinarily something like our parish ministers; and no wonder that the gifts of the court were too tempting to be rejected by needy theologians. When bishops were so numerous, they must generally have possessed very slender revenues. Even when the war with the Saxons had continued nearly three-quarters of a century, and when these pagan enemies had sadly shattered the British Church, it still retained a goodly supply of guardians of the episcopal order. At the Synod of Brevy in Wales, held about A.D. 520, one hundred and eighteen bishops [3] are reported to have been in attendance.

[1] "The Council of Arles consisted of bishops chiefly out of Gaul and Britain." Stillingfleet's *Origines Britannicæ*, p. 74, London, 1840. Stillingfleet makes a very weak attempt to explain away the testimony of Augustine, according to which there were 200 bishops at Arles. There were at this time 115 cities in Gaul. It is well known that early in the fifth century there were bishoprics in Gaul which subsequently disappeared. The ordinances of a council held in France early in the seventh century are subscribed by no less than seventy-nine Gallic bishops. Sismondi, *Histoire des Français*, i. 239, Bruxelles, 1847.

[2] Sulpitius Severus, *Sac. Hist.* lib. ii. Many modern historians speak of only three British bishops at Ariminum; whereas the statement of Sulpitius Severus is that, of all the British bishops at the Council, *only three* accepted of assistance from the Emperor during their stay there. The travelling expenses of all were, no doubt, defrayed. This writer also states that there were upwards of four hundred Western bishops at Ariminum.

[3] This statement is found in the oldest manuscript of the Life of St. David. See Stillingfleet's *Origines Britannicæ*, 356 and 358. Colgan, one of the most learned of our antiquarians, undertakes to maintain the truth of the statement. It would appear from this that village bishops were not extinguished in England in accordance with the canon of the Council of Sardica. See Todd's *St. Patrick*, 141, note, Dublin, 1864.

In these times of confusion, there were, no doubt, others in the country who did not sit in that assembly.[1]

The Arian controversy, which created so much agitation in the fourth century, awakened little discussion in England; and, though some of the British divines incurred the suspicion of heresy,[2] they appear, as a body, to have maintained an orthodox reputation. In the following century the Church was in greater danger from Pelagianism. The author of that heresy was a Welshman; and, though Pelagius probably never visited his native land after he became noted as an errorist, his views were soon extensively disseminated in South Britain; and the friends of the catholic faith, distrustful of their own capabilities, resolved to seek the aid of two eminent French theologians—Germanus of Auxerre and Lupus[3] of Troyes—to enable them to confront their opponents on the field of argument.[4] These bishops accordingly passed over into England, and gave a decided check to the progress of the new heresy; but, on their return home, its abettors recovered courage; and the bishop of Auxerre, accompanied by Severus of Treves, was obliged to make a second visit[5] before the triumph of the evangelical cause was secured. Nor was this the only service rendered by Germanus to the interests of truth in Britain. Perceiving the disadvantages under which the Church laboured in consequence of the low state of theological education, he induced two of his disciples—Dubricius and Iltutus—to undertake the training of candidates for the ministry.[6] The seminaries established at Caerleon and Llan-lwit in Wales[7]

---

[1] On a stone in a churchyard at the foot of some barren mountains five or six miles north-west of Buelt is a very ancient inscription in old characters—HIC JACET SANCTUS AVANUS EPISCOPUS. This was probably the bishop of the place. He is said to have lived in the beginning of the sixth century. *Itinerary of Arp. Baldwin through Wales in* A.D. 1188, by Giraldus de Barri, vol. i. p. 20, London, 1806.

[2] Gildas, *De Excid. Brit.* § 12.

[3] Lupus was brother to the famous Vincentius Lirinensis, and brother-in-law to Hilary, bishop of Arles. He was married to Pimeniola, Hilary's sister. Fuller, i. 49; Stillingfleet, 195. This mission of Germanus and Lupus is usually dated in A.D. 429.

[4] Bede, i. 17.   [5] About A.D. 446.   [6] Stillingfleet, 209.

[7] Fuller, i. 67, 69. There was another famous seminary at Bangor in North Wales, ten miles from Chester. Stillingfleet, 210. "The word *Bangor* in Welsh is simply an appellation for any college; and all the Christian societies among the Britons began to assume that epithet towards the close of the fifth century. . . Before that period the British Christians called their societies by the simple name

by these famous scholars served much to elevate the standard of clerical attainments, and long enjoyed extensive celebrity.

It is unnecessary to repeat the history of the subjugation of Britain by the Jutes, Angles, and Saxons. On the decline of the Roman power in England, the native inhabitants sought aid against their enemies, the Picts and Scots, from the fierce tribes settled along the opposite coasts of the Continent washed by the German Ocean; and their auxiliaries, proving more dangerous than their former foes, eventually established their dominion in the island. The triumph of these pagan freebooters, after a struggle of nearly a century and a half, well-nigh annihilated the Christianity of South Britain. The native Church still, indeed, maintained an existence in some mountainous or secluded districts, such as in Wales or Cornwall; and Welshmen regard the sixth century as the brightest period in their ancient annals. Then the famous King Arthur[1] signalized his valour in contests with Saxon foes; but the deeds of this true hero have been so absurdly magnified by his admirers that sober investigators have been provoked to question whether he ever figured elsewhere than in romance. Then, too, flourished his uncle David—the bishop of Caerleon—the traditions of whose piety and pastoral diligence have bestowed on him an immortal name; and then Gildas the Wise, reputed the earliest of British authors, committed to writing that piece of melancholy declamation[2] in which he mourns over the ruin of his country. Almost all the Christian ministers—driven from the lowlands—were shut up in Wales; and thus it was that, whilst spiritual darkness brooded over other parts of the country, the people of the Principality had "light in their dwellings." The light was indeed becoming dim; for the growing admiration of monasticism betokened the advance of superstition; and yet the religion even of a Welsh monk was incomparably superior to that brutish paganism by which it was in danger of being oppressed and superseded.

---

of Côr, a circle, or congregation. But, at the time above stated, they dignified the name by the additional epithet of Ban, high, superior, or supreme, that is to say Bangor—variously written in MSS. BanCor, Banchor, and Bangor. . . . Bangor Garmon is the College of Germanus at Llanveithin in Glamorgan." Gunn's *Preface to Nennius*, xxiv. note.

[1] The grave of this Welsh prince was discovered in A.D. 1189 in the Abbey of Glastonbury. See Sharon Turner's *History of the Anglo-Saxons*, i. 107, London, 1807.   [2] *Epistola de Excidio Britanniæ.*

The native Britons had made no attempt to evangelize the Anglo-Saxons; and, had they ventured on the undertaking, they must have proceeded in the face of no common difficulties; as wars of so long continuance between them and the new settlers had deepened national prejudices, and produced intense alienation. About the close of the sixth century a band of foreigners arrived in England and commenced the work of conversion. Gregory the Great, bishop of Rome, was the author of this mission. Before he reached the popedom, his attention had been drawn to the condition of the Anglo-Saxon colonists; and, in the ardour of his zeal, he had proposed to set out for Britain and preach to them in person; but the people of Rome refused to part with so useful and distinguished a citizen; and he was, in consequence, obliged to commit to others the execution of his benevolent designs. Soon after his appointment to the papal chair, he required Augustine, who then presided over one of the monasteries of the city, to gird himself for the task; and, in A.D. 596, the prior, in obedience to the order of his spiritual chief, departed, at the head of forty monks, on this expedition. When he had travelled as far as Lerins, in Gaul, he became so disheartened that he was on the point of giving up the mission in despair; but, stimulated afresh by the commands and exhortations of Gregory, he was induced to persevere. He had, indeed, little cause for discouragement. Furnished with recommendatory letters to the bishops and princes of France, he was sure of hospitable entertainment as he passed through the Gallic territories; and, on his arrival in England, he could reckon on the friendly offices of Bertha, wife of Ethelbert, king of Kent, the most powerful of the Anglo-Saxon sovereigns. Bertha, a descendant of Clovis, founder of the French monarchy, and daughter of Charibert, king of Paris, was a Christian; and it had been stipulated, at the time of her marriage, that she was to be protected in the enjoyment of the rites of her religion. An old chapel at Canterbury, partially spared by the conquerors when other buildings of the same description had been laid in ruins, was repaired for her accommodation; and a bishop, named Livdhard, was permitted to reside at court and superintend the celebration of her worship. Thus the pagan warriors had been already taught to tolerate Christianity.

Bede, the most learned of Englishmen, and born about three

quarters of a century after the baptism of Ethelbert, has supplied us, in his *Ecclesiastical History*, with an account of this memorable mission. His information is all the more satisfactory as he has embodied in his narrative a considerable portion of the correspondence which passed between Augustine and Pope Gregory. In A.D. 597, the missionaries reached the Isle of Thanet, a place then nearly half a mile from the mainland of Kent, but now connected with it by a small bridge spanning a rivulet. The king was immediately apprized of their arrival; and, predisposed by Bertha and others to give them a favourable reception, soon announced his intention of admitting them to an audience. But he deemed it prudent to deal cautiously with his ecclesiastical visitors. Suspecting that they might attempt to gain the mastery over him by magic, and hoping to break the spell, he met them in the open air. The manner in which Augustine and his companions approached Ethelbert was well fitted to impress the imagination of the ignorant pagan. The monks in their habits, and some of them who where priests in full canonicals, were arranged in the order of a solemn procession; a silver cross was born aloft as a banner; a picture, said to represent our Saviour, was displayed with equal ostentation; and the whole party moved along chanting a litany.[1] When the strangers advanced into the royal presence, Augustine addressed the king through an interpreter, assured him that he came to make known the way of salvation, and gave a brief exposition of the elementary articles of his faith. The monarch listened respectfully, admitted that the statements made to him were plausible; but suggested that, in a matter of such consequence, his conduct should be the result of mature deliberation. To show, however, that he was not unfriendly to the missionaries, he gave them permission to preach to his subjects, and undertook, for the present, to provide for their maintenance. Thus encouraged, Augustine and his friends applied with great diligence to the duties of their ministry; and, in a short time, Ethelbert himself submitted to baptism. Multitudes followed his example; and, on one occasion, no less than ten thousand persons received the ordinance.[2]

[1] Bede, i. 25.
[2] *Sancti Gregorii Magni Epistolæ*, Lib. viii. Epist. 30, *ad Eulogium Epis. Alexand.*

The tidings of success speedily reached Rome. A scheme for the establishment of a hierarchy in England, with two archbishops, each having twelve suffragan bishops, was forthwith settled in the mind of Gregory.[1] Augustine, who had laboured so effectually in the service of the Roman see, was constituted the first primate of Canterbury.[2] But there was another Church in the country which awakened his anxiety; and he could not feel at ease so long as it declined to recognize his papal master. Old British Christianity still survived in Wales; its rites were different from the Roman; and its professors, spurning the idea of Italian dictation, adhered with stubborn pertinacity to the ways of their forefathers. Through the influence of King Ethelbert a conference was held with the native clergy; and, on the condition that the Britons should relinquish some of their peculiar usages and conform to the Roman ritual, Augustine proposed a united mission to the Anglo-Saxons. One point which created much discussion at this meeting was the time of keeping Easter—a question which might have been easily settled had the disputants agreed to return to apostolic practice by giving up the observance as a remnant of Judaism. As it was, the decision of the controversy turned on the merits of different cycles, and therefore pertained to astronomers rather than divines. Augustine employed a new style of reckoning adopted at Rome about sixty or seventy years before,[3] whilst the British persisted in using a previous mode of computation. When, after lengthened discussion, no prospect of a settlement appeared, the Italian missionary proposed to arrive at a conclusion by appealing to the test of a miracle. A man reputed blind was brought into the meeting, and the Britons were challenged to prove the authority of their calendar by restoring him to sight. Even the eulogist of Augustine acknowledges that the Welsh divines reluctantly submitted to this ordeal;[4] and well might they have suspected

---

[1] Bede, i. 29.
[2] London appears to have been previously the metropolis. Canterbury was the capital of the kingdom of Kent, and hence it now became an archbishopric. The second archbishopric was erected subsequently at York; but, for a time, with the exception of Kent, in which a second see was erected at Rochester, a bishopric was co-extensive with a kingdom of the heptarchy. In the time of Theodore several new bishoprics were erected.
[3] Introduced by Dionysius Exiguus.
[4] Quod cum adversarii *inviti* licet concederent. Bede, ii. 2.

treachery; for the individual to be healed appears to have been a stranger as well as an Anglo-Saxon. When they failed to effect the cure, and when, in answer to Augustine's prayers, it was immediately accomplished, they still remained unconvinced. They agreed, however, to another meeting, at which a more numerous attendance was expected.

It is clear that the native clergy did not relish these conferences; and, had they not feared to provoke the wrath of King Ethelbert, they would perhaps have declined them altogether. Comparatively few of their leaders found it convenient to be present. Many monks from the monastery of Bangor in North Wales, with seven of their bishops, attended the second meeting;[1] a hermit whom they consulted had recommended them to mark carefully the deportment of Augustine, and to be very much guided in their proceedings by the spirit he displayed. They experienced no difficulty in acting on this advice. When the Welsh divines entered the assembly, the archbishop was there; but he did not condescend even to rise from his seat as he received their salutations. No good results could be expected from an interview commenced so inauspiciously. Both parties remained inflexible; and the primate, fairly losing his temper, began to bully and to denounce. "If," he exclaimed, "you will not join with us in unity, you shall from enemies suffer the vengeance of death."[2] The prediction was fulfilled; some time afterwards, North Wales was invaded by Ethelfrid, the pagan king of Northumberland; the monks of Bangor refused to wield the weapons of a carnal warfare; but, following their warriors, they stood on an eminence overlooking the field of battle, and lifted up their hands in prayer for the success of their countrymen. The unusual concourse attracted the notice of the enemy; who, made aware of their employment and deeming them more formidable than mailed champions, attacked them and put twelve hundred to the sword. Some Welsh writers maintain that

---

[1] Bede, ii. 2. These bishops appear to have been all from one district. At this period all the Christians in Britain did not probably much exceed fifty thousand. The statement put into the mouth of the abbot Dinoth on this occasion—that he and the bishops of his party were "under the jurisdiction of the bishop of Caerleon upon Usk"—is manifestly fabulous. See Fuller, *Ch. Hist. of Britain*, i. 90; and Lingard's *Anglo-Saxon Church*, 47.

[2] Bede, ii. 2.

Augustine instigated the massacre;[1] and the evidence adduced in his defence[2] does not completely relieve him from the dark imputation.

As the archbishop of Canterbury proposed a united mission to the Anglo-Saxons, we may safely infer that the British and Romish Christians did not differ essentially in doctrine. They disputed respecting discipline and ceremonies; and a number of the points of disagreement—such as that relating to the mode of clerical tonsure[3]—may seem to us very trivial. But it sometimes happens that great principles underlie discussions of little consequence in themselves; and the British divines evidently felt that the demands of Augustine involved a far larger amount of concession than was apparently required. These demands implied, in fact, the surrender of their ecclesiastical independence. The native clergy were, indeed, to be employed on a mission to the Anglo-Saxons; but it was understood that they were to be under the direction of Augustine;[4] and, to entitle them to the dubious privilege, they were to conform to the Roman way of keeping Easter, and to the Roman form of baptism.[5] It was not strange that they rejected such overtures. They refused to bow their necks to what they saw was a yoke of bondage. If the archbishop of Canterbury would treat with them only in the style of an autocrat—if he would not rise up to salute them even when they were arranging terms of agreement—what had

---

[1] The accusing evidence may be found in Fuller, i. 93, 94. According to Lingard (*Antiquities of the Anglo-Saxon Church*, p. 48, note), Augustine died in A.D. 605.

[2] It is very remarkable that the passage in Bede (ii. 2), which speaks of the death of Augustine as prior to the massacre is not found in the Saxon copies of his history. Hence it has been argued that it has been inserted subsequently to save Augustine's reputation. According to some authorities, such as Matthew of Westminster, the massacre occurred in A.D. 603, when the archbishop was still living; according to others, such as the *Annals of Ulster*, it happened in A.D. 613, or long after his death.

[3] The Britons shaved the entire front of the head from ear to ear; the Romans shaved the top of the head, thus leaving a circle of hair all round, representing, as they alleged, our Lord's crown of thorns. This priestly tonsure was of heathen origin. The priests of Isis and Serapis shaved their heads. See Bingham, vi. 4, § 16. Tonsure was introduced into the Christian Church in connection with monkery.

[4] Gregory had committed "all the bishops of Britain" to the care of Augustine. See Bede, i. 27.

[5] The Britons, it would appear, did not use the chrism in baptism.

they to expect if they once yielded to his dictation? Such, we know, was their actual reasoning. "If," said they, "he will not rise up to us *now*, how much more will he humble us and contemn us, if he once acquire jurisdiction over us?"[1] If the spirit of Augustine even imperfectly represented the spirit of his master Gregory, how much reason had they to fear the arrogance of that arch-prelate who ruled in Rome, and who, in mock humility, assumed the designation of "the servant of the servants of God?"

The conversion of England was completed within little more than eighty years after the arrival of the Romish missionaries. In preceding ages Christianity was embraced by many of the common people long before it became the religion of the court; but, among the Anglo-Saxons, the prince was often one of the earliest of the converts. Nor is it less worthy of note that, in five of these little Anglo-Saxon kingdoms, the progress of the new faith was greatly indebted to female influence. Bertha prepared her royal spouse for giving a kindly reception to the missionaries; and Ricula—mother of Sebert, king of the East Saxons, and sister of Ethelbert—formed a link of connection between her brother and a neighbouring prince, which facilitated the introduction of the Gospel into another state of the heptarchy.[2] Ethelburga, the daughter of Bertha and Ethelbert, was married to Edwin, king of Northumbria;[3] and her chaplain, the bishop Paulinus, who accompanied her to the North, prevailed on her husband and many of his subjects to make a profession of Christianity. Oswald, one of the successors of Edwin in Northumbria,[4] visited the court of Kynegils, king of the West Saxons, to seek his daughter in marriage; and, before his departure, he induced the young princess both to accept his hand and to embrace his religion. The conversion of the maiden was connected with the baptism of her father; and the men of Wessex were speedily added to the Church. Mercia long persisted in its paganism; and its king Penda was as cruel as he was courageous; but his

---

[1] Bede, ii. 2.

[2] The conversion of Essex took place about A.D. 604.

[3] This prince gave its name to Edinburgh (Edwinsburgh). He built the castle. Chalmers' *Caledonia*, 254. The present metropolis of Scotland was one of the frontiers of his kingdom. Northumbria was converted about A.D. 627.

[4] Oswald became king about A.D. 635, and in the same year Kynegils was baptized.

son and heir Peada, on a visit to the court of Oswio, the brother and successor of Oswald in Northumbria, was won over to the faith. The fair Alchfleda, the king's daughter, attracted him by her gentle influence; and engaged him to adopt her religion before she accepted him as her husband.[1] Edwin, king of Northumbria, persuaded Carpwald, king of East Anglia, to submit to baptism;[2] and Ædilwalch, king of Sussex—the last state of the heptarchy converted[3]—was admitted to the ordinance when sojourning at the court of Wulfhere, the brother and successor of Peada, king of Mercia. Wilfrid, a prelate expelled from his see in Northumberland,[4] was mainly instrumental in the conversion of the people of Sussex.

A candid review of the history of this mission of Augustine forbids us to believe that his wonderful success is to be entirely attributed to an outpouring of the Spirit of God. The account given of it by Bede furnishes very scanty evidence of any such visitation. The fickleness of the converts, and the levity with which, in several instances, a whole state relapsed into heathenism when a pagan prince succeeded to the throne, demonstrated that, at least in these cases, the truth had produced no very profound and lasting impression. Pious frauds were too much the fashion of the times; but they must always lessen our respect for those who had recourse to them; and their frequent performance by these English missionaries may well shake our confidence in their honesty. Augustine was unacquainted with the Saxon language—a disadvantage which must have greatly impaired his professional efficiency;—and if a functionary so indifferently qualified for his office claimed the possession of miraculous powers, it is the less remarkable that his pretensions were received with scepticism. At his first conference with the native clergy, when he sought credit for restoring a blind man to sight, we have seen how the Britons refused to yield to him, and evidently surmised imposture. The success which often

---

[1] Mercia was converted about A.D. 650.

[2] East Anglia was converted about A.D. 631.

[3] The conversion of Sussex took place about A.D. 678. The Isle of Wight is said to have been the last part of England which received the Christian faith.

[4] This ecclesiastic, who visited Rome and who was strongly attached to the papal interest, was distinguished alike by his taste, his genius, and his energy. He did much to improve ecclesiastical architecture in England. See Milman's *Latin Christianity*, ii. 80, 81.

crowned these efforts at delusion is to be ascribed to the gross barbarism of the Anglo-Saxons. When Ethelbert, king of Kent, and his nephew Sebert, king of the East Saxons, died, their little states renounced the Christian faith, and returned to the worship of Woden. The bishops settled there—Laurentius, successor of Augustine in the see of Canterbury, Mellitus of London, and Justus of Rochester—deemed the prospect hopeless; and determined to abandon the mission. Mellitus and Justus passed over into France; but Laurentius, at the last moment, contrived to recover his position. The night before his contemplated departure was spent by him in the church of Canterbury; and, on the following morning, he presented himself before Eadbald, the degenerate son of Ethelbert, with an affrighted countenance and lacerated shoulders. Saint Peter, he said, had appeared to him, had reprimanded him sternly for thinking of deserting his post, and had followed up his rebuke by administering a terrible flagellation. The apostles, in the days of their flesh, had not been wont to dispense such discipline; and one of their canons directs that a bishop must not be a striker;[1] but Eadbald, who was already more than half crazy,[2] listened with amazement to the startling tale, and accepted the scars on the back of Laurentius as ocular proof of its authenticity. The monarch was terror-stricken; he feared that, if he remained incorrigible, Peter might next commence operations on his own body; and, deeming it safer to give way at once, restored the archbishop of Canterbury to the place of which he had been deprived, and became himself a zealous disciple.

Augustine and his followers are entitled to only part of the credit of the conversion of England, as more than one half of the country was reclaimed from heathenism by missionaries from the Scottish monastery of Iona. On the death of Edwin of Northumbria, his subjects reverted to the idolatry of their ancestors; but when Oswald, a prince educated among the Scots, succeeded to the throne, Aidan, a bishop ordained in A.D. 635 by the abbot of Iona and his fellow presbyters,[3] became the apostle of the North of England. Mercia, comprehending all the midland counties, had hitherto remained pagan; and when its prince

---

[1] 1 Tim. iii. 5.
[2] Crebra mentis vesania et spiritus immundi invasione premebatur. Bede, ii. 5.
[3] See next Chapter of this Section.

Peada was converted at the court of Northumberland, he employed Scottish missionaries to introduce the Gospel into the kingdom. In A.D. 656, Diuma, a Scotchman, was ordained the first bishop of Lichfield by his countryman Finan, the successor of Aidan.[1] Essex, which had fallen back into heathenism on the death of King Sebert, was likewise evangelized by preachers from North Britain; and Cedde,[2] who had received a Scottish education, was ordained bishop of London by Finan. Fursey, an Irishman, contributed much to the restoration of Christianity in East Anglia.

The ministrations of Augustine and his colleagues were by no means so satisfactory in their results as the labours of the teachers trained at Iona. Four of the kingdoms of the heptarchy, converted by the agents of Rome, very soon returned to paganism; and Northern preachers, as we have seen, were largely instrumental in effecting their recovery; but no such extensive defalcations marred the progress of these Scottish missionaries.[3] Their mode of proceeding accounts for their more permanent success. The Romish monks aimed to impress the senses, and to lead captive the imagination, rather than to convince the understanding. They delighted in religious processions, in the display of pictures, in the exhibition of relics, in stories of nightly apparitions, and in mock miracles. The Scottish preachers sought to diffuse a knowledge of the Word of God, and to commend it by the light of its own evidence. They, too, were involved in various errors; and yet the purity of their lives and the assiduity with which they endeavoured to extend scriptural instruction are worthy of all praise. Bede, in spite of his Romish prejudices, could not but acknowledge their excellence; and, in his *Ecclesiastical History*, has left behind a lovely portrait of Aidan of Lindisfarne.[4] "It was," says he, "the highest commendation of his doctrine with all men that he taught no otherwise than he and his followers lived; for he

---

[1] Bede, iii. 21.

[2] St. Cedde and St. Chad, "St. Cedde, in Latin *Ceddus*, I believe the elder, born at London, where afterward he was bishop. . . . St. Chad, in Latin *Cedda*, born in Northumberland. . . . He was bishop of Lichfield." Fuller, i. 127.

[3] Essex, after its second conversion, relapsed partially into paganism, but was soon restored. See Bede, iii. 10.

[4] Or Holy Island in Northumberland.

neither sought nor loved anything of this world; but delighted in distributing immediately among the poor whatever was given him by the kings or rich men of the world. He was wont to traverse both town and country on foot, never on horseback, unless compelled by some urgent necessity; and wherever in his way he saw any, either rich or poor, he invited them, if infidels, to embrace the mystery of the faith; or, if they were believers, he sought to strengthen them in the faith, and to stir them up by words and actions to alms and good works. His course of life," continues Bede, "was so different from the slothfulness of our times, that all those who bore him company, whether they were shorn monks or laymen, were employed in meditation, that is, either in reading the Scriptures or committing psalms. This was the daily employment of himself and all that were with him wherever they went; and, if it happened, which was but seldom, that he was invited to eat with the king, he went with one or two ecclesiastics, and having taken a small repast, made haste to be gone with them, either to read or to pray."[1]

The different usages introduced by the Roman and Scottish missionaries among their English converts soon led to disputes and divisions. The Easter of one party not unfrequently varied some weeks from the Easter of the other; and, as the moveable feasts throughout the year depended on the paschal reckoning, the whole calendar was thus thrown into confusion.[2] In the hope of arriving at some amicable settlement, and of obtaining uniformity, a species of synod was held, in A.D. 664, at the nunnery of Whitby in Yorkshire. The abbess Hilda, a lady nearly allied to two of the royal families of England,[3] presided over this establishment, and took a deep interest in the deliberations.[4] King Oswio, with his son Alfrid and several bishops,

[1] Bede, iii. 5.

[2] The British cycle contained eighty-four years; that recently adopted at Rome only nineteen. Sometimes four weeks intervened between the Easter of the one party and the other.

[3] Lingard's *Antiquities of the Anglo-Saxon Church*, p. 120, Newcastle, 1810. She is said to have been grand-niece of Edwin, king of Northumbria.

[4] Fuller speaks of her as "moderatress" of the synod. *Church History of Britain*, i. 129. But King Oswio, who was present, no doubt presided. At a synod, held in A.D. 694 in Kent, as Fuller truly states, "five Kentish abbesses were not only present, but subscribed their names and crosses to the constitutions concluded therein. And we may observe that their subscriptions are not only placed before and above all presbyters, but also above Botred, a bishop, present in this great Council," i. 138. See Spelman, i. 190; and Hefele's *Christian Councils* by Clark, p. 24.

attended; and Wilfrid, already mentioned as the apostle of Sussex, was the great champion of the Romish observance. According to this disputant, Peter, who has the keys of the kingdom of heaven, was the author of the papal tradition. The Scottish divines admitted that none of their authorities had the same power as the prince of the apostles; and this statement decided the judgment of the royal auditor. "I must obey Peter," said Oswio, "otherwise I may find it impossible to get heaven's door opened when I seek admission."[1]

The Synod of Whitby did not, however, terminate the discussion. Though the Scottish bishop Coleman now resigned the see of Lindisfarne in disgust and returned to his own country, others who professed his sentiments retained their places and persisted in the use of their own ritual. New questions meanwhile arose to aggravate the bitterness of the controversy. The validity of the Scottish ordinations began to be impeached, and the more zealous advocates of the papal interest refused to accept imposition of hands from the successors of Aidan. The issue of the struggle did not long remain doubtful. The Scottish divines, whose usages were much the same as those of the hated Britons, were engaged in an unequal contest with fashion, power, and political intrigue. The Pope was now the spiritual guide of many of the crowned heads of Europe; the converted kings of England deemed themselves honoured by his patronage; he kept up a friendly correspondence with them; and gained them over completely to his interests. They soon indicated very unequivocally their ecclesiastical predilections. As several Irishmen or Scotchmen admitted to bishoprics had been ordained at Iona, and as thus, according to the views of the stricter Romanists, the episcopal succession in the Anglo-Saxon Church had been to some extent vitiated, the English princes resolved on the death of Deusdedit, archbishop of Canterbury, to send to the capital of Christendom a priest of their own selection, that, duly vested with archiepiscopal authority by the supreme pontiff, he might transmit the apostolic grace in all its purity to future generations.[2] Wighard, the individual chosen for this mission, died at Rome before his consecration; and a Greek monk, named Theodore, appointed to the vacant dignity by Pope Vitalian, was ordained by him to the primacy. Though a foreigner and the nominee of

[1] Bede, iii. 25.   [2] Bede, iii. 29.

the Italian prelate, Theodore may be justly ranked among the most distinguished of the archbishops of Canterbury. As a scholar he had few equals; he was profoundly acquainted with both Greek and Latin literature; and his knowledge of ecclesiastical law was minute and extensive. When he arrived in England in A.D. 669 he was sixty-seven years of age; but he was hale and vigorous; and in the succeeding twenty-one years during which he filled the primatial chair, he did much to promote the intellectual improvement as well of the clergy as of the people. He established schools throughout the country; and so great was his ardour as an educationist that, in a seminary under his own supervision, he himself gave instruction to the sons of the higher classes from all parts of England.[1]

Before the arrival of Theodore in Britain the influence of the Romish party preponderated; and, sustained by the support of the Anglo-Saxon kings, this prelate secured its undisputed ascendency. Chad, who had previously been ordained bishop of Lindisfarne, submitted to be *re-ordained* by him bishop of Lichfield;[2] and, in A.D. 673, at the Synod of Hertford, where he presided, the primate induced the bishops, and others there assembled, to agree to the observance of the Italian mode of keeping Easter. From this date the power of the old British Church continued to decline, until it was swallowed up by the dominant Romanism.

Before the close of the seventh century, Christianity was incorporated with the civil constitution of England. In A.D. 693, Ina, King of Wessex, promulgated a series of laws which illustrate alike his devotion to the Church and the rude spirit of his generation. According to one of these regulations, every infant was to be baptized within thirty days after birth; and in case of neglect the parents were to pay a penalty of thirty shillings[3]— a fine which in those days must have been ruinous to persons in humble circumstances. A master who required his slave to do any work on the Lord's Day was mulcted in a similar amount, and the slave was declared free. Kirk-shot, or Church cess, was established by this monarch.[4] Tithes, at first voluntary, were

---

[1] Bede, iv. 2. He is said to have introduced the use of the organ into the worship of the Church of England. Hook's *Archbishops of Canterbury*, i. 198. This instrument was yet unknown elsewhere in Europe.

[2] Bede, iv. 2. [3] Spelman's *Concilia*, i. 183, 186. [4] Spelman, i. 187.

subsequently converted into a legal demand. The bishops of the new hierarchy soon obtained large political power, and sat as constituent members in the Saxon Witena-gemot or Parliament.[1] Their wealth and the splendour of their palaces and equipages often excited the envy of the secular nobility.

The mission of Augustine to Britain forms an era in the history of the popedom. The brilliant success of the enterprise dazzled the catholic world; Gregory, by whom it was planned and patronized, was honoured with immense applause; and his great Italian bishopric derived from it additional lustre. So many kingdoms reclaimed from paganism produced so many kings to support the pontifical throne; and the members of the royal families of England soon became distinguished for their loyalty to the Western Patriarch. Many of them went on pilgrimage to the tombs of the Apostles, made princely presents to the Pope, and acquired vast credit with the people of Rome by the munificence of their charities.[2] As they passed from desolated England to the city of the Cæsars, no wonder that they were awe-struck as they gazed on its ecclesiastical pomp and its architectural grandeur. Though its noble structures had suffered much from the decay of time and the ravages of war, they still retained traces of their former glory; and, to eyes accustomed to behold the awkward wooden buildings and straw roofs of Britain, they must have appeared to possess almost celestial beauty. The English pilgrims, after receiving the papal benediction, returned home filled with admiration of the sights and scenes of the Eternal City, and prepared to exalt, in loftier strains than before, the claims of the successors of the prince of the apostles.

The establishment of Romanism in England prepared the way for its ascendency throughout the British isles. The friends of the Italian bishop gradually obtained a footing in adjacent regions already evangelized; and, in a few centuries, the Churches of Ireland and Scotland were persuaded to acknowledge papal jurisdiction. Small bishoprics disappeared; and the authority of the diocesan sometimes extended over a district as wide as the territory of a petty sovereign. In England, the division of the diocese into minor portions is said to have commenced in the

---

[1] Soames, *Anglo-Saxon Church*, p. 255, London, 1838.
[2] Among others, King Ina went to Rome, where he founded a Saxon school, and built a church adjoining it. These establishments were largely endowed.

days of primate Theodore.[1] A thane, or landed proprietor, who erected a church, was then recognized as its patron; and his estate became a parish. Shortly after the conversion of England, the Anglo-Saxons acquired distinction by their missionary zeal; and, as they had themselves been evangelized by the agents of Rome, they felt specially bound to uphold its pretensions. Passing over to the Continent—where they could labour with peculiar facility among tribes speaking their own language—they did much to extend the boundaries of the visible Church. Willibrord, a native of Northumbria, consecrated archbishop of Utrecht by Pope Sergius, is known as the *apostle of the Frieslanders*; and Winifrid, a native of Devonshire—who, early in life, took the name of Boniface [2]—has acquired the still higher designation of the *apostle of the Germans*. The anxiety of Boniface to enlarge the authority of the Pontiff was scarcely exceeded by his desire to make proselytes to Christianity; and the Irish missionaries preaching on the Continent, who persisted in their own observances, were treated with the utmost intolerance by this stern bigot. Supported by the political power of France, he threw some of them into prison, and greatly discouraged them in their labours.[3] The mission of Boniface to Germany was perhaps quite as serviceable to the bishop of Rome as the mission of Augustine to England.

Truth is a jewel which reveals its radiance even when dimly seen. Such is the Gospel. The teaching of Augustine and his fellow-monks was sadly obscured by superstition; but it exhibited some of the light of Christianity; and hence its vital power. The Anglo-Saxons felt its superiority to paganism; for its meretricious appendages did not altogether conceal its divine lustre. And though, as diffused by Boniface among the Germans, much of its real excellence was hidden, it still approved itself the power of God and the wisdom of God unto salvation. Ministers may hold many errors and display many personal infirmities; and yet, if they proclaim Christ as the Lamb of God that taketh away the sin of the world, they may labour success-

[1] Soames' *Anglo-Saxon Church*, p. 85; Lingard, p. 65.

[2] It has often been asserted that he received the name of Boniface when ordained bishop by Gregory II.; but this is a mistake. Several years prior to that time we find letters addressed to him as the *presbyter Boniface*. See *Bonifacii Opera*, i. 26, 27, ed. Giles, London, 1844.

[3] See *Murdock's Mosheim* by Soames, ii. 119, 120. Neander, v. 76, 79, 80.

fully. The great Apostle has said: "We have this treasure in earthen vessels, that the excellency of the power may be of God, and not of us."[1]

CHAPTER II.

ECCLESIASTICAL HISTORY OF SCOTLAND.

THE mists for which Scotland is proverbial may remind us of the cloud of obscurity which overhangs its early ecclesiastical annals. The account of its conversion towards the close of the second century under the auspices of King Donald must be classed with the fable of the conversion of England about the same period under the auspices of King Lucius; and, though we may so far credit the testimony of Tertullian as to admit that there were then Christians north of the great wall of Antoninus,[2] it would be easy to prove that their numbers were inconsiderable. The worship of the Church was, perhaps, publicly established in some of the southern districts of Scotland as early as the reign of Constantine the Great. In A.D. 314 a bishop of York attended the Council of Arles; and, as the whole region from the Clyde to Solway Frith was at that time subject to the Roman government, it is highly probable that, in an age of such religious activity, it was visited by the missionary, and brought, at least partially, under the influence of the Gospel. At a somewhat subsequent date we have direct evidence of the progress of the faith; for a native pastor, named Nynian, built at Candida Casa, or Whithorn, in Galloway, the first church of stone ever erected in North Britain.[3] This zealous and successful preacher, who

[1] 2 Cor. iv. 7.
[2] The southern part of Scotland between the Clyde and Solway Frith was long subject to the Romans, and in the fourth century received the name of Valentia. Caledonia, or North Britain, appears to have been so called from the fact that it was anciently covered with forests. "A dense thicket is in Welsh 'celyd,' in the plural number 'celyddon;' and Celyddon is to this day the British term for Caledonia, as preserved among the Cumbri of Wales. . . . The town of Dunkeld, said to have been once the capital of ancient Caledonia, is called in the language of the native Highlander 'Dunchaillein,' pronounced precisely as a Briton would pronounce his 'Din Chelyddon,' 'the city of the forests.'" M'Lauchlan's *Early Scottish Church*, 10, 11, Edinburgh, 1865.
[3] Bede, iii. 4.

afterwards proceeded still farther north[1] and acquired the honourable designation of *The Apostle of the Southern Picts*, died in A.D. 432.

The political condition of North Britain in the fifth century was not favourable to its religious improvement. When the Empire of the West began to stagger under the blows of the Gothic barbarians, its troops stationed in England were withdrawn for the defence of Italy; and the Picts and Scots, relieved from the presence of the Roman veterans, marched boldly southwards, and spread dismay and desolation all around them. So long as they remained under the fever of excitement created by these military expeditions, the voice of the heralds of the Prince of Peace could not well be heard by the fierce tribes bordering on the Roman frontier. But at length the Saxon power became quite too formidable for the northern warriors; and a variety of providences prepared them for listening attentively to the addresses of the missionary. In A.D. 563[2] a band of evangelists arrived among them, and entered on their labours under circumstances of much encouragement.

The leader of this movement was an Irishman, born in A.D. 521, at Gartan in the county of Donegal[3]—the far-famed Columba, better known by the name of Columbkille, or *Columb of the cell*. He was descended both paternally and maternally from celebrated Irish kings; and, though his royal lineage added greatly to his personal influence, he had other and better recommendations. He was an ardent student; as a scholar, he stood high among contemporaries; he possessed a sound judgment combined with much energy of character; his address was engaging, his stature lofty, and his countenance most pleasing; he was deeply pious; and a voice singularly sweet and powerful imparted a wonderful charm to his eloquence. About the middle of the third century, one of his ancestors, named Cairbre Riada, or Reutha,[4] had gained possession of the north-east corner of Ulster;

[1] "That Whithern was the see erected by Ninian over the Piks he converted is a gross error. Ailred tells us that it was his proper British see, long before he went to convert the Southern Piks, who lived, as Beda shews, south of the Grampian hills, or in Fifeshire," &c. Pinkerton's *Enquiry into the History of Scotland*, i. 74, Edinburgh, 1814.

[2] Bede has the date A.D. 565, but that given in the text is now generally accepted. See Lanigan, ii. 158; and *Ogygia Vindicated*, 166.

[3] Reeves' *Life of St. Columba* by Adamnan, Appendix to Preface, lxviii.

[4] From him a part of the county of Antrim is still called *The Route*.

and from him this territory, now forming part of the county of Antrim, obtained the designation of Dalriada.[1] In A.D. 503 [2] some of the posterity of Riada passed to the opposite shore of North Britain, and there succeeded in laying the foundation of another kingdom likewise known by the title of Dalriada. The authority of the Pictish rulers then prevailed north of the wall of Antoninus; but this new dynasty gradually encroached on their dominions; and, in A.D. 843, Kenneth, one of the Dalriadan chiefs—and also the grandson of Urgusia, a Pictish princess—wrested the sceptre from the hand of Wred, the last of the Pictish kings, and established his power over the whole of the country.[3] Before this event Ireland alone was called *Scotia*, or Scotland; but, some time afterwards, the name began to be applied to Caledonia—Hibernia being known as *Scotia Major*, or Scotland the Greater, and Caledonia as *Scotia Minor*, or Scotland the Less [4]—and, in the course of a few centuries, the title was transferred entirely to the land in which the descendants of Riada continued to retain possession of the sovereignty. Nor is it the least memorable fact connected with this department of our national history that the most illustrious crown in Christendom is at present worn by a lineal descendant of the Hibernian Prince Riada; for Queen Victoria, sprung from the royal family of Scotland, can point to a long succession of the kings of Ireland as her still more remote progenitors.[5]

The settlement of the Dalriadans in Cantyre [6] and the neighbouring districts prepared the way for the mission of Columbkille.

---

[1] That is, the portion or inheritance of Riada; for *Dal* in Irish means a share or portion, or the land possessed by a tribe.

[2] Chalmers' *Caledonia*, i. 274. Before, but less successfully, they attempted to obtain a settlement. See O'Conor's *Dissertations on the Ancient History of Ireland*, p. 197, Dublin, 1753; and *Ogygia Vindicated*, 103 and 163-5.

[3] Chalmers' *Caledonia*, i. 304. M'Lauchlan gives a somewhat different account of this portion of Scottish history. *Early Scottish Church*, p. 283. See, on the other side, MacGeoghegan's *History of Ireland*, pp. 213-214, ed. Dublin, 1844.

[4] O'Flaherty's *Ogygia*, part iii. 253; and *Ogygia Vindicated*, 295. See also Pinkerton's *Enquiry*, i. 116, Edinburgh, 1814.

[5] The famous stone which now sustains the coronation chair in Westminster Abbey is said to have been used originally at Tara by the Irish kings. It remained long at Scone in Scotland. M'Lauchlan's *Early Scottish Church*, p. 285.

[6] "In the Gaelic, *Cean* . . signifies a *head*, and *Tir*, *land;* so *Cean-tir* is literally head-land. . . . The analogous term in the Gothic is *Hœfde-lande.*" Chalmers' *Caledonia*, i. 274, note.

Loarn,[1] who in A.D. 503 became the first king of the Scottish Dalriada, was the great-grandfather of the Irish evangelist. The Dalriadans had been already converted to Christianity; and, as the head of the mission was a scion of their own royal house, they felt a peculiar interest in his undertaking. As a place for his settlement, Conal, his relative, the king of the newly-acquired territory, made him a grant of I or Hy,[2] a little island on the Western coast about three miles long and a mile broad, separated by a narrow channel from Mull. The success which crowned his first efforts emboldened Columbkille to persevere. The Pictish King Bruide, a prince of much consideration, was soon ranked among his converts. Hy lay on the outskirts of the Scottish Dalriada, and therefore some doubts existed respecting the right to the property; but the royal proselyte ratified its title, and thus quieted the fears of its new possessors.[3] The Irish preacher was now invited to pursue his labours among the subjects of Bruide;[4] the population, wherever he or his coadjutors travelled, exhibited a disposition to receive the message of salvation; and, among those who have earned renown in the field of missions, Columbkille has ever since been favourably known as *The Apostle of the Northern Picts.*

Even in the sixth century, Hibernia was celebrated as the land of saints and of scholars; and the number of Irishmen of noble lineage who then entered the ministry illustrates at once their religious zeal and the respect generally entertained for the clerical profession. The ordination of such a man as Columbkille must

[1] The Duke of Argyll is descended from this same stock, and hence his eldest son derives his designation of Marquis of Lorne. It thus appears that the Princess Louise and her noble husband are of the same royal lineage.

[2] "Adamnan's practice, with regard to the names of islands, is to put them in the adjective form agreeing with *insula;* and thus he deals with Hy on the sixty occasions where he makes mention of it. In all these instances the unmistakable reading in Cod. A is *Ioua Insula;* and the same prevails in Codd. C, F, S. The more modern manuscripts B and D, which are less precise in orthography, and very loose in the distinction of *n* and *u,* always read *Iona.*" Reeves' *Columba* by Adamnan, 258, 259, Dublin, 1857. "The I of the Gaelic was aspirated by the Saxon Bede into Hy." Chalmers, i. 319, note.

[3] Reeves' *Columba* by Adamnan, Appendix to Preface, lxxvi. and 151, and 434-6.

[4] "The title Bruide, Acu-punctus, the Pict, a name common to a long series of kings." *Additional Notes by the Hon. Algernon Herbert to the Irish version of Nennius,* xlv. The King was perhaps specially distinguished by the punctures of the painting-needle. This puncturing ceased on the introduction of Christianity; and, about the same time, the title Bruide disappears. *Ibid.* xlvi.

have been hailed by many with no common satisfaction. His rank, his talents, and his learning soon gave him weight among his countrymen; his ecclesiastical status invested him with additional importance in the estimation of a rude people; and the refusal of the chief monarch of the island, on a certain occasion, to respect the sacred character of the great churchman, is said to have brought on a civil war.[1] This affair involved him in much obloquy;[2] and, though the circumstances which led him to enter on the mission to North Britain have never been very lucidly explained, it is clear that he was blamed as the cause of at least one bloody battle; and it would appear that he was induced, in consequence, to withdraw from Ireland to a country where, far away from the whirlpool of politics, he would be at liberty to devote himself, with all his heart, to spiritual exercises.[3] At Hy he founded a religious institute over which he presided, as abbot, for thirty-four years. He was accompanied to this island by twelve of his friends, who were his associates in the care of the establishment, and who united with him in the observance of an ascetic discipline. At that time the rule of Benedict of Nursia, the second father of monasticism in the West, had been only recently promulgated;[4] as yet it was perhaps scarcely known in Britain or Ireland; and in several particulars it differed from the system of Columbkille. The abbot of Hy appointed his successor; and the head of the monastery belonged, almost invariably, to the kin or family of the founder.[5] Though required occasionally to practise severe abstinence, the monks were at other times permitted freely to partake of beef and mutton.[6] The rules of the monastery exhibit less of the spirit of routine than those by which the Benedictines were regulated; and the disciples of Columbkille were not inoculated with the superstition that prayer has peculiar efficacy when offered up on holy ground; for the abbot himself sometimes withdrew altogether from the building that, in the solitude of the desert, he might engage, with less restraint, in secret devotion.[7]

The special excellence of the monastery of Hy was, however, its educational character. The members of the fraternity were

[1] Reeves' *Columba* by Adamnan, 249.
[2] See Adamnan, iii. 3. See also Lanigan, ii. 150. [3] See Reeves, 247, 255.
[4] See Sec. I. Chap. IV. of this Period, p. 110. [5] Reeves, 342.
[6] Adamnan, ii. 29; Reeves, 355. [7] Adamnan, iii. 8; Reeves, 347.

taught that their lives could not, with impunity, be lost to society; that they were not to mope away existence in inactivity and silence; but that, as the soldiers of Christ, they must war a good warfare, as well against the world lying in wickedness as against indwelling corruption. Hy must, therefore, be a light shining in a dark place; and from it must radiate over Scotland the genial influence of the Gospel. The monastery was, in fact, a college where all the branches of learning then known were diligently cultivated; where astronomy was studied;[1] where Greek as well as Latin literature entered into the curriculum; where the sons of kings and nobles received tuition;[2] and where pious and promising youths were trained up for the sacred office. The abbots of Hy were famous for their erudition; and an extant production penned by one of the successors of Columbkille is still admired as an evidence of the classical culture of the seventh century.[3] But theology was the subject with which the attention of the teachers of the monastery was chiefly occupied; the Bible was their daily text-book; their pupils were required to commit much of it to memory; and there is good reason to believe that, had the Psalms been lost, there were brethren in Hy who could, without difficulty, have repeated them all, and thus supplied the Church with a new Psalter.[4]

About a hundred years after the death of the founder of the monastery, his life was written by Adamnan,[5] the ninth abbot; and though the narrative, dictated in the credulous spirit of the age, is filled with absurd tales of visions, miracles, and prophecies, it has made us acquainted with many interesting facts which illustrate the history of the times, and reveal the true character of Columbkille. Some of the information it supplies was obtained from individuals who had lived in Hy with the subject of the

[1] The Paschal Epistle printed by Ussher in his *Sylloge* is evidence of this; but it is not at all probable that Cummian, the author, was abbot of Hy. See Reeves, 199; Lanigan, ii. 109-397.

[2] Oswald, King of Northumbria, was educated there.

[3] Considering the age, Adamnan's *Columba* is written in excellent Latin. The public are greatly indebted to Dr. Reeves for his learned labours as its editor.

[4] Bede, iii. 5.

[5] Adamnan, or, as it is sometimes written, Adomnan, is an Irish diminutive of Adam. Under the effect of aspiration, Adam in Irish loses the force of its consonants, and assumes the various sounds of *Au*, *Eu*, *O*, and *Ou*. Hence, with the diminutive termination, Adamnan becomes *Eunan*. Reeves, 256. Adamnan, or Eunan, is commonly reputed the patron, if not the founder, of the church of Raphoe.

memoir, and who retained a vivid recollection of him; for the great Irish saint expired in presence of his monks only twenty-seven years before the birth of his biographer.[1] Cummian, surnamed The Fair, the seventh abbot, had previously drawn up an account of his famous predecessor; and this memorial, which has been transmitted in a separate form to our times,[2] is embodied in the work of Adamnan. Bede, in his History, has likewise noticed the abbots of Hy; and, as this laborious author flourished little more than a century after the days of Columbkille, his testimony is of high value. Very few of the later traditions relative to the ecclesiastical position originally occupied by the monastery of Hy can be accepted as trustworthy.

"That island," says Bede, "is always wont to have for its governor a presbyter abbot, to whose authority both the whole province, and even the bishops themselves, by an unusual constitution, owe subjection, after the example of their first teacher, who was not a bishop, but a presbyter and monk."[3] This sentence, evidently composed with uncommon care and expressed with much precision, has led to a keen controversy; and certain writers, blinded by prejudice, have sought earnestly to prove that it does not mean what it literally implies. They cannot believe that a presbyter-abbot ever was the ecclesiastical superior of the bishops of a whole kingdom; and, by referring to cases in which one individual must sometimes give way to another who is socially his inferior,[4] they have tried to show how, in accordance with the rules of Church discipline, the words of Bede may be susceptible of explanation. But all such sophistry is at once disposed of by the venerable historian, who was the most learned theologian of his age, and who assures us that the arrangement was "*unusual.*" It is perfectly apparent, as well from his statements as from other evidence, that the abbot, who was but a presbyter, ordained bishops, presided in Church councils, and

[1] That is, in A.D. 597. See Reeves, Appendix to Preface, xl.
[2] See Reeves, 199, note.
[3] "Habere autem solet ipsa insula rectorem semper abbatem presbyterum, cujus juri et omnis provincia, et etiam ipsi episcopi, ordine inusitato, debeant esse subjecti, juxta exemplum primi doctoris illius, qui non episcopus, sed presbyter extitit et monachus." Bede, iii. 4.
[4] Thus, Lloyd mentions the case of the Bishop of Oxford, who, when in the city, must give place to the Chancellor of the University. See Lanigan, ii. 256, who endeavours to get over the difficulty by alleging that this is "a singular case, *founded on the apostleship of St. Columba.*"

claimed supreme jurisdiction over all the episcopal dignitaries of the Pictish realm.

The ordination of bishops by Columbkille and his successors is the great question in dispute; and yet the most erudite antiquaries who deny to these abbots the exercise of this prerogative are prepared to admit that it was enjoyed by them in substance, though not in form. "The abbatial office," says the accomplished editor of Adamnan, "gave *all the jurisdiction* of the episcopate, *without its responsibilities;* and little more was left to the bishop than *the essence of his office*, the transmission of holy orders, with the personal reverence which was due to the holder of so important a commission."[1] Whilst the same writer asserts that "there were at all times bishops connected with the society resident at Hy," he concedes that their "acts were performed *on the responsibility of the abbot*,[2] or in the name of the community."[3] According to this view, "the essence" of the episcopal office is not worth the preservation; for a functionary who cannot act according to his own convictions of duty, and who must go through the solemn service of the laying on of hands in ordination as often as he is commanded by another, holds rather a pitiable position. We know, besides, that in the days of Columbkille and his immediate successors no such clerical puppet had a place in the monastery of Hy, for not a trace of his existence can be discovered; and an excellent witness avers positively that "in I there must ever be an abbot, *but not a bishop*, and all the Scottish bishops owe subjection to him, because Columba was an abbot and not a bishop."[4]

We learn from Bede himself that the rite of ordination was performed by the abbot and certain senior assistants. Speaking

---

[1] Reeves' *Columba* by Adamnan, 335.

[2] The apparent contradiction between this and the preceding statement illustrates the folly of attempting to explain away a perspicuous sentence.

[3] Reeves, 340. King candidly says: "We shall most safely interpret his (Bede's) words by understanding from them that, instead of the ordinary control exercised elsewhere over presbyters by bishops, such control over the bishops themselves was, among Columba's followers, vested in the presbyter abbot of Hy." *Memoir of the Primacy of Armagh*, 4, Armagh, 1854. Even Pinkerton admits that "the abbot of Hyona was in effect Primate of Scotland till the ninth century." *Enquiry*, ii. 271.

[4] *Anglo-Saxon Chronicle ad an.* 565. Jamieson has clearly shown that Ussher has made a mistake as to the testimony of the *Annals of Ulster* on this point. See Jamieson's *Historical Account of the Ancient Culdees*, 48-53, Edinburgh, 1811.

of the first successful Scottish missionary to Northumbria, in the seventh century, the historian observes that " from the college of these monks was Aidan *sent* to the province of the Angles . . . . having received the degree of the episcopate when Segenius, the abbot and presbyter, presided over the same monastery."[1] After some remarks on the excellence of the character of the new bishop, he then goes on to describe more minutely his election and ordination by " the assembly of the elders."[2] The members of this Council, as he reports, were so impressed with some striking proofs he had just given of his fitness for the work of an evangelist, that " *they determined he was worthy of the episcopal office, and that he should be sent to instruct the unbelieving and the ignorant,* it having been demonstrated that he was supereminently endowed with the gift of discretion, which is the mother of virtues; and *so ordaining him,* they sent him to preach."[3] When settled in England, the Scottish bishops ordained at Hy never scrupled to acknowledge that they derived their commission from presbyters; for, in A.D. 664, when Coleman of Lindisfarne at the Synod of Whitby was disputing against the Roman method of keeping the Paschal festival, he pleads the authority of the venerable men who had invested him with episcopal authority. " This Easter," said he, " which I am accustomed to observe, I received from my seniors *who sent me bishop hither.*"[4] Bede on this, as well as on other grounds, was strongly opposed to the Scottish discipline; and he doubtless refers, at least partially, to the objection arising from its presbyterial constitution when he tells us that, at a certain period of the seventh century, there

[1] Bede, iii. 5.   [2] " Conventu seniorum."
[3] "Quo audito, omnium qui consedebant ad ipsum ora et oculi conversi, diligenter quid diceret discutiebant, et ipsum esse dignum episcopatu, ipsum ad erudiendos incredulos et indoctos mitti debere decernunt, qui gratia discretionis, quæ virtutum mater est, ante omnia probatur imbutus; *sicque illum ordinantes*, ad prædicandum miserunt" (iii. 5). The pertinacity with which some have maintained that the abbot of Iona did not exercise the power of ordination is all the more remarkable when we consider that various ancient monastic rules expressly give this privilege to the head of a monastery. Thus, in the Rule of Aurelian, cap. 46, we have these words:— " Et quando (abbas) voluerit, ORDINANDI HABEAT POTESTATEM." Migne, *Patrol. Curs.* lxviii. 392. Aurelian was a French bishop, and the *contemporary of Columbkille.* Other evidences that abbots had the power of ordination in the fifth century and afterwards have been already adduced. See p. 105, note, Section I. Chap. IV. of this Period.
[4] " Pascha hoc quod agere soleo, a majoribus meis accepi, qui me huc episcopum miserunt." Bede, iii. 25.

was not, with one exception, "a single bishop in all Britain canonically ordained."[1] And Wilfrid, the great champion of Romish observance, when chosen to a vacant see, at first refused the appointment, "lest he should receive his consecration from the Scottish bishops, or from such as the Scots had ordained."[2]

Columbkille was well aware that an ordinary presbyter had a lower status than a bishop, and several parts of his *Life*, by Adamnan, clearly show that he recognized the distinction. But from these passages it has been inferred most illogically that he was prepared to admit his own inferiority, as a presbyter abbot, to a member of the episcopal order. On a particular occasion, a Munster bishop who visited Hy attempted, as is alleged, to pass himself off as a mere presbyter; and accordingly, when celebrating the communion at the request of Columbkille, instead of proceeding, as became his rank, to break the bread alone, he solicited his host's co-operation. The abbot, however, had the discernment to discover the quality of his guest, and immediately said to him: "Christ bless thee, *brother*,[3] break it alone, according to the episcopal rite. We know now that you are a bishop. Why have you hitherto endeavoured to conceal yourself, so as not to allow us to pay due respect to you?"[4] But this incident entirely fails to prove that the abbot admitted the official superiority of his visitor. According to ancient custom, if one bishop was in the church of another when the Lord's Supper was dispensed, he was permitted, as a matter of courtesy, to preside;[5] and had this ecclesiastic been in the presence of a dignitary of episcopal rank, he would have been entitled to act alone. Columbkille there-

[1] Bede, iii. 28.

[2] Ussher's *Religion anciently professed by the Irish and British*, chap. x.

[3] "Benedicat te Christus, *frater*." An ordinary presbyter would have addressed a bishop not as *brother*, but as *father*. See Bingham, ii. 2, § 7.

[4] Adamnan, i. 44. This incident proves the groundlessness of the statement, so persistently made, that a bishop at this time constantly resided in the monastery.

[5] See 19th canon of the Council of Arles, held A.D. 314. The following passage taken from the Ethiopic version of the *Apostolic Constitutions*, proves clearly that the conduct of Columbkille did not involve any admission of his ecclesiastical inferiority:—"If a bishop come, *a stranger*, let the bishop who is in the same station receive him, and let him sit with him, and let him *give him honour*. . . . *Entreat him that he offer up the sacrifice*. And if, through fear, he will not offer up the sacrifice, let them entreat him the more earnestly to give at least a blessing to the people."—*Didascalia*, by Platt, 97, London, 1834.

fore made no concession when he revealed the true character of
the stranger, and exhorted him to use his undoubted privilege.
The shyness of the Munster man evidently proceeded from awe
of the great abbot, and from an apprehension that a mark of
respect conceded elsewhere would have been withheld in a
monastery which enjoyed such extraordinary jurisdiction.

Another case mentioned by Adamnan, which has often been
adduced to show that the abbot did not exercise the power of
ordination, sustains apparently the very opposite conclusion.
A prince of infamous character, named Aidus,—the assassin of
several persons of rank, and among the rest of Diermit, the chief
monarch of Ireland,—had retired to a monastery subject to Hy,
and under the care of the presbyter Findchan. The wretch, who
could reckon on the pliancy of this abbot, wished, for some
reason not explained, to be ordained a presbyter; but knowing,
as we presume, that the sanction neither of Columbkille[1] nor of
the seniors of his own monastery could be obtained for the proceeding, Findchan sent for a bishop[2] of the neighbourhood to perform the service. The bishop employed seems to have been
of a very accommodating disposition; but as he was aware of
the evil reputation of the candidate, he refused to proceed without the co-operation of Findchan. The abbot, as Adamnan
informs us,[3] was obliged in consequence to lay his own right
hand *first*, " for confirmation," on the head of Aidus, and then

---

[1] It is probable that, in cases of ordination, the sanction of Columbkille was sought by the abbots under his jurisdiction. In this instance he authoritatively set aside an ordination where both an abbot and a bishop officiated.

[2] Various writers have maintained, as we have seen, in opposition to direct evidence to the contrary, that a bishop resided always in the monastery of Hy. There was obviously no such personage in this establishment, as the ordainer here required to be "*sent for*" (accito episcopo). Adam. i. 36. Cases can be quoted *in subsequent times* in which a bishop formed part of the monastic establishment (see Todd's *St. Patrick*, p. 53); but it is clear that in the fifth or sixth century the abbot himself could ordain. See p. 105, note. See also *Binii Concil*. i. 14, and Migne, *Patrol. Cursus*, civ. 175. Dr. Todd has entirely failed to show that a bishop was originally part of the establishment of the monastery of St. Martin at Tours. St. Martin himself was a bishop, so that the statement is not even probable. Bishops seem to have been introduced into monasteries on the Continent at a time when these foundations were seeking to escape from the control of the diocesan; and none of the examples adduced by Dr. Todd are earlier than the *eighth* century. See his *St. Patrick*, pp. 53, 55, 57. These monkish bishops were eventually suppressed.

[3] " Episcopus tamen non est ausus super caput ejus manum imponere, nisi prius idem Findchanus, Aidum carnaliter amans, suam capiti ejus pro confirmatione imponeret dexteram." Adam. i. 36.

the bishop completed the ceremony. When informed of this affair, Columbkille was exceedingly indignant; he pronounced the ordination a nullity, and declared that Findchan's hand, which had taken part in the profane transaction, would be smitten by the judgment of God. The legend states that the prediction was fulfilled: the unworthy hand rotted and fell from the body of the abbot while he was yet alive!

According to ecclesiastical regulations established elsewhere, a bishop, at the ordination of a presbyter, laid his right hand *first* on the candidate,[1] and the presbyters present imposed hands after him; but in this transaction the order was reversed, for the presbyter abbot took the lead and the bishop followed. The bishop was evidently an ecclesiastical tool employed to shift the responsibility from Findchan; but, at the eleventh hour, he refused to bear all the blame, and insisted that, though he repeated the official words, the abbot " for confirmation," or as expressive of his sanction, must take the initiative in the act of investiture. The right of Findchan to ordain is thus clearly implied.

Those who are so unwilling to acknowledge that Columbkille and his successors ordained bishops and presbyters seem to forget that they enjoyed a privilege usually exercised only by archbishops and popes; for they consecrated the Pictish sovereigns.[2] The inauguration of King Aidan, in A.D. 574, by the founder of the monastery of Hy, is particularly described by Adamnan, who tells us how the abbot " ordained "[3] the monarch by placing his hand on the royal head and by bestowing his sacerdotal benediction. It is admitted that Columbkille presided in synods where bishops were present;[4] and therefore a writer of the ninth century does not use words without understanding when he describes him as " the primate of all the bishops of Hibernia."[5]

[1] "Presbyter quum ordinatur, Episcopo cum benedicente, et manum super caput ejus tenente, etiam omnes presbyteri, qui præsentes sunt, manus suas juxta manum episcopi super caput illius teneant."—*Con. Carthag. Binii Concilia*, i. 553.

[2] Some of the French kings have been crowned by the Pope, others by an archbishop. The Archbishop of Canterbury is usually employed in the coronation of an English sovereign.

[3] "Imponensque manum super caput ejus, ordinans benedixit."—Adamnan, iii. 5.

[4] This privilege was inherited by his successors. Reeves mentions that "the *Topographical History of Tara Hill* records a synod at which Adamnan presided. *Life of St. Columba*, 179, note.

[5] "Omnium Hiberniensium episcoporum Primas." Notker Balbulus, who died A.D. 912. See Jamieson, 335.

The traditions relative to the ecclesiastical career of Columb-kille prior to his settlement at Hy are exceedingly obscure and unsatisfactory. Before leaving Ireland he founded conventual establishments at Durrow[1] and elsewhere; and the great Scottish institute was on much the same plan as these earlier monasteries: but he was no favourite with the bishops of his native country; and he was excommunicated by them in one of their synods before he entered on his mission to North Britain.[2] His obnoxious political proceedings have been assigned as the cause of his condemnation; but other circumstances seem to have conspired to provoke episcopal hostility; and it is not improbable that the jealousy entertained by the secular clergy towards the regulars—a feeling which subsequently created so much confusion throughout the whole Church—contributed to bring upon him this sentence of ecclesiastical proscription.[3] Columb-kille was a scholar; he was aware, no doubt, that the learned Jerome, one of the patriarchs of monasticism in the West, maintained the original identity of bishop and presbyter,[4] and that, even in the third century, the presbyters of Alexandria continued to inaugurate their chief pastors; he must have known, too, that abbots in other quarters of the Church had already been advanced to high honours and had been permitted to sit with the most distinguished prelates in the great councils;[5] and we may be sure that this "son of ancient kings" was well disposed to stand on his dignity, and to magnify his office. And if he asserted, as he unquestionably did, supreme control over the monasteries he founded; if he claimed a right, in conjunction with the monks, his fellow presbyters, to ordain the bishops sent out by them to evangelize the country; no wonder that he came into collision with the ecclesiastical authorities, and that he at length found himself excommunicated. But he obviously treated the sentence as an impotent demonstration, as we do not find

[1] Reeves, *Appendix to Preface*, lxxiii.
[2] Adamnan, iii. 3.
[3] It is noteworthy that at least one abbot who was present—Brendan of Birr—did not concur in the sentence. See Reeves, *Appendix to Preface*, lxxiv. A dispute relative to the possession of a Psalter or Gospel, which Columbkille had copied from the manuscript of a certain bishop appears to have entered into the controversy; but the story is very obscure. See Reeves, 248, 249.
[4] He is quoted by the Irish Cummian in his letter to the Abbot of Hy. See Ussher's *Sylloge*, *Epist.* xi. *Works* by Elrington, iv. 437.
[5] Thus in A.D. 449 the Abbot Barsumas sat in the Second Council of Ephesus.

that he ever sought its removal.[1] The brilliant success of his mission to Scotland appears to have silenced opposition—for who would have ventured to maintain that the man who had converted a whole kingdom and "ordained" a monarch, was incompetent to ordain a bishop or a presbyter? When he revisited Ireland a few years before his death, he was received with almost regal honours. And how singular that a country in which the right of presbyters to ordain was thus boldly exercised in the sixth century, became, in the sixteenth, one of the strongholds of Presbyterianism! How singular that Andrew Melville, a man also of noble lineage and of superior erudition, should be found, after so long an interval, establishing a principle asserted by Columbkille! And how remarkable that the ceremony performed by the Presbyter Abbot of Hy in the inauguration of King Aidan, should be substantially repeated, at the distance of a thousand years, by Robert Bruce, another Presbyterian minister, and another scion of royalty, in the coronation of the first Protestant Queen of Scotland![2]

Columbkille was contemporary with Kentigern, or St. Mungo,[3] so often described as the founder of the See of Glasgow. Kentigern died A.D. 601, so that he survived the first abbot of Hy about four years; but his claim as the founder of a Scottish bishopric is apocryphal, as it is well known that there are no traces of diocesan episcopacy in North Britain before the close of the ninth century.[4] The Irish and Scottish bishops of the days of Kentigern and Columbkille were indeed very different from our modern diocesans. Their representatives are rather to be found in our itinerant missionaries. Accompanied by a small clerical

---

[1] The legend that Columbkille desired to be made a bishop, that Etchen, his ordainer, committed a blunder, and made him only a presbyter, and that the saint then declined any farther ordination, is apparently an awkward attempt to account for the exercise of episcopal prerogatives by the presbyter abbot. See Lanigan, ii. 126.

[2] M'Crie's *Life of Melville*, i. 301, Edinburgh, 1824.

[3] It would appear that the word Mungo, in the ancient British language, conveys the idea of *dear friend*. "*Mwyngu*," says Chalmers, "signifies a courteous or mild person." *Caledonia*, i. 316, note.

[4] About that time the bishopric of St. Andrews was founded. Kellach, the first bishop, was living in A.D. 909. See Pinkerton's *Enquiry*, ii. 181, 182. But the system was not fully established until long afterwards. "The bishops of the Scots," says Camden, "exercised their episcopal functions everywhere without distinction to the time of Malcom III. about the year 1070, when their dioceses were confined to certain limits." See Jamieson, 345.

retinue of six or seven presbyters[1] and perhaps one deacon, they perambulated the country preaching the Word. The deacon acted in a somewhat menial capacity;[2] and whilst the bishop trained the more gifted presbyters for a higher office, they assisted him in various ways in the performance of his sacred functions.

The year A.D. 597, in which Columbkille died, is otherwise memorable as the time when the monk Augustine, under the direction of Pope Gregory, made his appearance in England. The success of the Romish missionary in South Britain led ultimately to a complete change in the ecclesiastical condition of both Scotland and Ireland. The Italian clergy could not brook any deviation from their ritual; they denounced the peculiar discipline and usages of other churches as a violation of Catholic unity; and the political power which they soon acquired, and which they contrived to manage most dexterously, enabled them at length either to gain over or to subdue the nonconformists. Even Adamnan, the abbot of Hy, and the biographer of Columbkille, when on a visit to the court of Aldfrid, King of Northumbria, was induced to agree to the Romish mode of keeping Easter; but, on his return home, he could not persuade his co-religionists to adopt his views, and, in consequence, retired from the monastery.[3] He revisited it, after a long absence, in A.D. 704; and died the same year[4] at the age of eighty. But Italian diplomacy in the end proved successful. Nectan, king of the Picts, was made a convert to Romish observance; and, in A.D. 716, the monks of Hy, who refused to follow the royal example, were expelled from the establishment. The monastery was afterwards more than once rifled by northern pirates; its reputation declined; and it was gradually stripped of the extraordinary privileges which it originally enjoyed. The island, once the scene of so much intellectual activity, still retains memorials of its mediæval glory; and is therefore still interesting to the tourist and the antiquary. There was a time when it was the favourite burying-place of royal personages; and the visitor is

---

[1] In ancient documents we find a bishop accompanied by six or eight presbyters, sometimes by three, and sometimes only by two. See King's *Memoir of the Primacy of Armagh*, 8, 12.

[2] He is represented as carrying water. Adamnan's *Columba*, ii. 1.

[3] He remained at this time seven years in Ireland. Reeves, *Ap. to Pref.* liii.

[4] Reeves, *Appendix to Preface*, xli. note.

reminded that it preserves the dust of Irish, Scottish, and Norwegian kings;[1] but the cathedral, the remains of which may well excite the admiration of the stranger, cannot claim to be nearly as ancient as the days of Columbkille.

The brethren of Hy have acquired celebrity under the designation of *Culdees*. The name—which cannot be traced farther back in ecclesiastical records than the beginning of the ninth century[2]—was also given to the inmates of conventual establishments in England, Wales, and Ireland.[3] It is apparently equivalent to "The religious"[4]—a title by which monks are still known. Even in the days of Bede, the polity of Hy and kindred institutions was of an "unusual order," conserving the remnants of a church constitution handed down from primitive ages. The Culdees were a fraternity, not of lay brothers, but of clergymen, who claimed and exercised the right of ordination, and who, by "the laying on of the hands of the presbytery," invested a goodly number of churchmen in the British isles with their ministerial commission. They therefore deserve the special notice of the ecclesiastical historian.

CHAPTER III.

IRELAND; AND PATRICK ITS APOSTLE.

THE history of man, as recorded in the Bible, is wonderfully corroborated by the traditions of all nations. Sceptical philosophers have tried to upset the authority of the Pentateuch, and to show that the inspired writers have misrepresented either the origin or the antiquity of our race; but it would be difficult to produce elsewhere such transparent specimens of sophistry, credulity, and wild theorizing, as are to be found in these attempts to overturn the divine testimony. Geology is only in

[1] Dr. Johnson's *Journey to the Western Islands.* Reeves, 232, 418.
[2] Jamieson's *Historical Account of the Ancient Culdees,* 354. See also Reeves, *Culdees of the British Islands,* p. 145, Dublin, 1864.
[3] Chalmers' *Caledonia,* i. 434; Reeves, *Culdees of the British Islands,* passim.
[4] According to some, Culdee is derived from two Irish or Gaelic words—*Ceile,* a servant, and *De* god. According to others, Culdee is a Gaelic word signifying a monk, or hermit, or any sequestered person. "As interpreted by the language to which this word belongs," says M'Lauchlan, "the Culdee was nothing else than *the man of the recess.*" *Early Scottish Church,* p. 176.

its infancy, and its votaries have often illustrated their inexperience by the folly of their speculations; but its facts demonstrate that man was formed exactly in the order of creation set forth in the sacred narrative. Whilst the Mosaic record bears internal marks of truth, it is also sustained by various kinds of collateral evidence. Its account of the deluge is confirmed by those wrecks of history which have floated down to us from all quarters in the shape of poetry and legend. Even the ancient names of seas, rivers, and mountains, assist us in tracing the route pursued by the dispersed builders of Babel; and point to Central Asia as the birthplace of the human family.

All existing memorials concur to prove that Western Europe was peopled from the East; and the language of the Celts, the earliest colonists, is still inscribed on the Seine and the Rhone,[1] the Alps, and the Apennines.[2] Ireland, where this tongue is yet spoken by a portion of the population, can produce records describing the succession of its kings extending back to a very remote antiquity; and though these documents contain many errors and absurdities, the reader may see that they often embody historical materials exaggerated or distorted in the course of transmission. According to them all, the island, at first uninhabited, was occupied by successive importations of strangers of oriental origin. Some of these, known as the Firbolgs or Belgæ, crossed from England—having previously migrated from Gaul; others, called the Tuath de Danan, or Northmen,[3] arrived from Scotland—where they had found their way from Scandinavia;[4] and others again, the Scots or Milesians, are said to have been colonists from Spain.[5] The Scots spoke the language now known

---

[1] The Seine—*Sequana*—from the Irish words, seac aban, *i.e.* the frozen river; the Rhone—*Rhodanus*—from roid aban, *i.e.* the swift river. Sir William Betham's *Gael and Cymbri*, 194, Dublin, 1834.

[2] "Ailp is an Irish word denoting a great mass. The Irish cenn sometimes assumes the form bean or bin, *pinna*, which appears in Welsh as *penn*." Reeves' *Columba* by Adamnan, 241, note. In Adamnan we have the words, "Ultra Alpes Peninas," iii. 23.

[3] Betham derives Tuath de Danan from the Irish words *tuat*—north, *de*—of, and *daoine*—people. *Gael and Cymbri*, 431. For another explanation see *Ogygia Vindicated*, p. 33.

[4] Stillingfleet's *Origines Britannicæ*, 252-254, London, 1840.

[5] This is vehemently denied by Pinkerton. See his *Enquiry*, ii. 47. He affirms that the Scots were Scythians who emigrated from Germany and Gaul. See *Ogygia Vindicated*, xxxi.

as Gaelic or Irish;[1] the Tuath de Danan used a different tongue, still preserved in the Welsh or Cumraig. About the beginning of the Christian era, the Scots or Milesians were the dominant race—a distinction for which they were indebted to their superior activity, enterprise, and intelligence.

In the time of Julius Cæsar Ireland was well known to the Greeks and Romans;[2] its situation is pointed out by their ancient geographers; and its ports are said to have been often visited by traders.[3] Several respectable writers, after a careful investigation of the subject, have adopted the conclusion that the Irish must have been acquainted with the use of letters before they were taught by Christian missionaries;[4] and if we admit that the Scots, like the Carthaginians, were of Phœnician ancestry,[5] the presumption in favour of the antiquity of their literature is considerably strengthened. Several facts attest that in remote times they were not greatly behind other nations in social progress. A water-mill for the grinding of corn was erected in the country about the middle of the third century;[6] and the prince who introduced this piece of valuable machinery appears to have maintained something like the dignity of a court, in connexion with a regular military establishment.[7] The island was then governed by a number of petty potentates, subordinate to a chief monarch whose royal residence was at Tara in Meath.

Christianity had acquired an influential position in England in the reign of Constantine the Great; and, as there was considerable intercourse between the countries, it is probable that the Gospel was then not unknown in Ireland. We have presumptive evidence, as well of the existence of a church, as of the use of letters in this remote region towards the close of the

[1] Pinkerton, ii. 139.
[2] See Sir William Betham's *Antiquarian Researches*, i. 12.
[3] Tacitus, *Life of Agricola*, 24.
[4] See *Transactions of the Royal Irish Academy*, vol. xviii. pt. 2, 46; O'Conor's *Rerum Hibernicarum Scriptores Veteres*, 1. xxix.; Todd's *St. Patrick*, 513.
[5] See Betham's *Gael and Cymbri*, chap. iii.; and Villanueva's *Ibernia Phœnicea*, Dublin, 1831.
[6] *Trans. Roy. Ir. Ac.*, xviii., pt. 2, pp. 150, 164. The famous Cormac O'Cuinn, or Cormac Mac Art, was now the chief monarch of Ireland. His general, or the "captain of his host," was Fin Mac Cumhail, the Fingal of Mac Pherson's *Ossian*.
[7] Pinkerton's *Enquiry*, ii. 77, 78.

fourth century; for Cœlestius, the noted heresiarch,[1] was an Irishman; and, when abroad, he is reported to have written to his parents in Hibernia—an intimation from which we may infer that there were individuals at home able to read his correspondence. But the earliest direct notice of Irish Christianity is furnished by a French writer of the fifth century, from whom we learn that in A.D. 431 Pope Celestine sent Palladius "to the Irish believing in Christ as their first bishop."[2]

These few words of the ancient chronicler throw much light on the ecclesiastical history of Ireland. They obviously imply that tidings of the spread of Christianity in the Western Isle had reached the capital of Christendom, and that the great Italian patriarch deemed it prudent to endeavour to establish his authority among the converts by placing a bishop of his own at the head of their hierarchy. The importance attached to the scheme is indicated by the rank of the individual selected to carry it into operation; for Palladius, ordained by Pope Celestine, had previously held the high office of archdeacon[3] at Rome. He was now probably about sixty years of age; tradition relates that he was a Briton by birth[4]—a circumstance which may have induced him the more readily to accept the appointment; and, with a goodly number of ecclesiastics in his train, as well as with an ample store of relics,[5] he set out for the scene of his intended ministry. But this attempt of the Pope to gain a footing in Ireland issued in a signal failure. Palladius was not well settled in the country when, according to reports current in after ages, the threats of a petty pagan chieftain, named Nathy, constrained him to take his departure. Driven from the Irish shore, he sailed for Scotland, where he met with little better encouragement; and at Fordun in Mearns, about a year after he had entered on the undertaking, a friendly fever put an end to his course.

[1] See Section II. Chap. III. of this Period, p. 181.

[2] Prosper, *Chronicon*. "Basso et Antiocho Coss. ad Scotos in Christum credentes ordinatus a Papa Celestino Palladius primus episcopus mittitur."

[3] Probus, i. 25; Lanigan, i. 200; *Ogygia Vindicated*, chap. xvi. Dr. Todd condemns the statement that Palladius was a Roman archdeacon as the invention of "some modern manufacturers of history;" and yet, according to his own testimony, it is made by a writer who flourished about A.D. 900, and "who probably derived his information from some now lost acts of still higher antiquity." See his *St. Patrick*, 276, 293, 294, Dublin, 1864.

[4] Lanigan, i. 33.   [5] Lanigan, i. 33.

The reason assigned for the failure of this mission is evidently most unsatisfactory. Nathy was not the chief monarch of Ireland, or even one of its provincial kings. His territory was not more extensive than a modern county—perhaps not much larger than a parish;[1] and it is absurd to say that Palladius was obliged to leave Ireland in consequence of the opposition of such an adversary. The account usually given of the subsequent proceedings of the Pope must also be acknowledged as very improbable. When Celestine, it is said, heard of the death of Palladius, he nominated Patrick to succeed him in the mission to Ireland. The enterprise had already been abandoned; and the death of the individual who had relinquished it as hopeless could scarcely have suggested the appointment of a successor. Nor is this the only difficulty connected with the reception of this ill-constructed tale. The Pontiff died in the spring of A.D. 432;[2] and it is almost certain that he was outlived by Palladius.[3] It is, at all events, evident that the report of the demise of his missionary could not have reached Celestine before the end of his pontificate. Thus, the story, that he nominated Patrick as the successor of Palladius, must be a fable.

It would appear that Palladius left Ireland for a reason much more substantial than that commonly assigned. He was sent by Celestine "to the Irish believing in Christ" as their "first" or chief bishop;[4] and the Irish Christians refused to receive him in any such character. Patrick, their great apostle, had already been labouring among them upwards of a quarter of a century; and neither he nor his coadjutors were prepared to submit to the supervision of this stranger from Rome. This

[1] Nathy is said to have been prince of Hy-Garchon, which, according to Colgan, was a maritime tract of the County Wicklow. According to some, Hy-Garchon was the same as Fotharta. See Lanigan, i. 40. Fotharta, at a somewhat later period, "constituted two lordships, namely Fotharta-Fea, now the barony of Forth in the County of Carlow, and Fotharta an Chairn, now the barony of Forth, in the County of Wexford." *Annals of the Four Masters* by O'Donovan, 2d ed. i. 333, note.

[2] On the 6th of April. Lanigan, i. 202.

[3] The *Annals of Innisfallen* state that Palladius remained a year in Ireland; and, according to some authorities, he died on the 6th of July, A.D. 432. See Lanigan, i. 44, 45. In those days many months must have elapsed before his death in Kincardineshire could have been known in Rome.

[4] That there were bishops in Ireland before either Patrick or Palladius admits of little doubt. See *Trans. Roy. Ir. Ac.* xviii. pt. 2, p. 47; Ussher, *Works*, vi. 345-354.

truth peeps out occasionally in a great variety of ancient documents. Thus, in the best and oldest Irish manuscript relating to Church history now preserved,[1] it is stated that "Palladius was sent by Pope Celestine *with a gospel for Patrick* to preach it to the Irish."[2] The volume here mentioned—probably a splendidly decorated copy of the four Evangelists—was a gift obviously intended to conciliate the popular missionary. In one of the oldest lives of Patrick still extant it is admitted that he was in Ireland *many years* before the arrival of Palladius.[3] Other evidences, yet to be considered, sustain the same conclusion. We shall first, however, notice the depositions of the primary witness—the testimony of Patrick himself.

This celebrated man, universally known as *The Apostle of Ireland*, has left behind him a piece of autobiography, entitled his *Confession*, in which, at the close of his life, he recapitulates the most prominent incidents of his remarkable career. The document possesses peculiar interest as being the earliest extant specimen of patristic literature produced by an author connected with the British churches. In addition to strong external proofs of its extreme antiquity,[4] it contains the clearest internal tokens of genuineness;[5] so that its claims have been acknowledged by

---

[1] The *Leabhar Breac, i.e. The Speckled Book*—"the oldest and best Irish MS. relating to Church history now preserved, or which perhaps the Irish ever possessed." Dr. Petrie on *Tara Hill*, in the *Tr. Roy. Ir. Ac.* xviii. pt. 2, 93. According to Petrie, the *Leabhar Breac* was written entirely in the twelfth century. *Tr. Roy. Ir. Ac.* xviii. p. 2, 104. According to others, it is a MS. of the latter end of the fourteenth or beginning of the fifteenth century. See Todd's *St. Patrick*, p. 176, and *Lectures on the MS. Materials of Ancient Irish History*, pp. 352, 353, where it is characterized by O'Curry as "the most important repertory of our ancient ecclesiastical and theological writings in existence." Some of the tracts which it contains appear to have been composed in the eighth century, and some are perhaps of a still earlier date.

[2] The reader may find the original in *Trans. Roy. Ir. Ac.* xviii. 103, pt. 2.

[3] "The interpolated version of his life by Probus sends Patrick to Rome to receive the apostolic blessing, after having preached unsuccessfully in Ireland many years before the mission of Palladius." Dr. Petrie on *Tara Hill, Tr. Roy. Ir. Ac.* xviii. pt. 2, 108, 109. The foundation of the monastery at Armagh is commonly assigned to A.D. 445, and yet it would appear from an old catalogue of those who presided over the establishment, that it was in existence in A.D. 429 or A.D. 430. See Lanigan, i. 315.

[4] A copy of it written towards the beginning of the ninth century, and preserved in the Book of Armagh, is still in existence.

[5] Some of these are pointed out by Dr. O'Conor, *Rer. Hiber. Scrip. Vet.* i. cxi. cxv. See also Lanigan, i. 80, 118.

the best critics of all denominations.[1] It was evidently written at a time when the Church was in a process of transition; when primitive simplicity had not been quite superseded by formalism; and yet when the monastic spirit threatened to interdict the marriage of the clergy. Patrick tells us in this memorial that he was himself the son of a deacon and the grandson of a presbyter;[2] but statements incidentally occurring show that another order of things was now prevailing, and that the discipline of the cloister was becoming exceedingly fashionable. He was born in the north of France—probably in Boulogne-sur-Mer;[3] and his native country was designated Britannia, or Britain, when the Confession was composed.[4] He informs us that, when nearly sixteen years of age, he was carried captive into Ireland; and that he remained there six years in slavery. This period of his life was the crisis of his religious history. He had been a gay and careless boy; he had neglected the advice of his spiritual instructors; but, in the day of adversity, the lessons of his childhood recurred to his recollection, and the seed sown began to bear good fruit. "The Lord," says he, "brought me to a sense of my unbelief, that at length I might remember my transgressions and turn with my whole heart to the Lord my God."[5] "I was daily employed in tending sheep, and often during the day I prayed, and the love of God more and more increased. . . . I used to remain even in the woods and on the mountain, and was wont to rise up before day to pray in snow, in frost, and in rain, and I felt no injury; nor was there any sluggishness in me, such as I now feel, because the Spirit was then ardent within me."[6]

[1] Among these may be mentioned Ussher, Ware, Tillemont, Lanigan, and Neander. That found in the Book of Armagh is obviously the genuine text—though having only about one-half the matter contained in other MSS. The additions have been made by interpolators to support a false chronology, and countenance certain fables relative to Bridget. The copy in the Book of Armagh has nothing as to objections against his ordination to the episcopate founded on acts done thirty years before. Tillemont was deceived by this spurious passage.

[2] Confession, i. 1. The references here given are to the chapters and numerals as found in Villanueva's edition, Dublin, 1835; but the translation sometimes follows a different text. Neither in Ware's edition, nor O'Conor's, is the Epistle divided into chapters.

[3] Lanigan, i. 93, 94. In his Confession Patrick speaks of Ireland as far away from his native country—language which he would not have used had he been a Scotchman born on the banks of the Clyde. He also mentions his Gallic brethren.

[4] Lanigan, i. 105, 107, 113-118.   [5] Confession, i. 1.   [6] Ibid. ii. 6.

Ireland.

Patrick eventually effected his escape from Ireland, and was restored to his parents; but, in consequence of the insecure condition of his native land—exposed to the incursions of the Francs, as well as of the Picts and Scots—he was again reduced to slavery. This second bondage was, however, only of two months' duration.[1] His parents, who appear to have been in comfortable circumstances, now hoped to enjoy his society for the rest of their days; but it was soon obvious that he was bent on becoming a missionary; and a singular dream which he had, when ruminating on the subject, confirmed him in his purpose. "I saw," says he, "in a vision of the night a man whose name was Victoricius,[2] coming as if from Ireland with innumerable letters, one of which he handed to me; and I read the beginning of the letter purporting to be the voice of the people of Ireland! And whilst I was reading the beginning of the letter, I thought at that very moment I heard the voice of those who were beside the wood of Foclud,[3] which is near the Western Sea; and they cried out thus, 'We entreat thee, holy youth,[4] to come and walk still among us.' And I was touched to the very heart, and could read no more; and so I awoke."[5]

When Patrick had this dream he could not have been much above thirty years of age, for he is addressed in it as a holy youth; and the designation of the individual who appeared to him bearing innumerable letters from Hibernia obviously inspired him with encouragement. To the ardent mind of the young Frenchman the title *Victoricius* was inspiriting.

---

[1] Confession, ii. 9.

[2] This name is evidently the foundation of all the fables respecting Patrick and the angel Victor. See *Life by Jocelin*, xv. xxi.

[3] Said to be Tirawley in the county of Mayo. Lanigan, i. 162. In this district Patrick's converts were more numerous than in any other part of Ireland. See Lanigan, i. 252.

[4] "Rogamus te, sancte puer, ut venias et adhuc ambules inter nos." He was but a boy when among them, and they still thought of him as such.

[5] Confession, iii. 10. The *Lives* of Patrick represent him as "*about* thirty years of age" at the time of this vision. See Lanigan, i. 160, 163. We have thus another confirmation of the chronology adopted in the text, for at the death of King Niall he was exactly thirty-two. The canonical age for the ordination of a bishop was thirty. See Lanigan, i. 164. About the time of his mission into Ireland, according to one account, Germanus sent with him an *aged priest*, named Segetius, to be the guide of his inexperience—and yet, according to current statements, Patrick was then entering on the sixtieth year of his age! See Todd's *St. Patrick*, 316.

Patrick knew well to whom that description was applicable. In his sixteenth year he had himself been led captive in the train of this Irish hero; and every one then living in the north of France could have told that the victor from Hibernia was no other than the chief monarch of the island—King Niall the Great, or Niall of the Nine Hostages. The people of Britain and of Gaul trembled at his approach; wherever he went, he carried victory along with him; and nine royal personages, as hostages, accompanied his march, and attested the power of the mighty conqueror. But why add ICIUS[1] to VICTOR? Patrick could also have explained the significance of that appendix; for the Irish monarch had often crossed the Ician sea in triumph, and had now perished in the arms of victory on its shore. An arrow from the quiver of a traitor had there terminated his career.[2] Patrick had long cherished the desire of labouring as a missionary in the land of his captivity; he soon heard of the death of the dreaded general; he was told that his surviving troops were about to return to Ireland; he probably conceived the idea of following the mourning host;[3] and, when brooding over the great enterprise, the ghost of Niall—a man named Victor Icius —appeared to him in a dream with innumerable letters of invitation from Hibernia.[4]

[1] The word is sometimes written *Icius;* sometimes, *Itius;* and sometimes *Iccius.* See Lemprière's *Classical Dictionary,* where it is written Icius, edit. London, 1815; and Smith's *Dictionary of Ancient Geography,* where it is Iccius and Itius. It is sometimes written Ictius. As Niall was called Victor-Icius, from the name of the sea where he was mortally wounded, so, in the ninth century, another Niall was called Niall-*Caille,* from the name of the river in which he was drowned. See MacGeoghegan's *History of Ireland,* p. 209, Dublin, 1844. In the thirteenth century another Niall was, for a similar reason, called "Bryan of the battle of Down." O'Donovan's *Four Masters,* vol. iii. 377, note at A.D. 1260.

[2] "The age of Christ, 405. After Niall of the Nine Hostages, son of Eochaidh Muighmheadhoin, had been twenty-seven years in the sovereignty of Ireland, he was slain by Eochaidh, son of Enna Ceinnseallach *at Muir-n-Icht, i.e.* the sea between France and England." *Annals of the Four Masters,* ad A.D. 405. Dr. O'Donovan, the editor, adds in a note: "This sea (Mare Icium) is supposed to have taken its name from the Port Iccius of Cæsar, situated not far from the site of the present Boulogne." If, at the time, Patrick was living at Boulogne he must have heard immediately of the death of Niall.

[3] When Dathy, his immediate successor, was killed at the foot of the Alps, the body was carried home to Ireland. See O'Donovan's *Annals of the Four Masters,* i. 129, note. It is not improbable that the body of Niall was also conveyed to his native land.

[4] There is another strange coincidence to be here noted. There was a Victori-

Ireland. 311

This interpretation of the Confession enables us at once to settle the chronology of the life of the Irish apostle. If Patrick, as there is every reason to believe,[1] came to Ireland immediately after the death of Niall the Great, he probably arrived in the country towards the close of A.D. 405. According to accounts which have been long current, his mission did not commence until seven and twenty years afterwards; but no reason whatever has been given for this extraordinary delay; and his own words convey the impression that he acted forthwith on what he regarded as a heavenly intimation.[2] The testimony of some of the earliest historical witnesses, though hitherto strangely overlooked, corroborates this interpretation. Thus Marcus, an Irish bishop who flourished in the beginning of the ninth century, informs us that Patrick came to Ireland in A.D. 405;[3] and Nennius, a Briton, who lived about the same period, repeats the statement.[4] Other circumstances lead us to infer that this is the true date of the commencement of his mission. According to the best authorities he was born about A.D. 373,[5] so that in A.D.

---

cius bishop of Rouen, who was the contemporary, and, it is said, the friend of Patrick. See Kelly's *Dissertations on Irish Church History*, note, p. 260, Dublin, 1864. In A.D. 404, Innocent I. writes a letter to him. See Dupin's *Eccles. Writers*, i. 337, edit. Dublin, 1723. Victoricius seems to have died shortly afterwards, perhaps in A.D. 405. He was not living in A.D. 409. See Migne's *Patrol. Cursus*, tom. xx. 438. It is not improbable that Niall and Victoricius died in the same year. Victoricius is said to have been distinguished by his missionary spirit.

[1] In the Confession Patrick thanks God that "after very many years the Lord gave him" to the people who called for him in the dream from the wood of Foclud. But this affords no proof that he did not immediately go to Ireland. Even, according to his biographers, he did not visit Connaught for years after his arrival in the country; and it is probable that he did not succeed there until a comparatively late period of his mission.

[2] In the copy of the Confession contained in the Book of Armagh he goes on to speak of his departure for Ireland immediately after describing his night visions. "I give thanks to God," says he, "who has comforted me in all things, *that he did not hinder me from the journey on which I had resolved.*" *Conf.* iii. 12. Lanigan remarks that "very little time seems to have elapsed between his promotion to the episcopacy and his repairing to Ireland," i. 179.

[3] *Introduction to the Irish Version of Nennius*, p. 19, Dublin, 1848.

[4] According to Nennius, Patrick was eighty-five years the apostle of the Irish! § 55. The text of the *History of the Britons* is very corrupt, and the statements contradictory.

[5] See Lanigan, i. 129, 130. Dr. Lanigan himself has adopted a different reckoning.

405 he was still in the vigour of youth;[1] and a late most acute and learned Roman Catholic historian has adduced good evidence to prove that he died in A.D. 465.[2] Traditions of the highest antiquity attest that he spent sixty years in Ireland;[3] and, as, between A.D. 405 and A.D. 465, there is exactly such an interval, we have thus another confirmation of the correctness of our computation. The testimony of the famous Marianus Scotus,[4] to the age of Patrick at the time of his death, supports the same conclusion. This learned Irishman, who flourished in the eleventh century, and who was minutely acquainted with the ancient history of his country, has informed us that the great Hibernian missionary expired at the age of ninety-two;[5] and it follows that Marianus must have believed that he was little more than thirty when he entered on his labours. If he was born in A.D. 373, the view now given sustains both these positions.

This version of the chronology of the life of Patrick solves a multitude of difficulties in which his history has been long involved. According to some of his oldest biographers he was ordained a missionary by Amator;[6] but the bishop of Auxerre of that name died in A.D. 418,[7] or fourteen years before his

---

[1] In the Confession he is made to say,—"You know, and God knows, how I have *lived among you from my youth* (a juventute mea)," v. 21. These words are not in the copy in the Book of Armagh, but the interpolater evidently believed that Patrick laboured from his youth as an Irish missionary.

[2] Lanigan, i. 362, 363. Since the time of Dr. Lanigan this point has been confirmed by additional testimonies. Thus, according to the Book of Armagh—in which it is stated that "from the passion of Christ to the death of Patrick there were 436 years," (Betham, ii. 288)—Patrick must have died about A.D. 466; as our Lord was crucified about A.D. 30. If these 436 years were current, not complete, time, the date would be A.D. 465.

[3] As the Hymn of Fiech, *Rer. Hib. Scrip. Vet.* i. *Proleg.* i. xciv.

[4] He was born A.D. 1028, and died about A.D. 1082. The last twenty-six years of his life were spent on the Continent. He was one of the most learned men of his time. There was another Irishman of the same name, his contemporary, who died at Ratisbon in A.D. 1088. See a paper by Dr. Reeves in the *Proceedings of the Royal Irish Academy*, vol. vii. 290, Dublin, 1862.

[5] Lanigan, i. 131; Ussher, *Antiq.* chap. xvii., *Works* by Elrington, vi. 443. The words of Marianus as quoted by Ussher are: "Sanctus Patricius Hiberniæ archiepiscopus, quum esset annorum nonaginte duorum, obiit. Quum esset annorum sexdecim, venditus est; sex annis vixit in servitute, in Romanis partibus; sexaginta annis in Hibernia prædicavit." The word *decem* seems to have here dropped out before *in Romanis partibus*. The text of Marianus is exceedingly corrupt, and a different reading is often adopted by his editors, but that above given, with *decem* supplied, bears internal marks of truth.

[6] Lanigan, i. 198.   [7] *Ibid.*

supposed appointment by Celestine; and no other Amator of the same age and country is now known. Ordinary accounts describe the Irish apostle as sixty years of age on his arrival in Hibernia; and, reckoning from the time when he was first carried away from his own country by King Niall, he must have been advanced in years at the death of Palladius; but his autobiography throughout conveys the impression that the most vigorous years of his life were devoted to the evangelization of Ireland. His biographers are sadly at a loss to explain his occupation from his boyhood until he reached threescore; and they absurdly relate how he spent thirty years in study preparing for his great work.[1] The good man himself repudiates these statements, for in his Confession, drawn up in his old age, he laments the defects of his early education.[2] He declares that, because of his ignorance, he long hesitated to attempt the preparation of the document. "I feared," says he, "that I should fall under the censure of men; because I had not studied like others."[3] The Confession shows that this is no vain apology; for the tract is written in miserable Latin, and almost every sentence attests that its author was illiterate. It is said that he attained the age of one hundred and twenty—a statement which may itself warrant very grave suspicions—and yet, those who contend for this almost unparalleled longevity, cannot satisfactorily explain how he spent the last thirty years of his career. Unable to supply incidents for this part of his history, many of them assert that it was devoted to contemplation![4] Here again the Confession supplies a contradiction, for it speaks of his life as a scene of constant labour. In the near prospect of dissolution, the old saint, in the spirit of a true martyr, indicates the perils by which he was even then encompassed. "Every day,"

---

[1] Betham, *Antiq. Res.* ii. 386; Lanigan, i. 164, 172. There are various other evidences that he was meanwhile in Ireland. Thus, the Church of Armagh is said to have been founded in A.D. 445; and the Church of Trim was erected twenty-five years before by Patrick. See Todd's *St. Patrick*, 470. According to another account he set out for Rome after having commenced his ministry in Hibernia; and, on his way, met St. Ciaran, or Kieran, to whom he announced a prediction that he would see him in Ireland *thirty years* afterwards. This second meeting with Kieran is said to have taken place shortly after the failure of the mission of Palladius—perhaps about A.D. 435 or A.D. 436. See Todd's *St. Patrick*, 326, 200. The story of Patrick's visit to Rome is manifestly a fabrication.

[2] Confession, i. 4.   [3] *Ibid.* i. 3.

[4] Lanigan, i. 353.

says he, "I brave the danger of being put to death, or entrapped, or reduced to slavery."¹

The sensation created on the Continent by the report of the success of Patrick was obviously the real cause of the mission of Palladius. King Niall was succeeded as chief monarch of Ireland by his nephew Dathy—a brave soldier who was employed during the greater part of his reign of twenty-three years in wars of foreign aggression. In A.D. 428, he was struck dead by lightning as he led his troops to the foot of the Alps.² Meanwhile Patrick was laboriously endeavouring to propagate the Gospel among the people of Hibernia; and many converts soon cheered the heart of the faithful evangelist. Though destitute of the advantages of a finished education, he was mighty in the Scriptures; he had an excellent command of the native language;³ he had a heart to feel and a hand to relieve; he was wholly devoted to his work; and his natural eloquence soon enchained crowds of admiring auditors. On the death of King Dathy, Laoghaire,⁴ the son of Niall the Great, succeeded to his father's throne; and, in the second year⁵ of the reign of this prince, Patrick contrived to gain admission to a national assembly, and thus enjoyed an opportunity of expounding the principles of Christianity to many of the chief men of the island. This conference evidently caused intense excitement; its importance may be inferred from the strange and exaggerated reports respecting it still preserved in Irish traditions; according to many of the biographers of Patrick, it accomplished the conversion of King Laoghaire; but, though it certainly failed to secure so influential a proselyte,⁶ it produced other valuable

---

¹ Confession, v. 23.

² *Annals of the Four Masters*, ad an. A.D. 428.

³ It has been remarked that the Confession was evidently written by one who thought in Irish. See O'Conor, *Rer. Hib. Scrip. Vet.* i. *Proleg.* cxv. note.

⁴ Pronounced *Leary*. He had a royal residence and fortress near Dublin known as *Dunleary*, i.e. the fort of Laoghaire—now Kingstown. Connellan's *Four Masters*, 267, note.

⁵ See Betham's *Antiq. Researches*, ii. 349, where "the *second* year of the reign of Laoghaire" is mentioned as the commencement of his "latest miracles." If Dathy died early in A.D. 428, the second year of Laoghaire commenced in A.D. 429. According to the *Chronicon Scotorum*, Dathy died in A.D. 427.

⁶ See *Trans. Roy. Ir. Acad.* vol. xviii. pt. 2, p. 52. Betham, *Antiq. Res.* ii. 356, 81-86. We may thus see the absurdity of the story that Patrick, in concurrence with Laoghaire and others, revised the laws of Ireland. In the preface

results; for, on this occasion, certain individuals of distinction embraced the faith of the preacher, and the Church now obtained something like a law of toleration.[1]

At the very time when Patrick was achieving these spiritual conquests, Germanus and Lupus, with their associates, were in England, opposing the Pelagian heresy. The good news from Hibernia was soon communicated to these strangers, and some of them probably crossed the Channel to take part in the prosperous mission.[2] Their companions on their return to the Continent disseminated the intelligence; and the tidings at length reached Rome. When the Pope heard of the marvellous success, he attempted to turn it to the account of the aggrandizement of his see; and accordingly sent Palladius to the Irish believing in Christ as their first or chief bishop. Such is obviously the true history of a transaction which legend and imposture have so much mystified.

The Hibernian apostle has often been confounded with a monk of the same name who flourished at the same period. This individual was called Sen-Patrick, or Patrick Senior—either on account of his great age, or because he was the abbot, or senior, of a monastery. He was in England as early as A.D. 425,[3] where he settled in Glastonbury; and when Germanus and Lupus came over from France to defend the cause of orthodoxy, he joined their party and gave them his support.[4] Shortly afterwards he removed to Ireland; where he resided many years; and where he was connected with the monastery of Armagh—an establishment over which he presided. This Patrick had a reputation for superior scholarship; and hence, in an old Irish poem, he is described as "Patrick of the prayers *who had good*

---

to the *Senchus Mor*, which has appeared under the direction of the "Commissioners for publishing the ancient Laws and Institutes of Ireland," the editor has given his sanction to this puerile legend.

[1] Betham, *Antiq. Res.* ii. 356, 359; *Trans. Roy. Ir. Acad.* xviii. pt. 2. 170.

[2] According to Heric of Auxerre, a writer of the ninth century, Germanus himself visited Ireland at this time. See Todd's *St. Patrick*, 318. The Scholiast on Fiace's Hymn states that St. Patrick accompanied Germanus to Britain in A.D. 429. This Patrick was probably Patrick Senior.

[3] See Collier's *Ecc. Hist. of Great Britain*, i. 20; Spelman's *Concilia*, i. 19. See also William of Malmesbury, *History of the Kings of England*, i. 2.

[4] It is admitted that he was with them in Britain on this occasion. See Lanigan, i. 180, 181. According to the ordinary statement he came with them into England and returned with them to Gaul.

Latin"[1]—an accomplishment by which he might have been easily distinguished from his great namesake. He has also been sometimes called the preceptor or tutor of the Irish apostle[2]— probably because he was employed by him in the education of youth, and as a teacher of candidates for the ministry.[3] When far advanced in life he returned to England; where he is said to have died on the 24th of August, A.D. 458, in the monastery of Glastonbury.[4]

Nor is the monk of Armagh the only individual who has been mistaken for the celebrated missionary. Palladius also, as early as the seventh century, began to be called Patrick;[5] and thus the incidents of three separate lives have been jumbled together in most perplexing confusion. We read in the biographies of Patrick, the apostle of Ireland, that he was the disciple of Germanus, and the nephew of Martin of Tours;[6] and it has been found impossible to reconcile many of the ordinary statements on this subject with what we otherwise know of his history;[7] but if Sen-Patrick or Palladius stood thus related to the bishop of Auxerre or the father of French monachism, the difficulty is at once explained. In this way, too, the current stories respecting Patrick's mission from Rome admit of a simple solution. These misconceptions are of ancient date; and there are good grounds for believing that they were encouraged and promoted by parties in the interest of the Pope, who cunningly sought to recommend Romish pretensions by pretending that they had the sanction of the great Irish evangelist.[8] Such attempts may be traced back

---

[1] O'Donovan's *Annals of the Four Masters*, i. 135.

[2] *Trans. Roy. Ir. Acad.* xviii. pt. 2, p. 95.

[3] It is not improbable that he also made Patrick himself better acquainted with the Augustinian doctrine; and thus we may account for the strong anti-Pelagian feeling which appears in the Confession.

[4] The *Annals of the Four Masters* place his death in A.D. 457. See also Lanigan, i. 131, and *Trans. Roy. Ir. Acad.* xviii. pt. 2, 112.

[5] Betham's *Antiq. Researches*, ii. 296, 388; *Trans. Roy. Ir. Acad.* xviii. pt. 2, 117. *Paddy*, the name still used vulgarly in Ireland for Patrick, is apparently a contraction for *Pallady*.

[6] See *Life* by Jocelin, chap. xxii.

[7] Martin of Tours died at an advanced age in A.D. 397; and Patrick is said to have been *four* years under his tuition. As Patrick returned from his first captivity in A.D. 395, this story cannot be correct. See Lanigan, i. 156, 170, 158, 171.

[8] The legend that Patrick died at the age of 120 may thus be explained. It was known that he had been sixty years in Ireland; but these sixty years began

almost as far as the time of the mission of Augustine to England; but, though it was no easy matter to expose the imposture so many years after the death of Patrick, and in an age when printed documents were unknown, there were parties in the country who vehemently suspected fraud, and protested that these new versions of the life of their apostle were opposed to their traditions.[1] An Irish writer of the seventh century, named Maccumachtheni, has candidly made this acknowledgment. In the preface to a Life of Patrick, addressed by him to Aidus, bishop of Sletty, who died in A.D. 698, he declares that "on account of the diverse opinions and *multifarious surmises* of *very many people*," and "the extreme difficulty of making out the narrative," no "certain track of history" in this matter had been "attained." "I shall endeavour," says he, "to explain these few, selected from the many actions of St. Patrick, my knowledge being small, *my authors doubtful*, and my memory treacherous."[2] We can attach little weight to a biography introduced with such credentials.

The Confession itself is in fact almost the only reliable memorial relating to Patrick to be found among all the documents of antiquity.[3] The information supplied even in this very valuable tract is rather vague and meagre. It furnishes, however, abundant light to show that the ordinary lives of the saint are a mass of impudent fabrications.[4] His career, as described by

---

to be reckoned from the year after the arrival of Palladius; and that his early captivity in Ireland might correspond with the reign of King Niall, it was necessary to make the apostle sixty years of age on his arrival as a missionary.

[1] Todd's *St. Patrick*, 401; Betham's *Antiq. Researches*, ii. 302, 403. By some this writer is designated Maccuthenius. See *Trans. Roy. Ir. Acad.* xviii. pt. 2, 109, 110. The corruption of Patrick's own Confession, attested by the difference between the copy in the Book of Armagh and later transcripts, is decisive evidence of a systematic attempt to mislead the public mind as to his history.

[2] In the *Proceedings of the Royal Irish Academy*, vol. viii. p. 269, there is a very able paper by Dean (now Bishop) Graves on the authorship of this preface.

[3] The tracts *De tribus habitaculis* and *De abusionibus sæculi* are obviously the works of another writer. The style has no resemblance whatever to that of the Confession. The letter to Coroticus may justly be suspected as spurious. The canons attributed to Patrick are manifestly of later origin. That quoted by Professor O'Curry (*Lectures on MSS. Materials of Ancient Irish History*, p. 373) is a barefaced forgery—of perhaps not much earlier date than the beginning of the ninth century.

[4] "Of all the Lives of our saint," says Dr. Lanigan, "*Jocelin's is the worst*, although it has been published oftener than the others." "Jocelin, one of whose

himself, is very different from the account given of him in these lying biographies. He wrought no miracles; he delivered no prophecies; he converted no chief monarch of Ireland. When he arrived in the country he found some Christians there already; but Druidism was dominant; and he was obliged slowly to make his way in the face of a most obstinate opposition. He was "in deaths oft;" he was more than once thrown into imprisonment;[1] he saw his disciples forced away into slavery: and yet none of these things moved him; for, upborne by a living faith, he continued to preach the Gospel in season and out of season. But he did not labour in vain. In a country thinly populated he had the satisfaction of baptizing thousands of converts;[2] he ordained many to the pastoral office; and among the members of the Church which he organized were not a few of the families of the inferior chieftains. At his death he had made a deep impression on the whole land; so that his memory should be cherished by all right-hearted Irishmen as their country's best and most ancient benefactor.

The negative testimony of the Confession as to his mission from Rome is ample and unequivocal. Had he received his authority from the Pope, a circumstance to which he must have attributed much importance would have been prominently noticed in this autobiography. But, though the document is of considerable length, and though it treats expressly of the origin of his great undertaking, it does not contain the most distant reference to any such appointment.[3] He evidently believed that he had far higher credentials—that he was sent by God Himself to evangelize Ireland. "The Lord aroused me, a fool," says he, "that with fear and reverence, and without murmuring, I should faithfully serve that nation to which the love of Christ transferred me."[4] It may, indeed, be said that he was too much guided by

---

patrons was the Primate Thomas O'Conor, mentions a disposal of lands . . . in virtue of which the right of them was transferred to St. Patrick and the see of Armagh. The Tripartite (Life), also *a compilation apparently patched up at Armagh*, has something to the same purpose." *Ecc. Hist.* i. 88, 222-3. Jocelin, who lived in the twelfth century, was a Cistercian monk of the monastery of Furnes who removed to Ireland.

[1] Confession, iv. 15.   [2] *Ibid.* ii. 6.
[3] *The Hymn of Fiech or Fiacc*, an Irish poem of great antiquity, detailing the principal incidents of the life of Patrick, is equally silent as to his mission from Rome.   [4] Confession, i. 5.

his dreams; but many others, as well as Pilate's wife[1] and the Irish missionary, have acknowledged their power; and philosophers have found it easier to deride tales told respecting them by men who cannot well be charged with superstition, than to explain how openings in Providence have been thus disclosed, secrets imparted, and coming events made to cast their shadows before.

The silence of the author of the Confession respecting a mission from Rome is singularly corroborated by the silence of other ancient writers respecting Patrick himself. Had he actually been sent from Italy to Ireland by the great Pontiff, an event of such consequence would have been registered by some contemporary chronicler. The appointment of Palladius by Celestine is twice reported by Prosper,[2] and the failure of his mission is kept in abeyance; and yet no notice is taken by this annalist of the marked success of Patrick. No father of the sixth century so much as records the name of the Irish evangelist. It is barely mentioned by Adamnan in his life of Columbkille.[3] In the voluminous works of Bede it occurs only once,[4] and even then in a passage of doubtful authority. In his Ecclesiastical History of England this author speaks of Palladius,[5] but ignores Patrick. No wonder that men of learning and integrity have been tempted to deny the existence of the Irish Apostle.[6] His Confession and the many traditionary evidences of his influence are sufficient to overcome doubts; but it must be acknowledged that the reasons which have been assigned for incredulity are weighty and plausible.

If we admit that Patrick was not sent to Ireland by Celestine, and that he gave no encouragement to Palladius on his landing in the island, the silence of so many writers can be satisfactorily explained. The conversion of Clovis, king of the Francs, little more than a quarter of a century after the death of Patrick, added immensely to the Papal power in the West; and every

---

[1] Matt. xxvii. 19. See also Gen. xl. 5; Dan. iv. 5.
[2] *Liber contra Collatorem*, cap. xxi.; and *Chronic. Patrologiæ Cursus* by Migne, li. 271, 595.   [3] *Præf.*, 2.   [4] In his *Martyrology*. See Ledwich, 60.
[5] *Ecc. Hist.* i. 13.
[6] See Ledwich's *Antiquities of Ireland*, 58, Dublin, 1803. It has of late been very much the fashion to deride this learned writer; but though, like others, he has committed several grave mistakes in the investigation of a difficult subject, he is vastly superior to many of his critics in candour and vigour of judgment.

Continental writer, not wishing to offend the mighty prelate, took care never to allude to the success of the Irish missionary. Had he been an agent of the Pope, his wonderful achievements would have been trumpeted in the metropolis of Christendom, and a constant intercourse would have been ever afterwards maintained between the Church of Rome and her Hibernian daughter; but, for ages, no correspondence whatever can be traced; no Italian writer refers to the labours of Patrick; and no Pontiff, in any encyclical epistle, inserts his name. Though Pope Leo the Great wrote such a multitude of letters;[1] though he was so remarkable for energy and vigilance; and though he filled the Roman chair for twenty-one years[2] at the very time when Patrick was proceeding so prosperously in the Western isle; he never penned a single line for his encouragement. Before the seventh century we have no traces whatever[3] of intercourse between Romish and Irish Christians. The Italian missionaries who then settled in England sought to commence a correspondence; but their advances were very coldly received. The Easter cycle was changed at Rome in the former part of the sixth century,[4] and the alteration was soon generally adopted on the Continent; but the Irish Church adhered to its own arrangements—a plain proof that it was not meanwhile subject to Italian supervision. Its mode of keeping Easter was peculiar, and had never been observed in Italy[5]—another evidence that Patrick, its apostle, had no commission from Pope Celestine. The Irish at first utterly refused to hold communion with the ecclesiastics sent into England by the bishop of Rome. "When the apostolic see," says one of these strangers, "sent us to these Western parts to preach to pagan

---

[1] Of these, nearly one hundred and fifty are still extant, many of which are addressed to bishops in Germany, Spain, and Gaul.

[2] From A.D. 440 to A.D. 461.

[3] It is now admitted by the most competent judges that Ussher was mistaken when he supposed that the first two letters in his *Sylloge* were written by Pope Gregory I. to Irish bishops. Letter I. appears to have been addressed to bishops, not in Hibernia, but in *Histria;* and Letter II. to bishops in *Iberia*, near the Black Sea. See Lanigan, ii. 292, 293; and Migne's *Patrol. Cursus*, lxxvii. 592, 1204. Though Gregory wrote so many hundred letters, it is a most significant fact that *not one of them was sent to Ireland*, and that at a time when his mission to England was attracting general attention.

[4] See Lingard's *Anglo-Saxon Church*, 36.

[5] Cummian expressly distinguishes the cycle which "our holy Pope Patrick" introduced from that established at the Council of Nice. See his letter, Ussher's *Sylloge*, Epistle xl., Works, iv. 440.

nations, we came into this island which is called Britain, without possessing any previous knowledge of its inhabitants. We held both the Britons and the Irish in great esteem for sanctity, believing that they proceeded according to the custom of the catholic Church; but, becoming acquainted with the errors of the Britons, we thought the Irish had been better; yet we have been informed by bishop Dagan coming into this island . . . that the Irish in no way differ from the Britons in their behaviour; for bishop Dagan, coming to us, not only refused to eat with us, but even to take his repast in the same house where we were entertained."[1]

Nor are these the only evidences that Ireland could not have been converted by missionaries from Rome. Many of the ecclesiastical usages introduced by Patrick were different from those of the Italian Pontiff and his adherents. Patrick did not practise the right of confirmation,[2] did not insist on the celibacy of the clergy,[3] did not conform to the Roman tonsure,[4] did not use the Roman liturgy,[5] and did not respect the laws sanctioned by the Pope relative to ordination and Church government.[6] But about the time of the conversion of the Anglo-Saxons by Augustine and his fellow-missionaries, the emissaries of Rome began to labour with the utmost assiduity to bring over the Irish to conformity; and, though at first they made little progress, they were not discouraged. The Irish Church was, however, the last in Western Christendom which succumbed to Italian domination; and the triumph of the Pope was not consummated until the twelfth century.

[1] Bede, ii. 4.

[2] In the copy of the Confession contained in the *Book of Armagh* there is no reference to confirmation. It was not practised in the north of Ireland even in the time of Malachy Morgair. See his Life by Bernard.

[3] Ussher's *Religion anciently professed by the Irish and British*, chap. v.

[4] Bede, iii. 26.

[5] Ussher's *Religion*, &c., chap. iv. At a much later period the Irish continued to reject auricular confession. See Ussher's *Works*, iv. 287.

[6] It is universally admitted that ordination by one bishop was practised in Ireland at the ordination of a bishop. Dr. Lanigan acknowledges that the disagreement between the Irish clergy and the Roman missionaries "would prove that St. Patrick did not come to Ireland direct from Rome." *Ecc. Hist.* i. 68.

x

CHAPTER IV.

DOCTRINE AND POLITY, LITERATURE AND PIETY, OF THE EARLY IRISH CHURCH.

THOUGH the Confession is the only ancient record to which we can safely appeal for information relative to the personal history of the famous Hibernian missionary, there is another memorial of great antiquity which illustrates his theological principles. It is a poem still extant in the Celtic language, and known as "The Hymn of Patrick."[1] This bold and spirit-stirring composition was a favourite with Christian Irishmen upwards of twelve hundred years ago: it was then sung by them with the highest enthusiasm; and a peculiar blessing was supposed to be attached to its repetition.[2] Nor is it difficult to account for its popularity. It brings before us the most exciting scene in the career of Patrick—his appearance in presence of King Laoghaire and the nobles of Ireland at the royal residence of Tara, to plead the cause of the Gospel against the priests of Druidism. The apostle, invoking the aid of the High and the Holy One, is represented as advancing, single-handed, to do battle with the powers of darkness. "At Tara to-day," says the Hymn, "may the strength of God pilot me;[3] may the power of God preserve me; may the wisdom of God instruct me; may the eye of God view me; may the ear of God hear me; may the word of God render me eloquent. . . . Christ be in the heart of each person to whom I speak; Christ in the mouth of each person who speaks to me; Christ in each eye which sees me; Christ in each ear which hears me."

This poem is perhaps the production of the abbot of Armagh —"Patrick of the prayers who had good Latin." It exhibits a degree of mental cultivation which cannot be traced in the Confession. But, whoever was its author, its great age is indisputable, as it is the oldest undoubted monument of the Irish language in existence.[4] The doctrine taught by Patrick may

---

[1] It may be found at length in the *Trans. Roy. Ir. Ac.*, xviii. part ii. pp. 57-67.
[2] *Ibid.* pp. 68, 69.
[3] Dr. Todd translates these words—"I bind to myself to-day the Power of God to guide me," &c. See his *St. Patrick*, 426, 427.
[4] *Tr. Roy. Ir. Academy*, xviii. pt. 2, 55.

here be distinctly recognized; for the Hymn virtually embodies the primitive creed of the Church of Ireland. Here is no invocation of Mary, no trust in relics, no confidence in personal righteousness. Christ alone was the hope of the Hibernian apostle.

Patrick acknowledged the supreme authority of the sacred volume; and yet he must have received Tobias and the books falsely ascribed to Solomon as inspired, for he quotes them along with the canonical Scriptures.[1] It can be shown, however, that the early Irish Church rejected the greater part of the Apocrypha.[2] Athanasius finished his chequered course about the time when Patrick was born; and the Arian controversy had fairly gone to rest before the young Frenchman had completed his first captivity. But there is abundant evidence that the author of the Confession was a zealous advocate[3] of the Nicene faith. Tradition relates that he taught the Irish how there could be a Trinity in Unity by holding up before them their own three-leaved shamrock; and in the Confession itself the doctrine is repeatedly inculcated.[4] It is equally clear that he believed in the Atonement, or, as it is called in his Hymn, "the virtue of Christ's crucifixion;" and he bears the most unequivocal testimony to the sovereignty of grace. "I was," says he, "like a stone that lay in the deep mire; and He who is powerful came, and, in His mercy, relieved me; and raised me up, and placed me on the top of the wall; and from thence I should cry aloud 'What shall I render to the Lord for so great benefits here and hereafter, which the human mind cannot estimate.'"[5] We have already seen how he relates his own spiritual history—thus bearing emphatic testimony to the necessity of regeneration; and he expresses his views of the way of salvation by quoting the memorable words —"He that believeth and is baptized shall be saved, and he that believeth not shall be damned."[6] In none of the works imputed to him does he make any reference to Purgatory;[7] and, when he

---

[1] Confession, 1-5, where he quotes from Tobias, Wisdom, and Ecclesiasticus.
[2] Ussher's *Religion of the Ancient Irish*, chap. i.
[3] He does not, it is true, use the word Homoousios or Consubstantial, but he distinctly recognizes the doctrine of "one God in the Trinity of the Sacred Name." Conf. i. 2.
[4] Confession, i. 2.; ii. 6. [5] *Ibid.* i. 5. [6] *Ibid.* iv. 17.
[7] In the tract *De tribus Habitaculis*, heaven, earth, and hell are the only places of existence recognized. The fact that this little work was so long attributed to Patrick shows what were the views entertained as to the character of his theology.

states that "we must account even for our slightest sins before the tribunal of the Lord Christ,"[1] he virtually rejects the idea of venial transgressions.

There is satisfactory proof that, in early times, the Irish clergy were permitted to marry;[2] and that, in the Eucharist, both the cup and the bread were given to the Irish laity.[3] It can also be demonstrated that, long after the days of Patrick, the dogma of transubstantiation was unknown. The Hibernian doctors thought for themselves; they believed the testimony of their own senses: they saw that the elements remained unchanged after the prayer of thanksgiving; and even in the ninth century, when the doctrine of their transmutation was asserted on the Continent in all its absurdity by Paschasius Radbert, his most powerful opponent was a learned Irishman—the famous Johannes Scotus Erigena. Commenting on the words of our Lord, "Do this in remembrance of me," one of the earliest of the Irish expositors employs the following decisive language:—"He left a remembrancer of himself to us, even as if one that were going a far journey should leave some token with him whom he loved, that, as oft as he beheld it, he might call to memory his benefits and friendship."[4]

The ecclesiastical polity established by Patrick in Ireland is deserving of attention, as it supplies an example of a system then passing rapidly into desuetude. Immediately after the organization of what was called the Catholic Church, the pastor of every little town had the rank of a bishop, and for a time these rural dignitaries enjoyed the same official authority as the prelates of the great cities. The canons adopted at Sardica in A.D. 343 led to a complete change in the Church constitution; for, by permitting deposed ecclesiastics to appeal to the Italian Pontiff,[5] he was virtually made the arbiter of Christendom; and,

---

[1] Confession, i. 3.   [2] Ussher's *Religion of the Ancient Irish*, chap. v.
[3] Thus a very ancient hymn, sung in the Irish Church whilst the communicants were participating, commences with these words:
"Sancti venite,
Christi corpus sumite;
Sanctum bibentes
Quo redempti sanguinem."
The Book of Hymns of the Ancient Irish Church, by J. H. Todd, D.D., part i. p. 43, Dublin, 1855.
[4] Sedulius on 1 Cor. xi., *Patrol. Cursus*, ciii. 151, Migne. Sedulius was born in the latter half of the eighth century.
[5] See Sec. V. Chap. 1. of this Period.

by forbidding the ordination of bishops in small cities,[1] comparatively few could henceforth gain admission into the episcopal order, so that the great prelates were invested with much more extensive authority. But in various districts these canons came very slowly into operation, as they could not be well enforced without the aid of the civil power; and in some places, such as Africa, they were quite neglected. In the north of France, towards the close of the fourth century, the Imperial Government was weak; and hence, probably, there was no interference with the existing village bishoprics.[2] It would seem that Patrick introduced into Ireland the ecclesiastical regulations of his own country, and thus we are to account for the extraordinary number of early Hibernian bishops.[3] We cannot reasonably reject the reports of a crowd of ancient authors who assure us that they amounted to several hundreds; for, when these historians wrote, this state of things was an anomaly, and they had therefore no temptation to exaggerate. Nennius, who flourished in the ninth century, affirms that the Irish Apostle erected 365 churches and ordained 365 bishops.[4] When the members of an ecclesiastical judicatory are scattered over an extensive territory, it seldom happens that many more than one-half are present at a meeting; and yet, a century after the death of Patrick—when the country was almost without roads, and when travelling from one part of the island to another must have been alike perilous and disagreeable—we read of 150 bishops assembled at the palace of Tara.[5] A document preserved in the *Book of Armagh*, and written long before the time of Nennius, affirms that "the number of bishops ordained by Patrick amounted to 450;"[6] and the *Annals of the Four Masters*[7] attest that he erected *seven* hundred churches and ordained *seven* hundred bishops. The *Irish Litany* of Ængus the Culdee—a production probably of the ninth cen-

---

[1] See Sec. III. Chap. III. of this Period.

[2] Boulogne, though but a village, is said to have had a bishop in the time of Constantine. See Lanigan, i. 96. These French village bishoprics afterwards disappeared.

[3] In Brittany, even as late as the sixth century, we find traces of resemblance to the constitution of the Church of Africa. Thus the primatial dignity was not attached to any particular see. See Thierry's *Conquest of England by the Normans*, p. 9, London, 1841.

[4] *History of the Britons*, § 54.

[5] *Book of Clonmacnoise*. See *Trans. Roy. Ir. Ac.* xviii. pt. 2, 126, 127.

[6] Sir W. Betham's *Antiq. Res.* ii. 351.   [7] Ad an. A.D. 493.

tury—enumerates no less than 141 places in Ireland where there were, or had been, *seven contemporary bishops*.[1]

It may be objected that the statements now given differ widely; but they are not therefore, as a whole, to be summarily set aside. They are all, perhaps, rough estimates, and they have obviously not been taken from any common registry; but it is noteworthy that the higher numbers are furnished by some of the most ancient and valuable authorities. At the period of the English invasion in the twelfth century, it has been computed that the entire population of Ireland scarcely exceeded 300,000;[2] and seven hundred years before, or in the time of the Hibernian Apostle, it was not nearly so considerable. A census of the island could not then have afforded a larger return than would at present be supplied by the Irish metropolis. It is thus apparent that, at a very early date, there was something like an adequate provision of ministers for the whole country.

In his ecclesiastical arrangements, Patrick proceeded on the principle that there should be a bishop, or spiritual overseer, for each congregation.[3] In his days the greater portion of the surface of the island presented a succession of forests and barren bogs; there was little husbandry; there were no towns of any magnitude; and the bishop often occupied a very humble position. His jurisdiction extended only over those to whose pastoral care he could personally attend; in a very poor country, his income was small; he is occasionally represented as endeavouring to eke out a subsistence by following the plough,[4] or engaging in some of the other toils of agriculture. An ancient Irish bishopric was something like a modern parish[5]—more extensive perhaps—but with only a fraction of its population. Thus, in the seventh

---

[1] Todd's *St. Patrick*, 32, 35.

[2] Sir Wm. Petty's *Political Anatomy of Ireland*, chap. v.

[3] Hence the number of churches built by him, according to various accounts, corresponded to the number of bishops he ordained.

[4] Bishop Etchen was ploughing when Columbkille visited him to receive ordination. Todd's *St Patrick*, 71. In A.D. 1179 there was an Irish bishop who had no other revenue than the milk of three cows. Reeves' *Antiquities of Down, Connor, and Dromore*, p. 162.

[5] Some have maintained that the old Irish bishops wandered about without any fixed sees; but this opinion is untenable. In ancient annals their names are connected with particular places, and tradition describes them as ministering in certain buildings. These buildings could not have itinerated.

century, there was a bishop of Connor[1] and a bishop of Rashee[2] or Ballycaston, now two adjoining parishes of the county of Antrim.[3] In the county of Clare, the three contiguous parishes of Kilmanaheen, Kilaspuglenane, and Kilmacreehy, had also formerly each a bishop.[4] A bishopric was sometimes limited to a small island with very few inhabitants. We read of the bishop of the island of Rathlin on the north coast of the county of Antrim,[5] and of the bishop of Innisboffin,[6] an island near the coast of Mayo. Even so late as the beginning of the twelfth century there are said to have been 300 bishops in Ireland.[7]

The constitution of the early Irish Church was decidedly popular. The bishop was elected by the clergy and people,[8] and the ecclesiastical government was conducted by synods in which there was a lay element, for princes and chieftains, as well as bishops, met for deliberation.[9] Some of the most important of these ancient convocations assembled at Tara, in a fort or stronghold, long known as the "Rath of the Synods."[10] Tara ceased to be the residence of the chief monarch about A.D. 565;[11] but for a considerable time afterwards this Rath was the meeting-place for such conventions.[12] It does not appear that the synods had always a fixed president. It is probable that, as in the Church of Africa, the senior bishop generally acted as chairman; Patrick himself, perhaps, was moderator for the greater part of his life; but in some instances we find distinguished strangers, such as Columbkille and Adamnan, occupying the seat of dignity.[13]

---

[1] Lanigan, iii. 412. *Annals of Four Masters*, ad an. 658, 537.

[2] Reeves' *Antiquities*, p. 68. *Annals of the Four Masters*, ad an. 617.

[3] We read of other bishops in the same county, as the bishop of Coleraine, the bishop of Armoy, and the bishop of Kilroot (near Carrickfergus). See Reeves' *Ecc. Antiq.* 75, 80, 60.

[4] See the account of the Union of Kilmanaheen, by the Rev. James Kelly, LL.D., archdeacon of Kilfenora, in Mason's *Statistical Account of Ireland*, vol. i. p. 489, Dublin, 1814.

[5] Lanigan, iii. 171.   [6] *Ibid.* iii. 79.

[7] Ledwich's *Antiquities*, 83.

[8] Ussher's *Religion of the Ancient Irish*, chap. viii.   [9] *Ibid.*

[10] *History and Antiquities of Tara Hill.*, Trans. Roy. Irish Acad. xviii. pt. 2, pp. 139, 150, 171.

[11] *Ibid.* 125.   [12] *Ibid.* 174.

[13] Reeves' *St Columba*, by Adamnan, 179, note.

According to legends long current, Patrick erected the city, as well as the archbishopric, of Armagh. Such statements supply materials for their own refutation. The building of towns formed no part of the duty of the great missionary; and an archbishop, or metropolitan, was unknown in Ireland for ages after the time when he flourished.[1] The story that he was the first Primate of Armagh cannot bear the slightest investigation. Several others, such as Patrick Senior, Secundinus, and Benignus, are said to have presided at Armagh while, according to the common chronology, he was yet alive—a contradiction which his biographers have endeavoured to obviate by a very silly explanation. The weight of the primacy, say they, was too great for him to sustain; and he sought to relieve himself by placing it on more vigorous shoulders. But, if the ordinary chronology be adopted, he survived his retirement nearly fifty years;[2] so that his "natural force" could not have been much abated at the period of his resignation. The fable of his primacy has evidently been fabricated to give éclat to the northern archbishopric; and other traditions invented for the same purpose are so transparently false that their forgery has been generally admitted.[3] The fame of Armagh appears to have commenced with the monastery founded there in the fifth century. When Germanus visited England a second time in A.D. 444, he was accompanied by several men of learning, some of whom passed over to Ireland, and probably became teachers in this establishment. These scholars either assisted in its erection, or added

---

[1] The Irish word *ard-epscop* "did not imply anything of jurisdiction, and is not synonymous in this respect with our present use of the term *archbishop*. It denotes only an eminent or celebrated bishop; and there is nothing in it inconsistent with the existence of several *ard* or chief bishops, at the same time in the same district." Todd's *St. Patrick*, 16. The old Irish gave very high titles to bishops in great repute for sanctity or learning. Hence we read of Donnell O'Heney "*archbishop of West Europe*," and of Hoey O'Kelly "chief head of the men of Meath and distinguished *bishop of all Ireland*." King's *Memoir of the Primacy*, 15, 16. Titles of this kind given on two or three occasions by Irishmen of the seventh century to the Pope have induced some to believe that they acknowledged his supremacy!

[2] See some of the difficulties stated in Lanigan, i. 315. See also O'Donovan's *Annals of the Four Masters*, i. 135, 147, 151.

[3] *Antiquities of Tara Hill.*, Trans. Roy. Ir. Acad. xviii. ii. 111. Dr. Todd admits that "archiepiscopal and diocesan jurisdiction was introduced" at "the close of the eleventh or beginning of the twelfth century." Todd's *St. Patrick*, 172. See also King's *Memoir of the Primacy of Armagh*, preface.

greatly to the reputation. Hence the origin of the story that the primatial see was erected in A.D. 445. The first ecclesiastics of distinction connected with Armagh were, not bishops, but abbots.[1] In this monastery candidates for the ministry were educated; Patrick "of the prayers who had good Latin" was, in all likelihood, its first superior; its earliest teachers were among the most eminent scholars in the country; and thus it soon acquired an influence and authority which it subsequently retained.

Had a fixed primatial see been deemed necessary in the ancient Irish Church, it would probably have been established at Tara—the seat of the chief monarch. A bishop resided there as early as the beginning of the sixth century;[2] and the Rath of the Synods supplies proof that the place, at a very early period, was a centre of ecclesiastical influence. But, for ages after the coming of Patrick to Ireland, the chief monarchs adhered to Druidism; Tara had meanwhile no educational institute to spread abroad its reputation; and neither the extraordinary learning nor the commanding eloquence of its bishops added weight to their position. In A.D. 565, when it was deserted as a royal residence, the crown of the chief monarch passed to the northern Hy Nialls;[3] and thus Armagh gradually increased in importance. It stood on classic ground, for it was in the immediate vicinity of Emania—the palace occupied by the kings of Ulster until the century before the arrival of Patrick;[4] and a fortress, which continued there for ages afterwards, contributed to its security.[5] The chieftain to whom the district belonged soon embraced Christianity;[6] the Church was liberally endowed by him; and, for many generations, the abbots of Armagh were all scions of the royal family of Ulster.[7] When Augustine and the other papal missionaries appeared in England, a correspondence was commenced between these new-comers and some of the Irish churchmen; Thomian of Armagh—reputed the most learned ecclesiastic in the Western Isle[8]—was particularly

---

[1] King's *Memoir of the Primacy*, preface.
[2] *Antiquities of Tara Hill.*, *Trans. Roy. Irish Acad.* vol. xviii. part ii. p. 224.
[3] Lanigan, ii. 198.
[4] Todd's *St. Patrick*, 472.
[5] O'Donovan's *Four Masters*, i. 210, note.
[6] Lanigan, i. 312.
[7] Todd's *St. Patrick*, 155.
[8] O'Donovan's *Four Masters*, i. 271, note.

courted by them; he was induced to adopt the Romish mode of keeping Easter; and, shortly after this time, the idea of asserting the ecclesiastical precedence of what began to be called "the see of Patrick" appears to have originated.

About the seventh century Ireland was so celebrated all over Europe for its piety that it acquired the honourable title of the "Isle of Saints." It was at the same period so distinguished for intellectual cultivation that youths, as well from the Continent as from England, flocked to its shores for education. Armagh was probably the seat of the oldest of its literary institutes. Shortly after the middle of the sixth century the monastery of Bangor, near Belfast, was founded by the Abbot Comgall;[1] and seminaries at Clonard, Clonmacnois,[2] and elsewhere, soon attained eminence. The rapid progress of the Irish Church was, no doubt, extraordinary; but a reference to the contemporary history of neighbouring nations reveals a variety of circumstances all tending to promote its prosperity. The northern parts of Gaul, exposed to the incessant incursions of the Francs, afforded no safe and peaceful settlement; some of its ecclesiastics were, in consequence, induced to follow the footsteps of Patrick into Ireland;[3] and as the pagan Saxons were now burning the churches of South Britain, rifling its monasteries, and reducing the whole country to a scene of desolation, not a few of the English clergy also sought refuge among their Hibernian brethren. Ireland was meanwhile free from foreign invasion, and in the enjoyment of an unwonted measure of internal tranquillity. Hence it was that it had so many devout inhabitants, so many excellent bishops, and so many illustrious seats of learning.

The spirit of missionary enterprise soon sprung up in the ancient Irish Church. Towards the close of the sixth century[4] Columbanus, a native of the south of the island, passed over into France, and endeavoured to diffuse the blessings of the Gospel among some of its semi-pagan inhabitants. That country, subdued by Clovis about a century before, was again divided into several states; and the wicked posterity of the founder of

[1] Lanigan, ii. 62.
[2] Lanigan, i. 465-6; ii. 52. Clonard and Clonmacnois were perhaps founded somewhat earlier than Bangor.
[3] Dollinger, ii. 24, 32; Lanigan, i. 492.
[4] About A.D. 590.

the French monarchy misgoverned these petty kingdoms. The appearance of Columbanus in Gaul attracted the attention of all classes; for he was recommended by a handsome person[1] and a dignified bearing, as well as by erudition and genius. At a time when classical knowledge was rare he was distinguished by his attainments in both Greek and Latin literature. But active benevolence and indomitable integrity were his most prominent characteristics; and, when admitted into the presence of barbarian princes, he exhibited sublime courage by testifying against the vices of these royal personages. Columbanus, like many others of his countrymen, attached undue importance to asceticism; he was himself a monk; and a certain rule still extant illustrates the species of discipline practised in the monasteries he established.[2] In A.D. 615, after a laborious career, he died at Bobbio, in the north of Italy, at the advanced age of seventy-two.[3]

Gallus, the disciple of Columbanus, is also entitled to honourable mention among the Irishmen engaged in missionary labours on the Continent. After having spent several years in France he settled in the neighbourhood of the Lake of Constance, and there preached with much success to a benighted population. He survived his master Columbanus thirty years; and the Canton St. Gall still perpetuates the name of this apostle of Switzerland. Kilian, or Killen,[4] who signalized himself as a missionary among the Franconians, was also an Irishman.[5] He is said to have been martyred at Wartzburg in A.D. 696.

The Irishmen engaged in missionary operations on the Continent exhibited an independence of thought and action very embarrassing to the adherents of the papacy. Accustomed at home to rites and ceremonies quite different from the Roman, these worthies, in not a few instances, refused to abandon their

---

[1] Lanigan, ii. 261.
[2] See *Patrol. Curs.* tom. lxxx. 209.
[3] Lanigan, ii. 295.
[4] There is mention of an earlier Killen who is said to have been made a bishop by St. Patrick. "The festival of St. Killen," says Lanigan, "was kept at Teballan on the 27th of May. . . . There are so many saints of the name of Killen that we cannot decide which of them he was." i. 270.
[5] Murdock's *Mosheim by Soames*, ii. 64. The story that he went to Rome to obtain the papal sanction is rejected by Neander, v. 47.

own ecclesiastical observances when they went abroad; and, regarding the Italian pontiff as nothing more than the most powerful bishop in the West, they declined either to acknowledge his infallibility or to submit to his dictation. They were willing to believe that Peter had at one time been connected with the Church of Rome; but they did not see why the Pope was therefore entitled to exclusive jurisdiction. They had no idea that Peter alone was the rock which supports the Church; for they seem to have believed that every true evangelist shares that honour. Hence one of their ancient hymns in praise of Patrick says of him; "He is constant in the fear of God and immoveable in the faith; the Church is built on him as on Peter; whose apostleship also he has obtained from God, and the gates of hell shall not prevail against him."[1]

Columbanus was not afraid to address the great patriarch of the West in language which must have astonished his Italian sycophants. Dissatisfied with the conduct of the court of Rome in reference to the question of the Three Chapters, he gave utterance to his indignation in a letter written with all the boldness of a Christian freeman. "That you may not lack apostolic honour," says this eloquent Irishman to Boniface IV., "preserve the apostolic faith; confirm it by testimony, strengthen it by writing, fortify it by synod, that none may justly resist you. . . . The Pastor of pastors is approaching; beware lest he find you negligent and beating your fellow servants with the blows of an evil example. . . . Dissemble, therefore, no longer: keep no longer silence. . . . It is your fault if you have deviated from the true belief and made void the primitive faith: your juniors deservedly withstand you, and deservedly they do not communicate with you until the memory of the wicked be taken away, and delivered over to oblivion. For if these things are certain rather than imaginary, the tables being turned, your sons are changed into the head and you into the tail—which is sad even to be mentioned. Therefore they also shall be your judges who have always preserved the orthodox faith, whosoever they may be, though they appear to be your juniors. . . . Rome is the head

---

[1] Hymn of Secundinus or Sechnall. This hymn is of very great antiquity; but there is no reason to believe that it was written, as some think, when Patrick was still alive.

of the churches of the world, *with the exception of Jerusalem*. . . . So long shall power remain with you as right reason shall remain; for he is the sure door-keeper of the kingdom of heaven who through true knowledge opens to the worthy and shuts against the unworthy. But if he act otherwise, he will be able neither to open nor to shut."[1]

But the predominating influence of Romanism all around them, and the untiring zeal with which the Benedictine monks laboured to extend papal authority, gradually made an impression even on these outspoken Irishmen. Their continued residence on the Continent reconciled them to many things which they viewed at first with impatience; as we pass down through the Middle Ages their protests wax feebler and feebler; and at length some of them become the most strenuous supporters of Romish supremacy.

There is extant an old catalogue of Irish saints drawn up, as it would appear, shortly after the time of Columbanus,[2] in which the writer represents the century after the arrival of Patrick in the country as the most illustrious period of its ecclesiastical history. "The first order of catholic saints," says this memorial, "was in the time of Patrick. And then all were bishops illustrious and holy, and full of the Holy Spirit, in number three hundred and fifty, the founders of churches. They had one Head Christ, and one leader Patrick, one ritual, and one celebration. Whoever was excommunicated by one church, all the others excommunicated. They did not reject the attendance and company of women, because, being founded on the rock Christ, they did not fear the wind of temptation. This order of saints continued during four reigns."[3] The antiquity of this document is universally admitted;[4] and yet it speaks with the highest satisfaction of a state of things very far from that now sanctioned by the majority of Irishmen. The Church of the Emerald Isle was most prosperous, according to this venerable witness, when it neither acknowledged the supremacy of the Pope nor insisted on the celibacy of the clergy—when its bishops were reckoned by hundreds—and when they were so bound

---

[1] *Epist. to Boniface IV*. This epistle appears to have been written in A.D. 613.
[2] See Todd's *St. Patrick*, 88.
[3] *i.e.* from A.D. 429 to A.D. 538.
[4] As by Ussher, Lanigan, and Döllinger.

together in a great ecclesiastical confederation that whoever was excommunicated by one church was excommunicated by all. The framers of the Solemn League and Covenant, assembled at Westminster in 1643, aimed to re-establish this primitive regimen; but their visions of Catholic uniformity yet remain to be realized.

SECTION V.

PROGRESS OF THE POPEDOM.

CHAPTER I.

PROGRESS OF THE POWER OF THE BISHOPS OF ROME FROM THE CONVERSION OF CONSTANTINE TO THE DEATH OF THEODOSIUS THE GREAT IN A.D. 395.

WHEN Constantine entered Rome as a conqueror, after the battle of the Milvian bridge, the Gospel had already made considerable progress in the great metropolis. The city at this time contained at least twenty-five churches;[1] but, though Maxentius had permitted the disciples to remain almost unmolested, they were still destitute of the safeguard of a legal toleration. Their chief pastor, Melchiades,[2] must have experienced no ordinary satisfaction when told that the victor was disposed to encourage Christianity. The conversion of Constantine produced, indeed, a wonderful change in the position of the Church of Rome. The proscribed sect at once rose into distinction; and its leader, whose life would have been imperilled, not long before, had he publicly appeared among his fellow citizens, was soon courted as an influential patron and dreaded as a powerful adversary. In A.D. 313, when the Donatists applied for redress to Constantine,[3] the Emperor appointed the bishop of Rome and a few of his brethren to examine the complaint. The assessors held their sittings in the palace of the Lateran. As Melchiades entered the princely residence, well might he marvel at the alteration in his circumstances; and yet little did he think that his successors were one day to occupy this royal mansion and to rule over the city.

A portion of one of the Nicene canons already quoted[4] throws some light on the position of the bishop of Rome in A.D. 325.

[1] See *Ancient Church*, 359, note.
[2] Or Miltiades.
[3] See Section I. Chap. V. of this Period, p. 118.
[4] Section III. Chap. III. of this Period, p. 244.

"Let the ancient customs be maintained which are in Egypt, and Libya, and Pentapolis," says this authority, "that the bishop of Alexandria rule over all these places, as is the custom in the parallel case of the bishop of Rome."[1] The limits of the jurisdiction of the Alexandrian primate are here defined; and an exposition of the canon, written towards the termination of the fourth century, points out, with precision, what were then considered the boundaries of the See of Rome. Rufinus, the author of this paraphrase, was born a few years after the meeting of the Council of Nice; he was a native of Italy and a presbyter of Aquileia; he possessed superior intelligence; and he may be regarded as a very competent interpreter of the meaning of the regulation. "Let the ancient custom be preserved at Alexandria and in the city of Rome," says this commentator—"the former attending to Egypt, and the latter to the *Suburbicarian churches.*"[2]

A great officer of state—"the vicar of the city"—presided over a section of the empire known by the designation of the *Suburbicarian provinces.* He had under his government the three islands of Sicily, Corsica, and Sardinia, and the whole of the southern part of Italy, including Naples and nearly all the territory which belonged, until lately, to Tuscany and the States of the Church.[3] The suburbicarian churches were obviously those within the bounds of the suburbicarian provinces; and, when the canon was framed, Rome was in the zenith of her glory, and these provinces were the very garden of the mistress of the world.

There were ten suburbicarian provinces;[4] and, under ordinary circumstances, there would, of course, have been ten archbishops; but, owing to his local position, the Roman chief pastor soon became the common primate of almost all the suburbicarian churches. Sicily and Sardinia, and perhaps Corsica, were the

[1] Canon vi.
[2] Rufinus, Migne, *Patrolog. Curs.* tom. xxi. 473.
[3] The view here given is that of Sirmond and others; but Cave disputes its accuracy, and endeavours to show that the suburbicary churches were confined within narrower bounds. See his *Dissertation on the Government of the Ancient Church*, chap. iii. § 3. On the other side see Gieseler, i. 256; and Stillingfleet, *Rational Account of the Grounds of the Protestant Religion*, pp. 411-15, London, 1681.
[4] *i.e.* ten provinces under the *vicarius urbicus.* See Kurtz, *Hist. of the Christ. Church*, 165.

only provinces which usually had separate metropolitans.[1] Rome was easy of access from the whole surrounding territory, as it was the point to which all the great roads converged; it was the place to which every one was attracted by its scenes of unremitting excitement, by business, or by family connexions; and, when synods met, the bishops of the central and southern parts of Italy often preferred to repair to it rather than assemble in their respective districts. Whilst, therefore, the Roman prelate was the spiritual governor of the greatest city of the empire, he was also the sole metropolitan of six or seven of its richest provinces. He possessed wealth which enabled him to support a social position higher than any other bishop; and he had contrived to concentrate in his own person an amount of power which placed him above any other metropolitan.

The Arian controversy added much to the influence of the Roman See. When orthodoxy was oppressed in the East it was protected in the West; Athanasius himself found an asylum in the old capital of the empire; and the great Italian primate repeatedly signalized himself as the assertor of Trinitarianism. The supporters of the Nicene Creed were so sensible of the value of his services that, in a council held at Sardica in A.D. 343, they concurred in the adoption of a canon which has ever since held a conspicuous place in the history of the progress of papal authority. According to this enactment, when an accused bishop had been tried and deposed by his provincial synod, he was at liberty to appeal to the Roman metropolitan; and this great churchman was thus empowered to take up a case already decided by the proper tribunal, to remit it for re-examination to any neighbouring ecclesiastical judicatory, and to appoint some of his own presbyters, to attend the trial as his deputies, and to take part in the investigation.[2]

This council of Sardica was convened by the joint authority of Constans and Constantius; but its members, finding it impossible to act together, separated into two bodies, and drew up contradictory canons. The decree just described was framed by the orthodox majority. In several places the Arian bishops had behaved most arbitrarily; and, without any just cause, had ejected the adherents of Athanasius. This regulation was accord-

[1] See Bingham, book ix. chap. i. sect. vi.
[2] Canon v. in the Greek and vii. in the Latin.

ingly intended to provide the means of redress. Pope Julius was the steady friend of the Alexandrian primate; and it was well understood that any appeal to him, by an advocate of the Nicene faith, would meet with most favourable consideration.

The Council of Sardica recognized the Roman prelate as, under specified circumstances, the general arbiter of the Western Church; and its regulations were calculated to add immensely to his influence. But its proceedings did not command the respect which they might otherwise have challenged; as it was considered a partisan assembly, or at least only the larger fragment of an ecclesiastical convention. Its decree warranting appeals to Rome was, indeed, a most unwise piece of legislation; for, whilst it attempted to make provision for a present difficulty, it placed a very dangerous amount of power in the hands of an individual, and thus threatened the whole discipline of the Church with permanent derangement. Its folly speedily became palpable. Liberius, the immediate successor of Julius in the Roman bishopric, commenced his episcopal administration by excommunicating Athanasius.[1] He subsequently, indeed, changed his course, and acted as the champion of orthodoxy; but, when banished by Constantius into Thrace, he again veered about, and subscribed the semi-Arian creed of Sirmium.[2] The reputation of the Roman see, as the conservator of orthodoxy, was thus sadly damaged. But, in a very few years, the apostasy of Liberius was forgotten; the bishopric recovered its prestige as the defender of the faith; and its pretensions were urged, by a crowd of interested eulogists, with reinvigorated effrontery.

The wealth of the Bishop of Rome even at this early period enabled him to wield vast influence. His revenues were already so extensive that he rivalled the opulent Roman nobles in the liberality of his expenditure and the splendour of his domestic establishment. In A.D. 366, when the episcopal chair became vacant, two ecclesiastics, Damasus and Ursinus,[3] contended for it with such eagerness that much blood was shed before the controversy was decided. The man who, on that occasion, did not scruple to step into his office over heaps of slain, has been canonized by the Church of Rome,[4] and has ever since been honoured by her as one of her most distinguished ornaments. A contem-

[1] Bower, *History of the Popes*, Liberius. [2] Sozomen, iv. 15.
[3] Or Ursicinus. [4] See *Roman Breviary*, 11th December.

porary pagan historian of high respectability, who has recorded this struggle, observes that the value of the prize sufficiently accounts for the violence of the rival candidates. "Damasus and Ursinus," says he, "in their immoderate anxiety to obtain the bishopric, formed factions and carried on the conflict with such asperity that their partisans proceeded to hostilities, involving the wounding and death of the combatants. The prefect Juventius, unable to extinguish or abate the tumult, was compelled to withdraw into the suburbs. The strenuous efforts of the partisans of Damasus ultimately secured the victory. In a Christian church—the Basilica of Sicininus,—were found one hundred and thirty-seven dead bodies; and the populace, who had been roused to a frenzy of ferocity, were with great difficulty restored to order. When I consider the splendour of Rome, I do not wonder that those who desire such rank and power, should strive with all possible exertion and impetuosity to realize their wishes; since, if they succeed, they are sure to be enriched by the presents of matrons, to be enabled, elegantly dressed, to appear abroad in a carriage, and to live so luxuriously that their feasts will be more sumptuous than royal entertainments."[1]

The Bishop of Rome did not derive his income from a state provision. The voluntary contributions of the faithful were amply sufficient to maintain him in a style of princely magnificence. The wealth of the civic aristocracy was enormous; and the more devout or superstitious lavished benefactions on the great prelate and his clergy. A well-informed ecclesiastic of that age has most graphically described the arts by which greedy churchmen imposed on the generosity of the Roman matrons. "The clergy," says he, "who ought to instruct and awe the women by a grave and composed behaviour, first kiss their heads, and then stretching out the hand, as it were to bestow a blessing, slily receive a fee for their salutation. The women, in the meantime, elated with pride, because they are thus courted by the clergy, prefer the freedom of widowhood to the subjection attending the state of wedlock. Some of the clergy make it the whole business of their lives to learn the names of the ladies, to find out their habitations, and to study their humour."[2] These

[1] Ammianus Marcellinus, xxvii. 3.
[2] Jerome, *Epist.* xxii. Migne, *Patrol. Cursus*, tom. xxii. 404, 414.

words may have been written partly under the influence of spleen; but Jerome here, in all likelihood, records proceedings of which he was personally cognizant. The Emperor was obliged to interfere and provide means for checking the rapacity of these schemers. A rescript of Valentinian I. ordains that the clergy shall not benefit, directly or indirectly, by any gift or devise made to them by any woman "to whom, under the pretext of religion, they may have attached themselves."[1] This law, which is dated July A.D. 370, was sent to Damasus, with orders that it should be read in all the places of worship at Rome.[2] It was followed up by other provisions of a similar character. The Church had already contrived to gain possession of such a large amount of property that the State began to take alarm, and deemed it necessary to curtail the right of inheritance which the clergy had enjoyed since the days of Constantine. Laws declaring the invalidity of wills in which legacies were bequeathed to ecclesiastics, and founded on the same principle as our statutes of mortmain, were accordingly enacted.[3]

Whilst the State was thus devising measures to prevent the rapid accumulation of ecclesiastical wealth, it was quite willing to conciliate the great bishop of the West by legislating for the increase of his ecclesiastical authority. The emperors remembered that this dignified churchman was their subject; and that, in cases of necessity, the power thus acquired by him could be made available for the support of their own political influence. Hence an extant rescript of Gratian and Valentinian II., drawn up apparently towards the end of A.D. 378, confirms and extends the Bishop of Rome's appellant jurisdiction. This law requires even metropolitans, when accused, to repair to the ecclesiastical capital of Italy, or to submit to trial before such judges as the Roman bishop chose to nominate.[4] The power conferred by the Council of Sardica was thus considerably enlarged; as ecclesiastics of almost the highest rank, when arraigned, were made amenable to a tribunal composed entirely of members selected by the Western Patriarch.

The pontificate of Damasus[5] is specially memorable as con-

[1] *Theod. Cod.* xvi. t. ii. 20.
[2] Bower, *History of the Popes*, Damasus. See also *Theod. Cod.* 1493, ed. Haenel, 1842.
[3] *Theod. Cod.* xvi. ii. 20 and 27.
[4] Gieseler, i. 257.   [5] A.D. 366 to A.D. 384.

nected with the progress of papal aggression. The appointment of what have been called *Apostolic vicars* may well be ranked among the most artful schemes of aggrandizement contrived by that ambitious and able churchman. The system was first inaugurated in Greece. From the days of Constantine, Illyricum, comprehending all Greece and several provinces on the Danube, with Sirmium for its capital, had belonged to the Western Empire;[1] but in A.D. 379,—when Theodosius was advanced to the sovereignty of the East—Greece and Dacia, under the designation of East Illyricum, were transferred to his dominion.[2] The Bishop of Rome now claimed ecclesiastical supremacy far beyond the bounds of the Suburbicarian provinces, and the Bishops of Illyricum acknowledged his pretensions; but this new arrangement awakened his anxiety, as it threatened to curtail the bounds of his jurisdiction. The Bishop of Constantinople—to whose care the Church in East Illyricum was apparently about to be transferred—was fast rising into power; and Damasus was most unwilling that the spiritual supervision of so large a territory should be consigned to an already formidable rival. As the bishops concerned had sided with Rome in the Trinitarian controversy, and as they were not particularly desirous to change their ecclesiastical chief, Damasus managed to retain them under his own authority. Thessalonica, the metropolis of Macedonia, was the principal city of the district now severed from the Western Empire; and Damasus appointed its bishop Acholius to act as his vicar throughout the whole of the dismembered territory. Some of the metropolitans consigned to the care of the new functionary were not, at first, altogether willing to recognize his supervision; as they had hitherto stood with him on a footing of equality; but, believing that the great prelate of the Eastern capital, as their near neighbour, would be a more dangerous overseer, they eventually submitted to the Roman vicar. Acholius, who had as yet been only the metropolitan of Macedonia, and who had no prospect of enjoying a better position under a new dynasty, was completely won over to the side of Damasus by this piece of ecclesiastical promotion.[3]

---
[1] Bower, *History of the Popes*, Damasus.
[2] Bingham, ix. ch. iv. sec. vii. Kurtz, 165.
[3] Bower, *History of the Popes*, Damasus.

Future occupants of the Roman See did not fail to turn to account the lesson taught by this successful experiment. In after times, when a powerful bishop in some quarter of the West seemed disposed to assert his independence, the great Italian prelate frequently contrived to disarm his opposition by conferring on him the appointment of papal vicar. The individual on whom this honour was bestowed thus obtained an enlargement of his jurisdiction, and was understood to represent the Roman Pontiff within the extended territory over which he exercised authority. By accepting the commission of vicar, he pledged himself to the support of the papal interest.

Another practice commenced by Syricius,[1] the immediate successor of Damasus, contributed greatly to augment the influence of the Roman See. This was the writing of letters purporting to be expositions of Church law. The first of these documents—known as the *Decretal Epistles*—was promulgated by Syricius in the very beginning of his episcopate. A letter had reached Rome from Himerius, a Spanish bishop, soliciting instruction on various points of ecclesiastical discipline. Damasus, to whom it was addressed, was now dead; but his successor submitted the communication to a meeting of his colleagues assembled, probably, on the occasion of his ordination; and, in a long reply, dictated with an air of authority, Syricius gave specific directions in reference to the several questions suggested by this Spanish correspondent. One of the inquiries of Himerius related to the propriety of clerical celibacy; and it is somewhat remarkable that the earliest decretal letter contains an injunction "forbidding to marry."

At a later period in the history of the papal see, it was alleged that the Italian patriarch had always authoritatively expounded the Apostolic faith and discipline to the bishops and people of the Catholic Church. The statement, which long passed uncontradicted, was apparently authenticated by a series of epistles claiming to be the official communications of the primitive pontiffs. These letters, treating of all manner of ecclesiastical questions, are couched in the language of command, and date from the very days of the Apostles. It is now generally admitted that they are wretched forgeries. They first saw the light shortly before the middle of the ninth century.[2] In ages of

[1] A.D. 384 to A.D. 398.   [2] See Bowden's *Life of Gregory VII.* i. 54.

ignorance they remained unchallenged; but the test of sober criticism has long since revealed the imposture. The letter of Syricius to Himerius is the earliest of the genuine decretals; and its appearance marks the increased activity and boldness of Romish ambition. The second Œcumenical Council, held in A.D. 381, had just raised the chief pastor of Constantinople above every other churchman except the great prelate of the West; and it was by no means improbable that another ecclesiastical vote would recognize the Eastern patriarch as *the first* spiritual dignitary in Christendom. The Roman bishop felt that he must employ all the resources of a vigorous diplomacy to avert such an alternative; and accordingly the occasional promulgation of official letters, broadly asserting his prerogatives, was among the expedients he adopted to preoccupy the public mind, and thus, indirectly to fortify his position.

In the middle of the third century, when the principle of the equality of all pastors was still maintained, the Bishop of Rome would have been stigmatized for impertinence had he ventured to issue one of these dictatorial manifestoes. At that time he exposed himself to scorn when he attempted to overbear his brethren by insisting on the validity of heretical baptism. But meanwhile a wonderful change had passed over the spirit of the Church. It was now admitted, throughout a large portion of the West, that, in cases of peculiar difficulty, it was expedient for ordinary prelates to consult the Bishop of Rome and to conform to his directions. As his church had enjoyed the ministry of apostles, it at length began to be known as *The Apostolic See;*[1] and, such were the special advantages of his position, that he was presumed to be more competent to expound all matters of apostolical tradition than any other ecclesiastic at least in Europe. The public mind was, therefore, not altogether unprepared to submit to the authority of the decretal epistles. They could scarcely be characterized even as officious; for, though professing to lay down the law of the Church, they were generally written in answer to some pressing application. Soon after they began to make their appearance, many perhaps imagined that the circumstances of the times demanded their continuance. When the Western Empire was dismembered by the Northern

[1] But long after the fourth century the seat of an ordinary bishop was called *an apostolic see.* See Bingham, book ii. chap. ii. sec. 3.

barbarians, existing ecclesiastical arrangements were thrown into confusion; and pastors could no longer regularly meet for consultation in their synodical assemblies. When, therefore, an emergency arose, and when an insulated bishop was obliged to apply for advice or instruction, he deemed himself singularly fortunate if he procured a letter of direction from a venerated prelate who possessed means of information to which very few others could have access.

The Roman bishop obtained facilities for adding indefinitely to his influence when recognised as the expounder of church law. The transition from the interpreter to the legislator could not be easily detected; and few would have the courage to dispute the deliverances of a judge of such reputed sanctity and of such undoubted power. His letters, which were widely circulated as soon as written, at once took a high place among ecclesiastical authorities; and in due time formed part of the canon law. Thus it was that he was permitted to announce, as the traditions of the Church, a crowd of doctrines and observances which often outraged common sense or contradicted the declarations of Scripture; but which, in not a few instances, were mainly calculated to perpetuate his own spiritual domination.

The Bishop of Rome was obviously very much indebted for his elevation to imperial patronage. Constantine the Great was an able statesman; without his sanction no ecclesiastical canon had any legal significance; and, as he took a deep interest in the proceedings of all the councils of his age,[1] he no doubt managed to secure the recognition of such a form of church polity as harmonized with his political arrangements. Hence, in his time, the framework of the Christian commonwealth was closely assimilated to the structure of the civil government; and the rank of a city determined the status of its ecclesiastical overseer. Constantine might not comprehend the discussions relative to the mystery of the Trinity; but he saw that his own influence could be brought to bear most effectively and readily on a church under the care of metropolitans. Had the country and village bishops[2] been preserved, and had all possessors of episcopal dignity been still permitted to occupy the same ecclesiastical level, the spiritual authority would have been in frequent con-

---

[1] See Sect. I. Chap. I. and Sect. III. Chap. IV. of this Period, pp. 71, 257.
[2] See Sect. III. Chap. III. of this Period, p. 245.

flict with the temporal; for the sovereign could not have easily controlled the movements of thousands of pastors of equal power acting together in their judicatories. But little more than a hundred metropolitans, many of whom could be restrained or overawed by three great primates, did not present the same difficulties. When Constantine embraced Christianity, no uniform system of ecclesiastical polity prevailed; for more than a century afterwards the Church of Africa retained its peculiar constitution;[1] and the extreme vagueness of the Nicene canon as to the powers of the bishops of Rome, Alexandria, and Antioch, betrays a consciousness that it would have been inconvenient to enter into more specific explanations. These three churchmen had long exercised considerable influence throughout the districts adjacent to their respective capitals;[2] this influence had been continually augmenting; and it was now converted into legal authority. The Nicene fathers imparted additional consistency and vigour to the whole hierarchical system. Whilst the Church now, for the first time, recognized the name of *metropolitans*, it also secured to them some of their most important prerogatives.[3] Constantine was an utter stranger to the principles of civil and religious liberty; but he desired the Church and the State to move on in harmony; and it doubtless appeared to him that the best means of preventing a collision was to place himself at the head of both, and to assimilate their organization. As he came into closest contact with the higher prelates, it was obvious that the greater amount of power he could secure to these dignitaries, he could the more conveniently manage the whole ecclesiastical machinery. The same reason induced so many of his successors to encourage the aggrandizement of the Bishop of Rome. Ages passed away before monarchs began to dread him as a rival; and meanwhile they conceived they could best concentrate their own authority by requiring other prelates to submit to supervision which they were still perfectly able to control. Hence, throughout the whole of the fourth century, the state favoured the Roman pontiff's aspirations; and, in A.D. 378, he made one of his greatest strides towards supremacy

---

[1] See Sect. I. Chap. V. of this Period, p. 128.
[2] It is evident, from the proceedings of the Melitians, that the pretensions at least of the Alexandrian primate were still disputed.
[3] See 4th, 6th, and 7th of the Nicene canons.

by means of the rescript of Gratian and Valentinian II. The same policy was pursued by Theodosius, who commanded all his subjects to conform their faith to that of "the Pontiff Damasus" of Rome, and of "Peter, Bishop of Alexandria."[1] Thus the Italian primate was set forth by the Emperor as the director of the doctrine of the Western Church.

The death of Theodosius the Great, which occurred in A.D. 395, was immediately followed by the final separation of the Eastern from the Western Empire. This event had a considerable influence on the position and prospects of the Bishop of Rome.

CHAPTER II.

THE PROGRESS OF THE POWER OF THE BISHOPS OF ROME, FROM THE DEATH OF THEODOSIUS THE GREAT TO THE FALL OF THE WESTERN EMPIRE.—A.D. 395 to A.D. 476.

THE lofty tone adopted by the bishop of Rome, about the beginning of the fifth century, has attracted the special notice of ecclesiastical historians. In A.D. 402, Innocent I., a man of imperious character, was called to occupy the papal chair; and during the nearly fifteen years of his eventful pontificate, the dignity of his see seemed ever present to his contemplation. It was not strange that the subject so much employed the thoughts of this haughty churchman. The East and the West were now under different sovereigns, and various circumstances indicated that the Patriarch of Rome would soon have to contend with the Patriarch of Constantinople for the ecclesiastical primacy. Innocent had the sagacity to perceive that, were he to rest the claims of his see on the social pre-eminence of its metropolis, he would urge an argument of transparent insufficiency; for, as the Western Emperor had transferred the seat of government to his palace at Ravenna, Rome was fast sinking into the condition of a provincial city; whereas Constantinople was the residence of the imperial court, and the capital of the Eastern Empire. Another cause must therefore be assigned for the superiority of the Western bishopric. It had long been currently asserted that the Church

[1] Baronius, ad. 380.

of Rome was founded by the Apostles Peter *and Paul;*[1] and though the statement is contradicted by the testimony of Scripture,[2] the spirit of the age was so favourable to papal usurpation that its truth was generally admitted. It was, indeed, at length discovered that Paul could not be conveniently associated with the apostle of the circumcision, and about this time he was dismissed from the legend.[3] It was now affirmed that Peter was the Prince of the Apostles, that he was entrusted by Christ with the care of the universal Church, and that the bishop of Rome, as his successor, inherited his primacy and jurisdiction. "Who does not know, or does not perceive," says Innocent, " that what has been delivered by Peter, the Prince of the Apostles, to the Church of Rome, and is still preserved there, ought to be observed by all? And that nothing should be added or introduced which has not this authority, or which may seem to be copied from any other quarter—especially since it is manifest that none instituted Churches in all Italy, Gaul, Spain, Africa, Sicily, and the interjacent islands, save those who were appointed to the sacerdotal office by the venerable Apostle Peter, or his successors. They do not read that in these provinces any other apostle appeared or is reported to have taught."[4]

At the time of the Council of Nice the bishop of Byzantium acknowledged the bishop of Heraclea as his metropolitan; but when the former city was enlarged and called Constantinople it speedily obtained ecclesiastical advancement. Every one could explain the cause of its promotion; and there were perhaps persons living at the death of the Emperor Theodosius who recollected the successive steps by which the Eastern patriarch reached the position secured to him by the second Œcumenical Council. It was otherwise with the bishop of Rome. The primatial importance of his see was covered with the mantle of a venerable antiquity, and an age of increasing superstition listened reverentially to his exalted pretensions. His more discerning partisans rather desired than believed his representations to be true; and those who could have demonstrated their folly recoiled from the ungracious task—for, if efficiently performed, it must have exhibited the weakness of the whole fabric of the hierarchy, as

---

[1] See Irenæus, iii. 3, § 2.   [2] Rom. i. 13, xvi.; Gal. ii. 7, 8.
[3] The text, Matt. xvi. 18, could not in any way be applied to Paul.
[4] *Epist.* xxv. *ad Decent.* Migne, *Patrol. Curs.* xx. 552.

well as exposed themselves to the displeasure of the proud patriarch. The wrath of the Roman prelate was not now expended in a mere outburst of passion; for he was supported by the sword of civil authority, and an assailant of his dignity might have reckoned on incarceration or banishment, if not on some more weighty infliction.

Had Byzantium been the scene of the martyrdom of one of the apostles, the Pope would not have ventured to expatiate so magniloquently on the prerogatives of Peter. But the history of New Rome supplied few sacred recollections; and Innocent well knew that he took up a position which his rival could not even pretend to occupy when he asserted his primacy as a divine right and an apostolic inheritance. Whilst he was advancing these high-flown claims it so happened that passing events contributed to augment his personal consequence. The death of Theodosius the Great was the signal for the invasion of the empire by the Gothic barbarians; and fifteen years afterwards that mighty city, which had so often spread terror to the ends of the earth, was sacked by the victorious Alaric. The pillage of the capital involved the ruin of its ancient aristocracy. "The great men, and the rich men, and the chief captains, and the mighty men,"[1] were swept away by the torrent of war. Many of the noblest families were suddenly reduced to beggary; many of their members were carried off as slaves; and very few citizens of distinction survived the terrible catastrophe. As Innocent was on a mission to the Emperor at Ravenna when Rome was captured, he had not the misfortune to witness its humiliation; and the Gothic warrior, though an Arian, would not permit his troops to injure any of the places of Catholic worship, or to appropriate any of their sacred vessels of gold and silver. When the enemy had retired, it appeared as if the Church alone had escaped the desolation, and as if the Pope were almost the only individual of rank or influence in Rome. From this date until he attained sovereign power he continued to be its chief citizen.

It has been already stated that the Roman princes, from motives of policy, promoted the formation of the Popedom; and now that the Italian patriarch had become so powerful, they deemed it prudent—more especially as their own authority was declining—to treat him with increased deference. Far beyond

[1] Rev. vi. 15.

the bounds of the suburbicarian provinces, the imperial officers insisted on submission to the bishop of Rome. But still Western Christendom was not quite prepared to bow implicitly to his dictates; and nowhere did he encounter so vigorous opposition as in Africa. The Donatist schism, as we have seen,[1] had narrowly directed public attention in that country to questions of polity and discipline; and the people and clergy had declined to adopt several of the changes introduced elsewhere into the ecclesiastical constitution. The doctrine of the primacy of Peter and of the divine right of the Pope had there very few cordial advocates. Even Augustine, the leader of the Catholics and the greatest theologian of his age, rejected, after mature consideration, the interpretation commonly given of the proof-text of Romanism— " Thou art Peter, and upon this Rock will I build my Church."[2] " Our Lord declares," says this father, " on this rock will I build my Church, *because* Peter had said ' Thou art the Christ, the Son of the living God.' On this rock *which thou hast confessed*, he declares, ' I will build my Church,' for *Christ was the rock* on whose foundation Peter himself was built, for other foundation hath no man laid than that which is laid, which is Jesus Christ."[3]

During the Pelagian controversy the African clergy more than once practically asserted their ecclesiastical independence. When Pelagius and Cœlestius ventured across the Mediterranean from Rome, their heresy was condemned, and its authors cut off by synodical authority from catholic communion. The African bishops then forwarded to Innocent an account of their proceedings, and requested his concurrence—not because they had any doubts as to the validity of their independent judgment, but because they believed that the approving testimony of so influential a prelate would impart additional importance and

---

[1] See Sect. I. Chap. V. of this Period.

[2] Matt. xvi. 18.

[3] " Ait Dominus, *Super hanc petram ædificabo Ecclesiam meam, quia dixerat Petrus, Tu es Christus Filius Dei vivi.* Super hanc ergo, inquit, petram quam confessus es, ædificabo Ecclesiam meam. Petra enim erat Christus : super quod fundamentum etiam ipse ædificatus est Petrus. Fundamentum quippe aliud nemo potest ponere præter id quod positum est, quod est Christus Jesus." *In Joannis Evang. Tractat.* cxxiv. § 5. *Patrol. Curs.* Migne, tom. xxxv. 1973. It is worthy of note that the above exposition of Matt. xvi. 18 was given after Augustine came into collision with the bishop of Rome in the Pelagian controversy. He had before adopted the Romish interpretation. See Neander, iii. 225.

publicity to their decision. "We have," said they, "anathematized Pelagius and Cœlestius, and *thought fit to acquaint you with it*, that to the decrees of Church rulers in our comparatively humble position might be added the authority of the Apostolic See."[1] Innocent was obviously somewhat puzzled by this application; for, as he was most jealous of his dignity, he did not care to appear merely to follow in the wake of these African Churchmen; but his character for orthodoxy was at stake; and some of his correspondents had informed him that he was actually suspected of favouring the heresy.[2] He contrived, however, to escape from the difficulty by assuming that the African fathers had referred the case to his final arbitration; and accordingly denounced Pelagianism. Zosimus, the succeeding Pope, did not act with the same prudence. During his pontificate, Cœlestius arrived in Rome, complained of the judgment of the African bishops, asserted his orthodoxy, and presented a confession of his faith. In this document he intimated that he was in doubt as to the doctrine of original sin, and affirmed that it did not form any part of the catholic creed. Zosimus approved of the production, and wrote to the African bishops complaining of the rashness with which they had pronounced judgment. In the lofty tone of ecclesiastical superiority he condemns their discussions on the subject of original sin as "silly controversies,"[3] and demands an explanation of their conduct. But the Africans were not to be thus intimidated. At a Council convened on the occasion they unanimously reaffirmed their former sentence, and condemned anew the disputed doctrine. The Pope himself was now obliged to yield, and at length withdrew his protection from the errorists. The African bishops were not, however, content to let the matter rest here; for, as they disapproved of the conduct of Pelagius and Cœlestius in applying to Zosimus for a reversal of their sentence, they passed a law condemnatory of all who should in future pursue the same course. "If any one," says this decree, "shall presume to appeal beyond sea, let no one in Africa receive him to communion."[4]

[1] "Hoc itaque gestum, domine frater, sanctæ Charitati tuæ intimandum duximus, ut statutis nostræ mediocritatis etiam apostolicæ Sedis adhibeatur auctoritas." August. *Epist.* clxxv., Migne, *Patrolog. Curs.* xxxiii. 760.

[2] August. *Epist.* clxxvii. Migne, *Patrol. Curs.* xxxiii. 764.

[3] "Inepta certamina." Zosim. *Epist.* ii. 7. *Patrol. Curs.* xx. 653.

[4] This regulation is also to be found in the Code of the African Church, cap. 28, 125.

Another transaction in which the African Church was concerned shortly after this period supplies a curious illustration of the arts by means of which the Italian prelate endeavoured to support his encroachments. A presbyter of Sicca in Numidia, named Apiarius, had for various crimes been deposed and excommunicated; but having, in the face of the canon just quoted, appealed to Rome, he was by Zosimus at once released from the sentence. Aware, after what had occurred, that it might be difficult to induce the African bishops to submit to such high-handed interference, the Pope tried by a piece of most disreputable trickery to secure their obedience. Knowing that the Sardican Synod had not been recognized in Africa, and that it was the only ecclesiastical authority which warranted the right of appeal to his tribunal, he attempted to pass off its canons as if they had been framed by the Council of Nice! When a deputation appointed by him, consisting of a bishop and two presbyters, appeared in Africa, and proceeded to produce these vouchers to a Synod before which they were pleading the cause of Apiarius, the assembly immediately demurred, alleging that the regulations now quoted were not to be found in their copies of the Nicene decrees. "It matters not," replied the deputation, "whether or not these canons are to be found in your copies, or indeed in any other. You must know that the canons and ordinances of Nice which have been handed down to us by tradition and established by custom are no less binding than those that have been conveyed to us in writing."[1] Intimidated by the power of the Pope, who, since the confirmation of his appellant jurisdiction by Gratian and Valentinian II., could confidently calculate on the assistance of the civil magistrate, the bishops were obliged to listen to this insolence without reply; but still they resolved to send messengers to Constantinople and Alexandria to obtain from these great Churches accredited copies of the Nicene canons. Meanwhile the affair of Apiarius was compromised; and the offending presbyter, on making certain acknowledgments, was restored to the ministry. But he soon afterwards committed crimes of a more aggravated character, and was again deposed and excommunicated. He betook himself, a second time, to the tribunal of Rome, where the sentence was once more summarily removed. Celestine, who was now Pope,[2] sent back

[1] See Bower's *Popes, Zosimus*.   [2] A.D. 422 to A.D. 432.

this worthless man to Africa, accompanied by a commission empowered to replace him in his former ecclesiastical position. Long ere this the messengers to Constantinople and Alexandria had returned to the African bishops bearing authentic copies of the Nicene decrees, exactly corresponding to those already in their possession—so that it was now useless to attempt, under a false name, to secure authority for the canons of Sardica. But, where argument failed, effrontery was not wanting. Before an African Synod the Papal commissioner stoutly asserted the innocence of Apiarius; and the trial had continued several days, when, to the astonishment of all and the confusion of the Roman advocate, the accused, smitten with remorse, made a full and free confession of his criminality. For very shame the Pope was now obliged to abandon his protegee; and thus this attempt to enslave the African Church was ingloriously defeated. The African bishops now renewed more stringently the canon prohibiting appeals beyond sea on any pretence whatever, and extending it to all classes of Churchmen. In a letter addressed on the occasion to Celestine, they employed language which must have been anything but grateful to the proud pontiff. "Would it not," said they, "be presumptuous in any of us to suppose or imagine that God will inspire *a particular person* with the spirit of justice, and refuse it to many bishops assembled in Council? And how can a judgment given out of the country and beyond sea be right, where the necessary witnesses cannot be present by reason of their sex, or their age, or some other impediment? As for your sending legates, we find no such ordinances in any council, nor in the writings of the fathers. As to what you have sent us by our colleague Faustinus as a canon of the Council of Nice, we must let you know that no such canon is to be found in the genuine and uninterpolated canons of that Council which have been transcribed and sent us by our fellow-bishop Cyril of Alexandria and the reverend Atticus of Constantinople. These copies we sent to Boniface,[1] your predecessor of worthy memory. We therefore earnestly beg you will send no more legates or ecclesiastics to execute your judgments here, lest you should seem to introduce worldly pride and arrogance into the Church of Christ."[2]

Notwithstanding the assistance of the State, the bishop of

[1] Bishop of Rome from A.D. 419 to A.D. 422.
[2] See the original quoted by Gieseler, i. 268, note.

Rome long found it difficult to secure submission beyond the suburbicarian provinces. Nowhere, except in Africa, did he meet with more resolute opposition than in Gaul. Pope Zosimus had an obstinate struggle with some of the bishops of that country when he attempted to interfere with their ecclesiastical arrangements by extending the jurisdiction of the bishop of Arles; and Proculus of Marseilles continued to the last to set at nought his authority and to disregard all his fulminations.[1] Nearly thirty years afterwards, Hilary of Arles refused to acknowledge the Italian patriarch's appellant jurisdiction; and Leo, who then filled the Papal chair, was obliged to throw himself on the civil power for support. In A.D. 445, at the instigation of this Pontiff, the feeble Emperor Valentinian III. issued an edict which confirmed and enlarged the authority granted, upwards of sixty years before, by Gratian and Valentinian II. The rescript, which on this occasion was addressed most appropriately to Ætius, the General of the troops in Gaul, declares that nothing must be attempted by the bishops, either there or elsewhere, "without the authority of the venerable Pope of the Eternal City."[2] It adds that "whatever the authority of the apostolic see has sanctioned, or will sanction, shall be a law for them and for all others."[3]

An appeal has been often made to this edict as if it introduced a new era in the history of the Popedom; and it must be admitted that it confers larger powers, and that it is more peremptory in its tone, than any preceding act of legislation; but its influence has been probably over-estimated. It merely gives another and more emphatic sanction to pretensions which the State was already pledged to uphold. But, as the Western Empire was now overrun by enemies and tottering on the verge of ruin, this law could have been only very partially enforced. Other circumstances contributed still more efficiently to place the papal authority on a stable foundation. Among these may be mentioned the jealousies and contentions of the great Eastern prelates. As the bishop of Rome was the only Patriarch in the West, he had nothing to fear from the intrigues of envious rivals; and the ecclesiastics whom he compelled to obedience were generally too

---

[1] Bower's *Popes, Zosimus.* Gieseler, i. 266.
[2] "Sine viri venerabilis papæ Urbis Æternæ auctoritate."
[3] "Sed hoc illis omnibusque pro lege sit, quidquid sanxit vel sanxerit apostolicæ sedis auctoritas." S. Leo. Mag. *Epist.* xi. *Opera*, tom. i. 638, ed. Migne.

feeble to embarrass him in his career of usurpation. But in the Eastern Empire the four Patriarchs of Constantinople, Alexandria, Antioch, and Jerusalem were employed in challenging each other's pretensions and checking each other's advancement. The Patriarch of Constantinople—the most influential of them all—was long engaged with the three others in embittered contests. His rapid elevation was peculiarly mortifying to his brethren of Alexandria and Antioch, as they were both thus placed a degree lower in the scale of ecclesiastical dignity. Chrysostom felt the effects of their galled ambition; and, when he submitted a statement of his wrongs to Innocent of Rome, the energy with which that prelate espoused his cause tended greatly to exalt the reputation of the Western bishopric. The Nestorian and Eutychian controversies, fomented by the rivalry of the bishops of Constantinople and Alexandria, were also extremely favourable to the growth of papal influence. When the victory was doubtful —as the bishop of Rome, by throwing his patronage into either scale, could decide the hesitating balance—each party applied to him for support; and meanwhile he obtained acknowledgments from both which increased his weight and secured his preponderance. In A.D. 451 his legates, associated with other dignitaries,[1] took a prominent part, for the first time, in an œcumenical council; and his letter condemnatory of Eutychianism was registered by the fathers of Chalcedon as a portion of the creed of the catholic Church. Leo the Great, the Pope who was thus honoured, and who continued to occupy his place for the unusually long period of twenty-one years,[2] was the ablest, most eloquent, and most ambitious of all the churchmen who had ever yet presided in the Roman bishopric. The doctrine that the Apostle Peter is the foundation of the Church, and that the chief pastor of Rome, as his successor, is the heir of his prerogatives, was inculcated by this pontiff with uncommon industry and boldness; and the arrogance with which his representatives in the Council of Chalcedon put forward his pretensions gave just offence to the assembled prelates. But, before the close of the proceedings, his pride received a most appropriate rebuke by a

---

[1] The Imperial commissioners occupied the chief place. See Binius, ii. 40. During some of the proceedings of the Council the Roman legates were not even present.

[2] From A.D. 440 to A.D. 461.

vote, passed almost unanimously by these ecclesiastical legislators. "Whereas," says this resolution, "the fathers with great propriety bestowed the chief honours on the see of old Rome, *because it was the Imperial city;* and whereas the one hundred and fifty fathers [1] beloved of God, actuated by the same motive, conferred *the like dignity* on the most holy see of New Rome—judging it reasonable that the city honoured as the seat of empire and of the Senate, and *equal in civil privileges* with ancient royal Rome, should be *equally distinguished also by ecclesiastical privileges,* and enjoy the second place in the Church, being next to old Rome—we ratify and confirm the same."[2] Another canon, corresponding to that which had been adopted upwards of a century before at Sardica in favour of the Roman bishop, was at the same time enacted. "If any one," says this regulation, "is wronged by his metropolitan, he is to be judged by the Exarch of the Diocese,[3] or by *the throne of Constantinople.*"[4] Thus the precedence of the Western primacy was reduced to a mere affair of courtesy, and the great Constantinopolitan prelate was placed exactly on a level with his Western brother.

The Italian Pontiff maintained that his see stood at an immeasurable distance above all other bishoprics, inasmuch as it was founded and occupied by the prince of the apostles. But here the doctrine of its primacy is expounded by a general council; and all such statements are quietly discarded as mere romance. The fathers of Chalcedon teach that the bishop of Rome had hitherto held the first place in Christendom simply because he was located in the first city of the Empire. Leo was intensely dissatisfied because they consistently carried out the principle involved in this interpretation by recognising the bishop of Constantinople as his ecclesiastical peer. As soon as the matter was mooted, his legates abruptly left the council; and at a subsequent session they entered their protest against the canon as unjust to "the Pope of the universal church."[5] Leo

[1] Of the General Council of Constantinople, held A.D. 381.
[2] Council of Chalcedon, Canon xxviii.
[3] See Sect. III. Chap. III. of this Period, p. 249.
[4] Council of Chalcedon, Canon xvii.
[5] Binius, tem. ii. 343. It is obvious from this and other statements that titles at least equivalent to that of universal bishop were given to the Pope long before the beginning of the seventh century. In this same Council of Chalcedon one of the Pope's legates speaks of Rome as "the head of all the churches" (caput

himself denounced it as null and void. As the Christian community was already torn by divisions, it was deemed prudent to endeavour to pacify the exasperated prelate; and, at the instigation of the Eastern Emperor, the bishop of Constantinople attempted to conciliate him by addressing to him a soothing and deprecatory letter. But the canon, notwithstanding, received the imperial confirmation; and thus openly commenced that strife between the Eastern and Western churches which forms so prominent a topic in the history of succeeding centuries.

The power of the bishop of Rome had obtained such a firm foundation before the Western Empire fell that his throne scarcely felt the shock of the overthrow; and the assaults of the barbarians on the crumbling fabric furnished him with some splendid opportunities for the display of his pontifical greatness. We have seen that, after the sack of Rome by Alaric, the Pope remained almost its only grandee; and, in A.D. 452, when the terrible Attila, King of the Huns, appeared in Italy, and threatened the city again with desolation, the bishop, at the head of a deputation, was commissioned to visit his camp, and to entreat him to desist from his enterprise. At this very time the barbarian chief had some reason for anxiety, as his army was in critical circumstances; and his own military skill might have dictated the course pointed out by the commissioners; but their application supplied him with a plausible apology for withdrawing from a dangerous position. His retirement, on payment of a large sum of money, was, however, currently attributed to the influence of Leo. It was alleged that the fierce Hun, who delighted in the designation of "The Scourge of God," was overawed by the majestic deportment, the saintly character, and the commanding eloquence of the Roman bishop. Three years afterwards, when Genseric plundered the ancient capital of Italy, Leo is said to have succeeded in moderating the rapacity of the savage Vandal. As the imperial power declined, the Pope gradually assumed a bolder and more imposing attitude. The

---

omnium ecclesiarum), Binius, ii. 41. Gregory the Great asserts erroneously that the title "universal" was given to the bishops his predecessors by the Council of Chalcedon. *Epist.* lib. v.; *Epist.* 18, Migne, *Patrol. Curs.* tom. lxxvii. 740. It is clear, from the above testimonies, that it was used at that time somewhat ostentatiously by the papal partizans. But other bishops of high authority were also called *universal.* See Gieseler, i. 254, 269; and Schaff, ii. 285, note.

barbarians, from motives either of policy or superstition, respected his sacerdotal dignity; and though they waged war against the Empire, it never seems to have occurred to them that the great bishop should be treated as an enemy. He was not directly dependent on the State for his support—as his revenue was derived, partly from the contributions of the faithful, and partly from landed possessions in various countries,[1] given or bequeathed to his predecessors, or purchased by the treasures of the Church; and as he had no reason to anticipate their confiscation, he had little personal interest in the maintenance of a sinking dynasty. Simplicius, who was Pope[2] at the time of the deposition of Augustulus, the last sovereign of the West, has left behind him a variety of letters in which he treats of the transactions of his age; but it is remarkable that he does not record the extinction of the Empire. It may be that he did not consider it expedient to notice the catastrophe; and it is quite possible that he experienced no inconvenience whatever from a change of masters. The breaking up of the old political fabric served rather to strengthen his relations with distant prelates. The hurricane of revolution destroyed much of the existing ecclesiastical organization, separating bishops from metropolitans and metropolitans from exarchs, and scattering some whole communities to the winds; and, in the meantime, not a few churches surrendered to him the remnants of their independence, preferring the shelter of his domination to the anarchy created by the political tempest. After the conquest of Africa by the Vandals, even the Church of that country, which had so long resisted his authority, is found patiently submitting to his jurisdiction. When the Western Empire fell, the influence of the Pope was established more firmly than ever; and the bishop of Constantinople was the only ecclesiastic in existence who appeared likely to disturb his dreams of ambition. Acacius, who then presided in the See of the Eastern capital, was a man of ability and address; and the zeal with which he asserted his dignity gave no little uneasiness to the Roman patriarch.

[1] As in Sicily, Gaul, and elsewhere.
[2] From A.D. 467 to A.D. 483.

CHAPTER III.

THE PROGRESS OF THE PAPACY FROM THE FALL OF THE WESTERN EMPIRE TO THE PONTIFICATE OF GREGORY THE GREAT, A.D. 476 TO A.D. 590.

THE growth of that spiritual despotism which eventually enthralled so many of the churches of Christendom commenced in the days of the apostles. "The mystery of iniquity doth already work," says Paul, "only he who now letteth will let, until he be taken out of the way."[1] It was the opinion of the early fathers that the Roman Empire was the power which *let*, or hindered, the revelation of Antichrist.[2] Whatever may be thought of this interpretation, it is certain that the influence of the bishop of the Italian metropolis continued to increase as the imperial authority declined. Long before the extinction of the Western Empire, Rome had ceased to be the residence of the court; and when the Pope became its chief citizen, his ambition was stimulated and fostered by the weakness of the existing government. We have seen that the circumstances of the times added greatly to his importance. His vast wealth enabled him to relieve the multitudes of poor to be found in a sinking capital; his person was invested, in popular estimation, with peculiar sanctity; when the irruptions of the barbarians created perplexity and peril, his advice was eagerly solicited and reverentially obeyed; and when it was necessary to implore imperial aid, or to deprecate the vengeance of the conqueror, the pontiff was expected to appear at the head of the deputation, and to exert the influence of his character and eloquence. Thus, even the disasters of his country conspired to augment his reputation. His power continued to increase notwithstanding the triumphs of the northern barbarians. When Augustulus, the last Emperor of the West, was set aside by Odoacer, king of the Heruli, this prince, though an Arian, respected the pontifical dignity; for he doubtless considered that his own throne would be more secure, could he conciliate the support of the Roman prelate. But if his Gothic kingdom was represented by one of the toes on the feet of the

---

[1] 2 Thess. ii. 7.
[2] See Tertullian's *Apology*, ch. 32.

great image seen by Nebuchadnezzar in his dream,[1] it must have been symbolized by a toe of clay; as, after a brief existence of little more than fourteen years, it was broken in pieces. Theodoric, king of the Ostrogoths, by whom it was destroyed, was, like Odoacer, an adherent of Arianism; he nevertheless asserted his right, as sovereign, to interfere in elections to the Popedom, and in one case was provoked to imprison an occupant of the Roman see;[2] but, as the supporters of the Nicene Creed formed an overwhelming majority of his subjects, he generally recognized the political expediency of cultivating the good opinion of the most powerful bishop in his territories.

After the deposition of Augustulus, the sovereigns of Constantinople claimed the inheritance of the Empire of the West; and the Gothic princes did not directly repudiate the tribute of a nominal allegiance. The Greek monarchs were exceedingly unwilling to relinquish this titular dignity; and, in the hope that the Italian pontiff might one day help them to obtain a footing on the banks of the Tiber, some of them courted most assiduously the favour of the great churchman. In A.D. 533, the Eastern Emperor, Justinian, wrote a letter to the Roman bishop, John II., in which, adopting the fulsome style already more than once employed by his predecessors, he consulted him as the judge of Catholic doctrine, and the index of Catholic unity.[3] Shortly afterwards his general Belisarius appeared, first in Africa, and then in Europe; triumphed over the Vandals and the Goths; and added several of the Latin provinces to the Eastern Empire. But the sovereignty thus acquired rested on a very insecure basis. Though the authority of the court of Constantinople was now acknowledged at Rome for nearly two hundred years, the Greek monarch still felt that it was unsafe to test too severely the loyalty of his Italian subjects—more especially as, throughout almost the whole of this period, his dominion was imperilled by the neighbourhood of the conquering Lombards. The Pope, who sometimes ventured to brave the displeasure of his Eastern master, was meanwhile gradually strengthening the foundations of his power and enlarging his pretensions. In a

---

[1] Dan. ii. 42.
[2] Pope John I. in A.D. 526. See Bower, *John fifty-second bishop of Rome.*
[3] In Elliott's *Horæ Apocalypticæ*, iii. 134, this letter is quoted as written at a great prophetic era. But its importance seems to be over-rated.

few instances, when he did not prove obsequious, the Emperor treated him with rigour;[1] but prudential considerations commonly preponderated; and the imperial letters to the occupants of the Roman See were ordinarily couched in the language of compliment or of flattery.

Whilst reasons of state were prompting the Greek sovereigns to pay court to the Roman patriarch, circumstances of a different nature were constantly augmenting his consequence. In the Arian controversy he added greatly to his credit by upholding Trinitarianism; and he was thus taught that his influence might be still farther promoted could he maintain his character as the defender of the faith. In most cases his position enabled him to be pretty sure of the ground he occupied in reference to any disputed dogma before he committed himself by a positive deliverance. As, with the exception of Pelagianism, all the heresies which had hitherto disturbed the Church originated in the East, he had ample time to investigate debated questions before giving his decision; and, as he was comparatively free from secular control, he could afford to pronounce an independent judgment. Thus it happened that almost every new heresy contributed to his fame. Shortly after the downfall of the Western Empire he was presented with a golden opportunity of exhibiting his zeal for orthodoxy. In A.D. 482 the Greek Emperor Zeno, harassed by the contentions which the Council of Chalcedon had rather aggravated than repressed, and believing that the discussion between the Monophysites and their adversaries had dwindled down nearly into a war of words, framed a Formula of Concord, designated the *Henoticon*,[2] with a view to promote a reconciliation. The Monophysite leaders, as well as the patriarch of Constantinople, and others, subscribed this document; and hopes were entertained that the Church, exhausted by strife, would at length enjoy a season of repose. But the bishop of Rome pertinaciously refused to sanction the compromise. He anathematized the great Eastern patriarch as a betrayer of the high trust committed to him, and denounced the Henoticon as a renunciation of Catholic verity. The communion between the Eastern and Western churches was now

---

[1] As in the case of Pope Vigilius, who died A.D. 555. The case of Pope Martin, who died in exile in A.D. 655, is another illustration.

[2] See Section II. chap. V. of this Period, p. 211.

interrupted for upwards of thirty years;[1] and at length the Greek Emperor, yielding to the intimidation of his orthodox subjects, was obliged to purchase a restoration of the ecclesiastical peace by submitting to the demands of the Roman pontiff, and acknowledging, without reserve, the decrees of the Council of Chalcedon.

During the continuance of this schism between the Eastern and Western churches, some of the most extravagant pretensions since advanced by the Italian pontiffs were first mooted. About A.D. 511, Ennodius, bishop of Ticinum, a flatterer of Pope Symmachus, broached the doctrine that the bishop of Rome judges in the place of God, and that he is subject to the jurisdiction of no earthly tribunal.[2] At the time, these statements were treated as mere gasconade; and long afterwards the Greek Emperor continued to exercise a species of ecclesiastical supremacy; but, at length, the assertions of such men as Ennodius were adduced as vouchers for the antiquity of pontifical prerogatives. A few years, however, before the bishop of Ticinum promulgated his reveries, an event occurred which led to a great change in the state of Western Europe, as well as to the enlargement and consolidation of pontifical authority. In A.D. 496 the celebrated king Clovis embraced Christianity. As the history of the conversion of this prince illustrates the spirit of the age, it is entitled to particular notice.

When Clovis became king of the Salian or Sicambrian Franks, the whole tribe did not consist of more than three or four thousand warriors. Clothed in skins of wild beasts, and devoted to war and hunting, they were only imperfectly acquainted with the elements of civilization. As they led a species of wandering life, they were very little attached, by local associations, to the superstitions of their ancestors; but the Gospel and the Roman power had been long connected in the thoughts of the barbarians; and, as Clovis desired the protection of a mighty tutelary guardian, he hesitated to pass over to the Church. He had witnessed the subversion of the Western Empire; and he imagined that

---

[1] From A.D. 484 to A.D. 519.

[2] "Aliorum forte hominum causas Deus voluerit per homines terminare; sedis istius præsulem suo, sine questione, reservavit arbitrio." The forged acts of a preceding council and some other spurious documents have been quoted in support of these sentiments. See Gieseler, i. 339.

its fall indicated the weakness of the God of the Christians. His wife Clotilda, a zealous Catholic, and niece of Gundebald, king of the Burgundians, had laboured diligently to effect his conversion; but, for a considerable time, all her exertions were unavailing. The issue of a battle with the Alemanni at length completely removed his scruples. In this engagement he had cried in vain for help to the gods of his forefathers; and at last, in an agony of despair, when his troops were giving way on all sides, he invoked the aid of the god of Clotilda. At this critical moment the tide of war began to turn, and the enemy fled before him. Clovis, now convinced of the power of the Saviour, openly embraced the Christian faith; and three thousand of his Frankish warriors forthwith followed his example.[1]

The conversion of Clovis bears a strong resemblance to that of Constantine. In both cases the same secular motives apparently predominated; but the subsequent career of the barbarian prince is much less reputable than that of the Roman Emperor. Remigius, bishop of Rheims, expounded the Christian system to Clovis about the time of his baptism; and yet the knowledge of the Gospel evinced by the royal proselyte reflected little credit on his episcopal instructor. When the prelate narrated to him the history of the crucifixion, the barbarian, who had no conception of its real significance, is reported to have uttered the unseasonable exclamation—"Had I been present at the head of my Franks, I would have avenged the wrong!"[2] As Clovis was no ordinary convert it was deemed expedient to celebrate his baptism in a style of unwonted magnificence. On the day appointed for the ceremony the king and the bishop proceeded in state to the scene of the solemnity: the way was strewn with flowers; the air was filled with perfumes; the houses of the city of Rheims were richly decorated; and the royal procession, under the cover of a splendid canopy, passed through the street which led to the cathedral. Clovis had heard of the glory of the celestial abodes, but he had never before beheld such an imposing demonstration; and, turning to Remigius, who walked beside him in embroidered vestments, asked in astonishment—

[1] *Gregorii Epis. Turonensis Hist. Franc.* ii. c. 31. Fredegarius doubles the number of the soldiers baptized. *Epitomata*, c. 21.

[2] *Hist. Franc. Epitomata per Fredegarium Scholasticum*, cap. xxi. Migne, *Patrol. Curs.* lxxi. 586.

"Good father, is not this the kingdom of heaven to which you have promised to conduct me?"[1] The subsequent career of the Frankish king supplied melancholy evidence that he had derived little spiritual benefit from his baptism. His reception of the Gospel was connected with no moral transformation; and his whole reign is a sad exhibition of ambition and covetousness, perfidy and cruelty.

The conversion of Clovis was fraught with important consequences as well to Gaul as to the papacy. Though but a petty sovereign he was the only prince in Europe who espoused the Catholic faith; for all the other kings professing Christianity, who ruled over the conquered provinces of the Western Empire, were the abettors of Arianism. The baptism of the Frankish conqueror was hailed with delight by all the friends of orthodoxy; and to none did it afford more cordial satisfaction than to the bishop of the ancient capital of Italy. He was not slow to perceive that it opened up to him a way by which he could extend and consolidate his power; and, in a letter addressed to the royal neophyte, he complimented the father of the "Catholic kings" and of the "eldest sons of the Church."[2]

When Clovis entered the Catholic Church he took a step which signally promoted his political advancement; as he at once secured the sympathy of all the orthodox bishops around him. At this time these dignitaries occupied a very influential position. Under the imperial administration they had been invested with a certain amount of political authority; but when the municipal government of the cities of the Western Empire was destroyed, episcopal privileges were still respected, and the catastrophe rather promoted the progress of ecclesiastical usurpation. As society was fast verging towards barbarism, superstition attached undue importance to clerical decisions; and churchmen, now almost exclusively the depositaries of the literature of the age, could direct the current of public opinion. When Clovis secured the support of the spiritual aristocracy, he virtually laid the foundations of the Frankish Empire. In all

---

[1] *Vita Sancti Remigii ab Hincmaro*, Migne, *Patrol. Curs.* cxxv. 1160. The account of Gregory of Tours suggests the probability of such an occurrence—"Totumque templum baptisterii divino respergitur ab odore, talemque ibi gratiam astantibus Deus tribuit, *ut æstimarent se paradisi odoribus collocari.*" *Hist. Franc.* ii. 31.

[2] *Patrol. Curs.* Migne, tom. lxxi. 1154.

the conquests he attempted he enjoyed the avowed or secret co-operation of his ecclesiastical friends; and the miraculous interpositions supposed to mark his prosperous career were generally nothing more than the development of well-contrived schemes devised by the clergy to accelerate his triumphs. Thus, a prince who commenced his reign as the ruler of a petty tribe of barbarians, at length swayed his sceptre over various districts beyond the Rhine, as well as the greater portion of the present French territory.[1] Every new victory added to the power of the Church, as well as to the glory of the founder of the Merovingian dynasty.[2]

It is said that this monarch presented to Pope Anastasius II. a crown of gold studded with precious stones;[3] but though such a statement may be discarded as apocryphal, it is beyond doubt that Clovis was most desirous to stand well with the Roman bishop. Nor was it strange that the pontifical favour was so eagerly coveted; for it was of vast importance to the aspiring adventurer. The yoke of the Arian kings was borne with reluctance by their orthodox subjects; and meanwhile the Catholic bishops had been prompted to cultivate a closer alliance with the chief pastor of Italy. In the divided and unsettled state of Europe no large council could assemble; questions urgently calling for solution were constantly recurring; and matters in dispute were often submitted for decision to the great Western patriarch. The practice commenced by Syricius, of issuing decretal epistles, was still continued; and, at a time when few were competent to conduct a theological discussion, much respect was paid to these carefully composed documents. By pursuing the system of appointing distinguished ecclesiastics in different parts of Europe as his vicars, the Pope also strengthened his

[1] The population of France was then very different from what it is in the nineteenth century. Sismondi reckons that a portion of territory, which now sustains eight millions, had not, in the days of Clovis, more than from six to eight hundred thousand inhabitants. *Histoire des Français, Prem. Par.* chap. v. i. 121, Bruxelles, 1847.

[2] As to the origin of this name, see Gibbon, chap. xxxv. note Q, p. 568, ed. London, 1836.

[3] Bower's *Popes*, Anastasius II. 49th bishop of Rome. This story, on various grounds, must be received with suspicion. According to Hincmar, in his *Life of Remigius*—perhaps the earliest authority on this subject—the crown was presented to Hormisdas: but he was not made pope until some years after the death of Clovis.

position; for, in this way, he at once flattered the vanity and disarmed the opposition of ambitious and influential prelates.

Nothing, perhaps, contributed more to papal aggrandizement than the course pursued by the Roman bishops in reference to appeals to their tribunal from the clergy or people of other churches. Their right to adjudicate in such cases, as has already been related, rested originally on the rather equivocal foundation of a canon of the Council of Sardica; but it had been subsequently fortified by the laws of the Empire; and it was frequently exercised without much regard either to justice or decency. The complainant could always reckon on a gracious hearing; and a favourable deliverance generally awaited his appeal.[1] Thus it was that all who laboured under any real or imaginary grievance were disposed to repair to the Roman judgment seat. So gross was the partiality shown to the appellant that the other party often rejected the award with indignation or scorn. A transaction which occurred about A.D. 570, and which illustrates at once the degeneracy of the times and the absurdity of the papal decisions, may here be narrated.

Two brothers, Salonius, bishop of Embrun, and Sagittarius, bishop of Gap, had been tried by a synod held at Lyons; and had been convicted, on the clearest evidence, of housebreaking, robbery, adultery, and murder.[2] They were accordingly deposed by a unanimous sentence; but, in the semi-barbarous condition to which France was then reduced, their crimes were regarded by many with indulgence; and, as they possessed considerable personal or family influence, they prevailed on King Guntram to permit them to appeal to the Roman Pontiff. When they reached the ancient metropolis of Italy they met with a kind reception from John III.; and, on the strength of their own testimony, the sentence of deposition was cancelled. The Pope wrote a letter to the king requiring him to restore them to their sees; and Guntram, who was favourable to the delinquents, acceded to the application.[3] But the French bishops were by

[1] Dr. Campbell asserts that "*for many centuries*, the judgment of the apostolic see, as it affected to be styled in contradistinction to others, was *uniformly* in favour of the appellant." *Lectures on Ecc. Hist.* Lect. xv. This statement is rather strong, as there were some exceptions. See Bower, Celestine 42d bishop of Rome, and Leo 44th bishop.

[2] Gregory of Tours, *Hist. Franc.* v. 21.

[3] Though not very scrupulous, Guntram gave the two bishops a severe rebuke

no means so complaisant. They could not exclude Salonius and Sagittarius from their bishoprics, as the offenders were supported by the civil power; but they resolutely refused to readmit them to their communion. In a short time events too clearly justified their resistance. The restored bishops, confiding in the protection of the Pope and king, indulged more freely than ever in lewdness and profanity; and at length in defiance of all propriety, took part in a war between the Burgundians and the Lombards. They are said to have been the first prelates who engaged in military operations; and, in the strife of arms, they acquired an unenviable notoriety by their bloody achievements. The scandal of their behaviour became at length so flagrant that the public voice indignantly demanded their punishment; and Guntram himself was obliged to interfere and shut them up separately in monasteries.[1]

It is apparent from this narrative that the bishop of Rome as yet possessed nothing like unchallenged or absolute authority throughout Western Christendom. The Gallic prelates peremptorily refused to submit to his award; and by force the offending brethren were prevented from attempting to take shelter a second time under the covert of his jurisdiction. But, notwithstanding such incidents, the influence of the great Italian ecclesiastic advanced apace. The Arian chiefs, who ruled over the dismembered provinces of the Western Empire, began at length to appreciate the advantages derived by the kings of the Merovingian dynasty from their connection with the head of the Catholic Church; and guided, perhaps, partly by the suggestions of political expediency, and partly by religious conviction, were induced, one after another, to renounce their heresy. The sixth century witnessed the rapid decline of Anti-Trinitarianism. Its political strength was greatly weakened when its most prominent abettors, the Vandals in Africa, and the Ostro-Goths in Italy, were overwhelmed by the victorious troops of the Greek Emperor Justinian. The Burgundians in A.D. 517, and the Suevi in A.D. 558, voluntarily embraced the Nicene creed; and in A.D. 589

---

before complying with the papal requisition. "Quod rex sine mora, *castigatis prius illis verbis multis*, implevit." Greg. Turon. v. 21.

[1] Gregory of Tours, v. 21. On the strength of other authorities, Bower has mentioned various incidents connected with this affair not noticed by Gregory. See his Life of John III. 60th bishop of Rome.

the Visigoths of Spain, with their king Recared, followed the example.[1]

The Lombards who invaded Italy in A.D. 568, and who made Pavia the chief town of their new kingdom, interfered for a time with the progress of the power of the Roman Pontiff. In A.D. 587, their king Autharis embraced Christianity under the form of Arianism. But this prince died in A.D. 590; and his widow Theodelinda, who is said to have been educated in the Catholic faith, soon secured its ascendency. Agilulf, duke of Turin, whom she married after the death of Autharis, succeeded him on the Lombard throne: the story that he became a convert to Trinitarianism may be a fable;[2] but there is no doubt that his son received Catholic baptism, and that, about the middle of the seventh century, Arianism had disappeared from among the Lombards.

The conversion of the Arian chiefs removed various impediments in the way of papal ambition. The boundaries of the Catholic Church were enlarged by the multitudes who followed their leaders into it; the counteracting influence of a hostile religious element was extinguished; and all these kings were added to the friends of the Roman bishop. He knew well how to avail himself of the patronage of such a goodly company of royal personages; and either by flattering their vanity, or appealing to their fears, or working on their superstition, he induced them to support him in his encroachments on the rights and privileges of the Churches subject to their dominion.

CHAPTER IV.

THE PONTIFICATE OF GREGORY THE GREAT.—A.D. 590 to A.D. 604.

A NEW era in the history of the Roman See commences with the pontificate of Gregory I. This prelate, who has been honoured with the title of *The Great*, filled the papal chair upwards of thirteen years. The appointment to the popedom had already been often vigorously contested, and the successful candidate had sometimes carried his election amidst confusion and blood-

---
[1] Gieseler, i. 355.
[2] See Robertson's *History of the Christian Church*, ii. 13.

shed; but Gregory is said to have neither solicited nor desired the dignity. The circumstances of the times, as well as his own temperament, led him to shrink from promotion. The Lombards, who were wasting the country, had spread terror to the very gates of Rome; the feeble exarch, who resided at Ravenna, had confessed his inability to protect the subjects of his Eastern master; the Tiber, which had recently risen to an unusual height, had created a general panic; the inundation, by destroying the wheat in the public granaries, had produced a scarcity of food; and a plague which was desolating the city had cut down, amongst its earliest victims, no less distinguished a personage than Pope Pelagius II. At this crisis all eyes were turned to Gregory, who had previously, on several occasions, signalized his zeal and ability in the public service. He was a scion of one of the noblest families of Rome, and many years before had been prætor, or governor, of the city. He had subsequently devoted his wealth to benevolent and religious objects, and, retiring to a monastery, of which he became abbot, had distinguished himself by the austerity of his asceticism. But in these times such a man could not be permitted to remain long in obscurity. The Pope found it necessary to send an embassy to Constantinople, and Gregory was obliged to come forth from his seclusion and undertake the mission. During a residence of some years at the imperial court he gained no small amount of diplomatic experience—an acquisition which he knew well how to turn to account in the high position he subsequently occupied. When he returned to Rome he withdrew once more into a monastery; but, on the death of Pope Pelagius, he was called by the unanimous suffrages of the laity and clergy to the vacant throne; and, after much apparent hesitation, he consented to become the bishop of the first see in Christendom.

When Gregory entered on his pontifical career the Church was in a most unpromising condition. Formality and will-worship prevailed. Had the new Pope possessed the true spirit of an ecclesiastical reformer, he might have greatly improved the tone of public sentiment; for the authority of his station, added to his reputation for intelligence and piety, enabled him to exert an immense moral influence. But the mind of Gregory was thoroughly besotted by superstition; and, instead of rising superior to existing prejudices or adventuring into the region of independent thought, he did more than any individual of his generation to promote the progress of ignorance and folly. From an early period of his religious life he cherished a silly admiration of relics; and when he reached Rome, on his return from his embassy to Constantinople, he congratulated himself no little because he carried with him what he believed to be an arm of the Apostle Andrew and the head of the evangelist Luke.[1] He listened with absurd credulity to tales of miracles performed by reputed fragments of the skeletons of saints; and when he presented a missionary, a bishop, or a prince with some alleged particles of the wood of the cross, or with a few grains of iron filed off chains said to have been worn by one or other of the primitive heralds of the Gospel, he imagined that he made a donation of unspeakable value. About this time the Greek empress—who had built a church in the Eastern capital, and who wished to impart surpassing sanctity to the edifice—requested the Roman bishop to supply her with some apostolic bones; but Gregory, unwilling that such treasures should be transferred to the city of a rival patriarch, assigned rather a startling reason for declining to accede to the application. "The bodies of the holy Apostles Peter and Paul are," said he, " so resplendent with miracles and terrific prodigies in their own churches that no one can approach them without great awe, even for the purpose of adoring them. . . . . It is the custom of the Romans, when they give any relics, *not to touch any portion of the body:* they only put into a box a piece of linen, which is placed near the holy bodies; then it is withdrawn and shut up, with due veneration, in the church which is to be dedicated; and as many prodigies are then wrought by it as if the bodies themselves had been carried thither."[2]

This veneration for relics silently promoted the ecclesiastical ascendency of Rome. The city, consecrated by so many martyrdoms, was supposed to possess spiritual treasures of peculiar excellence; and strangers from all parts of Europe, who flocked to it to visit the tombs of the apostles, were well pleased to bear home any little trinket to which superstition attached a factitious value. Bishops and princes were not unfrequently found among the pilgrims; and the Pope never failed to profit by the presence

---

[1] Bower, *Gregory, Sixty-third Bishop*.
[2] *Epist.* iv. 30, *Opera*, tom. iii. 701-2, Migne edit.

of distinguished foreigners. Nor was it singular that the natives of countries sunk in barbarism were filled with wonder when they appeared in the ancient capital of the world. Even in its decline, Rome still sat as "a queen;" its majesty was visible amid the ruins of its architectural magnificence; and the unlettered Franc or Burgundian who repaired to its shrines and gazed on the trophies of its pontifical grandeur, would not be slow to acknowledge the Western patriarchate as the mistress and the mother of all churches. Should he be so fortunate as to obtain the papal benediction, he would be furnished with a new motive to magnify the apostolic see; and, on his return to the land of his birth, he might be trusted as an advocate who would feel a personal interest in maintaining its pretensions.

The attainments of Gregory were of the most common-place description; for he was entirely unacquainted with oriental literature, and, as he himself tells us,[1] even ignorant of Greek; but in his own age he enjoyed the reputation of a man of learning, and he is the only Pope among the ecclesiastical writers known as the Four Great Latin Fathers.[2] Upwards of 800 of his letters are still extant,—a large portion of which are addressed to bishops, and relate to questions of Church discipline. Whilst these epistles attest his professional industry, they also betray his uncommon anxiety to maintain and extend the influence of the Roman See. His eye ranged over all Christendom; and he was ready to send a decretal epistle, containing warning or advice, wherever he had encouragement to interfere. His *Regula Pastoralis*, or work on the pastoral care, may be still perused with interest and advantage;[3] and his *Moralia*, or Exposition of the Book of Job, was so highly appreciated in his own time that it was read by some bishops in their churches. It is obviously the production of a serious and earnest commentator; but its popularity indicates a sadly vitiated taste, as it is a miserable specimen of biblical interpretation. According to Gregory, Job's friends denote the heretics; his seven sons, the twelve apostles; his three daughters, the laity adhering to the doctrine of the trinity; his seven thousand sheep, the same faithful people; and

---

[1] *Epist.* vii. 32; xi. 74.
[2] Ambrose, Jerome, Augustine, and Gregory. See p. 90, note.
[3] In ancient times a copy of this book was handed to every French bishop at the time of his ordination. Dupin, *Ecc. Writers*, i. 579.

his three thousand hump-backed camels, the depraved Gentiles.[1] It would be easy to extract anything from Scripture by such a system of exegesis.

Ecclesiastical writers have given very contradictory accounts of the spirit and policy of Gregory, and to some who have studied his history his character is an insoluble riddle. He has been canonized by the Church of Rome; and perhaps there never was a Pope who was better entitled to the honours of saintship; but many telling facts are adduced by those who accuse him of profound hypocrisy and insatiable ambition. The want of candour and consistency which he so often exhibited may be traced partly to the corrupt maxims of his age, and partly to his anomalous position. A *pious fraud* is now justly condemned as a contradiction in terms; but in the days of Gregory public feeling did not protest so indignantly against everything like ecclesiastical imposture, and, centuries before his time, there were churchmen who deemed it perfectly legitimate to dissemble and deceive with a view to promote the interests of religion. This Pope adopted the dangerous principle; and we may thus account for the monkish fables with which his writings are so absurdly interlarded. As a man of discernment who had mingled largely with the world, he could not have believed all his own extravagant legends of miracles and apparitions; but he perhaps expected that his reputation for sanctity would give them currency; and he may have imagined that these narratives would awaken the awe and establish the faith of an ignorant and superstitious generation. If he made such calculations he overrated popular credulity; as his *Dialogues*, in which such stories most abound, only excited the merriment of not a few of the ancients, and he was known at one time among the wits of Constantinople by the not very complimentary designation of "*Gregory Dialogue.*"[2] It may be that the constant yet unequal struggle between the ascetic and the pontifical spirit in this celebrated church dignitary was the real cause of most of his inconsistencies. As a monk, he thought himself contaminated when he took any part in the concerns of men; whilst, as a pope, he conceived that he should intermeddle with the affairs of all the churches all over

[1] *Moral.* lib. i. 14, 15.
[2] This name has by some been given erroneously to Gregory II. See Spanheim, *Hist. Ecc. Sec. Sext.* iv.

Christendom. For at least a century and a half—or since the time of Leo the Great—the papal pretensions had been promulgated with much industry and confidence; they had now become quite familiar to the public mind; and it is scarcely fair to charge Gregory with wilful dishonesty when we find him exalting his prerogative: he was no doubt persuaded that, as the successor of Peter, he had a right to assume a certain superiority over all other bishops; but he is often miserably entangled when he attempts to unite the humility of the cloister with the arrogant assumptions of the occupant of the great Western patriarchate. The apostolic see, according to Gregory, exercises its authority only for the punishment of offenders. Thus every prelate is subject to it from the moment that he commits a transgression; "but humility makes all bishops equal, when no fault challenges interference."[1] Here, with an affectation of meekness, the pontiff virtually proclaims himself the dictator of the Church. Theoretically all bishops hold a co-ordinate position; but, whilst the pope has really no peers, every one who offends him is at his mercy, and when condemned, can make no appeal against the sentence of this solitary and irresponsible arbiter.

Throughout the whole of his public life the conscience of Gregory was obviously ill at ease. He could appreciate the beauty of holiness and the spirituality of the requisitions of Scripture; and yet he enjoyed little of the peace of God which passeth all understanding. He considered the assurance of God's favour unattainable.[2] Though convinced that, as the successor of Peter, he acted under the warrant of a divine commission, he could not well reconcile his ideas of true godliness and the ordinary character of his official occupations. It is not therefore wonderful that he was an advocate of the doctrine of purgatory.[3] He was sensible of his exceeding sinfulness; but, as his knowledge of the way of salvation was at once inaccurate and indistinct, he realized very inadequately the power of a most holy faith; and he imagined that, beyond the grave, some new appliances are requisite to fit the redeemed sinner for the full glory of the beatific vision. He was the first writer who ventured to affirm that de-

---

[1] *Epist. Gregor.* lib. ix. 59.
[2] *Epist.* vii. 25.
[3] "Sed tamen de quibusdam levibus culpis esse ante judicium purgatorius ignis credendus est."—*Dialog.* iv. 39.

liverance from purgatory may be obtained by means of masses for the dead;[1] and he professed to be guided in this matter by strange communications transmitted from the abodes of departed spirits.[2] His doctrine was quite to the taste of his age, and in due time "the oblation of the host," for the mitigation of the sufferings of souls in purgatory, began to prove one of the most remunerative of ecclesiastical services.

In the primitive Church there were no liturgies properly so called; for every pastor conducted worship "according to his ability."[3] In the fourth century we hear, for the first time, of the reading of prayers;[4] and, as the hierarchical system acquired consistency and strength, set forms, sanctioned by the metropolitans, were generally adopted. Pope Vigilius, who flourished about the middle of the sixth century, tells us that the Roman liturgy was "received from apostolical tradition;"[5] but by this he probably means no more than that, in a church claiming the name of apostolical, the prayers in use had been handed down from generation to generation. Gregory altered and enlarged this service, so as to render it more attractive and imposing. In his *Sacramentary, Antiphonary,* and *Ordinal,*[6] the course of worship is minutely traced; the most popular forms of devotion are incorporated; and everything is done to gratify the ear, to dazzle the eye, and to light up the imagination. Even the gestures of the officiating clergy are noted down in the rubrical arrangements; their dresses, as well as the decorations of the altar, are prescribed; and, to captivate the lovers of pomp and music, a new mode of recitation, since known as the *Gregorian chant,* supplied its fascinations. There were few who could enjoy the simplicity of spiritual worship, and the magnificent service of Gregory quickly acquired celebrity. It was soon extensively adopted; and it thus exerted no inconsiderable influence in augmenting the renown of the Roman bishopric. The

---

[1] Si culpæ post mortem insolubiles non sunt, multum solet animas etiam post mortem sacra oblatio hostiæ salutaris adjuvare."—*Dial.* iv. 55.

[2] *Dial.* iv. 55.

[3] Justin Martyr, *Apol.* ii.

[4] Le Brun contends that no liturgy was *written* till the *fifth* century. This is perhaps rather late a date.

[5] Vigil. *Epist. ad Eucherium.*

[6] These works appear to have been considerably altered since the time of Gregory.

successors of Gregory laboured with art and industry to introduce it into distant churches; and their zeal was quickened by the consideration that every step of progress involved a recognition of their ecclesiastical supremacy. In several instances their efforts to promote ritual uniformity provoked the most determined opposition; but, after a struggle of upwards of five hundred years, the Roman liturgy was established throughout almost every part of Western Christendom. When originally framed it was understood by the worshippers, as it was written in the vernacular tongue;[1] but meanwhile new languages appeared; and when, after the lapse of ages, it was adopted nearly over all Europe, it had become unintelligible to the whole population. In some of our Protestant liturgies it is partially translated.[2]

There is no evidence that Gregory's support of monachism was dictated by any far-sighted political sagacity; but it is certain that he and his successors—who prudently followed his example—thus created, to a great extent, that widespread attachment to their see which was long its most popular bulwark. In A.D. 529, or about eleven years before the birth of this pontiff, the famous Benedict established, at Monte Cassino, in South Italy, a monastery on a new principle. Idleness had become the reproach of the ascetics; and, to remove the scandal, this abbot required his monks to devote a certain time daily to some industrial occupation.[3] His system at once became popular, and the Benedictines quickly spread themselves over Italy, France, and other countries. Gregory warmly recommended their discipline, signalized himself as a vigilant guardian of their rights and privileges, and, in a biography still extant, celebrated the self-denial, the sanctity, and the miracles of the founder of their order. The fraternity did not prove ungrateful for these papal favours. Wherever they settled they carried with them their loyalty to Rome; they were the most enthusiastic advocates of the claims of the alleged heirs of Peter; and, as they

---

[1] Latin continued to be spoken in France in the seventh century. A song in Latin, written on a victory of Clotaire II. in 662, and obviously intended for circulation among the people, is still extant. See Hallam's *Middle Ages*, ii. 348, 349.

[2] "By a comparison of our Book of Common Prayer with his (Gregory's) *Sacramentary*, it is evident that almost all the collects for Sundays and the principal festivals in the Church of England were taken out of the latter."—Milner's *History of the Church of Christ*, cent. vi. chap. 8.

[3] See Sect. I. Chap IV. of this Period.

rapidly acquired influence, they contrived, in ages of ignorance, to leaven the public mind all over the West with a profound veneration for the popedom.

The renunciation of Arianism by the Lombards—who began to pass over to the Catholic Church shortly after the death of King Autharis, in A.D. 590—shed special lustre on the administration of Gregory; and the conversion of England added still more to the glory of his pontificate. The British mission was a project he had long cherished, and he had at one time been with difficulty prevented from engaging personally in the enterprise; the agents eventually employed all belonged to a Roman monastery of which he was the founder; he supplied the expenses of the undertaking; and it was conducted throughout exactly according to his directions. The monk whose name has ever since been most prominently connected with it was not permitted to pass unrewarded. Augustine became the first archbishop of Canterbury, and was otherwise distinguished by the highest marks of ecclesiastical favour. Before this time the Pope had occasionally presented a piece of episcopal finery, called a pall[1] or pallium, to bishops whom he delighted to honour.[2] Gregory seized on the auspicious occasion of the inauguration of the new English primate to give éclat to the donation. From this period it became more common for the Italian patriarch to grant the pall to metropolitans; and the sums at length paid to him for this bauble, by all the great prelates of the West, at once proclaimed their subjection to Rome, and proved a steady source of supply to the pontifical treasury.

Neither the high position of the Roman Church towards the close of the sixth century, nor the reputation of its bishop for talent, piety, and energy, prevented the great Eastern patriarch from aspiring to ecclesiastical supremacy. The character of John of Constantinople somewhat resembled that of Gregory;

---

[1] "It was originally only a stole wound round the neck with the ends hanging down behind and before."—Palmer's *Orig. Litur.* ii. 406.

[2] The earliest example of the giving of the pall by the Pope is said to occur in A.D. 501, when Symmachus presented it to the bishop of Laurea in Pannonia. See Gieseler, i. 344, note 35. But the letter of Symmachus is of very doubtful authority. See Dupin, i. 528. Macarius of Jerusalem, who flourished early in the fourth century, is said to have been the first bishop who wore a pall. The garment was given to him by the Emperor Constantine the Great. Theodoret, *Ecc. Hist.* ii. 27, at the beginning.

he was surnamed *The Faster*, because of his severe asceticism; but a soul full of ambition lodged in the tenement of an emaciated body. The circumstances of the times encouraged him to attempt to wrest the first place in the Church out of the hands of his Western competitor. The Council of Chalcedon in A.D. 451 had declared, as we have seen,[1] that "the fathers gave the primacy to the elder Rome as being the imperial city," and "equal privileges" to New Rome because it "was honoured with the sovereignty and senate." John conceived that, according to the principle here laid down, the Roman bishopric had long since lost its right to precedence among the sees of Christendom. The Western Empire had fallen; its old capital was now but a provincial town under the government of the Exarch of Ravenna; and Constantinople was the residence of the court and the imperial metropolis. John therefore maintained that he was entitled to stand at the head of the ecclesiastics of the empire; and much to the vexation of the Roman pontiff, styled himself *Universal* Bishop and *Universal* Patriarch. A Council recently held in Constantinople had sanctioned the assumption of these titles; and the Greek emperor Maurice, somewhat dissatisfied with the course pursued by Gregory when endeavouring to maintain peace in Italy, had concurred in their recognition. The Western patriarch, who regarded their assumption as fraught with danger to his see, most earnestly protested and expostulated. Bent on exhibiting a startling contrast to the spirit of his rival, he described himself, with an affectation of humility, "the servant of the servants of God,"—a designation which has since become part of the papal nomenclature.[2] It was on this occasion that Gregory used the words, so often quoted with effect against the claims of his successors—"I confidently affirm that whoever calls himself Universal Priest, or desires to be so called, in his elation is *the precursor of Antichrist*.[3] Let Christian hearts reject the *blasphemous name*."[4]

[1] See Chap. II. of this Section, p. 355.

[2] The title was not appropriated by the Popes until the eleventh century. It was used by bishops and others before the time of Gregory. See Robertson's *Hist. of the Christian Church*, ii. pt. i. 10, note. We find it frequently adopted in the eighth century by Boniface, the apostle of Germany. See his *Works*, by Giles, i. 38, 52, 63, 70.

[3] "Ego autem fidenter dico quia quisquis se universalem sacerdotem vocat, vel vocari desiderat, in elatione sua Antichristum præcurrit."—*Epist.* vii. 33.

[4] *Epist.* v. 20, Migne ed. See also v. 21.

The pertinacity of the Eastern patriarch galled the pride of Gregory, and provoked him to give utterance to his indignation in terms of unmeasured vehemence. But the arguments he urged against the use of the odious designation may well suggest doubts as to his candour, and furnish grounds for impeaching his consistency. It is clear that his opposition to John was dictated by official jealousy, and not by any abstract objection to the dignity of universal bishop; for he himself, as the successor of Peter, virtually claimed that position.[1] The title had been already sometimes given to the Roman patriarch;[2] and, a few years afterwards, it is said to have been formally bestowed on Pope Boniface III. by the Emperor Phocas.[3] But an apprehension that the Eastern sovereign was determined to deprive him of his ecclesiastical precedence haunted the mind of Gregory; and the most humiliating passage in the history of the Roman prelate is that which describes his indecent exultation when he heard of the murder of his imperial master. Maurice, though deficient in generosity and energy, was a prince otherwise respectable; and Gregory himself, in his letters, often extols him in strains of inflated eulogy.[4] But when he and his children were butchered by the monster Phocas, the Roman pontiff rejoiced over his fall, and addressed a most complimentary epistle to the loathsome usurper. The first words of this message of congratulation—" Glory be to God in the highest"—express its jubilant spirit throughout. "We are delighted," says the Pope

---

[1] "Petro principi apostolo totius ecclesiæ cura commissa est." *Epist.* v. 20. "Cunctarum ecclesiarum injuncta nos sollicitudinis cura constringit." *Epist.* vii. 19.

[2] See Chap. II. of this Section, p. 355.

[3] According to Baronius this occurred in A.D. 606. But Boniface was not made Pope till A.D. 607. See Bower, *Boniface 65th bishop.* Many interpreters of prophecy regard A.D. 606 as a great era in the history of the Popedom—but apparently without any foundation. It is certain that the Church of Rome was not then, for the first time, advanced to any position which it had not before occupied. Even the statement made by Baronius—that Phocas bestowed on Boniface the title of universal bishop—is not very clearly authenticated. See *Mosheim* by Murdock and Soames, ii. 82; and Hallam's *Middle Ages,* i. 520-1, note.

[4] "Omnipotens Deus longa vobis et quieta tempora tribuat, et pietatis vestræ felicissimam sobolem diu in Romana republica florere concedat." *Epist.* v. 30. "Cum sincera in vobis, Christianissime principum, velut emissum coelitus jubar, fidei rectitudo resplendeat." *Epist.* vi. 16. See also *Epist.* vi. 65; vii. 6; viii. 33, Migne edit.

to Phocas, "that *the benignity of your piety* has attained to the imperial eminence. Let the heavens rejoice, and let the earth be glad—and let the whole community, *heretofore so sadly afflicted*, exult in your benignant deeds."[1] This correspondence convicts Gregory at once of the grossest insincerity and of the vilest adulation.

False religion hardens the heart as well as enfeebles the intellect; and this distinguished prelate is a melancholy specimen of its debasing influence. He wanted neither warmth of affection nor vigour of mind; but his understanding was prostrated and all his kindlier feelings disappeared when he was under the spell of the demon of superstition. He considered an attempt to remove the primacy from Rome as a sin not to be forgiven; he regarded the Emperor Maurice, who appeared to be not indisposed to encourage the project, as the very incarnation of iniquity; and he hailed the miscreant Phocas, by whom the hated prince was put to death, as a Deliverer from heaven. No wonder that such a man was suspected as an enemy to the cultivation of general literature, and that he has been accused, though unjustly, of the destruction of the Palatine library.[2]

Gregory possessed a large share of the unpolished eloquence of his age, and he has perhaps never been equalled by any other pope as a laborious and earnest preacher. His personal influence in Rome, during the time of his pontificate, was unbounded. Without the name, he virtually wielded the power of a petty sovereign. He provided for the defence of the city; supplied the poorer inhabitants with food; and, on one occasion, excited the displeasure of the Greek Emperor by concluding a treaty of peace with the Lombards on his own authority.[3] His birth, his family connexions, his reputation as a saint, his natural shrewdness, his ability as a public speaker and a preacher, and his amazing diligence as a writer and a correspondent, all contributed to add to his weight in the community; so that he was, beyond comparison, the most influential prelate who had occupied the papal chair since the fall of the Western Empire. He can scarcely be said to have invented many new errors; but he

---

[1] *Epist.* xiii. 31.
[2] This story rests upon a tradition of the twelfth century. See Neander, v. 194-5, note.
[3] *Epist.* v. 40.

did much to strengthen, or to stimulate into fresh activity, almost all the false principles that were already in operation. The darkness of the Middle Ages was now fast enveloping the Church; and his decisions, whatever they might be, were generally permitted to pass unchallenged. He had a great share in the aggrandisement of the papacy; and, in every history of the system, he should, undoubtedly, be acknowledged as one of its master-builders.

CHAPTER V.

PROGRESS OF THE PAPACY FROM THE DEATH OF GREGORY THE GREAT TO THE ESTABLISHMENT OF THE POPE AS A TEMPORAL SOVEREIGN.—A.D. 604 TO A.D. 755.

LONG before the fall of the Western Empire the Church had degenerated. Monachism emasculated the intellect; the hierarchical spirit repressed freedom of thought; and the settlement of the barbarians in the conquered provinces completed the ascendency of ignorance. Many educational institutes perished amidst the confusion of war; many books were destroyed; and literature was neglected. The taste for reading declined; and the means of its cultivation, where it still continued to be cherished, were procured with increasing difficulty. Paper, manufactured from a plant which grows along the banks of the Nile, had heretofore been exported in considerable quantities to Italy, France, and other countries; but, when Alexandria was taken by the Saracens in A.D. 640, the intercourse between Egypt and the West was interrupted; and the usual supply of papyrus was no longer conveyed to Europe. Parchment, almost the only writing material still available, brought a high price; and books became scarce and expensive. The appearance of a new work often involved the destruction of another of superior value; for the productions of the old classic authors were obliterated to provide parchment for puerile ecclesiastical legends. Whatever literary culture existed was confined almost entirely to the clergy; and yet the attainments of the most accomplished dignitaries of the Church were miserably meagre. At a synod held in Rome by Pope Agatho in A.D. 679, a deputation, consisting of bishops, presbyters, and others, was appointed to visit Constantinople, and maintain there the Catholic doctrine in opposition to Monothelitism. The parties sent on this mission were, no doubt, the best to be found; but though the Roman pontiff was always exceedingly unwilling to disparage the gifts of the Western clergy—more especially when communicating with the East—he is constrained on this occasion to apologize for the deficiencies of his representatives. Agatho candidly tells the Greek Emperor that little was to be expected from the skill of the commissioners. "We have sent them," says he, "not because we place any confidence in their learning . . . for how can a full knowledge of the Scriptures be found among men who live in the midst of heathens, and who, with extreme difficulty, earn their daily bread by bodily labour."[1] Learning could not flourish when even bishops were obliged to toil with their own hands to procure a subsistence.[2]

In these unsettled times the clergy, particularly in Italy, were often in difficulties; but it would be incorrect to infer that poverty was the normal condition of the episcopal order. Many of the bishops lived in affluence; in some countries they were almost all persons of high birth; and, though qualified neither by character nor education for their office, it presented sufficient temptations, in the way of rank and emolument, to induce them to undertake its responsibilities. The state of the inferior clergy was, in general, most deplorable. As the ministers of religion could not be decently required to become soldiers, warlike princes interdicted their vassals from entering, without their express sanction, into the service of the Church; but, the restriction did not extend to those who were in bondage, and the ecclesiastical ranks were largely recruited from the numerous slave population. In some places the children of the serfs, who cultivated the estates of the great prelates, formed a considerable proportion of the candidates for the clerical profession. These alumni of the Church retained, in after life, much of the feeling of servility which belonged to their original condition; and continued to be

---

[1] Migne, *Patrol. Cur.* tom. lxxxvii. 1164.

[2] "At this time (from A.D. 685 to A.D. 715) seven successive Pontiffs—John V., Conon, Sergius, and John VI., John VII., Sisinnius, and Constantine, were either Greeks or Syrians—a fact that we can ascribe only to the want of theological scholars in Rome, or to the influence of the Byzantine Court." Döllinger's *Hist. of the Ch.* iii. 110.

treated most ignominiously by their episcopal masters. But they did not all submit with equal patience to indignity; and there were cases in which councils listened to their complaints, and interfered for their protection. Thus, in A.D. 675, the Council of Braga in Spain censured those bishops who were in the habit of administering the discipline of flagellation to their clergy; and who compelled their deacons, like beasts of burden, to carry them in processions.[1] The people could not be expected to honour ministers subjected to such degrading treatment by their episcopal guardians.

The laity were now sunk in still deeper ignorance than their spiritual instructors. Few were able to read; and still fewer were acquainted with the art of penmanship. It was not, therefore, strange that they ceased to possess influence. From the time of the apostles downwards, the members of the Church had been in the habit of choosing its office-bearers; but, as indifference and formality increased, the privilege was less and less appreciated; and, in these dark ages, the people at length permitted themselves to be entirely denuded of the right of election. When a prelate died, even the ecclesiastics of the diocese were often denied a voice in the appointment to the vacancy, especially if the wealth of the see tempted the king to claim the presentation. Councils sometimes interposed and tried to adjust the disputes relative to the patronage of bishoprics, by assigning to the clergy and people the right of *election*, and to the sovereign the right of *confirmation*; but arbitrary princes easily found pretexts for disregarding such decisions. Meanwhile the authority of the pope was gradually advancing. The bishops preferred the supervision of a great prelate at a distance, who could know little of their movements, to the jurisdiction of metropolitans at home whose vigilance was quickened by the periodical meetings of provincial councils. Owing to various causes, such meetings became less and less frequent. Revolutions sometimes dismembered dioceses so as to disturb the relations between metropolitans and suffragans;[2] and as many princes viewed with jealousy the proceedings of church conventions, apologies were contrived for their postponement or discontinuance. Thus it

[1] *Binii Concilia*, t. ii. pars. ii. 560. When slaves became churchmen they acquired their liberty, *Con. Tolet. Non.* xi.; *Patrol. Curs.* tom. lxxxiv. 438.
[2] Guizot's *History of Civilization*, ii. 48, Bohn's edition.

was that the power of metropolitans declined, that synods were at length very rarely congregated,[1] and that the pope silently secured the position of an ecclesiastical arbiter.

Whilst the great Italian patriarch was obtaining acknowledgments of his supremacy from so many bishops in the West, he was barely willing to tolerate the yoke of the Eastern Emperor. The Greeks had a singular taste for investigating obscure theological questions of a speculative character; and, when they happened to differ, they conducted their discussions with much of the violence of a partisan warfare. Their rulers had not always the good sense to discourage these metaphysical disputations. Instead of confining themselves to their legitimate functions, the Greek sovereigns were, in fact, ever and anon adding fuel to the flame of theological contention by entering keenly into the controversies of the Church, and by attempting to crush their opponents with the weight of their civil authority. On such occasions the bishops of Rome repeatedly proved the most untractable of their subjects. When the doctrine of the One Will in Christ was first promulgated, Pope Honorius was induced to give it the sanction of his approbation;[2] but his successors pursued a different course, and incurred the imperial displeasure by firmly rejecting Monothelitism. Pope Martin, by whom it was most bitterly opposed, assembled a council at Rome, in A.D. 649, which anathematized a number of the more prominent abettors of the fashionable heresy. This proceeding was highly resented by the Greek monarch, who caused Martin to be seized, carried prisoner to Constantinople, and finally banished to a region bordering on the Black Sea. In that inhospitable district, then inhabited by a pagan population, he died soon afterwards.[3]

The sufferings of Martin awakened general sympathy; and, when he finished his career, he was honoured as a martyr. His party boasted that he had contended for the faith with unflinching constancy, and that he had fallen a victim to the pride of a tyrannical sovereign. Whilst his fate irritated the Western subjects of the Greek Emperor, it tended to elevate the papacy in public estimation. The Roman see had been sadly scandalized

---

[1] "In the course of the sixth century, there were held in Gaul fifty-four councils of every description; in the seventh century, only twenty; in the first half of the eighth century, only seven, and five of these were held in Belgium, or on the banks of the Rhine." Guizot's *Hist. of Civilization*, ii. 49.

[2] See Sect. II. Chap. V. of this Period, p. 214. [3] *Ibid.* p. 215.

by the heresy of Honorius; but its ancient reputation, as the bulwark of orthodoxy, was restored by Martin. This pontiff, who had acted, in the first instance, with much arrogance, displayed, in the day of adversity, no common magnanimity and resolution; and the Italian Church has recognized her obligations to him by enrolling him as a saint in her calendar.

Other events soon contributed to extend the boundaries of papal authority. The conversion of Britain by agents from Rome prepared the way for the establishment of the Italian ritual in several countries where Christianity had hitherto been scarcely known. Towards the end of the seventh century and the commencement of the eighth, English churchmen displayed great missionary zeal, and laboured with remarkable success on the continent of Europe. The language of the Anglo-Saxons then differed little from that spoken by the people of Friesland and the North of Germany, so that the British preachers could at once make themselves intelligible to the natives of these regions. By far the most famous and effective of the missionaries was a monk of Devonshire, named Winfrid or Boniface[1]— whom we have already mentioned when treating of the ecclesiastical history of England.[2] This indefatigable man, who has been called the apostle of the Germans, left his native country about A.D. 715, and laboured nearly forty years among the Hessians, the Thuringians, and the various tribes settled upon the banks of the Rhine. During this period he thrice visited Rome, where he was uniformly greeted by the pope with a cordial welcome. In A.D. 738, he had baptized no less than 100,000 converts.[3] After passing through various stages of ecclesiastical promotion he was finally advanced to the dignity of archbishop of Mayence. In A.D. 755, he fell a prey to the ferocity of some savage Frieslanders, who murdered himself and a faithful band of fifty-two assistants, when preparing to administer the rite of confirmation to a company of neophytes.

Boniface was well entitled to all the honours bestowed upon him by the Roman pontiff, for he did more than any other bishop in the Middle Ages to place papal authority on a firm foundation in France and Germany. When ordained to the episcopal office

---

[1] He probably took the name of Boniface when he became a monk.
[2] See Sect. IV. Chap. I. of this Period, p. 286.
[3] *Epist.* xlvi. Bonif. *Opera*, i. 96, 97, ed. Giles.

by Gregory II. in A.D. 723, he entered into a remarkable engagement. Standing over the grave of Peter, he vowed[1] to the apostle, to Pope Gregory, and to his successors, that he would continue in the unity of the catholic faith, and always conform to the usages of that church which, as he believed, had received from the Lord God the power to bind and to loose. Should he learn that priests or bishops acted contrary to the ordinances of the fathers, he pledged himself to hold no intercourse or communion with them, and to oppose them to the best of his ability. Should he fail in putting a stop to their proceedings, he promised to give immediate information to his apostolic master.[2]

This oath betrays the fears which now disturbed the mind of Pope Gregory. Certain Irish missionaries,[3] who had no idea of recognizing his supremacy, were labouring assiduously in Germany; and their success threatened to be detrimental to the interests of the Roman see. Boniface was accordingly required to watch their movements, and to obstruct their progress; and,

[1] The oath was drawn up in Latin, and was in these words: "Promitto ego Bonifacius Dei gratia episcopus, tibi, beate Petre Apostolorum Princeps, vicarioque tuo beato Gregoriæ Papæ, et successoribus ejus, per Patrem et Filium et Spiritum Sanctum, Trinitatem inseparabilem, et hoc sacratissimum corpus tuum, me omnem fidem, et puritatem sanctæ fidei Catholicæ exhibere, et in unitate ejusdem fidei, Deo operante, persistere, in quo omnis Christianorum salus esse sine dubio comprobatur, nullo modo me contra unitatem communis et universalis ecclesiæ, suadente quopiam, consentire, sed, ut dixi, fidem et puritatem meam atque concursum, tibi et utilitatibus tuæ ecclesiæ, cui a Domino Deo *potestas ligandi solvendique data est*, et prædicto vicario tuo atque successoribus ejus per omnia exhibere. Sed et si cognovero, Antistites contra instituta antiqua Sanctorum Patrum conversari, cum eis nullam habere communionem aut conjunctionem; sed magis, si valuero prohibere, prohibeam; si minus, hoc fideliter statim Domino meo Apostolico renuntiabo. Quod si, quod absit, contra hujus professionis meæ seriem aliquid facere quolibet modo, seu ingenio, vel occasione, tentavero, reus inveniar in æterno judicio, ultionem Ananiæ et Saphiræ incurram, qui vobis etiam de rebus propriis fraudem facere præsumpsit: hoc autem indiculum Sacramenti Ego Bonifacius exiguus episcopus manu propria scripsi, atque ponens supra sacratissimum corpus sancti Petri, ita ut præscriptum, Deo teste et judice, feci sacramentum, quod et conservare promitto." *Sanct. Bonifacii Opera*, ed. Giles, ii. 9, 10, London, 1844.

[2] The latter part of the oath bears a strong resemblance to that taken by the Pope to the Greek Emperor. See Neander, v. 61, note.

[3] One of these, Clemens, refused to recognize the authority of fathers or councils. Boniface denounces him as living "in adultery" because he had a wife and two children. *Bonifacii Epist.* lvii. Virgil, another Irishman with whom Boniface came into collision, appears to have believed in the existence of antipodes. He seems at length to have conformed to the Romish discipline, as he became bishop of Salzburg.

should they prove too formidable, to notify the danger forthwith to his pontifical employer. An oath of this description had long before been exacted from the bishops of Italy;[1] but its extension to countries beyond the Alps marks an important step in the progress of papal usurpation. The bishop of Rome could fully estimate the immense accession of power it secured to him; and he did not relax his efforts until all the prelates of the West were bound to his throne by a like solemn obligation.[2]

In A.D. 732, Boniface was appointed apostolic or papal vicar; and the whole of Germany was thus placed under his ecclesiastical supervision. His authority was sustained by the civil power; for he enjoyed the patronage, first, of Charles Martel, the great captain of his age, and afterwards of his sons Carloman and Pepin—the former of whom became eventually a monk, and the latter the father of a new dynasty of Gallic sovereigns. He gratefully acknowledges the assistance received by him from these illustrious personages. "Without the support of the king of the Francs," says he, "I could govern neither the people, nor the priests and deacons, nor the monks and nuns; nor, were it not for his commands and the fear he inspires, could I prevent the Germans from practising their pagan rites and impious idolatries."[3] Boniface founded several new bishoprics; and divided Bavaria into four dioceses—Saltzburg, Freisingen, Ratisbon, and Passau.[4]

When Boniface was made apostolic vicar, synods had almost ceased to meet. War and other causes had subverted many of the old ecclesiastical arrangements; metropolitans had, to a considerable extent, lost their influence; and the greatest laxity of discipline everywhere prevailed. Boniface sought to bring about a reform by the revival of Church judicatories, and by adding to the authority of primates. But all the while he aimed at the exaltation of the power of Rome; so that the restoration of synods was but another step in the progress of papal aggression. The synod was no longer a free assembly where every

---

[1] Neander, v. 60; Lingard's *Antiq. of Anglo-Sax. Church*, p. 447, Newcastle, 1810.
[2] Hallam, *Middle Ages*, i. 522.
[3] *Epist.* xii. *Bonif. Opera*, i. 39, ed. Giles.
[4] Gieseler, ii. 11.

bishop was at liberty to act according to his independent judgment; but a meeting in which the apostolic vicar or some other eminent church dignitary occupied the chair, and to which he dictated decisions. As he was backed by the royal authority,[1] the auditory listened submissively to his awards. Some of these deliverances were, no doubt, salutary; but they were not the spontaneous results of unshackled discussion; and, as they were often adopted with apathy, if not reluctance, they were seldom very vigorously carried into execution. They were all conceived in a spirit intensely hierarchical. A council held about A.D. 743, over which Boniface presided as apostolic vicar, acknowledged the supremacy of the Roman see, promised subjection to Saint Peter and his Italian representative, and ordained that every metropolitan, at the time of his appointment, should apply to the Pope for a pallium.[2] By means of these synods, which met in obedience to the civil ruler, Boniface extended his influence over both the French and German Churches, and thus contrived to bring the most powerful monarchy in Europe completely under the yoke of the Western pontiff.

The metropolitans and the monks soon became the two main pillars of the papacy. The metropolitans consecrated the bishops, who governed the inferior clergy; the monks, by the agency of superstition, ruled the masses of society. The policy of Boniface bound the metropolitans firmly to the pontifical chair. They were obliged to apply to the great Western patriarch for the pallium; their election was void without his confirmation; and they were pledged to obey him by an oath of the utmost stringency. The monasteries were gradually exempted from the jurisdiction of the bishops, and placed under the direct supervision of the alleged heir of Saint Peter. Their inmates were at length known as the most zealous assertors of papal prerogative; and, as they possessed much influence, they were able to give a tone to public opinion. When Boniface in A.D. 744 founded the

---

[1] The name of the "Prince of the Francs" stands at the head of these regulations, and they are represented as "promulgated" by Boniface. See his *Works* by Giles, ii. 11, 22, 28. It is expressly stated that "the consent" of those who attended these councils was all they had to do with the proceedings—"*Omnes venerabiles sacerdotes Dei, . . . prioris synodi decreta consentientes firmaverunt.*" *Concil. Liptinense.* "*Propterea nos una cum consensu episcoporum decrevimus.*" *Concil. Sucssionense.* Migne, *Patrol. Curs.* lxxxix. 809, 825.

[2] *Epist.* lxiii. *Bonif. Opera*, i. 140, ed. Giles.

famous monastery of Fulda,[1] he induced Pope Zachary to take it under his own immediate inspection.[2] Such a privilege had, it is said, never before been granted to a distant convent;[3] but, in due time, others were admitted to it; and, in the end, all such institutions in the West enjoyed the direct patronage and supervision of the powerful Italian prelate. Thus his influence in the Latin Church became unbounded.

Though Boniface holds so prominent a place among those concerned in establishing Romish domination, it would be a mistake to infer that he was prompted entirely by secular motives or by the spirit of an ecclesiastical partisan. As an honest and earnest missionary he maintained and promoted the Church principles in which he had been educated. Early prejudices continued throughout life to blind his understanding, and to exert an evil influence on his conduct. In dealing with those whom he deemed errorists he did not confine himself to the legitimate weapons of exhortation and argument. When such means failed, he had recourse to threats, invoked the aid of the civil power, and threw his opponents into prison. But he cannot be denied the praise of consistency and conscientiousness. Hence we find him expostulating with the Pope himself, protesting against the charges exacted for the pall by his officials,[4] and denouncing the horrid profligacy connected with pilgrimages to Rome.[5] In his old age he transferred the care of the archiepiscopal see of Mayence to his disciple Lull, and prosecuted his evangelistic labours among the Frieslanders. Though he attached undue importance to human rites and ecclesiastical traditions, he could appreciate something higher and holier. His habitual study of the Word of God supplies evidence of his spiritual enlightenment. "What is there," said he, "which old men can with greater sobriety pursue, than the knowledge of the

[1] In Hesse. In this work he employed his faithful disciple Sturm. Fulda had soon four thousand inmates.
[2] *Epist.* lxxvii. *Bonif. Opera*, ed. Giles, i. 187. The genuineness of this letter has been challenged, apparently without much reason. In A.D. 743, Zachary is said to have granted the same privilege to Monte Cassino. Waddington, *Hist. of the Church*, 378, note, London, 1833.
[3] There were, however, cases in which monks were subject, not to the bishop of the diocese, but to another more remote. This practice is said to have commenced in Africa. See Gieseler, i. 348, note.
[4] *Zacharia Epist.* vi. 2. Migne, *Patrol. Cur.* tom. lxxxix. 928.
[5] *Bonifacii Epist.* lxiii. *ad. Cuthbertum.*

Holy Scriptures, which will guide the vessel of the soul without danger of its being shipwrecked in a storm, until it arrives at the coast of the very fair land of paradise, where it will be admitted to share for ever the happiness of the angels above?"[1] When advanced in life, he requested his friend, the English bishop Daniel, to send him the book of the prophets written in very distinct characters by the abbot Winbert. "You cannot," said he, "transmit to me a greater consolation in my old age."[2] The history of this extraordinary man demonstrates that there may be much real excellence mingled with much superstition; but it also admonishes the Church not to permit her respect even for the most painstaking and devoted ministers to seduce her from the plain paths of evangelical truth and purity.

Whilst Boniface was labouring so assiduously to establish the supremacy of the Pope, the progress of political events tended to the same consummation. Public attention had been directed, by the spread of Mohammedanism, to the obligations of the second commandment—as the Saracens were most unsparing image-breakers; and the Greek Emperor, Leo the Isaurian, became convinced that the current practice of the Church involved an outrageous violation of the divine law. But instead of first endeavouring to impart his convictions to his subjects, so that whatever measures he adopted might be sustained by the verdict of their approbation, he attempted, by arbitrary edicts, to accomplish a religious reformation. In A.D. 726 he issued a proclamation forbidding the worship of images, and commanding that all such objects, with the exception of the representation of Christ on the Cross, should be removed out of the churches. Whilst this imperial order created much commotion in the East, it led, almost immediately, to the final separation of Rome and the adjacent territory from the Greek Empire. Its publication in Italy called forth two letters from Pope Gregory II. to Leo, such as have rarely been equalled even in the annals of papal insolence. "Go into the schools where children learn their letters," writes Gregory to the Emperor, "and say: 'I am the overturner and breaker of images,' and they will instantly fling their tablets at your head, so that the simple will make you understand what the wise can by no means teach you. . . . You threaten and say: 'I will send to Rome and break in pieces the

---

[1] *Epist.* iv. ed. Giles.   [2] *Epist.* xii.

image of Saint Peter. I will take care, too, that the pontiff Gregory shall be brought to me from thence in chains, as Martin was brought by order of one of my predecessors.' . . . If you provoke us with such insolence and persist in your threats, it is not necessary for us to descend to a trial of strength with you. The Roman pontiff can retire four and twenty stadia into the region of Campania (to the first fortress of the Lombards), and then, you may pursue the winds. . . . The eyes of all the West are fixed on our humility, . . . and they revere as a god upon earth the Apostle Peter whose image you threaten to throw down and destroy. . . . I beseech you, for the Lord's sake, to desist from your rash and puerile doings. . . . If you send any to overturn the image of Saint Peter, we take you to witness that we are innocent of the blood which must be shed."[1]

The author of this haughty letter was obviously prepared for rebellion. The edict requiring the demolition of images was successfully resisted; the representative of Leo in Italy lost his life in a popular tumult; and Rome and the exarchate ceased to pay tribute to the Eastern Emperor. About A.D. 730 the citizens of the ancient capital of the West attempted to restore their old republican institutions; and, from that date, they virtually ceased to recognise the authority of their former sovereign, though, for some time longer, they did not formally withdraw from his jurisdiction.[2] The king of the Lombards now took possession of the exarchate of Ravenna, and was proceeding to make himself master of Rome, when a still more powerful monarch was induced to interpose, and put a stop to his career of ambition. The record of this transaction forms one of the most remarkable passages in the history of the Popedom.

In France the nominal rulers, the princes of the Merovingian line, had become political nonentities. The real power was vested in a functionary called the Mayor of the Palace; and the office, which had been lately held by Charles Martel—the hero who had saved his country from the dominion of the Saracens—had descended to his son, the celebrated Pepin. This ambitious soldier did not feel inclined to continue the pageant of a titular superior; but—not to give too rude a shock to the pre-

[1] *Epist.* xii.; *Patrol. Curs.*, Migne, tom. lxxxix. 516, 519, 520.
[2] Even for some time after the Pope became a temporal prince, the claims of the Eastern Emperor were not entirely ignored.

judices of his age—he deemed it prudent to employ the Church to consecrate his usurpation. By a meeting of the French nobility, held in A.D. 751, the Pope was accordingly requested to state whether, without any breach of the divine law, a brave people might not set aside a useless sovereign, and appoint, as his successor, one who had already attested his ability to reign by a brilliant succession of public services? Though the Roman bishop Zachary does not appear to have profoundly studied the principles of constitutional freedom, or to have considered very fully the obligations of the oath of allegiance which the Francs had already taken, he well knew the answer which promised to be most advantageous to himself, as well as most agreeable to his interrogators; and he had no difficulty in meeting the question with an affirmative solution. The French king Childeric was, in consequence, deposed; and, in A.D. 752, Boniface, archbishop of Mayence, acting under a commission from the Pope,[1] anointed Pepin on the day of his coronation.

The new sovereign had soon a splendid opportunity of exhibiting his gratitude. Rome was closely pressed by the Lombards; and their king Aistulphus appeared determined at all hazards to secure its possession. Zachary was now dead; but his successor, Stephen III.,[2] a prelate no less sagacious than energetic and intrepid, at once perceived that Pepin was the only prince in Christendom who could afford him effectual aid; and he embraced the bold resolution to cross the Alps, and to make a personal appeal to him for assistance. In the face of great difficulties he accomplished his purpose; and his mission proved successful. On this occasion Stephen repeated the coronation of the French monarch,[3] and absolved his new subjects from their oath of allegiance to Childeric. Pepin now marched into Italy with a powerful army, overthrew the Lombards, and delivered Rome. But he had not long returned home when Aistulphus made an effort to recover his lost ground; and the Pope found himself and his fellow-citizens encompassed by an army of Lombards. Stephen once more appealed to his French protector; and in

---

[1] *Eginhardi Ab. Annal. ad an. DCCL.* Migne, *Patrol. Curs.* t. civ. 373. Eginhard, who was educated in the Court of Charlemagne, died A.D. 840.

[2] By some he is called Stephen II. as his immediate predecessor, who was also named Stephen, and who survived his election only a few days, was not consecrated. Stephen I. was Bishop of Rome from A.D. 253 to A.D. 257.

[3] *Eginhardi Ab. annal. ad an DCCLIV.*

several most pressing letters, the last of which was written in the name of the Apostle Peter,[1] entreated his interference. Pepin marched into Italy a second time, defeated Aistulphus, and conferred on Stephen the sovereignty of Rome, the Pentapolis,[2] and the exarchate of Ravenna. Thus in A.D. 755, the Pope became a temporal potentate;[3] and thus were founded those "states of the Church" of which, notwithstanding so many European revolutions, some vestiges remained till 1870.[4]

The first pope who was a temporal potentate had the same name as the first Christian martyr;[5] and it is rather remarkable that the year in which Stephen III. died exactly completed the first half of the interval between the birth of Christ and the Reformation.[6] At this time a large proportion of the errors which disfigure Romanism had been more or less fully developed. The doctrine of justification by faith alone was supplanted by the doctrine of human merit; and the intercession of Christ was well nigh forgotten amidst prayers to the saints and to the mother of God. The term transubstantiation was still unknown, and the dogma which it announces had not yet been formally propounded; but the institution of the Supper was, to a great extent, stripped of its original character; and the germs of the delusions which have since prevailed respecting it had appeared. The oath administered to Boniface, when ordained to the episcopal office by Pope Gregory, aimed ostensibly at the preservation of the unity of Christendom; and yet, whilst this celebrated formula emphatically recognizes the "ancient ordinances of the

[1] *Epist.* v. *Patrol.* tom. lxxxix. 1004.
[2] "The confederation of the five cities Pesaro, Rimini, Fano, Umana (Numana?) and Ancona," Döllinger, iii. 111.
[3] If, as there is reason to believe, John was banished to Patmos in A.D. 89, and if he had the Apocalyptic visions in that year, the Pope became a temporal prince exactly 666 years afterwards. See *Ancient Church*, 168, note. Stephen obtained possession of the keys of the cities given to him by Pepin towards the end of the year 755. Sismondi, *Histoire des Français*, i. 357, Bruxelles, 1847.
[4] The troops of Victor Emmanuel, King of Italy, took possession of Rome on the 20th September of that year.
[5] It is somewhat singular that the official title of this ecclesiastical monarch signifies the *third crown*. The triple crown was not worn by the Pope till long afterwards.
[6] He died April 29, A.D. 757. But the birth of Christ took place about three years before the commencement of the vulgar era. See *Ancient Church*, 32-35. The year 1517 is commonly adopted as the date of the Reformation. But $1517 + 3 = (757 + 3) \times 2$.

holy fathers," it ignores the authority, if not the existence, of the Scriptures. The Church had long before given its sanction to persecuting principles;[1] and Romish missionaries such as Boniface now felt no scruple when perpetrating deeds of intolerance. It is a most significant fact that the Pope was indebted for his position as an earthly sovereign to his support of the worship of images. Though among the rulers of the nations he was only a "little horn,"[2] or a petty monarch, his power was not to be measured by the extent of his territories; for he was "diverse"[3] from other royal personages; as he was supposed to possess attributes of peculiar and tremendous potency; and the acknowledgment of his pretensions gave him an ascendency over all his fellows. Though the question submitted to Zachary by the French nobles was merely a case of casuistry, papal advocates subsequently urged that it recognized his right to depose kings,[4] and that such a right was virtually asserted when the Pope released the subjects of Childeric from the obligations of their oath of allegiance.[5] "In this horn were eyes like the eyes of man, and a mouth speaking great things."[6] Such a description applies exactly to the Bishop of Rome, for with unceasing vigilance he has ever been looking out for opportunities of aggrandizement; he asserts that he is the overseer of the Catholic Church; and all his utterances proclaim the vastness of his pretensions.

The Pope became a temporal prince at a time when a concurrence of events held out to him the promise of further advancement. The Eastern Church had been kept for centuries in the turmoil of controversy, and the Saracens had, for upwards of a hundred years, been weakening its strength and curtailing its boundaries. The Greek Empire had been sadly shattered by the khalifs; the sees of Antioch and of Alexandria, by the triumphs of Mohammedanism, had lost much of their importance; and the patriarch of Constantinople could no longer hope to contend successfully for the dignity of universal bishop. His master, the emperor, had once swayed the sceptre over both the West and

[1] See Sect. I. Chap. V. of this Period, p. 127.
[2] Dan. vii. 8.   [3] Dan. vii. 24.
[4] This argument was used by Gregory VII.
[5] Stephen is said to have formally freed Pepin himself from his oath of allegiance. Murdock's *Mosheim* by Soames, ii. 137.
[6] Dan. vii. 8.

the East, and under his auspices he might have cherished the hope of ecclesiastical supremacy; but almost all the West had renounced the imperial yoke, and the diminished frontier in the East was defended with increasing difficulty. The Pope had ever been the only patriarch in the West, so that here he had no reason to dread a rival, and at this time his position was peculiarly influential. The Saracens, whose progress had long inspired him with alarm, had been completely checked in their career of conquest; and the very year in which Stephen III. was put into possession of his little kingdom[1] witnessed the commencement of the dismemberment of the Mohammedan Empire. Britain, France, and Germany, as well as other countries, acknowledged Stephen as their chief bishop; and the greatest prince in Europe was bound to the pontifical chair by the strongest ties of interest and gratitude.

What a change had passed over the Church during the revolutions of six hundred years! A little after the middle of the second century the bishop of Rome, almost for the first time, emerges into notice. Anicetus, one of the predecessors of the popes, then welcomed Polycarp, pastor of Smyrna, to "that great city" which had dominion "over the kings of the earth."[2] Anicetus was the obscure leader of a proscribed sect; his very life was in continual jeopardy; and if he escaped persecution, it was because he was contemned as insignificant or commiserated as helpless. He could do nothing without the concurrence of his little company of presbyters; he prayed "according to his ability," and he preached with exemplary diligence. When he requested Polycarp to preside at the administration of the Lord's Supper, the venerable Asiatic presbyter cheerfully complied with his invitation. Had the same request been now repeated to a pastor accustomed to the simplicity of apostolic ordinances, he would have been obliged to decline the task as utterly impracticable. The primitive worship had been superseded by a gorgeous ceremonial; free prayer, such as that uttered by Polycarp or Anicetus, had been supplanted by the "Canon of the Mass;" and no one, without having been specially trained to the per-

---

[1] In A.D. 750 the Abbassides, a new dynasty of Khalifs, supplanted the Ommiades. Gibbon, chap. lii. In A.D. 755 Spain revolted, and Abdalrahman, of the race of the Ommiades, was established on the throne of Cordova.

[2] See *Ancient Church*, 322, 554.

formance, could have attempted to conduct the celebration. In the city where Paul had been martyred, the Pope now sat on a throne, and the whole adjacent territory acknowledged the authority of the mitred sovereign. The successor of Anicetus now claimed to be king of the Church as well as king of Rome, and he might be already distinguished among the potentates of the earth by a "look more stout than his fellows."[1] Anicetus was honoured because he laboured in the Word and doctrine; but Stephen III. could not well devote himself to such service, as he was cumbered with the cares of a secular administration. The Pope has now entered on a new era of existence, and "the great words which the horn spake"[2] must henceforth occupy much of the attention of the ecclesiastical historian.

[1] Dan. vii. 20. [2] Dan. v. 11.

APPENDIX.

APPENDIX.

PERIOD I. SECTION I. CHAP. III. NOTE, p. 8.

Letter of the late Dr. Cureton.

IMMEDIATELY after the appearance of the second edition of *The Ancient Church*, a copy of it was sent to the late Rev. W. Cureton, D.D., Canon of Westminster—the well-known author of various publications relating to the Ignatian Epistles. It was considered only due to that distinguished scholar to call his attention to a work in which he was so prominently noticed, and in which various arguments were adduced to prove that all the letters he had edited are utterly spurious. In a short time that gentleman acknowledged the presentation of the volume in a most kind and courteous communication, which will be read with special interest by all who have studied the Ignatian controversy. I give the letter entire—just as it reached me.

DEANS YARD, WESTMINSTER, *Sep. 24th*, 1861.

DEAR SIR,—I beg to thank you very much for your kindness in sending me a valuable contribution to Ecclesiastical History in your book, *The Ancient Church*, which I found here upon my return to London two or three days ago. How much would it contribute to the promotion of charity and the advancement of the truth were all who combated the opinions and views of another to give him the means of seeing what was written fairly and openly, and not to endeavour to overthrow his arguments without his knowledge. This will indeed ever be the case when truth is sought for itself, and no personal feelings enter into the matter.

I have read your chapters on Ignatius, and you will perhaps hardly expect that I should subscribe to your views. It is now about twenty years since I first undertook this inquiry, and constantly have I been endeavouring to add some new light ever since. I once answered an opponent in my present brother canon, Dr. Wordsworth, but since that time I have never replied to any adverse views—but have only looked to see if I could find anything either to show that I was wrong or to strengthen my convictions that I was right. And I have found the wisdom of this, and have had the satisfaction of knowing that my ablest opponents, after having had more time to inquire and to make greater research, have of their own accord conformed to my views and written in their support.

I attach no very great importance to the Epistles of Ignatius. I shall not draw from them any dogma. I only look upon them as evidence of the time to certain facts, which indeed were amply established even without such evidence. I think that in such cases we must look chiefly to the historical testimony of facts; and you will forgive me for saying that I think your arguments are based upon presumptive evidence, negative evidence, and the evidence of appropriateness—all of which, however valuable, must tumble to the ground before one single fact. You notice that Archbishop Ussher doubted the Epistle to Polycarp. But why? simply because its style (not having been altered by the forger) was different from the rest. But you know he says there was more *historical* evidence in its favour than for any of the rest. It thus becomes an argument in support of the Syriac text instead of against it. Can you explain how it happens that the Syriac text, found in the very language of Ignatius himself, and transcribed many hundreds of years before the Ignatian controversy was thought of, now it is discovered, should contain only the *three Epistles* of the existence of which there is any historical evidence before the time of Eusebius, and that, although it may contain some things which you do not approve, still has rejected all the passages which the critics of the Ignatian controversy protested against? You go too far to say that Bentley rejected the Ignatian Epistles—he only rejected them in the form in which they were put forth by Ussher and Vossius, and not in the form of the Syriac. So did Porson, as Bishop Kaye informed me—but he never denied that Ignatius had written letters—indeed the very forgeries were a proof of true patterns which were falsified.

A great many of the ablest scholars in Europe, who had refused to accept the Greek letters, are convinced of the genuineness of the Syriac. But time will open. Believe me, yours faithfully,

WILLIAM CURETON.

THE REV. DR. KILLEN.

Since this letter was written, ecclesiastical literature has sustained a severe loss in the death of its amiable and accomplished author. Though Dr. Cureton has here expressed himself with due caution, his language is certainly not calculated to reassure the advocates of the Ignatian Epistles. Their most learned editor in recent times—so far from speaking in a tone of confidence respecting them—here admits that he attached to them "no very great importance." Though he had spent twenty years chiefly in their illustration, he acknowledges that he was constantly endeavouring "to add some new light" for his guidance. To him, therefore, the subject must have been still involved in much mystery.

It is noteworthy that, in the preceding letter, he has not been able to point out a solitary error in the statement of the claims of these epistles as presented in *The Ancient Church*. He alleges, indeed, that the arguments employed are "based upon presumptive evidence, negative evidence, and the evidence of appropriateness;" he confesses that these proofs are "valuable;" but, though he contends that they must all "tumble to the ground before *one single fact*," he has failed to produce the one single fact required for their overthrow.

Dr. Cureton had obviously not been previously aware that Dr. Bentley, the highest authority among British critics, had rejected the Ignatian Epistles. Had he been cognizant of that fact, when he wrote the *Corpus Ignatianum*, he would have candidly announced it to his readers. The manner in which he here attempts to dispose of it is certainly not very satisfactory. He pleads that, though Bentley condemned as spurious the letters edited by Ussher and Vossius, he would not have pronounced the same decision on the Syriac version recently discovered. Why not? This Syriac version is an edition of *the same epistles* in an abbreviated form. If Bentley denounced *the whole* as a forgery, it seems to follow, by logical inference, that he would have pronounced the same verdict on the half or the third part. Dr. Cureton is mistaken when he affirms in the preceding communication that his Syriac version has rejected *all the passages* against which "the critics of the Ignatian controversy" had protested. The very contrary has been demonstrated in *The Ancient Church*. A large number of the sentences which had provoked the most unsparing criticism are retained in the Curetonian edition. It is right to add that Archbishop Ussher more than "doubted" the Epistle to Polycarp. He discarded it altogether. Without hesitation he set it aside as spurious. Whilst he disliked its style, he felt that it wanted other marks of genuineness. He evidently expresses his own opinion when he says of it—"Augustodunensis Honorius, in libro de Luminaribus Ecclesiæ, (cui Hieronymianum scriptorum catalogum, in epitomen a se redactum, inseruit) epistolam ad Polycarpum in censu scriptorum Ignatii *plane prætermittendam* esse judicavit: ita videlicet verbis Hieronymi acceptis, ac si nulla peculiaris ad Polycarpum data, intellecta hic ab eo fuisset epistola ; sed illa ad Smyrnæos retenta . . . Quam sane Hieronymi mentem fuisse, *ego omnino non dubito.*" (*Dissertatio*, cap. ii. *Ussher's Works*, vol. vii. 97, 98, ed. Elrington. See also *Cor. Ignat.* introd. p. 51.)

Had Dr. Cureton re-examined the chapters on the Ignatian controversy in *The Ancient Church*, he must have seen that the question as to the origin of *the three epistles* had already received a solution. It is there stated : " An island in the Ægean sea has been confounded with *Syria*, the Eastern Province ; and the error has led to the incubation of the whole brood of Ignatian letters. . . . The first edition of them appeared, not at Troas or Smyrna, but in Syria or Palestine. . . . There is every reason to believe that, as edited by Dr. Cureton, they are now presented to the public *in their original language*, as well as in their original form." (*Ancient Church*, 408, 407.) From three, these letters multiplied to fifteen, and the enlarged copies made their appearance in Greek and Latin.

Any one who studies the two chapters on the Ignatian Epistles in *The Ancient Church* must see that what is there urged against them is something more than "presumptive evidence, negative evidence, and the evidence of appropriateness." It is shown that their anachronisms, historical blundering, and false doctrine clearly convict them of forgery. But it is unnecessary to pursue this subject ; as, though *The Ancient Church* has now been many years before the literary public, no one either at home or abroad has attempted to answer its arguments.

INDEX.

ABBASSIDES, 146, 393.
Abbesses, 282.
Abbot, 105, 110, 208, 329.
Abdalrahman, 393.
Abraham, 131, 137.
Abrogation, 138.
Abu Bakr, 133, 138, 145.
Abu Talib, 130, 133.
Abyssinia, 73, 111.
Acacius, 357.
Academy, Royal Irish, Proceedings of, 62.
Achamoth, 34.
Acholius, 341.
Acolyte, 48.
Adam, 137.
Adamnan, 288, 290, 292, 298, 301, 319, 327.
Ædesius, 73, 111.
Ædilwalch, 279.
Ægean Sea, 248.
Ægiali Islands, 248.
Ælia Capitolina, 249, 250.
Æneid, 21.
Ængus, the Culdee, 325.
Ætius, 353.
Æons, 34, 35.
Africa, Church of, 66, 113, 128; North, 123, 146; population of, 125; peculiarities of Church of, 327; Pope opposed by clergy of, 349-352; Proconsular, 23, 61, 114, 128.
Agatho, 215, 216, 379, 380.
Agilulf, 367.
Agonistici, 122.
Aidan, 280-3, 295; King, 298, 300.
Aidus, 297.
Ailred, 288.
Aistulphus, 390.
Akoimetoi, 106.
Alaric, 95, 348, 356.
Alban, 268.
Alchfleda, 279.
Aldfrid, 301.
Alemanni, 362.
Alexander, bishop of Alexandria, 166, 168; Severus, 11, 18, 25.
Alexandria, 54-5, 79, 103, 146, 167, 171, 244, 249, 336.
Ali, 133.
Alps, 303.
Amator, 312.
Ambo, 228.

Ambrose, 79, 90, 92-5, 97, 99, 100, 107, 222, 229.
Ambrosiaster, 86.
Ammianus Marcellinus, 339.
Ammonius, Saccas, 11; the monk, 197.
Anastasius, 194, 364.
Anatolius, 210.
Ancyra, 245.
Andrew, the Apostle, 5, 369.
Angles, 53.
Anicetus, 393.
Annals of Ulster, 277; of Four Masters, 325.
Annunciation, 238.
Anomœans, 175.
Anthropology, 178.
Antichrist, 52, 57, 376; bishop of Rome, 57.
Antioch, 22, 37, 48, 54, 82, 108, 249; Council of, 172, 173.
Antiphonary, 373.
Antoninus, Pius, 17, 53; wall of, 287, 289.
Antony, 100, 103, 107.
Antrim, 327.
Anulinus, 117.
Apennines, 303.
Apiarius, 351-2.
Apocalypse, 51, 57, 148, 154, 159.
Apocrypha, 151-3, 323.
Apollinaris, 175; Apollinarians, 175, 176.
Apostles, 4, 47, 48; Creed, 31.
Apostolic Canons, 8.
Apostolic Constitutions, 8; Ethiopic version of, 296.
Apostolic Fathers, 9.
Apostolic See, 343.
Aptunga, 114, 120.
Aquileia, 214.
Arabia, 73, 131, 135.
Arcadius, 81.
Archbishop, 328.
Archdeacon, 114, 115, note.
Archilamens, 269.
Archimandrite, 105.
Architecture, Christian, 227.
Ard-epscop, 328.
Argyll, Duke of, 290.
Arian Controversy, 70, 85, 165-178; Arianism, 103, 117; decline of, 366.
Aristocracy, Pagan, 80.
Ariminum, 268, 270.
Arius, 166-7, 170, 260; death of, 171.

2 c

Armagh, 308, 313, 315, 328; Book of, 312, 321, 325.
Armenia, 24, 72.
Arnobius, 12.
Arsenius, 170.
Artemon, 36.
Arthur, King, 272.
Ascetic life, 106.
Asia Minor, 111; Central, 303.
Aspect, 204.
Asylums, 82.
Athanasian Creed, 85.
Athanasius, 85-6, 90, 97-8, 100, 107, 152, 162, 169-70, 173, 176, 194, 221-2, 265.
Athens, 22.
Atticus, 352.
Attila, 356.
Auditors, 259.
Augusti, 96.
Augustine, 90, 95, 97, 107, 113, 124, 126, 153, 162, 178, 182-3, 185-6, 189, 191-2, 193, 226, 229; the monk, 273-4, 277, 285, 301, 321, 375.
Augustulus, 81, 357, 358.
Aurelian, 19; the abbot, 295.
Autharis, 367, 375.
Autun, 118.
Ayesha, 145.

Babel, 58.
Babylon, 58.
Bagai, 123.
Baldwin, Archbishop, 271.
Ballycaston, 327.
Bangor, 271, 275, 277, 330; its meaning, 271; note, 272.
Baptism, 39, 45, 46.
Baptismal controversy, 39, 40.
Baptistery, 228.
Baradæus, Jacobus, 211, note.
Barnabas, companion of Paul, 49; Epistle of, 8, 13.
Baronius, 91, 119, 216, 377.
Barrow, 127.
Barsumas, 208, 290.
Baruch, 152.
Basilicæ, 67.
Basil the Great, 87-8, 99, 105, 249; Rule of, 109.
Basilides, 34.
Basiliscus, 211, 212.
Bede, 84, 273, 277, 284, 293, 319.
Beersheba, 141.
Bel and the Dragon, 152.
Belcher, Sir Edward, 62.
Belfast, 330.
Belgæ, 303.
Belisarius, 213, 359.
Bellarmin, 253.
Benedict, 105, 109-10, 291, 374.
Benignus, 328.
Bentley, 399.
Bertha, 273, 274, 278.
Betham, Sir William, 146, 303-4, 312-3.
Bethlehem, 90, 91, 183.

Bible, 150.
Bibliotheca Sacra, 107.
Bingham, 164, 208, 248.
Binius, 120, 198, 208, 248, 254, 263, 355.
Bishops, 55, 128; Bishop of bishops, 56; of Rome, 107; preaching, 232; as judges, 245; their number, 125, 128, 248; who could not write, 262; number at Carthage, 124, 125; in Africa, 128; village, 325.
Bobbio, 331.
Boniface, 286, 352, 376, 383-5; the IV., 332; the III., 374.
Botred, 282.
Book of Common Prayer, 374.
Boskoi, 108.
Boulogne, 308, 310, 325.
Bower, 353, 359.
Braga, Council of, 381.
Brendan of Birr, 299.
Brevy, Synod of, 270.
Bricknell, 259.
Britain, 24, 61, 120; Britons, 273; Brittany, 325.
Bruce, Robert, 300.
Bruide, 290.
Buddha, 35.
Bunsen, 230.
Burgess, 87.
Burgundians, 362, 366.
Byzantium, 250, 347, 348.

Cæcilian, 114-5, 117, 120-1, 126.
Caerleon, 271, 272, 276.
Cæsarea, Creed of Church of, 168; bishop of, 250.
Cæsars, 60.
Cairbre Riada, 288, 289.
Caledonia, 287, 289.
Caliphs, 138.
Callistus, 10.
Calpe, 146.
Camden, 300.
Campania, 110.
Campbell, Dr., 365, note.
Candida Casa, 287.
Candlemas, 238.
Canon of the N. T., 97; of Scripture, 151; of the Mass, 232; of Nice, 335.
Canterbury, 273, 275; archbishop of, 275, 277, 283, 298.
Cantors, 229.
Cantyre, 259.
Captives, 28.
Carloman, 385.
Carpocrates, 34.
Carpwald, 279.
Carthage, 24, 40, 146; Council of, 98, 121, 155, 188, 189; Church of, 113, 114, 115; Carthaginians, 304.
Casæ Nigræ, 116, 118.
Cassian, 96, 97, 107, 190, 191, 199.
Cassino, Monte, 110, 374.
Catacombs, the, 23.
Catechumens, 228.
Catholic, Church, 55-7, 113, 122, 126,

Index. 403

154, 163; Catholics, 131, system, 55; bishops, 113; unity, 126, 242, 251.
Cave, 87, 119, 175, 244, 249, 336.
Cedde, 281.
Celestine, 199, 305, 319, 320, 351.
Celibacy of clergy, 321.
Cerdon, 34, 53.
Ceremonies, heathen in Christian worship, 71.
Cerinthus, 34.
Chad, 281, 284.
Chalcedon, 153, 160, 244, 254, 259, 376; Council of, 211-3, 261, 354, 355.
Chalmers, 259.
Chancel, 227.
Chant, Gregorian, 229, 373.
Chapters, The three, 212-3, 332.
Charibert, 273.
Chest of the Apostleship, 145.
Childeric, 390.
Chorepiscopus, 128, 245-6, 248.
Chosroes, 142.
Chrestus, 120.
Christ, His ministry, 1-4; prophecies relating to Him, 29, 30; Christians, morality of, 25-6.
Christmas, 237.
Chronicle, Anglo-Saxon, 294.
Chrysaphius, 206, 210.
Chrysostom, 88-90, 152, 160, 161, 223, 354.
Church and State, 116, 122.
Circumcelliones, 122-4.
Cirta, Synod of, 116.
City of God, 95.
Clare, 327.
Clarkson, 178.
Claudia, 267.
Clement, of Rome, Epistle of, 8, 13, 153, 156, note; of Alexandria, 10, 99.
Clementine Homilies, 8.
Clergy, 339.
Clonard, 330.
Clonmacnoise, 325, 330.
Clotilda, 362.
Clovis, 273, 319, 336, 361-5.
Clyde, 287.
Cœlestius, 129, 181, 188, 190, 305.
Codex, Vaticanus, 156; Alexandrinus, 156; Sinaiticus, 156.
Cœnobites, 104, 105, 106; Cœnobium, 104.
Coins, 66.
Coleman, 283, 295.
Colgan, 270.
Collier, 267.
Collyridians, 241.
Cologne, 118.
Coleraine, 327.
Columbanus, 330-1, 332-3.
Columbkille, 288, 290-3, 296, 299, 301, 326, 327.
Congall, 330.
Commodus, 18.
Commonitorium, 191.
Communicants, 259.

Conference with Donatists, 124-6.
Confessions of Augustine, 182.
Confessors, 257.
Confession of Patrick, 307-8, 321.
Confirmation or Chrism, 234, 321.
Congregationalism, 47.
Constance, 331.
Constans, 73, 74, 122, 174.
Constantia, 170.
Constantine the Great, 19, 61-2, 65-8, 70-1, 117, 121, 162, 172, 176, 242-3, 257.
Constantine Pogonatus, 215, 264.
Constantinople, 171, 249, 341, 347, 355; Council of, 176, 259.
Constantius Chlorus, 19, 61, 268; Son of Constantine, 73-4, 86, 172, 175.
Copts, 211.
Corinth, 22, 50; Church, government of, 50.
Cormac O'Cuinn, 304.
Cornwall, 272.
Cornelius of Rome, 40.
Coroticus, 317.
Corsica, 336.
Coss, 131.
Councils, 382, 386; General, 252-266.
Co-standers, 259.
Country bishops, 245.
Covel, 240.
Creed, Nicene, 176.
Crispus, 70, 83.
Crosier, origin of the, 239.
Cross, sign of the, 38, 45, 62, 63, 163; finding of the, 241.
Crown, Triple, 391, note.
Culdees, 294, 302.
Cummian, 120, 292-3, 299, 320.
Cumraig, 304.
Cureton, Dr., 8, 24, 397-400.
Custom, 244.
Cybele, 238, note.
Cycle, Roman, 275, 282; British, 282.
Cyprus, 35, 251.
Cyril of Jerusalem, 86-7, 152; of Alexandria, 96-7, 197-8, 199, 203, 212, 352.
Cyprian, 11, 12, 40, 114, 119, 179.

Dacia, 341.
Dagan, bishop, 321.
Dalmatius, 74, 203, 248.
Dalriada, 289, 290.
Damascenus, 97.
Damascus, 22, 338.
Damasus, 85, 90, 107, 145, 152, 338-9, 340.
Daniel, the monk, 105; the prophet, 152.
Dathy, 310, 314.
David, St., 270.
Deacons, 47.
Decalogue, 219, 226-7, note.
Decius, 18; persecution of, 102, 103.
Decretals, 85, 342.
Demiurge, 34.
Demosthenes, 156, 157.
Devonshire, 286.
Deusdedit, 283.

Didascalia, 296.
Didymus, 91.
Dinoth, 276.
Diocletian, 19; persecution of, 19; his wife, 25, 60, 61, 65.
Diermit, 297.
Diognetus, Epistle to, 9.
Diocese, 249.
Dionysius Exiguus, 84, 275.
Dioscorus, 208, 247.
Diospolis, 184, 188.
Dinma, 281.
Docetæ, 33.
Doctrine of the Church, 29-32.
Döllinger, 231, 333.
Domitian, 16.
Donatus, 116, 118, 119, 124; Donatists, 113-129, 192, 268.
Donald, King, 287.
Donegall, 288.
Dorner, 167, 173, 177, 201.
Dress of Christians, 27.
Druids, 224, 318; Druidism, 322, 329.
Dubritius, 271.
Dunkeld, 287.
Dupin, 98.

Eadbald, 280.
East in Prayer, 163.
Easter, 236, 239, 275, 282, 295, 301, 320, 330.
Ebion, 34.
Ecclesiastical Writers, 82.
Ecclesiasticus, 98, 152, 159, 323.
Ecthesis, 214, 215, 217.
Edessa, 24.
Edinburgh, 278.
Edwin, 278, 280.
Eginhard, 390.
Egypt, 22, 104, 146, 244.
Elders of the people, 48, 113, note.
Eleutherius, 267, 269.
Eliberis, Council of, 223.
Elizabeth, 259, note.
Elliott, 81, 359.
Elrington, 120.
Emania, 329.
Embrun, 365.
England, Ecclesiastical History of, 267-287.
Ennodius, 361.
Ephesus, 49, 50, 54; Council of, 190, 202, 250, 259, 261.
Ephræm Syrus, 87.
Epiphanius, 84, 91, 163, 222.
Epiphany, 237.
Episcopacy, 47.
Eremites, 103.
Erigena, Johannes Scotus, 324.
Essenes, 102.
Essex, 281:
Etchen, 326.
Eternal City, the, 353.
Eternal Generation, 166.
Eternal Life, 187.
Ethelbert, 273-276, 280.

Ethelburga, 278.
Ethelfrid, 276.
Eucharist, 45, 46, 104, 114, 235, 236, 324.
Euchites, 108.
Eudoxia, 89.
Euelpistus, 248.
Ennan, 292.
Eutyches, 147, 206, 207, 209; Eutychianism, 83, 206-209, 213, note, 261.
Eutychius, 212.
Evagrius, 84.
Evangelists, the Four, 3; Primitive, 4, 6.
Exarch, 249, 355.
Exorcism, 45.
Exorcist, 48.
Expositors, 98.
Ezekiel, 148.

Family piety, 26.
Fathers, the, 8-14; apostolic, 9.
Faster, the, 376.
Fasting on the Lord's Day, 226.
Fausta, 70.
Faustinus, 352.
Felicissimus, Schism of, 40, 41, 56.
Felix, 114, 115, 120.
Fiacc's Hymn, 315, 318, note.
Fifeshire, 288.
Finan, 281.
Finchan, 297, 298.
Fingal, 304.
Firbolgs, 303.
Flamens, 269.
Flavian, 206, 208, 209.
Fleury, 167.
Florentius, 248.
Foclud, 309, 311.
Fordun, 305.
Forms of Prayer, 230.
Four, first, Councils, 164, 254, 259.
France, 24.
Franconia, 331.
Frauds, pious, 279, 371.
Fredegarius, 362.
Freisingen, 385.
Freislanders, 387; apostle of, 286.
Frumentius, 73, 111.
Fulda, 387.
Fulgentius, 95.
Fuller, 267, 277.
Fursey, 281.

Gabriel, 131, 137, 145.
Gaelic, 304.
Galerius, 19, 63.
Gallienus, 19, 25, 253.
Galloway, 287.
Gallus, 19, 331.
Gangra, 104.
Gap, 365.
Gartan, 288.
Gaul, 61, 118, 119, 127, 270.
Gelasius, 232, 235.
Genseric, 356.
Geoffrey of Monmouth, 269.
Geology, 302.

Index. 405

George, 174.
Germans, Apostle of the, 286.
Germanus, 271, 309, 315, 328.
Germany, 108.
Gibbon, 130, 142, 248.
Gibraltar, 146.
Gieseler, 336, 356, 367.
Gildas, 272.
Giraldus Cambrensis, 269, 271.
Gladiators, 27.
Glasgow, 300.
Glastonbury, 272.
Gnostics, 33-35, 67, 179.
Godfathers and godmothers, 234.
Goode, 161.
Gospels, 158.
Goths, 24, 72, 111, 176.
Gottschalk, 246.
Grampians, 288.
Grant, 204.
Gratian, 79, 124, 340, 346, 351.
Graves, Bishop, 317.
Gregory Thaumaturgus, 12; of Tours, 84, 362-363; the Cappadocian, 173; the Great, 85, 90, 96, 98, 153, 164, 285, 232, 273, 301, 320, 367-379, the Second, 85; the Third, 85; the Illuminator, 72; of Nyssa, 87.
Gregory Nazianzen, 87-88, 90, 152, 249, 261.
Growth of the Church, 21-25.
Guizot, 381, 382.
Gundebald, 362.
Guntram, 365.

Hadrian, 16, 53, 249.
Hagar, 141, 142.
Hagenbach, 85.
Hallam, 374.
Halloween, 238.
Hannibalianus, 74.
Haruspices, 65, 66.
Heathenism, suppression of, 69, 74.
Hebrew Bible, 151, 152, 157.
Hebrews, Epistle to, 159.
Hefele, 119, 208, 245, 253.
Hegira, 138, 140.
Helena, 241, 250.
Helios, 65.
Henoticon, 211, 212, 270, 360.
Henry, 269.
Heptarchy, the, 281.
Heraclea, 250, 347.
Heraclius, 214.
Herbert, Hon. Algernon, 290.
Heresy, 33-38, 57.
Heric of Auxerre, 315.
Hermas, Shepherd of, 8.
Hermits, 103.
Hermogenes, 34.
Herod the Great, 1.
Herodotus, 155.
Heros, 184, 188.
Hertford, Synod of, 284.
Heruli, 358.
Hessey, Dr., 221, note.

Heteroousians, 175.
Hexapla of Origen, 11.
Hibernia, 289.
Hierarchy, Rise of the, 52, 242-252.
Hilarion, 105, 107.
Hilary of Poictiers, 86, 97, 152; Pope, 86; of Arles, 86, 353; the Deacon, 114, 191.
Hilda, 282.
Himerius, 342.
Hincmar, 364.
Hippo, 124, 178, note.
Hippolytus, 10.
Hira, Mount, 132.
Hislop, 238.
Histria, 320.
Holy Island, 281.
Holy water, 44.
Homoiousios, 173.
Homoousios, 168, 173, 323.
Honorius, 81, 125, 216, 382.
Horæ Apocalypticæ, 81.
Hormisdas, 364.
Hosius, 174, 254, 256, 257, 258.
Humanitarianism, 41.
Hunneric, 128.
Hy, 290.
Hy-Garchon, 306.
Hy-Nialls, 329.
Hyginus, 54, 58.
Hymeneus, 34.
Hymn, of Patrick, 322.
Hypatia, 197.
Hysteria, 132.

I or Hy, 290.
Ibas of Edessa, 212.
Iberia, 73, 320, note.
Ignatian Epistles, 8, 397-400.
Illiterate Prophet, 131.
Illyricum, 23, 341.
Iltutus, 271.
Immersion at Baptism, 45.
Ina, King, 224, 284, 285, note.
Incense, 44.
Incorrect phraseology introduced, 32.
India, 24, 73.
Indulgences, 260, note.
Infants baptized, 45, 187, 233, 234; fine for neglect, 284.
Innisbollin, 327.
Innisfallen, Annals of, 306.
Innocent I., 85, 184, 188, 346, 354.
Innocents, feast of, 238.
Inspiration, 160.
Instrumental Music, 43.
Iona, 106, 280, 281, 290.
Ireland, 285, 302-320, 322-331.
Irenæus, 9, 161.
Isidore of Seville, 53, 96, 224, 231; of Pelusium, 96; the monk, 181.
Isis, 277.
Islam, 133, 136.
Isle of Saints, 330.
Israelites (Clubs), 123.
Israfil, 144.
Istria, 214.

Jacobites, 211.
James, the Apostle, 5.
Jamieson, 294.
Japan, 102.
Jeremiah, 152.
Jerome, 54, 90, 91, 97-99, 107, 152, 153, 162, 183, 339, 340.
Jerusalem, 22; church of, 47; bishop of, 250.
Jesus Christ, 1, 29, 30, 134, 137; likeness of, 240.
Jewish Dispensation, 57; Jews, 197.
Job, 161, 370.
Jocelin, 317, 318, note.
John, the Apostle, 6, 16, 51, 57, 159; of Damascus, 97, 153; of Jerusalem, 184; of Antioch, 202, 204; Pope, 359, 365.
Jortin, 65, 241.
Josephus, 2; Joseph of Arimathea, 267.
Jovinian, 91.
Judicatum, 213.
Judith, 98, 152, 159.
Julia Mammæa, 11.
Julian, the Apostate, 75-77, 86, 123, 176, of Eclanum, 190.
Julius Cæsar, 304; Pope, 338.
Justina, 93.
Justin Martyr, 9, 62.
Justinian, 84, 212, 213, 359, 366.
Justus, 280.
Jutes, 272.

Knaba, 130, 131, 135, 140, 141, note.
Kaled, 145.
Kelly, 311, 327.
Kellach, 300.
Kenneth, 289.
Kennett, 63.
Kent, 273, 274, 275, note.
Kentigern, 300.
Khadija, 130, 131, 133, 140, 142.
Khalif, 145, 146.
Kieran, 313.
Kilaspuglenane, 327.
Kilian or Killen, 331.
Kilmacreehy, 327.
Kilmanaheen, 327.
Kilroot, 327.
Kincardineshire, 306.
King, 294, 301.
Kirk-shot, 284.
Kiss of peace, 45; kissing the foot, 239, note.
Koran, 130, 133, 134, 137, 140, 145.
Koreish, 129.
Kurtz, 172, 258.
Kynegils, 278.
Kyrie Eleison, 240.

Labarum, 62.
Lactantius, 83, 97.
Lady Day, 238.
Lanigan, 293, 305, 317, 329.
Laodicea, 153, 155, 159, 160; Council of, 98, 223, 245.
Laoghaire, 314, 322.

Lapsed, the, 18, 20, 260.
Lardner, 152.
Lateran, first Council of, 215.
Latin spoken, 374.
Lauræ, 104; Laurea, 375.
Laurentius, 280.
Lazarus, 184, 188.
Leabhar Breac, 307.
Leary, 314.
Le Brun, 373.
Lectors, 164.
Ledwich, 319.
Lee, Dr., 160.
Leo, 1., 85, 209, 231, 320, 353, 354; the Isaurian, 388.
Lerins, 273.
Lesbos, 247.
Leydecker, 128.
Liberatus Diaconus, 207, 208.
Liberius, 174, 338.
Libya, 244, 336.
Lichfield, 281, 284.
Licinius, 66-9, 70, 170.
Lindisfarne, 281, 283, 284, 295.
Lingard, Dr., 277, 282.
Litanies, 240, 274.
Liturgy of the heathen, 44, 231; Liturgies of the Church, 230, 231, 373.
Liudhard, 273.
Llan-lwit, 271.
Lloyd, 293.
Loarn, 290.
Locusts, 148.
Logos, 37, 195.
Lombards, 359, 366-7, 378, 389, 375.
London, 275, 281.
Lord's Day, 42, 65, 218-227, 284.
Lordship in the Church, 58.
Lord's Supper, 39, 45, 234-5.
Louise, Princess, 290.
Lucius, 267, 269, 287.
Lucilla, 114, 115.
Lull, 387.
Lupercalia, 239.
Lupus, 271, 315.
Lustral water, 78-9, 228.
Lutherans, 260.
Lyons, Church of, 17, 23; Synod of, 365.

Macarius, 123, 375.
Maccabees, 98, 151, 159.
Maccamachtheni, 317.
Macedonius, 175; Macedonians, 175, 176.
Macgeoghegan, 289.
Mâçon, Council of, 224.
Magnentius, 74.
Majorinus, 115, 116, 118.
Malcolm III., 300.
Manes or Manichæus, 37, 131; Manichæanism, 37, 41, 179.
Manna, 220.
Marcellinus, 125.
Marcellus, 175.
Marcian, 210.
Marcion, 34, 53, 57.
Marcus, 34, 311; Aurelius, 17, 18, 23.

Index. 407

Marinus, 118, 120.
Mar Jacob, 24.
Marianus Scotus, 312.
Marius Mercator, 95.
Mark the Evangelist, 22.
Marriage, 101.
Marseilles, 107, 190, 353.
Martel, Charles, 146, 385, 389.
Martin of Tours, 84, 107, 297, 316 ; Pope Martin I., 215, 360, 382.
Martyrdom, 32 ; martyrs, 236.
Mary, worship of, 23, 323 ; mother of Christ, 201 ; note, 196, 201, 211, 241 ; said to be buried at Ephesus, 202 ; mother of God, 194, 200, 259 ; not immaculate, 185, note.
Mass, origin of the name, 229, note ; for the dead, 236, 370.
Masters, Annals of the Four, 325.
Maternus, 118.
Matins, 109.
Matter, 33.
Matthew of Westminster, 277.
Maurice, 247, 377, 378.
Maxentius, 61, 64, 113, 117, 335.
Maximian, 124.
Maximin, 18, 103.
Mayo, 327.
M'Lauchlan, 287, 289, 302.
Mearns, 305.
Mecca, 130, 131, 136, 138, 139, 145.
Medina, 138, 140, 141, 145.
Melchites, 211, note.
Melitius, 166 ; Melitians, 244, 345 ; Meletius, 256.
Melito of Sardis, 152.
Mellitus, 280.
Melville, Andrew, 309.
Memnon, 202.
Mensurius, 113, 114, 126.
Mercia, 278, 280.
Merivale, 125, note.
Merovingians, 364, 366, 389.
Mesopotamia, 24.
Messiah, the, 29, 30.
Methymna, 248.
Metropolis, 243 ; metropolitan, 56, 128, 244, 251, 252, 337.
Milesians, 303.
Milevi, 84, 188.
Miesrob, 73.
Migne, 86, 97, 106, 108-10, 116, 188, 295, 363.
Milan, Edict of, 64, 120 ; Synod of, 174, 175.
Miller, Dr. Samuel, 114.
Mills, 144, 146.
Milman, 66, 73, 106.
Milner, 186, 374.
Miltiades or Melchides, 118, 119, 335.
Milvian Bridge, 61-4, 335.
Minervina, 83.
Minucius Felix, 12, 62.
Miracles, 6, 7, 25 ; mock, 262.
Mitre, origin of the, 239.
Mitylene, 248.

Mœsia, 24.
Mohammed, 129 ; Mohammedanism, 129-149.
Monday, 129, 142.
Monica, 182.
Monophysites, 131, 211, 214, 259.
Monothelites, 214 ; Monothelitism, 259.
Montanists, 41, 122, 154 ; Montanus, 35, 36, 131.
Morgan, 181.
Moralia of Gregory, 370.
Morris, 87.
Moses, 137, 141.
Moslems or Mussulmans, 133, 145.
Mosque, 139.
Mull, 290.
Munster, 296, 297.
Murdock, 204.
Mysteries of the heathen, 46 ; of the Church, 228 ; of iniquity, 358.

Najran, 131.
Naples, 336.
Natalius, 36.
Nathy, 305, 306.
Nave, 227.
Nazarenes, 38.
Neander, 65, 116, 203, 308.
Nectan, King, 301.
Nectarius, 88.
Nennius, 290, 311, 325.
Neo-Platonists, 99.
Nero, persecution by, 16, 22.
Nestorian controversy, 193-205 ; Nestorius, 193-4, 195, 199 ; his death, 204.
New Testament, 97.
Niall, King, 309, 310, 314.
Nice, Council of, 67, 70. 72, 112, 162, 168, 177, 223, 250, 256, 257.
Nicolas of Myra, 261.
Nicomedia, 19, 71, 167.
Nile, 169.
Noetus, 36.
Non-residence, 196.
Northumberland or Northumbria, 276, 278, 286, 295, 301.
Notker Balbulus, 298.
Novatian, 40, 56 ; Novatians, 41, 166, 197, 214 ; Novatianism, 121, 194.
Number of monks and nuns, 106.
Numidia, 114, 115, 123.
Nunneries, 106.
Nursia, 109, 291.
Nynian, 287.

Oath of Boniface, 384.
Obedience of monks, 110.
Ocatz, 131.
Ockley, 138, 146.
O'Conor, 289, 304, 307.
O'Curry, 307, 317.
Odoacer, 81, 358, 359.
O'Donovan, 310, 329.
Œcumenical Councils, 87, 253.
O'Flaherty, 289.
Ogygia, 288, 289.

O'Heney, 328.
Oil in baptism, 163.
O'Kelly, 328.
Old Testament, 98.
Omar, 138, 146.
Omniades, 146, 393.
Optatus, 84, 113, 115, 118, 124, 162.
Orange, Council of, 191.
Order of sitting in Councils, 255.
Ordination *per saltum*, 93; by the abbot, 105, 294, 321; ordinal, 373.
Orestes, 197.
Organs, 229-30, note, 284.
Origen, 10, 11, 13, 91, 92, 99.
Original sin, 179, 185.
Orosius, 183, 184.
Orphans, 28.
Ostrogoths, 359, 366.
Oswald, 279, 280, 292.
Oswio, 279, 282, 283.

Pachomius, 104, 106, 107.
Paddy, 316.
Paganism, 78, 80.
Palestine, 104, 109.
Pall or Pallium, 375.
Palladius, 305-7, 315, 316, 319.
Palmer, 161, 230, 231.
Pannonia, 90.
Pantheon, 238, note.
Paper, 379.
Paphlagonia, 104.
Paphnutius, 105, 112.
Paraclete, 37, 134.
Paradise of Mohammed, 143, 144.
Parchment, 379.
Paris, 273.
Parmenian, 124.
Parthia, 24.
Particular Redemption, 186, 191.
Paschal Controversy, 39.
Passau, 385.
Passive Obedience, 20.
Patriarchs, 249, 252.
Patrick, Apostle of Ireland, 307, 315-7, 319-20, 321.
Patripassians, 36.
Plato, 33; Platonism, 177.
Paul, the Apostle, 5, 6, 22, 49, 347; of Samosata, 36, 37; Father, 258, note; Paulus the hermit, 103, 107.
Paulinus, 181, 278.
Pavia, 367.
Peada, 279, 281.
Peasantry called Pagans, 78.
Pelagius, 129, 181, 184, 188, 190, 194; Pelagians, 192; Pelagian controversy, 178-193; Pope, 214, 368.
Penance, 32, 260.
Penda, 278.
Penitential, 97.
Penitentiary, the, 18.
Pentapolis, 244, 336, 391.
Pentecost, 21, 237.
People of the Book, 135, 147.
Perceval, M. Caussin de, 129, 138.

Periclyte, 134.
Persecutions, of the Church, 14-21; patronized by Augustine, 192.
Persia, 72, 145.
Persons in the Godhead, 31; in the Mediator, 204.
Petavius, 222.
Peter, the Apostle, 5, 280, 346-7; 1st Epistle of, 49; his name, 56; See of, 56, 198; of Alexandria, 346.
Pepin, 385, 389.
Petrie, Dr., 307.
Petty, Sir Wm., 326.
Philip, the Apostle, 6; the Arabian, 18; Bardanes, 216.
Philippians, 50.
Philoppopolis, 173, 247.
Philo the Jew, 2.
Phocas, 377, 378.
Photinus, 175.
Phygellus, 34.
Picts, 272; Apostle of southern, 288; of northern, 290.
Pictures, 241.
Pighius, 216.
Pilgrimages, 242; farewell, 141.
Pillar saints, 108.
Pimeniola, 271.
Pinkerton, 288, 294, 300, 303.
Plate, Church, 114, 115.
Platonism, new, 75, 78.
Plenary Inspiration, 160.
Pliny, 16, 231.
Poictiers, 146.
Polycarp, Epistle of, 9, 50, 393, 399.
Polychronius, 262, 263.
Pontifex Maximus, 239.
Population of England, 269; of Ireland, 326.
Porson, 398.
Porter, 48.
Potter, Archbishop, 114.
Pope, the, 145.
Posthumian, 246.
Præfectus Urbis, 248.
Prætorian Guards, 61.
Prayers for the dead, 23, 241; for the Emperor, 27; standing, 223; of the soldiers, 230; at councils, 256.
Praylus, 188.
Preachers, how maintained, 6; preaching, 232, 233.
Presbyters, 55; married, 104; preach, 232; without votes in synods, 365; presbytery, 47.
Presbyterians, 260.
Prideaux, 102, 130.
Primate, 114, 246.
Primian, 124.
Probus, 307.
Proclus, 196.
Proculus, 353.
Progress of the Church, 60-80.
Prophets, 47.
Proselene, 248.
Prosper, 91, 95, 191, 305, 319.

Index. 409

Prostrators, 259.
Psalmody, 43, 229; psalms, importance of the, 165.
Pudens, 267.
Purgatory, 23, 323, 372.
Pusey, 176, 254, 269.

Quarrels of the bishops, 251.
Queen Victoria, her descent, 289.

Radbert, Paschasius, 324.
Ramadan, 144.
Raphoe, 292.
Rashee, 327.
Rath of the Synods, 327, 329.
Rathlin, 327.
Ratisbon, 385.
Ravenna, 189, 348, 368.
Reader, 48, 164.
Rebaptism, 119.
Recared, 367.
Red Sea, 111.
Reeves, 288, 290, 292, 301, 312, 326.
Regeneration, 46, 234.
Regula Pastoralis of Gregory, 370.
Relics, 241.
Remigius, 362.
Reticus or Reticius, 118, note.
Retractations of Augustine, 97.
Revelation, 155.
Review, Edinburgh, 63.
Rheims, 362.
Rhone, 303.
Riada, 289.
Richard of Cirencester, 269.
Ricula, 278.
Rimini, 174, 255, 268.
Robber Synod, 207, 210, 262.
Robertson, 367.
Rochester, 275, 280.
Rock, the, 349.
Rodwell, 139, 144, 145.
Rome, 22, 244, 336; Church of, its extent, 51, 249; Epistle of Church of, 50; prelacy begins at, 53, 252; Babylon, 57; Papal, 58; synod at, 118.
Roman Liturgy, 231, 232, note.
Route, 288.
Routh, 119.
Rufinus, 83, 91, 92, 97, 336.
Ruling elders, 114, note.

Sabbath, 42, 218, 219, 220.
Sabellius, 36; Sabellianism, 166.
Sacrament, use of the word, 45.
Sacramentary, 373.
Sacrifices, 29.
Sagittarius, 365, 366.
Sale, 139, 144.
Salian Francs, 361.
Salonius, 365, 366.
Salzburg, 385.
Samosata, 36, 253.
Sarabaites, 108.
Saracens, 138, 146, 379.
Sardica, 173, 245, 247, 253, 268, 324, 351, 352.

Sardinia, 336.
Saturday, 38.
Saturnalia, 237.
Saturninus, 34.
Saxons, 272; East, 278; West, 278.
Scandinavia, 303.
Schaff, 85.
Schism of the Donatists, 113-116.
School of Antioch, 206.
Scotia Major, 289; Minor, 289.
Scotland, 24, 285, 287-302; Scots, 272, 303.
Scriptures, the, 19, 26, 32, 43, 109, 150-165; read by the laity, 161; of more authority than Councils, 162.
Scythians, 303.
Sebert, 278, 280, 281.
Secundinus or Sechnall, 328, 332.
Secundus, 144.
Sedulius, 324.
Segenius, 295.
Segetius, 309.
Seine, 303.
Seleucia, 174, 337.
Semi-Arianism, 177.
Semi-Pelagianism, 190, 191.
Senchus Mor, 315, note.
Seniors, 113.
Sen-Patrick, 315, 328.
Serapis, 79, 277.
Sergius, Pope, 286.
Seventy, the, 4.
Severus of Treves, 271.
Sharon Turner, 269, 272.
Shinar, 58.
Sicca, 351.
Sicily, 92, 120, 336, 357.
Sicininus, 339.
Simon Barjona, 56; Magnus, 34.
Simeon, the Stylite, 108.
Simplician, 93.
Simplicius, 357.
Singing, 241.
Siricius, 85.
Sirmium, 341.
Sirmond, 336.
Sismondi, 270, 364, 391.
Slaves, 26; made clergy, 380, 381.
Soames, 285, 286.
Socrates, 83, 112.
Solemn League and Covenant, 334.
Solway Frith, 287.
Sonnah, 138.
Soothsayer, 65.
Sozomen, 83, 102, 111.
Spain, 6, 22, 61, 120, 303.
Spelman, 119, 120, 267.
Sponsors, 206.
Sprenger, 129, 131, 132, 133.
Sprinkling at baptism, 45.
St. Andrews, 300.
Standing when communicating, 45; at prayer, 260.
Stanley, 62, 161, 167, 176.
States of the Church, 336.
Stephen III., 390, 391.
Stillingfleet, 229, 270, 303, 336.

Stridon, 90.
Stylites, 108.
Subdeacons, 48.
Suburbicarian Provinces, 336.
Suevi, 366.
Sulpitius Severus, 84, 270.
Sunday, 65, 219.
Suras, 133, 145.
Surplices, 44, 240.
Susanna, 152.
Sylloge, Ussher's, 320, note.
Sylvester, 256.
Symbols, the Eucharistic, 46.
Symmachus, 361, 375.
Synagogue, 48.
Syncletica, 106.
Synods, 327.
Syracuse, 120.
Syria, 104, 108, 109, 145.
Syricius, 342, 343, 364.

Tacitus, 2.
Tara, 289, 298, 304, 307, 322, 327, 329.
Tarik, 146.
Te Deum, its origin, 229, note.
Temple of Jerusalem, attempt to rebuild, 77.
Tenedos, 247.
Tertullian, 9, 13, 62, 161, 179, 252, 287.
Text, preaching from a, 43.
Thane, 286.
Thanet, Isle of, 274.
Thaumasius, 197.
Theatre, 27.
Thebes, 103.
Theodelinda, 367.
Theodora, 212, 213.
Theodore, 97; of Mopsuestia, 204, 212; of Canterbury, 224, 283, 284, 286.
Theodoret, 83, 97, 98, 160, 212, 261.
Theodoric, 96.
Theodosius the Great, 79, 80, 81, 82, 88, 92, 93, 94, 176; the Second, 198; 202, 210, 223, 261, 341, 346.
Theodotus, 36.
Theophilus, 72, 80, 89, 197.
Therapeutæ, 102.
Thessalonica, 22, 93, 341.
Thierry, 325.
Thirty-nine Articles, 193.
Thomas, the Apostle, 5.
Thomian, 329.
Thrace, 24.
Tiberius, 2, 65.
Ticinum, 361.
Tickets, 20.
Tillemont, 113, 118, 123, 308.
Timothy, the Evangelist, 6, 50.
Tirawley, 309.
Tiridates, 72.
Tithes, 284, 286.
Titus, the Evangelist, 6, 50.
Tobit, 98, 152, 159; Tobias, 323.
Todd, Dr., 267, 270, 297, 305, 322.

Tome, the, 209.
Tongues, gift of, 7.
Tonsure, 277, 321.
Tours, 146.
Tractoria, 190.
Tradition, 161.
Traditor, 116, 120.
Trajan, 16.
Transubstantiation, 324.
Treffry, 166.
Trent, 266.
Trim, 313.
Trinity, 31, 86, 144, 166, 172, 176, 323.
Trullan Synod, 153.
Tuath de Danan, 303, 304.
Turin, 367.
Twelve, the, 4.
Type, the, 214, 215, 217.
Tyre, Synod of, 170, 171.

Ulphilas, 72, 176.
Ulster, 329; annals of, 277, 294.
Unanimity in Councils, 258.
Unction, 45, 234.
Unitarians, 36; Mohammed a Unitarian, 144.
Universal Bishop, 355, note, 376.
Urgusia, 289.
Ursinus, 338, 339.
Ussher, 120, 292, 296, 308, 399.
Utrecht, 286.

Valentia, 287.
Valens, 79, 104, 176, 223.
Valentine, 34, 35, 54.
Valentinian, 78, 79, 124, 176, 223, 340; the Second, 340, 346, 351, 353; the Third, 353.
Valeria, 25.
Valerian, 19.
Valerius, 189.
Vandals, 192, 366.
Vatican Council, 253, 255, 256.
Vestal Virgins, 102.
Vestibule, 227.
Vicar of Christ, 57; of God, 145.
Vicarius Italiæ, 248.
Vicars, Apostolic, 341.
Victoria, Queen, 289.
Victoricius, 309, 310, 311, note.
Victor Vitensis, 128.
Victory, statue of, 63, 64; altar of, 79.
Vienne, Church of, 17, 23.
Vigilantius, 91.
Vigilius, 213, 217, 360; of Tapsus, 85; Pope, 373.
Vigils, 109.
Villanueva, 304, 308.
Village bishops, 128, 246, 251, 325.
Vincent of Lerins, 96, 181, 271.
Virgil, 156.
Virginity, 163.
Visigoths, 367.
Vitalian, Pope, 283.
Vitringa, 49.
Vossius, 398.

Index. 411

Votum Consultativum, 265, note.
Vulgate, 91.

Waddington, 105, 176, 261.
Wales, 270, 271, 272, 275, 276.
Ware, Sir James, 308.
Wartzburg, 331.
Water, holy, 78, 79, 228, note; Mill, 304.
Wax tapers, 44, 240.
Wesley, 46.
Westminster Confession, 193.
Wessex, 284.
Whitby, 282, 283, 295.
Whithern, 287, 288.
Whitsuntide, 237.
Wicklow, 306.
Widows, 28.
Wiggers, 179, 184.
Wighard, 283.
Wight, Isle of, 279.
Wilfrid, 279, 283, 296.
Will, one, 214.
Willibrord, 286.
Wine of the Eucharist mixed with water, 45.

Winifrid, 286, 383.
Winter Solstice, 237.
Wisdom, 98, 152, 323.
Witena-gemot, 285.
Woden, 280.
Wolf, 72.
Worship, places of, 25, 44; of the Church, 42, 227-241; of images, 388.
Wred, 289.
Writers, ecclesiastical, 8, 82.
Wulfhere, 279.
Wulfilaich, 108, 109.

Xavier, Francis, 102.

Yathreb, 135, 136, 137, 138.
York, 61, 275, 287; Yorkshire, 282.
Yule, 239, note.
Zachary, 85, 387, 392.
Zeid, 133.
Zemzem, 141.
Zeno, 211, 212, 360.
Zephyrinus, 10.
Zosimus, 127, 188, 189, 190, 191, 350, 351, 353.

ERRATA.

Page 33, line 8 from the foot—*dele* "eternal and."
,, 43, note 4, line 3 from the end—*for* μιᾶ *read* μία.
,, 201, line 24 from top—*for* "Constantine" *read* "Celestine."

The Works of St. Augustine.

EDITED BY THE REV. MARCUS DODS, M.A.

MESSRS. CLARK have much pleasure in publishing the first issue of Translations of the Writings of St. Augustine:

THE 'CITY OF GOD,'

IN TWO VOLUMES.

Translated by the Rev. Marcus Dods, M.A.

They believe this will prove not the least valuable of their various Series, and no pains will be spared to make it so. The Editor has secured a most competent staff of Translators, and every care is being taken to secure not only accuracy but elegance.

The Works of St. Augustine to be included in the Series are (in addition to the 'City of God'):—

All the Treatises in the Pelagian, and the four leading Treatises in the Donatist Controversy.

The Treatises against Faustus the Manichæan; on Christian Doctrine; the Trinity; the Harmony of the Evangelists; the Sermon on the Mount.

Also, the Lectures on the Gospel of St. John, the Confessions, a Selection from the Letters, the Retractations, the Soliloquies, and Selections from the Practical Treatises.

All these works are of first-rate importance, and only a small proportion of them have yet appeared in an English dress. The Sermons and the Commentaries on the Psalms having been already given by the Oxford Translators, it is not intended, at least in the first instance, to publish them.

The Series will include a Life of St. Augustine, by Robert Rainy, D.D., Professor of Church History, New College, Edinburgh.

The Series will probably extend to Sixteen or Eighteen Volumes. The Publishers will be glad to receive the *Names* of Subscribers as early as possible.

Subscription: Four Volumes for a Guinea, *payable in advance*, as in the case of the Ante-Nicene Series (24s. when not paid in advance).

It is understood that Subscribers are bound to take at least the books of the first two years. Each Volume will be sold separately at (on an average) 10s. 6d. each volume.

The second issue will be ready in a few months, and will probably comprise:—The Volume on the Donatist Controversy, translated by the Rev. J. R. King, Vicar of St. Peter's in the East, Oxford; and the First Volume of the Treatises in the Pelagian Controversy, translated by Rev. Peter Holmes, D.D., Rural Dean, etc., Plymouth.

They trust the Subscribers to the Ante-Nicene Library will continue their Subscription to this Series, and they hope to be favoured with an early remittance of the Subscription.

T. and T. Clark's Publications.

LANGE'S
Commentaries on the Old and New Testaments.

MESSRS. CLARK have now pleasure in intimating their arrangements, in conjunction with the well-known firm of SCRIBNER AND Co., of New York, and under the Editorship of Dr. PHILIP SCHAFF, for the Publication of Translations of the Commentaries of Dr. LANGE and his *Collaborateurs*, on the Old and New Testaments.

Of the OLD TESTAMENT, they have published the

COMMENTARY ON THE BOOK OF GENESIS, One Volume,
imperial 8vo, to which is prefixed a Theological and Homiletical Introduction to the Old Testament, and a Special Introduction to Genesis. By Professor TAYLER LEWIS, LL.D., comprising Excursus on all the chief subjects of Controversy.

COMMENTARY ON PROVERBS, ECCLESIASTES, AND THE SONG OF SOLOMON, in One Volume. By OTTO ZÖCKLER, D.D., Professor of Theology at Greisswald.

COMMENTARY ON JEREMIAH AND LAMENTATIONS, in One Volume. By Dr. C. W. E. NAGELSBACH.

Other Volumes on the Old Testament are in active preparation, and will be announced as soon as ready.

Messrs. CLARK have already published in the FOREIGN THEOLOGICAL LIBRARY the Commentaries on St. Matthew, St. Mark, St. Luke, and the Acts of the Apostles.

They had resolved to issue that on St. John only in the imperial 8vo form; but at the request of many of their Subscribers they will publish it (without Dr. Schaff's Additions) in Two Volumes, demy 8vo, uniform with the FOREIGN THEOLOGICAL LIBRARY, which will be supplied to Subscribers at 10s. 6d.

There are now ready (in imperial 8vo, double column),

COMMENTARY ON THE GOSPEL OF ST. JOHN, in One ·Volume. By J. P. LANGE, D.D. Translated, Revised, Enlarged, and Edited by Rev. Drs. YEOMAN and SCHAFF.

COMMENTARY ON THE EPISTLE OF ST. PAUL TO THE ROMANS. By J. P. LANGE, D.D., and F. R. FAY. Revised, Enlarged, and Edited by Dr. SCHAFF.

COMMENTARY ON THE EPISTLES OF ST. PAUL TO THE CORINTHIANS. By C. F. KLING, D.D.

T. and T. Clark's Publications.

Lange's Commentaries on the Old and New Testaments
—*CONTINUED.*

COMMENTARY ON THE EPISTLE OF ST. PAUL TO THE
GALATIANS, by OTTO SCHMOLLER, P.D. EPHESIANS, PHILIPPIANS, and COLOSSIANS, by KARL BRAUNE, D.D. In One Volume.

COMMENTARY ON THE EPISTLES TO THE THESSA-
LONIANS, by Professors AUBERLEN and RIGGENBACH. On the Epistles to TIMOTHY, TITUS, and PHILEMON, by Professor VAN OOSTERZEE. On the Epistle to the HEBREWS, by C. M. MOLL, D.D. In One Volume.

COMMENTARY ON THE EPISTLE OF JAMES, by Prof.
VAN OOSTERZEE. On the Epistles of PETER, by C. F. FRONMULLER, Ph.D. On the Epistles of JOHN, by K. BRAUNE, D.D. On the Epistle of JUDE, by C. F. FRONMULLER, Ph.D. In One Volume.

The New Testament is thus complete, with the exception of the Commentary on the Book of Revelation, which is in progress.

The Commentaries on Matthew, in one volume; Mark and Luke, in one volume; and on Acts, in one volume, may be had uniform with the above if desired.

Each of the above volumes (three on Old Testament and five on Epistles) will be supplied to Subscribers to the FOREIGN THEOLOGICAL LIBRARY and ANTE-NICENE LIBRARY, or to Purchasers of complete sets of Old Testament (so far as published), and of Epistles, at 15s. The price to others will be 21s. each volume.

Dr. Lange's Commentary on the Old and New Testaments is the combined labour of a large number of the most able and distinguished scholars and divines of Europe, who have spared no pains to make it the standard commentary of Christendom. Dr. Schaff is being assisted by several of the most eminent scholars in the United States, among whom are Professors Shedd, Yeoman, Hackett, Kendrick, Day, Drs. Poor, Schaeffer, and Tayler Lewis, and has made large and valuable additions, comprising nearly one-third more matter than the original German. It thus combines the united evangelical scholarship of Europe and America, and is a commentary truly scholarly and learned, yet popular, orthodox, and sound in the evangelical sense, while it is unsectarian and liberal, and catholic in spirit and aim, combining with original research the most valuable results of the exegetical labours of the past and the present, and making them available for the practical use of the clergy and the general good of the Church. No minister's or layman's library will be complete without it.

'It is with no common feelings of gratification that we note the progress of this truly noble work of Dr. Lange's through the press. There is no commentary in our language at all to compare with it in fulness, availableness, and scholarly care. . . . Those who have been turned away from buying or using it by reason of its bulk, or its look as a compilation, have lost much thereby. The series combines in quite an unexampled way original scholarship of the first order, with doctrinal and homiletical matter of a very rich and varied character.'—*Presbyterian.*

T. and T. Clark's Publications.

Ante-Nicene Christian Library.

A COLLECTION OF ALL THE WORKS OF THE FATHERS OF THE CHRISTIAN CHURCH, PRIOR TO THE COUNCIL OF NICÆA,

EDITED BY THE

REV. ALEXANDER ROBERTS, D.D.,

Author of 'Discussions on the Gospels,' etc.,

AND

JAMES DONALDSON, LL.D.,

Rector of the Royal High School, Edinburgh, and Author of 'Early Christian Literature and Doctrine.'

MESSRS. CLARK are now happy to announce the near completion of this Series. It has been received with marked approval by all sections of the Christian Church in this country and in the United States, as supplying what has long been felt to be a want, and also on account of the impartiality, learning, and care with which Editors and Translators have executed a very difficult task.

The whole Series will be completed in Twenty-four Volumes, of which Twenty-two are ready, and the remaining Two will be published as early as possible.

Each Work is supplied with a good and full Index; but, to add to the value of the completed Series, an Index Volume is preparing for the whole Series, which will be sold separately to those who may desire it, at a moderate price; and the complete Series (exclusive of General Index), in Twenty-four Volumes, will cost Six Guineas.

The Subscription for 1st, 2d, 3d, 4th, 5th, and 6th Years is now due—£6, 6s.
The Subscription to the Series is at the rate of 21s. for Four Volumes when paid in advance (or 24s. when not so paid), and 10s. 6d. each Volume to Non-Subscribers.

The Publishers, however, do not bind themselves to *continue* to supply the complete Series at this rate.

Single Years cannot be had separately, with the exception of current year, unless to complete sets, but *any Volume* may be had separately, price 10s. 6d.

The Homilies of Origen are not included in the Series, as the Publishers have received no encouragement to have them translated.

T. and T. Clark's Publications.

ANTE-NICENE CHRISTIAN LIBRARY—*continued.*

The Works are arranged as follow:—

FIRST YEAR.

APOSTOLIC FATHERS, comprising Clement's Epistles to the Corinthians; Polycarp to the Ephesians; Martyrdom of Polycarp; Epistle of Barnabas; Epistles of Ignatius (longer and shorter, and also the Syriac version); Martyrdom of Ignatius; Epistle to Diognetus; Pastor of Hermas; Papias; Spurious Epistles of Ignatius. In One Volume.
JUSTIN MARTYR; ATHENAGORAS. In One Volume.
TATIAN; THEOPHILUS; THE CLEMENTINE RECOGNITIONS. In One Volume.
CLEMENT OF ALEXANDRIA, Volume First, comprising Exhortation to Heathen; The Instructor; and a portion of the Miscellanies.

SECOND YEAR.

HIPPOLYTUS, Volume First; Refutation of all Heresies and Fragments from his Commentaries.
IRENÆUS, Volume First.
TERTULLIAN AGAINST MARCION.
CYPRIAN, Volume First; the Epistles and some of the Treatises.

THIRD YEAR.

IRENÆUS (completion); HIPPOLYTUS (completion); Fragments of Third Century. In One Volume.
ORIGEN: De Principiis; Letters; and portion of Treatise against Celsus.
CLEMENT OF ALEXANDRIA, Volume Second; Completion of Miscellanies.
TERTULLIAN, Volume First: To the Martyrs; Apology; To the Nations, etc.

FOURTH YEAR.

CYPRIAN, Volume Second (completion); Novatian; Minucius Felix; Fragments.
METHODIUS; ALEXANDER OF LYCOPOLIS; PETER OF ALEXANDRIA; Anatolius; Clement on Virginity, and Fragments.
TERTULLIAN, Volume Second.
APOCRYPHAL GOSPELS; ACTS AND REVELATIONS, comprising all the very curious Apocryphal Writings of the first Three Centuries.

FIFTH YEAR.

TERTULLIAN, Volume Third (completion).
CLEMENTINE HOMILIES; APOSTOLICAL CONSTITUTIONS. In One Volume.
ARNOBIUS.
DIONYSIUS; GREGORY THAUMATURGUS; SYRIAN FRAGMENTS. In One Volume.

SIXTH YEAR.

LACTANTIUS. Two Volumes.
ORIGEN, Volume Second (completion). } *Shortly.*
EARLY LITURGIES AND REMAINING FRAGMENTS.

CLARK'S
FOREIGN THEOLOGICAL LIBRARY.

ANNUAL SUBSCRIPTION:
One Guinea (payable in advance) for Four Volumes, Demy 8vo.
When not paid in advance, the Retail Bookseller is entitled to charge 24s.

N.B.—Any two Years in this Series can be had at Subscription Price. A single Year's Books (except in the case of the current Year) cannot be supplied separately. Non-subscribers, price 10s. 6d. each volume, with exceptions marked.

1 8 6 4—
Lange on the Acts of the Apostles. Two Volumes.
Keil and Delitzsch on the Pentateuch. Vols. I. and II.

1 8 6 5—
Keil and Delitzsch on the Pentateuch. Volume III.
Hengstenberg on the Gospel of John. Two Volumes.
Keil and Delitzsch on Joshua, Judges, and Ruth. One Volume.

1 8 6 6—
Keil and Delitzsch on Samuel. One Volume.
Keil and Delitzsch on Job. Two Volumes.
Martensen's System of Christian Doctrine. One Volume.

1 8 6 7—
Delitzsch on Isaiah. Vol. I.
Delitzsch on Biblical Psychology. 12s.
Delitzsch on Isaiah. Vol. II.
Auberlen on Divine Revelation.

1 8 6 8—
Keil's Commentary on the Minor Prophets. Two Volumes.
Delitzsch's Commentary on Epistle to the Hebrews. Vol. I.
Harless' System of Christian Ethics. One Volume.

1 8 6 9—
Hengstenberg on Ezekiel. One Volume.
Stier on the Words of the Apostles. One Volume.
Keil's Introduction to the Old Testament. Vol. I.
Bleek's Introduction to the New Testament. Vol. I.

1 8 7 0—
Keil's Introduction to the Old Testament. Vol. II.
Bleek's Introduction to the New Testament. Vol. II.
Schmid's New Testament Theology. One Volume.
Delitzsch's Commentary on Epistle to the Hebrews. Vol. II.

1 8 7 1—
Delitzsch's Commentary on the Psalms. Vols. I. and II.
Hengstenberg's History of the Kingdom of God under the Old Testament; and probably
Delitzsch's Commentary on the Psalms. Vol. III.

Lange on St. John's Gospel, Two Volumes (supplemental to regular issue), 10s. 6d. to Subscribers.

MESSRS. CLARK have resolved to allow a SELECTION of TWENTY VOLUMES (or *more at the same ratio*) from the various Series previous to the Volumes issued in 1868 (see *next page*),

At the Subscription Price of Five Guineas.

They trust that this will still more largely extend the usefulness of the FOREIGN THEOLOGICAL LIBRARY, which has so long been recognised as holding an important place in modern Theological literature.

T. and T. Clark's Publications.

CLARK'S FOREIGN THEOLOGICAL LIBRARY—*Continued.*

The following are the works from which a Selection may be made (non-subscription prices within brackets):—

Dr. E. W. Hengstenberg.—Commentary on the Psalms. By E. W. HENGSTENBERG, D.D., Professor of Theology in Berlin. In Three Volumes 8vo. (33s.)

Dr. J. C. L. Gieseler.—Compendium of Ecclesiastical History. By J. C. L. GIESELER, D.D., Professor of Theology in Göttingen. Five Volumes 8vo. (£2, 12s. 6d.)

Dr. Hermann Olshausen.—Biblical Commentary on the Gospels and Acts, adapted especially for Preachers and Students. By HERMANN OLSHAUSEN, D.D., Professor of Theology in the University of Erlangen. In Four Volumes demy 8vo. (£2, 2s.)

Biblical Commentary on the Romans, adapted especially for Preachers and Students. By HERMANN OLSHAUSEN, D.D., Professor of Theology in the University of Erlangen. In One Volume 8vo. (10s. 6d.)

Biblical Commentary on St. Paul's First and Second Epistles to the Corinthians. By HERMANN OLSHAUSEN, D.D., Professor of Theology in the University of Erlangen. In One Volume 8vo. (9s.)

Biblical Commentary on St. Paul's Epistles to the Galatians, Ephesians, Colossians, and Thessalonians. By HERMANN OLSHAUSEN, D.D., Professor of Theology in the University of Erlangen. In One Volume 8vo. (10s. 6d.)

Biblical Commentary on St. Paul's Epistle to the Philippians, to Titus, and the First to Timothy; in continuation of the Work of Olshausen. By LIC. AUGUST WIESINGER. In One Volume 8vo. (10s. 6d.)

Biblical Commentary on the Hebrews. By Dr. EBRARD. In continuation of the Work of Olshausen. In One Volume 8vo. (10s. 6d.)

Dr. Augustus Neander.—General History of the Christian Religion and Church. By AUGUSTUS NEANDER, D.D. Translated from the Second and Improved Edition. In Nine Volumes 8vo. (£2, 11s. 6d.)
This is the only Edition in a Library size.

Prof. H. A. Ch. Havernick.—General Introduction to the Old Testament. By Professor HAVERNICK. One Volume 8vo. (10s. 6d.)

Dr. Julius Müller.—The Christian Doctrine of Sin. By Dr. JULIUS MÜLLER. Two Volumes 8vo. (21s.) New Edition.

Dr. E. W. Hengstenberg.—Christology of the Old Testament, and a Commentary on the Messianic Predictions. By E. W. HENGSTENBERG, D.D., Professor of Theology, Berlin. Four Volumes. (£2, 2s.)

Dr. M. Baumgarten.—The Acts of the Apostles; or the History of the Church in the Apostolic Age. By M. BAUMGARTEN, Ph.D., and Professor in the University of Rostock. Three Volumes. (£1, 7s.)

Dr. Rudolph Stier.—The Words of the Lord Jesus. By RUDOLPH STIER, D.D., Chief Pastor and Superintendent of Schkeuditz. In Eight Volumes 8vo. (£4, 4s.)

Dr. Carl Ullmann.—Reformers before the Reformation, principally in Germany and the Netherlands. Translated by the Rev. R. MENZIES. Two Volumes 8vo. (£1, 1s.)

Professor Kurtz.—History of the Old Covenant; or, Old Testament Dispensation. By Professor KURTZ of Dorpat. In Three Volumes. (£1, 11s. 6d.)

Dr. Rudolph Stier.—The Words of the Risen Saviour, and Commentary on the Epistle of St. James. By RUDOLPH STIER, D.D., Chief Pastor and Superintendent of Schkeuditz. One Volume. (10s. 6d.)

Professor Tholuck.—Commentary on the Gospel of St. John. By Professor THOLUCK of Halle. In One Volume. (9s.)

Professor Tholuck.—Commentary on the Sermon on the Mount. By Professor THOLUCK of Halle. In One Volume. (10s. 6d.)

Dr. E. W. Hengstenberg.—Commentary on the Book of Ecclesiastes. To which are appended: Treatises on the Song of Solomon; on the Book of Job; on the Prophet Isaiah; on the Sacrifices of Holy Scripture; and on the Jews and the Christian Church. By E. W. HENGSTENBERG, D.D. In One Volume 8vo. (9s.)

T. and T. Clark's Publications.

CLARK'S FOREIGN THEOLOGICAL LIBRARY—Continued.

Dr. John H. A. Ebrard.—Commentary on the Epistles of St. John. By Dr. JOHN H. A. EBRARD, Professor of Theology in the University of Erlangen. In One Volume. (10s. 6d.)

Dr. J. P. Lange.—Theological and Homiletical Commentary on the Gospel of St. Matthew and Mark. Specially Designed and Adapted for the Use of Ministers and Students. By J. P. LANGE, D.D., Professor of Divinity in the University of Bonn. Three Volumes. (10s. 6d. each.)

Dr. J. A. Dorner.—History of the Development of the Doctrine of the Person of Christ. By Dr. J. A. DORNER, Professor of Theology in the University of Berlin. Five Volumes. (£2, 12s. 6d.)

Lange and Dr. J. J. Van Oosterzee.—Theological and Homiletical Commentary on the Gospel of St. Luke. Specially Designed and Adapted for the Use of Ministers and Students. Edited by J. P. LANGE, D.D. Two Volumes. (18s.)

Professor Kurtz.—The Sacrificial Worship of the Old Testament. One Volume. (10s. 6d.)

Professor Ebrard.—The Gospel History: A Compendium of Critical Investigations in support of the Historical Character of the Four Gospels. One Volume. (10s. 6d.)

Lange, Lechler, and Gerok.—Theological and Homiletical Commentary on the Acts of the Apostles. Edited by Dr. LANGE. Two Volumes. (21s.)

Dr. Hengstenberg.—Commentary on the Gospel of St. John. Two Volumes. (21s.)

Professor Keil.—Biblical Commentary on the Pentateuch. Three Volumes. (31s. 6d.)

Professor Keil.—Commentary on Joshua, Judges, and Ruth. One Volume. (10s. 6d.)

Professor Delitzsch.—A System of Biblical Psychology. One Volume. (12s.)

Professor Delitzsch.—Commentary on the Prophecies of Isaiah. Two Volumes. (21s.)

Professor Auberlen.—The Divine Revelation: An Essay in Defence of the Faith. One Volume. (10s. 6d.)

Professor Keil.—Commentary on the Books of Samuel. One Volume. (10s. 6d.)

Professor Delitzsch.—Commentary on the Book of Job. Two Volumes. (21s.)

Bishop Martensen.—Christian Dogmatics. A Compendium of the Doctrines of Christianity. One Volume. (10s. 6d.)

Dr. J. P. Lange.—Critical, Doctrinal, and Homiletical Commentary on the Gospel of St. John. Two Volumes. (21s.)

And, in connection with the Series,—

Shedd's History of Christian Doctrine. Two Volumes. (21s.)
Macdonald's Introduction to the Pentateuch. Two Volumes. (21s.)
Hengstenberg's Egypt and the Books of Moses. (7s. 6d.)
Ackerman on the Christian Element in Plato. (7s. 6d.)
Robinson's Greek Lexicon of the New Testament. 8vo. (9s.)
Gerlach's Commentary on the Pentateuch. Demy 8vo. (10s. 6d.)

The above, in 105 Volumes (including 1871), price £27 11s. 6d., form an *Apparatus*, without which it may be truly said *no Theological Library can be complete*, and the Publishers take the liberty of suggesting that no more appropriate gift could be presented to a Clergyman than the Series, in whole or in part.

*** *In reference to the above, it must be noted that* NO DUPLICATES *can be included in the Selection of Twenty Volumes: and it will save trouble and correspondence if it be distinctly understood that* NO LESS *number than Twenty can be supplied, unless at non-subscription price.*

Subscribers' Names received by all Retail Booksellers.

CHEQUES on COUNTRY BANKS under £2, 2s. must have 6d. added for Bank charge.

LONDON: (*For Works at Non-subscription price only*) HAMILTON, ADAMS, & CO.

www.ingramcontent.com/pod-product-compliance
Lightning Source LLC
Chambersburg PA
CBHW020536300426
44111CB00008B/686